opposing viewpoints

SOURCES

death/dying

opposing viewpoints

SOURCES

death/dying

vol. 1

David L. Bender, *Publisher*
Bruno Leone, *Executive Editor*
M. Teresa O'Neill, *Senior Editor*
Claudia Debner, *Editor*
Bonnie Szumski, *Editor*
Lynn Hall, *Editorial Assistant*
Pat Jordan, *Editorial Assistant*

Carl M. Kjellstrand, M.D., F.A.C.P., *Consulting Editor*
Professor of Medicine and Surgery
University of Minnesota Medical School, Minneapolis

Introduction by
Robert Fulton, Ph.D. *Professor of Sociology*
Director, Center for Death Education and Research
University of Minnesota, Minneapolis

greenhaven press, inc.

577 Shoreview Park Road
St. Paul, MN 55126

"Congress shall make no
law. . . .abridging the freedom of
speech, or of the press."

first amendment to the US Constitution

contents

foreword

"It is better to debate a question without settling it than to settle a question without debating it."

Joseph Joubert (1754-1824)

The purpose of Opposing Viewpoints SOURCES is to present balanced, and often difficult to find, opposing points of view on complex and sensitive issues.

Probably the best way to become informed is to analyze the positions of those who are regarded as experts and well studied on issues. It is important to consider every variety of opinion in an attempt to determine the truth. Opinions from the mainstream of society should be examined. But also important are opinions that are considered radical, reactionary, or minority as well as those stigmatized by some other uncomplimentary label. An important lesson of history is the eventual acceptance of many unpopular and even despised opinions. The ideas of Socrates, Jesus, and Galileo are good examples of this.

Readers will approach this anthology with their own opinions on the issues debated within it. However, to have a good grasp of one's own viewpoint, it is necessary to understand the arguments of those with whom one disagrees. It can be said that those who do not completely understand their adversary's point of view do not fully understand their own.

A persuasive case for considering opposing viewpoints has been presented by John Stuart Mill in his work *On Liberty*. When examining controversial issues it may be helpful to reflect on his suggestion:

> The only way in which a human being can make some approach to knowing the whole of a subject, is by hearing what can be said about it by persons of every variety of opinion, and studying all modes in which it can be looked at by every character of mind. No wise man ever acquired his wisdom in any mode but this.

Analyzing Sources of Information

Opposing Viewpoints SOURCES includes diverse materials taken from magazines, journals, books, and newspapers, as well as statements and position papers from a wide range of individuals, organiza-

tions and governments. This broad spectrum of sources helps to develop patterns of thinking which are open to the consideration of a variety of opinions.

Pitfalls to Avoid

A pitfall to avoid in considering opposing points of view is that of regarding one's own opinion as being common sense and the most rational stance and the point of view of others as being only opinion and naturally wrong. It may be that another's opinion is correct and one's own is in error.

Another pitfall to avoid is that of closing one's mind to the opinions of those with whom one disagrees. The best way to approach a dialogue is to make one's primary purpose that of understanding the mind and arguments of the other person and not that of enlightening him or her with one's own solutions. More can be learned by listening than speaking.

It is my hope that after reading this anthology the reader will have a deeper understanding of the issues debated and will appreciate the complexity of even seemingly simple issues on which good and honest people disagree. This awareness is particularly important in a democratic society such as ours where people enter into public debate to determine the common good. Those with whom one disagrees should not necessarily be regarded as enemies, but perhaps simply as people who suggest different paths to a common goal.

The Format of SOURCES

In this anthology, carefully chosen opposing viewpoints are purposely placed back to back to create a running debate; each viewpoint is preceded by a short quotation that best expresses the author's main argument. This format instantly plunges the reader into the midst of a controversial issue and greatly aids that reader in mastering the basic skill of recognizing an author's point of view. In addition, the table of contents gives a brief description of each viewpoint, allowing the reader to identify quickly the point of view for which he or she is searching.

Each section of this anthology debates an issue, and the sections build on one another so that the anthology as a whole debates a larger issue. By using this step-by-step, section-by-section approach to understanding separate facets of a topic, the reader will have a solid background upon which to base his or her opinions. Each year a supplement of twenty opposing viewpoints will be added to this anthology, enabling the reader to keep abreast of annual developments.

This volume of Opposing Viewpoints SOURCES does not advocate a particular point of view. Quite the contrary! The very nature of the anthology leaves it to the reader to formulate the opinions he or she finds most suitable. My purpose as publisher is to see that this is made possible by offering a wide range of viewpoints that are fairly presented.

David L. Bender
Publisher

introduction

*"Death comes equally to us all, and
makes us all equal when it comes."*

John Donne, 1572-1631

Death is a universal experience for the human
race. It is shared by all nations and all cultures for all
times. As the American psychologist Herman Feifel
has so colorfully observed, "death resides in the
bowels of all men." Such imagery helps to remind
us, private citizens as well as professional caregivers,
that all living things die and all human relationships
end in separation.

Nations experience death differently. As with an
individual, a nation's culture and history provides a
unique context for the inevitable encounter with
death. The focus of concern, however, at any given
time varies, reflecting the particular issues that have
emerged within different countries. The "death
awareness" movement over the past two decades in
the US, for example, has brought attention to the
manner in which individuals and institutions denied
both the prospect and reality of death. The practice
of death avoidance was shattered, however, by the
1969 publication of Elisabeth Kübler-Ross's book *On
Death and Dying*, which not only rediscovered the
problems of the dying in America's health care
system, but also recognized and helped illuminate the
problems that denial presented to caregivers in
public institutions.

Spain today, for instance, is confronted with a
burgeoning secularism and, as a Catholic country, is
wracked with controversy over the question of
abortion. In Sweden, the euthanasia issue is foremost
in the minds of many and is heatedly debated, while
England contends with the voluntary suicide movement. The different problems surrounding dying and
death that are presently being addressed in the US as
well as around the world serve to challenge our intellect and resourcefulness at the same time that they
inform us of our common humanity.

The many issues and problems associated with dying and death today have taken on new significance
as the circumstances of life have changed. Progress
in medical science and the general enhancement of

life since the turn of the century, for example, has
greatly increased the proportion of elderly persons in
society. The consequence of this development is that
death is now primarily the experience of the aged. Of
those who will die this year in the United States,
two-thirds will be 65 years of age or older.

The context in which dying and death are experienced in the US has also undergone a significant
change. More than 70 percent of the deaths in 1980
took place outside the home in either a hospital or
nursing home setting. The trend toward increased
hospitalization and institutionalization of the
chronically ill or dying patient can be expected to
continue even with the advent of hospice care.

These changes that are overtaking the US and
indeed the industrialized world, are also having a
direct, and frequently deleterious, effect on family
relations. Today's elderly, whether they live in
Stockholm, London, Tokyo, or New York, are increasingly retired from work and often live physically removed from their children and grandchildren.
Geographical mobility and urbanization as well as
secularization deprive the elderly of traditional family and community assistance.

Family relations have also been directly affected by
contemporary mortality and the new social patterns
and attitudes that are emerging across all modern
industrialized societies. Prolonged separation of the
elderly, due to hospitalization or residential change
for instance, serves to reduce family and friendship
contacts as it weakens social and emotional commitments. With a sense of having "lived out one's
life," the death of an elderly person today need not
affect the emotional life of his or her family to the
same degree it once might have. This does not mean,
of course, that when an elderly parent or relative
dies, grief is absent. Rather, the degree or extent of a
survivor's grief appears to depend upon many factors, not the least of which is the nature and intensity
of the social bond itself.

The topics that are addressed in this anthology (abortion, euthanasia, suicide, definition of death, grief, the funeral, care of the dying, and life after death) testify to the profound impact that these various questions have upon our lives. Their impact, however, has been both differentially experienced and perceived. Our pluralistic society with its diversity of religious traditions and racial and ethnic populations, variable life styles and unique life experiences cannot help but generate a divergence of opinion regarding these several issues. The editors of Greenhaven Press are to be commended for organizing this compendium in the manner that they have and for presenting without comment the substance of the disagreements that have emerged. These debates are certain to continue. The answers to the questions of Who shall live and who shall die? What social and economic support should be offered our elderly citizens? Who should receive an organ transplant? What rights does a women have over her own body? and Does a person have the right to commit suicide?—to say nothing of the time honored question Is there life after death?—are answers not to be found in established rules of law or by fiat or revelation. They will be found, if at all, in the hearts and minds of men and women as they struggle to resolve the competing claims and emotional demands that these issues make upon their lives.

Robert Fulton, Minneapolis, Minnesota,
August 1984.

"The charge that abortion equals murder is demagoguery. A fetus is no more a human being than an acorn is an oak tree."

The Case for Abortion

Caroline Lund and Cindy Jaquith

"For years women have been under constant pressure to have children. Our culture teaches us that we are not complete women unless we have children. Our husbands and boyfriends encourage us to bear children as proof of their masculinity. Contraception is almost always our responsibility. Contraceptives that are known to be safe are not always effective; contraceptives that are known to be effective are not always safe....

"Other pressures compel some of us not to have children. If we are unmarried, we become social outcasts by bearing children. Those of us who are poor and live on welfare know that opponents of welfare want to limit the size of our families. We are pressured to use contraceptives or be sterilized; each time we have another child the meager allowance per child gets even smaller. Population control advocates tell us that overpopulation is the reason our environment is polluted....

"We want control over our own bodies. We are tired of being pressured to have children or not to have children. *It's our decision.*"

Thus begins a pamphlet put out by Women vs. Connecticut, a group of over 1,000 women who have filed a suit challenging the constitutionality of the Connecticut abortion law. This quote from the introduction to their pamphlet expresses the goals of their struggle, and it is a good summary of the feelings of thousands of women across the country who are fighting... toward gaining control over their bodies and their lives.

Sentenced to Forced Breeding

The right of women to control their own reproductive lives could easily be provided by the advanced technology of this society. And yet this society has consciously denied this right to women. "Instead," writes Evelyn Clark from Boston Female Liberation, "it sentences its female population to a life of forced breeding or to suffer the consequences of social stigma, psychological and physical maiming or death."

This simple, just demand of women has created a furor of debate and opposition from all quarters—more than over any other single women's liberation demand. Religious people, politicians, doctors, hospital administrators, antiabortion organizations, and even individuals, like Norman Mailer, are mobilizing across the country in an attempt to stop women from winning this demand.

The fact that the opponents of women's liberation have chosen this issue as the focal point of their counterattack on the women's movement emphasizes the importance of the abortion issue. We are obliged to meet this attack head-on and escalate our fight for the repeal of all abortion laws.

In some areas, the hierarchy of the Catholic Church has used Sunday masses to try to convince their members to oppose abortion, even passing out petitions against abortion repeal to the congregation and stipulating that no one could leave without signing the petition. The Catholic hierarchy has used its great tax-free wealth to provide free headquarters to such organizations as the "Right to Life Committees," complete with free telephones and priests to staff the offices. In Washington, D.C., the ultraright group "Sons of Thunder," dressed in their uniform of khaki shirts and red berets, invaded a new Washington abortion clinic to protest the abortions performed there. These antiabortion groups exist in many areas of the country: the Massachusetts Value-of-Life movement, the Houston Solid Rock League of Women, the California Coalition for Life, the Pittsburgh Women Concerned for the Unborn Child, and the Minnesota Citizens Concerned for Life, to list some of them.

Caroline Lund and Cindy Jaquith, "Abortion on Demand: A Woman's Right" from *Abortion: A Woman's Right,* edited by Linda Jenness, Caroline Lund, and Cindy Jaquith. Reprinted by permission of Pathfinder Press. Copyright 1971.

When one looks at this array of opponents of the right of women to abortion and at their arguments, it becomes clear that in the fight for abortion women are challenging all the religious and mystical prejudices, traditions, and institutions of class society.

Arguments Against Abortion

The arguments against women's right to control their own bodies could be listed in three main categories: (1) abortion is murder; (2) legalizing abortion would encourage sex, which is sinful, especially for women; (3) abortion would take away men's power over women to make them pregnant. These objections stem from some of the most fundamental ideological underpinnings of class society—such false concepts as the necessity for the repression of sexuality, the belief that women are naturally inferior and ought to be submissive to men, and the concept that fulfillment for a woman must come primarily from motherhood. Until the past few years, the weight of these prejudices kept us silent, suffering the burden of unwanted children or mutilation at the hands of backstreet abortionists because we were too ashamed of our own bodies and sexual functions even to *talk* about abortion, much less protest the denial of our rights.

"All you have to do is take a look at the miserable conditions in orphanages to see how much the people who run this country actually care about protecting the lives of the young."

Let's look at the first charge—that abortion is murder and should therefore be classified as a criminal act. Illustrating this approach is a letter from the New York Catholic hierarchy that was sent to all parish priests in New York state and quoted in the March 25, 1971, *Village Voice*. The letter compared "killing of unborn children" to Nazism, and demagogically said, "Each day [abortionists] grow wealthier from the killing of unborn children—some of whom have been heard to cry as they were dropped into surgical trash cans. . . .P.S. Please read this letter at all the Masses on Sunday."

The charge that abortion equals murder is demagoguery. A fetus is no more a human being than an acorn is an oak tree. The emotion-laden word "murder" is used to obscure the real issues involved: the rights, the safety, and the whole course of life of pregnant women. It is absurd to equate the "rights" of the fetus to the rights of a pregnant woman.

In order to be consistent, anyone who contends that abortion is murder must also oppose any method of contraception which kills a fertilized egg, because

that would also involve killing a "potential human being." And what about killing the egg or the sperm? Furthermore, recent biological research has found that the fertilized egg is not the only cell which can develop into a human being. According to Roy U. Shenk, a scientist who is involved in studies of the ability of cells to develop into complete animals, "Increasing evidence is accumulating that almost any cell of an organism is totipotent—that is, capable of producing another complete, genetically identical organism."

The Religious Opposition

Both the Church and common law have been completely inconsistent in their judgments on abortion. British common law in the thirteenth century set "ensoulment" of the fetus at the time of quickening (approximately five months), and abortion before quickening was either completely legal or widely tolerated, both in England and in the U.S. until 1803. In 1588, Pope Sixtus V issued a papal decree that all abortions were murder, but in 1591 Pope Gregory, who succeeded Sixtus, reversed this ruling. In 1803, British common law was changed, outlawing abortion before or after quickening. In the 1820s, the U.S. began to enact its first abortion laws, and by the late 1860s abortion before or after quickening was outlawed except to save the life of a pregnant woman.

Obviously, whatever the specific reasons for changing their minds, the churches and the ruling classes of Europe and the U.S. have ruled on whether or not women have the right to abortion on the basis of expediency—not on the basis of any "higher moral law." The history of abortion laws shows that the judgment that "abortion is murder" does not come from any god, but from men, who have changed their minds on the basis of such things as the desire to increase the birth rate in order to have more workers for industry or more cannon fodder for armies.

The charge that abortion is murder has been used to cover up the real motivations behind outlawing abortion: the desire to force women to be breeders, and the desire to uphold the institution of the patriarchal family by punishing women for any sexual activity outside of marriage through forcing them to raise an "illegitimate" child.

Most of the people shouting the loudest for "the right to life," and the "protection of life," demonstrate their complete hypocrisy when it comes to protecting the "right to life" of children already born, or protecting the lives of the thousands of women who die each year from backstreet abortions....

All you have to do is take a look at the miserable conditions in orphanages to see how much the people who run this country actually care about protecting the lives of the young. And they care nothing about driving women to despair and suicide by forcing them to bear and raise unwanted children.

Men Ignore Women's Fear

The male priests, politicians, and doctors who are shouting the loudest against women having the right to control their bodies have no idea what the fear of pregnancy and forced motherhood means to a woman. They have no concern for the torment and constant worry that for women accompanies any sexual activity, because it is they who must face the possible consequences. They have no idea of the despair that untold numbers of women have suffered from having their whole lives determined by the responsibility to care for one child after another.

The feminist movement is saying that women have the right to be free of this crushing burden, to be sexual beings without that fear, and to be able to devote our lives to any area we may choose. This right to control our own bodies is a necessary step in the struggle of women to win complete liberation.

And this freedom for women will also mean greater freedom for children, because they will all be wanted. It is the feminist movement that is fighting for the protection of lives—of women, men, and children—not the antiabortion forces, who weep crocodile tears over the ''rights of the fetus'' as a justification for the oppression of women....

A Positive Sexual Revolution

As the struggle for abortion demonstrates, women's liberation is part of a more general sexual revolution. Not a ''sexual revolution'' in the perverted sense of increasing promiscuity and the exploitation of women as sexual objects, but rather a revolution involving the affirmation of sexuality along with human dignity—for both men and women. A revolution involving the rejection of dominance and submissiveness, which is the content of the exploitative, dehumanizing distortion of sexuality common in our society. A revolution which affirms the right of each individual to control her or his body and life, free of laws or customs which attempt to enforce irrational, mystical precepts.

The liberating effects of this revolution can be seen already in the change in women's attitudes concerning abortion and concerning their bodies and sexual lives in general. We are standing up and raising our voices in protest, refusing to bend to feelings of guilt and shame over our sexuality that this society tries to inculcate into us in a myriad of different and subtle ways. The abortion struggle is reaching thousands of women, helping to liberate their minds from the fear of struggle, creating a new kind of woman who will not be afraid to struggle against all aspects of her oppressed status.

The ruling class in this country recognizes the implications of granting women the right to control their own bodies, and is trying to waylay this movement in any way it can. They are attempting to confuse the issue of abortion to hurt the movement in two specific ways. One is to associate population control with abortion, and the second is to try to get away with merely reforming abortion laws rather than repealing them and establishing free abortion clinics.

Population Control Not the Issue

Population control has nothing to do with the interests of women; in fact population control is contradictory to women achieving the right to control their own bodies. It is a theory of the ruling class, designed to deflect attention from the real causes of the evils of the capitalist system. The problem is not that there are too many children, but the fact that, because of private property, the great wealth of this world is not available to or controlled by the people who produce that wealth, but is owned privately by a small number of rich families.

''Population control is contradictory to women achieving the right to control their own bodies.''

Through population-control measures, politicians propose that the state should determine for people in some way that they should have fewer children. Most often this is directed against Black, Chicano, Puerto Rican and Native American people, as well as people on welfare. At the bottom of population-control theories there often lies racism and an attempt to lay the blame for racial oppression and poverty on poor people themselves. The victim is made into the criminal.

The women's movement must fight against any association of population-control measures with the struggle for the right to abortion, because these measures are against the interests of women and will serve especially to narrow the support to be won from Third World women, poor women, and Catholic women. Women do not want anyone deciding for them either to have children or not to have them. *We* want to decide. Hence the demand of the women's movement for ''no forced sterilization.''

Politicians who support this system are trying to divert the abortion movement away from the concept of women's right to control their own bodies and lives—and mixing abortion bills with population-control measures is the perfect way to do this. In this way they are trying to blunt and stifle the dynamic of women demanding control over their lives and over the institutions affecting them.

Some women within the feminist movement have

suggested that since the ruling class may try to use the legalization of abortion in order to control population, the women's movement should give up on the fight for abortion. But exactly the opposite is the case. If we give up the fight for our right as women to control our own bodies, this will make it all the easier for the antiabortion forces to triumph, or for the population-control "experts" to be able to control our lives in another form.

"The restrictions in reform abortion laws are often masked as 'protections' for women, but they all have the purpose of limiting the woman's right to decide whether or not she wants an abortion."

The best way to keep women from being the victims of population-control measures, such as forced sterilization, is to build the strongest possible movement for the right of women to control their own bodies. This will help to build our confidence in our rights, and we will not submit out of shame to a forced sterilization or accept laws restricting our right to decide.

Reforming of Laws

The other tactic politicians are using to try to appease and disorient the movement for abortion is reform laws which include various restrictions on the right of women to abortion. If they cannot have abortions outlawed completely, for instance, Catholic Church officials have stated that they hope to at least restrict as much as possible the ability of women to get abortions. Said Monsignor McGovern of the archdiocese of New York, "Anything less than abortion on demand is better than nothing." Also, politicians hope to absorb and blunt the movement by convincing more conservative sections of the women's movement to throw their energies into building support for reform laws, on the basis that they would at least make things a little better for women, rather than struggling for the full and just demand for the repeal of all abortion laws.

The restrictions in reform abortion laws are often masked as "protections" for women, but they all have the purpose of limiting the woman's right to decide whether or not she wants an abortion. Some of the most restrictive reform laws limit abortion to cases of rape or cases where there is a chance that the fetus may be born mentally or physically deformed. Some require that the woman appear before a committee of a number of doctors and convince them that she should be given the right to abortion....

There are other, less blatant restrictions which have been proposed in many states. One would require that the woman be a resident of the particular state for a certain period of time. But why should out-of-state women be denied this right? This is simply a way of appeasing opponents of abortion, who charge that legalizing abortion will turn their state into an "abortion mill." Would these people object to a "tonsillectomy mill," with people coming to their state from all over the country for tonsillectomies?

The restriction that abortions must be performed in hospitals has the effect of limiting the right to abortion to wealthy women because of the high cost of hospital care.

Time Restrictions

Another common restriction is a time limit—usually from twelve to twenty-six weeks of pregnancy—after which a woman cannot have an abortion. But if a woman has the right to control over her own body, why should this control be limited to a certain period of time? This restriction reflects an attempt to maintain some control over women's bodies. As the president of the Greater New York Hospital Association said regarding the proposal to cut down the New York time limitation from twenty-four to twenty weeks, "Twenty weeks should be enough time for a woman to come to a decision." And if she doesn't come to a decision sooner? Then the idea is, she should be punished by having to bear the child.

The authors are revolutionary socialists active in the Women's Liberation Movement. Caroline Lund is a staff writer for The Militant *and author of* The Family: Revolutionary or Oppressive Force? *Cindy Jaquith is the national secretary of the Young Socialist Alliance.*

"Even if [the fetus] is to be considered merely a woman's 'property' and not the 'person' that the anti-abortionists claim, control over property is not absolute."

The Case Against Abortion

Bernard N. Nathanson with Richard N. Ostling

We are sometimes told that abortion is necessary because of world overpopulation. This article deals with the United States, not the developing nations, which face different cultural, economic, and medical situations from our own. Overpopulation is simply no reason to advocate widespread abortion in a nation like the U.S., and we are not going to end starvation in Ethiopia by aborting in Manhattan.

An aside on this matter of population control: It is intriguing to me that even extreme sectors of the American abortion movement do not advocate it as a primary contraceptive technique but rather as a "fallback" (a precious little euphemism) if birth control fails or is not used. There is a medical paradox here. The Pill produces a death rate far in excess of that in first-trimester abortions, yet few pro-abortionists have had the integrity or the courage to advocate abortion as "just another" birth-control method. Does not some recondite human repugnance for abortion lurk here?...

Pro-abortion spokesmen too often treat alpha [the fetus] as merely a chunk of tissue or an ordinary organ of the mother's body, rather like an appendix that is snipped off. One writer of this persuasion even likened alpha to the cells that flake off every morning when we brush our teeth. The biological facts of the matter will be described subsequently, but let me simply state here that this whole line of argumentation is biological nonsense, unworthy of the people who have advocated it. Alpha is an entity like no other within the woman's body. . . .

The Woman and Her Doctor

How many times have we heard this one? The "woman and her doctor" alone ought to decide on abortion. Even the Supreme Court swallowed this.

This is a clever way of subtly implying professional scrutiny and endorsement for an abortion, but the phrase is wholly spurious. All one needs to do is look at the New York newspapers, where this allegedly "medical" service is advertised alongside "Madame Marie, Indian Reader," "Weight Loss—Amazing Breakthrough!" and "SINGLE? Looking for someone special?" One author has stated that abortion is no more a medical issue because doctors do it than is capital punishment a matter of electrical engineering because an electric chair is used.

Quite obviously, the mother and the mother alone makes the decision, except in the small percentage of abortions that involve true medical indications. Physicians have no special moral wisdom to impart on such non-medical decisions.

I must agree with Daniel Callahan's remarks against abortion as "medical": It may be very beneficial for a woman, but unless her life is threatened, "an abortion cures no known disease and relieves no medically classifiable illness." "It may be merciful and it may be wise," but medicine does not classify a procedure as "therapeutic" when "it is not notably therapeutic for the fetus" and has a "100% mortality rate."

We are told that laws against abortion were a plot by male chauvinists to oppress women, or in the less hysterical version, that men can never understand what the pregnant woman suffers. But one day as a mother who had just given birth signed the routine consent form for a circumcision that would inflict considerable pain on her newborn boy, I asked myself: On this account, ought we not require that the father sign consent? How could a woman know what it is to have part of your penis cut off?

James Mohr's historical book points out that the original nineteenth-century feminists were universally opposed to abortion, even after antisepsis had made it a safer procedure. They considered it yet another outrage that had been inflicted upon women by men who forced them to have abortions.

Daniel Callahan objects to the argument about "men legislating for women" because abortion, child-bearing, and child-rearing have consequences for everyone in our society, of both sexes. For that matter, as a "women's issue," abortion works against the pro-choicers in that virtually every U.S. poll over the past decade has shown that women are significantly more anti-abortion than men are....

Social Panacea

If the anti-abortionists would blame every social malady on abortion, the pro-abortionists propose it as the *solution* to all manner of social ills. But now that we have had several years of open abortion, what maladies have been alleviated? Liberalization has certainly brought benefits to individuals, but where is the society-wide evidence that it has reduced the welfare rolls, the curse of poverty, or illegitimacy and child abuse? (Actually, as mentioned already, reported child abuse has *risen* noticeably since abortion was legalized, and so have illegitimate births, despite the availability of abortion as an alternative.)

The "Unwanted Child"

The specter of child abuse is used as part of a broader pro-abortion argument, that every child born into this world must be "wanted," and that social evils will result if they are not. I have some important philosophical objections to the "unwantedness" line, but will limit myself here to matters of simple logic.

"Unless her life is threatened, 'an abortion cures no known disease and relieves no medically classifiable illness.'"

Would that all children were wanted. But projections of future harm from present emotions are totally unreliable. At some point in pregnancy, many children are temporarily "unwanted." For that matter, offspring are often "unwanted" at certain moments after they are born. An unwanted alpha does not always end up as a resented baby. As for battered children, there is no solid evidence that unwantedness during pregnancy produces battering. Rather, battered children appear to be the result of mistreatment of the parents when they themselves were children. Contrary to the stereotype, battering is not a problem limited to the poorer families that are of particular concern to the (usually more affluent) abortion advocates. As noted above, if anything, the statistical reports would lead one to conclude that liberal abortion laws, not strict ones, foster child abuse.

The "unwanted child" is also a myth. If alpha is carried to term, it will never be "unwanted" because of the hopeless shortage of babies available for the long list of childless couples who earnestly want to adopt them. So alpha need be "unwanted" only for the nine months between conception and birth. Adoption is difficult for the unwed mother, and more so for the widow, divorcee, or wife who becomes pregnant out of wedlock. The point is that an option does exist if we do judge alpha's survival to be even more important than the difficulties of the unwillingly pregnant woman.

Psychiatric Scare Tactics

No less than their opponents, the pro-abortionists indulge in pop psychology. The adoption solution, just mentioned, is portrayed as an unutterable trauma for the natural mother, or the psychological harm to a woman refused abortion is painted in lurid terms. Clinical proof of this is, on the whole, lacking. (For ample detail on psychological studies on both sides, see Callahan's *Abortion: Law, Choice and Morality*.) Just as I granted to the anti-abortionists, it is inarguably true that refusal of abortion or giving up of babies for adoption placement may occasion regret or remorse, mixed perhaps with more optimistic thoughts about the life that the mother has authored and preserved. But sadness is not sickness, nor a psychosis. There may indeed be emotional turmoil. This is true of all major life decisions and events, normal pregnancy and childbirth among them. The difficulties of life, however, are not psychiatric pathology and do not provide justification for a procedure if, on other grounds, it is judged to be unethical.

Women's Control Over Their Bodies

Leaving aside for the moment the question of whether alpha is merely "part" of the mother's body like an appendix, this principle is wrongheaded in any event. Civilized societies do not permit women absolute control over their bodies; they do not sanction such things as mutilation of one's own body, drug abuse, prostitution, or suicide. Even if alpha is to be considered merely a woman's "property" and not the "person" that the anti-abortionists claim, control over property is not absolute—statutes against cruelty to animals are legitimate, including the animals that the violator owns. We cannot grant women absolute control over alpha without consideration of abortion on its own terms.

The broader claim is to the "right to privacy," which N.A.R.A.L. figured correctly was the only one that would work for us in the courts. We cited in particular the *Griswold v. Connecticut* ruling striking down anti-birth-control laws on privacy grounds. Justice Blackmun also cited that case in guaranteeing a "right to privacy" on abortion in 1973, but John Hart Ely of the Harvard Law School has pointed out that in *Griswold* the court reasoned that enforcement of the birth-control ban would have been impossible without outrageous government prying into the privacy of the home. With abortion, the conception may occur in private, but the abortion itself is ''in public''— in a clinic or hospital—with various outsiders in attendance. Each act of abortion (but never each use of contraception) must be registered with the government.

There are, after all, good invasions of privacy. Society requires the white majority to respect the rights of the black minority. It does not grant parents total physical control over their offspring *after* birth, legislating against child abuse. Government intervenes in bodily privacy in the control of communicable diseases, and is even willing to violate parents' control and their explicit First Amendment right to religious liberty in medical-legal disputes where life is at stake (e.g., forced blood transfusions for underage Jehovah's Witnesses, or various medical procedures for children of Christian Scientists).

In the contemporary situation, the woman's ''control over her body'' offers her a number of options other than abortion. She can choose sexual continence, or if not continence, then contraception, or if not contraception, then sterilization; or if none of these, she can take control in making sure that the man in her life makes such a choice.

The Coathanger

The favorite button of the pro-abortionists is the one showing the coathanger, symbol of the self-induced abortion and the carnage that results from it, or the similar problem of botched illegal abortions done by ''back-alley butchers.'' This is a fundamental argument; one that moved us deeply in the late '60s, and one that could justify non-medical abortion even if no other argument stood up.

How many deaths were we talking about when abortion was illegal? In N.A.R.A.L. we generally emphasized the drama of the individual case, not the mass statistics, but when we spoke of the latter it was always ''5,000 to 10,000 deaths a year.'' I confess that I knew the figures were totally false, and I suppose the others did too if they stopped to think of it. But in the ''morality'' of our revolution, it was a *useful* figure, widely accepted, so why go out of our way to correct it with honest statistics? The overriding concern was to get the laws eliminated, and anything within reason that had to be done was permissible. Statistics on abortion deaths were fairly reliable, since bodies are difficult to hide, but not all these deaths were reported as such if the attending doctor wanted to protect a family by listing another cause of death. In 1967, with moderate A.L.I.-type laws in three states, the federal government listed only 160 deaths from illegal abortion. In the last year before the Blackmun era began, 1972, the total was only 39 deaths. Christopher Tietze estimated 1,000 maternal

deaths as the outside possibility in an average year before legalization; the actual total was probably closer to 500.

The death of 500 women, or even 39, is a matter of the most serious concern, but this is hardly an overwhelming death rate among the millions of women of childbearing age. Depending upon the value that is placed upon alpha, it might be lopsided for a society to consider only the 500 women and ignore the 1,000,000 alphas that are legally extinguished each year.

''Abortion was revolutionized. . .through suction curettage in 1970. . . .If abortion is ever driven underground again, even non-physicians will be able to perform this procedure with remarkable safety.''

Apart from deaths, there were the walking wounded of the abortion injustice. Their sufferings were very real to me and to other physicians in the reform movement. In the old days there would be two or three critically ill patients in our ward from infected botched abortions at any one time, and the same in the ward of every other hospital. For this reason obstetrics-gynecology used to be a sobering specialty, and this was a major reason why its practitioners gradually accepted the change. In the middle of too many nights we had gotten a call that a woman was ''miscarrying'' in early pregnancy. When we would appear bleary-eyed to examine the seriously ill woman it would turn out that, one way or another, she had been ''started.'' Those were bleak nights indeed.

Carnage Eliminated

Why, then, do I now dismiss the whole carnage argument? Simply because technology has eliminated it.

The practice of abortion was revolutionized at virtually the same moment that the laws were revolutionized, through the widespread introduction of suction curettage in 1970. (Even before this, antibiotics and other advances had already dramatically lowered the abortion death rate.) Instead of scraping the soft wall of the pregnant uterus with a sharp instrument, the operator vacuums it out with a plastic suction currette. Though it is preferable that this be done by a licensed physician, one can expect that if abortion is ever driven underground again, even non-physicians will be able to perform this procedure with remarkable safety. No woman need die if she chooses to abort during the first twelve weeks of pregnancy. Largely due to suction curettage, the total of deaths from all abortions (legal and spontaneous "miscarriage" as well as the illegal abortions, which decreased markedly after legalization) was only 25 by 1976. Even without a suction machine, a simple combination of catheter and syringe can produce enough suction to carry out a safe early abortion.

"The 'unwanted child' is also a myth. . . . Carried to term it will never be 'unwanted' because of the hopeless shortage of babies available for the long list of childless couples."

As for the self-induced abortion, by thrusting a coathanger or other dangerous object into the womb, this will also be a thing of the past. Compounds known as prostaglandins can now be used to bring on contractions and expel alpha, and would readily be available for do-it-yourself abortions in vaginal suppository form. Prostaglandin suppositories would not provide a full abortion in most cases, but they would "start" the woman, and she could then go to her doctor to have her uterus cleaned out. Prostaglandins in general are safe for the mother's system, and besides that, there is no evidence that anything other than a spontaneous miscarriage has occurred. There are no signs of instruments in use, and the woman can command medical attention on a legitimate and legally safe basis. They may sound rather cynical, but this is what would now happen in practice if abortion were illegal.

There may be many other reasons or cases under which abortion is desirable, but this most emotional of the arguments, the one which swayed me more than any other, is now wholly invalid and obsolete.

Bernard N. Nathanson and Richard N. Ostling are co-authors of the landmark book Aborting America. *A former abortion advocate, Mr. Nathanson claims his views changed after he witnessed the ravages of abortion.*

"[The obstetrician] simultaneously cares for two patients, the mother and infant; each has an individual right to life."

A Fetus' Right to Life Must Be Protected

Joseph R. Stanton

Recently, before the Congress of the United States, prestigious organizations of Medicine and Science have recorded their acceptance of abortion. As part thereof, they necessarily dissemble and obscure the painfully and tediously acquired knowledge of the centuries. "No one knows or can know," they would have us believe, "when a protectable human life begins." Thus, there continues to unfold in the public domain subversion of medicine's traditional role of protection of all human life from its authentic beginning to its natural death.

Already the perceptive can see that toleration of the extinction of the defective "fetus" before birth has weakened the defense of the impaired child at and after birth. Joseph Fletcher, the situation ethicist, tells us that infanticide at and after birth is the moral equivalent of "post natal abortion," that there is really no difference between the two. A burgeoning literature even now develops defending infanticide. The dehumanization essential for toleration of abortion and infanticide even now reaches out to encompass aging and impaired human beings at life's end.

Can Sanctity of Life Be Defended?

What does one write to a new generation of emerging doctors about medical ethics and the sanctity of human life, born and unborn? Can that concept of life's sanctity, so revered in the ideal and honored in the past, be defended in the modern age? What should be the response of the doctor, faithful to the ideals of the Hippocratic tradition, and rejecting its abandonment by those who, under the guise of social expediency, would jettison a noble past? Is it yet to be the wave of the future that only the planned, the genetically perfect, and the wanted are entitled to the loving concern of a caring society?

Joseph R. Stanton, speech presented in Ford Hall Forum in Massachusetts on November 1, 1981.

As abortion has been in and out of human history since ancient times, so too opposition to abortion has been "a near constant in human history." Yet, opposition to abortion has not enjoyed a favorable press since the U.S. Supreme Court's Roe and Doe decisions of January 22, 1973 decriminalized abortion.

The "quickened" child "in ventre sa mere" was unquestionably protectable under the common law from the time of Blackstone. Yet the modern re-write of history would have one believe that anti-abortion laws protecting the unborn on the statute books of all 50 states until 1973 were put there because the procedure of abortion was so dangerous; that legislators were acting only to protect maternal health; that there was no legislative concern for the entity within the womb. How paradoxical it is that the A.M.A., which in 1859 held abortion to be "the unwarrantable destruction of human life," in 1981 appears in the lists as a proponent of abortion. No less shocking than the abandonment of the unborn by organizations of Medicine has been the co-equal abandonment by the institutions of Law. Indeed, the subversion of the elites in obstetrics and the law was essential for any advancement of abortion.

Constitutional scholars continue to condemn the mechanism by which the Supreme Court of the United States abandoned the rights of the unwanted unborn. It did this under a rubric which discovered, after some 190 years, a right to privacy *in penumbra* of the Constitution which seven justices tell us encompasses a right to abortion. Thus, some 10,000,000 abortions in the last 10 years were legitimated. The American Bar Association has been the willing handmaid in defense of "the right to choose"—the abortion rite—which now justifies more abortions than live births in Washington, D.C., the nation's capital, and in New York City.

Judith Blake, the demographer, had written in 1971 that liberalized abortion would not come about through the pressure of public opinion. Indeed, she suggested it could only occur through Supreme Court actions invalidating the constitutionality of state laws prohibiting abortion. This was unquestionably the genesis of the Roe v. Wade and Doe v. Bolton cases, the Supreme Court ruling which overturned all state abortion laws.

Questioning Life's Beginning

Preparatory groundwork had been accomplished by abortion promoting organizations including the National Association for the Repeal of Abortion Laws, Planned Parenthood, the Association for the Study of Abortion, and the Population Law Institute through a complaisant media. Fundamental to changing public perceptions about unborn human life was the casting of doubt about when human life begins. Quickly, the biologically known became the unknowable. "When do *you* think human life begins?" evoked a panoply of speculative answers which includes human life starting at any time from fertilization through "quickening" and birth to three years post natally.

The second strategic thrust of the abortion activists was to portray opposition to abortion as primarily a religious view, held essentially by one religious group. Its logical corollary was that in a pluralistic society no sectarian religious view had any right to be encoded on the law books of the land. The fact that the original anti-abortion laws in America were passed as a result of A.M.A. urging and encoded by essentially Protestant legislatures was deviously obscured.

"A human being begins his existence when a spermatozoan fertilizes an egg cell."

Against this background, a review of some of the evidence on the beginning of human life is in order. Unless we are to burn the books in our medical libraries, and turn our backs on biologically and genetically knowable facts, such a review may serve to strengthen the resolve of those in Medicine and its allied arts to be only life serving and never life destroying.

Individual Right to Life

Long before it became medically chic to ask the question, "When *Does* a Human Life Begin?", the late Dr. Alan Guttmacher, who subsequently became an ardent proponent of abortion, authored a book. In that book, dedicated to his mother and titled, *Pregnancy and Birth, a Book for Expectant Parents,* Dr. Guttmacher wrote: "A facet that makes the obstetrician's burden unique in the whole field of medicine is his double obligation; he simultaneously cares for two patients, the mother and infant; each has an individual right to life."

Of life's beginning, Dr. Guttmacher wrote: "The essential step in the initiation of a new life is fertilization, the penetration of the ovum by a spermatozoan and the fusion of the two cells into a single cell." Dr. Guttmacher fully knew when an individual human life began. Indeed, he concludes his book: "If these pages have instructed, advised or encouraged, the author is well rewarded. To your baby not yet born, he wishes a triumphant entrance into the universe."

Now was this view of the beginning of human life an aberration peculiar to Dr. Guttmacher? Let us examine a portion of the evidence in medical libraries.

T. Dobzhansky in his book, *Evolution, Genetics & Man,* Wiley, 1961, wrote: "A human being begins his existence when a spermatozoan fertilizes an egg cell."

Salvatore Luria in *36 Lectures in Biology,* MIT Press, 1975, writes: "A fertilized egg generates a baby in nine months, an adult in 15 years."

L.B. Arey in *Developmental Anatomy,* Saunders, 1974, writes: "The formation, maturation and meeting of a male and female sex cell are all preliminary to their actual union into a combined cell, or zygote, which definitely marks the beginning of a new individual."

B.M. Patten in the widely studied textbook, *Human Embryology,* 3rd Ed., McGraw-Hill, 1968, writes: "It is the penetration of the ovum by a spermatozoan and the resultant mingling of the nuclear material each brings to the union that constitutes the culmination of the process of fertilization and marks the initiation of the life of a new individual."

If you have been reading about the hearings on the Human Life Bill before the Sub-Committee on the Separation of Powers in the U.S. Senate in Washington, you will know that the prestigious National Academy of Sciences states: "The proposal that the term person shall include all human life has no basis in our scientific understanding."

Dr. Leon E. Rosenberg from Yale, where the motto bears the legend *Lux et Veritas,* offered the U.S. Senate this illumination. "I know of no scientific evidence which bears on the question of when actual human life exists." He then states: "The notion embodied in the phrase 'actual human life' is not a scientific one, but rather a philosophic and religious one."

As a graduate of Yale's Medical School, and long ago an intern in its hospital in surgery, gynecology, and obstetrics, I wrote to the Dean and President Giammatti at Yale, and told them that in my four years in their institution no one had ever taught that in human pregnancy the conceptus was not both alive and human. President Giammatti replied to me on August 26, 1981. "In his testimony at the Senate hearings, he, (Rosenberg), was not purporting to be presenting the Yale University point of view on this or any other matter.''

Dr. George M. Ryan, Jr., current head of the American College of Obstetricians and Gynecologists, also denies the findings of biology and his chosen specialty, and the painfully acquired insights of human knowledge, accumulated over the centuries. ''The issue of when life begins,'' said Ryan, ''is not a question that can be answered strictly scientifically.'' Now, what is a medical student to think of Ryan's bald statement as he reads the following in A. Sheinfeld, *Heredity in Humans*, Lippincott, 1972. ''Heredity is what makes us what we are as members of a particular species—in our case, human beings. When a woman is pregnant, we know definitely that she is not going to give birth to a little elephant, kangaroo, mouse or bird, but to a human baby.'' ''The conception of a new baby takes place the instant a sperm from the father enters and fertilizes the egg waiting in the mother.''

Or yet again, Keith Moore's book, *The Developing Human*, Saunders, 1974. ''Development is a continuous process that begins when an ovum is fertilized by a sperm and ends at death. It is a process of change and growth which transforms the zygote, a single cell, into a multicellular adult human being.'' ''Zygote—this cell results from fertilization of an ovum by a sperm and is the beginning of a human being.''

Youngest Human Ever Photographed

Hundreds of thousands of Massachusetts children have travelled to the Science Museum in Boston to view the human life exhibit there. Funded by the Hood Foundation, it has taught the known facts of human development before birth. In the exhibit is a picture of the two cell human enbryo from the Carnegie Institute of Embryology in Washington. It bears the legend, ''This remarkable photograph taken by Doctors Hertig and Rock of Boston, shows the two cell human embryo, the youngest human ever photographed.'' Do we now tell those children, ''Sorry, you were being deceived.'' Do we burn the books in the medical libraries at Yale, Harvard, Columbia and assorted way stations?

The American College of Obstetricians and Gynecologists, which in 1981 doesn't know when human life begins, in cooperation with *Redbook* Magazine, published a book, *The Expectant Mother* (Pocket Books, Simon and Schuster, 1969). Twenty-three distinguished professors of obstetrics and members of the college are contributors to this widely circulated volume. They constantly use the terms embryo, fetus, infant and unborn child interchangeably. In the appendix, they give definitions of terms. While they fail to define baby, they do define embryo. It is ''the unborn baby during the first three months gestation. After three months, it is called fetus.''

Let me cite two or three quotations from that book.

Dr. Emmanuel Freedman, Chairman of the Department of Obstetrics and Gynecology, Michael Reese Hospital and Chicago Medical School. ''Everyone knows that a mother's abdomen enlarges as her unborn baby grows. But a surprising number of women are unfamiliar with the uterus—the remarkable organ inside the abdomen that contains the baby during its nine months of life before birth.''

The First Six Days

Virginia Apgar, M.D., celebrated for the Apgar scores, writes: ''The nourishing of a baby begins almost at the instant of union between the egg of the mother and the sperm of the father. During the first week of life, or to be precise, the first six days, the food for the newly forming infant comes from the egg itself.

''I suggest that. . .'experts' currently denying the humanity and individuality of the human unborn are allowing their personal bias for abortion to obscure and obfuscate the scientific fact that abortion is the taking of a human life.''

Incidentally, Dr. Lee Buxton, Professor of Obstetrics at Yale, opens his chapter, ''The Unborn Baby's Movements,'' with the following. ''One of the great thrills of a woman's pregnancy occurs when she first feels her unborn baby move within her body.'' He further writes that occasionally ''as early as 10 weeks after conception, a mother feels the fluttering of her tiny baby's limbs.''

It is perfectly obvious that in Dr. Buxton's chapter in this book, and in Dr. Rosenberg of Yale's statement to the Sub-Committee on the Separation of Powers, they are both talking about the same entity. It is likewise obvious that one of them is wrong. I suggest that Dr. Rosenberg and other ''experts'' currently denying the humanity and individuality of the human unborn are allowing their personal bias for abortion to obscure and obfuscate the scientific fact that abortion is the taking of a human life. Is it too much to demand that a national policy implemented by doctors over 1.2 million times a year should be based on honesty, not falsehood and dissembling?

In present abortion practice, totalling an officially recorded 1,157,776 cases in 1978, 74% of those abortions were carried out on women who were single or unmarried at the time of the procedure. 48% of that, over 1,000,000 abortions, were carried out after the eighth week of pregnancy.

Now at the end of the eighth week of human

development all the organ systems of a human being have already differentiated. Dr. Guttmacher describes that stage of development as follows: "Face completely formed, arms, legs, hands and feet partially formed, stubby toes and fingers. From this time on looks very much like a miniature infant. Its length is one and one-fifth inches long."

The fetus, at this stage of development, possesses a brain giving off brain waves. Indeed, E.E.G.'s have been recorded at least as early as 43 days. Describing work by Japanese scientists, Dr. Hamlin from the Massachusetts General Hospital reported in the *Journal of the American Medical Association* in 1964: "Thus at an early prenatal stage of life the EEG reflects a distinctly individual pattern that soon becomes truly personalized." The heartbeat is also there. Indeed, the first beats in the circulatory system occur at 21 days. Together with Dr. O'Connell of Boston in 1974, I recorded, by ultrasound, the human heartbeat at 10 weeks after conception, and I understand it can now be done easily as early as eight weeks.

The Human Heartbeat

We use the absence of brain waves as a sign that human life has ended, so also the human heartbeat. Why has there been such reluctance by so many to recognize the early presence of brain waves and EKG as signifying indeed and in fact an individual human life's presence? Dr. Arnold Gesell of Yale in his book *The Embryology of Behavior,* 1947, Harper & Row, writes: "And so by the close of the first trimester the fetus is a sentient moving being. We need not speculate as to his psychic attributes, but we may assert that the organization of his psychosomatic self is well under way."

So much for the humanity of the unborn child. Let us now consider two problems that I believe demand a response from every medical student and physician and everyone who cares or should care about human life.

"America is capable of less pragmatic and expedient solutions than abortion."

The U.S. Supreme Court in the abortion decisions arbitrarily divided human pregnancy into three trimesters of three months each, and said:

"(a) For the stage prior to approximately the end of the first trimester, the abortion decision and its effectuation must be left to the medical judgment of the pregnant woman's attending physician.

(b) For the stage subsequent to approximately the end of the first trimester, the State, in promoting its interest in the health of the mother, may, if it chooses, regulate the abortion procedure in ways that are reasonably related to maternal health.

(c) For the stage subsequent to viability the State, in promoting its interest in the potentiality of human life, may, if it chooses, regulate, and even proscribe, abortion except where it is necessary, in appropriate medical judgment, for the preservation of the life or health of the mother."

The Court said: "The State may, if it chooses, regulate and even proscribe abortion except...." It made it optional whether the State would protect life when an admittedly viable human being exists. The Supreme Court fudged the issue of viability which it said occurred somewhere between 24-28 weeks.

Specifically, Justice Blackmun wrote: "Viability is placed at about seven months (28 weeks), but may occur earlier even at 24 weeks." Yet today we can save younger and younger premature babies.

Margin of Viability

Dr. Stubblefield has written: "The margin between viability and non-viability is a dynamic one and has been shifted downward by scientific progress in neonatology." *(Archives of Surgery* Vol. 110, pg. 790, July 1975) He also has written that "the obstetrician cannot accurately predict fetal weight in utero. He can attain the date of the last menses from the patient, but this datum has in the past been misleading." Doctors make what is a guesstimate of the duration of the pregnancy, and that guesstimate can be off by two or three weeks. This has inevitably led to the abortion of viable babies.

What I report to you is America's dirty little secret. Dr. Willard Cates, Head of the Abortion Surveillance Center at the U.S. Center for Disease Control, estimates that between four to five hundred live births occur in abortions each year. That's more than one every day. It happens in every major city, many of these born premature infants are simply allowed to die by neglect. In Florida, in Chicago, Illinois, in Phoenix, Arizona, and in Wilmington, Delaware, there are documented instances of untreated aborted babies who have survived.

Damaged Infants

You become a citizen of this land by birth or by naturalization. What is to be society's answer to those born and living, and some of them badly damaged, infants? Often, they are just left untreated to die. That, not infrequently, causes emotional problems for the nursing personnel involved, and the serious suggestion has been made that what the nurses and attendants really need is therapy sessions to ventilate and integrate all this into their healing mission. None of the official organizations of medicine or law have expressed concern over this problem. Yet, were a similar situation occurring with baby seals or puppy dogs, I suggest to you the public outcry would be instantaneous and massive. I raise the question, is an unwanted living human infant of lesser account than whales, seals, or puppy dogs? If it is of lesser account, what does it say about American society and about each of us?

Finally, abortion is leading to a cheapening of respect for born human life—particularly if born with a defect.

In this International Year of the Disabled, I point out that we have spent literally billions of dollars in accordance with public law to guarantee equality of access and educational opportunity to the disabled. Formerly, disabled children at birth called out immensely dedicated effort to support and sustain and improve their lives. Now, non-treatment, sedation and starvation unto death are seriously proposed as treatment, both here and in Great Britain. (*Lancet*, November 24, 1979, pgs. 1123-24)

"Medical students and physicians today do have a clear choice either to defend and serve all human life. . .or. . .to become accomplices in [its] betrayal and destruction."

Joseph Fletcher writes: "The question of whether infanticide is ever justifiable, and if so when, can be approached more appreciatively if we begin by locating infanticide on the total map of induced death," and "we have already suggested that there is no ethical difference between active and passive ways of inducing death." In support of "Infanticide the induced death of infants," Fletcher writes, "it is reasonable to describe infanticide as post-natal abortion." (Fletcher, J., pgs. 13-17, M. Kolb, *Infanticide and the Value of Life*, Prometheus Press 1978).

Judith Blake, the demographer, wrote in 1971 (*Science* Vol. 171, pgs. 540-548) that liberalization of the abortion laws would not come about through a popular demand because the demand was not there. "A Supreme Court ruling," she wrote, "concerning the constitutionality of existing state restrictions is the only road to rapid change in the grounds for abortion."

The Supreme Court of the United States obliged with the fateful Roe and Doe decisions of 1/22/73, in what Mr. Justice White in his dissent characterized as "an exercise of raw judicial power."

10,000,000 Abortions

Since that date, some 10,000,000 abortions now stain our national honor as we exercise what John D. Rockefeller III in 1966 was the first to term, "Freedom of Choice." "Freedom of Choice" means Freedom for Feticide, the elimination of the "unwanted unborn." It has not been a blessing to this land. It has cheapened respect for human life before as well as after birth. Its erosive evil has compromised the ideals and practice of the elites in law and medicine to the detriment of both professions. It has stirred the impulse for public toleration of the infanticide of born children, who have Trisomy 21 or Mongolism, or the condition known as meningomyelocele.

It has not decreased by one iota the problem of teenage pregnancy or venereal disease. Indeed, induced abortion is a procedure of whose long term consequences Dr. Stubblefield has written, "There is little information as to the effect of curettage procedures performed in the mid-trimester upon later pregnancy."

For so large a population of teenage young women to have been exposed to a procedure which may directly affect their subsequent reproductive health without a sure knowledge of the possible adverse consequences is crassly violative of sound medical practice.

Surely, America is capable of less pragmatic and expedient solutions than abortion. Millions of Americans share this view, and paraphrase and make their own words spoken by another American on another great moral issue almost a century and a quarter ago. "We are in earnest; we will not retreat; we will not equivocate; we will not yield a single inch in the defense of innocent life, born or unborn; we will be heard!" We are the pro-life movement in America.

Medical students and physicians today do have a clear choice either to defend and serve all human life, born and unborn, or, by silence and collaboration, to become accomplices in the betrayal and destruction of human life. The Hippocratic tradition needs worthy followers that it be passed undiminished to succeeding generations. That choice, and how *you* respond to it, is perhaps the most crucial challenge you face.

Joseph R. Stanton is a medical doctor and a member of the Human Life Foundation, a pro-life organization.

"Humans without some minimum of intelligence or mental capacity are not persons, no matter how many of their organs are active, no matter how spontaneous their living processes are."

A Fetus Is Not Entitled to Human Rights

Joseph Fletcher

Seeing how the humanhood and abortion issues surface everywhere in biomedical ethics, I want to take a more sharply focused look at both questions.

For some of us "human nature" is fixed, a given entity; for others, the human organism and psyche are malleable and adaptable. T.E. Hulme said, "Man is an extraordinarily fixed and limited animal whose nature is absolutely constant." To the contrary, Ashley Montagu explains that babies are not born with a human nature, only with more or less capability of *becoming* human. In the same vein the Spanish philosopher Ortega y Gasset concluded that people have no nature; they have only their histories.

Actually, we have to ask whether it is human life we put first or *personal* life? If it is personal human life, then our first-order concern is with certain qualities and capacities, not just human life as such. In short, may we use 'a human life' and 'a person' interchangeably? The philosopher Henry David Aiken calls it "fetishism" to believe that a fetus is already a person. But is he justified in saying so? This question is of the greatest practical importance in making decisions about such matters as the terminally ill and when to let the patient go, in dealing with irreversible coma, and whether we ought to "save" what are called monsters at birth. When we quote the Socratic maxim Know thyself, what *is* the self, the person? Not to know what we mean by these key terms is simply to flounder around when we talk about moral decisions.

Abortion provides a test. Ethically the core issue is whether an embryo or fetus is a human being, and if so, in what sense we call it that. How we assess the morality of abortion follows from how we answer this question.

For example, a Catholic lawyer says flatly, "One person's freedom to obtain an abortion is the denial of another person's right to live." He believes that a fetus is a person or has a person's rights. There is no argument, of course, about a human fetus being of the species *Homo sapiens*; it is easily recognizable biologically. Nor is there any question of its being alive. Cell division is proceeding. But what about claims of personhood or humanhood for a fetus? If every human fetal organism is a person, and if we think it is immoral to end such forms of human life unnecessarily—at least when self-defense or the common security is not at stake—we will logically look upon abortion at will as immoral. If, on the other hand, we do not regard uterine life as human in the sense of a personal being, we will not believe its termination is "murder"—that is, we won't see it as taking the life of an innocent person. The nonpersonal view of fetuses fits in with the morality of elective abortion or abortion on request, as well as with therapeutic abortion for medical reasons.

The ethical issue is dramatized in a truly tragic situation in a Nazi concentration camp. A Romanian woman doctor secretly aborted three thousand Jewish women in the camp because if the medical report showed them to be pregnant, they would be incinerated—sent to the ovens. If we believe that a fetus is a person, it would follow that the doctor, by killing three thousand human beings, saved three thousand others and prevented the murder by the Nazis of all six thousand. On the nonpersonal basis we would say only and quite calmly that three thousand persons were rescued from a terrible death. (The United States Congress agreed with the latter interpretation. The doctor was admitted to residence and citizenship in America as a war hero.)

The most basic issue is whether a fetus is a person or not. This in turn poses the question, What's the *essence* of a person? Along with it goes the related question, When does this essential element emerge, whatever it is? The question of what a person is

Chapter 10 of *Humanhood* by Joseph Fletcher. Buffalo, NY: Prometheus Books, 1979. Copyright © 1979. Reprinted with permission.

hinges on whatever is held to be the essence. There would be room for some variety of opinions on additional factors, the other things which make for the fullness or optimum of a person. The decisive problem is to identify the essential thing, the *sine qua non,* that without which there is no person. And to find this key is to get pretty close to answering the question about "when" a person is.

"The most sensible opinion is Plato's, that a fetus becomes a person at birth— after it is expelled or drawn from the womb, its umbilical cord is cut, and its lungs start to work."

What are the factors or components which people have suggested is the essential one? There are three of them, basically. Some argue that life is the essential element in a person's being; whenever and as long as we are alive, as long as life is present, they say, a human organism is a person. This would mean that a person exists at fertilization, when growth gets started, and continues to exist through the whole complex biological continuum. Indeed, *before* fertilization oöcytes and sperm are "alive." Death is not complete until the cessation not only of bodily functions but even of cell activity. This opinion identifies the person with life, making the two coexistent or even one and the same. It is the doctrine behind recent agitation to prohibit tests and research with live abortuses, even though there is no possibility of the fetus surviving and even though the knowledge to be gained by obstetricians and pediatricians could save the lives or health of many children yet to be born. It is a radical and sad consequence of an absolute sanctity-of-life ethic.

The Soul Makes the Person

A second notion is that, not life, but the soul makes a person. In this camp we find two different ideas about the soul's entrance into the living tissue. While they both agree that it enters somehow before the birth of the individual, some guess or believe that the soul or *animus* enters after conception, probably in the second trimester ("delayed animation") and others guess it enters with fertilization ("immediate animation")—thus coinciding, in the latter case, with the *life* theory. An obvious absurdity of this latter doctrine is that it means the soul or person of identical twins has been split in two, since after fertilization they separated from a common cell mass or single fertilized ovum. Triplets, quadruplets, and so on, add to the absurdity of the ensoulment-at-fertilization doctrine. Aristotle, Augustine, and Aquinas held to the late ensoulment theory and

therefore justified abortion, at least in the first trimester; Tertullian, the great heretic, declared for the fertilization idea, and his opinion finally became the official Catholic teaching in 1869, when abortion was condemned at any stage. (The papacy has never actually said when the soul is infused; rather, it has decreed that people must play it safe by acting *as if* the soul were infused at fertilization.)

The third opinion is that the essence of a person is reason, the rational function, the *ratio.* In this view everything depends on the mental capability of the individual. This is not to say that reason is everything; feeling is an important part of mental function, too. But without intelligence the feeling alone is subhuman. The cerebral has to undergird the visceral. Before cerebration comes into play, or when it is ended, in the absence of the synthesizing or *thinking* function of the cerebral cortex, the person is nonexistent; or, put another way, the life which is functioning biologically is a nonperson. This nonpersonal condition can be seen both in the protoplasm at the start of life and in the "human vegetable" which is sometimes all that remains at the end.

The Definition of a Human

Humans without some minimum of intelligence or mental capacity are not persons, no matter how many of their organs are active, no matter how spontaneous their living processes are. If the cerebrum is gone, due to disease or accident, and only the mid-brain or brainstem is keeping autonomic functions going, they are only objects, not subjects—they are *its,* not *thous.* Just because heart, lungs, and the neurologic and vascular systems persist, we cannot say a *person* exists. Noncerebral organisms are not personal.

The Harvard Medical School's *ad hoc* committee accepted the "brain death" definition, but it is too undiscriminating. So is the Kansas statute modeled on it, and the recent (1972) ruling of the Italian Council of Ministers. It is not the death of the *brain* that counts. What is definitive is the absence of cerebration or "mind" even though other brain functions continue. A human vegetable is not a person, not truly a human being. It goes without saying, of course, that the loss of the cerebral function must be determined to be irreversible.

According to this third view, perhaps something like a score of twenty on the Binet scale of I.Q. would be roughly but realistically a minimum or base line for personal status. Obviously a fetus cannot meet this test, no matter what its stage of growth.

Nor can a fetus have any of the other traits that make for the full *humanum* or personal quality, such as curiosity, affection, self-awareness and self-control, memory, purpose, conscience—none of the distinctive transbiological indicators of personality. The fetus-is-a-person doctrine is of necessity the most argumentative one because it has to defend an arbitrary assertion. The nonpersonal view is under no such strain. It asserts nothing not in evidence, and therefore it really does not have to be defended or make a case for itself.

The Potential Vs. the Actual

Antiabortion agitators often say, "Well, anyway, there is a *potential* in the fetus for all of these things that make up a person; for example, the morphon or rudimentary physical basis of mind is present by the eighth month." This is tantamount to admitting that a fetus is in fact *not* a person. And to argue (which is what this is—*arguing*) that the potential is the actual is like saying that an acorn is an oak or a promise is its fulfillment or a blueprint is a house. The "as if" argument is a prolepsis which tries to wipe out the vital difference between what is and what could be. Thomas Aquinas was at least right to distinguish between human life *in potentia* and *in sit* (actual) and to assign personal status only to the latter, after several months' gestation.

The plain inescapable fact, as a chemist might say, is that we have no litmus paper test for the presence of a person. Jean Rostand, the French biologist, puts it this way: "It must be said that these differing opinions are held by people who are equally sincere, have the same level of morality, and sometimes even profess comparable philosophical doctrines." Any attempt to impose a single "doctrine" on those who do not share it is ethically intolerable. We are driven to admit that, if anybody wants to believe a fetus is a person at conception or whenever it is "ensouled," he is entitled to. It is a kind of mental Mexican stand-off.

The only possible moral test of these rival views lies in their consequences. When beliefs or nonempirical opinions, neither of them being falsifiable, contradict or clash with each other, the only possible way to choose between them morally is in terms of their consequences if they are followed out logically in practice. The one which results in greater good for people is the correct one. On this basis there is an open and shut case for abortion, obvious and overwhelming; it can be justified very often, sometimes for reasons of human health, sometimes for reasons of human happiness.

Furthermore, the question of *when* the person comes into existence, the timing, has never found any general agreement or any convincing evidence favoring one opinion over others. In the past people have argued variously that this event or "moment" is at (1) fertilization, (2) the blastocyst or implantation stage, (3) the first heartbeat, (4) the phenomenon of "kicking" or "quickening," (5) viability—when the fetus might maintain its life outside the womb (sometime in the third trimester), and finally (6) birth. Here, too, we have no litmus paper test, no diagnostic criteria. When the Grand Mufti of Jerusalem says the "moment" is the 120th day of pregnancy, like the theologians who used to say it was forty days in the case of males and eighty days for females, we can only try to keep a straight face.

A Person at Birth

The most sensible opinion is Plato's, that a fetus becomes a person at birth—after it is expelled or drawn from the womb, its umbilical cord is cut, and its lungs start to work. This has been the opinion held down through the centuries in the common law tradition. It was not until the nineteenth century that abortion was for the first time made a crime—although, be it noted, only against the state because of the supposed loss of a much needed citizen, soldier, or worker. Crowded subways and expressways, growing lists of hard-core unemployment in the midst of highly productive industrial and agricultural machinery—these things make the "public interest" of a century ago archaic.

Later on, some groups began to claim that abortion is a crime against the *fetus* as well as against the state, with the result in America that new laws began to prohibit termination of pregnancy for any reason other than to save the woman's life or, in a few states, her health. In spite of these new statutes, however, no prosecutor has ever returned an indictment for murder in any abortion case before the courts. In cases of miscarriage no birth certificates are made out, and abortions of such fetal tissue are not entered into the vital statistics. Pregnant women traveling abroad have not been required to carry two passports, one for themselves and one for the fetus. Miscarried embryos at a primitive stage are not baptized.

"If we adopt the sensible view that a fetus is not a person, there is only one reasonable policy and that is to put an end to compulsory pregnancy."

On and on we could go, pointing out similar lapses or discrepancies between what people preach and what they practice. In 1972, before the Supreme Court's decision in January 1973, spokesmen for the Right to Life Movement carried around a fairly fully formed human organism, superficially, and displayed it for the shock effects ("homunculus reaction") on uncritical and impressionable people in audiences. When they were asked if the fetus had been baptized or entered into the birth statistics, christened with a name, and "Why hasn't this child, as you call it, been buried with respect"—their replies were only mumbles, not even clear words.

For some time legislators and courts have been revamping those Victorian laws in a return to the main tradition, to the view that a fetus is not a person or what American lawyers call a "Fourteenth

Amendment person." The chief reason for the postnatal definition of a person in the law is that any other doctrine is necessarily only a matter of private faith or belief, and it is morally unjust to impose private beliefs upon others who do not share them. To do so violates the First Amendment of the Constitution which guarantees religious freedom and freedom of thought.

Abortion — A Historic Position

The United States Supreme Court on January 22, 1973, declared that it is unconstitutional for any state to forbid abortion in the first trimester, which only reaffirms the historic position of Western civilization. The question *when* a pregnancy should be terminated for health reasons is a medical one, the Court explained, and not a proper government function.

> *"To condemn. . . both the termination and the* prevention *of unwanted pregnancies. . . is an antisexual and inhumane morality."*

This decision knocked down restrictive statutes in forty-six of the fifty states of the Union. It means that freedom of abortion may not be regulated in the first six or seven months—but after the first six months the state would be *allowed* but not *required* to limit abortions. The Court rejected any assignment of *personal* status to the fetus at any stage, and allowed only that a government might find a public interest in *potential* human life, and even then not until the fetus has become capable of survival independent of the maternal body. It has no rights.

In any case, in the last analysis it remains the patient's choice, on the principle of consent, as in any other medical or surgical treatment. This freedom of choice coerces no physician into doing an abortion nor any patient into having one. The Court did not enter into the ethical-moral question, it is true; yet by finding for the nonpersonal view of fetal life, it put the focus where it really belongs, and more profoundly affected the moral issue than any court judgment for hundreds of years.

Choice of Four Positions

Only if we can decide where we stand on these issues can we decide where we stand on the morality of terminating pregnancies. In practical policy terms, there are four positions to choose among, and our choice will depend on what we decide about the status and quality of the fetus. (1) We can condemn abortion altogether, or at most only justify it to save the pregnant woman's life. (2) We can favor a limited permissiveness to prevent ill health, to prevent defective babies, or to prevent the product of rape or incest. This is a policy of compulsory pregnancy but with escape clauses. (3) We can approve of abortion for any reason prior to the ability to survive outside the womb—possibly on the grounds of social needs or some question of justice, although these grounds are not so apparent as they were when we lacked enough labor power and needed lots of soldiers. (4) We can oppose any and all forms of compulsory pregnancy, making the ending of pregnancies, like their beginning, a private or personal matter.

If we adopt the sensible view that a fetus is not a person, there is only one reasonable policy, and that is to put an end to compulsory pregnancy. The ethical principle is that pregnancy when wanted is a healthy process, *pregnancy when not wanted is a disease*—in fact, a venereal disease. The truly ethical question is not whether we can justify abortion, but whether we can justify compulsory pregnancy. If our ethics is of the humane brand we will agree that we cannot justify it, and would not want to.

Many sensitive people who support abortion in principle nevertheless see it as a sad, even tragic, action. In this view abortion is a reason for regret, but not for remorse or moral guilt. To deplore abortion is *a fortiori* a strong reason to advocate contraception. To condemn both—both the termination and the *prevention* of unwanted pregnancies—is an antisexual and inhumane morality. (This is what the official Catholic teaching does, except that it allows "natural" birth control by "rhythm," which helps to understand the grass roots revolt of Catholics who defy their church's ban on contraceptives and sterilizations.)

Joseph Fletcher is emeritus professor of social ethics and moral theology at the Episcopal Theological School and visiting professor of biomedical ethics at the School of Medicine, University of Virginia. He is a humanist and the author of many books on ethics including Moral Responsibility, Morals and Medicine, *and* The Ethics of Genetic Control.

"What is beyond debate . . . is the need for a human life amendment. It is the only way to provide legal protection for the life . . . of the unborn."

Abortion Is a Legal Issue

Charles DeCelles

It is estimated that 1.5 million abortions are performed yearly in the United States. For every 70 babies allowed to live, 30 fetuses lose their lives through a systematic medical attack on the physical integrity of their person. What do American Catholics do in the face of such information, which they would be hard pressed to interpret in any other way than that of a continuous holocaust? They can assist pregnant women to carry their unborn children to term. They can try to educate the public regarding the sanctity of human life. But is that all that they can do? Should they not also fight for a human life amendment and, ultimately, for legislation that would prohibit the destruction of fetuses?

Few Catholic liberals, if any, deny their conservative co-religionists the right to attempt the passage of a constitutional amendment on behalf of the unborn. But, more than likely, they do not themselves positively favor antiabortion legislation. A small but vocal minority actually oppose an amendment. Most liberals stand aloof from the legal battle. They lend their brethren no support. The result is an amendment stalemate.

I am of the opinion that the time is ripe for liberals and conservatives to initiate a concerted prolife push. My appeal in this essay is mainly to Catholic, intellectual, mainstream liberals. I would have them rethink their position on the amendment issue. If they find they can support at least a modified amendment, they should assist the prolifers to clarify their own antiabortion views and to formulate an amendment that would stand a realistic chance of public acceptance. I also appeal to conservatives to enter into dialogue with liberals so that they might expand their horizons on the abortion issue, and to cooperate with them in the forming of a conservative-liberal ecumenical coalition on behalf of the unborn. Men and women of compassion and concern, after enlightening dialogue, must labor together for the accomplishment of good.

Ecumenical Coalition Needed

There is simply no way that a human life amendment can become a reality unless it is supported by an ecumenical coalition, with both liberal and conservative backing. The main reason for this is that a constitutional amendment requires for passage a two-thirds majority from both Houses of Congress. It also needs ratification by three quarters of the states. A human life bill has been proposed which, among other things, would assert that human life begins at conception. Such a bill could perhaps succeed without much support from liberal groups, since it would require to become law only a simple majority in Congress. If passed, however, it would enjoy a precarious existence, because it could at any time be toppled by the Supreme Court. A constitutional amendment, by contrast, as part of the U.S. Constitution, would stand above the Supreme Court whose sole task it is to "interpret" the Constitution. A simple law cannot, therefore, be regarded as the human life ideal. The ultimate goal must be a constitutional amendment followed, if necessary, by prolife legislation. Catholics campaigning alone for such an amendment hardly have a prayer. Catholic conservatives by themselves, forget it. Bread for the World recently succeeded in pushing through Congress a bill to establish a giant grain reserve to be tapped in the event of international famine. It succeeded because it enjoys a diversified membership and because it joined forces with American farmers. Coalitions work and the wider the better.

The wisdom of uniting behind a prolife amendment as well as behind prolife legislation revolves around the question of the humanity of the embryo-fetus. Scientific evidence supports the notion that human life begins early in pregnancy, if not from conception itself. Eleven weeks after the ovum is fertilized every organ system of the body is operative. From that point on, they but grow and mature. At only 10 weeks the human body is completely formed. With the use of an ultrasonic stethoscope, the heartbeat of an unborn baby eight weeks from conception can be heard. It actually starts beating at less than four weeks. The blood it pumps is different from that of its mother. The brain of an embryo six weeks old emits waves that can be measured on an electroencephalogram. From the moment of fertilization, the zygote—a cell distinct from either parent—contains the complete genetic blueprint of a fully developed human being. The only ingredients lacking for the perfection of maturity are time and nutrition.

When Life Begins

Of course, medical arguments have emerged contradicting the position that human life begins with conception or even early in pregnancy. For instance, it is pointed out that until about the 14th day, individuality has not been achieved. The conceptus can yet divide to form identical twins. Again, up to the fifth month, the surface of the fetus's brain is structurally akin to that of lower animals.

Because science in dialogue with other disciplines, such as philosophy is uncertain precisely when the human life begins, prolifers maintain that the embryo-fetus should be treated as though it were human from the first moment when it might reasonably be regarded as human, namely, fertilization. In this they reflect traditional Catholic teaching. They, therefore, tend to eye every abortion as murder, since the willingness to kill what might be a human being embodies the disposition of a murderer.

The prolifers quite logically favor the legal prohibition of abortion. Recently their position has been bolstered by the views of a former abortionist, Bernard N. Nathanson, M.D. Dr. Nathanson is a well-known obstetrician and gynecologist. Co-founder of the National Association for Repeal of Abortion Laws (now the National Abortion Rights Action League), Dr. Nathanson was at one time the most prominent physician engaged in the struggle to repeal abortion laws. For a year and a half he headed the Center for Reproductive and Sexual Health, the busiest and largest abortion clinic in the world. In 1974, he admitted to having presided over 60,000 deaths. After years of soul-searching, he wrote a book entitled *Aborting America,* published in 1979 (from which incidentally we have gleaned many of the ideas presented in this essay), in which he states: "The obvious scientific conclusion is that alpha (author's terms for human-embryo-fetus) is demonstrably an independent human entity (life). The obvious moral conclusion is that alpha's destruction cannot be

justified unless, on clear medical grounds, the mother's life is at stake. A life is a sound humanistic basis on which to sanction the intentional destruction of human life; nothing else is....

"What if the biological findings are not as conclusive as they appear to me? In Western medical ethics and cultural tradition, one of the cornerstones is that if you are unsure whether life is present, you give it the benefit of the doubt. Civilized societies cannot afford to destroy even what might be a human life, except under unusual circumstances.... A judge's charge to a jury asks only that its conclusion be 'beyond a reasonable doubt' not a 'virtual certainty'. To me, we have virtual certainty in the matter of alpha, but certainly we are beyond reasonable doubt."

"Evil consequences do not invalidate a good law, any more than good consequences justify an evil law."

A few years ago all 50 states could boast of laws to protect alpha. No more. In 1973, the U.S. Supreme Court made a clean sweep of all state laws banning abortion during the first two tri-mesters of pregnancy. Why? Because the unborn child is not a human being in the eyes of the law. A woman's right to "privacy" therefore takes precedence over the unborn's claim on life. The Court even determined that the states cannot uphold laws destined to protect the lives of viable fetuses, if the well-being of the mother is at stake. A woman can thus undergo an abortion during the ninth month of pregnancy, if she can convince her physician that the birth of her child would cause her undue distress and therefore endanger her health.

An Amendment for the Fetus

It is therefore the considered opinion of many lawyers that the only way to afford legal protection to the unborn is to amend the Constitution. A human life amendment would—or could, depending on its content—establish the unborn child as a human being in the eyes of the law and therefore guarantee him all the rights granted to persons by the Constitution of the United States and its amendments. The individual states would then be able to enact detailed laws regulating the practice of abortion, so as to protect the life and well-being of the unborn child, as well as those of the mother.

If a human life amendment should be supported, what kind? Many conservative Catholics have rallied behind the Helms-Dornan Human Life Amendment, which states: "The paramount right to life is vested in each human being from the moment of fertilization without regard to age, health or condition of dependency." The question of course is: Can an ecumenical coalition rally behind a formula that assumes that a human being exists at the moment of fertilization and that makes no specific allowance for a termination of pregnancy in the case of rape or to save the life (or the quality of life) of the mother? Maybe yes and maybe no. A lot could depend on how the amendment is read.

"Although, from one perspective, abortion laws restrict a woman's freedom, from another, they enhance it."

The Helms-Dornan Amendment, or one similar to it, which speaks about the right to life being vested in each person from fertilization onward, would clearly not outlaw the so-called indirect abortion where no harm at all is intended to the fetus but where the fetus is removed because it is in the middle of an urgently needed operation. Examples are a cancerous uterus and an ectopic pregnancy. An "abortion" in these cases is simply the by-product of a life saving surgical intervention. Such an amendment might require, however, that every reasonable effort be made to save the child's life, for instance, by transplanting him or her into a real or artificial womb, if that be medically feasible. The Catholic Church has traditionally recognized indirect abortion as morally acceptable though regrettable.

Nor can an amendment of the Helms-Dornan variety be construed as automatically prohibiting true, that is, direct abortions intended to save the mother's life or the quality of it, when that quality is tantamount to life itself. In this country mature human beings are defended with the full force of the Constitution, and yet self-defense killings are tolerated, as last resorts. The same Constitution would undoubtedly protect the mother against her unborn child, should that child become, from a medical perspective, a mortal aggressor. We should add, however, that with today's advances in medicine and surgical procedures and with the advent of new, improved psychiatric drugs, such a situation is more fantasy than reality.

Rape and Abortion

What about pregnancies resulting from rape? Would an amended Constitution tolerate the expulsion of the fetus in that kind of situation? Possibly. Suppose you suddenly found yourself artificially attached to a stranger whose life you had in no way committed yourself to protect. He had annexed himself to you because his kidneys had failed, and his only hope of survival lay in temporarily sharing yours. Would it be illegal for you to detach him and send him on his fateful way? I don't think so. So likewise, constitutional law would probably not compel a mother to retain within her womb an embryo-fetus that she was not responsible for, even if the Helms-Dornan Amendment were passed. The Christian ethics of love would dictate that she do so, but not the law.

These reflections notwithstanding, many liberals, both Catholic and non-Catholic, would still not support a Helms-Dornan type of amendment. While they generally maintain a qualified condemnation of abortion, they do not consider it wise to legislate against it. Their arguments have merit but can be reasonably rebutted.

The liberal Catholic is concerned about the negative consequences to the woman of antiabortion legislation. He reasons that if a woman is really bent upon obtaining an abortion, she will procure one whether it is legal or not. If abortion is illegal, however, she may have recourse to an incompetent and unscrupulous back-alley abortionist. As a result she may seriously endanger her life. This argument has a forceful ring to it, but is not without major flaws. When abortion was illegal throughout the country, perhaps one to two hundred thousand abortions were done annually. In 1973, the first year in which abortion on demand reigned in the United States, 615,831 abortions were performed. Seven years later 1,550,000 human fetuses lost their lives through a variety of abortion procedures. The illegal status of abortion dissuaded many women from having an abortion. Secondly, the number of deaths among women who underwent illegal abortions has been grossly and deliberately exaggerated by the pro-abortion camp. According to Dr. Nathanson, The National Association for Repeal of Abortion Laws in 1969 claimed that women were dying from illegal abortions at a rate of ten thousand annually. They knew, however, that the figure was roughly two hundred. Thirdly, evil consequences do not invalidate a good law, any more than good consequences justify an evil law. The fact that some women may be permanently injured or may even die as the result of illegal abortions, is not cause to legalize the destruction of fetal life. Thieves, muggers and bank robbers are killed daily when they circumvent the law. Yet no one would recommend legalizing thievery, mugging and bank robbing.

Enforcing Abortion Law

Many Catholic intellectuals oppose anti-abortion laws on the grounds that they cannot be enforced. It is of course true that abortion laws could never be perfectly enforced. But that is hardly a reason for not legislating against abortion. If it were, every law would have to be dissolved, because no law can be perfectly enforced. How enforceable are perjury laws or drug laws? Right now the nation is experiencing a cocaine epidemic which is taking the lives of prominent American citizens. Not many people are screaming for the legalization of drug trafficking.

Income tax laws are not about to be repealed, even though tax evasion is incomparably more widespread than illegal abortion used to be.

People who argue that abortion laws are unenforceable forget that pre-1973 anti-abortion legislation was generally adhered to. Many women who were inclined to abort abided by the law. Potential abortionists, too, were deterred. Laws are to some extent self-monitoring. The fact that they exist keeps numerous individuals from circumventing them. They exert moral and societal pressure, not to mention inspire some fear. Whatever the reason, there are children alive today who never would have seen sunlight, if it had not been for anti-abortion laws. When anti-abortion laws exist, women are also much more likely to take the precautions necessary to avoid unwanted pregnancies.

What is more, the laws of a country articulate the values for which that nation stands, regardless of whether they are enforceable or not. Our civil rights laws are something to be proud of. Along with the Constitution, they witness eloquently before the world the conviction of the American people that every individual human being has inestimable worth. So, too, would a prolife amendment coupled with anti-abortion legislation.

Question of Freedom

Another reason it is considered unwise to legislate against abortion is that abortion laws unnecessarily curtail the freedom of women, given the fact that no absolute certitude exists as to when human life begins. Admittedly, freedom of action constitutes a fundamental human right, one indispensable to a democratic society. But human freedom is not an absolute. Necessarily, there are limits imposed upon it, especially when probable, or at least possible, human life is at stake. Child abuse laws, laws requiring the registration of hand guns and laws prohibiting driving while under the influence of alcohol—which have become very strict in recent years—are certainly restrictive, yet they are welcomed by society. Like abortion laws they aim directly at the protection of human life.

Although, from one perspective, abortion laws restrict a woman's freedom, from another, they enhance it. Many women who choose to abort the child within their womb do so out of compulsion. They may be driven by uncontrolled emotions, or by pressures from their family or society. They obtain an abortion only to regret it the rest of their lives. If abortions were illegal, they might effectively be protected from acting in a way contrary to their fundamental makeup.

It is sometimes argued that anti-abortion legislation discriminates against poorer women. These do not enjoy the means to board a plane and fly to Europe to undergo their desired surgery, as affluent women do. Granted there is injustice here. Yet, the solution is

not to get by without abortion laws, but to uncover ways of enforcing such laws equitably and thoroughly. Some criminals, with sufficient funds, are able to elude the long arm of the law by permanently exiling themselves in countries with which the United States has no extradition agreement, and thereby go scot free. This is no reason for not prosecuting the remaining criminals caught within this country.

The Inequities of No Legislation

Actually the worst inequalities are found not with anti-abortion laws, but with their absence. In general hospitals today, physicians and nurses on one floor are expending enormous energy trying to salvage the life of one imperiled fetus, whereas on another floor the snuffing out of the life of an equally advanced fetus is taking place through meticulous surgical procedure. That's discrimination.

A major argument voiced by Catholic liberals against condemning abortion by law is that there is lacking a consensus for such condemnation. Americans do not agree as to when human life begins. They are not in accord that abortion should be outlawed, especially not from the onset of pregnancy. Hence, to pass a prolife amendment would be to impose upon the whole country the opinions of a minority.

"Another possibility is an amendment that would offer a graduated protection to the embryo-fetus.... Hence, the cause needed to justify a termination...at 20 weeks would be far greater than...at one week."

This argument is fraught with weaknesses. In the first place, while all Americans do not agree that a person comes into being with conception, more opt for this event as marking the initiation of human life than any other. Moreover, relatively few people favor abortion on demand. An April 1975 Gallup survey reveals that 50 percent of the American population hold that human life begins with conception. About 15 percent consider that it starts with quickening; less than 13 percent with viability; less than 15 percent with birth. A Gallup poll released Jan. 22, 1978, disclosed that, whereas 55 percent of all Americans favor legalizing abortion under certain circumstances, only 22 percent approve of abortion on demand. A 1982 poll conducted in Maine indicated that more than 75 percent of its residents favor making abortion illegal in all or nearly all circumstances. Only 1.5 percent approve of legal abortions during all nine months of pregnancy.

In the second place, it is false to assume that law cannot rightfully clash with substantial public opinion, especially when that opinion conflicts with the view of the world community. There are instances when law forms national opinion and anticipates public morality. This was true in the case of legislation condemning racial bigotry and dueling. As regards abortion, the major religions of the world condemn it as immoral. For the most part, Islam prohibits abortion as a serious evil. Hinduism has traditionally disallowed abortion, considering it one of three acts for which a woman may be condemned as an outcast. The other two are murder of husband and murder of a Brahman. Buddhism, which abhors the destruction of all life, prohibits it. Orthodox Judaism recognizes abortion to be a crime under the Noachidic Code, binding on all human beings. It tolerates it only to protect the life and health of the mother. World Christianity condemns abortion generally. *The Common Cathechism*, a comprehensive statement of the Christian faith, produced by an international team of 40 distinguished Protestant and Catholic theologians, states that: "The Christian churches have pronounced themselves unambiguously on this point." It quoted the Second Vatican Council as follows: "From the moment of conception life must be guarded with the greatest care, while abortion and infanticide are unspeakable crimes." It goes on to say: "Apart from those borderline cases in which a choice has to be made between the life of the mother and the life of the child ("medical grounds"), the Christian will find himself unable to agree to a termination of pregnancy in other circumstances. . . ."

Abortion Is Violence

Some Christian liberals who personally abhor abortion and see it as grievous sin do not think it should be outlawed, because it is not the function of society to legislate morality but to establish justice and maintain peace. They are absolutely right. No one should be tossed in jail for the commission of private sins. Homosexuality between consenting adults should ordinarily not be outlawed. People should be punished for crimes, that is, actions injuring or destroying society and its members. What these liberals forget, however, is that abortion is not a private sin. It is a deliberate act of violence against an unborn child. True peace does not coexist with destructive violence.

One unspoken argument of the Catholic intellectual against abortion legislation is that it represents a return to the past. Nothing could be further from the truth. The progressive unfolding of history coincides with growth in humankind's recognition of the essential dignity of the human person, and with general sensitivity in social ethics. In ancient Rome, the father of the family wielded absolute authority over his offspring. He could abort them in the womb or sell them into slavery. The church successfully combatted these injustices. It also fought against infanticide, child sacrifice, combat to the death in the arena and political torture. In pre-Islamic Arabia, female children, considered practically worthless, were often buried alive in the desert sands, if rations were short. The Qu'ran, however, condemned this barbaric practice: "Slay not your children, fearing a fall to poverty." In the United States, for well over a hundred years, Blacks were treated as subhumans. White masters could mutilate or kill them with impunity. The Supreme Court, in the Dred Scott decision of 1857, is believed by some to have declared them nonpersons. That state of affairs was altered, in part, by the passage of a constitutional amendment, when America's ethical sensitivity had become more refined. The passage of a human life amendment today would be indicative, on the part of this nation, of a still more refined social conscience.

> *"Some Christian liberals who personally abhor abortion. . .do not think it should be outlawed, because it is not the function of society to legislate morality."*

Can we conclude from all this rebutting that the ethically sensitive person should favor and even work toward the passage of a human life amendment that would protect the embryo-fetus from the moment of fertilization? Yes. And he should do so immediately, if it were realistic to hope for the passage of such an amendment. Unfortunately, it is not, not right at the moment. The Helms-Dornan type of Amendment would make the swallowing of the day-after pill and the use of intrauterine devices unconstitutional acts. How many American's could or would accept that? Perhaps the majority, eventually. But not right now. The ethically sensitive person would, therefore, do well to aim for compromise legislation. Compromise legislation is better than no legislation at all. James Doyle writes in *Pastoral Life* (June 1980): "In the effort to have legislation and public policy that contain what is possible and feasible, we may at times have to tolerate a situation more permissive of abortion than our moral principles would dictate."

The Progression of Cell Division

In a spirit of realistic compromise, therefore, perhaps an amendment could be proposed which would protect the embryo-fetus not from the moment of fertilization but from the 14th day. By this time, cellular differentiation has occurred: The cells of the conceptus, previously endowed with open-ended potentiality, have been programmed to develop into specific organs or parts of the body. The individuality of the conceptus is thus established. The phenomenon of twinning through cellular division can no longer take place. James Diamond, M.D., argues forcefully in a *Theological Studies* essay (1975), that the conceptus should not be viewed as human, that is, as an ensouled person, prior to the 14th day. In his opinion, animation probably occurs between the 14th and the 23rd day after fertilization. During this period, the embryo begins to draw nutrition from outside itself, by means of a placenta implanted in the mother's uterine wall. Previously, it lived off its own substance, thus cannibalizing itself. A cardio-circulatory system also emerges. In some future year, if and when public sentiment has shifted more substantially in favor of human life, a new amendment could be proposed which would protect life from conception.

Another possibility would be an amendment that would by-pass the whole issue of when human life begins but would set the stage for prolife legislation by asserting that the Constitution does not guarantee a woman the right to have an abortion. The Hatch-Eagleton Amendment voted on in the Senate in 1983 and defeated embodied this idea. Its precursor—The Hatch Amendment—had an additional clause that made it far better. Both Congress and the states would be given the power to legislate against abortion, with the national laws binding upon all Americans, except where state laws offered more protection to the unborn child.

> *"Perhaps an amendment could be proposed which would protect the embryo-fetus not from the moment of fertilization but from the 14th day."*

The type of amendment that an ecumenical coalition should work toward is negotiable—although it must be one that all parties can live with in conscience. The amendments offered here are just examples. What is beyond debate so far as an ultimate goal is concerned, it seems to me, is the need for a human life amendment. It is the only sure and permanent way to provide legal protection for the life and integrity of the unborn.

The Moral Imperative

Responding to this moral imperative does not absolve one from the obligation of treading other paths to save the lives of the unborn, paths which might produce tangible results immediately. On the other hand, volunteering one's services to Birthright or supporting Lifeline does not excuse a person for throwing in the towel on the pursuit of a prolife amendment, just because the cause looks hopeless. The Christian never despairs of justice triumphing.

The Birmingham campaign for integrated busing at times looked futile to Martin Luther King, but he persisted. He trusted in a Transcendent Force that guides history and works through men to establish justice. In *Stride Toward Freedom* he wrote: "Whatever the name, some extra-human force labors to create harmony out of the discords of the universe. There is a creative power that works to pull down mountains of evil and to level hilltops of injustice. God still works through history His wonders to perform." King's trust was vindicated. Would not the labor and trust of a conservative-liberal human life coalition, ecumenical in breadth, be ultimately vindicated? One hopes sooner rather than later.

Charles DeCelles is professor of religious studies at Marywood College in Scranton, Pennsylvania.

"We believe that one must not legislate something for which there is no moral consensus."

Abortion Should Not Be a Legal Issue

The New Republic

There is no more vexing jurisprudential question than the enforcement of morals. Society wishes to promote certain moral values; one of the instruments for doing so is the law. Unfortunately, the law has more than just an educative function; it has a punitive one as well. Are we justified in punishing transgressions against moral standards, even when the behavior involved is not deemed injurious to others?

A classic formulation of this problem arose twenty-five years ago in Britain, when the Wolfenden Commission recommended the legalization of homosexual behavior between consenting adults. That sparked a spirited debate, led on one side by Patrick Devlin and on the other by H.L.A. Hart. In *The Enforcement of Morals* Lord Devlin argued that the state is justified in seeking to legislate prevailing morality. As the last twenty-five years of legislation regarding homosexuality, pornography, and, to a lesser extent, drug taking have shown, Mr. Hart's side won.

But the issue is not so easily disposed of. In the United States today the battleground has shifted to the more difficult case of abortion. Abortion is more difficult because it is far less clearly injurious to no one. One might expect that such a morally complex issue would result in a commensurately sophisticated debate. It hasn't. The abortion controversy was inflamed by the Supreme Court decision in 1973, *Roe v. Wade*, which struck down state laws restricting or outlawing abortion. Ever since, the debate has been monopolized by the more extreme exponents of the two sides.

Pro-Choice Arguments

On one side, the strident pro-choice advocates (the euphemisms chosen by each side are themselves

indications of their intolerance: pro-choice and pro-life; who stands against choice or life?) argue that abortion is a simple question of privacy and of "a woman's control of her own body." If there is no moral difference between abortion and removal of a tumor, it follows that there should be no more societal interest in regulating the one than the other. (As any woman who has had an abortion—whether she has misgivings about it or not—can testify, the experience is never merely medical.) The attempt has been made to subsume the issue entirely under the rubric of women's rights, not only to tap into growing support for the women's movement and to portray anti-abortionists as animated by an archaic denial of women's rights, but also to blur the distinction between this issue and, say, equal pay for equal work.

On the other side we find an equal desire for obfuscating simplification. In the last Congress, the leaders of the anti-abortion crusade, Senators James East and Jesse Helms, tried to overturn *Roe v. Wade* by asking Congress to declare that life begins at conception, a notion which has been the subject of dispute throughout much of Jewish and Christian history, which was not part of the English common law, and which entered into general practice in the United States only in the late nineteenth century. One of the principal difficulties with the East proposal was that it would accord the rights and privileges of a citizen of the United States to a sixty-four-cell blastocyst. Such absurdities do not deter zealots.

Any debate that forces one to choose between the view that the fetus is a citizen and the view that the fetus is a tumor is a bad one. Between the judgment that abortion is murder and the judgment that abortion is mere surgery is the more sensible—and sensitive—view that many people, including both supporters and opponents of the Supreme Court decision, hold: that the fetus has some of the

"The Abortion Perplex," *New Republic*, July 11, 1983. Reprinted by permission of THE NEW REPUBLIC, © 1983, The New Republic, Inc.

attributes of human life and acquires more and more of them as it approaches birth; and abortion, therefore, by ending this potential, partial life, is a serious and ethically problematic procedure. The core of the sin, if we may call it that, is carelessness: carelessness in the making of life on one hand, and of preventing it on the other.

Carelessness With Life

Carelessness is contagious. It is a short step, and one that has already been taken, to carelessness with the life of an infant born imperfect. In the recent "Baby Doe" case in Indiana, the courts allowed parents to let their Down's Syndrome infant die, when he could have been saved by a simple operation. In a recent article in *Human Life Review*, an anti-abortion publication, President Reagan tries to frame the abortion issue as a choice between the "sanctity of life ethic and the 'quality of life' ethic." Things are not that easy. Infanticide is not abortion. All of life is lived on a slippery slope, yet the law must and does draw lines. It is one thing to say that the habitual performance of a morally dubious behavior can lead to a state of mind in which morally wrong behavior becomes possible. But that in no way leads to the conclusion that the law should deal with the two behaviors in the same way. Those who believe that Baby Doe should not have been allowed to die are not forced to the conclusion that abortion should be prohibited. But they are forced to look at the social consequences of a decade of legal abortion.

"We have misgivings about the morality of abortion, but we do not want to see them written into law."

Roe v. Wade led not only to an increase in the number of abortions, but to its acceptability. Today 1.6 million abortions are performed yearly in the United States, meaning that one out of every three pregnancies ends in an abortion. With the abolition of legal sanction, it is inevitable that social sanction is eroded as well. The mass availability of abortion has, almost by necessity, transformed it into an acceptable—if not the most economical—form of birth control. (In countries where the traditional resistance to such a view has been even more methodically eroded, abortion rates are astonishingly high. Recent demographic studies suggest that in the Soviet Union there are about two to three abortions for every live birth.)

Legislating Morality

The law *is* a teacher. But it is not the only teacher. The child growing up today receives daily lessons in sexual and moral carelessness from the mass media,

from advertising, from schools. And in a larger historical sense, freedom is to blame; carelessness is its companion, perhaps even its price. *Roe v. Wade* itself was grounded in the notion of "liberty" in the Due Process Clause of the Fourteenth Amendment, which the court interpreted as mandating a "right to privacy." The debate over *Roe* has revolved around the question of whether or not the framers of the Constitution (or the Fourteenth Amendment) really intended a constitutional right to privacy. But this historical point seems to us less relevant than the sociological one: in a society that has performed the miracle of continually expanding the realm of freedom, it is to be expected that people should come to feel a right to unmolested action even in increasingly morally problematic areas. It was this state of affairs that was ratified by the Supreme Court decision of 1973, and reaffirmed by the powerful new *Akron* ruling of the Supreme Court this month.

Since 1973 many legislatures have tried to limit the effect of *Roe* by nibbling at it from the edges. *Roe* permitted abortion, but also recognized a compelling state interest in promoting the health of the mother and the potential life of the fetus. It restricted the implementation of these two interests to the second and third trimesters for maternal health, and to the period after fetal viability (roughly the third trimester) for protecting the potential life of the fetus. Using the first provision, the city of Akron passed a regulation which, in the name of protecting the mother's health, imposed restrictions and certain procedural obstacles to abortions occurring beyond the first trimester. These included the requirement that they be performed in a hospital; that there be a twenty-four-hour waiting period between the time of decision and the time of abortion; that the woman be given a list of particulars about the risks, dangers, and alternatives by her doctor, and so on. The Court, while granting in principle the permissibility of regulation which presents minimal obstacles to obtaining an abortion and is meant to protect the health of the mother, ruled that these provisions seemed more intent on influencing the woman's decision in a particular way than on preserving her health. By declaring all the regulations unconstitutional, the Court reaffirmed its original position and rejected any suggestion that it had either not intended or not anticipated the consequences of *Roe*. With *Akron* it declared that it will not tolerate a legislative circumvention of its original ruling.

Illegal Abortions Repugnant

We have misgivings about the morality of abortion, but we do not want to see them written into law. We therefore support the Akron decision. For one thing, the social costs of outlawing abortions are enormous. The argument is familiar and does not need extensive restatement: the deaths and maimings of women in botched, illegal abortions; the nightmare of innocent women forbidden to end pregnancies caused by rape or incest; the anguish of families with unwanted children; the burdens (and poverty) of women forced to bear children they cannot provide for. But more importantly, we believe that one must not legislate something for which there is no moral consensus. It may be true that the original decision legalizing abortion helped to weaken that consensus—we have now become used to the social efficiency of abortion—but there is no going back. There comes a point in the moral evolution of society when the law by itself can no longer restore the previous order. And if the law strays too far from existing morality, it serves only to promote lawlessness and contempt for legal norms, without in any way significantly solving the problem it purports to address.

"The attempt to enforce a legal standard vastly more severe than the prevailing moral standard. . . .is. . . .a self-defeating exercise in coercion."

We learned that lesson with Prohibition. It was, though most people don't like to admit it, an enormous public health success. The rates of hepatitis and other related illnesses were reduced. Yet it proved such a social catastrophe that it had to be repealed. It might perhaps be preferable to live in a society where alcohol (or pornography or abortion) didn't exist. But in a society where they carry the taint of sin but not of crime, the attempt to enforce a legal standard vastly more severe than the prevailing moral standard considers just is worse than futile. It becomes a self-defeating exercise in coercion.

We agree with the Court that a woman has a legal right to an abortion, though we would hope it is a right that will never be exercised routinely. We look forward to the day when those who oppose abortion will give up the legal battle by which they intend to use the coercive powers of the state to enforce their norm, and instead use moral suasion to promote the view that abortion, while no longer a crime, is not morally neutral either.

The New Republic *is a weekly journal of opinion that focuses on liberal politics and literature.*

"A simple restoration of 'personhood' to the unborn child, without exceptions, should prevent the states from legalizing any abortions."

A Human Life Amendment Is Needed

Charles E. Rice

In recent years, the abortion question has become one of the most controversial moral and political issues to receive public debate in the entire history of our nation.

Up until the last two decades, there has been no question about abortion. Until recently, abortion has always been considered completely wrong—a social, moral, legal and religious evil.

The "legal" murder of unborn children by abortion is now considered legitimate by so many people only because of the serious moral and religious decay in our society coming at the same time as rapid advances in medical science.

Since public debate began on the abortion question, many attempts at a "solution" have been made by courts and legislatures. None of these "solutions" has ever been accepted by the forces on either side of the question.

The most current "solution" to the abortion dilemma is the 1973 U.S. Supreme Court ruling which sets forth standards which the individual states must follow in legislating abortion.

Pro-life, anti-abortion groups in America disagree with the Supreme Court's 1973 decision. Many such groups believe that the only acceptable solution to the abortion question is a Human Life Amendment to the U.S. Constitution.

American Life Lobby (ALL) supports the Human Life Amendment.

These questions and answers have been prepared by ALL in an attempt to explain fully the Human Life Amendment and to show why it is the only answer to the abortion question that is acceptable for our country.—Mrs. Judie Brown, president, ALL

1. What is the essence of the 1973 Supreme Court ruling, and how has that ruling affected abortion practices?

Charles E. Rice, "A Human Life Amendment Is Necessary to Halt 'Legal' Murder of Millions," *Conservative Digest*, March 1981. Reprinted with permission of The Cashel Institute, University of Notre Dame Law School.

Answer: In its 1973 abortion decisions, the Supreme Court ruled that the unborn child is not a person within the meaning of the Fourteenth Amendment and that therefore the unborn child is not entitled to the right to life protected by that amendment. In providing guidelines, the Court allows the states to impose no prohibition at all on abortions performed during the first two trimesters of the pregnancy. During the third trimester, the Court held, the states could prohibit abortions except in cases where the abortion is sought to preserve the life or health, physical or mental, of the mother.

Since no restrictions are allowed on abortion in the first two trimesters, and since "mental health" is such an elastic criterion, the net effect of the Supreme Court rulings is to require the states to allow elective abortion at every stage of pregnancy until birth.

2. What is the remedy for the Supreme Court decisions that mandate such elective abortions?

Answer: The ultimate remedy for the Supreme Court decisions is an amendment to the U.S. Constitution. The amendment must accomplish the following three objectives:

• Expressly, or by clear implication, restore "personhood" to the unborn child with respect to his right to live;

• Apply the protection of the Constitution to the unborn child from the beginning of life, that is, from the moment of fertilization;

• Permit no exceptions.

3. Why shouldn't we be satisfied with a law that would stop most abortions, even if it allowed some abortions to continue?

Answer: Every year we "legally" kill by abortion innocent human beings in numbers equivalent to the combined populations of Kansas City, Minneapolis and Miami—at least 1,300,000. Because of the horrible dimensions of this mass slaughter, there is a tendency in some areas of the pro-life movement to favor whatever will promise an immediate reduction of the killings, even if that reduction is at the price of permanently legalizing abortion on a smaller scale. Those who insist, on the contrary, that the right to life must be restored, without exceptions, may appear to be heartless and more devoted to an abstract principle than to the saving of innocent lives. In fact, the Supreme Court rulings on abortion leave no alternative but to support a no-compromise, no-exception constitutional amendment that would prohibit all abortions. Such an amendment, named the Helms-Dornan Amendment after its cosponsors, has already been proposed in Congress.

4. Why shouldn't abortions to save the life of a mother be permitted under the law?

Answer: There are no situations where abortion is medically or psychiatrically justified to save the life of the mother. (See Wilson, "The Abortion Problem in the General Hospital," in Rosen, *Abortion in America* (1967), and Whitehead, *Respectable Killing: The New Abortion Imperative.*) We must be careful, however, to distinguish cases such as the cancerous uterus and the ectopic or tubular pregnancy. If a pregnant woman has a cancerous uterus and, to save her life, it is necessary to remove the uterus and the operation cannot be postponed until the baby is born, then the uterus may be removed even though such an operation results in the death of the unborn child. Similarly, when a fertilized ovum lodges in the fallopian tube and begins to grow there, the damaged portion of the tube, containing the developing fetus, may be removed surgically where it is clearly and imminently necessary to save the life of the mother.

"There are no situations where abortion is medically or psychiatrically justified to save the life of the mother."

Such operations as these are considered moral even under Catholic teaching. (See Ethical and Religious Directive for Catholic Health Facilities, National Conference of Catholic Bishops, 1971, paragraphs 10-17.) Morally, these operations are considered indirect abortions, and they are justified by the principle of the double effect, since the death of the child is an unintended effect of an operation independently justified by the necessity of saving the mother's life. They do not involve the intentional killing of the unborn child for the purpose of achieving another objective, such as the preservation of the mother's health or life. Morally, therefore, such operations may be justified. Legally, they are not considered to be abortions at all. There has never been a prosecution even attempted in this country based on the removal of such a condition, even

where the mother's life was not immediately threatened. There is no need, therefore, to provide a specific exception for such cases in a constitutional amendment prohibiting abortions.

Apart from such cases as the ectopic pregnancy and the cancerous uterus, there is no medical or psychiatric justification for terminating a pregnancy. But even if there were, a constitutional amendment should not legalize abortion in such cases. For example, if two people in the middle of the ocean are on a raft that can hold only one person, the law does not permit one to throw the other overboard, even to save his own life. (See Regina vs. Dudley and Stephens, 14 Q.B.D.273, 15 Cox C.C. 624, 1884; and U.S. vs. Holmes, 2G Fed. Cases 360 (No. 15,383), C.C.E.D., Pa., 1842.) Otherwise, might would make right. In maternity cases, the duty of the doctor is to use his best efforts to save both of his patients, the mother and her child. He should not be given a license to kill either of them intentionally.

5. Why shouldn't abortions be permitted to preserve a mother's health or when amniocentesis shows that the child will be born with serious defects?

Answer: If an exception should not be made where the life of the mother is concerned, it follows that an exception should not be made for any lesser reason. To allow abortion to prevent injury to the mother's mental or physical health (where her life is not in danger) is to allow killing for what ultimately amounts to convenience. And to kill an unborn child because he may be born defective is to do exactly what the Nazis did to the Jews whose lives they regarded as not worth living.

6. But why shouldn't abortions be allowed to those women who become pregnant by rape or incest?

Answer: The woman who is raped has a right to resist her attacker. But the unborn child is an innocent nonaggressor who should not be killed because of the crime of the father. More to the point, since a woman has the right to resist the rapist, she also has the right to resist his sperm. There are nonabortive measures that can be taken, consistent with the law and even with Catholic teaching, promptly after rape, which are not intended to abort and which will prevent conception. However, once the innocent third party to a rape, the unborn child, is conceived, he should not be killed. The duty of the state and society in all cases of "troubled" pregnancies is to mobilize resources to solve the problems constructively with personal and financial support. A license to kill is not a constructive solution.

Incest is a voluntary act on the woman's part. If it were not, it would be rape. And to kill a child because of the identity of his father is no more proper in the case of incest than it is in the case of rape. Again, the positive solution of support should be pursued—not legalized murder by abortion.

7. Why is it so important for a Human Life Amendment to provide for granting the legal status of "personhood" to the unborn child?

Answer: In Roe vs. Wade, the basic 1973 abortion ruling, the Supreme Court held that, if the personhood of the unborn child is established, the pro-abortion case "collapses, for the fetus's right to life is then guaranteed by the [Fourteenth] Amendment." This is because the law does not permit one person to kill another innocent person even to save the life of the killer. As the Supreme Court itself noted in Roe vs. Wade:

> When Texas urges that a fetus is entitled to Fourteenth Amendment protection as a person, it faces a dilemma. Neither in Texas nor in any other state are all abortions prohibited. Despite broad proscription, an exception contained in Article 1196, for an abortion procured or attempted by medical advice for the purpose of saving the life of the mother, is typical. But if the fetus is a person who is not to be deprived of life without due process of law, and if the mother's condition is the sole determinant, does not the Texas exception appear to be out of line with the amendment's command?

It seems clear from these statements of the Court that a simple restoration of "personhood" to the unborn child, without exceptions, should prevent the states from legalizing any abortions, even when they are claimed to be necessary to save the life of the mother. Such a result is consistent with the common law, under which the principle of necessity does not justify anyone taking the life of an innocent nonaggressor even to save his own life. The Helms-Dornan Amendment implicitly but clearly restores "personhood" to the unborn child without any exceptions. The amendment provides:

> The paramount right to life is vested in each human being from the moment of fertilization, without regard to age, health or condition of dependency.

It is true that the Helms-Dornan Amendment would not prevent the state legislatures and the Supreme Court from applying, incorrectly, the law of necessity so as to permit abortion to save the life of the mother. But no constitutional amendment on any subject can be drawn so as to be immune to misconstruction. The recent history of the Fourteenth Amendment is evidence enough on that point. The object of a Human Life Amendment should be simply to restore to the unborn child the same right to live which is enjoyed by his older brother and his grandmother. Even the Supreme Court acknowledged in Roe vs. Wade that such recognition of personhood would prevent the legalization of abortions even where claimed to be necessary to save the life of the mother.

8. Wouldn't it be better to have a Human Life Amendment with limited exceptions so as not to invite courts and legislatures to write their own more far-reaching exceptions?

Answer: It has been argued by some that to write an amendment without exceptions is to invite the states and the Supreme Court to write their own exceptions, which could be practically unlimited. But this contention is unsound. It argues that if you write in just one little exception, the states and the Court will not be able to add others. This is wholly unrealistic. To argue that writing one exception into the amendment will prevent the Supreme Court from adding others is to rely on the Court's adhering to the canon of legislative drafting, "expressio unius est exclusio alterius"—which means that the inclusion of one excludes others not mentioned. This canon of interpretation, however, is merely presumptive and has been disregarded by courts on numerous occasions. Curiously, those who favor exceptions on this theory rest their case on the expectation that the Court will strictly adhere to this merely presumptive guide to construction while they wholly disregard the more basic concepts of personhood and necessity which were even acknowledged by the Court in Roe vs. Wade. Advocates of an exception are sure the Court will disregard that very basic concept under which a restoration of personhood would prevent all abortions while they assume that, if one exception is written in, the Court will feel itself bound by the merely presumptive rule of "expressio unius" and will go no further.

"If the personhood of the unborn child is established, the pro-abortion case 'collapses, for the fetus' right to life is then guaranteed by the [Fourteenth] Amendment.'"

In fact, it is impossible to draft any exception clause which will not open the door to psychiatric abortions and, in ultimate practice, to abortions on request. Even the most limited exception would be broadly interpreted. For example, on the televised "MacNeil-Lehrer Report," April 22, 1980, Dr. Michael Burnhill of the National Abortion Federation said that even an exception limited to abortions that would endanger the life of the mother would permit him to perform whatever abortions he thought were "medically necessary." These would include abortions to preserve the mother's "health," which he defines as "a condition in which one can actively participate in one's total life, that you are not a cripple or an invalid." On a practical level, the recent experience with the Hyde Amendment indicates that when pro-lifers concede one exception, they disarm themselves and become incapable of resisting the arguments of those who would extend the exceptions to cover such cases as rape and incest. The preferable alternative is to restore personhood to the unborn child with respect to his right to live, without exceptions.

9. But isn't it good tactics to include exceptions in an amendment to make sure it will gain broad support?

Answer: No. Those in the pro-life movement who traffic with exception clauses are trying to gain support from those who favor "only a few" abortions. But such people are worthless as allies, since they are basically opposed to an authentic pro-life position and since they are practically incapable of resisting the expansion of their exceptions. On the contrary, the pro-life movement is only as strong as its refusal to compromise. In fact, there are no cases where a legal abortion is necessary even to save the life of the mother. The removal of a cancerous womb or an ectopic pregnancy is not an abortion in legal terms, and therefore no exception clause is necessary to authorize such operations, which are permitted even under Catholic teaching.

"The real issue is whether life is a gift of God or of the state."

Agreeing on amendment language is a problem mainly for those who are trying to carry water on both shoulders. If you want leeway for some abortions, or if you favor the intrauterine device or morning-after pill, which are early abortifacients, you will have trouble with the language, and you will end up with an "anything goes" amendment.

Those who propose exceptions to the right to live present themselves as pragmatic realists. But in fact, the only practical solution here is one that adheres to principle. If an amendment with exceptions to the right to live were ever passed by Congress and sent to the states for ratification, *it would have to be actively opposed by all who regard the right of innocent life as nonnegotiable.* Such an amendment would never be ratified over the opposition of the strongest elements in the pro-life cause. To write into our Constitution a license for the intentional destruction of innocent life would be to adopt the jurisprudence that underlay the Nazi extermination of the Jews. This we can never allow.

10. What is really at stake in this matter of making exceptions to the right to live?

Answer: The real issue is whether life is a gift of God or of the state. Innocent life is nonnegotiable precisely because it comes from God. The governing principles were stated by Pope John Paul II in his homily at the Capitol Mall on October 7, 1979: "I do not hesitate to proclaim before you and before the world that all human life—from the moment of conception and through all subsequent stages—is sacred, because human life is created in the image and likeness of God. Nothing surpasses the greatness or dignity of a human person. . . . Let me repeat what I told the people during my recent pilgrimage to my homeland: 'If a person's right to life is violated at the moment in which he is first conceived in his mother's womb, an indirect blow is struck also at the whole of the moral order, which serves to ensure the inviolable goods of man. Among these goods, life occupies the first place. The Church defends the right to life, not only in regard to the majesty of the Creator, who is the First Giver of this life, but also in respect of the essential good of the human person.'" On a more specific level, the Declaration on Procured Abortion, issued with the approval of Pope Paul VI in 1974, said, "A Christian can never conform to a law which is in itself immoral, and such is the case of a law which would admit in principle the liceity of abortion. Nor can a Christian take part in a propaganda campaign in favor of such a law, or vote for it."

It is long past time for the pro-life movement to stop apologizing for itself and to affirm without compromise that life is a gift of God and not of the state. Our duty is to protect the right to live of each and every child of God.

Charles E. Rice is professor of law at the University of Notre Dame Law School and coeditor of The American Journal of Jurisprudence. *Among his books are* Freedom of Association, the Vanishing Right To Live, *and* Abortion: The Theory and Practice of the Secular State.

"The American people, irrespective of their position on abortion, would be making a great mistake to permit a church to write its theological views...into the Constitution."

viewpoint **8**

A Human Life Amendment Violates Constitutional Rights

John M. Swomley Jr.

The Roman Catholic bishops of the United States are currently campaigning for passage of an amendment to the Federal Constitution which would write Catholic doctrine into constitutional law. They want to change the traditional American position that a person legally exists at birth to their theological position that a person exists from the moment of conception. The Fourteenth Amendment to the Constitution makes birth a prerequisite to citizenship and gives it to "persons born or naturalized in the United States."

The connection between personhood and birth undoubtedly comes from the second chapter of Genesis, which states that "man became a living being" when God "breathed into his nostrils the breath of life." In other words personhood exists when a child is able to breathe on his or her own apart from the oxygen delivered through the uterus. There is also a practical reason. The moment of birth is known; the moment of conception is speculative. Retired Supreme Court Justice Tom Clark has asserted that "the law deals in reality, not obscurity—the known rather than the unknown. When sperm meets egg, life may eventually form, but quite often it does not. The law does not deal in speculation."

The Catholic bishops made no issue of the legal assumption that personhood begins at birth until the Supreme Court decision of 1973 removing abortion from the criminal code. Thereafter they have demanded an amendment which would give to an embryo or fetus from the moment of conception due process of law and equal protection by the law. Such an amendment sponsored by Sen. James Buckley (C-NY) says the word person "applies to all human beings, *including their unborn offspring at every stage of*

John M. Swomley Jr., "Theology and Politics," *Church and State,* the publication of Americans United for Separation of Church and State. Reprinted with permission from the November 1976 issue.

their biological development...."

These amendments come directly from Catholic sexual and medical ethics which not only prohibit abortion but also birth control devices such as the intrauterine device (IUD) and "morning after pills" which function after conception. The traditional Roman Catholic position is that sexual relations are a biological function whose purpose is procreation. The conception and birth of children are part of the natural process instituted by God. Therefore parents may not choose the number of children they will have. The Roman church has viewed the practices of contraception and abortion as interference with the processes of nature and therefore sinful. This position is not rooted in the Bible, but comes from the Greek philosophy of nature known as Natural Law. There is no mention of birth control or abortion in the Bible.

Protestant View

By contrast, the major Protestant churches do not view sex as necessarily sinful or place virginity or celibacy on a higher plane. Nor is it simply a biological function. It has been created by God as an expression of love in which men and women may engage without any necessary relation to birth. Protestants do not believe that Jesus Christ set them free from the ancient Jewish Law only to bind them by some other legalism derived from Greek philosophy. They generally have understood God as acting within human beings to set us free and to enable us to assume responsibility for ourselves, our environment and our future. This means that the number of children is the responsibility of the parents. God's grace is involved in the free choice of husband and wife to have or not to have children. The choice by some persons not to have children is not a sin.

Protestants do not identify God's natural order with a pre-scientific period where infant and adult death rates were high because of disease and ignorance. If

God's natural order includes medicine, surgery and psychiatry to prolong and enhance life, it also includes those same medical approaches when they prolong or enhance the life of a woman for whom a specific birth would be dangerous. The mere fact of conception does not mean that God wills a childbirth. The occurence of miscarriages and stillbirths suggest that every conception is not intended to result in the birth of a baby.

Jewish View of Abortion

A Jewish scholar, Rabbi Israel R. Margolies, notes that in his tradition "there is no law of nature or of God that requires" that the expression of love through sexual intercourse "must perforce lead to conception and birth. It is a man and a woman who must decide whether or not they wish their union to lead to the birth of a child, not the church or the synagogue, and certainly not the state."

Catholic authorities now also accept sexual intercourse as having a purpose of expressing love in addition to procreation, but they have not abandoned the idea that any action is forbidden which "proposes . . . to render procreation impossible" (*Ethical and Religious Directives for Catholic Health Facilities*, Nov. 16, 1971).

The second basis for the proposed constitutional amendments comes out of papal teaching. Pope Pius XII on October 29, 1951, said: "Now the child, even the unborn child, is a human being in the same degree and by the same title as its mother . . . So, . . . to save the life of the mother is a most noble end, but the direct killing of the (unborn) child as a means to that end is not lawful." This means that it is better for both mother and fetus to die than it is to save the life of the mother through a direct abortion.

"The first major objection to the proposed amendment is that it would interfere with the religious liberty of non-Catholics."

Judaism generally views the fetus as part of its mother, and just as a person may choose to sacrifice a limb or organ of his body in order to be cured of a worse malady, so may the fetus be removed for the sake of the mother. Isaac Klein, a Conservative rabbi, elaborated a rule of Maimonides against a "pursuer" which is apparently comparable to the law of self-defense: "Since the child causing a difficult birth and threatening the woman's life 'is regarded as one pursuing her and trying to kill her' it may rightly be aborted."

Protestants generally do not believe that a human person is present at conception. The soul is not infused. Instead, the fetus is a potential person with a developing unity of body, mind and spirit. Protestants do not baptize a miscarried or aborted fetus but baptize only after birth. Roman Catholics according to Canon 747, do baptize a fetus even if doubtful about its life.

Abortion and Religious Liberty

In view of these doctrinal differences the first major objection to the proposed amendment is that it would interfere with the religious liberty of non-Catholics. A church has a right to teach its members that a person exists from the moment of conception and that it is a sin to expel a fertilized egg, embryo or fetus from the mother. The religious liberty of everyone is at stake, however, if a politically influential church hierarchy can impose such church doctrine upon a pluralist society that does not accept its theological assumptions. Even the religious liberty of its own members has been denied when a church that cannot persuade them voluntarily to refrain from abortion asks the state to restrain or punish them by criminal law. The records of the Chicago Planned Parenthood Association prior to the Supreme Court decision reveal that 2,000 Roman Catholic women during a 12 month period were sent to New York for abortions. They represented more than 40% of the women sent to New York from that area, a higher percentage than Jews or Protestants.

Churches have the same rights as others to argue for or against abortion, but the American people, irrespective of their position on abortion, would be making a great mistake to permit a church to write its theological views about conception or sex into the Constitution. It is not necessarily an evasion of the issue when a politician says he is against abortion but opposes a Constitutional amendment prohibiting it. In a secular state, governments should adopt laws against abortion only if it adversely affects the public health or welfare, and not because church leaders regard it as sinful.

There is a second ethical question raised by the proposed constitutional amendment. Can the problem of abortion be dealt with by law?

Legal Abortion and Public Safety

At first glance it would seem that the Roman Catholic bishops are protecting the lives of unborn babies by proposing a constitutional amendment. Exactly the opposite is true. Prior to the Supreme Court decision, experts, according to *Time* magazine of March 9, 1970, estimated that as many as one million illegal abortions took place in the U.S. each year. The *Kansas City Times* reported an interview with a man who had no medical degree who had performed 30,000 illegal abortions since he began in 1933. No law can prevent women from having abortions if they are determined to end a pregnancy. The attempt to prevent abortions is unenforceable unless individual pregnant women are to be kept under constant surveillance and their homes subject to unannounced invasion. What the law can do is prevent hospitals and doctors from performing medically safe abortions.

After the Kansas law permitting abortions went into effect I interviewed Dr. William Cameron, a professor of obstetrics at the Kansas University Medical Center. He indicated that when abortion was illegal they always had a ward of 20-30 beds full of patients who had practiced abortion on themselves and had come to the hospital with blood poisoning or other serious self-injury. "Now," he said, "we almost never have a case like that." The Cook County hospital in Chicago, prior to the Supreme Court decision, admitted each year about 4,000 women for medical care following illegal abortions. After the decision they had fewer than five such cases a month.

In Latin America, where both law and religion prohibit abortions, there is one abortion for every two live births and in Uruguay, three abortions to each actual birth, according to Alice S. Rossi of the U.S. Public Health Service. In practice Catholic authorities around the world seem more concerned with a theologically acceptable law than with the actual problem of abortion. They do not encourage particularly effective alternatives to abortion.

Rights of Parents and Family

A third major ethical question posed by the proposed constitutional amendment relates to the rights of parents and the family. The amendment would give women no right to preserve their own lives if endangered by pregnancy. This is not simply an issue of women's rights since the husband has a concern for his wife's life; and so do their children. If Vatican legalism with respect to fetal rights were inserted in the Constitution it would triumph over the rights of the husband, wife and children of an existing family.

Dr. Edward Rynearson, a physician at the Mayo Clinic, said to a group of Methodist clergy some years ago: "I want you to think of this happening to your 16 year old daughter. Visualize her as having been kidnapped by a group of men, held prisoner in a cabin for ten days, and repeatedly raped. It was later found that she was pregnant. What would you want for your daughter? Never mind the statistics or your moralizing. What would you really want?" Under the proposed amendment she would have to have the unwanted baby.

Episcopal Bishop George Leslie Cadigan said in 1971:

"It is at once the glory and the burden of each of us that we are called upon to make such difficult personal decisions according to our consciences. When we deny that liberty to any one of our number, we give away a part of our own birthright. When, more specifically, we condemn a woman for making

an independent judgment according to her own conscience, relating to her reproductive life, we denigate her personhood.

"The 'rightness' or 'wrongness' of abortion as the solution of a problem pregnancy is not the critical issue here. The issue is the larger ethical one: can any one of us stand in the role of judge for the personal decisions of others? What robes shall he wear? Greater than the debatable immorality of terminating an undesired pregnancy is the immorality of refusing a woman access to medical help when she has determined that she needs it."

"If Vatican legalism with respect to fetal rights were inserted in the Constitution it would triumph over the rights of the husband, wife and children of an existing family."

The response of the Catholic bishops to such ideas as permitting women to follow their consciences is that abortion is murder and the law cannot tolerate murder. Abortion is neither murder nor any other form of homicide, because the victim of a homicide must be a human being who has been born and is alive. Just as the digging up of a sprouting acorn is not the same as cutting down an oak tree, so it is incorrect to speak of terminating a pregnancy in its early stages as murder. If the ending of fetal life were murder, then it would not have been permitted to save the life of the mother as it was throughout the United States prior to the Supreme Court decision. Even the Catholic bishops who think of it as murder were not prepared to try women for murder after a self-inflicted abortion. If the planned ending of pregnancy were murder then a miscarriage due to negligence would be a homicide punishable by law. Instead the state has left the prevention of spontaneous abortions or miscarriages entirely to the medical profession.

Religious Liberty

Opposition to abortion does not necessarily mean advocacy of a constitutional amendment prohibiting it. Nor does opposition to such an amendment imply approval of abortion. The basic reason for opposing an amendment which defines personhood as beginning at conception is religious liberty. When millions of Jews, Protestants and other Americans, including many Catholic laypersons, live by a different sexual and medical ethic than that of the Catholic bishops, it is not the business of the government to interfere in the private sexual relations of human beings and force them to reproduce contrary to their consciences. Is such a position anti-

Catholic? Not at all. Every church is a better church
if it wins the loyalty or obedience of its people
instead of relying on the government to enforce
church teaching.

*John M. Swomley Jr. is a professor of Christian social
ethics and philosophy at the St. Paul School of Theology
in Kansas City, Missouri.*

"The legalization of abortion has been accompanied by a decline in deaths and complications among American women of childbearing age."

viewpoint 9

Legal Abortion Has Improved Public Health

Willard Cates Jr.

In the public health annals of the United States, the chapter on developments in abortion over the last decade is a record of exceptionally rapid change. In that time, during which abortion ceased to be a clandestine procedure and began to be practiced under normal medical conditions, we have come to know more about it than any other surgical operation.

The purpose of this article is to describe objectively what we know about the effect on public health of the increased availability of legal abortion. The morality of abortion is a controversial topic, and the statistical data brought together here do not address that issue.

No direct count of the number of illegal abortions has ever been possible. Estimates have been made by various means, such as local surveys with the randomized response technique, extrapolations from deaths and hospitalizations, and retrospective projections based on numbers of births and legal abortions. Through these approaches, most estimates of illegally induced abortion in the United States in the 1960's range between 200,000 and 1,200,000 a year....

Deaths and Complications

Illegal abortions caused sizable numbers of deaths and complications among American women. For example, in 1965, 235 deaths, or 20 percent of all deaths related to pregnancy and childbirth, were attributed to abortion. Complications from abortion accounted for nearly 20 percent of pregnancy-related admissions to municipal hospitals in New York and California during the 1960's; the average length of stay of these patients was 4 days.

During the 1970's the United States passed through three stages with regard to the availability of legal abortion: until the middle of 1970 legal abortion was generally not available; from mid-1970 through early 1973 it was available in some regions; since 1973 it has been generally available throughout the nation. The number of reported legal abortions increased from approximately 22,000 in 1969 to over 1.5 million in 1980. Initially the increase in legal abortions was accompanied by a progressive decline in the estimated number of illegal abortions. Thus, most of the initial increase in legal abortions was due to a corresponding drop in illegal abortions.

This shift from illegal to legal abortions has had a documented effect on deaths of women of reproductive age. In 1965, even before the availability of legal abortion, deaths of women from all types of abortion began to decline more rapidly than other causes of death related to pregnancy and childbirth. One reason may be the introduction of more effective contraception at that time. Between 1965 and 1970 oral contraceptives and intrauterine devices were used by an increasing percentage of married women, and this was associated with a decline in unwanted fertility during those years. Another possibility, suggested by Tietze, is that illegal abortions may have shifted from the non-medical to the medical sector and become safer.

Decline in Deaths

The decline of abortion mortality rapidly accelerated in 1970 and generally continued through 1976. This accelerated decline further suggests that legal abortions were primarily replacing illegal abortions. If legal abortions had been replacing term births, then deaths to women from abortion should have increased relative to deaths from other pregnancy-related causes. Instead, the opposite occurred.

A clearer view of these trends [is] based upon records started in 1972 by the Centers for Disease

Willard Cates Jr., "Legal Abortion: The Public Health Record," *Science*, Vol. 215, pp. 1586-1590, 26 March 1982. Copyright © 1982. Reprinted with permission.

Control (CDC) in which abortion-related deaths are separated into three categories—legally induced, illegally induced, and spontaneous. In 1972 there were 90 abortion-related deaths; in 1979 there were 29. Through 1976 the highest proportion of the decline was in the illegal category, where the number of deaths decreased from 39 to 2. The reduction in illegal-abortion mortality had a distinct temporal association with the increasing availability of legal abortion.

During the initial years of CDC's surveillance of abortion-related mortality, the number of deaths after legally induced abortion increased slightly, consistent with the increasing number of such abortions performed. In 1976, however, the number of deaths from legally induced abortion decreased precipitously, and it has remained lower than in the initial years despite a continuing increase in the number of legal abortions performed. Thus, the death-to-case rate for legal abortion has declined.

"The legalization of abortion has given clinicians the opportunity to learn different surgical techniques and to manage the immediate complications associated with these techniques."

Morbidity trends for abortion in recent years parallel mortality trends. Studies performed at national, state, and local levels show that hospitalization of women with complications resulting from abortion has decreased. Estimates based on the Hospital Discharge Survey from 1970 to 1977 show a general decline in number of patients with complications from other-than-legal abortions; the greatest part of this decline occurred in 1973, the year of the Supreme Court decisions striking down state laws prohibiting abortion. Individual hospitals on both the east and west coasts have registered similar declines.

Legal abortion has lower morbidity and mortality rates than does pregnancy continued to term. From 10 to 15 percent of term births are by cesarean section, whereas only .07 percent of first-trimester abortions entail intra-abdominal operations, and second-trimester abortion methods lead to major surgery in only .1 to .2 percent of cases. Thus, the risk of having to undergo major surgery for a complication of a legal abortion is approximately 1/100 that of carrying a pregnancy to term. The rates of severe psychiatric sequelae are lower for women who obtain legal abortions than for those who have normal pregnancies and a live birth. The risk— adjusted for age and race—of dying from an abortion induced during the first 15 weeks of pregnancy is one-seventh the risk of dying from pregnancy and childbirth.

The risk to the woman of continuing rather than terminating her pregnancy may be still greater when the pregnancy is unwanted. Women with negative attitudes toward their pregnancies have higher postpartum infection and hemorrhage rates than women with more favorable attitudes. Possible mechanisms for the poorer obstetric outcomes associated with unwanted pregnancies include a direct stress-mediated influence on catecholamines, less concern by the woman for proper prenatal care, and differences in clinical management of labor and delivery.

Development of Abortion Expertise

The increased availability of legal abortion since 1970 has influenced the safety of abortion methods and the skill of clinicians. The sixfold increase in the number of legal abortions performed has led to rapid development of technology. The most influential change has been the widespread adoption of the vacuum aspiration technique (suction curettage), which replaced the traditional scraping technique (sharp curettage) as the primary means of terminating pregnancies. In 1970 suction was used in 54 percent of cases, sharp in 46 percent. By 1978 suction curettage accounted for 90 percent of all abortions by curettage; of curettages done at 12 weeks or earlier, 96 percent were by suction.

Another improvement has been the recognition that curettage techniques can terminate pregnancies at 13 weeks' gestation or later more safely than the alternative methods; thus, delaying an abortion through the 13- to 16-week interval, as is required for the instillation of abortifacients into the uterus, is no longer considered necessary. Before legal abortion was available, performing curettage on a pregnant uterus after 12 weeks was thought to be too dangerous. Once abortion became legal, comparative studies could be undertaken, from which we have learned that curettage techniques, especially through 16 weeks' gestation, are safer than instillation procedures.

The legalization of abortion has given clinicians the opportunity to learn different surgical techniques and to manage the immediate complications associated with these techniques. Before legalization very few pregnancy-termination procedures were taught in routine obstetric and gynecologic training programs. The only experience with uterine evacuation for residents in training usually came from performing sharp curettage on a nonpregnant uterus for diagnostic purposes or when removing residual uterine tissue after a routine miscarriage. These procedures are different from those required for evacuating a pregnant uterus.

The increase in physician training and experience may be one factor in the decrease in deaths related to legally induced abortion after 1975. The death-to-case rate for legal abortion has decreased from 6.2 per 100,000 in 1970 to 1.5 in 1979. Improvements in anesthesia technique, use of better methods of dilation, reductions in the use of hysterotomy or hysterectomy for purposes of abortion, greater willingness to reevacuate a uterus if retained tissue is suspected, and physician familiarity with other abortion complications all may have contributed.

Delivery of Abortion Services

The increasing availability of and requests for abortion services have also led to two changes in when and where they are rendered: first, women obtaining legally induced abortions are doing so at progressively earlier gestational stages; second, most abortions are now being performed in nonhospital facilities, the so-called freestanding clinics. These two factors concurrently influence the safety, convenience, and cost of abortions.

Gestational stage is an important factor in complications after induced abortion. In 1970 nearly one-fourth of all abortions were performed at 13 weeks or later. By 1978, fewer than one in ten were performed at later than 13 weeks, and more than half were done before 8 weeks. This trend has contributed to reducing the number of deaths and complications.

Before the legalization of abortion, the term "in-hospital" was generally used to refer to legal abortion procedures. In 1970 having a legally induced abortion frequently required at least 2 days in hospital, the first for preoperative evaluation, the second for postoperative recovery. Even in 1973 more than 60 percent of all abortions were performed in hospitals. During the last 6 years the situation has reversed itself. By 1980 more than 70 percent of abortions were performed in freestanding clinics, without any hospitalization, and about half of those performed in hospitals were on an outpatient basis.

Costs of Medical Care

Before 1969, if it could be obtained a medically indicated abortion performed in a hospital was likely to cost more than $500. For this reason women of high economic status were more likely than other women to obtain such abortions. Today the charge for a uterine evacuation performed in a clinic is usually no more than $150. The average room charge for 1 day in a hospital is alone more than the cost of an abortion by suction curettage in a clinic. Curettage to terminate pregnancies of more than 12 weeks' duration costs approximately one-half as much as the instillation procedures formerly used.

The increased availability of legal abortion has also reduced the cost to society of treating abortion complications. The saving in public expenditures for treating infected or incomplete abortions is estimated at $30 per abortion. Assuming a national decrease in morbidity similar to that in mortality, we may estimate a 75 percent reduction in complications and a saving thereby of approximately $20 million annually.

Formation of American Families

Marriage and childbearing patterns have been measurably influenced by legal abortion; so has the formation of American families. Before 1969 trends in marriage rates among states with different levels of legal abortion services were similar. Beginning in 1970, states with high ratios of legal abortions to live births began exhibiting significant declines in marriage rates, especially among teenage women, which were not experienced in states with lower legal-abortion ratios. Liberalized abortion apparently provided teenagers with a new alternative to marriage precipitated by premarital pregnancy. Such marriages are less stable than those of their contemporaries who postpone childbearing.

"The availability of amniocentesis and selective abortion has allowed couples to undertake pregnancies they might not otherwise have considered or to continue pregnancies that they would have otherwise terminated."

Legalization of abortion has been found to be temporally associated with a decline in out-of-wedlock birth rates in New York City, California, Oregon, and the United States as a whole. More than 85 percent of teenagers obtaining abortions were unmarried. States with the highest teenage and overall childbearing rates had the lowest abortion-to-live-birth ratios.

In American families at known risk of genetic anomalies, the availability of amniocentesis and selective abortion has allowed couples to undertake pregnancies they might not otherwise have considered or to continue pregnancies that they would otherwise have terminated.

Decision-Making About Reproduction

Many family planning providers have developed elaborate counseling protocols to aid women with unwanted pregnancies in making decisions about them. In a survey of a random sample of abortion providers in 1976, 98 percent of clinics and 60 percent of hospitals reported offering pregnancy counseling services; 100 percent of clinics and 60 percent of hospitals provided contraceptive counseling.

The increasing use of legal abortion is associated with an increasing use of contraception beyond that related to increased sexual activity. Four different methodologic approaches have supported this inference. First, longitudinal studies of women who have had abortions show that the percentage using contraception increases immediately after abortion, and contraception is still being used at least 6 months afterwards.

Second, national studies of reproductive behavior conducted between 1965 and 1975 found an increasing percentage of married women using contraception even as legal abortion was becoming more widely available. The largest incremental annual increases, 3 percent per year, occurred between 1973 and 1975.

"Shady practices and incompetence have been attacked by both abortion providers and those opposed to abortion."

Third, the national patterns of increasing sexual activity and declining birth rates indicate that women are becoming increasingly able to control their fertility through either contraceptive practice or abortion. The proportion of never-married teenagers having unprotected intercourse decreased by one-half between 1971 and 1979. In 1976, among young unmarried women who became pregnant unintentionally those who had an abortion were more likely to have been using contraception than were those who did not have an abortion.

Fourth, between 1960 and 1974 the national conception rates actually decreased, if allowances are made for the number of illegal abortions performed in earlier years. A study in New York City showed a decline in the conception rate also during the first 3 years that legal abortion was available.

Unethical Practices

The extent of shady practice in the abortion field is not precisely known, but the relatively low overall rates of morbidity and mortality after legal abortion would indicate that it is not widespread. Nevertheless, isolated examples of questionable clinical practices have received media attention.

Investigations in four cities (Detroit, Los Angeles, Chicago, and New York) have found occasional instances such as "pregnancy counseling" agencies that use high-pressure tactics and false information to induce women to go to a subsidiary abortion facility; "abortion" procedures performed on women who are not pregnant; operations performed by unlicensed personnel—either non-physicians masquerading as physicians or physicians who have lost their license to practice; and facilities operating without state licenses and falsifying required medical records.

One practitioner allegedly performed intentionally incomplete abortions which would require a second procedure, so that he could bill for two separate operations; a patient died of infection resulting from retained products of conception. Another physician performed vaginal hysterotomy procedures in his private office; he was not equipped to handle operative emergencies that occurred and two women died from these procedures. Both physicians were found guilty of criminal offenses.

Early in the 1970's, use of outdated or unproven methods by some clinicians led to sporadic clusters of deaths and complications. For example, intrauterine placement of a "super coil" to terminate second-trimester pregnancies had high complication rates. This specific procedure was abandoned, but as late as 1977 a death was reported from implantation of a foreign body in a legal abortion attempt.

Shady practices and incompetence have been attacked by both abortion providers and those opposed to abortion. Responsible abortion providers have cooperated with investigative organizations to identify the problem practitioners and have developed model standards to improve their already relatively safe procedure. Groups opposed to abortion have highlighted the isolated events as representative of the quality of medical care given by abortion providers and have used them to promote regulation of all abortion services.

Future Childbearing

Recent headlines have reported that women who have had induced abortions, especially those who have had multiple abortions, have an increased risk of adverse events in future desired pregnancies. These preliminary reports have led some to predict an epidemic of miscarriages, prematurity, and low-birth-weight infants.

Unfortunately, the best available data addressing this issue do not enable us to estimate the risk, if any. Scientific studies in the United States are inconsistent about whether one abortion or even multiple abortions were associated with increased rates of adverse reproductive outcomes in subsequent desired pregnancies. Of the eight studies currently published, two have found a significant association of a single induced abortion with undesirable features of subsequent childbearing; the others have found either no association or such a small one that chance could have accounted for it. Two published studies have related multiple induced abortions to a threefold higher ratio of miscarriage, but one preliminary report from Hawaii says that this finding could not be confirmed.

Several studies outside the United States have demonstrated significant associations implicating a particular abortion procedure, especially the practice of sharp curettage. Since variations in abortion methods produce different short-term complications, they might also be expected to have different effects on long-term obstetric sequelae. For example, traditional sharp curettage frequently involves wider dilatation than current suction procedures. If the manner or width of dilatation, rather than the number or method of evacuation procedures, influences future pregnancies, use of laminaria for preoperative cervical dilatation might reduce risks.

Differences among the characteristics of women studied also produce conflicting results. For example, parity has an important effect on pregnancy outcome, with first births being at higher risk of preterm delivery than subsequent births. Thus, investigations in which first births to women with a previous abortion are compared with second births to women with a previous term birth will tend to find more complications among the abortion group, because of the difference in parity.

Breast Cancer

Whether induced abortion is associated with subsequent development of breast cancer is another question about which there is growing concern. Previous international investigations have shown that a woman is at lower risk of developing breast cancer if she gives birth at a young age. However, only full-term pregnancies afford this protection. With first pregnancies that terminate within 4 months there appears to be an increased risk of breast cancer. Unfortunately, these earlier studies did not differentiate between induced and spontaneous abortion.

"The increasing availability and utilization of legal abortion in the United States has had an important public health impact."

A recent investigation in Los Angeles found that in certain circumstances the risk of breast cancer in young women was more than doubled if they had had either an induced or a spontaneous abortion. Two specific conditions were involved: (1) the abortion had occurred before 3 months' gestation and (2) the women were nulliparous at the time of the abortion. A biologic explanation for a possible positive association between early abortion and breast cancer, and a negative association between early age at first childbearing and breast cancer, might involve variations in breast tissue during different intervals of pregnancy. Early in pregnancy, rapid proliferation of breast tissue might render more cells susceptible to neoplastic stimuli (tumor initiation) or might hasten the growth of malignant cells (tumor promotion). The protective effect of continuing a pregnancy to term could be due either to breast cell differentiation later in pregnancy or to a permanently altered estrogen profile during the later states, or both.

While data from this investigation are consistent with earlier findings, the case-control designs raise questions of ascertainment bias. Specifically, might women with breast cancer be more likely to remember or admit previous abortions than a comparison group would be? Also, women in the Los Angeles study had their cancers diagnosed before age 32. The incidence of breast cancer at this age is very low, about 20 per 100,000 women. Whether or not any association between abortion and breast cancer occurs later in life has not been ascertained. If that association is not found, then the effect of abortion on breast cancer incidence, if any, would be very small. Further investigations may cast light on these important questions.

Conclusion

To summarize, the increasing availability and utilization of legal abortion in the United States has had an important public health impact. The data clearly indicate that the legalization of abortion has been accompanied by a decline in deaths and complications among American women of childbearing age. It led to the rapid development of technological advances and clinical expertise in pregnancy-termination procedures. It stimulated development of more convenient, low-cost outpatient health services. Legal abortion has also brought with it new concerns—for example, about whether abortion has adverse effects on future desired pregnancies and whether it increases the risk of breast cancer in certain women. Accurate information will help policy-makers, medical practitioners, and those most directly concerned— women of childbearing age—to make rational decisions about this subject.

Willard Cates Jr. was deputy director of the Family Planning Education Division of the Center for Disease Control in Atlanta, Georgia. He presently works with the Venereal Disease Control Division, Center for Prevention Services of the same agency.

"Legalizing abortion has not wiped out abortion deaths. Deaths and near deaths from legal abortions are still being documented."

viewpoint**10**

Legal Abortion Has Not Improved Public Health

Matthew J. Bulfin

I would like to share with you today some of the thoughts that have occurred to me since the Supreme Court Decision of January 22, 1973. As an obstetrician I sincerely believe that everyone deserves a birthday.

A lady lawyer speaking before the Canadian Bar Association in Montreal drove this point home most cogently. Elizabeth Robson, of Burlington, Ontario told the assembly that had she been conceived these days, abortion might have put an end to her. Born with a very severe birth defect, she nevertheless overcame her serious disability, graduated from law school and became a highly successful and respected attorney. She said, "If I had not had the right to have been born, all those other rights would have been useless to me because I wouldn't have been here to enjoy them. Who is going to say to those who come like me: 'You are not the right kind of person we want in the world so you have no right to live'?" Attorney Elizabeth Robson received a resounding applause and a standing ovation from the assembly of Canadian attorneys.

Our role as physicians is to protect and preserve life—yet only in my specialty of Obstetrics and Gynecology are we now being asked to destroy it.

Baby as Property

The Supreme Court ruled on January 22, 1973, that an unborn baby is the property of the owner (mother) and she can have the baby killed at her request because of social distress, or for that matter, for any or no reason at all.

The most recent Supreme Court decision in January, 1979 now goes even further in that it gives full legal protection to the doctor who chooses to do abortions in the second and third trimester of

Matthew J. Bulfin, M.D. Speech presented at the ACOG Nurses District Meeting, Ft. Lauderdale, Florida, May 1979.

pregnancy. The doctor who bungles the abortion attempt at an advanced stage of pregnancy can no longer be penalized if the baby should be born alive. The physician cannot be forced to use the abortion technique most likely to save the baby's life should it be born alive. For all practical purposes, the Supreme Court has removed almost all restrictions on abortions and have declared open season on the unborn.

The fall out from this latest Supreme Court ruling has already occurred. The defense in the Dr. Waddill trial in Orange County, California is expected to stress this ruling as it will help in the possible exoneration of Dr. Waddill for his alleged strangling of Baby Girl Weaver in a hospital nursery following the baby's birth after a bungled saline abortion.

Abortion Because of Vacation

Shortly after the January 1973 Supreme Court decision I saw a 23 year old girl, pregnant for the first time; after having examined her and having heard the baby's heart beat loud and clear, I mistakenly congratulated her. She told me she wanted an abortion. It evolved that she and her husband had won a 3 week all expense paid trip to Europe and her due date would be in conflict with their European travel. She was seemingly grateful for the Supreme Court decision as it made everything legal and right for them. Needless to say she left my office and went elsewhere.

In a world in which adults control power and money, the unborn is at a disadvantage, being small, naked, nameless and voiceless. He has no one except sympathetic adults to speak up for him and defend him.

The Supreme Court has decreed death for the unborn, but they've delegated the doctor to perform the deed. They've commissioned him their executioner. The Supreme Court orders the annihilation of thousands of unborn, but they wash their hands of the blood of the abortionist. They decreed it a private matter between the woman and her physician.

No Enforceable Restrictions

The Supreme Court's abortion on demand decision is so sweepingly liberal that there are practically no restrictions that can be enforced. I recently had to hospitalize a 17 year old girl at Holy Cross Hospital who was critically ill with a large pelvic abscess following a legal abortion in Miami. She had her uterus perforated during the procedure and suffered much disability during the 2 weeks subsequently. She had the abortion done without parental consent and without their knowledge. When she became ill she was too afraid to tell them, and she would not return to the clinic because it was a "butcher shop." She pleaded with me not to tell her parents what her real problem was.

Fortunately, with large doses of intravenous antibiotics, she recovered. But had she died, her parents would probably have a million dollar lawsuit against that abortion clinic. Minors must have parental consent even to have their ears pierced—but for abortion—No.

"Deaths and near deaths from abortion complications are numerous in the United States today."

Legalizing abortion has not wiped out abortion deaths. Deaths and near deaths from legal abortions are still being documented in the United States today.

Many well-meaning people have joined the pro-abortionist lobby because they have been revolted by the horrendous tales of back street abortions. Grisly talk about unsavory operations, grubby kitchen tables, coat hangers and knitting needles used on terrified girls, leads the kindly listener to vehement opposition, and the entirely wrong assumption that this will be brought to an end with legalized abortion.

In a two year period 29 women—many of them teenagers, died in New York state following legal abortion complications. There may have been more. The number of women who have died in other states from legal abortion complications is conjectural. But the number of deaths, when tabulated, could be startling.

Is Legal Safer?

Let me give you some reasons why it is questionable whether legal abortions in many areas of the country are really safer than illegal ones. Most states fail to regulate abortion clinics. The lack of regulations permits a level of medical care so low, that in one Detroit clinic, an ex-convict with no formal medical training performs all types of abortion, both early and late.

In a three month Detroit Free Press investigation of a dozen Detroit area abortion clinics, the major findings were:

1. Five of the clinics were prepared to perform an abortion on a Free Press reporter who was not pregnant.
2. Four of the clinics perform abortions on women more than 12 weeks pregnant—a most unsafe procedure.
3. One Detroit woman died following her abortion at a small Detroit hospital.
4. Only one clinic provided even a semblance of abortion counseling.
5. No one knows how many serious complications occur as Michigan does not require that doctors report legal abortions.
6. One woman required 12 operations, including a hysterectomy, following an abortion in a Detroit clinic.
7. Abortion referral agencies advertise on radio and charge the patient $75 for referring her to an abortion clinic.
8. In Pontiac, Michigan, a woman reporter who knew she was not pregnant, stopped the doctor at the last minute from performing the procedure. When asked why he was ready to operate on a patient who was not pregnant, the doctor told the reporter that he gives refunds to those patients who are not pregnant—after the operation.

Starting on November 12, 1978 the Chicago Sun Times ran a 22 day series of front page articles on abortion clinic abuses in the Chicagoland area.

Chicago's Thriving Abortion Clinics

Five months before the *Sun-Times* and the Better Government Association began the first in-depth investigation of Chicago's thriving abortion business since the U.S. Supreme Court legalized abortion on January 22, 1973. They found:

— Dozens of abortion procedures performed on women who were not pregnant and others illegally performed on women more than 12 weeks pregnant.
— An alarming number of women who, because of unsterile conditions and haphazard clinic care, suffered debilitating cramps, massive infections and such severe internal damage that all their reproductive organs had to be removed.
— Incompetent and unqualified doctors, including moonlighting residents, medical apprentices and at least one physician who has lost his license in one state and faces revocation in Illinois.
— Doctors who callously perform abortions in an excruciating 2 minutes, when they should properly take 10 to 15 minutes, and doctors who don't even wait for pain-killing anesthetics to take effect.

— Referral services that, for a fee, send women to a disreputable Detroit abortionist, whose dog, to one couple's horror, accompanied the nurse into the operating room and lapped blood from the floor.

— Clinics that either fail to order critical post-operative pathology reports, ignore the results or mix up the specimens.

— Dangerously shoddy record keeping by aides who falsify records of patients' vital signs and scramble or lose results of crucial lab tests.

— Counselors who are paid not to counsel but to sell abortions with sophisticated pitches and deceptive promises.

Super Citizens with Right to Kill

Mildred Jefferson in her testimony before the Senate Sub-Committee on Human Life Amendments testified that the doctor and pregnant woman have been elevated to the rank of super citizens with the private right to kill by contract.

Seven justices of the Supreme Court have undertaken to practice medicine without a license by dictating what should comprise the medical judgment in the abortion decision. Without indicating when the life of the abortion target begins, the court has established a time table for allowing its willful end.

The Supreme Court decision is used as an excuse for some doctors to use no medical judgment in the abortion decision, but to serve as medical technicians performing abortions on demand.

At the same time, the Supreme Court has ruled that the state may not interfere in the abortion decision in the first three months; thus subjecting women to all the same risks of the previously illegal abortion practices. They are subject to operations at the hands of those doctors who do not face the scrutiny of peer review or the credentials committee. The patient does not even know the operator's ability to handle complications arising from the abortions.

Battering the Unborn

Parents who batter their children are being prosecuted by state attorneys across the country. Some are receiving jail sentences. The mother who batters her unborn child to death by abortion procedure is now fully protected by the courts.

Most people—and especially women who may be weighing an abortion decision—do not like to admit to themselves that abortion actually kills someone. And it is for that reason that we witness the extraordinary lengths to which proponents of abortion will go to obscure what it is that actually takes place during an abortion. It is neither novel nor surprising. What is novel, and sadly disappointing, is to observe medical professionals either actively participating in, or indifferently tolerating, the distortion, dissemblance, or avoidance of scientific fact which is so much a part of the pro-abortionist position.

For the physician, the life process is a continuous one, and observation of the patient must start at the earliest period of life. The whole thrust of present medical teaching is in support of the notion that the child in its mother is a distinct individual in need of the most diligent study and care and that he is a patient whom science and medicine treat, just as any other person. The young mother-to-be talks and asks about her baby. She doesn't ask about ''it'' or her ''thing''. Only the pro-abortion forces do that.

This concept is exemplified best by the work of Dr. Liley, a New Zealander, the world's foremost pediatrician to the unborn. Dr. Liley devised the first method for transfusing unborn infants in the mother's womb, and he thus saved the lives of thousands of Rh sensitized infants with his techniques which are now used all over the world. He has reaffirmed on his world lecture tours the fact that he is dealing with the same baby before and after birth and his clinical approach to these children is simply a matter of whether he can look after them more safely in the uterus or out of it.

Life-Saving Techniques Misused

He is extremely dismayed and unhappy that the techniques he invented for diagnosing and treating diseases of the unborn infant are now being perverted toward the selective extermination of the unborn rather than the treating and curing of these infants.

''Very often the doctors who do the abortions never see their complications. The complications are seen in the emergency rooms of hospitals.''

A striking example of the type of perversion Dr. Liley refers to can be cited rather graphically.

In a past issue of *Contemporary Obstetrics and Gynecology* two university research obstetricians are describing what is happening within the uterus of a woman five months pregnant who is about to be aborted by the saline instillation method. ''Once'', the researcher relates, ''I had a blood vessel lined up with my fetoscope (an optical instrument for visualizing the inside of the uterus) and was just about to strike with my needle when out of nowhere came this little hand and knocked the needle away. I think it was coincidental, but who knows?'' That baby was fighting for his life.

Every obstetrician should know that the unborn is very sensitive to touch and pressure and sustained pressure will produce evasive action which, in fact, can be utilized when we wish to modify the baby's position for diagnostic or therapeutic purposes—for example, in amniocentesis.

Let me talk a bit about abortions beyond the third month. Saline abortions came into popularity when it was discovered that the baby could be killed inside the mother's womb by injection of saline poison—the infant convulses and dies.

Previously, hysterotomy was the procedure of choice for terminating second trimester pregnancies. The uterus would be incised, the bleeding could be controlled because visualization was good, but the removal of a perfectly normal, heart beating, limbs waving baby from the uterus to be left to die is a most repugnant and deeply disturbing experience for the nurses, and operating room personnel. Now, however, saline abortion allows the killing of the baby inside the uterus out of public view, so to speak. It's seemingly, to some of these people, not as offensive.

Saver and Executioner

These type abortions especially have all types of horrendous ramifications. The obstetrician can well become schizophrenic. How can he be both life saver and executioner at the same time? How can one obstetrician work frantically to save the life of a 2 lb. 4 oz. infant born prematurely to a mother who desperately wants her baby to live? How can this same obstetrician, maybe that very day, instill the poisonous saline into the uterus of another woman with a baby identical in size and development, and watch that baby convulse and die in her uterus? Or should he use the prostaglandins for her second trimester abortion he may very likely be confronted with a normal baby born alive whom he may now choose to allow to die—Dr. Waddill in California is alleged to have strangled the baby in a similar situation.

"Our American Association of Pro Life Obstetricians and Gynecologists will continue to monitor abortion catastrophes and complications and publicize them."

With more than a million abortions having been done last year in the United States, the new subspecialty of exterminative medicine may be on the horizon. Deaths and near deaths from abortion complications are numerous in the United States today....

Abortion Complications

Some malpractice carriers will not insure doctors who do abortions because of the multiplicity of physical, mental and legal complications that may evolve years later.

The immediate complications following induced abortions which are given by various authors as ranging from 3% to 25%—are really only the tip of the iceberg. The latent morbidity, which cannot be fully assessed this early, is much more significant. This morbidity will become apparent during the course of subsequent pregnancies with stillbirths, prematurity problems—exsanguinating maternal hemorrhages from old cervical lacerations, and uterine ruptures. These events will definitely occur and the obstetrician who cares for these patients must be prepared to cope with them.

Very often the doctors who do the abortions never see their complications. The complications are seen in the emergency room of hospitals or in the offices of gynecologists closest to the patient's home. It is this unfortunate physician who is called upon to manage the complication who is at a tremendous disadvantage. Abortion records are notoriously poor and inadequate and tissue examinations of aborted specimens are non-existent in many clinics. Record keeping for abortion cases is evidently discouraged in many of the places where abortions are done.

What can obstetricians do to stop this senseless onslaught on human life?

I urge my colleagues to speak out. More than 800 obstetricians and gynecologists have joined our new American Association. It seems incongruous that any obstetrician trained to safeguard the mother and her unborn would deliberately choose to depart from this joy giving specialty to one of death and destruction. A pathologist in Miami told me that if our Association could dissuade one young obstetrician from doing his first abortion, we would be on the right road. One abortionist told my pathologist friend that his first abortion was a sickening experience. He felt the needle stick the baby and he felt the baby jump and convulse in the uterus as the poison saline solution was injected. His second and third abortions did not bother him nearly as much, because he prepared himself for what to expect. He has done hundreds since then.

Abortion and Child Abuse

Our new association is also refuting headlines such as these:
"Abortion cuts the numbers of abandoned infants."
"Abortion is Safer than Childbirth."
Jonathan Lanman, M.D., of the Population Council proudly proclaimed "Abortion cuts numbers of abandoned infants", to the American Pediatric Society meeting in San Francisco. The Journal of the American Medical Association gave this story top billing.

Abortion proponents after having endorsed the killing of hundreds of thousands of the unborn have seen fit to conclude that because of their good work, less babies are abandoned. It's great to die in the uterus as a fetus before you get old enough to be abandoned as an infant.

It seems incongruous and pitiful that in our own area in Broward County Florida, more than 5,000 abortions are done each year, mostly because the pregnancy is a temporary inconvenience to the mother. At our hospital the obstetricians do no abortions at all and have a long list of adoptive parents who desperately desire to adopt but can find no babies to adopt and give their love to. There should be some way to bring all these parties together without sacrificing one human life.

The most effective means that I have today to dissuade girls from having abortions is the small fetal doptone that I use at my office every day. It is now easy to pick up strong fetal heart beats at 2 to 2½ months pregnancy. Girls who hear their baby's heart beat at this early stage often become supporters of the Pro Life movement.

Reverence for Life

As physicians and human beings, we would do well to follow the example and teachings of that famous medical missionary, Dr. Albert Schweitzer, who said, "If a man loses reverence for any part of life, he will lose his reverence for all life."

"Girls who hear their baby's heart beat. . . often become supporters of the Pro Life movement."

Our American Association of Pro Life Obstetricians and Gynecologists will continue to monitor abortion catastrophes and complications and publicize them. We are striving to encourage the providing of adequate care and living needs for the patient who cannot bring herself to destroy her unborn. We will continue to give support to obstetricians and hospital administrators who refuse to allow social abortions and abortions of convenience in their hospitals. We must educate the American public and our legislators and show them what abortion really is. It is not to be equated with birth control.

I have learned well that those who take the trouble to investigate abortion thoroughly will hardly ever campaign for it.

Matthew J. Bulfin, M.D., is president of the American Association of Pro Life Obstetricians and Gynecologists. Physician members of this organization oppose abortions, perform no abortions, and take no part in arranging abortions.

"As we learn to detect more imperfections. . .will we in fact be losing more than we gain?"

Overview: Prenatal Screening

Graham Chedd

Parents come to this hospital clinic in Stony Brook, New York, where doctors can tell months before their babies are due whether the infants are the victims of potentially severe defects of the spinal cord and brain. Unlike the more costly and potentially dangerous genetic screening procedures that involve withdrawing fluid from the womb, the program here begins with an innocuous blood test for a chemical warning called alphafetoprotein or AFP. And unlike other screening programs that look for specific birth defects in small, high-risk populations, this one is designed for every pregnant woman. No couple is any less likely than another to have one of the thousands of children born each year with these neural tube defects.

Scientists say AFP screening may be the first of many simple checks for defects in all fetuses, the beginning of a large-scale quality control program for children that is already raising a host of ethical, emotional, and economic questions. Couldn't these tests eventually be used to justify the elimination of babies with what are relatively minor disorders? Perhaps no one is more aware of the dilemma posed by AFP screening than James Macri, the prenatal expert who runs the program and who is himself the father of a child with a neural tube defect. "I do this testing to inform families," he says, "and to prepare them for all the options."

Neural Tube's Formation

Toward the end of the first month of pregnancy, when the human fetus is still less than an inch long, a platelike structure along its back curls upward like a sheet of paper being formed into a roll. The resulting neural tube is the precursor of the backbone, spinal cord, and brain. Should the tube fail

to close securely for some portion of its length, the future development of the fetus is impaired. An opening at the top end of the neural tube results in the fetus failing to develop a normal brain. Such a fetus, should it come to term, is born with anencephaly and rarely survives more than a few hours or days. A defect lower in the neural tube can lead to the exposure outside the body of the spinal cord and nerve bundles. At birth the opening can be surgically closed, but the baby is paralyzed below the waist and commonly cannot maintain proper bladder and bowel control. Many babies with such open neural tube defects—called spina bifida—also suffer from hydrocephaly, water on the brain. This can be controlled with the aid of a permanently implanted shunt that drains the excess fluid in the brain away to the heart or abdomen. As well as these physical handicaps, many spina bifida children suffer from mental retardation.

The prognosis for infants with spina bifida is a matter for debate. Some paint an uncompromisingly bleak picture of the disease and note that less than half of all babies with moderate to severe open neural tube defects survive two years. They also note the hardships—both economic and emotional—faced by spina bifida victims and their families when these children survive into adulthood. This group favors prenatal diagnosis.

On the other side are those who point to the extreme variability of the disease, arguing that those least affected have only minor physical impairment and normal mental development. Aggressive therapy has improved the quality of the victim's life, they say. And above all, afflicted children—perhaps especially because they are afflicted—are capable of both loving and being loved. Members of this group, many of them parents who have learned to cope with the disease with the help of organizations like the Spina Bifida Association of America, are much more circumspect about screening. They worry about

Graham Chedd, "Who Shall Be Born?" *Science 81,* January/February 1981. Reprinted by permission of SCIENCE 84 Magazine, © the American Association for the Advancement of Science.

creating an atmosphere in which people who have learned to live with the disease feel that perhaps they should never have been born.

Opposing Views of Prenatal Diagnosis

This confrontation is not unique to spina bifida, of course; it reflects opposing views of the merging technology of prenatal diagnosis. Until now only pregnant women known to be at a higher than normal risk for specific diseases have been screened before birth—women over the age of 35, for example, who are at a greater risk for Down's syndrome; or Jewish women of eastern European descent, who suffer a greater incidence of the fatal, degenerative Tay-Sachs disease. But while neural tube defects do show up at different rates in different groups, in general the risk is spread throughout the entire population, threatening one or two pregnancies in every thousand. The cause of the disease is unknown; as a consequence, spina bifida seems to strike quite unpredictably. Every pregnancy must be regarded as a candidate for AFP screening.

"The chances of a normal fetus being aborted by its parents because of a mistaken diagnosis are now very small."

In 1972 David Brock and Roger Sutcliffe of Western General Hospital in Edinburgh discovered a correlation between abnormally high levels of AFP in amniotic fluid and pregnancies leading to anencephaly and spina bifida. A year later, reasoning that pregnancies could be screened for neural tube defects by determining levels of AFP in a sample of maternal blood, Brock and a group of colleagues developed a sophisticated but highly reliable measuring technique using immunological agents tagged with radioactive tracers.

AFP is manufactured mainly in the liver of a fetus. When the fetus urinates, AFP passes into the amniotic fluid in which the fetus floats. However, a fetus with a neural tube defect pours higher than normal amounts of AFP into the amniotic fluid—and eventually the mother's blood—through the opening in its spine. By the 16th to 18th week of pregnancy, the level of AFP is high enough to measure in the mother's blood. Unfortunately the high level could also indicate many other factors, some known, some unknown. In fact, a neural tube defect is one of the least likely causes of high AFP measurement.

AFP and the Normal Fetus

For example, because a normal fetus continues to excrete AFP as it grows older, a misjudgment of the age by even a week or two can result in an AFP measurement that suggests a neural tube defect.

According to Macri, whose Neural Tube Defect Lab at the State University of New York at Stony Brook is one of the most successful screening programs in the country, most AFP blood levels considered high are caused this way. If the pregnant woman is carrying twins, both of them excreting AFP, the measurement would also falsely suggest a fetus with spina bifida or anencephaly. And there are many other still poorly understood reasons why AFP levels can be high.

All these instances are "false positives," suggesting a fetus is affected when it isn't. Because Macri and his colleagues have set a fairly low cutoff point for a positive result, they are able to catch 90 percent of all open neural tube defects. But the inevitable concomitant of their low cutoff point is a high number of false positives. So if 1,000 women are tested, 50 will have a positive AFP, suggesting they may be carrying a fetus with a neural tube defect when, in fact, only one or two of them are.

What happens to those 50 women? First, another AFP blood test is run, which will clear about 20 women. The remaining 30, still with high AFP levels—and more anxious than ever now that their odds of carrying an affected fetus have been shortened from about 500 to 1 to about 15 to 1—undergo an ultrasound examination. This relatively straightforward and widely available procedure uses the reflection of sound waves to determine the fetus' head diameter and thus its age. It also can reveal twins. Of the 30 women undergoing an ultrasound examination, 15 will be cleared, most of them because the fetus each is carrying is older than it was thought to be.

For the remaining 15 women, however, the odds of carrying a fetus with a neural tube defect are now down to 7 to 1. They must undergo amniocentesis, the procedure in which a three-inch needle is inserted through the abdominal wall into the amniotic fluid and some of the liquid is drawn off. Fetal cells in the fluid can be tested to diagnose Down's syndrome and Tay-Sachs disease, among others; the fluid, of course, also contains AFP. The more direct AFP measurement possible from the amniotic fluid allows most of the 15 women remaining from the original 1,000 to be cleared.

For those who remain, the odds favor an affected fetus. But still there is room for error; for example, any fetal blood contaminating the sample could drastically raise AFP levels, a possibility that can be excluded with a repeat amniocentesis. To further reduce the chance of a wrong diagnosis, two more tests are possible: a highly sophisticated ultrasound examination, which in the hands of a few experts— including one at Macri's lab—can actually reveal the lesion characteristic of spina bifida; or a new chemical test, also used at Stony Brook, in which the amniotic fluid is analyzed for the presence of the enzyme acetylcholinesterase, which appears to be a reliable indication of a neural tube defect.

Provided all these tests are run, Macri says the chances of a normal fetus being aborted by its parents because of a mistaken diagnosis are now very small. That does not mean that the screening program will not lead to the loss of normal fetuses, however. Amniocentesis, while generally safe for both mother and fetus, is not risk free. Macri concedes that up to one percent of all women undergoing amniocentesis suffer miscarriages, though others believe the true miscarriage rate to be somewhat higher. That means that if 100,000 undergo the AFP screening, 1,500 will have to undergo an amniocentesis, which will identify 180 fetuses with open neural tube defects in time for the women to consider aborting them, as almost all in that position do, or at least in time to prepare for the difficulties that lie ahead. But as a result of the procedure, between 10 and 20 normal fetuses will be lost through miscarriage. Moreover, 5,000 women, by having high AFP levels, will enter a maze from which there are several exits, each more anxiety-provoking and expensive to reach than the one that preceded it, until in the end the great majority will be told it was all a false alarm. In less comprehensive programs some women may be so frightened early on that they have abortions even though later tests would have cleared them.

In Britain the consensus is that even considering the negative side of the equation, AFP screening is useful and desirable. Two years ago, when it was considering licensing the radioimmunoassay materials for sale to laboratories in the United States, the Food and Drug Administration seemed to agree. But then the Spina Bifida Association of America and later Ralph Nader's Health Research Group, various anti-abortion organizations, the American College of Obstetrics and Gynecology, and the American Association of Pediatrics intervened, causing the FDA to reconsider its options.

AFP Opinions Voiced

Last summer in Washington the FDA and the National Center for Health Care Technology organized a meeting to air some of the differences of opinion about the AFP test. Few at the meeting doubted the desirability of going ahead with screening programs; the question was how, or, as it was called at the meeting, the "full vs. half-a-loaf" issue. Everyone agreed that, ideally, a full loaf of service should be available to women undergoing AFP screening, including knowledgeable, sympathetic counselors who can explain and perform the testing procedure and the full range of backup diagnostic tests, such as amniocentesis and ultrasound. But many at the meeting argued that half a loaf—just the AFP blood test itself—was better than nothing. Despite the problems that the rapid, widespread, and only minimally restricted introduction of AFP screening might generate, they claimed the alternative—the birth of from 3,000 to 6,000 children with open neural tube defects each year—is worse.

Macri was among those who urged caution. He continues to do so today. "Anyone who preaches the half-a-loaf philosophy is asking a mother to make a decision based on inadequate information," he says, "and I can't imagine how anyone can do that." He believes that the favorable experience of the British and of regional programs like his in the United States have been due to tight and careful supervision. As an example of what can go wrong under the half-a-loaf philosophy, Macri envisions what might have happened to Julie Magnani, a recent patient at Stony Brook. Although her blood contained elevated levels of AFP, further analyses proved them to be false positives and she gave birth to a normal baby boy. "If that same woman is out in Utah or down in Tennessee, away from a regional program, she is not going to have the benefit of informed advice. She's going to terminate a perfectly normal pregnancy."

"In the end it might cost a woman several hundred dollars to be told that nothing is wrong."

The FDA now agrees with the whole-loaf approach. Regulations proposed in November for the sale of AFP materials to laboratories are designed to limit the availability of the test to physicians participating in comprehensive screening programs. Manufacturers would be required to monitor the use of the materials and report to the FDA on test results and the choices parents make based on them. Further, specially trained counselors would have to be available to fully brief women on the implications of the test, the nature of open neural tube defects, and the options available, including abortion, if the fetus is shown to be affected. Each woman would have to acknowledge in writing that such a briefing had been given.

The Costs of AFP

The proposed regulations do not settle many other problems raised by AFP screening, among them the question of cost. A woman can be offered the AFP blood test for $20, but the expenses mount as later tests become necessary: $80 for an ultrasound exam and another $75 at Macri's clinic for amniocentesis, for example. In the end it might cost a woman several hundred dollars to be told that nothing is wrong. Currently not all medical insurance policies have provisions for prenatal testing. What will become of a woman who takes the first test and then discovers that the next one will cost $80, the next $75—amounts she cannot afford? How many will drop out midway through the tests with fears about their pregnancies that they cannot allay? Then, too, there is the question of paying for the abortion of an affected fetus. To complete all the diagnostic steps and then abort an affected fetus could cost close to $1,000. Is AFP screening, along with the option of avoiding the birth of a severely handicapped baby, to be reserved only for the affluent?

The Ethics of AFP

But the most difficult question surrounding AFP screening and future broad-based genetic testing has little to do with economics or regulatory considerations. As we learn to detect more imperfections and eliminate more fetuses, will we in fact be losing more than we gain? It is a question that's powerfully framed every week at a clinic 300 miles from Stony Brook in Washington, D.C.

In the middle of the pastel yellow waiting room on a Monday afternoon, a young mother sits with her son, Andrew, a two-and-a-half-year-old with a large round face, big brown eyes, and a joyful smile. His mother boasts that Andrew demonstrated the intellectual capacity of a four-year-old on a recent intelligence test. Lifting him momentarily, she reveals the only outward signs of a health problem: Andrew's legs droop lifelessly. Spina bifida has paralyzed them.

Here at Georgetown University Hospital's spina bifida clinic, parents learn to cope with and care for their handicapped children. Few of them have undergone AFP screening, but every one of them who was asked said that it wouldn't have changed a thing.

"Every day Andrew does or says something that makes me thank God I have him," says his mother, beaming. "He's a blessing."

Graham Chedd is a contributing editor of Science 81.

"We decided that termination of the pregnancy was the only course. Every person deserves a fair chance at a good life, and this child wouldn't have that chance."

Aborting a Handicapped Fetus Is a Private Decision

Julie K. Ivey

On a Thursday morning early in March while doing my housework, I had a wonderful feeling of contentment. Usually I hate those tedious domestic tasks, but this morning I was spending extra time on them, and enjoying every minute of it.

I had a few good reasons to be happy. Our daughter, Jennifer, would be four years old on the fifteenth of the month, and Jim and I were planning an exciting party for her with all the little friends she wanted to invite. Also, I was almost five months pregnant with my second child whom I could feel moving and kicking inside of me. These two children were especially important to us because we had been infertility patients for six years and had been told it was unlikely we'd ever have children. Then, after eight years of marriage, the miracle we had prayed for occurred, and Jennifer was born. Now, it had happened again. We were on our way to having the family we wanted to make our lives complete.

As I counted my blessings that morning, I was certain I had another one to count. Any day now we expected the results of the amniocentesis I'd undergone—it's a test that's usually performed on pregnant women over thirty-five and other high-risk patients to detect abnormalities in the fetus. When I became pregnant with Jennifer, I was twenty-nine. At that time Jim and I learned that because we both had spinal disorders, our risk of bearing a child with spina bifida—a severe defect of the central nervous system—was increased to 2 percent. So, for this reason we decided to go ahead with the test just for reassurance. The results told us Jennifer would be fine, and we expected the same kind of reassurance this time around. I was anticipating the call from the doctor, who would tell us, "You have a normal, healthy baby."

Just as I finished cleaning the bathroom, the telephone rang. "Good," I thought, "it's either Jim, or the doctor with our news."

A person's life can be turned into a nightmare with just a few words. My obstetrician was on the line, informing me that the results of the amniocentesis indicated the baby was severely abnormal, with forty-seven chromosomes instead of the normal forty-six. Trembling and on the verge of hysterics, I immediately called our geneticist who confirmed the child was afflicted with Klinefelter's Syndrome, a disorder that affects males only. He explained that Klinefelter children may appear outwardly normal, but they have inner abnormalities of the reproductive system caused by an extra sex chromosome received at the moment of conception that results in abnormally developed sex organs. There is some breast development, the voice tends to be high-pitched, there is a lack of normal male hair growth, and Klinefelter males are sterile. Moreover, they can be mentally retarded, ranging from moderate to severe. This abnormality is a fluke—the incidence of Klinefelter's Syndrome is one in six hundred for live-born males. Nothing can be done medically to correct it. Our geneticist advised that the abnormality was so severe and so devastating that abortion, as soon as possible, should be the only consideration.

Denying the Truth

Somehow I managed to maintain my composure on the phone, but once I hung up, I fell apart. Our baby, our special creation, was to be taken away from us. It couldn't be true. This was a child Jim and I had conceived; there couldn't possibly be anything so seriously wrong with it. These things happen to other people—strangers—not to us.

It was a crank call, that's what it was. Or there had been a mistake in the test. Or the doctor had confused my test results with another patient's. They weren't talking about my baby.

I hugged my abdomen protectively. I paced up and down, crying, repeating to my baby, "Nothing is going to happen to you. Nobody is going to take you away from me." I loved this fragile little wisp of life, so innocently moving inside me, and I cursed the unmerciful God who would let such a thing happen, wondering what I had done that was so horrible to warrant such a punishment.

I needed help, I needed Jim, but I couldn't bring myself to call him at work. He loved this child as much as I did; we had to be together when he received the news.

I managed to live through the day until Jim came home. After much discussion and soul-searching, we decided that termination of the pregnancy was the only course. Every person deserves a fair chance at a good life, and this child wouldn't have that chance. He would also be an outcast, the object of stares and pity, perhaps even ridicule. He would never be a playmate for Jennifer; instead he'd be a lifelong burden, a burden we had no right to place on her. We had a responsibility to provide Jennifer with as normal and happy a childhood as possible, and we would be failing in that responsibility if we brought this child into the world. We knew we couldn't cope with the havoc and devastation that visits families with children who are severely deformed and retarded.

Preventing Suffering

Still, I questioned whether we had the right to end the child's life, and a friend said, "Julie, if God had wanted this child to be born, He wouldn't have made it possible for you to know it was going to be abnormal. God made it possible for you to know so that you could save one human being from a lifetime of suffering and pain. It's God's will."

It was this thought primarily, these words of reassurance, that made it possible for us to proceed with the abortion; I kept thinking it was God's will. Heartbreaking as it was, we had to give up our baby. It had to be done.

I made only one request of the doctors: that they spare me further agony by performing the abortion while I was totally anesthetized, so I wouldn't be aware of what was happening. My one request was to be denied. The obstetrician gently explained that a pregnancy so advanced—nearly five months—could not be terminated by any of the simpler methods used for a first-trimester pregnancy. A pregnancy at this late stage, he said, had to be terminated through induced labor and vaginal delivery, a method known as saline evacuation. This procedure begins with the extraction of some amniotic fluid from the uterus; the fluid is replaced with a saline (salt) solution that causes the fetus to die promptly, and subsequently—anywhere from twelve to forty-eight hours later—induces labor. Although this is the most traumatic method of terminating a pregnancy because of the

extended time factor and because the woman has to undergo labor and delivery, it is by far the safest and the most commonly used for second-trimester pregnancies. It is much safer than a cesarean section, which in my desperation I had requested.

And so, I was to go into labor and delivery in exactly the same manner as if a child were to be born. Only I wouldn't be taking a baby home in my arms from the hospital—I would deliver a dead fetus.

By now I was totally dependent on Jim's strength. I feared being left alone, and only he seemed to be able to calm me when the baby kicked or turned somersaults and I would burst into tears. We were facing a tremendous loss and we grieved equally, but he understood that the child who was to be aborted was in my body, and that this particular anguish we could not share.

Emotional Ordeal

On Monday morning Jim took me to the hospital, where I was admitted to out-patient surgery. Even for the few minutes it took me to change from my street clothes into a hospital gown I could not be left alone. I panicked, started trembling and stumbled out of my dressing room crying that I had to have my husband with me. The sympathetic nurse brought him to me immediately. He held my hands, talked to me of Jennifer, how beautiful she was, knowing that the thought of her would give me courage to proceed. He kissed me, hugged me tightly, and wished out loud that he could take my place so I could be spared the ordeal.

"Neither Jim nor I felt any desire to see the fetus. . . . The geneticist would examine it and report that it had an abnormally small head—a sure sign of mental retardation."

The procedure itself took only a few minutes. Cramping set in immediately, then subsided over the next few hours until there was no cramping at all. I was released from the hospital and allowed to return home until labor began; my obstetrician predicted it would commence sometime Tuesday night. He offered one consolation: Labor and delivery of such a small fetus would be shorter and less intense than for a full-term baby.

When I arrived home I slept, with the aid of tranquilizers the doctor prescribed, and when I awoke I felt only a heaviness, as though everything in my body had dropped. There was no longer any movement inside me. Most nights the baby's restless stirrings had lulled me to sleep with thoughts of little booties and lullabies I'd soon sing, but tonight there were only the strange stillness and abnormal heaviness within me.

Tuesday was a long, tension-filled day for Jim and me. We made arrangements for a friend to care for Jennifer on Tuesday night and Wednesday. Jim didn't leave my side for a moment for fear I'd go into labor during his absence. The heaviness was still with me, and I experienced some difficulty moving around, though no pain. I thought: I'm carrying around a dead baby. I have no right to be wearing maternity clothes. Maternity clothes are like a badge of achievement, and I have achieved nothing.

Contractions Begin

The doctor's prediction was correct. At 3 A.M. on Wednesday morning I awoke with mild contractions. Since they were so weak, I decided to let Jim continue sleeping and to occupy myself with sewing Jennifer's birthday dress while I timed them. Jennifer's party had become the focus of my life, my goal, something to look forward to.

"We know we made the right decision; we have no regrets."

I sewed for about an hour and, when the contractions were five minutes apart, called the hospital, even though I was still in no pain. I was advised to go there as soon as possible. Jim drove at record-breaking speed.

I was admitted immediately. There were no forms to be filled out—they were expecting me. I was taken in a wheelchair to a room in the gynecological ward where delivery would take place with the assistance of nurses specially trained to handle such circumstances. Periodically, my obstetrician came in to check my progress. I was assured that pain medication would be administered at my request, but warned that it would slow down the contractions and extend the ordeal. But when the contractions became intense I panicked. I didn't want to feel anything—couldn't cope with this simulation of natural delivery. I couldn't forget that there was nothing natural about it, that I would be leaving the hospital empty-handed. So I asked for medication and, as I had been forewarned the contractions slowed down. When its effects wore off, I made a decision: I would experience the full force of the contractions and get it over with as soon as possible.

Ten Hours of Labor

It was nearly ten hours of labor before anything really started happening. Jim had kept vigil at my bedside all night—nothing, not even hunger, could pry him away. At one o'clock Wednesday afternoon the contractions began to get increasingly severe. I

felt a need to urinate; however, once in the bathroom I was unable to and complained of a terrible pressure. The nurse was certain this was it, that the pressure indicated imminent delivery. She assisted me back to the bed and instructed me to push with all my might, she holding one of my hands and Jim the other. I pushed until the pressure and pain became unbearable. I cried out, "It's no good, nothing is happening." She urged me to go on, not to give up, that it would soon be over. I tried again and felt a sudden burst, a gush of fluids and then immediate relief from all pain and discomfort.

"Thank God. Thank God it's all over," I cried. And then I learned I had not yet delivered the fetus. All that had happened was that the membranes had ruptured and released the amniotic fluid.

With the rupture of the membranes, contractions stopped, and it was necessary to put a drug in my I.V. to cause my uterus to resume contractions. Once they began, I was instructed to push during each contraction. I gripped Jim's hand and gave a push.

"It's happening," I cried. "It's happening!" Within seconds the room was filled with nurses administering to my needs. I delivered the fetus, and the placenta followed shortly thereafter.

Neither Jim nor I felt any desire to see the fetus; we had already discussed this and felt strongly that we didn't want to have the visual reminder. Later that evening the geneticist would examine it and report that it had an abnormally small head—a sure indication of mental retardation—an abnormally small chin, low-set ears and small gonads.

When it was over, I felt so well, as though I had never been pregnant, had not just a few minutes earlier delivered the fetus. This curious feeling of well-being was accompanied by a peacefulness, a strange tranquility. Possibly it was because I had carried a dead baby around inside me for almost two days and was relieved it was over. Possibly it was because I had done what had to be done. Actually, it was merely the eye of the storm.

As soon as my obstetrician pronounced me fit to go home, I jumped out of bed, got dressed and left the hospital without a moment's delay. The ordeal was behind us; now we could return to our little girl and resume the business of living. Or so we thought. It never occurred to us that, having carried a child for almost five months, my body would react as though I had a baby, a baby it was prepared to receive and nourish. My breasts filled with milk and became painful. My arms longed for a baby to cradle. I felt desolate, empty, as though a part of me were missing.

Depression and Doubt

The only thing that kept me functioning as a reasonably sane person during the next few days was planning Jennifer's birthday party. It became my reason for living. As long as I remained involved in a frenzy of activity I didn't have to face up to reality; I could live within the narrow vacuum of my own creation. Everyone else recognized the lifeline I was desperately grasping, except me.

When the party day passed and the excitement was over, it was time to resume our everyday routine. Jim returned to work, Jennifer to school. I was alone for the first time. Suddenly I felt lost in my own home, driven to seek an escape. But it wasn't my home I wanted to escape, it was myself. I'd lost the lifeline; now what would I cling to for survival? It was then that I fell completely apart.

I had never known the depths of depression, the utter despair that can drive a person to suicide. My descent from sanity into this bottomless, abysmal pit was so rapid and so totally demoralizing that I no longer wanted to live. I castigated myself with a single-minded ferocity, becoming the object of self-hate.

Why had I ended my baby's life? All those rational reasons of an earlier time eluded me. Without my baby I wasn't complete. I wanted to put an end to my misery. I refused Jim's help and, so wrapped up in my piteous wretchedness, became oblivious to *his* needs for comfort. Friends who sensed my emotional upheaval tried to reach out to me but I refused them, too, permitting nothing to penetrate my agony, silently crying out for my lost baby, my only possible salvation.

"The passage of time has a healing effect; somehow, you find yourself surviving."

Yet somehow I managed during those days to complete the absolutely necessary tasks a mother and wife must perform. I know that I at least provided Jim and Jennifer with their meals. And I suppose I should be grateful for those mundane tasks, because they provided an interlude during which other feelings surfaced, such as my love for my family. Could I knowingly inflict pain on Jennifer? And what about Jim? After all, he had lost as much as I had. Nor could I hurt my mother, father, sister, my friends who had been so supportive—all the people I loved and who loved me.

Violent Nightmares

I then cried out for help. I called my obstetrician, who prescribed antidepressants that were helpful. I accepted the comfort Jim held out to me and the kindness of my family and friends. I forced myself to read in an attempt to keep my mind off my problems. I took Jennifer out to lunch every day when she got home from school so I'd be forced to look presentable and get out of the house.

The passage of time has a healing effect; somehow,

you find yourself surviving. Each day at dusk I gave thanks that I'd gotten through another day; each morning after a fitful sleep, I felt grateful that another long night was over. I had violent nightmares and would wake up screaming. What they were about I don't quite remember, except for the fleeting impression of a little boy. Gradually they lessened in intensity and frequency, so that now I no longer have them.

Jim and I have spent many hours talking about the baby. We know we made the right decision; we have no regrets. And though we know it's impossible to forget what happened, we were making a conscious effort to think of the ordeal as a thing of the past, and to plan, with hope, for the future. We are young and healthy, and the geneticist has assured us that we will be able to have all the children we want. We will have more children, and we will have a son to take the place of the one we lost.

Julie K. Ivey is a Virginia-based freelance writer who is currently working on a novel.

Aborting a Handicapped Fetus Should Not Be Allowed

Anna Marie Dahlquist

"You're definitely pregnant," the obstetrician announced, confirming my joyful suspicions. Now that I was out of the chilly, antiseptic examining room, I settled back to relax in the comfortable black leather chair in his office. Meanwhile, pencil in hand, he glanced over my medical records.

"What a nice doctor," I thought as I looked at his round, jovial face. I was glad another young mother had recommended him to me when we moved to our present home.

"Age thirty-eight," he remarked casually as he read my chart. "You know, California law requires me to tell every patient over thirty-five about the risks of bearing a child with Down's syndrome. This condition occurs when an extra chromosome is present at conception, and it results in certain physical traits in the child, as well as in mental retardation."

I felt myself getting nervous as the doctor continued, "There's only a slight chance of a mother in her twenties having a baby with Down's syndrome, one in a couple of thousand. But the risk increases sharply with age. For a woman in her late thirties, there's a likelihood of one in every few hundred. In her early forties, the chance is one out of every 100, increasing to one in forty by the time she reaches her mid-forties."

By now I was grasping the padded arms of the chair very tightly. "State law," he continued, laying my chart down on his desk, "also requires me to inform you of the availability of amniocentesis. This is a test in which a small amount of amniotic fluid is removed and examined to determine whether Down's syndrome is present. You can be tested either at Stanford or Cal. And if the fetus is abnormal, then you can have an abortion."

"Then you can have an abortion!" The words reverberated in my ears like a thunderbolt. Every muscle in my body tightened as I tried to respond as calmly as I could.

"Well, I don't believe in abortion, so I'm not interested in having the test! I'd rather raise a mongoloid child than have an abortion."

Law and Morality

The obstetrician leaned forward in surprise. "Most women can't wait to see if their babies are okay. They rush right down to Stanford! Of course, most of them get good news. Out of 100 women tested recently, only five had abortions. But the test isn't always 100 percent accurate. One of those aborted fetuses was found to be normal, although the amniocentesis had indicated otherwise.... But it's my duty to inform you of the available services. Then you can decide what to do."

I calmed down as the interview continued. But as my husband, Richard, drove me home, I was seething inside: "The very idea! A state law that requires patients to know where they can get an abortion! What will be next? A law requiring amniocentesis itself in women over thirty-five? And then a law requiring abnormal fetuses to be aborted?"

Later on, as the baby grew and moved within me, I began to think of the risks the doctor had mentioned. Richard and I both had been single for some years; I was thirty-three when we met and thirty-four when we married. Two years later, our little girl had been born. And now Richard and I so much wanted a companion for her! We had been praying for more than a year that God would give us another child. When we first suspected pregnancy, it had seemed like the answer to our prayers!

"But what if the baby *is* afflicted with Down's syndrome?" I asked myself. "It might tie me down for years! Could the doctor possibly be right, along

Anna Marie Dahlquist, "Then You Can Have an Abortion," *Eternity*, March 1981. Reprinted by permission of the author.

with so many politicians and women's magazines? They all seem to assume a woman has a right to decide whether or not she wants to give birth to a child she has already conceived."

What would it be like to raise a mongoloid child? I knew three Christian couples with Down's syndrome babies. I thought about how, without exception, they had stated, "This child has been a blessing to our family." In each case, they had said, the family had been drawn closer together, and the older children had learned gentleness and patience through the relationship.

Celebrating Down's Syndrome

I thought of the dozen young men I had seen at an amusement park recently. Their short, stocky frames and distinctive features had indicated to me at once that they were all Down's syndrome cases. Bounding out of their institution's bus with all the gusto of nine-year-olds, they had climbed aboard the little trains and race cars with such enthusiasm that I could not help feeling a sense of celebration rather than sorrow. Certainly the few "special" children I knew in this category had a real ability to be affectionate and also to enjoy life.

"How could I, or anyone else, I asked myself, even consider breaking that commandment just to make life a little easier and less demanding?"

"Yes," I thought, "such a child might be a burden, but surely not an unbearable one. And wouldn't it be better for our little girl to grow up with a retarded brother or sister, than with no brother or sister at all? Wouldn't it help teach her to be loving, sharing, and responsible?"

But beyond all the practical implications, there stood the law of the Lord: "Thou shalt not kill." How could I, or anyone else, I asked myself, even consider breaking that commandment just to make life a little easier and less demanding?

During the next few months, the risk of bearing a child with Down's syndrome did not often cross my mind. My husband and I had committed the matter to the Lord and knew that he could give the necessary grace if and when we needed it. I knew beyond any doubt that I would abide by the words that had come to my lips in my initial reaction: "I'd rather raise a mongoloid child than consider an abortion."

Christian leaders today seem to be divided on this issue. Some argue that compassion for the mother should not require her to bring a retarded child into the world. Others feel retardation is not a valid grounds for abortion. John R.W. Stott writes, "The Christian conscience rebels against the notion that an unborn child may be destroyed because his birth would be a 'burden' to the mother or her family."

Perhaps it could be argued that most theologians have not experienced the situation firsthand. They know nothing of the pain and sorrow a mother faces when she is told her infant will never be normal.

How does it feel? Dale Evans, recently interviewed by Dr. James Dobson on his "Focus on the Family" radio program, told of the heartache she experienced when doctors told her that her baby was afflicted with Down's syndrome. Yet she states, "Knowing what I know now, I would not abort a Down's syndrome child. Our child blessed us and taught us things we would never have learned in any other way."

In my own case, all fears for our child were needless. Elizabeth Joy, born when I was thirty-nine, is a healthy, mischievous, normal toddler.

Nevertheless, I am glad the doctor made me stop to consider the possibility of giving birth to a retarded child. Facing the issue made me realize more fully how deeply committed I am to the belief that only God has the right to terminate human life, even if that life is still in the womb and possibly afflicted with some abnormality.

Anna Marie Dahlquist lives in Kingsburg, California.

"If the prospective life of defective newborns is bad we are doing them a favor to let them die."

Infant Euthanasia Is Morally Acceptable

Richard B. Brandt

The *legal* rights of a fetus are very different from those of a newborn. The fetus may be aborted, legally, for any reason or no reason up to twenty-four or twenty-eight weeks (U.S. Supreme Court, *Roe v. Wade*). But, at least in theory, immediately after birth an infant has all the legal rights of the adult, including the right to life.

The topic of this paper, however, is to identify the moral rights of the newborn, specifically whether *defective* newborns have a right to life. But it is simpler to talk, not about "rights to life," but about when or whether it is *morally right* either actively or passively (by withdrawal of life support measures) to terminate defective newborns. It is also better because the conception of a right involves the notion of a sphere of autonomy—something is to be done or omitted, but only if the subject of the rights wants or consents—and this fact is apt to be confusing or over-simplifying. Surely what we want to know is whether termination is morally right or wrong, and nothing can turn on the semantics of the concept of a "right."

What does one have to do in order to support some answer to these questions? One thing we can do is ask—and I think myself that the answer to this question is definitive for our purposes—whether rational or fully informed persons would, in view of the total consequences, support a moral code for a society in which they expected to live, with one, or another, provision on this matter. (I believe a fully rational person will at least normally have some degree of benevolence, or positive interest in the welfare or happiness of others; I shall not attempt to specify how much.) Since, however, I do not expect that everyone else will agree that answering this question would show what is morally right, I shall, for their benefit, also argue that certain moral

Richard B. Brandt, "Defective Newborns and the Morality of Termination," from *Infanticide and the Value of Life*, edited by Marvin Kohl. Buffalo, NY: Prometheus Books, 1978. Reprinted with permission of Prometheus Books.

principles on this matter are coherent with strong moral convictions of reflective people; or, to use Rawls's terminology, that a certain principle on the matter would belong to a system of moral principles in "reflective equilibrium."

Historic Basis of Infanticide

Historically, many writers, including Pope Pius XI in *Casti Connubii* (1930), have affirmed an absolute prohibition against killing anyone who is neither guilty of a capital crime nor an unjust assailant threatening one's life (self-defense), except in case of "extreme necessity." Presumably the prohibition is intended to include withholding of food or liquid from a newborn, although strictly speaking this is only *failing* to do something, not actually *doing* something to bring about death. (Would writers in this tradition demand, on moral grounds, that complicated and expensive surgery be undertaken to save a life? Such surgery is going beyond normal care, and in some cases beyond what earlier writers even conceived.) However the intentions of these writers may be, we should observe that historically their moral condemnation of all killing (except for the cases mentioned) derives from the Biblical injunction, "Thou shalt not kill," which, as it stands and without interpretation, may be taken to forbid suicide, killing of animals, perhaps even plants, and hence cannot be taken seriously.

Presumably a moral code that is coherent with our intuitions and that rational persons would support for their society would include some prohibition of killing, but it is another matter to identify the exact class to which such a prohibition is to apply. For one thing, I would doubt that killing one's self would be included—although one might be forbidden to kill one's self if that would work severe hardship on others, or conflict with the discharge of one's other moral obligations. And, possibly, defective newborns would *not* be included in the class. Further, a decision has to be made whether the prohibition of killing is *absolute* or only *prima facie*, meaning by "prima facie" that the duty not to kill might be outweighed by some other duty (or right) stronger in the circumstances, which could be fulfilled only by killing. In case this distinction is made, we would have to decide whether defective newborns fall within the scope of even a prima facie moral prohibition against killing. I shall, however, not attempt to make this fine distinction here, and shall simply inquire whether, everything considered, defective newborns—or some identifiable group of them—are excluded from the moral prohibition against killing.

Prospective Quality of Life

Suppose that killing a defective newborn, or allowing it to die, would not be an *injury*, but would rather be doing the infant a favor. In that case we should feel intuitively less opposed to termination of newborns, and presumably rational persons would be less inclined to support a moral code with a prohibition against such action. In that case we would feel rather as we do about a person's preventing a suicide attempt from being successful, in order that the person be elaborately tortured to death at a later stage. It is no favor to the prospective suicide to save his life; similarly, if the prospective life of defective newborns is bad we are doing them a favor to let them die.

"The burden of care for a defective infant, say one born with spina bifida, is huge . . . The cost of surgery alone . . . has been estimated to be around $275,000."

It may be said that we have no way of knowing what the conscious experiences of defective children are like, and that we have no competence in any case to decide when or what kind of life is bad or not worth living. Further, it may be said that predictions about a defective newborn's prospects for the future are precarious, in view of possible further advances of medicine. It does seem, however, that here, as everywhere, the rational person will follow the evidence about the present or future facts. But there is a question how to decide whether a life is bad or not worth living.

In the case of *some* defective newborns, it seems clear that their prospective life is bad. Suppose, as sometimes happens, a child is hydrocephalic with an extremely low I.Q., is blind and deaf, has no control over its body, can only lie on its back all day and have all its needs taken care of by others, and even

cries out with pain when it is touched or lifted. Infants born with spina bifida—and these number over two per one thousand births—are normally not quite so badly off, but are often nearly so.

The Happiness Criterion

But what criterion are we using if we say that such a life is bad? One criterion might be called a "happiness" criterion. If a person *likes* a moment of experience while he is having it, his life is so far good; if a person *dislikes* a moment of experience while he is having it, his life is so far bad. Based on such reactions, we might construct a "happiness curve" for a person, going up above the indifference axis when a moment of experience is liked—and how far above depending on how strongly it is disliked. Then this criterion would say that a life is worth living if there is a net balance of positive area under the curve over a lifetime, and that is bad if there is a net balance of negative area. One might adopt some different criterion: for instance, one might say that a life is worth living if a person would *want* to live it over again given that, at the end, he could remember the whole of it with perfect vividness in some kind of grand intuitive awareness. Such a response to this hypothetical holistic intuition, however, would likely be affected by the state of the person's drives or moods at the time, and the conception strikes me as unconvincing, compared with the moment-by-moment reaction to what is going on. Let us, for the sake of the argument, adopt the happiness criterion.

Is the prospective life of the seriously defective newborn, like the one described above, bad or good according to this criterion? One thing seems clear: that it is *less* good than is the prospective life of a normal infant. But is it bad?

Balancing Enjoyment and Boredom

We have to do some extrapolating from what we know. For instance, such a child will presumably suffer from severe sensory deprivation; he is simply not getting interesting stimuli. On the basis of laboratory data, it is plausible to think the child's experience is at best boring or uncomfortable. If the child's experiences are painful, of course, its moments are, so far, on the negative side. One must suppose that such a child hardly suffers from disappointment, since it will not learn to expect anything exciting, beyond being fed and fondled, and these events will be regularly forthcoming. One might expect such a child to suffer from isolation and loneliness, but insofar as this is true, the object of dislike probably should be classified as just sensory deprivation; dislike of loneliness seems to depend on the deprivation of past pleasures of human company. There are also some positive enjoyments: of eating, drinking, elimination, seeing the nurse coming with food, and so on. But the brief enjoyments can hardly balance the long stretches of boredom, discomfort, or even pain. On the whole, the lives of such children are bad according to the happiness criterion.

Naturally we cannot generalize about the cases of all "defective" newborns; there are all sorts of defects, and the cases I have described are about the worst. A child with spina bifida may, if he survives the numerous operations, I suppose, adjust to the frustrations of immobility; he may become accustomed to the embarrassments of no bladder or bowel control; he may have some intellectual enjoyments like playing chess; he will suffer from observing what others have but he cannot, such as sexual satisfactions, in addition to the pain of repeated surgery. How does it all balance out? Surely not as very good, but perhaps above the indifference level.

"Society has an interest, at certain crucial points, that may not be served by doing just exactly what is for the lifelong interest of the newborn."

It may fairly be said, I think, that the lives of some defective newborns are destined to be bad on the whole, and it would be a favor to them if their lives were terminated. Contrariwise, the prospective lives of many defective newborns are modestly pleasant, and it would be some injury to them to be terminated, albeit the lives they will live are ones some of us would prefer not to live at all.

Consenting to Death

Let us now make a second suggestion, not this time that termination of a defective newborn would be doing him a favor, but this time that he *consents* to termination, in the sense of expressing a rational deliberated preference for this. In that case I suggest that intuitively we would be *more* favorably inclined to judge that it is right to let the defective die, and I suggest also that for that case rational persons would be more ready to support a moral code permitting termination. Notice that we think that if an ill person has signified what we think a rational and deliberated desire to die, we are morally better justified in withdrawing life-supporting measures than we otherwise would be.

The newborn, however, is incapable of expressing his preference (giving consent) at all, much less expressing a rational deliberated preference. There could in theory be court-appointed guardians or proxies, presumably disinterested parties, authorized to give such consent on his behalf; but even so this would not be *his* consent.

Nevertheless, there is a fact about the mental life of the newborn (defective or not) such that, if he could

understand the fact, it seems he would not object—even rationally or after deliberation, if that were possible—to his life being terminated, or to his parents substituting another child in his place. This suggestion may seem absurd, but let us see. The explanation runs along the lines of an argument I once used to support the morality of abortion. I quote the paragraph in which this argument was introduced.

> Suppose I were seriously ill, and were told that, for a sizeable fee, an operation to save "my life" could be performed, of the following sort: my brain would be removed to another body which could provide a normal life, but the unfortunate result of the operation would be that my memory and learned abilities would be wholly erased, and that the forming of memory brain traces must begin from scratch, as in a newborn baby. Now, how large a fee would I be willing to pay for this operation, when the alternative is my peaceful demise? My own answer would be: None at all. I would take no interest in the continued existence of "myself" in that sense, and I would rather add the sizeable fee to the inheritance of my children. . . . I cannot see the point of forfeiting my children's inheritance in order to start off a person who is brand new except that he happens to enjoy the benefit of having my present brain, without the memory traces. It appears that some continuity of memory is a necessary condition for personal identity *in an important sense.*

My argument was that the position of a fetus, at the end of the first trimester, is essentially the same as that of the person contemplating this operation: he will consider that the baby born after six more months will not be *he* in any *important* and *motivating* sense (there will be no continuity of memory, and, indeed, maybe nothing to have been remembered), and the later existence of this baby, in a sense bodily continuous with his present body, would be a matter of indifference to him. So, I argued, nothing is being done to the fetus that he would object to having done if he understood the situation.

Memory Is Essential

What do I think is necessary in order for the continuation of my body with its conscious experiences to be worthwhile? One thing is that it is able to remember the events I can now remember; another is that it takes some interest in the projects I am now planning and remembers them as my projects; another is that it recognizes my friends and has warm feelings for them, and so on. Reflection on these states of a future continuation of my body with its experiences is what makes the idea motivating. But such motivating reflection for a newborn is impossible: he has no memories that he wants recalled later; he has no plans to execute; he has no warm feelings for other persons. He has simply not had the length of life necessary for these to come about. Not only that: the conception of these things cannot be motivating because the concept of some state of affairs being motivating requires roughly a past experience in which similar states of affairs were satisfying, and he has not lived long enough for the requisite conditioning to have taken place. (The most one could say is that the image of warm milk in his mouth is attractive; he might answer affirmatively if it could be put to him whether he would be aversive to the idea of no more warm milk.) So we can say, not merely that the newborn does not want the continuation of himself as a subject of experiences (he has not the conceptual framework for this); he does not want *anything* that his own survival would promote. It is like the case of the operation: there is nothing I want that the survival of my brain with no memory would promote. Give the newborn as much *conceptual* framework as you like; the *wants* are not there, which would give significance to the continuance of his life.

The Newborn Is Indifferent

The newborn, then, is bound to be *indifferent* to the idea of a continuation of the stream of his experiences, even if he clearly has the idea of that. It seems we can *know* this about him.

The truth of all this is still not for it to be the case that the newborn, defective or not, gives *consent* to, or expresses a preference for, the termination of his life. *Consent* is a performance, normally linguistic, but always requiring some conventional *sign*. A newborn, who has not yet learned how to signalize consent, cannot give consent. And it may be thought that this difference makes all the difference.

In order to see what difference it does make in this case, we should ask what makes adult consent morally important. Why is it that we think euthanasia can be practiced on an adult only if he gives his consent, at least his implied consent (e.g., by previous statements)? There seem to be two reasons. The first is that a person is more likely to be concerned with his own welfare, and to take steps to secure it, than are others, even his good friends. Giving an individual control over his own life, and not permitting others to take control except when he consents, is normally to promote his welfare. An individual may, of course, behave stupidly or shortsightedly, but we think that on the whole a person's welfare is best secured if decisions about it are in his hands; and it is best for society in the normal case (not for criminals, etc.) if persons' own lives are well-served. The second reason is the feeling of security a person can have, if he knows the major decisions about himself are in his own hands. When they are not, a person can easily, and in some cases very reasonably, suppose that other persons may well be able to do something to him that he would very much like them not to do. He does not have to worry about that if he knows they cannot do it without his consent.

The Moral Importance Of Consent

Are things different with the newborn? At least he, like the fetus, is not yet able to suffer from insecurity;

he cannot worry about what others may do to him. So the second reason for requiring consent cannot have any importance in his case. His situation is thus very unlike that of the senile adult, for an adult can worry about what others may do to him if they judge him senile. And this worry can well cast a shadow over a lot of life. But how about the first reason? Here matters are more complex. In the case of children, we think their own lives are better cared for if certain decisions are in the hands of others: the child may not want to visit the dentist, but the parents know that his best interests are served by going, and they make him go. The same for compulsory school attendance. And the same for the newborn. But there is another point: that society has an interest, at certain crucial points, that may not be served by doing just exactly what is for the lifelong interest of the newborn. There are huge costs that are relevant, in the case of the defective newborn. I shall go into that problem in a moment. It seems, then, that in the case of the newborn, *consent* cannot have the moral importance that it has in the case of adults.

On the other hand, then, the newborn will not *care* whether his life is terminated, even if he understands his situation perfectly; and, on the other hand, consent does not have the moral importance in his case that it has for adults. So, while it seems true that we would feel better about permitting termination of defective newborns if only they could give rational and deliberated consent and gave it, nevertheless when we bear the foregoing two points in mind, the absence of consent does not seem morally crucial in their case. We can understand why rational persons deciding which moral code to support for their society would not make the giving of consent a necessary condition for feeling free to terminate an infant's life when such action was morally indicated by the other features of the situation.

A Better Life in Exchange

Let us now think of an example owing to Derek Parfit. Suppose a woman wants a child, but is told that if she conceives a child now it will be defective, whereas if she waits three months she will produce a normal child. Obviously we think it would be wrong for the mother not to delay. (If she delays, the child she will have is not the *same* child as the one she would have had if she had not delayed, but it will have a better life.) This is the sole reason why we think she should delay and have the later-born child.

Suppose, however, a woman conceives but discovers only three months later that the fetus will become a defective child, but that she can have a normal child if she has an abortion and tries again. Now this time there is still the same reason for having the abortion that there formerly was for the delay: that she will produce a child with a better life. Ought she not then to have the abortion? If the child's life is bad, he could well complain that he had been injured by deliberately being brought to term. Would he complain if he were aborted, in favor of the later normal child? Not if the argument of the preceding section is correct.

But now suppose the woman does not discover until after she gives birth, that the child is seriously defective, but that she could conceive again and have a normal child. Are things really different, in the first few days? One might think that a benevolent person would want, in each of these cases, the substitution of a normal child for the defective one, of the better life for the worse one.

Cost and its Relevance

It is agreed that the burden of care for a defective infant, say one born with spina bifida, is huge. The cost of surgery alone for an infant with spina bifida has been estimated to be around $275,000. In many places this cost must be met by the family of the child, and there is the additional cost of care in an institution, if the child's condition does not permit care at home—and a very modest estimate of the monthly cost at present is $1,100. To meet even the surgical costs, not to mention monthly payments for continuing care, the lives of members of the family must be at a most spartan level for many years. The psychological effects of this, and equally, if not more so, of care provided at home, are far-reaching; they are apt to destroy the marriage and to cause psychological problems for the siblings. There is the on-going anxiety, the regular visits, the continuing presence of a caretaker if the child is in the home. In one way or another the continued existence of the child is apt to reduce dramatically the quality of life of the family as a whole.

It can be and has been argued that such costs, while real, are irrelevant to the moral problem of what should be done. It is obvious, however, that rational persons, when deciding which moral code to support, would take these human costs into account. As indeed they should: the parents and siblings are also human beings with lives to live, and any sacrifices a given law or moral system might call on them to make must be taken into account in deciding between laws and moral codes. Everyone will feel sympathy for a helpless newborn; but everyone should also think, equally vividly, of all the others who will suffer and just how they will suffer—and of course, as indicated above, of just what kind of life the defective newborn will have in any case. There is a choice here between allowing a newborn to die (possibly a favor to it, and in any case not a serious loss), and imposing a very heavy burden on the family for many years to come.

Continuing a Marginal Life

Philosophers who think the cost to others is irrelevant to what should be done should reflect that we do not accept the general principle that lives should be saved at no matter what cost. For instance, ships are deliberately built with only a certain margin of safety; they could be built so that they would hardly sink in any storm, but to do so would be economically unfeasible. We do not think we should require a standard of safety for automobiles that goes beyond a certain point of expense and inconvenience; we are prepared to risk a few extra deaths. And how about the lives we are willing to lose in war, in order to assure a certain kind of economic order or democracy or free speech? Surely there is a point at which the loss of a life (or the abbreviation of a life) and the cost to others become comparable. Is it obvious that the continuation of a marginal kind of life for a child takes moral precedence over providing a college education for one or more of his siblings? Some comparisons will be hard to make, but continuing even a marginally pleasant life hardly has absolute priority.

There are two questions which must be answered in any complete account of what is the morally right thing to do about defective newborns.

The first is: If a decision to terminate is made, how soon must it be made? Obviously it could not be postponed to the age of five, or of three, or even a year and a half. At those ages, all the reasons for insisting on consent are already cogent. And at those ages, the child will already care what happens to him. But ten days is tolerable. Doubtless advances in medicine will permit detection of serious prospective defects early in pregnancy, and this issue of how many days will not arise.

Second, the argument from the quality of the prospective life of the defective newborn requires that we decide which defects are so serious that the kind of life the defective child can have gives it no serious claim as compared with the social costs. This issue must be thought through, and some guidelines established, but I shall not attempt this here.

One might argue that, if the newborn cannot rationally care whether its life ends or not, the parents are free to dispose of a child irrespective of whether he is defective, if they simply do not want it. To this there are two replies. First, in practice there are others who want a child if the parents do not, and they can put it up for adoption. But second, the parents are *injuring* a child if they prevent it from having the good life it could have had. We do not in general accept the argument that a person is free to injure another, for no reason, even if he has that person's consent. In view of these facts, we may expect that rational, benevolent persons deciding which moral code to support would select one that required respect for the life of a normal child, but would permit the termination of the life of a seriously defective child.

Active and Passive Procedures

There is a final question: that of a choice between withdrawal of life-support measures (such as feeding), and the active, painless taking of life. It seems obvious, however, that once the basic decision is made that an infant is not to receive the treatment necessary to sustain life beyond a few days, it is mere stupid cruelty to allow it to waste away gradually in a hospital bed—for the child to suffer, and for everyone involved also to suffer in watching the child suffer. If death is the outcome decided upon, it is far kinder for it to come quickly and painlessly.

Richard B. Brandt was educated at Denison, Cambridge, and Yale Universities. He taught at Swarthmore College and is now a professor at the University of Michigan. He is the author of Ethical Theory, Hopi Ethics, *and* A Theory of the Good and the Right.

"The sanctity of life ethic which now spreads its tattered mantle of protection over newborn defective infants must be upheld."

viewpoint **15**

Infant Euthanasia Is Immoral

Eugene F. Diamond

Speaking as the official American witness at the Nuremberg doctors' trials, Dr. Leo Alexander commented on the genesis of the medical atrocities revealed during the proceedings. "Whatever proportions these crimes finally assumed, it became evident to all who investigated them that they had started from small beginnings. The beginnings at first were merely a subtle shift in emphasis in the basic attitudes of physicians. It started with the acceptance of the attitude, basic in the euthanasia movement, that there is such a thing as a life not worthy to be lived." Today we can see the same shift in attitude occurring in American medicine. We can see the substitution of a "quality of life" ethic for a "sanctity of life" ethic and a discarding of our Hippocratic traditions in favor of the cost-benefit morality of the new technocracy.

Death as Treatment

Three recent events document and confirm this drift in medical ethics towards the acceptance of death as a treatment of choice—events that are liberally commented on by several other scholars in this volume. The first was the case of a mongoloid infant at Johns Hopkins University Medical Center, given notoriety by its dramatization in *Who Shall Survive?*, a film produced by the Kennedy Foundation. The second milestone was the 1973 publication of *Moral and Ethical Dilemmas in the Special-Care Nursery* by Drs. Raymond Duff and A. G. M. Campbell. This article chronicled the treatment of forty-three handicapped infants whose deaths were associated with the discontinuance or withdrawal of various forms of treatment. Some of these infants were born dying with untreatable maladies; some, however, were born with treatable

conditions such as meningomyelocele and Down's syndrome with duodenal atresia who were denied treatment because of considerations of their prospective "quality of life."

The third milestone was the publication of proceedings of the Sonoma Conference on ethical issues in neonatal intensive care. The twenty participants in this multidisciplinary conference included pediatricians, psychologists, social workers, professors of community medicine, medical economists, attorneys, and bioethicists. Among the questions asked of the panel was: "Would it ever be right to intervene directly to kill a self-sustaining infant?" Two considerations about this question are crucial. First, to "intervene directly" indicates that what was at question was an act of positive killing, not passive euthanasia. Second, the question was directed at a "self-sustaining" infant—not one whose vital processes are maintained by a respirator or pacemaker. The response, given this understanding, was astounding: seventeen of the twenty conferees responded in the affirmative, two in the negative, and one individual was uncertain. The shockwaves from Sonoma were widely felt, and Dr. Paul Ramsey has devoted a chapter in his *Ethics at the Edges of Life* to an analysis of this epoch-making conference. It was as if a mirror had been held up to the various professions involved in neonatal care to reveal a Dorian Gray-like deterioration in ethics that we had not before sensed. Unwittingly, the medical profession had stepped onto the "slippery slope" in cases such as that documented in *Who Shall Survive?*, apparently failing to realize where this step might lead us.

Quality of Life

The consequences of introducing the "quality of life" ethic to treatment of the handicapped are better understood when a case such as that of the Johns Hopkins infant is more closely examined. The patient was a two-day-old, full-term male, a second-born to a married, middle-income Protestant couple in their twenties, parents of a normal two-year-old girl. The pregnancy was uneventful except for excess amniotic fluid accumulation and delivery was normal. Greenish vomiting began shortly after birth and there was slight abdominal distension and moderate dehydration, but no evidence of cardiac abnormalities. The infant had mongoloid facies and features and an X-ray of the abdomen showed intestinal obstruction. The clinical impression was Down's syndrome and duodenal atresia.

After discussion with the parents, a decision was made not to operate to repair the obstruction due to the duodenal atresia. All feeding and fluids were withheld and the child eventually died, after fifteen days, from starvation and dehydration.

"Traditional medical ethics has obviously had exquisite difficulty in making a distinction between one's duty to a retarded child and one's duty to a normal child."

It is important to examine the rationalization involved in such medical management in order to understand the implication of this new development in medical ethics and its significance for the profession and the society as a whole. The rationale is not easy to understand and a short ten years ago would have been considered monstrous and unacceptable. Perhaps we can begin to understand if we break the elements of the physical problem down. Suppose first that the infant in question had neither Down's syndrome nor duodenal atresia. Obviously, the physician could not kill the child and nursery personnel could not fail to nourish him or her. Our law makes it clear that the parents' dominion over children does not extend to willful acts or negligence which will harm the child. No exception to this rule is made in the event that a child is born with a handicap. In the case of a child born with Down's syndrome but without duodenal atresia, most would agree that medical personnel would certainly be obligated to nourish and treat the child. Indeed, if nurses or physicians were to concur in a decision of the parents not to feed such a child, they would be guilty of active participation in a killing act and not just an omission.

Parents Forced to Give Consent

Now suppose that the child was born normal except for duodenal atresia. This defect can be corrected by an operative procedure with an approximate survival rate of 98 percent. The pediatrician cannot fail to recommend an operation in such circumstances, nor can a surgeon fail to operate. Parents who refuse to consent to such an operation would almost certainly be compelled to do so by legal action.

Finally, consider the case of the "Johns Hopkins" baby: born with both Down's syndrome and duodenal atresia. Here, for some reason, there is a change in the rules and apparently in a physician's duty as well. The physician's duty obviously derives from the physician-patient relationship. Traditional medical ethics has obviously had exquisite difficulty in making a distinction between one's duty to a retarded child and one's duty to a normal child. It has held, if anything, that there was a greater obligation to the retarded. Thus, if I have the obligation to care for a child without Down's syndrome, how can I avoid my obligation to the child with Down's syndrome? And if I have a clear obligation to care for the child with Down's syndrome, does not that obligation compel me to perform a duty which I am physically capable of performing? In this case, am I not obligated to perform a virtually risk-free operation? These would seem like rhetorical questions expecting the answer "yes," and yet, I do not hear a strong affirmative reply from my profession and I wonder why. Is it because of a judgment that I have passed on the child with Down's syndrome that places him in an isolated, unheard position as he tries to incur my obligation to him? If so, I should then ask, Who is this mongoloid child and by what authority may I treat him as if he does not have the rights of other children?

Children with Down's syndrome do far better at home and only a small percentage should ever be institutionalized. Most of these children should not be placed away from home—and will not be if the pediatrician and obstetrician perform properly. The Down's syndrome child who has broken his mother's heart will usually mend it again in two or three years.

Allowing Parents to Grieve

There is no avoiding, of course, the initial reaction of grief. The parents should be allowed active grief without detachment. They should, however, recognize the baby as their own and should have physical contact with it. One of the recurrent mistakes made is that of the obstetrician who says, "Don't take him home or you will become attached to him." First of all, becoming attached to your own child is not necessarily a bad development. Secondly, this attachment does not begin with taking the baby home. The mother has already been "attached" to this baby for nine months. He was a presence within her from the earliest weeks and a more profound and intimate presence as he began to move, to grow, to accompany her to bed, to go literally everywhere with her.

If parents see the physician treat the Down's child as he would any other child, they draw their strength from him. One disadvantage for the physician is that the descriptive terminology used in describing the features of the child with Down's syndrome is often pejorative. Such children are described as having a "Simian" foot or a "Simian" crease, a "Mongoloid" facies, a "saddle" nose, a "spade" hand and so on. When the doctor describes her baby in terms usually reserved for foreigners or monkeys, it is not surprising that the mother will hesitate to welcome it into her home.

Rights of the Handicapped

When we examine the handicapped child under the law it is clear that there is no legal authority to support this derogation of rights of the handicapped or retarded. If there was ever a doubt that the retarded have rights, those doubts have been categorically removed. Article II of the United Nations Draft Convention on the Rights of the Child, to be presented to the U.N. General Assembly in 1982, states that the "Parties to the present Convention recognize the right of a mentally or physically disabled child to special protection and care...and shall extend appropriate assistance to such a child. A disabled child shall grow up and receive education in conditions designed to achieve his fullest possible social integration." Over the past two decades, the federal courts in the United States have responded to the nontreatment and abuse of handicapped and retarded persons in state hospitals. In the 1965 St. Elizabeth's hospital case in Washington, D.C., it was ruled that "the Retarded must be cared for and trained, not just kept in custody." This standard was also applied in the Pennhurst case in Pennsylvania in 1972. In an Alabama case, a federal court held that these rights "are present ones and must not only be declared but secured at the earliest practicable time." It is inconsistent with the holdings in these cases for a physician to deny treatment—to the extent of withholding *food* and *water*—to an infant because of his or her handicapped condition.

Choosing Starvation

How is it possible, then, that these rights have been violated and abridged in this case? What are the factors that have conditioned public acceptance of the fact that medical personnel chose to starve this baby to death rather than to go to court to compel restorative surgery? The most important factor, in my opinion, has been the development of large amniocentesis programs funded by the March of Dimes or by federal agencies. The development of these programs and the acceptance of abortion as a means to "prevent" the occurrence of handicaps such as Down's syndrome has led to the creation of a

"free fire zone" during which mongoloid children may be killed by abortion during the late-middle and last trimester. There are no restrictions on aborting Down's syndrome children even after viability. Such a practice naturally leads to the possibility of abandoning such infants if they survive prenatal screening and are born alive. Recently a pediatric journal published an article entitled "The Prevention of Mongolism through Amniocentesis." I wrote a letter to the editor pointing out that the only way to prevent mongolism was at conception by preventing the fertilization of a 24-chromosome gamete by a 23-chromosome gamete, or better yet by preventing nondisjunction during meiosis. Aborting a child with Down's syndrome only prevents his birth. The editor refused to publish the letter, calling me a "religious fanatic." Presumably he was referring to genetics as a religion, which it well may become.

"Our preoccupation with materialism and our consequent acceptance of death as a treatment of choice threatens the integrity of the medical profession as one devoted to healing."

Just as the sacrifice of newborn infants with Down's syndrome is the logical extension of the abortion of viable infants with Down's syndrome, the rationalization of withholding care for newborns establishes the precedent for neglecting older children with Down's syndrome. In the early 1970s, Congressman Walter Sackett of the Florida legislature, a physician, introduced a "Death With Dignity" bill, ostensibly aimed at allowing individuals to execute a "living will." Congressman Sackett, however, in his testimony before Senator Church's Special Committee on the Aging in 1973, betrayed an underlying motive in proposing his bill. This motive was to promote what he described as "a major change in American law." He disclosed that the "first step" of allowing individuals to execute their own living will was to be followed by a "second step" of allowing next of kin to execute living wills on behalf of individuals and a "third step" of allowing physicians to execute the living will when next of kin were not available. He suggested that as many as 90 percent of institutionalized mental defectives in Florida might qualify for elimination under the provisions of steps two and three. Sackett also proposed that the retarded be evaluated by the criteria of cost-benefit analysis. "Now where is the benefit," he asked, "in these 1,500 severely retarded, who never had a rational thought?" Such patients, he stated, should be allowed to die by withholding all medical treatment; for example, by not treating adolescents with Down's syndrome if they contract pneumonia.

Cost-Benefit Analysis Appalling

Sackett's proposals are not an isolated phenomenon, but rather represent the encroachment of cost-benefit analysis upon traditional medical doctrine. This intrusion of government economists into medical care and planning has in my opinion been an important factor affecting society's attitudes towards treatment of the handicapped. Jonathan Swift describes the Lilliputians as believing that Gulliver's watch was his god because he consulted it before making important decisions. In the American technocracy the computer has become this kind of god. Predictably, in a land of conspicuous consumption, computer technology has reached its zenith in the area of marketing and finance. Most billing is done by computer and the computer always has the instant answer to the great American question, "How much will it cost?" No important decision is made without a cost-benefit analysis and what used to be called basic verities are now rejected on the scales of economy.

"Protests on behalf of parents' rights in the making of lethal decisions affecting their newborn children are particularly inappropriate when one knows the circumstances under which such decisions are usually made."

A recurring theme in medicine today, consequently, is the notion of the "finite health dollar." We are told that, if we could only divert the money spent on the custodial care of retarded children into research or nutrition, we would soon have cures for these afflictions and many other social ills as well. What proponents of this line of thinking obscure is the fact that caring for retarded children, and funding research to prevent future handicaps, are not mutually exclusive. Who can say that in a $2 trillion economy we cannot achieve both goals by shifting our priorities? Given the relatively slight cost of the needed care and research, we can probably do whatever we set our minds to do in this realm.

Yet if we set our minds in another direction, the consequences for our medical profession and our society will be tragic. Our preoccupation with materialism and our consequent acceptance of death as a treatment of choice threatens the integrity of the medical profession as one devoted to healing. We should have realized this earlier, because of the horror brought on by another society of recent unhappy memory that employed violence as a weapon in its pursuit of "order" and "perfection." In that society efficiency and bloodletting were caught up in the vortex of the Holocaust. In the vanguard of the Holocaust were those who wore a caduceus alongside their swastikas and who provided the expertise, even the genius, for the implementation of final solutions.

Quality vs. Sanctity of Life

A third important factor that has led to our shifting attitudes on the treatment of handicapped infants has been the attempt to substitute the "quality of life ethic" for the "sanctity of life" ethic in medicine. Applying this ethic to the child with Down's syndrome and duodenal atresia, we need only declare that life is not worth living unless it can be lived without handicaps. From this cult of perfection, then, we derive a new definition of death. Death becomes living with handicaps. To repair the duodenal atresia would only prolong the "living death" of Down's syndrome.

It is possible that this alleged compassion for the handicapped may be entirely misplaced. There is no evidence that the handicapped child would rather not go on living. As a matter of fact, handicapped persons commit suicide far less often than normal persons. An interesting study was done at the Anna Stift in Hanover, Germany, a center where a large number of children with phocomelia, due to thalidomide, are cared for. Psychological testing on these children indicated that they indeed value their lives, that they are glad that they were born and that they look forward to the future with hope and pleasant anticipation.

We are listening to the wrong experts. Mass screening programs to detect genetic defects, the intrusion of the cost-benefit approach to treatment decisions, and adherence to the quality-of-life ethic have all promoted infanticide in America. I have, however, taken my own poll on the Johns Hopkins case and have come up with some interesting statistics. When left with the choice between surgery and starvation, the parents, grandparents, and siblings of children with Down's syndrome vote overwhelmingly for surgery as do pediatricians who subspecialize in the care of the retarded. Nurses and other primary physicians cast a majority vote for surgery and only surgeons and educators are unsure. (One surgeon described the withholding of food and water for two weeks as "conservative management.")

Destroying Status of Physicians

This journey, above and beyond its cost in human life, may destroy the status of physicians as a trusted, learned profession. Every time we let something like the Johns Hopkins case happen, we all lose something. What we lose is a little of what sustains us, a little of what holds us together. We become more as technocrats, less of a learned profession. If a physician becomes preoccupied with the social and public good, who will protect the individual rights of the patient?

Consider the case of the nurse in Decatur, Illinois, who had to conceal water on her person when she visited a mongoloid infant suffering in his twelfth day without nourishment. The water was merely to moisten the baby's eyes so that he could, at last, close his dessicated eyelids. To her, no doctor will have status again.

We continually try to convince ourselves that this new ethic of death is demanded by the difficulty of caring for the handicapped infant. Seldom stated, however, is the fact that there are fewer handicapped children being born as a result of improved prenatal care, viral vaccines, and the control of drugs given to pregnant women—or that infinitely more can be done to rehabilitate handicapped children than we could a generation ago or even a decade ago or even five years ago. "Our success has been our undoing," we tell one another with perverted logic. We are convinced that when we could do nothing for any child, there were no agonizing decisions. How simple it was to talk to parents of children with meningomyelocele in the 1940s. Shunts and other surgical methods being unknown, there was little other alternative to committing such children to institutions. There, shielded from the eyes of the public and most of the medical profession, the answers came automatically. Little heads blew up like watermelons and tiny increments of pressure finally built up to a point where they turned off vital centers. Enteric organisms poured out of incontinent sphincters into ruptured meningeal sacs and there were very few drugs to control the infections.

Human Potential Subjective

Theoretically, it is probably true that we should not sustain a life that is totally without any potential for human experience or relating, at least not by extraordinary means. Two questions arise in the application of this standard. First of all, do we really mean that there is no person who can relate to the human being in question? Second, does the agency that applies that standard—parent, physician, committee—have sufficient expertise to accurately relate the defective person to the norm or standard for withholding life support? These are extremely important questions. The psychological profile of persons present when the defective infant is born will differ greatly from that of the caretakers who would be expected to assume long-term responsibility for follow-up care. Acute-disease hospitals and their personnel, especially in intensive-care units, are accustomed to instant gratification in applying therapeutic modalities. Dramatic corrective surgery, resuscitative brinksmanship, and rapid turnover of patients are their daily expectation. They are inclined to have a low frustration tolerance and to doubt the validity of large investments of professional time and energy to realize small returns of stable or slightly altered function. Those whose daily life involves the care of mentally retarded or other chronically handicapped children, however, are a different breed altogether.

The Reality of Institutions

For ten years I visited at the Misericordia Home in Chicago, usually with a contingent of medical students. Severely retarded and pathetically handicapped children populated this institution along with a larger, less-retarded group of mongoloid children. Each child, ambulatory or not, was fully dressed, including shoes and stockings, each morning. The institution was immaculate. Someone in the institution was capable of relating closely to every child, and, as we made rounds, at every bedside there would be a staff member, usually an aid or a nurse, who could tell us the child's history. Severe hydrocephalics and markedly obtunded, neurologically damaged children were called by name and regarded as individuals. Their needs were appreciated and even anticipated. Their disease-related irascibility was understood, explained away, and assuaged by acts of comfort.

Almost all the students came away with the impression that something very human, and medically dramatic, was happening in that institution. Certainly, there are those unfortunate patients who in the act of dying cannot escape from measures that merely prolong their death. To withdraw treatment from such a patient is quite different from suggesting that someone now dying can be judged as having a quality of life that precludes their ever relating to another human being at a meaningful level. If there are persons in this latter category, who truly cannot relate to another human being, they are few and far between. To use them as a paradigm for the withholding of medical care as an ordinary option is so susceptible to misinterpretation as to be dangerous and counterproductive. In fact, all attempts to circumscribe and isolate examples of "quality of life" criteria for sustaining medical care seem to reemphasize the superior workability of the traditional "sanctity of life" criteria for medical decision making. If one stands at the bedside or the cribside convinced of the irreducible value of every human person, he is, in the practical order, much better equipped to make rational and humane decisions in his patient's best interests.

Parents' Rights Inappropriate

Protests on behalf of "parents' rights" in the making of lethal decisions affecting their newborn children are particularly inappropriate when one knows the circumstances under which such decisions are usually made. What parent is really free in making such a decision? Deeply in mourning for the perfect child she planned on, who is now irretrievably lost, the mother faces a phalanx of professionals who are usually strangers in an unfamiliar, stainless, even hostile hospital environment. Her husband usually defers to her wishes, and her wishes are usually determined by the way the circumstances are presented. If the need for immediate care is separated, as it should be, from the long-term prognostic implications of survival, she will usually opt for that care. She should not be isolated from the knowledge that the society will accept its appropriate legal obligation to share the long-term burden in most instances.

While it is true that ordinary and extraordinary means are relative and dependent on circumstances, it is also true that what is ordinary for an affluent, intelligent child cannot be extraordinary for a poor, retarded child. If a low-risk operation for intestinal obstruction is indicated in an otherwise normal child, it is indicated in a mongoloid child. If a shunt is indicated for the only child of affluent professionals, it is also indicated for the comparably handicapped child born to welfare parents with other normal children. The defective child who will enter a loving home deserves no more from his physician than the defective child who will enter a deprived or broken home.

Sanctity of Life Principle Needed

The importance of maintaining the highest regard for the sanctity of life can only really be appreciated in the context of the kind of society in which we live. The dominating realities of the American system as they are brought to bear upon the weak, the handicapped, and the dispossessed have very little to do with the recent explosion of scientific knowledge. The real jeopardy posed by the last quarter of the twentieth century is not that we will ignore technological advancement and cling to the obsolete. Rather, it is that this society has become committed to violence as a solution to problems posed by economic considerations. With a birthrate below replacement and with the mean age of the population constantly increasing, the next focus will unquestionably be upon the "quality of life" of the aged. The official position of our federal government condones violent death for sacred unborn life throughout pregnancy. Not content with killing the fetus, the medical profession has proposed to perform nonbeneficial research assaults on him in anticipation of his demise.

If we are to reclaim protection for the unborn child, we cannot concede the logical extension of the abortion mentality into the nursery. The sanctity-of-life ethic which now spreads its tattered mantle of protection over newborn defective inants must be upheld. It is really protecting all of us.

Eugene F. Diamond is professor of pediatrics for Strich School of Medicine at Loyola University. He is past president of the Illinois chapter of the American Academy of Pediatrics and a member of the editorial boards of Spina Bifida *and* Journal of Pediatric Social Work.

"For years doctors have been allowed to conceal, behind their claim of 'medical judgment,' a doctrine for taking life that cannot arise from anything in their field of competence."

The Sanctity of Life Principle Forbids Infant Euthanasia

Hadley Arkes

Why is it that the terms of our public discourse—and our familiar canons of reasoning—are suddenly suspended whenever we are faced with the questions of medical treatment for newly born children? There was nothing especially complicated or esoteric about the regulations that were recently announced by the Department of Health and Human Services: hospitals were required to post, in their maternity wards and nurseries, a notice that the "discriminatory failure to feed and care for handicapped infants in this facility is prohibited by federal law."

But the American Academy of Pediatrics challenged those regulations in a federal district court, and its position was upheld, for the moment, on a procedural ground: the administration failed to persuade the court that it was acting quickly "to protect life from imminent harm" and that it was reasonable to forgo, in this case, the usual waiting period for public comment before new rules are put into effect.

Still, when this procedural issue is finally resolved, the question of substance will remain. On that point Judge Gerhard Gesell managed to express—quite early, and quite gratuitously—his hostility to the measures of the administration.

From the remarks of the judge and the reactions of the public commentators, one would gather that the administration had addressed a problem too inscrutable to yield to ordinary language or to the judgments of the law. Ellen Goodman worried, with many doctors, that the regulations would not allow a distinction to be made between the child handicapped by Down's syndrome and the child handicapped by the absence of a brain, or by other afflictions so profound that his prospects were

hopeless. For the critics, these were matters properly left to the "medical" judgment of doctors and to that delicate, private relation between a physician and his patients.

The Medical Question

It has become a common reflex among doctors these days to regard any matter as a "medical" question if physicians are somehow involved in it. But with the benefit of more strenuous reflection it should become apparent that the new regulations raise no question that is distinctly "medical." Nothing in the regulations would foreclose the need for doctors to make assessments, from one case to another, on the condition of patients and the prospects for treatment. What the new regulations reach are those cases in which the afflictions of the child could be treated practicably by surgery; where the doctors and the parents would agree to operate; but where the decision is made, nevertheless, to hold back medical treatment *because* the child is retarded or "handicapped."

Discrimination Against the Handicapped

The judgment, at that point, does not pivot on any medical issue but on a question of "principle": Is there something in the very condition of being retarded which establishes that people *deserve* to perish or that they have a lesser claim to live? Does the presence of infirmities justify a policy of withholding from the "handicapped" services or benefits that should not be affected by their disability (such as their access to education)?

When stated in this way, it should be evident that the principle engaged here is the same principle that has underlain our statutes on the treatment of the handicapped. And that is in fact the provenance of the new regulations: they were drawn by the administration under the authority of the Rehabilitation Act of 1973. To my knowledge, none

Hadley Arkes, "'Baby Doe': It's Not a 'Medical' Question," *The Washington Post*, April 17, 1983. Reprinted by permission.

of the critics who find the regulations dangerously imprecise has ever raised a question about the clarity of that statute—or of the law that has been built up now for a decade in protecting the "handicapped" from all species of unwarranted harms and exclusions.

Of course, the notion of being "handicapped" cannot be free of ambiguity. But it hardly raises problems of interpretation that are any graver than those generated by other statutes, which have not excited anything near the same alarms. Can we define, after all, everyone who is part of a "minority" that suffers "racial discrimination"? Would a preference for people with "Spanish surnames" extend to the child of Mendoza, but not to the child of Mendoza's sister, who married a man named Flynn? Is a restaurant a facility involved in "interstate commerce," even when it is separated from the highway by a dirt road, and when it seeks no interstate business? Ellen Goodman, who thought the language of the new regulations fatally sweeping and categorical has not apparently suffered any discomfort over the Equal Rights Amendment, which would ban, in a categorical, sweeping way, all discriminations based on sex (even though its proponents have been quick to assure us that they do not mean to go quite that far).

"Pediatricians apparently think it is legitimate to withdraw medical care from the retarded, for the same reason that they have been willing to honor the decisions made by parents to end the life of the infant in the womb."

Suppose for a moment that the new regulations had declared that "it is prohibited by federal law to withhold treatment from infants on the basis of their race." Is it imaginable that the American Academy of Pediatrics would now be in court arguing that rules of this kind interfere with the "medical" judgment of doctors and the privacy of their patients?

The academy is more likely to recognize that the regulations express a *principle*, and that the principle cannot be affected, in its validity, by the variety of personal experiences that are brought into view from one case to another: no set of novel circumstances, no "medical" facts disclosed in any case, can possibly bear on the question of whether it is right or wrong to withhold treatment on the basis of race. And what can be said here in regard to race would have to be said, with equal force, in regard to the withholding of medical treatment from the retarded or handicapped.

The doctors are no doubt aware that parents who

withhold food or medical care from their children would be subject to prosecution even if they starved their children in the privacy of their homes. The physicians must understand then, as well as anyone else, that when the law "interferes" with this disposition of the parents, it does not interfere with anything the parents have a "private right" to do. And what is not within the privacy rights of the parents surely cannot be brought within that domain when the action shifts to a hospital and the collaboration of doctors.

If the pediatricians and their friends have been made uncomfortable by the new regulations, it is not because the administration has invaded a sacred sphere of privacy or encroached on "medical" judgment. The problem for the doctors, rather, is that the administration is challenging precisely, in principle, the moral understanding on which they have been willing to redefine their missions as doctors.

The American Academy of Pediatrics has good reason now to believe that most of its members do indeed reject the principle behind the law: in one national survey of pediatricians, carried out in 1977, 85 percent of the doctors in the sample expressed their willingness to withhold surgery for children with Down's syndrome if that were the preference of the parents. More recent surveys suggest that this perspective has retained its dominance.

The pediatricians apparently think it is legitimate to withdraw medical care from the retarded, for the same reason that they have been willing to honor the decisions made by parents to end the life of the infant in the womb who is thought to have Down's syndrome. For years doctors have been allowed to conceal, behind their claim of "medical judgment," a doctrine for taking life that cannot arise from anything in their field of competence. What they feel now, in these new regulations, is the sting of reproach; and in this case, the law has directed that reproach to the proper place.

Hadley Arkes is currently the William Nelson Cromwell professor of jurisprudence at Amherst College. His articles frequently appear in Human Life Review.

"The sanctity with which we endow all human life often works to the detriment of those unfortunate humans whose lives hold no prospect except suffering."

viewpoint **17**

The Sanctity of Life Principle Is Unrealistic

Peter Singer

The ethical outlook that holds human life to be sacrosanct—I shall call it the "Sanctity-of-life view"—is under attack. The first major blow to the sanctity of life view was the spreading acceptance of abortion throughout the Western world. Supporters of the sanctity-of-life view have pointed out that some premature babies are less developed than some of the fetuses that are killed in late abortions. They add, very plausibly, that the location of the fetus/infant—inside or outside the womb—cannot make a crucial difference to its moral status. Allowing abortions, especially these late abortions, therefore does seem to breach our defense of the allegedly universal sanctity of innocent human life.

A second blow to the sanctity-of-life view has been the revelation that it is standard practice in many major public hospitals to refrain from providing necessary life-saving treatment to certain patients. Although this practice applies to geriatric patients and those suffering from terminal illness, the most publicized and also the potentially most significant cases have been severely defective newborns. In Britian, Dr. John Lorber has quite candidly described his method of selecting which babies suffering from spina bifida should be given active treatment, and he has indicated, with equal candor, that in his view the best possible outcome for those not selected is an early death.

Non-Treatment of Down's Syndrome

The decision not to treat an infant with Down's syndrome has also been publicized. In April 1982, in Bloomington, Indiana, the parents of an infant with Down's syndrome and in need of corrective surgery refused permission for the surgery to be performed. Few details are available because the court ordered the records sealed, but the court refused to intervene

or to take the child out of his parents' custody.

Although many doctors would sharply distinguish the active termination of life from a decision not to treat a patient for whom the forseen outcome of this decision is the death of the patient, the distinction is a tenuous one, and the claim that it carries moral weight has been rejected by several academic philosophers. Hence, the acceptance of nontreatment in these situations is rightly perceived as a further threat to the sanctity-of-life view.

Some respond to this situation with a sense of alarm at the erosion of our traditional ethical standards. We already have, these people tell us, one foot on the slippery slope that will lead to active euthanasia, then to the elimination of the mentally feeble and of the socially undesirable and finally to all the atrocities of the Nazi era. To pull back from this abyss, we must renew our commitment to the most scrupulous respect for all human life, irrespective of its quality.

It is in keeping with this response that shortly after the verdict was handed down in the Bloomington case, the Reagan administration issued, through the Department of Health and Human Services, a "Notice to Health Care Providers" stating that is unlawful for a recipient of federal financial assistance to withhold from a handicapped infant any medical treatment required to correct a life-threatening condition, when the treatment is not medically contraindicated and would be given to an infant who was not handicapped.

Infant's Lives May Be Awful

Seen from a distance, this notice appears to put doctors in the absurd situation of having to keep alive the most grossly defective infants, for whom life is either quite valueless—because the infant is forever incapable of any conscious experience whatsoever—or else a positive burden, because it is a life of pain and discomfort without the redeeming

Peter Singer, "Sanctity of Life or Quality of Life?" *Pediatrics,* July 1983. Copyright American Academy of Pediatrics 1983.

death/dying 73

value of a rational awareness of self or others. Even Lord Justice Templeman, who in a recent English case concerning an infant with Down's syndrome ordered that surgery be performed, did not wish to go so far. He allowed that in a case in which the life of the infant would be "demonstrably awful" there would have been grounds for allowing a child to die. The Reagan administration, it would seem, wishes infants to be kept alive even when their life will be "demonstrably awful."

> "If we can put aside the obsolete...notion of the sanctity of all human life, we may start to look at human life as it really is: at the quality of life that each human being has or can achieve."

Is the erosion of the sanctity-of-life view really so alarming? Change is often, in itself, alarming, especially change in something that for centuries has been spoken of in such hushed tones that to question it is automatically to commit sacrilege. There is little evidence, however, to support the application of the slippery slope argument in this context. Cultures have practiced forms of infanticide or euthanasia—Ancient Greece, the Eskimos—have been able to hold the line around those categories of beings that could be killed, so that the lives of other members of these societies were at least as well protected as the lives of citizens of the United States, where the culture officially accepts no limits to the sanctity of human life.

Whatever the future holds, it is likely to prove impossible to restore in full the sanctity-of-life view. The philosophical foundations of this view have been knocked asunder. We can no longer base our ethics on the idea that human beings are a special form of creation, made in the image of God, singled out from all other animals, and alone possessing an immortal soul. Our better understanding of our own nature has bridged the gulf that was once thought to lie between ourselves and other species, so why should we believe that the mere fact that a being is a member of the species Homo sapiens endows its life with some unique, almost infinite, value?

Race Supremacy and Defective Infants

Once the religious mumbo-jumbo surrounding the term "human" has been stripped away, we may continue to see normal members of our species as possessing greater capacities of rationality, self-consciousness, communication, and so on, than members of any other species; but we will not regard as sancrosanct the life of each and every member of

our species, no matter how limited its capacity for intelligent or even conscious life may be. If we compare a severely defective human infant with a nonhuman animal, a dog or a pig, for example, we will often find the nonhuman to have superior capacities, both actual and potential, for rationality, self-consciousness, communication, and anything else that can plausibly be considered morally significant. Only the fact that the defective infant is a member of the species Homo sapiens leads it to be treated differently from the dog or the pig. Species membership alone, however, is not morally relevant. Humans who bestow superior value on the lives of all human beings, solely because they are members of our own species, are judging along lines strikingly similar to those used by white racists who bestow superior value on the lives of other whites, merely because they are members of their own race.

Ironically, the sanctity with which we endow all human life often works to the detriment of those unfortunate humans whose lives hold no prospect except suffering. A dog or a pig, dying slowly and painfully, will be mercifully released from its misery. A human being with inferior mental capacities in similarly painful circumstances will have to endure its hopeless condition until the end—and may even have that end postponed by the latest advances in medicine.

Families of Defective Children

One difference between humans and other animals that is relevant irrespective of any defect is that humans have families who can intelligently take part in decisions about their offspring. This does not affect the intrinsic value of human life, but it often should affect our treatment of humans who are incapable of expressing their own wishes about their future. Any such effect will not, however, always be in the direction of prolonging life—as the wishes of the parents in the Bloomington case, and in several other recent court cases, illustrate.

If we can put aside the obsolete and erroneous notion of the sanctity of all human life, we may start to look at human life as it really is: at the quality of life that each human being has or can achieve. Then it will be possible to approach these difficult questions of life and death with the ethical sensitivity that each case demands, rather than with the blindness to individual differences that is embodied in the Department of Health and Human Services' rigid instruction to disregard all handicaps when deciding whether to keep a child alive.

Peter Singer is an Australian professor who is currently with the Monash University Center for Human Bioethics. He has written articles on a wide range of issues and is the author of the book Animal Liberation.

"The surviving child's life at home might have such a detrimental effect on the family that the child, too, would suffer excessively."

Infant Euthanasia Should Be the Parents' Choice

Raymond S. Duff

Having worked for many years in a neonatal intensive care unit and having interviewed staff and parents of children in neonatal intensive care and chronic care facilities in numerous states from Maine to Hawaii, I will describe conditions I have observed. From these observations and literature review, I will present an opinion about family counseling and deciding care of severely defective children. I believe this opinion reflects accurately the feelings of almost all parents, clergy, and social workers, most nurses, and more than 80% of pediatricians.

By using professional and family standards for assessing biologic conditions, quality of child and family life, and treatment alternatives, most health professionals and parents resist keeping alive children with anencephaly, trisomy 13, and others with an extremely bleak or hopeless prognosis; they are unenthusiastic about treating children with trisomy 18 and others with an equally poor prognosis. Most of these children have lethal conditions. If they do not, they are sometimes sedated and given skilled nursing and parental care as they wither and die. That is always sad. By strict interpretation of law, it is also illegal, but no action is taken because few believe that any other alternative makes sense. At the other prognostic extreme are most infants who are admitted to nurseries. All are treated. No question about fighting for their lives is ever raised. In a third category is a minority of "borderline" children—those with spina bifida, Down's syndrome, severe prematurity, brain damage, and miscellaneous others. Informants in my travels indicate that physicians and nurses in all nurseries treat borderline children, usually very willingly. These informants estimate that 5% to 15%

of neonatologists strongly believe that practically all of these children should be treated. In discussing treatment with parents, such physicians commonly present Hobson's choice, and most parents accept it because it seems reasonable and because the doctors seem kind and sincere. Those few parents who object to treatment are given friendly or, if necessary, unfriendly persuasion. Some physicians do not hesitate to ask parents: "Why do you want us to kill your baby?" "Are you fit parents?" "Can you defend yourself in court?" The threat of internal guilt and of public notoriety resulting from court action brings most parents into line. Parents who want to resist are further handicapped by ignorance of existing ethical guidelines in nurseries (these are not stated) before their child is born. Also, they have practically no chance of a favorable court hearing unless they have abilities to recruit knowledgeable legal counsel and to present convincing alternative medical opinion very quickly. Such abilities are rare; they are found most often among parents who are nurses, social workers, or physicians having prior knowledge of alternatives. Besides all this, most courts guided primarily by laggardly homicide laws are reluctant to accept low quality of child life or great family burdens as reason for nontreatment.

Aggressive Treatment Preferred

Generally, health professionals are very tolerant of aggressive treatment because they and parents are more comfortable with the good appearance of optimistically discussed treatment, and there is genuine satisfaction in lowering morbidity and mortality rates and even in "incomplete solutions." As a result, there is strong bias toward treatment. But the reported reasons for treating are varied: "Since the prognosis is always a little uncertain, we must always treat." "Treating is morally right." "We have to treat. I'm not an executioner." "Parents cannot tolerate the guilt of letting their child die." "We

Raymond S. Duff, "Counseling Families and Deciding Care of Severely Defective Children: A Way of Coping with 'Medical Vietnam,' *Pediatrics*, March 3, 1981. Copyright American Academy of Pediatrics 1981.

won't learn if we don't treat." "We have to avoid setting a bad example for the staff. They must be geared to fight for life. That is our only hope." "That's nursery policy." "That's hospital policy. We have to avoid trouble with the law." Staff often recognize that some of these reasons have nothing to do with the child's interests. However, the rigors of disease and treatment can be concealed easily behind the benevolent mask of a crusading ethic. Optimism is highly valued, skepticism suppressed; diseases and treatment are usually hidden from public view; and people are awed and often terrorized by death, that final, rather objectionable state. Discussion of these issues in intensive care facilities is likely to be minimal, awkward, and resisted.

> *"Treatment may brutalize the child, and yet promise little except better understanding of disease, some good technical practice for the staff, . . . and income."*

Risking unpopularity, some people reason that while nontreatment appears more unfair to the child, in fact sometimes it is not. Treatment may brutalize the child and yet promise little except better understanding of disease, some good technical practice for the staff, consistent staff orientation to fighting (albeit blindly) against disease and death, and income. The surviving child's life at home might have such a detrimental effect on the family that the child, too, would suffer excessively. Deprived of a loving home, the severely handicapped child's life in a series of foster homes or an institution would be too miserable. Choosing death sometimes is viewed as an act of love because some life can only be wrongful.

Risking One Person's Life for Another

The fact that the best interests of children are almost always inextricably linked to those of families demands special consideration. In defining and securing the child's best interests (whatever they are), the central (often sacred) role of the family must be acknowledged and supported even though the resulting decisions occasionally risk violating one or another of numerous, perhaps conflicting, moral, religious, or legal doctrines. Since one cannot prudently ignore the family's limitations and interests even if considering only the child's interests, responsible decision makers cannot avoid some "tragic choices"—that is, at times knowingly sacrificing, perhaps unfairly, one person's good or life in order to protect another's. With a sense of balance, irony, and tragedy it is understandable,

right, and common that the family's interests are sacrificed to benefit the child. With a similar sense, the converse may be true particularly when the child may benefit little even though the family sacrifices much. Separating interests of children from those of families by foster home or institutional care are reasonable alternatives to home care or death in many situations, but not all. Since such choices are already "beyond the best interests of the child," family advisors tend to resist these, and they usually feel that institutionalization is a last resort. Even in better institutions where severely defective human beings are "warehoused," conditions are so unavoidably detrimental to any child's interests that it is easy to understand why some loving parents either keep their child at home despite great burdens or sorrowfully choose death for their child and perhaps eventually feel little or no guilt for it. Indeed, some have reported feeling guilty for not helping their child die. At what level of prognosis, then, and under what social circumstances may the family's interests come before the child's when the child's biologic life is at stake? My reasons for differing with Fost about who should resolve this sticky issue require further elabortion.

Regarding emotionally troubled parent's abilities to assimilate information, practically all discerning clinical observations by families, social workers, nurses, and physicians indicate that generally they do so very well. Being emotionally troubled does not make parents unintelligent nor does it prevent them from using the intelligence they have. This is demonstrated by the fact that parents are emotionally upset (as Fost emphasizes) precisely because they have a painfully adequate general understanding of the situation. True, parents cannot assimilate and understand all the technical data (which even experts only partly understand and about which they often disagree), but that is not necessary for them to make informed judgments about care unless it is assumed that the primary aim is to serve technology rather than people. Furthermore, parental understanding of all the nuances in ethical debates about care is not necessary either unless it is assumed that the primary aim is to serve one dogma or another rather than the purposes which people themselves in their inner beings find most sacred. It is only necessary that parents be reasonably knowledgeable of the personal and social meaning of biologic circumstances to themselves and their children in a moral order which they (parents) have helped to create and urgently need to continue creating in order to adapt. Benfield's work indicates that greatly stressed parents are capable of sharing difficult decisions and that they and hence their children may benefit if they do so.

Child and Parent Interests

When the child's interests conflict with those of the

parents (as they usually do in any case) and the parents have power over the child, is the resolution likely to favor the parent's interests and neglect the child's? While there is no simple answer here, several observations are pertinent. The initial reaction of most parents at birth is, "Don't let our baby die. Make him live." Firm rooting of a parental death wish for a defective child usually takes days, at least; and it is never free of ambivalence. In human and other species, there is a powerful altruism which defends and nurtures the young. This commonly restrains parents because they fear guilt if they make a bad choice for death *or* life. (This second alternative is usually overlooked because crusading professionals do not listen enough.) These altruistic forces serve as a balance against selfish tendencies to let a child die unfairly or to keep a child alive only to support the illusions of parents. Some parents who are aware of very poor prognosis report deep religious convictions that they should allow their child to die. But, sensing staff bias and feeling vulnerable to attack by cynics, they keep that to themselves.

"Hospital and governmental representatives generally must be more sensitive to the utilitarian issue of high costs and low benefits than are families who are more likely to be concerned about their duty to their child."

Most parents in turmoil separately or together contemplate the family's lot and that of their abnormal child day and night. They often talk about their views with each other and with family, friends, health professionals, clergy, and others. Out of the shock, rage, sorrow, guilt, denial, depression, anxiety, and exhaustion, frequently leavened by some laughter and some prayer, they often find or create new strength. And they may even discover some profound, life-transcending meaning which has value above all else in deciding care. Those who counsel carefully with families are privileged to learn about such meaning, to transmit it on occasion from family to family, and thus to improve decision making for children and support for families.

However, such contemplation by families may be disregarded. I have been told by parents, nurses, social workers, and physicians that nursery policy is shaped by two main forces, neither rooted consistently in the values of families. The first is medical opinion which in a minority of instances represents a rigid "moral entrepreneurship." Whether or not such rigid moral policy exists in the

nursery, institutional leaders (administrative, medical, and nursing) as a second and much stronger force commonly compel it upon the nursery. These leaders emphasize the appealing ethics of the crusade against disease and death and point out their obligation to observe homicide laws. This avoids controversy and protects institutional license and finances and jobs. It also discourages identifying children who have borderline or poorer prognoses, and it inhibits facing up to the issues of that status when recognized. Institutional leaders may insist upon court review of nontreatment, and they may proscribe behavior which "mercifully helps a child along" (toward death). No professional group or hospital that I know of has ever stated a patient centered policy like:

> We aim to serve your interests through thick and thin. Especially when the outlook is poor, we will discuss conditions and options carefully with you and with those closest to you. Living well to the end of life is the same as dying well, and that can be done best only on terms which make good sense to you. We are partners with you in a deliberative forum where deciding care is a shared responsibility.

Rigid Policies

If nursery policy is rigid, life for nurses and physicians is difficult, for social workers it is miserable, and for many children and families it is a nightmare. Staff members often leave if no changes seem possible, and they are likely to be replaced by those who will go along with prevailing policies. But there is no escape for children and families. Families can use their religious and other *supports* to help them adjust to decisions made by others, but often they cannot use their religious and other *values* to help shape those decisions. Hospital chaplains at a recent meeting of the New England Hospital Assembly sadly acknowledged the truth of that statement in the care of most chronically or terminally ill persons of any age (D. Eaton, personal communication, 1980).

Separating decisions for care from those of long-term custody in order to escape conflict of interest may protect some children by increasing the power of the profession or the courts over families. But this suggestion is simplistic and misleading because in real life professional, legal, economic, personal, family, religious, and social interrelationships are enormously complex. Altering custody arrangements may frustrate parent-child "bonding" which is extremely important for all children. Besides, any pretense that anyone can make conflict-free decisions is a dangerous illusion. There is great potential for conflict of interest in hospital committees, regulating agencies, and courts because these parties have some agendas far removed from the child's and family's interests. For example, because of the importance of distributive justice, hospital and governmental representatives generally must be more sensitive to the utilitarian issue of high costs and low benefits than are families who are more likely to be concerned about their duty to their child, normal or abnormal. Courts must be more concerned about legal doctrine than about particular child or family problems and needs. It is reported, for example, that one judge guided by law ordered treatment which he personally believed should not have been given. Moreover, the conflict of interest which physicians regularly face can be a major problem. They have a long history of *using* the sick to learn about diseases, to transmit knowledge, and to make a living, all being important "latent" functions which often are in competition with the "manifest" function of patient care. Furthermore, institutionalizing optimism, so common and self-serving among scientists, may prompt behavior which is detrimental to the public interest.

Counselors and Parents

Counseling and support of families cannot be effective in artificial, vacuous isolation from the often agonizing deliberations about the care of their defective children. Yet, like adversaries, some counselors ignore the views of parents. These counselors isolate and fight against parents rather than respectfully join them as an ally in an effort to puzzle out what choice is least tragic. This antagonism may wreck a family's integrity, even its religious or other ethos. While thus compounding the agonies of families and forcing them into helplessness, health professionals may escape their own agony and responsibility by turning such decisions over to committees or courts. Yet, the medical profession, hospital committees, social agencies, and courts have limited powers to rescue and in many situations none at all. Moreover, if decision makers are disinterested or unagonized, decisions may be made casually. But casually coerced life preserving may be wrong as well as right, and in great social crisis casually coerced dying may easily become an ugly policy of unagonized decision making.

Of course, it would be naive to assume that all families will always act altruistically in caring for their children. They will not and often cannot. And sometimes they should not because there are legitimate competing interests. Only if the family selects a course which goes too far toward sacrificing their child's interests and seeking their own should paternalism be invoked. Of course, what is "too far" is a very difficult assessment to make. Here, Fost implies repeatedly (but for some reason does not state) that if parents and their advisors decide to let borderline children die, they are neglecting the child's best interests and violating the law. But there is no consensus about the child's best interests, and, as already noted, these cannot be defined abstractly by committees or courts. Also, by suggesting that the

legal decisions in the rather anomalous Saikewicz and Edlin cases be applied in the medical context (and conveniently ignoring Quinlan), Fost seems to want to scare practitioners into compliance with his ethical position by warning of possible prosecution for criminal liability if they do otherwise. Yet he acknowledges that if they do not comply (and most do not because very often, as described before, that does not make sense), such prosecutions are unlikely. I and numerous others can attest, although with some discomfort, that he is correct in that observation.

Who Should Make Decisions

From many informal contacts with lawyers and judges thus far, I sense a prominent feeling among them that complex human predicaments should be resolved by those who understand them best: patients, families, and their advisors. If the patient is incompetent, the family and the responsible physician should decide care, taking into account the views of the patient (if known), their own views, the opinions of assorted health professionals, and those of whatever religious or other advisors they find useful. If they act upon carefully made decisions, I believe the law will give them protection. However, some persons surely will threaten to use the law against those whose behavior displeases them. This cannot be avoided because, as Manning noted, "The work of doctors in the termination of care, in the allocation of death, will press hard not only on man's resistance to change, but also upon his single most sensitive nerve—his instinct for self-preservation and his well-founded distrust of the homicidal proclivities of his fellow man.

"We may prudently place some limits on our increasingly vast powers to make the unfit survive especially when we know we cannot make them well...or effective citizens."

There is another major problem. Passing responsibility for deciding care more and more to committees or the courts would give away or destroy a central ethos of the profession along with that of the family. I refer to the profession's responsibility, in working with individual patients and their families, to establish a standard of conduct for itself and to assert the freedom to do what it considers best. Without this ethos, medicine could no longer be called a profession and might be impotent precisely when strength is most needed to help people in those tragic predicaments which most likely can only be aggravated by societal intrusion. If the profession developed and applied this ethos explicitly, it would give guidance to the law. And it should do this since health professionals, being close to people who suffer, know more about human disease and suffering than do those in law. There are some individual exceptions, of course, and there is a debate between law and medicine as to which profession should be primary in guiding decisions about the care of incompetent persons.

Since courts are obliged (rightly) to focus on laws applicable to all people and since they use an adversary approach to debate (none other in courts apparently being superior), they must be slow to act and often rigid. They are unlikely to understand the sensitive feelings and complex inner values (some religious in nature) of individual family members and to act in harmony with them. Such failure is noncaring, will stifle creativity, will disrupt adaptation, and will foster helplessness. Of course, routinely deciding care in courts might be a happy dream for lawyers in our litigious society.

Making the Weak Survive

In complex predicaments, what is lawful is not necessarily right, and what is unlawful is not necessarily wrong. Truly caring, responsible people must examine these ambiguities. For example, in harmony with "natural law" such as "survival of the fittest," we may prudently place some limits on our increasingly vast powers to make the unfit survive especially when we know we cannot make them well or reasonably comfortable or effective citizens. I do not argue for the strong against the weak. I only wish to point out that we should try to minimize tyranny: of the strong over the weak and of the weak over the strong. It must be remembered too that the weak do not necessarily benefit by efforts made in their behalf. Persons who claim to represent the weak may be acting also or even only out of medical, moral, legal, political, or economic self-interest. The potential for exploitation is enormous because to live effectively all people must make great efforts to subdue the ever-present internal terror of suffering, disability, and death. Medical technology when misused as ritual to mask terror only adds to it.

I and others believe that patients (when able) and those closest to them (often including religious counselors) must have a major voice in deciding what constitutes practical, sensible help and minimal tyranny. Otherwise, serving rigid legal doctrine and using modern medical technology, the profession of medicine and the public will become trapped increasingly in a kind of "medical Vietnam," rightly claiming some gains which sometimes will be dramatic; but wrongly inflicting great harm, wastefully consuming enormous resources sorely needed elsewhere, and immorally covering up the results. We should use the courts sparingly, and we should not necessarily apply the court's decision in

one biologic instance to another like it because doing so would ignore human, social, and religious uniqueness and creativity. The primary aim of medicine is personal and social, not biologic, nor is it religious or legal. And the profession of medicine in addition to recognizing its own limits often must keep some socially useful or necessary legal and religious doctrines a little distance away.

The chief difficulty in Fost's approach, if I understand it correctly, is that he seeks to set aside the family too quickly. With that, the most practical religious, humanitarian, and philosophical values needed to deal with complex tragedies as they exist in real life would be lost. His approach is a confused paternalism which emphasizes and may even encourage human weakness and malice. It stresses to illogic extremes the need for people to be protected against themselves by other people. It threatens to weaken families and health professionals by disrupting the ethos of both. Fost's approach would result in rescuing some children who probably should be rescued and some who probably should not. Since it is comforting to look only upon the good side of this equation, Fost's approach may appear most safe. In fact, it might lead us "safely" to cynicism and despair.

There should be less paternalism, not more. In proposing an approach to this earlier, we placed moderate confidence in the strength and benevolence of parents and their advisors despite our inflexible belief in the tendency to sin. This approach humbly acknowledged tragedy: the limits of families, professionals, and society in attempting to rescue the severely afflicted. It also noted irony and self-interest as well as benevolence in professional behavior. This approach to counseling families and deciding care of borderline children, although probably used commonly, is little talked about. In place of dialogue, there is often evasion, pretense, and tyranny. Choosing death may or may not be bad in particular instances, but it always can be given a bad appearance; and some have made the most of that. I admit that the alternative I have emphasized is perilous and it makes us squirm. I regret that, but not much. Agonized decisions probably are best for borderline children and their families; they offer some chance for growth and for trust and hope whether the choice is for life or for death.

Raymond S. Duff is professor of pediatrics at Yale University. For most of his professional life, his time has been divided between caring for children and doing research and testing in behavioral aspects of medicine.

"The community should assist the handicapped individual and his family in integrating their handicaps into their daily lives."

viewpoint **19**

Parents Should Accept Their Handicapped Infant

Karen Metzler

The quality of life for an infant born with a birth defect is established long before its conception. Society's attitudes toward diseased, disabled, or disfigured individuals mirror its attitudes toward life and death. Many social and environmental factors that influence individual action and feeling grow from the initial confrontation between one person and another person who is handicapped. Infanticide for those afflicted with a severe handicap is the ultimate negative reaction; it results from other less dramatic but still debilitating actions against persons that are handicapped: prejudice and discrimination in education, employment, daily activities, and personal relationships.

The psychosocial circumstances surrounding the birth of a defective infant relate directly to the issues of death and dying. In birth and death, one is confronted with questions concerning the meaning and value of human life.

A newborn's injured condition reminds us of human vulnerability, the ultimate realization of which is death. Society, through its individual members, may wish for the death of the imperfect infant: it is a biological mistake, which those perceiving it wish they could erase.

The desire for the death of an imperfect infant may persist even when there is a good prognosis for survival or intellectual development. Death becomes desirable as a means of escaping suffering for the infant; however, the suffering continues on the part of the parents and society, and the form it takes is the realization of failure.

If an infant born with a birth defect should survive, he still represents a failure to realize the ideals of perfection and perfectability. In a society that idealizes and idolizes the body beautiful, athletic achievement,

mental development, and upward mobility, a person who is handicapped threatens the sense of security of those who encounter him, because he is supposedly unable to attain what society considers success and a good life (an "inability" reinforced by prejudice and discrimination).

Those persons who are most doubtful about their own ability to meet societal standards tend to compare others as well to the social demands for success and acceptance. They often become the persons who reject the handicapped individual the most; yet all, even the most secure and mature, sigh in relief that they are not handicapped and hope it never happens to them, although disability is always possible in human life.

Lack of Personal Contact With Handicapped

Attitudes and assumptions about these handicapped individuals were propagated through fears, fantasies, and misinformation, instead of knowledge and fact. The lack of personal contact, due primarily to the limited opportunities for participation in society's mainstream, caused barriers of prejudice to be built against persons who are handicapped. Society's basic attitudes toward the handicapped emerged: if they were acknowledged as persons, they were objects of curiosity; if their painful difference caused a hesitant awareness of their condition, they became objects of fear.

This fear often leads to the rejection and isolation of a birth-defected infant. Even from the time of its birth, parents may refuse to take the child home with them, and, if he is taken home, he is a statistically greater risk for neglect and abuse than are normal children. Parental response to their child establishes his psychosocial life and can determine the quality of the infant's future.

The mother-infant bond, the infant's first attachment to and relationship with another person, is based largely on physical contact, and an infant's

Karen Metzler, "If There's Life, Make It Worth Living," *Infanticide and the Value of Life,* edited by Marvin Kohl. Buffalo, NY: Prometheus Books, 1978. Reprinted with permission of Prometheus Books.

physical attractiveness influences his desirability and affects the mother's ease in contact with him. If the infant has medical complications, the mother may be reluctant to touch and hold the child, even after being given permission by attending medical personnel. Nonattachment between mother and infant may occur even in the presence of nonvisible disabilities, such as in the instances of cardiac difficulties. Emotional withdrawal by parents who do not otherwise abandon their child may result from fear that the infant will die, a fear based on the physical and medical realities facing the child.

The child itself is born into a preexisting family unit that has developed its own interpersonal dynamics and history. An infant who is handicapped becomes an added stress on the members of each family. While a couple may have expected to become parents, neither have been prepared for the responsibilities of dealing with a handicapped child. With the development of amniocentesis parents could gain additional time to prime themselves emotionally for a birth-defected infant but, confronted with the unanticipated reality of the birth of a defective child, the parents will react in a manner consistent with their own personalities and their own experiences with illness and disability.

Society Dictates Parental Response

The basis of parental response is grounded in the prevailing social attitudes and assumptions about those persons who are handicapped, to which is added the parents' own personal reactions of guilt and anger at bringing a defective child into the world. The handicapped child as a biological entity does not determine the responses of his parents or others in general, but his birth places the event within a psychosocial context.

"Society reacts to the infant on the basis of his handicap and the family is similarly stigmatized."

For example, the child of a young couple has been born with a cleft lip. The mother had a brother with the same defect, but the new father, with no prior experience of illness or handicaps, was left emotionally devastated at the baby's birth. As a counter-example, another couple, who, throughout childhood experiences positive encounters with retarded individuals, were more able to accept their child who was born with Down's syndrome.

Although grandparents and extended family members may be inaccessible, due to the mobility and frequent relocation of today's society, they also influence parental response and acceptance of a birth-defected child. The parents of the child may feel that his imperfections have caused them to be seen as failures in the eyes of their parents. Extended family members, grandparents, and the parents themselves may feel frustrated in their new roles; the child's condition negates the realization of their hopes and plans for him, particularly if he is a first-born child. Then, if the infant remains an only child, the fulfillment of the parents' various emotional needs that are related to their offspring becomes equally frustrated.

Incorporate the Defective Infant

Other children in the family must also incorporate the birth-defected infant into their own personal development and lifestyles. They must cede expectations of perfection for the infant and be supported and prepared for the effects their handicapped sibling will have on them as individuals, and on the family as a whole. Further disruptions in family routines, should the birth-defected newborn require further hospitalization, must be anticipated and dealt with, and the other children need more reassurance, as they learn to cope with strained family resources of money, time and attention.

Society reacts to the infant on the basis of his handicap and the family is similarly stigmatized. In facing such stigmatization, the parents' response to their newborn child who is handicapped establishes the foundation for the reactions of their other children, their families, and their friends. The normal developmental needs of all the children must be considered; so, the child that is handicapped must neither consume all of his parents' time and attention, nor become the scapegoat for family problems not necessarily related to him and his handicap.

The success with which the other family members deal with their individual feelings, the feelings of others within the family group, and the feelings of the handicapped child himself determines how effectively the child is welcomed and accepted as a natural part of the family. To achieve these goals, and to assure that the infant has as normal a childhood as possible, family counseling and contact with other families having children with similar problems are often beneficial in maximizing the quality of the later life of the child who is handicapped.

Medical Personnel and the Infant

A constant feature in the life of a handicapped individual, and one that also influences his normal development, is the frequent contact with a myriad of medical personnel. Doctors, nurses, and other health-related professionals are also people, and they experience the same natural feelings that other human beings do when confronting an individual who is handicapped. The initial feelings of discomfort, shock, anger, denial, and depression, common to everyone, may be worked through by all and result in feelings of acceptance and compassion.

The significant and crucial difference between the reactions of medical personnel and the reactions of other societal members to a person who is handicapped is that health-related professionals have made a deliberate personal decision to enter a field where they encounter disease, disability, and disfigurement daily. Too often, however, particularly in dealing with a birth-defected infant, medical personnel avoid contact with the handicapped individual and his family, in an attempt to protect themselves from experiencing the natural human feeling of discomfort. In addition, the medical profession's role-model is that of "healer," which carries the implied responsibility of "curing" the patient. However, in instances of chronic illness and disability and birth defects, a total and perfect cure may be unobtainable in terms of the current level of medical technology, knowledge, and skill. In such cases, medical personnel should emphasize the comforting and compassionate aspects of their professional roles, instead of stressing the curative role, in their care of their patient.

"The concept of normalcy needs to be revised so that it no longer negates the personhood of the individual."

Intellectual understanding and knowledge are not all that is sufficient to enable medical personnel to react easily and supportively toward those persons who are handicapped. The experience and awareness of one's own gut-level feelings, even those deemed socially unacceptable, and the recognition that medical personnel are not exempt from experiencing such negative feelings gradually lead to the ability to see beyond the handicap and into the human being.

Counseling and Support Needed

The natural feelings of helplessness and hopelessness that surface first at the birth of a defective infant may prompt others to avoid both the child and his family, just when emotional support is vital. If the infant should die, either naturally or as a result of withholding life-supportive measures, medical personnel should not terminate their involvement with the family. Instead, they should offer follow-up counseling and support to the family.

Some persons, in order to avoid the extensive demands of a habilitation program for the infant, suggest infanticide in those few cases where such a choice exists. The ultimate denial and rejection of the newborn implicit in infanticide does not free its

advocates from the emotional impact of disease, disability, and disfigurement.

At some point in life, all persons encounter the handicapped, no matter how brief or superficial their contact might be. Attention and effort should be directed toward the development of society's ability and capacity to acknowledge uncomfortable feelings, in order to increase the potential for acceptance of and comfort with handicapped persons. Compassionate and understanding encounters with those who are disabled foster the movement toward greater integration and participation of handicapped individuals in the mainstream of society.

There is neither a guarantee that any human being will be born free of disease, disability, or disfigurement, nor any assurance that one will remain unimpaired throughout his life. A five-year-old, normal at birth, may be struck by a car and left paralyzed; a teen-ager may be permanently injured in a diving accident. Many healthy, able-bodied young men, doing military service for their country, may return as disabled veterans to face the social conditions that limit the handicapped. Cancer victims, even those cured or in remission, are denied insurance and employment opportunities because of the persistence of other people's fears that they may be "tainted," or that cancer necessarily results in an untimely death. Burn victims endure the inability to be freely mobile and visible in the community, because of others' reactions to seeing them.

Not all Defects Occur at Birth

Many defects are not immediately noticeable at birth. Cerebral palsy, epilepsy, deafness, birth traumata such as a lack of oxygen affect the child's later development. Then too, there is the inescapable reality that thousands of children, healthy at birth, are destined to become battered children, the victims of emotional and physical abuse that may sometimes result in permanent disability or death.

Individuals afflicted with any of these conditions are as subject to social negativity and frequent medical interventions as the infant born with a noticeable birth defect. Since persons with facial disfigurements are the least accepted social group, and since any impairment is usually linked with mental retardation, despite the fact that most handicaps neither impair social function nor impede intellectual development, it becomes apparent that the mere existence of a handicap, whatever its cause, elicits prejudice and negative social response.

The possibility of being afflicted with a handicapping condition from a variety of causes remains a reality for persons of all ages. For some handicaps, there are cures at the present time; others are not medically remediable. Handicaps must be seen within their social context: while the medical model focuses strictly on an isolated individual and his physical symptoms, a more holistic view of handicapping conditions is necessary. Because designations such as *normal* or *exceptional* are socially defined and determined, persons who have been successfully rehabilitated from a medical standpoint still retain the social stigma of being handicapped; thus, they still encounter prejudice in the form of reduced opportunities, educational neglect, and vocational and interpersonal rejection.

Normalcy Needs Revision

The concept of normalcy needs to be revised so that it no longer negates the personhood of the individual. Exceptionality should refer only to a child's developmental rate, rather than to his whole being. The birth-defected infant becomes an exceptional child that has developmental needs and a rate of development beyond the minimum standard range designated by society as a comparative measurement of its children's progress. This definition of exceptionality allows a child to be ahead of, behind, above, or below the social norm.

The norm and the direction of deviation from it remain the standard criteria by which society evaluates its members. Persons of recognized achievement, talents, or genius differ from the average American, but, since they symbolize the actualization of man's potential, they are desired and revered by society. The handicapped, however, symbolize human vulnerability and limitation, and they differ from social norms in a negative manner. Were they socially recognized as contributors to the general welfare, they would be valued in a positive frame of reference.

Society perceives handicaps as negative qualities, and so disease, disability, and/or disfigurement become socially unacceptable; thus, the handicapped individuals are subjected to fear, denial, avoidance, and pity when they confront society.

The Handicapped Inspire Vulnerability

The fear experienced in encounters with the disabled reminds individuals of their personal vulnerability, and challenges their ability to successfully cope with a handicap within the context of their own lifestyle. Attitudes and actions that reflect a lack of awareness of the special needs of the handicapped indicate denial. Avoidance is demonstrated when the handicapped person is shunned as a partner, friend, employee, or mate; its extreme manifestation is segregation for the handicapped in institutions isolated from the mainstream of society. When fund-raising campaigns feature poster childen or other handicapped individuals, their appearance and disabilities evoke pity. Society's members respond with monetary contributions or token material kindnesses but not human companionship.

The poor societal conditions that exist for the individuals who are handicapped in our society should not determine whether birth-defected infants are allowed to live or die. The excessive medical expenses, social stigmatization and isolation, limited educational opportunities, and unemployment or underemployment that face the handicapped are man-made social problems that need to be redressed for all individuals who are affected, instead of being denied or avoided in those instances where a choice of life or death is possible.

While the quality-of-life for handicapped children and adults can be improved, their presence in our society emphasizes the need for responsivity and flexibility in meeting the requirements of all its members. The community should assist the handicapped individual and his family in integrating their handicaps into their daily lives, and society should provide the handicapped with opportunities to fully develop their potential.

The array of different opportunities for development makes us unique from each other; but the denial of opportunity can limit the quality of life. People are what we make of them and what we help them make of themselves.

At the time of birth we are not aware of what the future holds for an infant. Necessary changes effected by society could result in a more equitable quality of life for all handicapped persons. However, the real issues are not merely the infant's ability to have a "quality life" and an awareness of future capabilities, but rather the need for a social reappraisal of what qualities should be a part of human experience and the concomitant acceptance of the handicapped in the mainstream of society.

Karen Metzler was born with spina bifida and other medical problems. She has nearly grown up in the hospital, having undergone an estimated fifty-eight operations including an amputation of her right leg. She graduated magna cum laude from Baldwin Wallace College and works as a health care consultant and lecturer.

"A bias in favor of perfect mental and physical health seems to enter into the thinking of many doctors and a life in which such health is not possible is thought to have little value."

Physicians Encourage Infant Euthanasia

Rosalyn Benjamin Darling

The question of withholding treatment from a patient whose life is judged no longer valuable is most likely to arise at the endpoints of the life cycle: early infancy and old age. While active euthanasia is illegal, the decision not to treat a patient who is terminally ill or whose chances for a normal life are felt to be poor has in many instances received positive legal sanction, and sometimes religious and social endorsement as well. As a sociologist, I am interested in these decisions because they stem from the social roots of decision-makers and have consequences for society.

An important question, then, is: how are such decisions made? Often cases are decided on an individual basis rather than in categorical terms—if a couple does not wish to bring its Down's syndrome baby home, they may instruct the physician not to perform intestinal surgery necessary for the child's survival. However, in the case of myelomeningocele (spina bifida), sets of guidelines have been established by physicians, so that only those children that meet certain predetermined criteria are given the surgery necessary to preserve life.

What is the sociological basis for the establishment of such criteria? One way of exploring that question is to examine the physician's definition of the situation, as it derives from a more general medical world-view. The physician's view in such cases may not conform to the layman's, particularly the patient's family. The ethical implications of these differing definitions should be of concern to decision-makers and those who guide decision-makers toward various courses of action or non-action in such cases.

Research on Families

My research in this area originated with the presumption that physicians and parents who must

Rosalyn Benjamin Darling, "Parents, Physicians and Spina Bifida," *Hastings Center Report*, August 1977. Reproduced with permission of the Hastings Center Report, © Institute of Society, Ethics and the Life Sciences, 360 Broadway, Hastings-on-Hudson, NY 10706.

decide whether or not to treat infants with serious birth defects should be guided by concrete information about the consequences of such decisions. Thus, my study was originally designed to investigate the problems and adjustments of families who had children with spina bifida living at home. Because the physician directing the spina bifida clinic I intended to use as the basis for my sample objected to the project on the grounds that such multi-problem patients had been "bothered enough already" (he never actually asked them if they would object to participating), I eventually drew my cases from the files of the genetic counseling service at a university medical center. As a reflection of the nature of the defects represented in the files, my final sample included, in addition to spina bifida, other serious defects such as Down's syndrome, severe cerebral palsy, congenital blindness, and some other forms of moderate to severe psychomotor retardation.

Twenty-five children ranging in age from three weeks to nineteen years were randomly chosen for in-depth study. Their families were initially contacted by the pediatrician-geneticist they already knew. I then interviewed both parents of each child, except four cases, where only the mother was available. The interviews were conducted in the subjects' homes and generally lasted only from two to five hours. Almost all the parents were very cooperative and seemed genuinely interested in the project. A few expressed great satisfaction at having the opportunity to talk about their problems, since they felt that friends, relatives, and doctors were not always interested in listening to them.

In the course of the study, the majority of the parents expressed dissatisfaction with their doctors and other professionals who worked with their children. As a result, I became interested in learning more about the physician's point of view and interviewed a random sample of fifteen local pediatricians. These interviews focused on techniques of informing parents about their children's problems and the physician's feelings about treating handicapped children in their everyday practices, two problem areas that had been pinpointed by the parents.

The Parents' Perspective

Almost without exception, all the parents I interviewed defined their situation in a positive manner. They did not generally express unqualified enthusiasm but neither did they see themselves as unfortunate victims of tragedy. The positive attitude of these parents is at first somewhat surprising, given the widespread societal stigma toward the physically and mentally handicapped. As Edwin Lemert, Erving Goffman, and others have noted, those members of society who are "different" or do not conform to an arbitrary set of expectations are branded as morally inferior and subjected to prejudicial treatment in their everyday interactions. The parents in my sample seemed to draw support for their positive definitions of their children from small groups in which they had immersed themselves, especially family, friends, and parents' associations. Many had become friendly with other parents of handicapped children. By far, though, the most important influence on parental attitudes seems to have been interaction with *the child himself*. Similar findings have been reported elsewhere. Margaret Voysey, for example, has shown that the parents of a group of chronically ill children in Britain tended to define their situations in the terms of normal parenthood and to receive social support for their definitions.

"One mother noted that whenever her severely handicapped son (now ten years of age) was ill she had to fight to get treatment for him against the advice of physicians who believed he should be allowed to die."

Doctors seem to be significant in shaping parental definitions *only* when they offer or share in a positive definition of the child as a person. Commonly, parents become hostile toward doctors and medical definitions. Many of the parents I interviewed reported changing doctors when they were dissatisfied with the care their children received. Such changes were generally made quietly, however, so that the rejected physician was probably not aware of his patients' dissatisfaction. Several parents reported lengthy searches for a physician willing and eager to treat their children, and many complained about doctors who responded to their retarded

children as nonpersons. One mother noted that whenever her severely handicapped son (now ten years of age) was ill she had to fight to get treatment for him against the advice of physicians who believed he should be allowed to die. She knew that the boy was not likely to reach adulthood, but as long as he seemed content, she emphatically felt that he should live as long as possible.

I asked all the parents if they would have wanted their child to be conceived if they had known in advance that the child would be handicapped. Most, but not all, agreed that they would not have wanted the child to be born. The severity of the child's handicap seemed not to be correlated with parents' responses, and some parents of children with the most extreme handicaps felt strongly that they would have wanted their child to be born, even if they had known of the problem in advance.

Parents' Attitudes Toward Children

Among those who would not have conceived the child, all felt that once the child was born, its life was valuable. Some admitted at first wishing that the child would die, but changed their minds as they grew to love the child. Many parents said, "I would rather have this child than no child at all." The father of one child with an extreme form of psychomotor retardation remarked, "I can't imagine life without her....The thing I dread most is her death. We know we will lose her someday, and that is the worst thing." The parents of a child paralyzed, deformed, and incontinent from spina bifida stated that their daughter had brought them great joy. In fact, the mother was pregnant at the time of the interview and had no intention of having amniocentesis since she would not abort a spina bifida child. While she hoped that her unborn child would be normal, she felt that another child like her daughter would be better than no child at all. In general, these parents seemed to agree that although their initial definition of the situation at the birth of their child was one of tragedy, with time they had come to alter that definition, to the point, in some cases, of feeling sorry at not having rejoiced when their child was born.

Some professionals in the field, particularly those with a psychoanalytic orientation, might question these findings. Psychoanalytic theory suggests that the birth of a handicapped child produces feelings of guilt in parents. Guilt, in turn, supposedly gives rise to various "defense mechanisms" such as "denial" and "projection." By this reasoning, all or most parents of defective children may be seen as nonaccepting. Even those who *seem* to be coping well are frequently accused of "overnormalization," "overcompensation," "overidealization," or "well-disguised rejection."

The psychoanalytic argument is not supported empirically by most of the writers who present it. Parental actions are simply assumed to be based on guilt. *All* parents probably engage in some amount of autistic distortion in evaluating their children. Tillie Worchel and Philip Worchel found that parents of retarded children rated their children's *normal* siblings as better than "most other children," while they rated their retarded children as slightly less favorable than most children. Overevaluation, then, may be even more prevalent among parents of normal children who have no reason to feel "guilty." No one is suspicious of a parent who is proud of a normal child, but bragging about the accomplishments of one's handicapped offspring typically becomes defined as "denial."

> *"The negative reactions of these physicians toward severely handicapped children conforms with medical judgments to withhold necessary treatment from these children as newborns."*

Certainly the picture that most parents presented to me was not all positive. Many candidly admitted that, if given a choice, they would not have wanted their children to have been born. The typical parental attitude I found might best be described as "realistic acceptance." All the parents would have preferred a normal child but they were still able to love the defective child they had. Although one might argue about deeply hidden unconscious motivation, these parents' attitudes seem entirely understandable given our cultural norms about family life. Parents are socialized to love their children by various agencies in society, and as Voysey has demonstrated, the same socialization model prevails whether families have handicapped or normal children.

The Physician's View

Most of the doctors I interviewed did not share these parents' views. Although some did not object to treating children with serious defects, most did not welcome such patients. As one remarked,

> It's hard to find much happiness in this area. The subject of deformed children is depressing. Other problems I can be philosophic about. As far as having a mongoloid child...I can't come up with anything satisfying about it, I can't think of anything good it does. It's not fun or pleasant, it's somebody's tragedy. I can find good things in practically everything—even dying—but birth defects are roaring tragedies.... Death doesn't bother me, but the living do. Maybe if I was trained differently I'd have a different outlook.

The doctors I interviewed repeatedly cited the inadequacy of medical training in this area. Socialization in medical school, which stresses the treatment of acute illness, does not adequately

prepare physicians for dealing with chronic conditions and certainly does not suggest to them that such conditions could possible have any positive effects.

The doctor quoted above also noted that he "liked problems as a resident" but does not "enjoy sick kids anymore." All of the pediatricians echoed this view in one way or another, describing their feelings at the birth of a handicapped child variously as "sad," "uncomfortable," "inadequate," or "terrible." Several expressed wonder at physicians who devote their entire careers to the treatment of children with severe congenital problems, stating that they could see no rewards in such a practice. Clearly, all the pediatricians to whom I have talked have a bias in favor of healthy children.

Physicians are often reinforced in their views by the feelings that parents concur in their definitions of the situation. John Lorber, a leading British doctor, comments, for example, that most parents of newborns with spina bifida accept his criteria as a basis for refusing treatment to their babies. However, parents are probably highly suggestible in this situation and likely to accept a clear-cut alternative presented by an authority figure—the physician. Some of the doctors I interviewed cited instances of parents who, hostile at first, later returned to thank them for suggesting that their child be placed in an institution or be allowed the correctness of their handling of the situation. Of course, as I indicated earlier, many parents are not as satisfied as their doctors believe them to be. As Eliot Freidson and others have noted, in American culture, the physician has been seen as an awesome and powerful figure, and as a result, patients have often accepted treatment that does not satisfy them. And although they expressed numerous misgivings about their childrens' medical treatment, none of the parents I interviewed had ever complained to a doctor directly.

Guidelines for Treating Spina Bifida

The negative reactions of these physicians toward severely handicapped children conforms with medical judgments to withhold necessary treatment from these children as newborns. A bias in favor of perfect mental and physical health seems to enter into the thinking of many doctors, and a life in which such health is not possible is thought to have little value. This bias has become institutionalized in the case of the current precedent-setting treatment policy for spina bifida.

Spina bifida is one of the most serious human birth defects. The defect commonly involves a deformity of the spine known, in its most severe form, as myelomeningocele. It is typically accompanied by an abnormal accumulation of fluid in the head, or "hydrocephalus." Until the introduction in 1958 of the shunt, an effective treatment for hydrocephalus, most victims died early in infancy. Since that time, the defect has generally been treated through surgical closure of the lesion on the child's back, shunt-control of any accompanying hydrocephalus, and various measures for dealing with complications that might arise, such as infection. Even with vigorous treatment, however, a certain number of patients do not survive.

Various follow-up studies cite different rates of survival for treated spina bifida children, with mortality rates ranging from zero to 65 percent. In addition, most of those who survive have some consequences, ranging from minor physical deformity to severe paralysis, incontinence, and mental retardation. Lorber found, for example, that in a large series of survivors 3 percent had no handicap, 15 percent had a severe physical handicap with moderate mental retardation, and 12 percent were profoundly retarded with gross physical handicaps.

"A life defined by physicians as intolerable might come to be defined in a very different manner by parents."

The birth of a spina bifida child creates many problems for the family. First, the child is often separated from its mother at birth and transferred to a special nursery or hospital for the first of a long series of in-patient stays. One study found, for example, that by age four, the average spina bifida child had had six hospital admissions for neurosurgical, orthopedic, urological, or other care, creating financial, transportation, child care and emotional difficulties for the families. In addition, these children need frequent out-patient visits for physiotherapy, urine checks, and appliance fittings.

Selective Treatment

Although the less seriously affected spina bifida patients can expect to lead fairly normal lives, the quality of life of the more severely handicapped victims has been questioned. As a result, Lorber has advocated a policy of *selection* of cases to be treated based on a set of criteria including the degree of paralysis present at birth, the presence or absence of hydrocephalus, the presence or absence of spinal deformity, and the existence of associated gross congenital anomalies of major birth injuries. Lorber also suggests, although he does not consider in detail, the possibility of "social" criteria such as illegitimacy. Thus, those that are likely to be paralyzed and incontinent or retarded are denied treatment. Lorber suggests that such selection is best done soon after birth when the emotional involvement of parents and doctors is weakest.

The selection policy has since been followed in many hospitals here and abroad although the morality of the position continues to be questioned. The establishment of criteria for the "right to life" is felt to be possible in the case of spina bifida, since findings at birth seem to have some predictive value for the future medical condition of the patient. Such guidelines might be more difficult to set for defects such as Down's syndrome, where the presence at birth of various physical stigmata is not necessarily indicative of future intellectual development.

Aside from larger moral questions about "right to life," several immediate problems are raised by the policy of selective treatment. First, a few severely handicapped patients manage to survive without operation. Gordon Stark and Margaret Drummond comment,

> There is no doubt, however, that parental acceptance of these infants, who, having been mourned, return like Lazarus from the grave, is prejudiced. Nevertheless, only one has not been discharged home.

The situation is made more complex when parents want their child institutionalized. In Connecticut, for example, a child with hydrocephalus will not be accepted for custodial care without shunt surgery. These partially treated children are more likely to survive, but their existence is likely to be considerably restricted by their uncorrected orthopedic difficulties, as well as from an open or only partially closed lesion. John Freeman has argued that the large minority who live without any surgery at all pose nursing problems because of head enlargement and the open back lesion. Further, the death of many untreated patients is slow and painful. (Other writers have mentioned the possibility of such techniques as "subcaloric feeding" to hasten the process.) Freeman argues that since active euthanasia is illegal, the only humane course is to treat virtually every child. He wonders, however, about the long-range effects of active early treatment of these children and their families:

> It has been said that the infants we treat will grow up to curse us, that the adolescent who is ambulatory only in massive braces and crutches, or is in a wheelchair, with an ideal loop and an ever precarious shunt, when facing the difficulties of marriage and employment will hardly be thankful for the investment of time, effort, and money expended in bringing him or her to that state.

Physicians, such as Lorber and Freeman, have been trained as healers; their basic mission is to *cure*. A worldview that primarily involves sick people who get better may not leave room for the chronically ill or incurable patient, whose defect cannot be "fixed." Even if spinal surgery is performed on a myelomeningocele child, he may still never walk, and a Down's syndrome baby whose intestinal blockage is relieved will be retarded nonetheless. The rewards, then, for physicians, of treating such patients are perhaps not as great as those stemming from making a baby "normal" through their actions. The "action" orientation that Freidson ascribes to practicing physicians often "works" in the case of acute illness, reaffirming the doctors' faith in their healing abilities. One study found that when doctors were asked which aspects of their careers they found most satisfying they usually noted "good therapeutic results or a large percentage of successful cases." The action orientation does not seem to prevail in the spina bifida situation, since a "successful" outcome is not possible. "Success," in this view, seems somehow to be equated with complete normalcy of function, and the chronically ill or disabled present a moral dilemma to the physician so oriented.

A Plea For Informed Decision

As my findings have indicated, a life defined by physicians as intolerable might come to be defined in a very different manner by parents. These findings call into question Lorber's medical criteria for the selection of myelomeningocele cases for treatment. Several social criteria could perhaps be added. A number of writers have reported correlations between parental acceptance of their handicapped children and such factors as religion, social class, having had other (normal) children, and presence of supportive friends and relatives. However, *no* pre-established criteria can adequately suggest the emergent, interactional nature of "adjustment": parents typically learn to value and love their children as they live with them.

The decision to treat or not to treat them, then, is always something of a gamble. Life is uncertain, but does this inherent uncertainty give physicians the right to deprive parents of a child they are likely to grow to want? Perhaps, in addition to being informed of the potential difficulties, parents ought to be made aware of the possible rewards of raising such a child, and be encouraged to participate in decisions about whether to treat or not. Currently, under the pressure of medical authority, parents consent to such decisions with very limited information. They are also generally unaware of the bias behind the physician's recommendations (as indeed, the physician himself may be unaware of his underlying values).

Doctors have argued that decisions to treat or not to treat must often be made in great haste and that immediately after the birth of a handicapped child, parents are often in a state of shock. The parents I interviewed agreed that they were emotionally upset when their children were born. Almost all, however, felt that one of their greatest needs at the beginning was for more information. In fact, much of their anxiety often stemmed from not knowing the truth. The mother of the spina bifida child quoted earlier remembered waking after her daughter's birth to be told only that her baby was desperately ill and that she had to sign a consent for surgery. Others reported asking questions that were not answered. These parents may have been upset, but they were not irrational.

Even when giving truly informed consent, however, parents are handicapped by lack of time to consider their decision fully. For this reason as well doctors have an obligation to be as fully informed as possible in helping parents arrive at a decision. They certainly ought to be made aware that some parents have the feelings and values expressed by the respondents in my study. Perhaps, too, in the limited realm of education in medical schools, students could be better prepared for dealing with the chronically handicapped if "success" in medicine were redefined. Future doctors might be more responsive to the needs of some patients if they would sometimes abandon the overwhelming need to "cure."

One doctor I interviewed held a view very close to that of the parents and quite unlike that of the other doctors. He had had two siblings with myelomeningocele, one who died early and one still alive. He remarked that watching his sister grow up showed him how a handicapped person could lead a happy life and observed,

> Maybe, there is too much expectation these days that things are to be perfect. There is nothing inherently wrong with having to face problems in life. People can learn to accept problems....

Those who have lived with the handicapped seem to reject any necessary incompatibility between being handicapped and leading a worthwhile life, a conclusion that ought to be taken in account by those charged with making decisions about the "right to life" of infants with birth defects.

Rosalyn Benjamin Darling is special lecturer in sociology at Central Connecticut State College. The research for the study described in this viewpoint was supported in part by a grant from the University of Connecticut Research Foundation.

"The successes of the modern, regionalized, high-technology intensive care nursery are real and well publicized. Its failures and risks,... are just as real."

viewpoint 21

Physicians Hopelessly Prolong Infant Suffering

Peggy and Robert Stinson

The following article is an excerpt from the book, The Long Dying of Baby Andrew. *The book is written by the parents of an infant born with incalculable defects. Written in a diary format, it is a vivid testimony to the parents' confrontation of, and feelings toward, the doctors that prolonged their infant's life.*

Saturday, February 12, Robert Stinson

We were barely awake this morning when Peg said we had to *do* something, go down there and confront them, make them take us seriously. I felt my old sinking feeling, but she had such a look of desperation I knew we had to go.

About 9 I called the IICU [Infant Intensive Care Unit] and asked for Craft, but the nurse said he was not in the unit and was probably at home. What followed might have been funny if I were not frustrated by a long history of expectations being so regularly discounted. I asked for Craft's home number and was told to wait a minute. Silence. Then the nurse came back and said they did not have his home number. "What do you mean you don't have it," I said. "He's in charge of the unit this month."

"I'm sorry, Mr. Stinson."

"Look," I said, "if you don't want to give it to me, then say that. At least be honest. Don't lie to me."

"I'm not lying to you, Mr. Stinson. You can call the main operator, and if *she* wants to give you the number, she will." I hung up.

Then I dialed the main operator. "Hello," I said. "This is Dr. Stinson. I need to get in touch with Dr. David Craft right away. Do you have his home telephone?" That did it.

"Yes, doctor, I have it here."

I called him and said we had to talk about Andrew

in a major way. "Things have come to a head for us." Unexpectedly, Craft was sympathetic, not disturbed at being called at home, willing to come in. We agreed on 11 o'clock. We dropped Jenny at Rossis', telling them only that we "had to go to the hospital."

Confronting the Doctor

On the way down we went over Peggy's notes about what we wanted to say. How can we impress upon Craft the seriousness of Andrew's crisis and ours? To him Andrew is a case, interesting. To us, in a way that has pushed far beyond the figurative, Craft's "case" has become a slow destroyer. How can we get him to look us in the eye and talk to us about Andrew the way he talked about him to Nielsen? How can we get him to be honest about Andrew's condition, Andrew's prognosis, Andrew's fate, and how *they* decide these things? How can we get Craft into our world and how can we get into his?

By the time we reached PHC [the institution where Andrew was hospitalized] we had discussed Andrew, Craft, ourselves, and Jenny so thoroughly that I felt more intensely aware of the depth and range of our family's collapse—including Andrew's—than ever. Which tells me one thing, anyway: I *have* avoided a good deal of the crisis. Is that a pathology or a therapeutic self-protection? Whatever the answer to that, going up in the elevator I felt what we and Craft were about to say to each other was going to be the most crucial exchange yet with any of them. If the three of us could face each other just once and admit that Andrew—and babies like him wherever they are—are on a frontier of not just human viability but medical science as well, and if we could admit, then, that there is nothing simple and automatic about decisions for life and death in IICUs then maybe we could *together* establish a reasoned course for our baby.

Strains on Our Lives

I spoke first when the three of us sat down in the conference room, and as I started through the catalogue of the crisis's dimensions, I worried that it might seem just that: a catalogue, rationally presented, each element in its place. The strain on our marriage; Jenny's little regressions and our neglect of her; Andrew's deterioration; disastrous relations between us and the hospital. At first I was aware that my very presentation hardly made me appear to be falling apart. Yet I knew he would see by the sheer accumulation and the obvious interconnectedness of medical, financial, and social effects that it was time to talk again the way we talked in early January the first time we met.

"When parents refuse consent for treatment, we have to be the child's advocate."

Nothing. An hour of mere talk. And it was not my calm but Craft's steady and finally insulting resistance to our trying to find out—to *know*—what they decide for Andrew and how they decide it that set the tone.

Craft insists on defining the problems to us with convenient simplicity. Andrew and his pathologies are the only focus, and he insists they are minimal. He needs the respirator to live but, technically, his breathing is only assisted by it, and he does take some breaths himself. When he can't be fed normally they can manage his nutrition intravenously with the new technique of hyperalimentation, which solves all feeding and growth problems experienced by premature babies. And the infection is simply a puzzle. I told him, again, I thought he was seeing these as separate problems, whereas, to us, they seemed to describe a pattern of deterioration. His reply, as on Wednesday, was "you could look at it that way," but, as on Wednesday, that admission did not lead him to any larger conclusion. We were still on square one.

Andrew's Condition

I came back to the effect of the infection. Craft replied that one blood culture had shown up negative—free of E. coli [*Escherichia coli*, bacteria]—but said also that it's possibly an aberration and that repeat cultures over several days are the only test. Andrew had "a little sore on his leg" from one of the needles, and that may have contributed to the continuing infection, he said, but it's healing nicely. I still wanted to know, since Nielsen talked about destruction of blood platelets and other things, what the long-term effect might be. Again he said he did not know, could not even speculate, because he had

never seen an infant like Andrew live this long with a dangerous infection. You don't know, I thought, but you'd like to find out. "Isn't Andrew's life a kind of experiment, then?" I asked. Craft really bridled. "Our concern here is for the health of each patient," he said. I couldn't make him see that health care and research are inextricably mixed and that health care in a hospital like this could be a mask—a partial truth—which covers, however unintended, the research which is just as much a reason for PHC's being.

And if we were not getting anywhere with the medical aspects, he seemed unwilling to see even the relevance of other dimensions: our family, our finances. They are pathologies, too, but, like Andrew's, they are discrete and discretely treatable. Have we a family we can fall back on? Have we seen a marriage counselor? None of these problems is a reason to rethink Andrew's. It is Craft's assumption that bothers me. He did not argue with us, he did not give us what we came down for, an honest, extraordinary, substantive discussion of everything Andrew is: a medical, ethical, legal, social dilemma. We told him things about ourselves which we have told no one else. But he assumes their irrelevance from the start. He made me feel a sense of "methinks thee protests too much" for raising the broader dimensions at all. It's as though PHC is an entirely different world from the one I normally inhabit. Logic, even common sense, seem different here. I feel small and even a little mean for saying things which are normal and obvious when I think them at home or say them to Peg or Joel.

Hospitals Vary in Care

After a while Peg tried to get him to admit as a general proposition that doctors and hospitals do vary in how far they pursue infants in Andrew's condition.

"Well, I don't know about that," he said. "We have standards in medicine. I don't think the approach is different."

"Are you saying every doctor and every hospital evaluates these things and decides to keep going or not in exactly the same way?"

Craft's blank expression.

"Parents have a right to know what kind of hospital they are putting their children into and what kind of ideology the doctors have."

Craft replied that the policy of all hospitals is to provide "proper care" for each infant.

"But what about when parents and hospitals disagree on what is 'proper care'?"

"When parents refuse consent for treatment, we have to be the child's advocate. When Jehovah's Witnesses refuse consent for blood transfusions for their children, we get the courts to overrule them."

We argued for a while about the accuracy of comparing Andrew's case to the refusal of a standard blood transfusion. Peggy: "It's not as if we got involved by accident with the hospital that believes in blood transfusions." She was still trying to talk about the nature of the difference between PHC and Community, between Nielsen and Farrell; the problem of moving by mistake from a hospital where what you want is moral and legal to a hospital where what you want is immoral and illegal.

Legal Consent

Craft either didn't see the point or didn't choose to acknowledge it; he argued testily instead that blood transfusions aren't "standard" or risk-free either but that some risk is an acceptable necessity of any medical treatment. He didn't see why any of this was "relevant" anyway: "you already signed a legal consent to Andrew's treatment."

We had to acknowledge that was so. It was equally "irrelevant" to try to protest the conditions under which we signed it, the inexplicit nature of the consent—that no one made clear what we were agreeing to.

How then do they make their decisions that we had "consented" to before they were ever made? "How do you decide when to turn off equipment or when not to turn it on?" Peggy asked.

"Every case is different."

"Do you have an explicit policy?"

Craft didn't insist on "brain death" as Carvalho had, but neither would he say just what the considerations were. "Does the IICU make decisions then that are technically to the left of the law?" He "couldn't comment on that sort of question," he said. Peggy asked him for a written statement of the units policy in making life/death decisions; he said he'd "see what I can do."

I said, "We've heard that you and Dr. Farrell don't agree on how far to go in these cases." I wanted to give him an opening, something more specific without violating Jeff's or Nielsen's confidences.

"No, there's no real disagreement. We are all together here."

"But you *once* had a different view of Andrew than your colleagues?"

"Well, no. Maybe I think about these issues a little more often."

Depleting Our Resources

At one point, struck, I think for the first time by how long this could go on, I told Craft I did not think even our major medical insurance would cover a "foreseeable future" hospitalization. "Will they take our house and everything we have and make us declare bankruptcy?" I asked. I guess I wanted to shock him into seeing how extensive and unrealized the consequences of his pursuit were, but he shocked me instead. "I guess they will," was all he said. I don't think he meant to shock. Rather, my guess is that the social or financial consequences of his work, being literally beyond the glass walls of the IICU, are

just not real to him. The unit is sterile and intensive in more ways than one thinks.

Craft asked if we wanted to talk to the Chief of Medicine. "I should tell you, though," he added, "that he would not tell you anything different." I thought of Nielsen's comment yesterday that the higher up they go at PHC the more conservative they get.

Peg tried one last time to find out why Craft thought that Andrew was "doing all right," that there was hope for his future. He cited the "Vanderbilt study" again and said that anyway the technology being used to "salvage" Andrew was so new there can be no reliable follow-up studies yet: "We don't have the answers because we are on a frontier here." Peg said: "How awful to *be* the one who is on the experimental edge." And her crying became hysterical. I put my arm around her and said, more to myself than to either of them, that there was no point in continuing. Silence. Awkward getting up, putting on coats. Craft at the door: "Shall I wait to hear from you?" I just said the very truest thing I could in reply: "I don't know what we are going to do now."

Sunday, February 13, Peggy Stinson

Why do I even believe anymore that something will happen, that something can be done?

Craft is no use, the residents have rotated again, Perlman is gone, no one tells the truth, no one understands what we keep trying to say.

It's out in the open now that visiting Andrew is seen as cooperation. Keeping in routine contact undermines the credibility of our dissent. Throws whole days into turmoil for no useful end. Special conferences are stonewalled.

"He asked again if I didn't feel guilty raising the question of when the respirator could be turned off and I screamed at him...'Can't you understand that it's what YOU are doing that I believe is wrong'?"

This week has done it—how can we go back to PHC? It's not so much a strike as a lockout.

The Craft conversation was the end of the line. Craft was our only hope for honest conversation with someone in power. Our only hope for being able to influence someone who could change anything. Just the fact that he came in at all to see us on a Saturday morning shows a certain decency, but that was as far as it went. Once he got there, he was the proverbial stone wall.

I got really hysterical this time. He asked again if I didn't feel guilty raising the question of when the respirator could be turned off and I screamed at him this time, "Can't you understand that it's *what YOU are doing* that I believe is wrong?"...

Medical Bills

The summer following Andrew's death was nonetheless busy with the legacies of his crisis. Bills began to come in the mail from doctors we had never heard of and from the hospital itself, including one day a bill ("please remit immediately") for $25,157. A later statement set hospital costs at $104,403.20. Weeks of tedious negotiations about medical insurance lay ahead....

The successes of the modern, regionalized, high-technology intensive care nursery are real and well publicized. Its failures and risks, its moral controversies, its potential to harm rather than help, are just as real. A more widespread facing up to some of these problems could help not only the many thousands of babies and their families whose fate it will be in the years ahead to need neonatal intensive care, but also all the rest of us who face the prospect of hospitalization and death in this age of highly specialized, often depersonalized medicine.

The following is a summary of Andrew's medical problems:

    Summary diagnosis includes:

    Prematurity 24 to 26 weeks
    Apnea prematurity
    Escherichia coli sepsis
    Urinary tract infection
    Rickets and numerous fractures
    Ventricular Septal Defect
    Resolved Grade II retrolental
       fibroplasia
    Question of central nervous
       system bleeds
    Bronchopulmonary dysplasia
    Failure to thrive
    Question of enlarged ventricles
    Pulmonary artery hypertension
    Social considerations

Peggy Stinson is a part-time teacher with a graduate degree in German language and literature.

Robert Stinson is an associate professor of history at Moravian College and is the author of Lincoln Steffens.

"In cases of disagreement, doctors should ask the courts to appoint a guardian and determine the patient's rights."

Overview: The Legality of Euthanasia

John A. Robertson

Some of the hardest questions in the care of the critically ill arise with patients who are not competent to make choices about their treatment. Patients may lack the capacity to consent because of mental retardation, mental illness, senility, brain damage, or major organ failure. Their incompetency may be irreversible or temporary. They may also be terminally ill or in no danger of dying if properly treated. Finally, incompetent persons differ in their level of awareness. Some are comatose, while others are conscious and interact with others.

Since such patients cannot consent, there is no ready benchmark for knowing when treatment can be stopped. Vigorous treatment and prolonged life is not in the interest of all incompetent patients. When it is burdensome and has no compensating benefit, it can, and should, be withheld. At the same time, vigorous treatment that prolongs life with minimal suffering should be provided if incompetent patients are to be shown equal respect.

Competing Interests

In practice, doctors and families have had considerable discretion in deciding when treatment on such patients is to be terminated. But their decision may be motivated by competing interests, or by incomplete information; they also may be moved by the intense stress of critical illness. Since incompetent patients are entirely dependent and vulnerable, there is a danger that the needs of others will control, rather than those of the patient.

Since the courts are just now grappling with the task of defining the rules that apply to the continuation of treatment on incompetent persons, the law here is particularly uncertain. Most states have not yet enacted laws or decided cases in this

area. The few cases that have been decided—in New York, New Jersey, and Massachusetts—are thus very influential and are likely to be followed by other states. Yet these cases have answered only a few of the many legal questions that arise. This chapter discusses the law that is now developing.

Question: Does a critically ill incompetent patient have a right to be treated?

Answer: Yes. As long as the treatment will benefit the patient by relieving discomfort or by extending his life for a significant period of time and is not excessively burdensome, he has a right to be treated. The mentally impaired have the same right to treatment as the mentally normal. A person does not lose the right to necessary medical care just because she is retarded, mentally ill, senile, comatose, terminally ill, or otherwise incompetent, even though some patients in each of those categories may at some point have treatment legally stopped.

Doctors who have undertaken to care for a patient who is, or has become, incompetent, have a duty to treat the patient as long as treatment is beneficial. An intentional or negligent failure to provide proper treatment would constitute abandonment of the patient, and as with competent patients, could lead to civil liability, criminal sanctions, or disciplinary proceedings against the doctor.

Question: When does an incompetent patient's right to treatment end?

Answer: It depends. Treatment may be stopped when it will no longer benefit the patient, either because it does not provide a longer or better quality of life, or because its burdens seem excessive. It is often said that such treatments can be withheld because they are "extraordinary" or "heroic." Since these terms incorporate a conclusion about whether the benefits of treatment to the patient are justified by its burdens and do not directly tell us which medical treatments are required, it is better to address directly, the question of benefits and

From John A. Robertson's *The Rights of the Critically Ill.* Copyright 1983, American Civil Liberties Union. Reprinted with permission from Ballinger Publishing Company.

burdens.

In assessing benefits to the patient, the pain and suffering of the treatment itself, as well as the resulting state or quality of life, will be considered. Thus, a treatment that would prolong a very impaired life and be itself very painful, would probably not be required. On the other hand, treatments that keep patients alive without undue suffering, but do not relieve incompetency, cannot be withheld, just because the patient is mentally retarded or senile.

Equal Respect

The law's basic approach to treatment decisions for incompetents is a patient-centered one that gives primary regard to the needs and interests of the incompetent patient, rather than the needs and interests of families, doctors, and society, with whom the patient's interests may conflict. The patient's diminished ability, mental status, or social worth, are not valid grounds for ignoring his interests. Equal respect for persons requires that incompetent patients not be denied treatment to serve the interests of others.

"An intentional or negligent failure to provide proper treatment would constitute abandonment of the patient."

The courts, however, have not yet agreed on the test or standard for determining the patient's interests. Massachusetts and New Jersey, the states with the most experience in this area, have adopted the substituted judgment test for determining what should be done for an incompetent patient. This test attempts to treat the incompetent patient as a choosing individual, by asking what he would choose if cognizant of his interests and able to communicate his choices. But unless the patient when competent had expressed a preference on the subject, it is difficult to infer any choice for an incompetent patient other than that which would protect his current best interests, viewed in his particular circumstances as a critically ill incompetent patient.

A less confusing approach, when there is no prior expression of preference, to the substituted judgment procedure of asking what the patient would choose if competent, is to ask directly whether treatment, in light of the additional life it makes possible and the burdens it entails, serves the patient's interest. Indeed, when properly understood, the best interests and substituted judgment tests should reach identical results, for an incompetent patient, if competent and able to make rational choices, would choose what would best serve his interests.

The situations in which an incompetent person's right to treatment ends, will thus depend on whether or not, under the substituted judgment or a best interests test, he would find medical treatment to be in his interest. This will depend on the facts of each case—diagnosis, prognosis, treatment alternatives, therapeutic discomforts, and the prospect of recovery—rather than on the type of treatment proposed. In some cases, an incompetent patient might have a right to have respirator care, while in others, he has a right to have it discontinued. In any event, the courts are likely to respect the judgments of physicians and families who stop treatment on the basis of good faith assessments of what an incompetent patient would choose or what would best save his interests. The following questions discuss, more specifically, situations in which treatment may no longer serve the interests of an incompetent patient, and therefore may be stopped.

Question: May treatment be stopped on an incompetent patient who is irreversibly comatose?

Answer: Yes. The *Quinlan* case, which is likely to be followed by other courts, held that patients who are irreversibly comatose, or in a persistent vegetative state, are deemed to have no further interest in living, and therefore can have necessary medical care stopped.

In *Quinlan*, a twenty-two-year-old unmarried woman suffered irreversible brain damage and became comatose. Because some brain function remained, she was still legally alive, and with treatment, could live indefinitely. The doctors described her as being in a "chronic persistent vegetative state," with no cognitive or sapient functioning, and no possibility of recovery.

After several months in a comatose condition, Ms. Quinlan's parents asked the doctors to discontinue the respirator. The doctors refused, claiming that it was their professional duty to maintain the patient's life as long as possible. Ms. Quinlan's father then asked a court to appoint him her guardian so that he would have legal authority to refuse further care. The trial court refused this petition, and he appealed to the New Jersey Supreme Court which, in a landmark decision, held that necessary medical care could be withheld from a chronically vegetative patient.

The court concluded that if Ms. Quinlan were competent, she would have a right to stop the respirator, because the state's interest in preserving life would be insufficient to overcome the patient's interest in avoiding a prolonged existence in such a debilitated condition. It then held that the competent patient's right to decline care "should not be discarded solely on the basis that her condition prevents her conscious exercise of the choice. Instead, the privacy right of incompetent persons could be protected by permitting "the guardian and family...to render their best judgment...as to whether she would exercise it in these circumstances.

Since the family judged that a person in that situation would not want further care, a request to stop the respirator would be upheld.

Vegetative Patient

Thus the court, in effect, ruled that doctors and families could stop treatment on a chronically vegetative patient, because it is reasonable to think that the patient, if competent and able to express a preference, would make the same decision. While it may be argued that a patient in a comatose state would choose, if able to speak, to go on living, the substituted judgment test need not be followed so strictly. When the person's interests are so slight that the concept of harm or benefit hardly appears to be relevant, the wishes of the family and society may appropriately be followed.

The *Quinlan* decision is likely to be followed by other courts. In the *Matter of Eichner,* for example, New York trial and appellate courts used a theory similar to that used in *Quinlan,* to uphold their decision to disconnect a respirator on an eighty-year-old man who had suffered a cardiac arrest and subsequent brain damage during a hernia operation. The New York Court of Appeals affirmed, on different grounds, that there was clear evidence that the patient had previously, when competent, asked that his life not be prolonged if he ever ended up like Karen Quinlan. When proof of a prior wish to stop treatment on irreversibly comatose patients is absent, it is likely that courts in other states will follow *Quinlan.*

Question: May treatment be stopped on incompetent patients who are terminally ill?

Answer: It depends. Terminal illness is a vague term that covers a range of illnesses and prognoses. A person can be terminally ill in the sense that he is suffering from an incurable illness, but may not die for months, or even years. In other cases of terminal illness death may be literally imminent and occur in a few hours or days. The important questions then, for determining when treatment can be stopped on an incompetent patient said to be terminally ill are: (1) how intrusive and painful the life-prolonging treatment is; (2) how long it will prolong the person's life; and (3) what the quality of that additional life will be. In some cases, the treatment will be so intrusive and painful, and the additional life it makes possible so impaired or painful, that one could reasonably say that judging from the patient's perspective, the treatment is not in his interest (hence, would not, under the substituted judgment test, be chosen by the patient if competent and able to speak). In such a case, treatment could legally be stopped, and indeed to provide it could be said to violate the patient's right not to be treated.

In other cases, however, the extended life will be well worth the burdens that the treatment making it

possible impose. In that case, treatment must be provided, regardless of the patient's future mental status and social worth, for it serves the patient's interest (hence, would be chosen by him under the substituted judgment test if the patient were competent and able to choose).

Worth the Burdens

A case illustrating these principles is the *Saikewicz* case from Massachusetts. Joseph Saikewicz, a severely retarded male (IQ about 15) of sixty-seven, who had spent most of his life in a state institution, was diagnosed as having acute myeloblastic monocytic leukemia, a cancer of the blood. Most adults in that situation would consent to a course of chemotherapy that would not cure the disease, but possibly prolong life for about four to thirteen months. Without chemotherapy, the patient would probably die within a few months.

"Treatment may be stopped when it will no longer benefit the patient."

The doctors sought court approval to withhold chemotherapy. The trial court agreed that treatment would not be in the patient's interest because it involved significant side effects and discomfort. The patient would not be able to understand what was happening to him, and would have to be forcibly restrained to have chemotherapy administered. The pain and suffering involved in the treatment would outweigh the benefit of a few additional months of life in such a state, and therefore was not in Saikewicz's best interest. The Massachusetts Supreme Judicial Court affirmed the decision. It applied the substituted judgment test and found that if Saikewicz were competent to express his preferences, he would, in light of his mental and physical prognosis, choose to reject therapy, because the pain, discomfort, and suffering of treatment would outweigh any possible benefits.

On the other hand, situations do arise in which a terminally ill incompetent person could benefit from treatment, which thus must be provided. Competent patients who are dying will often want life-prolonging treatment, at least for a while. Patients who are incompetent might also have an interest in staying alive. This is most apt to be true where the patient might recover competency, or if permanently incompetent, is conscious and able to relate to others. (It is unlikely where the terminally ill patient is comatose or severely brain damaged.) Relatively painless treatments that will allow incompetent patients to live for several weeks or months would ordinarily be in their interest, just as it would be in the interest of a competent patient. For example, a mentally retarded person with cancer has a right to surgery, chemotherapy, and radiation therapy, even if it will not prevent death. His right to treatment ends only when he no longer benefits from the treatment sufficiently to justify the pain and discomfort of the therapy.

"Equal respect for persons requires that incompetent patients not be denied treatment to serve the interests of others."

A 1981 New York case shows that the courts will sometimes require treatment of a terminally ill incompetent patient. John Storar, a profoundly retarded fifty-two-year-old man who had been institutionalized since he was five, suffered from an advanced stage of bladder cancer. He was treated with radiation therapy, but the cancer metastasized to his lungs, and the doctors estimated that he would die in two to six months. He also began losing massive amounts of blood, which necessitated blood transfusions every eight days. His mother, a seventy-seven-year-old widow, requested that the transfusions be stopped. They were painful, required physical restraints, and only prolonged the pain of his dying. The director of the facility in which he lived requested judicial approval for further treatment. The trial court found that "Storar's best interest will be served by terminating the transfusions and that this would be. . .Storar's preference were he able to make a decision and articulate it," and ordered the transfusions stopped. The New York Court of Appeals reversed the decision and ordered Storar to be treated. It found that the transfusions, which did not appear to involve excessive pain, would not cure the cancer, but would prevent a more immediate death from loss of blood. Any pain Storar would have to endure was thus justified by the continued life it made possible.

The court concluded its analysis:

> Although we understand and respect his mother's despair, . . . a court should not . . . allow an incompetent patient to bleed to death because someone, even someone as close as a parent or sibling, feels that this is best for one with an incurable disease.

Question: May treatment be withheld from an incompetent patient who is not terminally ill?

Answer: It depends. Under the principles of *Quinlan* and *Saikewicz*, incompetent persons cannot be denied medical care solely because they are mentally incompetent and experience a life that some people think lacks meaning. Treatment can be withheld from incompetent patients only when treatment will not be beneficial. Since incompetent patients generally are assumed to benefit from continued life

without pain, it often will be in their interest to be treated and to go on living. As long as they retain consciousness they are legally entitled to the same care that incompetent patients in those circumstances would receive.

However, there are several situations in which the courts have found, or could find, that further treatment is not in the patient's interest, even if the patient were not terminally ill and could live indefinitely if the treatment were provided. One such situation, typified by the *Quinlan* case, is where the nonterminally ill incompetent patient is comatose, or so severely damaged that awareness of others is not possible. The courts are likely to rule that existence in such a diminished state serves no interests of the patient, and therefore under the judgment and best interests tests could be omitted. Whatever the validity of this reasoning, courts faced with such situations are likely to follow *Quinlan* and *Eichner* and rule that further treatment is no longer in the vegetative patient's interest and can be omitted.

Where the non-terminal incompetent patient is conscious and likely to remain so, there will be far fewer situations in which non-treatment and an early death would appear to be in his interests. The strongest case for non-treatment would be if the patient's condition entailed such suffering that death were preferable, or if the life-prolonging treatment were itself painful and the life it made possible was of such poor quality that it could be reasonably said that the incompetent person, if able to choose, would forego additional life rather than undergo such treatment. A typical case presenting this issue is the question of when renal dialysis may be stopped on a retarded or senile person. Although dialysis requires two or three six hour treatment sessions a week, it is a treatment which many people tolerate for years. Given its capacity to prolong a person's life for months or years, in many cases it will be in the incompetent person's interest to receive it.

Incompetent Patients

Finally, incompetent patients facing amputation of gangrenous limbs may not be terminally ill, but may be reasonably found in some cases to have, from their own perspective, no further interest in life. Competent patients are generally free to reject amputation when in their judgment the resulting life is not a sufficient good to outweigh the burden of the operation and the resulting impairment. The courts have generally assumed that if the patient is incompetent, the amputation should be ordered, on the assumption that continued life is in the patient's interest. But if the substituted judgment or best interest test is properly applied, amputation should not necessarily be ordered. Amputation may not necessarily serve the patient's interest, because it will merely prolong living in a situation of pain, discomfort, and impairment that may outweigh, from the patient's perspective, any corresponding benefit from living. Or, amputation might be inconsistent with past expressions of how he wanted to be treated when incompetent, and there is no reason to think that he has changed that preference in a finding of incompetency. In the *Quackenbush* case, for example, a finding of incompetency should not necessarily have led to an order for the amputation, because a nonambulatory life in a nursing home for Quackenbush could conceivably have caused him more harm than benefit.

In other situations, amputation could be found to serve the incompetent patient's interests and be chosen by him under the substituted judgment test if he were able to choose. As in all decisions concerning incompetent patients, however, courts must look at a situation from the patient's perspective. The inevitability of death, and the degree of patient awareness are important factors, but they do not automatically determine when treatment no longer serves the patient's interests.

Question: May treatment be stopped on a critically ill person who is senile?

Answer: It depends. Many people think that at a certain stage of senility, life is no longer meaningful for the person or worthy of respect, and that necessary medical treatments can be stopped. Indeed, studies have reported that it is common practice in some hospitals and nursing homes to withhold antibiotics and other necessary treatments from elderly patients.

The legality of such practices, however, can be questioned under the principles outlined in this chapter. The key question is whether treatment is, from the patient's perspective, in her interest because of the prolonged life it makes possible and hence likely to be chosen if she were competent to choose. Senility, even chronic senility, does not necessarily mean that that person will not benefit from a prolonged life, and therefore that all medical treatment can be stopped. An elderly nursing home patient may have an interest in being treated with antibiotics for pneumonia, even though it will only allow her to exist some months longer in a state of senility. On the other hand, it may not be in her interest to have her life prolonged if the medical treatments essential to do so are extremely burdensome and painful.

Substituted Judgment

The most recent guidance from the courts on how the substituted judgment test applies to senile patients, occurred in the *Spring* case. Earle Spring, a seventy-eight-year-old man who had been an active outdoorsman, was chronically senile and living in a nursing home. He suffered from total kidney failure and had to be taken thrice weekly to a dialysis center for a six-to-eight hour session to purify his blood.

Sometimes he became obstreperous and kicked the attendants and often had to be sedated or strapped down. His son petitioned to be appointed guardian to authorize that the dialysis be stopped. Without dialysis Mr. Spring would soon die; with it, he might have survived for as long as five years. The courts upheld the termination of dialysis on the ground that in the view of Spring's wife and son, he would, if competent, have made the same decision.

This result is difficult to justify in terms of Spring's best interest, since the benefit to him of additional life would seem to outweigh the burdens of dialysis. The case shows the errors that can arise when decisions about incompetent patients are made indirectly through the substituted judgment test, rather than approached directly by focussing on the patient's best interests.

Question: May doctors withhold nourishment and antibiotics from incompetent patients denied other forms of treatment?

Answer: It depends. Medical treatment, such as respirators, surgery, chemotherapy, and dialysis, may legally be stopped or withheld from incompetent patients on the ground that it is not in their interest. (Under the substituted judgment test, the patient, if he is competent to choose, would reject the treatment.) Withholding such treatments, however, may not always lead to the patient's death. Some patients will survive for long periods after seemingly essential treatments such as respirators are stopped, as occurred in the *Quinlan* case. An important question is whether other, less invasive forms of medical care, such as intravenous or nasogastric feeding and antibiotics, may also be stopped.

"The courts are likely to respect the judgments of physicians and families who stop treatment on the basis of good faith assessments of what an incompetent patient would choose."

The courts have not yet ruled on this question, though murder charges have been brought against two Los Angeles physicians who ordered that all feeding and fluids be stopped on an irreversibly comatose patient who continued to live after his respirator was withdrawn. The answer will depend on how they apply the substituted judgment or best interests tests and assess the interests of patients in those situations. Under these tests it would probably be legal to stop feeding and antibiotic treatment if the prolonged life that treatment made possible was not in the patient's interest, as might occur if the patient were chronically vegetative or imminently dying. If further life, no matter how easily obtained, is not good for the patient, then any means that prolongs life, including nutrition and antibiotics, could be withheld.

Nontreatment Decisions

On the other hand, if the basis for stopping treatment is its intrusive, painful, or burdensome nature, and not the mere fact of life extension, then medical treatments that do not impose those burdens, but could extend life, could not legally be withheld. Thus, nutrition and antibiotics, which ordinarily do not involve such burdens as to make the additional life they provide undesirable, would be legally required.

"The law does not permit active euthanasia even when the patient is competent and consents."

Unfortunately, the courts have not always made clear the precise basis of their nontreatment decisions—whether it was the harm from life extension itself, or the harm from the medical means utilized. In *Quinlan,* for example, it was not clear whether the respirator could be stopped because the chronic vegetative state that it made possible was itself a harm, or whether the burden and discomfort of total dependence on a respirator made any additional life worthless. However, the court did seem to emphasize the severe impairment of the comatose condition more than the burdens of the respiratory care. If this reading of the case is correct, then nasogastric and intravenous feeding could also be legally stopped, for they allow the state of severe impairment to continue.

In other cases, however, such as *Saikewicz* and *Spring,* the decision appeared to be based on the burdens that the treatments in question entailed, and not merely the fact of continued existence. Since providing food and antibiotics usually do not entail such heavy burdens, it is unlikely that the courts would allow those forms of life-support to be withheld from Earle Spring or Joseph Saikewicz.

Question: Do family members have a right to stop treatment on an incompetent person?

Answer: No. Only a competent patient or a court-appointed guardian have a legal right to stop treatment. The doctor's duty to give or withhold care depends upon the right of the incompetent person. If the treatment will be beneficial, the patient has a right to be treated. If the treatment will not serve the patient's interests, the doctor's obligation to treat ends. Ordinarily the doctor's assessment of these issues must be approved by the incompetent patient's

guardian or legal representative. The family has no independent rights of their own in the treatment decision.

Often, however, doctors regard the family as if it had the legal authority to decide on the treatment of the incompetent patient. Doctors may ask the spouse or next of kin to consent to decisions to give or stop treatments. If the family refuses, the doctor is not obligated to follow their wishes, and should determine what best serves the patient's interests, for the family has no right to harm an incompetent person. In one such case, a seventy-nine-year-old former banker, incompetent from senility, needed simple surgery to replace the battery in his pace-maker. His wife refused permission because "he knows nothing," has no memory, and he "is turning into a vegetable." The trial judge correctly applied the applicable principles and appointed a guardian to authorize whatever treatment was "necessary to protect his health and life," since further life in his condition was apparently in his interests, and the spouse had no right to prevent it.

Blood Transfusions

In another case, a blood transfusion was given over the objection of the husband of a Jehovah Witness because it could independently be determined that treatment was in the patient's interests. There was evidence that the patient herself would not consent to a transfusion, but did not believe she would be damned if this was done. Since the treatment would provide a healthy normal life, it could be reasonably inferred that it would be in her interest. Similarly, in the *Storar* case, a mother's determination that her adult retarded son would not, if competent, choose to have blood transfusions replace blood lost due to bladder cancer, was overridden on the ground that the patient's interest would be best served by treatment.

Question: Must the doctor get the consent of the family before treating or withholding care from an incompetent patient?

Answer: No. As the previous answer shows, such consent is not legally required, unless a relative has been appointed guardian of the patient and has the authority to decide on treatment. Where there is a guardian doctors should never act without getting the guardian's consent. In such cases, it is wise to inform the family of the situation as well, so that they may consult with the guardian or even challenge his decision if they think it does not serve the patient's interests.

Often, however, patients incapable of consenting will not be officially declared incompetent and have a guardian appointed. As a practical matter in those cases, rather than go through the formalities of having the patient be declared incompetent and appointing a family member as guardian, doctors will get the family's consent to stop treatment. The family's decision, however, is not legally binding on the doctor. If they refuse to give their consent, treatment can still be legally stopped if it is no longer in the interests of the patient. Similarly, treatment can still be legally provided over the family's objection if it will benefit the patient. However, when the family disagrees with the doctor's view of the patient's interests, the doctor should ask that a guardian be appointed and that a court approve any disputed medical decision. Although judicial approval is not legally required, it will minimize the possibility of suits and is generally advisable.

It is also important to recognize that family agreement with the doctor's decision does not automatically protect the doctor against legal liability (though it greatly reduces the chances of a suit). If the doctor's decision is challenged legally, as might occur in a criminal prosecution for unlawful termination of care or a civil suit on behalf of the deceased brought by a friend or a member of the family who disagreed with the course chosen, the legal effect of relying on the next of kin is unclear. The question will be whether the interests of the incompetent patient were reasonably protected. If they were not, then the consent of the family will not protect the doctor. However, if the interest of the incompetent are unclear, and the doctor has consulted the next of kin to try to ascertain what is best, the courts may well find that the doctor has pursued a reasonable course of action and will not be held liable.

Question: What if the family members disagree among themselves about the proper treatment of an incompetent patient?

Answer: If the incompetent patient has a guardian, family disagreement with the guardian's decision will have no legal effect. However, they could try to influence the guardian or even challenge his actions legally, claiming that they are not in the best interests of the patient.

If, as is more likely, no guardian has been appointed, the family has no legal right to make any decisions about the patient's treatment. Family disagreement over treatment should not stop the physician from making decisions that serve the interests of the patient. Practically speaking, however, in cases of disagreement, doctors should ask the courts to appoint a guardian and determine the patient's rights. A court faced with such a situation should focus on the interests of the incompetent patient and appoint a guardian most likely to protect them.

Amputation Recommended

One such situation arose in the *Nemser* case. Sally Nemser was an eighty-year-old widow living in a nursing home who suffered from heart disease, a stroke, and pneumonia. When her foot became gangrenous, her doctor recommended amputation to save her life. The woman did not want the operation, but, in her doctor's view, she did not understand the nature of the surgery and therefore was not competent to refuse. Her three sons disagreed over treatment. One, a doctor, objected to the surgery on medical grounds. The other two were in favor of it, and petitioned the courts to appoint them guardians to consent to the operation. The court found that Mrs. Nemser was incompetent, but refused to appoint a guardian to consent to the surgery, finding that because of the medical risks and low chances of success, amputation was not in her interests.

"The court, in effect, ruled that doctors and families could stop treatment on chronically vegetative patients."

In another case, a nephew disagreed with the decision of a husband and son to go along with the refusal of a blood transfusion by a questionably competent Jehovah's Witness. The patient had lost considerable blood from microcytic anemia and needed transfusions to stay alive. The court resolved the question by focusing on the interest of the woman. Finding that she was terminally ill and unlikely to live long even with the transfusion, the court refused to order the transfusion.

Question: Must doctors and family go to court to stop treatment on incompetent patients?

Answer: No. Court approval is legally optional. Doctors, hospitals and families sometimes ask courts to decide whether they may stop treatment on incompetent patients. They do so to have a guardian appointed, to settle disputes among the family or between the doctor and family about the proper course of action, or to protect the doctors and hospital from legal liability. Since resort to the courts can have substantial costs for all parties, it should occur only when other alternatives for resolving the situation have failed.

In some instances, as a result of misunderstanding or uncertainty in the law, lawyers have advised going to court without sufficient reason to justify the resulting stress to patients and families. Some lawyers, for example, have interpreted the *Saikewicz* case as requiring doctors to obtain judicial approval to stop treatment. Yet no court has made judicial approval for terminating treatment mandatory, although some courts, such as those in Massachusetts, have said that only a court can give a doctor legal immunity for his actions. (Massachusetts does require prior judicial approval for nontreatment decisions for institutionalized persons and wards of the state who have no family members willing to be involved in the decision.)

Indeed, even the courts that have required judicial approval for advance immunity, have made it clear that court action is not always necessary. The legality of stopping treatment depends upon whether the incompetent patient has a right to be treated, and not on whether a court has first approved the decision. This assessment depends, in turn, on whether the treatment will, from the incompetent patient's perspective, serve his interest, and hence satisfy the best interest or substituted judgment tests. If the family and doctors make the correct decision about the patient's interests, their actions do not become illegal just because a court has not approved it in advance.

Advance Judicial Approval

However, advance judicial approval has certain advantages for all parties concerned. The assessment of the patient's best interest if he were competent is often complex, requiring information about, and trade-offs among, several factors. Resort to the courts might protect patients by assuring that their rights were properly understood and that decisions are made on an adequate factual basis. It may also assure doctors that they can give or stop treatment without fear of legal liability, and will eventually clarify the rules for nontreatment decisions. When doctors are uncertain about their obligations, or want to avoid risking legal liability, seeking judicial approval—though not legally required—might be the best course of action. In emergencies a prompt judicial decision, with few of the formalities of typical court proceedings, can usually be arranged, though it can have substantial costs for the patient and family, and should not be done if there are reasonable grounds for the course of action chosen.

"Advance judicial approval has certain advantages for all parties concerned."

An example of an unnecessary use of the courts occurred in a New York case involving a 41-year-old diabetic who had lost his sight and both legs and wanted to stop the dialysis treatment keeping him alive. He was found competent by two psychiatrists, and with the approval of his family and religious advisors signed refusal of consent forms prepared by the hospital. Rather than accede to his request, however, the hospital sought a court order to continue treatment, apparently out of fear of legal liability. After holding a hearing in the patient's room, the judge eventually ruled that the patient had a right to discontinue dialysis. Given the well-established right of a competent patient to refuse care, and in New York, under *Eichner*, to give permission in advance to stop treatment if he becomes incompetent, the hospital seemed to have no reasonable grounds for seeking court approval of the patient's decision. Their refusal to honor the patient's lawful request increased enormously the stress which the patient and family were experiencing. Going to court in such cases may even lead to suits against the hospital, since a disgruntled family could then sue the hospital for intentional infliction of emotional distress, or for battery and false imprisonment on behalf of the patient.

Question: Must hospital ethics or prognosis committees approve decisions to stop treatment of incompetent patients?

Answer: It depends. Hospitals could institute review procedures for terminating care of incompetent patients which doctors, as a condition of employment or staff privileges, are obligated to follow. Doctors who do not comply could be disciplined or have their admitting privileges suspended. In addition, failure to consult a committee that is regularly consulted by other doctors could be viewed as unprofessional conduct and increase the chance of criminal or civil liability.

Legally, however, the courts have not required committee approval, though they have indicated that this could provide doctors with immunity from later suits. In the *Quinlan* case, for example, a doctor who turned off a respirator on a chronically vegetative patient could not be criminally or civilly liable if a hospital ethics or prognosis committee had first confirmed that there was ''no reasonable possibility of Karen's ever emerging from her present comatose condition to a cognitive, sapient state.''

Although not legally required, hospitals and doctors can protect themselves, as well as their patients, by creating such committees. Given the uncertain legal status of many nontreatment decisions, the possibility of error and bias, and the sophisticated judgments required by the substituted judgment test, doctors and hospitals will be in a better position to defend public criticism and legal challenges if they have set up such committees. The committees need not have ultimate decision-making authority. They can be consultative, and resort to them made optional. A doctor who follows their advice will be on firmer legal ground in a later legal challenge than one who has acted on his own.

Question: Can family members and doctors be sued for terminating treatment of incompetent patients?

Answer: Yes. However, liability will depend upon whether the action was legally justified. This would be a violation of the rights of incompetent patients if further treatment is in their interest and would be chosen by them if they were competent.

Legally, persons who withhold necessary medical care that they have a legal duty to provide, or who actively kill another, may be guilty of homicide, as well as be open to civil liability. Doctors have a legal duty to treat their patients as long as treatment will benefit them, and as long as they have not arranged for adequate alternative care. Family members may also have a legal duty to provide treatment or a duty not to interfere with, or prevent a doctor from treating the incompetent patient; otherwise, criminal charges for homicide could be levied against the family, doctors, and nurses. Civil liability for abandonment or wrongful death is also possible, though damages will usually be small and suits on this ground rare.

As a practical matter, however, it is highly unlikely, but not impossible, that criminal charges would be brought against doctors and families who discontinue the treatment of incompetent patients. Passive euthanasia of incompetent patients appears to be widespread in hospitals and nursing homes, much of which may be unlawful because the patient still had an interest in living. However, with a few exceptions, no doctor or family has ever been prosecuted for stopping treatment on critically ill incompetent patients. Civil suits are also rare. However, the rarity of prosecution should not lead doctors and families to ignore its possibility. Suits may be rare because people are not aware of the extent of the practice, and no one is available to represent the deceased patient's interests. In more flagrant cases, suits, or even criminal charges, could be brought. For example, a nurse who disconnected several terminal patients from respirators was prosecuted for manslaughter in Baltimore. She was not convicted because the jury believed her defense that the patient was already brain dead when the disconnection occurred. Had there not been evidence of brain death, she might have been convicted. In another case the Los Angeles District Attorney filed murder charges against two physicians who ordered all feeding stopped on an irreversibly comatose patient who had been taken off a respirator.

Question: Can doctors or families actively kill patients on whom treatment may be stopped?

Answer: No. The law does not permit active euthanasia even when the patient is competent and consents, and even when the patient will otherwise linger in a state of great suffering. When the patient is incompetent and his wishes are unknown, the reasons against active euthanasia are all the stronger, for the possibility of mistake is greater. Even if treatment can be legally stopped because it is not in the patient's interest, and doctors may administer drugs to relieve pain that might, as a wide effect, also depress respiration and hasten death, they may not actively kill a dying or critically ill incompetent patient in order to spare him from further suffering.

It is possible that killing incompetent patients by injecting drugs does occur in some cases, though its incidence is unknown and far lower than that of passive euthanasia of such patients. Doctors, as well as families and friends, might engage in the practice, usually for "humanitarian" reasons. Prosecutions have been rare, usually because it is done secretly, or is approved by those aware of it. When such cases do surface, prosecution usually occurs because many people disapprove of active killing. Prosecution, however, will not always lead to conviction. In the United States, doctors have been prosecuted for homicide on two occasions for allegedly actively killing terminal patients (a few prosecutions have also occurred in Europe). In one case, a doctor allegedly injected air bubbles, and in the other, potassium chloride, in order to kill terminal cancer patients who would soon expire anyway. Although the juries could have legally convicted the doctors if the patients were alive when the injections occurred, in both cases the doctors were acquitted. Similarly, in a 1981 Massachusetts case, a nurse was acquitted of homicide when she claimed that she had administered a lethal dose of morphine to a nonterminally ill cancer patient in good faith, according to a doctor's orders. On the other hand, persons who have drowned or suffocated a chronically ill family member have been convicted.

Question: Is euthanasia of incompetent patients ever legal?

Answer: It depends on how one defines euthanasia, the means used, and the situation of the incompetent patient. The term *euthanasia*, which literally means a good or happy death, usually refers to a decision to bring about a person's death earlier than would otherwise occur in order to benefit the patient. The legality of the practice depends upon whether the person's death is actively or passively caused, whether it is voluntary or involuntary, and whether death serves the patient's interests.

As this chapter has shown, passive euthanasia of incompetent patients by stopping essential medical treatments—a form of involuntary or nonconsensual euthanasia—sometimes is lawful and sometimes is not, depending on whether the benefits of treatment to the patient outweigh the burdens, and thus would be chosen by the patient if competent to choose. Active euthanasia, or directly killing an incompetent patient, is never lawful, even if passive euthanasia of the patient would be.

John A. Robertson is a professor of law in the law school and of medical ethics in the medical school at the University of Wisconsin. He is the editor of Rights of the Critically Ill, *an American Civil Liberties Union handbook.*

"Mercy killing is justified in the case of a terminal patient who is in great pain without hope of relief."

The Case for Euthanasia

Daniel C. Maguire

About two million people die each year in the United States, and the American culture has finally decided to take note of this fact. Death in our day is having its belated due. It is slipping out from under denials and disguises and bursting into explicit, obsessive, and, at times, pornographic recognition. This is a thanatology boom in colleges and in print and there are random reports from the lecture circuits that the subject of death is now outdrawing the perennials—sex and politics.

Though there are many levels and facets to this revolutionary shift in death-consciousness, the overall meaning is probably one of gain and health and not of decadence and morbidity. Only in a mature culture can death be received and accepted as a natural companion of life. The death pre-occupation we are witnessing is probably a clumsy but significant rite of passage. At the very least, it might exonerate Americans from the British historian Arnold Toynbee's charge that, for Americans, death is un-American and an affront to every citizen's inalienable right to life, liberty, and the pursuit of happiness. But, more than that, it affects and may well have epochal meaning for Western culture. Western civilization is Faustian in the sense that it is impatient with limits. It is a *can do* and *will do* civilization. Its paramount accents are on action and power. Small wonder that it has been so slow to come to grips with death, which is, after all, the very ultimate in passivity, impotence, and limit.

Whatever the long-term cultural significance of our current concern with death, however, there are shorter-term questions which are now urgently addressing the moral consciences of mortal men. Basically, they arise from the fact that man is the only animal who knows he is going to die and who

also knows he can bring about his own death. Only man can be troubled, like Hamlet, about the relative advantages of death over continued living. Before the prospect of death, man is, in the most poignant sense of Sartre's phrase, "condemned to freedom." He may allocate his own death or passively await its arrival. He may have death by chance or death by choice. He may also, in a reflective way, allocate death for others when he judges that certain values outweigh the need or right of others to remain alive. Indeed, history shows that men have chosen death for other men with a rather formidable liberality. Men have also chosen to bring their own lives to a voluntary close. But it is no gentle irony that humans have traditionally been much quicker to justify the killing of others than the killing of self.

Willful Death-Dealing

At any rate the problem of willful death-dealing has taken on new urgency because of revolutionary developments in medical science, the laggardly state of the law, and important shifts in moral outlook.

Science, which once basked in the illusion that it was somehow "value-free," is suddenly up to its neck in value-loaded questions. Medicine becomes more and more involved with problems of ethics as it is repeatedly forced to ask itself if it *may* do what it suddenly and often surprisingly *can* do.

And, speaking of the surprising, medicine, which has been making all these quantum leaps in our century, suddenly finds itself bereft of an agreed-upon definition of death, which, by any standard, is a very fundamental problem. "When you are dead, you are dead" is no longer a truism, since death is now seen not as a "moment" but as a process and indeed as a very manipulable process. The current terms "brain death" and "heart death" suggest an unsettling distinction, especially since you can have one without the other. Furthermore, in days of primitive medicine, death was often the solution for many of "nature's mistakes" and tragedies. Now medical technology can forestall the solution that death once would have brought in those cases where death would have been thought a blessing. As Sir Theodore Fox told the Royal College of Physicians in 1965, "Though cures are getting commoner, so too are half-cures, in which death is averted but disability remains." The inability to define death, and the ability to create situations where death would appear to be preferable, are parts of the perplexing yield of scientific medical progress.

Prehistoric Man

For most of his history, man has been a rather short-lived creature, especially when compared with some of the other warm-blooded creatures. Scholars can only estimate the average length of life for our prehistoric ancestors by studying fragmentary data and by observation of contemporary groups whose conditions probably approximate those of prehistory. According to these estimates, prehistoric man lived on the average about eighteen years. In those medically and socially brutish days survival beyond forty was a rare achievement. Longevity mounted, however, but slowly. Professor Monroe Lerner of Johns Hopkins writes:

> With the rise of the early civilizations and the consequent improvements in living conditions, longevity must surely have risen, reaching perhaps 20 years in ancient Greece and perhaps 22 in ancient Rome. Life expectancy is estimated to have been about 33 years in England during the Middle Ages, about 35 in the Massachusetts Bay Colony of North America, about 41 in England and Wales during the nineteenth century, and 47.3 in the death registration states of the United States in 1900....

The quest for immortality marches on. An important ethical question, however, is asked by physician J. Russell Elkinton: "When Adam and Eve ate of the fruit of the Tree of Knowledge, they lost their immortality. Do we really want it back?" What would be the quality and meaning that people would find in protracted life? Law professor Bayless Manning writes about the day when people can be kept alive for 150 to 200 years:

> Somewhere along the way, consciously or unconsciously, explicitly or implicity, society will have to make some basic decisions about the allocation of economic resources as between human beings of advanced years and those who are younger....We have not begun to consider the violent social dislocation that would be brought about if a large fraction of the population were to be kept alive for significantly longer periods of time.

Defective Children

Is it not possible that people will sense that there is truly a time for living and a time for dying and that future man will have the decision of death taken off his organism and put onto his will? Are not the pressures for shaping a moral position on death by choice mounting with every medical advance? Could

we not also expect that as infant mortality goes down and disease is further vanquished and population pressures on the earth's resources increase, there will be special challenges to the right to life of defective children? Note the words of Millard S. Everett in his book *Ideals of Life:*

> My personal feeling—and I don't ask anyone to agree with me—is that eventually, when public opinion is prepared for it, no child shall be admitted into the society of the living who would be certain to suffer any social handicap—for example, any physical or mental defect that would prevent marriage or would make others tolerate his company only from a sense of mercy....Life in early infancy is very close to nonexistence, and admitting a child into our society is almost like admitting one from potential to actual existence, and viewed in this way only normal life should be accepted.

The British jurist, Glanville Williams, also discusses the program of "involuntary euthanasia" for defective infants. Noting that the Euthanasia Society of America included this idea in its original program, he observes that "the legalization of euthanasia for handicapped children would bring the law into closer relation to its practical administration, because juries do not regard parental mercy-killing as murder." He also notes: "The proposal certainly escapes the chief objection to the similar proposal for senile dementia: it does not create a sense of insecurity in society, because infants cannot, like adults, feel anticipatory dread of being done to death if their condition should worsen." Thus, what to some is unthinkable has been thought and written. Medical power with every victory over disease creates conditions that stir up moral questions about death by choice.

"If it was thought that the child's death would indeed have been a mercy, could it not have been accelerated by increasingly large doses of morphine?"

Medicine cannot distinguish between good death and bad death. As medicine has developed, it is geared to promoting life under all circumstances. Death is the natural enemy of the healing science.

Death as a Friend

Death, however, can at times be a friend. It can at times be a welcome deliverance from a situation that has ceased to be bearable. Pneumonia has been referred to as "an old man's friend," since it often served, in days of simpler science, to shorten the old man's final agony. Actually, it was death that was the friend; pneumonia merely gave access to it. Now, of course, pneumonia usually can be contained and the old man lingers on in agony.

Dr. Eliot Slater, editor-in-chief of the *British Journal*

of Psychiatry, puts it in blunt language: "Death performs for us the inestimable office of clearing up a mess too big to mend; if we are going to intervene, then we must have at least some hope of doing this ourselves." What Dr. Slater is unambiguously saying is: if diseases such as pneumonia can be friends, why can we not be? Is it not within man's inherent moral freedom to recognize instances when death would be a blessing and to bring it about in ways that would be even more merciful than a bout of pneumonia? (Pneumonia is, by no reckoning, a pleasant friend.)

"It is possible that death might be seen as preferable to the kind of life this child could have."

Look at another example of the inverse side of medical progress. Sometimes patients with a terminal illness will be unable to take nourishment by mouth. In these cases they are now fed intravenously. Sometimes the intravenous feeding is not a friend. Consider this case:

> A cancer patient is in extreme pain and his system has gradually established what physicians call "toleration" of any drug, so that even increased doses give only brief respites from the ever-recurring pain. The attending physician knows that the disease is incurable and that the person is slowly dying, but because of a good heart, it is possible that this agony will continue for several weeks. The physician then remembers that there is one thing he can do to end the suffering. He can cut off intravenous feeding and the patient will surely die. He does this and before the next day the patient is dead.

Many of the older theologians approved of discontinuing the intravenous feeding in this kind of case.

Discontinuing Oxygen

Or what of the obligation to maintain the use of an oxygen tent? Ethicists have long since granted that it is moral to discontinue the use of oxygen in certain circumstances where death will inevitably follow. Thus Charles McFadden, a conservative moralist, writes: "If one were to think of recourse to oxygen as a *permanent* means of surviving I feel certain it should be classified as an *extraordinary* measure, which would not be morally binding."

There are other cases where nature taking its own course would seem to be the best doctor. Consider the case of a diabetic patient who has been using insulin for years and who develops an inoperable and very painful kind of cancer. By continuing with the insulin, the patient may live many months in agony. By discontinuing the insulin the patient would lapse into coma and die painlessly. Here is a case where diabetes would appear to be a friend.

Interestingly, this case was considered by Catholic moralists some years ago—in a very conservative period of Catholic moral theology—and reasons were found that might justify this action. There was a stern view that the patient would have to continue using the insulin since it was a normal medicament. Gerald Kelly, however, was not so sure. He noted that ordinary means to preserve life must be taken when there is a "reasonable hope of success." Regarding the rigorous opinion, Kelly said: "I no longer consider this solution as certain because I am not sure we are justified in stating that the patient must prescind from the cancer in determining her obligation of using the insulin."

Moral Men

And what of the patient suffering from a similar cancer who does not have the "blessing" of diabetes? Must moral man await the good pleasure of biochemical and organic factors and allow these to determine the time and manner of his demise? Putting it in religious language, can the will of God regarding a person's death be manifested only through disease or the collapse of sick or wounded organs, or could it also be discovered through the sensitive appreciations and reasonings of moral men?

There is, of course, a big difference between not using insulin or not treating pneumonia, and overdosing a patient to accelerate the death process. The failure to use ordinary means (antibiotics, insulin, oxygen) when they are available and necessary for life, and when death results from their deliberate nonuse, gives new vigor to the old question of whether the prohibition against all direct action to terminate life is hermetically closed. Though omission and commission are different realities with a potential for radically different moral meanings, they have a suggestive similarity in that in both cases, someone is dead who would have been alive if a different decision (to act or not act) had been made.

Some of the most difficult cases in point which medical progress has thrown at us involve children. Moralist Paul Ramsey of Princeton University presents one of the questions that medicine is putting to morals: "Should cardiac surgery be performed to remove the lesions that are part of the picture in cases of mongolism, from which many mercifully died before the brilliant developments of recent years?" Obviously, this is a very real question for many persons. At Johns Hopkins University Hospital, the parents of a mongoloid baby requiring surgery for survival refused to give permission. This case is not, by any means, unique but it received national attention in the fall of 1971. It took the baby fifteen days to succumb, during which time the hospital staff had to watch the infant struggle unsuccessfully for life. Many moral and legal questions were raised by this one incident. Should the parents have been made to take the child home and bear the pain of standing the death watch that their decision inaugurated?

Should the state have taken legal charge of the baby away from the parents and then authorized the operation, or should a court order have overruled the parents' decision? If it was thought that the child's death would indeed have been a mercy, could it not have been accelerated by increasingly large doses of morphine? In other words, should a certain amount of commission be added to the fundamental omission of the operation?

15 Days of Torture

Though the death of this child *may* have been a mercy, the dying was not. In fact, is this not a case where the omission might have been immoral without the act of overdosing to shorten the final fifteen days of torture? In other words, maybe omission was harder to justify in this case than commission. Or is the entire question of opting for this baby's death morally repugnant? Professor Arthur J. Dyck of Harvard Divinity School would seem to think so, since he refers to this very incident to show that those who reject out of hand any comparison of what happened in Nazi Germany with what we could expect here had better take heed. Dyck sees the Johns Hopkins case as "murder."

Dr. Warren Reich, a senior research associate at the Kennedy Center for Bioethics at Georgetown University, posed a hypothetical case at the meeting of the International Congress of Learned Societies in the Field of Religion in September, 1972. The case involved a girl, Missy, who was born with spina bifida with meningomyelocele of the lumbar spine. Spina bifida refers to an opening in the spine and meningomyelocele is a condition in which portions of the spinal cord, as well as meninges and spinal fluid, have slipped out through the spinal opening and are enclosed in a sac. The child lacked reflex activity in both legs and could not control her anal or urinary sphincters. She had club feet.

Hydrocephalus, "water on the brain," develops in 90 percent of these cases. To treat that, a "shunt" has to be surgically inserted to drain the cerebrospinal fluid from the brain into the heart or peritoneum. Even with a shunt, the child would have a fifty-fifty chance of being mentally retarded. Missy's complications might eventually require surgical procedure which would allow her urine to drain into a bag which she would wear on her abdomen permanently. Bowel control would be a lifelong problem for her. Kidney failure is a constant danger and the most common cause of death for children with this affliction. Broken bones and burns are the frequent lot of such children also, due to problems in mobility and sensation.

Lifetime of Extraordinary Care

In the panel discussion of this case, Dr. Harmon Smith of Duke University Divinity School noted that until ten years ago, about 80 percent of such babies

died and that today 75 percent survive. Thus, again, medical advance brings on troubling new moral questions. Should this baby have been allowed to die from the meningitis that would normally ensue in such cases? Or should the doctors have begun at once what would be for the child a lifetime of extraordinary care? The panel (which, along with Reich and Smith, included Dr. Eric Cassell of Cornell Medical School) considered only these two options.

In the discussion, it was suggested to the panel that there were other options, such as the direct termination of life. This was an option that no member of the panel would even consider. "I find it is absolutely incredible, even in a mere debate, to consider this a serious alternative in a group of moralists and theologians," said Professor Smith. The other panelists agreed that this line should never be crossed. But why is it so clear that these two alternatives exhaust the moral possibilities of the described case and that the path of direct termination is beyond the pale?

First of all, it is not clear that meningitis would be an efficient "friend." As Dr. Reich pointed out, babies have been known to survive the meningitis and live a number of years without being aware of anything and requiring a great amount of physical care. Thus the problem could be intensified by mere omission and reliance on the disease to achieve the desired results. Furthermore, as one of the doctors in the audience pointed out in this discussion, death by meningitis in such cases is not normally serene. Disease in this instance may not come to the aid of ethics.

"If diseases such as pneumonia can be friends, why can we not be?"

There can be good reasons offered to keep a child like this alive. Advances are being made in the treatment of nearly all the symptoms of this affliction. It may even be argued that if people do not take a chance on life for such children, medicine will not be able to learn all that it needs to conquer and prevent this disorder. It may be further argued that we should be extremely cautious about opting for death for a child. Caution is further indicated by the basic fact that a decision is being made for another person.

Death May Be Preferable

Given the realities of the case as described, however, it is possible that death might be seen as preferable to the kind of life this child could have. The moral question then is whether the death should be entrusted to the imminent disease or whether it could be brought on by the administration of drugs or whether a compromise could be found whereby the drugs are used to comfort and to weaken in coordination with the meningitis. In the current state of legal and moral debate, the latter possibility would offer the advantage of protective ambiguity. There is no precise way of knowing whether a drug is accelerating death as it relieves discomfort, since the unrelieved discomfort might accelerate death too and since the degree of immunity to the drug is a variable. Still, this flight to ambiguity would represent a retreat from the question: can it be moral and should it be legal to take direct action to terminate life in certain circumstances?

"Pneumonia has been referred to as 'an old man's friend,' since it often served. . .to shorten the old man's final agony."

Another of the terrible new powers of medicine is its ability to prolong life at a vegetative level. Take the case of a patient whose spontaneous brain activities are limited to those arising from the brain stem which controls breathing and circulation. Such a creature can be kept alive with stimulants and nourishment for a long period of time. Does it make good sense to do so?

Infinite Time on Respirator

In fact, patients with hopelessly damaged brains can be kept alive for indefinite periods through the use of respirators which keep the heart and lungs pumping. In these cases, the brain may by any definition be dead. Cases have been known where autopsy later revealed that the brain had even liquefied. A California doctor reports the case of a patient with irreversible brain damage who was maintained for eight years. Tubes for feeding and release of wastes kept the body going in a state of no mental response. "You could have taken a lighted match and held it against his eye and he still wouldn't have known you were there," the doctor said. The cost of the patient's care over those eight years came to $300,000. If the tubes had been taken away, he would have died completely within seventy-two hours.

Moral questions arise out of such bizarre cases: is merely physical, vegetative life sacred, or is it life that is actually or potentially personal that is sacred? What could justify prolonging life like this unless the body was being sustained in anticipation of organ transplantation? Should we try to cure a severely brain-damaged child or adult who contracts pneumonia or appendicitis? Does a man have a right to give a paired organ such as a kidney for transplant if there is a possibility that he may need that organ

someday and die if the remaining kidney should fail? May a dying person offer one of his healthy organs even though this will weaken him and speed up his death?

The British attorney Mary Barrington writes: "Death taken in one's own time, and with a sense of purpose, may in fact be far more bearable than the process of waiting to be arbitrarily extinguished. A patient near the end of his life who arranged his death so as, for example, to permit an immediate transfer of a vital organ to a younger person, might well feel that he was converting his death into a creative act."

The determination of death twenty-five years ago was not a very difficult job. If the patient's heart stopped beating and he stopped breathing, he was pronounced dead. Sometimes death was verified by electrocardiogram. Sometimes too there was an injection of a drug like epinephrine (adrenaline) to produce a few more heartbeats. But death was a rather definitive and definable moment.

Old Criteria Too Simple

Today, the old criteria have been robbed of their simplicity. Prompt cardiac resuscitation can restore a normal heartbeat in many cases, and mechanical assistance can keep a heart going that has lost all spontaneous capacity to pump. In some cases, as we mentioned, the brain could be quite dead and yet respirators could keep cardiovascular and respiratory functions going.

In some cases where the cerebral cortex has been destroyed, the brain stem continues for a time to regulate heart and lung functioning. The question that arises is: can a "man" with a beating heart (maintained by lingering brain stem control) be declared dead if the cerebral cortex is clearly dead? Should we, in a word, move to brain death as opposed to heart death as the real death? The unique importance of the brain would seem to support this view.

Agreement on Brain Death

An agreement on brain death might present itself as the obvious solution, but here, as anywhere, facile solutions are suspect. There is the practical problem of how to determine that a person is dead of brain and therefore dead. The most promising means for discovering brain life or its absence could appear to be the use of the electroencephalogram (EEG). A flat EEG might seem to be a clear-cut criterion for brain death. It is not. Persons with flat EEG's for several hours have been known to recover. Furthermore, persons with flat EEG's have been observed to continue breathing for up to six hours. Lower body temperatures and other factors can also affect the readings of the EEG. There are, however, other ways of supporting the judgment that death has overtaken the brain which medical science is exploring.

Dr. Julius Korein, professor of neurology at the New York University School of Medicine, distinguishes between brain death (death of the entire brain including brain stem) and cerebral death. He concludes that when cerebral death has been determined, the physician should pronounce the patient cerebrally dead and suggest the discontinuation of cardiovascular and pulmonary support systems. In other words, cerebral death is death. It is his opinion that "advances in medicine have accelerated development of techniques that will allow the physician to define and diagnose cerebral death with accuracy and rapidity in an appropriate hospital setting." If this is true, the concept of cerebral death may be the best that can be done by way of bringing up-to-date the detection of death.

Perhaps a case could best illustrate the need for the nature of a new definition of death. It concerns a twenty-year-old man who suffered a complete shattering of his cerebral cortex in an automobile accident four years previously.

> Since then only the brain stem has sustained life. All thought and feeling have been erased, and he has not moved a single muscle of his body since the accident. But he is in "excellent health," although he feels no stimulus of any kind, from within or without. Once an angular blond youth of sixteen, he is now a baby-faced "brunette" seemingly ten years old. He is fed through an in-dwelling nasal tube.

Whether To Bury a Breathing Corpse

It would seem obvious that such a situation requires a declaration of death. Death, in other words, should be declared even before the breathing stops, and even if a respirator is going to keep the body oxygenated for purposes of organ donation. The problem of whether or not we would bury a breathing corpse, or whether or not a funeral parlor would receive one, is not a practical difficulty. Even if the brain stem has some life in it, the withdrawal of all support will quickly silence the lingering signs of life.

"In general, in our law, there is no obligation to be a Good Samaritan."

But what of the organs of the cerebrally dead? If we pull the plugs and allow the patient to die fully—heart, lungs, and even brain stem—we might also have waited so long that asphyxia will have damaged all organs for potential transplant. Dr. Henry Beecher asks about the situation in which a decision has been made to turn off the respirator while the heart is, with this mechanical aid, still beating. His question is: "What difference does it make whether the heart is stopped by inexorable asphyxia or by removal?" The question can also be asked about a case in which

the heart is still beating by reason of brain stem functioning although cortical activity is entirely extinguished. Could this patient be declared dead so as to make it possible to keep him (it) breathing for purposes of transfer of tissue? Beecher is worried about the waste of needed organs as a consequence of timid and *passe* definitions of death. By his calculations, over 10,600 kidneys for approximately 7600 needy kidney recipients and 6000 livers for 4000 potential liver recipients could be made available in the United States each year. He believes that what is radical is not redefining death so as to save these tissues, but rather the waste of them.

But to tie the definition of death to the organ needs of others might build a conflict of interest in the medical profession which is not in the best interests of the departing patient. The specter of organ piracy might come to dwell over the deathbed. But if it can be seen that the cortically brain dead patient is departed, not departing, it should be possible to devise sufficient safeguards to ensure that organ needs do not hasten the declaration of death.

Euthanasia by Omission

In a survey of 250 Chicago internists and surgeons, 156 responded to a questionnaire asking: "In your opinion do physicians actually practice euthanasia in instances of incurable adult sufferers?" Sixty-one percent affirmed that physicians actually practice it, at least by omission, or what is sometimes called passive euthanasia. What is most revealing, however, is that 72 percent said the practice should not be legalized. Thus, although it occurs, they think, in the practice of a majority of their colleagues, it should not be permitted.

Professor Diane Crane of Johns Hopkins University asserts that "some doctors resort to 'invisible acts' in which patients' lives are deliberately shortened by manipulating dosages of pain-killing drugs." Most doctors who do this are at great pains to maintain the invisibility of their actions. There are some instances of high visibility, however: Dr. Walter W. Sackett, a Miami general practitioner, admits publicly that he has allowed patients to die "hundreds of times" during his thirty years of medical practice. What is more, the outspoken Dr. Sackett estimates that 75 percent of all doctors have made similar allowances on one or more occasions. For this reason, Sackett, who is also a member of Florida's state legislature, has been trying to push a "death with dignity" bill through the legislature. He has had no success so far. He claims that he finds major support for his bill among the elderly. "They fear the prolongation of dying," he says, "more than death itself."

Passive Euthanasia

Perhaps Sackett is drawing the long bow in estimating the incidence of at least passive euthanasia; the statistics of bill-pushers are always worth a second check. But then again there might be no exaggeration in his figures. Louis Lasagna, M.D., argues that decisions on lengthening or shortening life are unavoidable for doctors. "There is no place for the physician to hide," he says. He will constantly run into situations where he will have to choose between a treatment that provides less physical and mental stress but shortens life, and one that will surely prolong life, but at the cost of much suffering. Lasagna mentions a survey that shows that about a third of all doctors feel that mercy killing is justified in the case of a terminal patient who is in great pain without hope of relief or recovery. (He notes that the figure is close to 40 percent for Protestants and Jews and 7 percent for Roman Catholics.) He adds that many physicians covertly practice euthanasia in the case of children born with gross congenital abnormalities by not resuscitating the child at birth.

> *"Some doctors resort to 'invisible acts' in which patients' lives are deliberately shortened by manipulating dosages of pain-killing drugs."*

Dr. Lasagna comes out in favor of "euthanasia," suggesting the possibility of committees made up of medical and nonmedical members, including "perhaps" representatives of the patient's family. He concedes that the taking of life is an awesome business but that safeguards are conceivable which could prevent abuse of procedure.

Back in 1957, Pope Pius XII, no radical in the field of ethics, addressed the question of whether a respirator can be turned off if the patient is in a final and hopeless state of unconsciousness. The Pope reasoned that the respirator in these circumstances is not morally obligatory, and therefore it can be turned off. He recognized that this action causes "the arrest of circulation," but he said it is nonetheless licit.

The Law Is Murky

Many American physicians feel that this position is reasonable and permissible under American law. Many more are not so sure, and one can sympathize with their uncertainty. Lawyer William Cannon considers the matter of "pulling the plug" under American law and comes up with this conclusion: "If it is concluded to be an omission, the law is murky at best. If, however, it is concluded to be an affirmative act, the law has a ready charge: Murder in the first degree." In other words, "pulling the plug" might be murder, in Cannon's opinion. The area of omission in the law then is, as Cannon allows, "murky," to say the least.

In general, in our law, there is no obligation to be a Good Samaritan. But what of a physician who does not bring aid? For some omissions, physicians are liable in much the same way they would be for unpermitted operations or positive malpractice. If a doctor is out wining and dining and gets a call that a patient has suddenly become critically ill from pneumonia, the doctor must drop everything and go, or see that another doctor goes. If he does not respond to the call he is liable criminally and civilly should death ensue. In this case, omission is punishable. And, since motive does not matter in this criminal law, if the doctor arriving at the bedside failed to give the needed aid because he knew that his old patient would be better off out of his misery and because he knew further that the patient had been longing and praying for death—it is the same as if he had stayed out on the town and not answered the call. Or is it?

Professor Bayless Manning is probably accurate when he says that "decisions are predominantly being made by thousands of doctors in millions of different situations and by undefined, particularized, *ad hoc* criteria." This state of affairs is not something desirable under law for it leaves things to the vagaries of a "rule of man" instead of providing for the fairness and consistency of a "rule of law."

Daniel C. Maguire, a professor of theology, teaches Christian ethics at Marquette University in Milwaukee. He is the author of Death by Choice, The Moral Choice *and* A New American Justice.

"Euthanasia could make the sick elderly a ready target for an unwholesome social policy. . . . Let euthanasia be seen for what it is: a tragic attempt to patch up a morbid society."

viewpoint **24**

The Case Against Euthanasia

Jonathan Gould and Lord Craigmyle

This [article] seeks to examine the general ethical aspects of euthanasia on a basis which we believe will be acceptable to those who do not subscribe to a formal faith, notwithstanding that many of our arguments are drawn from lines of thought traditional in Christian philosophy. . . .

Much of the discussion has been blurred by the vague use of the term 'euthanasia'. There is no ethical merit in prolonging the process of dying, but it is false logic to equate the active termination of life with allowing someone to die peacefully without extraordinary efforts at resuscitation. Much stir was caused some time ago when instructions were issued in a hospital that patients above a certain age should not be resuscitated; these instructions were misguided because they were given as a general ruling, without consideration of individual circumstances, which can be judged only by the doctor attending the patient at the relevant time. . . .

The indefinite prolongation of life when the patient has no prospect of ever again being able to maintain his own life, or no prospect of leading a life rewarding to himself even with artificial aid, is in fact a travesty of sound medicine: it makes a mockery both of life and of the process of dying.

Principle of Double Effect

There is further clear distinction between using means for the relief of suffering which may, as a secondary result, shorten life, and actively ending life. Here the guide is the principle known as the principle of double effect. It is a principle commonly misunderstood, but one which in fact guides doctors whenever the problem of undesirable side effects arises with any treatment. And not only doctors: very many of our acts have more than one foreseeable consequence; if one foreseeable consequence is undesirable we have to weigh up whether or not to do the act we have in mind. There are four criteria:

1) the act itself must be morally good, or at least neutral;

2) the purpose must be to achieve the good consequence, the bad consequence being only a side effect;

3) the good effect must not be achieved by way of the bad, but both must result from the same act;

4) the bad result must not be so serious as to outweigh the advantage of the good result.

In practice these criteria can involve difficulties in judgement, but the ignoring of these criteria does not ease any problems; it merely permits evasion.

The use of medicaments with the intention of relieving pain is good, and if by repeated pain-relief the patient's resistance is lowered and he dies earlier than he would otherwise have done, this is a side effect which may well be acceptable. More often than not life will not be shortened in this way, because the benefit of rest and sleep and an untroubled mind will do the patient more good than heavy sedation will do him harm. On the other hand, to give an overdose *with the intention that the patient should never wake up* is morally wrong. It is killing. The protection of life is not only the concern of the churches, it is deeply entrenched in law. It was one of the accepted arguments against the death penalty that a man might be mistakenly convicted of a crime. Essentially the same consideration must be given to any man who has done no wilful harm, and Kamisar rightly put the question, 'What is the need for euthanasia which leads us to tolerate the mistakes, the very fatal mistakes, that will inevitably occur?'

Duty to Relieve Suffering

This principle of double effect has long been acknowledged as valid by the Catholic Church: although it has only been strictly formulated as a general principle in the last century or so, its origins go back to the time of St. Thomas Aquinas, who stated the principle clearly in connection with self-defence. Thus the authors of the Euthanasia Society's *Plan for Voluntary Euthanasia* are wide of the mark when they write: '*Even the Roman Catholic Church has recently agreed* that where a human life is ending in great suffering it is the doctor's duty to relieve that suffering, even though the means taken may shorten life. It is blurring the all-important clear definition of the term euthanasia when later on the same authors state: 'If that policy shortens the patient's life, even by a few hours, the doctor is, in fact, practising euthanasia, although not strictly *voluntary* euthanasia.' What the doctor is doing is to relieve his patient's suffering. As a secondary effect he may be securing for his patient euthanasia in the literal sense of an easy death, but he is very certainly *not killing* his patient, that is, he is not practising euthanasia in the sense for which legislation is sought. . . .

"To give an overdose with the intention that the patient should never wake up *is morally wrong. It is killing."*

What the various efforts to introduce euthanasia legislation have aimed at has been the legalisation not of the right to die—a palpable absurdity—but of the right to kill. This, even with the patient's consent and at his request (anyway supposedly so) is a very different matter. 'The *direct* ending of a life, with or without the patient's consent, is euthanasia in its simple, unsophisticated and ethically candid form' writes J. Fletcher [in *Euthanasia and the Right to Death* edited by A. B. Downing and Peter Owen]. His further sentence in this connection: 'A decision *not to* keep a patient alive is as morally deliberate as a decision to *end* life' strikes strange. Of course a decision to do a wise or good act is as deliberate as a decision to do a foolish or wicked act, but that does not make the two acts morally equal. The reader of that sentence might be forgiven for inferring that in its author's opinion, because the two decisions are equally deliberate, they are either equally culpable or equally praiseworthy, which clearly they are not. The same remark will strike doubly strange to the reader who pursues his study of that book into the next chapter, for there he will find George P. Fletcher emphasising strongly the distinction between causing harm and permitting harm to occur.

To relieve pain and stress remains the doctor's first task, and he has plenty of means to help him, whether the patient's suffering is physical or mental. The medical conquest of distress is still not complete, but even so the Euthanasia Society has this to say

about hospitals for terminal illnesses: 'Most of these hospitals are staffed by dedicated women belonging to some religious order, many of whom are also trained in nursing. Experience has shown that in the sympathetic and sometimes surprisingly cheerful atmosphere created by these women. . .they (the patients) are able to face death when it comes with a quiet mind—unafraid. Even if euthanasia were permissible to these patients probably very few would wish to avail themselves of it.'

The authors of the pamphlet say that these circumstances are exceptional, because there are few such terminal hospitals, and this fact is used as support for the legalisation of euthanasia. What an indictment against our society, to propose killing people because there is not enough sympathy for them. If the old are a burden on their relations, the solution is to make proper provision for them. . . .

An Ugly Business

In those cases where a patient 'merely exists', it is not he who suffers but those around him. In the words of the Euthanasia Society's spokesman: 'Dying is still often an ugly business', but where should we end up once we admitted the principle that a man may be killed for the benefit of someone else?

Medical judgement is fallible and, with ever-increasing medical skill, conditions may be curable tomorrow that are incurable today. To this argument the Euthanasia Society retorts that 'the remote possibility of making a mistake is not a reason for doing nothing'. The safeguard mentioned in that context is—or at least in the 1962 pamphlet was—'that patients will seldom seriously consider the termination of life before such gross damage has been done to vital organs that recovery is out of the question'; but this point has lost its validity since a declaration in advance was incorporated into the Euthanasia Society's proposals.

Once a patient has signed a declaration [declining treatment to prolong life], possibly even before he has signed it but when he knows the family expects him to do so, pride or a false sense of duty may prevent him, despite his distress, from changing his decision even though he has changed his mind. Such change of mind may be due only to a natural fear of death now the patient actually has to face it, but it may equally well be due to an experience of conversion or recovery of faith. There are certainly many instances known of this, so that clearly the spiritual state of a patient must not be assumed to remain static during a terminal illness. Moreover, where the patient's mind is clouded but still receptive, or his expression is impaired, how could an independent assessing doctor become aware, or be made aware, of a change of mind? The ethical point at issue here is that in the circumstances the doctor has no access to information from the patient on which he can conscientously base a decision which is both professionally and ethically sound.

A patient might be suffering from an incurable disease but still be capable of leading a gratifying life for a long time; who would decide, and by what criteria, when he was to be liquidated? For cases like carcinoma of the throat with difficulty in swallowing and breathing, the Euthanasia Society argues that, though few express it, 'we cannot know how many have harboured that wish (for release) secretly'. To this, it must be answered that we do not know either how many fear the end, and might fear it more if they had signed declarations and wondered at what stage their 'Will' might be executed.

Supporters of euthanasia urge that the quality of life is more important than the quantity. This slogan misleads many people: what is meant by quality? What criteria can be used to judge it, and by what possible standards can anybody assess the level of quality below which life is worthless?

Lord Ailwyn argued . . . that those who believe in an after-life should agree that a suffering mortal be given the right to be wafted painlessly into it. Followed to its logical conclusion this would lead to the obviously absurd inference that Christian babies should be killed as soon as they are baptised, as that would guarantee their going straight to heaven.

Suicide by Proxy

The opposition to the legalisation of euthanasia stems from the realisation that permissive legislation would end in the encouragement of what is, in fact, in Lord Cork and Orrery's phrase, 'suicide by proxy' Of course there are some who not only defend but extol suicide and consider the 'indoctrination' against it to be regrettable. The law of the land no longer allows prosecution for attempted suicide, but in abstaining from prosecution it does not express approval: in practice it treats attempted suicide as evidence of mental disturbance. Suicide pacts, and any encouragement to or help with a suicide, are still offences in law. Flew, in his essay on 'The Principle of Euthanasia', states that he is concerned primarily with general principles and is not discussing—except perhaps quite incidentally—'any questions of comparative detail'. Such a position is untenable: these general principles cannot be separated from practicalities. Whenever risk of error or abuse exists, as it certainly would in the practice of euthanasia, the question must be asked, 'How compelling is the need to implement the principle?'—particularly so when the soundness of the principle is itself in doubt.

The supporters of euthanasia consider that the doctor-patient relationship would not be damaged if euthanasia were available. In *A Plan for Voluntary Euthanasia* (1962) this was one of the 'Arguments commonly employed against euthanasia' which the authors sought to refute. On page 24 they state:

The legalisation of euthanasia would tend to undermine the confidence of patients in their doctors, and would even lead some patients to fear that euthanasia might be used without their consent.

Comment

On the contrary, the safeguards in the proposed Bill should help to allay such fears. And many people approaching old age would certainly find comfort in the assurance that their doctor would be sympathetic to their request for relief if a terminal illness should bring unbearable suffering. Medical men are not infrequently asked to give such an assurance.

Relief of Suffering

Scrutiny of this statement shows that use of the term 'relief' is ambiguous and perhaps euphemistic. If 'relief of suffering' only is meant, then the proponents of euthanasia are asking no more than is common, decent medical practice. If, however, 'relief' means the deliberate and intentional ending of life, why do they not say so, for this is an entirely different matter? Why obscure the difference?

Confidential Talk with Dying

The patient trusts his doctor to care for him to the best of his ability. However hard-pressed a family doctor may be, he will find time for a confidential talk with his dying patient. Knowing the family background, he will more quickly arrive at sound conclusions than another doctor, and his encouragement and comfort will be more easily accepted by his patient. But if the doctor had undertaken to observe his patient's requests, even though the doctor had grounds for regarding these requests as no longer relevant or applicable, then the doctor would be in a position where he could no longer freely serve the best interests of his patient. This is an example of the type of damage that could be done to the doctor-patient relationship from the doctor's point of view: the implications could be far-reaching.

"What an indictment against our society, to propose killing people because there is not enough sympathy for them!"

There might be tensions anyway in the home of an incurably ill man, but there is a great difference between those which the healthy relatives may have to bear in struggling with their mixed emotions, and the tensions which might arise between the patient and those surrounding him through a petition for euthanasia, or perhaps more often by a failure to petition. Particularly, children of vulnerable age would suffer from the effects of the discussions that would necessarily go on in a family before such a decision was made, and which it would be impossible to conceal from them. Obviously, so long as there is no provision in law for a petition for death, forecasts of what might happen if there were must be speculative. Nevertheless, such speculation can be fairly based on clinical observation, and such observation shows that there is more concern on the part of relatives that a patient should not be allowed to linger on in 'unnecessary suffering' than there is on the part of the patient himself.

Underlying Thought

Underlying the whole controversy is a difference of approach to the value of human life. On the one hand the tradition, not only of Christendom but of all civilised people, gives to human life a respect above that accorded to animal life, and of a different sort: on the other hand there are those who dismiss this respect as misplaced. Thus J.R. Wilson writes: 'We are all supposed to feel some deep inherent reverence for human life', the implication being not only that some poeple do not feel such reverence, but also that there is at least an element of superstition in such feeling. To accept that line of thought is to reduce men to the stature of animals—a notion offensive to common sense. 'People take the experience of killing very easily indeed; it is the disapproval of society which bothers them', the same author adds. Taken together with the preceding thought, it seems that Wilson considers it enlightened to feel free to kill, and old-fashioned to disapprove of killing. These quotations illustrate the type of thinking which underlies the case for euthanasia.

"We do not know either how many fear the end, and might fear it more if they had signed declarations and wondered at what stage their 'Will' might be executed."

However closely and carefully an Act might be framed in order to ensure that euthanasia was committed only in certain strictly defined circumstances, those circumstances would in practice be read into every conceivable case by those who wished to practice euthanasia, while those who declined could be denounced as failing to implement the law of the land, or to give patients 'their rights'.

Though no forecast concerning the long-term consequences of a Voluntary Euthanasia Act can be infallible, the suspicion that the voluntary aspect of it would not last long is certainly not to be dismissed as scaremongering. . . . More recently, the Earl of Listowel, though pleading for voluntary euthanasia only, added the ominous words ' . . . we cannot wish to preserve an anonymous individual who has been stripped of personality and reduced by incessant pain or physical deterioration to the animal or vegetable level'. Lord Listowel is here putting forward a highly

coloured picture of a rare case, but is putting it forward as if it were commonplace. Moreover, as should be clear from what has been said earlier, the perpetuation of a merely breathing body is not currently good medical practice.

Abandoning Sanctity of Life

Once the principle of the sanctity of human life is abandoned, or the propaganda accepted that to uphold it is old-fashioned, prejudiced or superstitious, the way is open to the raising of—and the satisfaction of—a demand for so-called euthanasia for severely handicapped children, the mentally sub-normal, the severely crippled, the aged, and ultimately for all who are a burden on the community services and the public purse.

Medicine—and thus its practitioner—is essentially concerned with the relief of pain and suffering and the furtherance of the well-being of the individual. For this reason, whenever the doctor is involved (and he is necessarily involved in this matter) his approach must be an individual one. Nevertheless there is no antithesis between the ultimate good of the individual and that of society. To those who believe in the brotherhood of man, whether from religious or humanist considerations, such an antithesis must appear as a contradiction in terms.

The small families of the 1920's and 30's have left us in the 1960's and 70's with a high proportion of elderly people. Euthanasia could make the sick elderly a ready target for an unwholesome social policy—indeed their destruction might improve the appearance of the population statistics. Let euthanasia be seen for what it is: a tragic attempt to patch up a morbid society.

Jonathan Gould is a psychiatrist in England. Lord Craigmyle is secretary of the Catholic Union of Great Britain. They are the authors of Your Death Warrant *which is the published outcome of a 1968 study group on euthanasia that was set up as a joint venture by the Catholic Union of Great Britain and the Guild of Catholic doctors.*

"The patient is allowed to die instead of being maintained as a laboratory specimen."

Euthanasia Is Humane

Gilbert Cant

George Zygmaniak, 26, . . . as he lay in a hospital bed last month in Neptune, N.J., paralyzed from the neck down because of a motorcycle accident, felt that he was a broken piece of machinery. He was ready to go. He begged his brother Lester, 23, to kill him. According to police, Lester complied—using a sawed-off shotgun at close range. Lester, who had enjoyed an unusually close relationship with his brother, has been charged with first-degree murder.

Last December Eugene Bauer, 59, was admitted to Nassau County Medical Center on Long Island with cancer of the throat. Five days later he was in a coma and given only two days to live. Then, charges the district attorney, Dr. Vincent A. Montemarano, 33, injected an overdose of potassium chloride into Bauer's veins. Bauer died within five minutes. Montemarano listed the cause of death as cancer, but prosecutors now say that it was a "mercy killing" and have accused the doctor of murder.

The two cases underscore the growing emotional controversy over euthanasia ("mercy killing") and the so-called right to die—that is, the right to slip from life with a minimum of pain for both the patient and his family. No one seriously advocates the impulsive taking of life, as in the Zygmaniak shooting. A person suddenly crippled, no matter how severely, may yet show unpredictable improvement or regain at least a will to live. Whether or not to speed the passage of a fatally ill patient is a far subtler question. The headlong advances of medical science make the issue constantly more complex for patients and their families, for doctors and hospitals, for theologians and lawyers.

The doctor's dilemma—how long to prolong life after all hope of recovery has gone—has some of its

roots in half-legendary events of 2,400 years ago. When Hippocrates, the "Father of Medicine," sat under his giant plane tree on the Aegean island of Kos, euthanasia (from the Greek meaning "a good death") was widely practiced and took many different forms. But from beneath that plane tree came words that have been immortalized in the physician's Hippocratic oath, part of which reads: "I will neither give a deadly drug to anybody, if asked for, nor will I make a suggestion to this effect."

Down the centuries, this has been interpreted by most physicians to mean that they must not give a patient a fatal overdose, no matter how terrible his pain or how hopeless his prospects. Today many scholars contend that the origin of this item in the oath has been misinterpreted. Most likely it was designed to keep the physician from becoming an accomplice of palace poisoners or of a man seeking to get rid of a wife.

The most emphatic opponents of euthanasia have been clergymen, of nearly all denominations. Churchmen protest that if a doctor decides when a patient is to die, he is playing God. Many physicians still share this objection. However much they may enjoy a secret feeling of divinity when dispensing miraculous cures, to play the angel of death is understandably repugnant. Moreover, as psychoanalysts point out, they are chillingly reminded of their own mortality.

Medicated Manslaughter

At a recent conference chaired by the Roman Catholic Archbishop of Westminster, Dr. W.F. Anderson of Glasgow University, a professor of geriatric medicine, called euthanasia "medicated manslaughter." Modern drugs, he argued, can keep a patient sufficiently pain-free to make mercy killing, in effect, obsolete. Perhaps. There is no doubt, however, that a panoply of new techniques and equipment can be and often are used to keep alive people who are both hopelessly ill and cruelly debilitated. Artificial respirators, blood-matching and transfusion systems, a variety of fluids that can safely be given intravenously to medicate, nourish and maintain electrolyte balance—these and many other lifesavers give doctors astonishing powers.

Until about 25 years ago, the alternatives facing a doctor treating a terminally ill patient were relatively clear. He could let nature take its sometimes harsh course, or he could administer a fatal dose of some normally beneficent drug. To resort to the drug would be to commit what is called active euthanasia. In virtually all Western countries, that act is still legally considered homicide (though juries rarely convict in such cases).

"So stern a guardian of traditional morality as Pope Pius XII declared that life need not be prolonged by extraordinary means."

On the record, physicians are all but unanimous in insisting that they never perform active euthanasia, for to do so is a crime. Off the record, some will admit that they have sometimes hastened death by giving an overdose of the medicine they had been administering previously. How many such cases there are can never be known.

Now, with wondrous machines for prolonging a sort of life, there is another set of choices. Should the patient's heart or lung function be artificially sustained for weeks or months? Should he be kept technically alive by physicochemical legerdemain, even if he has become a mere collection of organs and tissues rather than a whole man? If a decision is made not to attempt extraordinary measures, or if, at some point, the life-preserving machinery is shut off, then a previously unknown act is being committed. It may properly be called passive euthanasia. The patient is allowed to die instead of being maintained as a laboratory specimen.

Legal Purists

While legal purists complain that euthanasia and the right to die peacefully are separate issues, the fact is that they are converging. With the increasing use of extraordinary measures, the occasions for passive euthanasia are becoming more frequent. The question of whether terminal suffering can be shortened by active or passive means is often highly technical—depending on the type of ailment. Thus the distinctions are becoming blurred, particularly for laymen.

No dicta from ancient Greece can neatly fit the modern logistics of death. Until this century, death

was a relatively common event in the household, particularly among farm families. Today more than 70% of deaths in American cities occur in hospitals or nursing homes. Both medical care and death have been institutionalized, made remote and impersonal. In major medical centers the family doctor is elbowed out by specialists and house physicians who have their elaborate and expensive gadgets. The tendency is to use them.

Life at All Costs

"The idea of not prolonging life unnecessarily has always been more widely accepted outside the medical profession than within it," says a leading Protestant (United Church of Christ) theologian, University of Chicago's Dr. James Gustafson. "Now a lot of physicians are rebelling against the triumphalism inherent in the medical profession, against his sustaining of life at all costs. But different doctors bring different considerations to bear. The research-oriented physician is more concerned with developing future treatments, while the patient-oriented physician is more willing to allow patients to make their own choices."

House-staff physicians, says Tufts University's Dr. Melvin J. Krant in *Prism*, an A.M.A. publication, "deal with the fatally ill as if they were entirely divorced from their own human ecology. The search for absolute biological knowledge precludes a search for existential or symbolic knowledge, and the patient is deprived of his own singular humanism." The house staff, Krant says, assumes "that the patient always prefers life over death at any cost, and a patient who balks at a procedure is often viewed as a psychiatric problem."

Technical wizardry has, in fact, necessitated a new definition of death. For thousands of years it had been accepted that death occurred when heart action and breathing ceased. This was essentially true, because the brain died minutes after the heart stopped. But with machines, it is now possible to keep the brain "alive" almost indefinitely. With the machines unplugged, it would soon die. In cases where the brain ceases to function first, heart and lung activity can be artificially maintained. While legal definitions of death lag far behind medical advances, today's criterion is, in most instances, the absence of brain activity for 24 hours.

The question then, in the words of Harvard Neurologist Robert Schwab, is "Who decides to pull the plug, and when?" Cutting off the machines—or avoiding their use at all—is indeed passive euthanasia. But it is an ethical decision—not murder, or any other crime, in any legal code. So stern a guardian of traditional morality as Pope Pius XII declared that life need not be prolonged by extraordinary means.

But Pius insisted, as have most other moralists, that life must be maintained if it is possible to do so by ordinary means—that is, feeding, usual drug treatment, care and shelter. This attitude is supported by history. It would have been tragic, in 1922, to hasten the end of diabetics, for the medical use of insulin had just been discovered. Similar advances have lifted the death sentence for victims of hydrocephalus and acute childhood leukemia. But such breakthroughs are rare. For the aged and patients in severely deteriorated condition, the time for miracles has probably passed.

Faced with a painful and tenuous future and an all-too-tangible present crisis, how does the doctor decide what to do? Does he make the decision alone? Dr. Malcolm Todd, president-elect of the American Medical Association, wants doctors to have help at least in formulating a general policy. He proposes a commission of laymen, clergy, lawyers and physicians. ''Society has changed,'' says Todd. ''It's up to society to decide.'' The desire to share the responsibility is reasonable, but it is unlikely that any commission could write guidelines to cover adequately all situations. In individual cases, of course, many doctors consult the patient's relatives. But the family is likely to be heavily influenced by the physician's prognosis. More often than not, it must be a lonely decision made by one or two doctors.

Some conscientious physicians may not even be certain when they have resorted to euthanasia. Says Dr. Richard Kessler, associate dean of Northwestern University Medical School: ''There's no single rule you can apply. For me it is always an intensely personal, highly emotional, largely unconscious, quasi-religious battle. I have never said to myself in cold analytic fashion, 'Here are the factors, this is the way they add up, so now I'm going to pull the plug.' Yet I and most doctors I know have acted in ways which would possibly shorten certain illnesses—without ever verbalizing it to ourselves or anyone else.''

Drawing the Line

Kessler's ambivalence is shared by Father Richard McCormick of Loyola University's School of Theology. There are cases, McCormick observes, where the line is hard to draw. One example: a Baltimore couple who let their mongoloid baby die of starvation by refusing permission for an operation to open his digestive tract. The operation might have been considered an ordinary means of treatment, if the child had not been a mongoloid. ''In cases like that,'' says McCormick, ''you're passing judgment on what quality of life that person will have. And once you pass judgment that certain kinds of life are not worth living, the possible sequence is horrifying. In Nazi Germany they went from mental defectives to political enemies to whole races of people. This kind of judgment leads to the kind of mentality that makes such things possible.''

For cases where the line is unclear between ordinary and extraordinary means, Roman Catholic theology offers an escape clause: the principle of double effect. If the physician's intention is to relieve pain, he may administer increasing doses of morphine, knowing full well that he will eventually reach a lethal dosage.

Dying with Dignity

When Sigmund Freud was 83, he had suffered from cancer of the jaw for 16 years and undergone 33 operations. ''Now it is nothing but torture,'' he concluded, ''and makes no sense any more.'' He had a pact with Max Schur, his physician. ''When he was again in agony,'' Schur reported, ''I gave him two centigrams of morphine. I repeated this dose after about twelve hours. He lapsed into a coma and did not wake up again.'' Freud died with dignity at his chosen time.

''If the physician's intention is to relieve pain, he may administer increasing doses of morphine.''

Dr. Schur's decision was, in the end, relatively easy. More often, there are unavoidable uncertainties in both active and passive euthanasia. Doctors may disagree over a prognosis. A patient may be so depressed by pain that one day he wants out, while the next day, with some surcease, he has a renewed will to live. There is the problem of heirs who may be thinking more of the estate than of the patient when the time to pull the plug is discussed. Doctors will have to live with these gray areas, perhaps indefinitely. Attempts to legalize active euthanasia—under severe restrictions—have failed in the U.S. and Britain but will doubtless be revived. The fundamental question, however, is humane rather than legal. To die as Freud died should be the right of Everyman.

Gilbert Cant is a journalist whose articles have appeared in The New York Times Magazine *and* Good Housekeeping.

"To deprive the deformed, the mentally ill and those who suffer from incurable disease, of their lives. . .is a crime which offends all humanity."

Euthanasia Is Inhumane

Terence Cardinal Cooke

The theme of this Congress—Health and the Quality of Life—prompts me to offer a number of reflections concerning the question of "values, both changing and unchanging in the field of health." I am thinking particularly of the basic principles that underlie the phrase—*The Quality of Life.* In recent years, there has been considerable attention focused on improving the quality of life for all Americans. This has generated a new spirit of ecological concern, as well as an effort in law and social policy to improve the total environment in which our lives are lived. At the same time there arises a real danger—and that is, the serious threat of deciding that some lives are not of sufficient quality to merit society's concern and protection.

If there is to be a real quality to life, there first must be full recognition of the dignity inherent in every human life. Whatever might arise to modify or redefine values which are changeable, we must never lose sight of those values which are changeless. And paramount among these changeless values is the essential God-given dignity present in every human life at every stage and in every condition. Whatever winds of change may alter one philosophy or another, human life *is* an all important value as it comes from the Hands of God.

Reverence for Life

A society such as ours which prides itself on the affirmation of the equality of all must constantly be on its guard to protect that equality for each. It cannot allow respect for life to be removed from even the smallest segment of our population. We cannot—we must not—allow any human being to stand outside the pale of our respect for life.

Albert Schweitzer, who gave so much of his own life for others, phrased it very movingly when he

Terence Cardinal Cooke, address delivered to the First Annual American Health Congress in Chicago, August 8, 1972.

said: "If a man loses his reverence for any part of life, he will lose his reverence for *all* life."

I am very concerned lest in some ways we are losing part of our reverence for life. In the dynamics of American society today, this essential and changeless value is indeed assaulted in the pressure cooker of social change. Although I believe that human life begins at the moment of conception, I have seen the destruction of that life legally sanctioned in parts of our country, including, I am sad to say, my own state of New York, where legalized abortion has already claimed almost a half million innocent lives.

We have seen the tragedy of the destruction of life in many warn-torn parts of the world.

We have seen the death of mind and body and spirit suffered by so many through the evil of drug abuse.

We have seen oppressive limitations placed on the lives of the poor and the lower middle class by inadequate housing, education, employment, and yes, even inadequate health care.

We have seen far too many men, women, and children suffer—and we have seen the value and the very basic respect for their human lives threatened and assailed. Yet we believe that the right to life is a sacred and inalienable right, and we hold this truth to be changeless.

Every man, woman and child has dignity; every life has dignity. That dignity must not only be recognized, it must also be protected.

A particular opportunity to protect the God-given dignity of life is available to all of you in the field of health care. For you, death is a constant, always near at hand in your work. You see it come swiftly and unexpectedly; you see it come slowly and lingeringly. But come it does and you sense its presence. As much as anyone, and more than most, you deal with the incurably ill, the elderly and the dying.

Americans recently have become more sensitive to

the subject of dying. The media, state legislators, community organizations, all have expressed interest in the dignity of the incurably ill and the dying. Our society's concern for the quality of life has been broadened to encompass a special concern for the dignity of death. But it seems to me that as yet the meaning of the phrase, *death with dignity*, has not been fully explored.

Death with Dignity

There are some who equate "death with dignity" with allowing a person to die comfortably when death is inevitable. But, there are others who mean by "death with dignity" the direct termination of a person's life.

I believe that directly to take one's own life or to permit another person to do is contrary to nature and against the law of God. I also believe that to deprive the deformed, the mentally ill and those who suffer from incurable disease, of their lives, as though these people and their lives are somehow inferior in value and in dignity, is a crime which offends all humanity.

"If a man loses his reverence for any part of life, he will lose his reverence for all life."

The philosophical principles behind the euthanasia movement are utilitarian and materialistic and they run contrary to the Judaeo-Christian tradition which respects the sacredness and dignity of all human life.

Model Bill?

Recently, a so-called model bill was introduced in one of our state legislatures providing that "If any person is disabled and there is no (immediate family)—death with dignity shall be granted—if in the opinion of three physicians the prolongation of life is meaningless." But who is to decide the definition of the key terms of the proposed statute—when is a man disabled, and who is to decide when life ceases to be meaningful? This bill would have destroyed innocent life through the application of a totally materialistic and utilitarian misconception of the quality of life, masked and sugar-coated in the language of seemingly humane terminology. Although the Florida bill was defeated in Committee, it was only a recent skirmish in the new wave of attacks against life itself in our nation.

Legislation similar to this had already been enacted in Germany in 1943 when Pope Pius XII said what needs to be repeated today in America:

"We see the bodily deformed, the insane and those suffering from hereditary disease at times deprived of their lives, as though they were a useless burden to society. And this procedure is hailed by some as a new discovery of human progress, and as something that is altogether justified by the common good. Yet what sane man does not recognize that this not only violates the natural and Divine Law written in the heart of every man, but flies in the face of every sensibility of civilized humanity?"

God-Given Gift

The American Declaration of Independence testifies to values that are changeless and it speaks of life as an inalienable right. Basically, the Declaration of Independence states that the human right to life is beyond recall by anyone—individuals, physicians, or legal statutes.

Human life is a God-given gift. It is an innate right bestowed by the Creator. If there is to be any real *death* with dignity, every person's innate right to *life* must be respected. But in our technological society, there is a tendency to adopt a limited view of man, to see man only for what he does or produces and to overlook the source of man's dignity—the fact that he is made in the image of God and that, from the moment of conception to the moment of death, he is worthy of the full support of the human family of which he is a member. No reason, however allegedly humanitarian, can deny that right: not medical reasons, not family reasons, not social reasons, not reasons of alleviating suffering. No one can or should take innocent human life.

The current interest in euthanasia is related to recent remarkable advances in the field of medical science. Modern discoveries of "miracle drugs" have tempered the ravages of tuberculosis, influenza and pneumonia,—once the leading causes of death in our country. Refined medical skills and technical advancements have also aided in the control of fatal diseases and the consequent prolongation of life. At the same time, while the life expectancy of man has doubled in the past one hundred years in our land, the specter of dying from long-term degenerative illnesses such as heart disease and cancer is an ever increasing reality. Nevertheless, we cannot overlook the fact that the continuing progress of medical science and technology offers to patients so afflicted the hope of newly discovered cures. Furthermore, prolonged treatment of the dying patient immeasurably aids the medical profession to comprehend and hopefully one day conquer presently incurable diseases.

Responsibility of All

As members of one human family we are reminded that there is a responsibility on the part of all of us to insure that there is dignity both in living and in dying. In the case of the incurably ill, the dying, those suffering terminal disease, there is much that we can do that will harmonize with the respect due the individual and yet alleviate his pain, both physical and mental.

It goes without saying that if the patient reasonably desires extra-ordinary medical procedures, they should not be denied him. And, of course, in no case would it be justifiable to withhold ordinary medical procedures from any patient. Euthanasia or "mercy killing" in all its forms is contrary to nature and against the law of God.

"Euthanasia or 'mercy killing' in all its forms is contrary to nature and against the law of God."

There is no doubt that at times the application of these principles may be difficult and perplexing, but these problems cannot be solved apart from moral principles and changeless spiritual values.

To a very real degree we all share one another's burdens and responsibilities. Whether we be legislators or jurists, physicians or surgeons, nurses or technicians, attorneys or counselors, ministers or priests, we cannot retreat from invoking moral principles in dealing with the complex and grave problems which confront our society today. Those who for even the most humanitarian of reasons would relegate to men or to institutions the decision as to who will live and who will die run counter to the whole civilized tradition of Western man. The right to life is a fundamental, a basic right inherent in each individual. It comes from no man or no institution; it can be taken away by no man or no institution. Too much is at stake—the future of our nation, the welfare of our families and the hope of a tomorrow for young and old.

Changeless Value: Life

Real "death with dignity" respects each individual as he approaches death. It provides that he be subjected to no unnecessary procedures. It allows for alleviation of his pain. It gives to him the opportunity to put his house in order spiritually and temporally and to be at peace.

The changeless value which I urge that we all support is described by Moses in the Old Testament as follows: "I have set before you life and death....therefore choose life that you and your descendants may live." (Deut. 30, 19)

I hope and pray that our leaders and our society will heed those words of a great Hebrew prophet and indeed choose life, thus really bringing the blessings of the true quality of life to a generation which shall remain faithful to this most basic of human values.

Terence Cardinal Cooke, a cardinal in the Roman Catholic Church, became the Archbishop of New York in 1968. He led a rigorous campaign against legalized abortion. Cardinal Cooke died of leukemia in October 1983.

"A passive 'good death'...means withdrawing supportive measures in terminal cases."

Refusing Treatment Ensures Good Death

Lawrence Mosher

The right to die with dignity is as fundamental as the right to live with dignity. Yet American medicine, which honors this right in word, often abridges it in deed—not out of malice, but as an ironic by-product of medical technology that critics say turns mercy into unintended cruelty.

Where nature has failed, machines are succeeding. There are devices to breathe for patients who cannot breathe, to feed those who cannot swallow, to cleanse the blood of those whose kidneys have failed, to ring out help for those who cannot cry out.

Wondrous devices all, but not entirely beneficent. For this technology is forcing cruel choices upon the doctors and nurses in hospitals and nursing homes where, increasingly, Americans go to die.

More and more, persons who are deeply distressed by technology's ability to prolong life are asking: At what point is prolonging life not merciful but inhumane? Does medicine too often prolong not life but the act of dying? And, most significant, shouldn't each of us have the right to decide *for himself* his own time to die?

Miracles Bring Complications

One need only walk through one of those bleak, silent nursing homes where the aged go to die, or glance at the gleaming intensive-care equipment found in any good hospital, to discover the poignancy and point of these questions. Medical science has surely wrought miracles. But is also has changed and complicated our way of coping with death and dying.

The terminal patient "may cry for rest, peace, and dignity," writes Chicago's Dr. Elisabeth Kubler-Ross, a pioneer in this long-ignored subject, "but he will get infusions, transfusions, a heart machine, or tracheotomy if necessary. He may want one single

person to stop for one single minute so that he can ask one single question—but he will get a dozen people around the clock, all busily preoccupied with his heart rate, pulse, electrocardiogram, or pulmonary functions, his secretions or excretions, but not with him as a human being."

Such medical expertise is a blessing for patients with future potential. But what of the terminally ill? The brain-damaged? The cancer-ravaged? The elderly debilitated by chronic, painful disease?

A Perversion of Values

"We have somehow got on to a vitalistic tack that has made simple biological continuance the absolute good," says the Rev. Robert B. Reeves, Jr., Protestant chaplain at New York City's Presbyterian Hospital. "And it seems to me that this is a perversion of the Judeo-Christian value system. When illness brings a person to a state in which he is less than a free person,...then what is most valuable and precious is gone and we may well feel that his mere continuance by machine or drugs is a violation of him as a person."

But our culture does not agree. One California doctor recalls a patient with irreversible brain damage who was maintained for eight years with a catheter in his bladder. "Every eight hours a nurse would poke a tube down his throat and shoot some food in. You could have taken a lighted match and held it against his eye and he still wouldn't have known you were there."

The patient required three special nurses. His room cost $700 a month. His eight-year expenses came to almost $300,000. "All you had to do was pull out the tubes and stop feeding him," the doctor continues. "He would have died within 72 hours without any pain."

But the tubes were not pulled out; few doctors would dare. Yet the physician, Dr. Theodore C. Bauerlein, did allow another patient to die. He was a

Lawrence Mosher, "When There Is No Hope, Why Prolong Life?" *National Observer*, March 1972. Reprinted by permission of the *National Observer*, © Dow Jones & Company, Inc., 1972. All Rights Reserved.

70-year-old Episcopal bishop who could not swallow because of brain damage.

"One day he asked me, 'Will I ever be able to swallow again?'" Dr. Bauerlein recounts. "'No, bishop, you won't,' I said. 'You'll have to be fed with a tube.' 'Then why don't you let me die?' he asked. 'Well, if that's your wish, okay,' I said. So I gave him enough medication to ensure no pain, and in five days he was dead."

"The overwhelming majority of elderly persons polled did not want their lives prolonged by medical 'heroics.'"

Dr. Bauerlein, a gastroenterologist, said he was accused of practicing euthanasia for letting a woman suffering from cirrhosis of the liver die. "I didn't kill her; I permitted her to die," he says. "I stopped dialysis, withdrew the respirator, and ended intravenous feeding.

"I may not take life, but I don't have to sustain life under all circumstances either. I think most doctors agree with this, but they are afraid to admit it. Very few doctors will come out and state this publicly because they fear malpractice suits and public censure."

Death increasingly occurs in larger metropolitan institutions, where doctors do not know their patients and have had no opportunity to gain the confidence of relatives. As Dr. Kubler-Ross observes: "Dying nowadays is more gruesome in many ways. It is more lonely, more mechanical, and more dehumanized."

Medicine's Roulette Wheel

Hospital chaplains have a unique view of this, which they are beginning to express more forthrightly. Says Clarence Collins, a Protestant chaplain at New York City's Bellevue Hospital: "Medical schools are creating very competent technicians who view the body as a highly sophisticated machine. Disease is the infinite challenge, and medicine is a contest, a game; they talk about it in terms of probabilities. . . . So it's inevitable that in a clinical situation they fail to appreciate that sickness is an aspect of human experience too."

In Bellevue's neurological intensive-care unit, head nurse Linda Weisenbach tells of a comatose cerebral-thrombosis victim on whom one doctor ordered a blood-flow test after other doctors had given up hope. In this test, catheters are threaded through the blood vessels of the neck and into the brain to measure oxygenation there. Such exams are part of a national research project on cerebral death.

Mrs. Weisenbach recalls that the doctor said, "'Listen, we're going to do blood-flow studies on So-and-so.' I said, 'No, you don't have permission.' The doctor chuckled and said, 'Well, he's not in any position to give permission.'" She nevertheless succeeded in preventing the studies.

"I'm for this (national) study," the young nurse explains, "but not if it interferes with a patient's dignity in dying. I don't think we have. . .I may be wrong, but I just don't think we have that right. Suppose someone just sat there and held his hand. You know, wouldn't that make us more human? Cramming an endotracheal tube down a 78-year-old man's throat, or banging away and shocking him to make his heart start so he can 'live' for another 24 hours in abject misery, is wrong. And it degrades us as well as the patient and his family."

Heroism Over Humanity

Most doctors are traditionally ill at ease with death and dying; in fact, one theory says that medicine draws those who fear death most. Certainly death can arouse a doctor's sense of defeat and guilt, "an unreasoned, gut feeling that his professional acumen was not what it should have been," as Dr. Roland Stevens of Rochester, N.Y., puts it.

The doctor must re-evaluate this attitude, argues Dr. Stevens, a surgeon who champions the death-with-dignity cause at the University of Rochester Medical School where he teaches. "He must learn that humane considerations sometimes supersede scientific technique."

Dr. Stevens says hospital intensive-care units are particularly insidious violators of the right to die with dignity. In them, he says, "a small crowd of highly competent specialists, each with his supporting team of technicians, shares the control of a patient's destiny." Some results, Dr. Stevens maintains, "can only be described as more heroic than humane."

The head nurse of Bellevue's surgical intensive-care unit echoes Dr. Stevens. Says **Valerie Lezoli, 26:** "It's very rare that our patients die peacefully. Most have cardiac arrests, and an attempt is made to resuscitate them. Bellevue is a teaching institution; the doctors have to learn. Most of the time I can go along with it because a lot of these patients can be saved.

"But those who are very old, or who have terminal cancer, or whose brain is irreversibly damaged, these patients have a right to die peacefully. They should get their pain medication and just be left to die. But most of my house staff don't feel this way."

Death Taboo Is Disappearing

Bellevue's chief resident codes patients "DNR"—do not resuscitate—when he decides that they are beyond hope, Miss Lezoli says. But she says this coding isn't always allowed.

Sometimes an intern or resident will attempt resuscitation just for the experience, says Miss Lezoli.

Sometimes, when no doctor is around, it will be a nurse, frequently Miss Lezoli herself. But if the patient has clearly expressed his wish to die peacefully, she says, "I go out of my way" to let him.

The taboo that death is too morbid to discuss is disappearing. In 1965 Dr. Elisabeth Kubler-Ross, then an assistant professor of psychiatry at the University of Chicago, conducted research on dying, aided by students from the Chicago Theological Seminary. One result was her classic book, *On Death and Dying,* in which she develops a philosophy of therapy for the dying.

Another indication of changing attitudes is the growth of the four-year-old Euthanasia Educational Fund, New York City. An offshoot of the Euthanasia Society of America, the fund carefully limits itself to promoting *passive* euthanasia among doctors, lawyers, and the public.

A passive "good death," according to the fund, means giving a dying patient sufficient medication to relieve pain even if it tends to shorten life. It also means withdrawing supportive measures in terminal cases with intractable pain or irreversible brain damage.

The recent surge in public response to the fund has "flabbergasted" its executive director, Mrs. Elizabeth T. Halsey. Letters, almost all favorable, now roll in at 25 a day. Membership, only 600 in 1969, is more than 5,000.

Material for Discussion

A Baptist minister in Fairview Park, Ohio, writes that he plans to preach favorably on the subject. The School of Nursing at West Virginia University wants 150 copies of a tract. A sociology professor at the State University of New York at Brockport seeks material for discussion; a doctor in Hallandale, Fla., does too.

More interesting, perhaps, are the requests from law firms for copies of the fund's "living will." The three-paragraph form is not legally binding, but it does put in writing the signer's attitude toward death and dying.

"If there is no reasonable expectation of my recovery from physical or mental disability," it reads, the signer requests to "be allowed to die and not be kept alive by artificial means or heroic measures." The fund has distributed 40,000 of the living wills so far, Mrs. Halsey says.

The Foundation for Thanatology (thanatology means the study of death) is another new group calling for a change of attitude toward death. Started by Dr. Austin H. Kutscher, a professor at Columbia University's School of Dental and Oral Surgery, it is trying to get medical and nursing schools to teach students how to deal with dying patients and their families.

Dr. Kutscher reports progress is slow. He can list almost in one breath the schools that teach seminars on dying. Notable examples are Columbia, Tulane, Einstein, and Tufts University in Boston.

Many medical students appear to favor passive euthanasia. In two recent surveys at the University of Washington, 90 per cent of the fourth-year students endorsed it. More surprising, 46 per cent favored "positive" or active euthanasia.

Most physicians favor and practice passive euthanasia, according to a 1969 survey by the University of Washington's Dr. R.H. Williams. He polled members of the Association of American Physicians and the Association of Professors of Medicine.

Courts Say Yes and No

By no means do all doctors or theologians approve of passive euthanasia. "If euthanasia were legalized, the next logical step would be the legalization of genocide and the killing of social misfits," asserts Dr. Fred Rosner, director of hematology at New York City's Queens Hospital Center. "And who can make the fine distinction between prolonging life and prolonging the act of dying?"

"Hospital intensive-care units are particularly insidious violators of the right to die with dignity."

Passive euthanasia has provoked few malpractice suits. But in Miami last summer Florida Circuit Court Judge David Popper ruled that a patient could refuse painful treatment even if it meant quick death.

Dr. Orlando Lopez brought the case to clarify whether he could be charged with aiding a suicide if he granted his patient's request to stop treatment. The patient, a 72-year-old Cuban exile, suffered from hemolytic anemia, which destroys the red blood cells. Dr. Lopez said he would have to remove her spleen or continue painful transfusions. Judge Popper ruled that a person "has the right not to be tortured."

Another Florida physician, Dr. Walter W. Sackett, Jr., has been trying since 1968 to amend the state constitution to include the right "to die with dignity." He hasn't succeeded, but he says he's making headway.

Two Patients, Two Precedents

More recent court decisions have split on the right-to-die issue. Last January New York City's Cornell Medical Center won court permission to install new batteries in a 79-year-old man's pacemaker over his wife's objections. "He is turning into a vegetable; isn't death better?" the wife asked. But State Supreme Court Justice Gerald P. Culkin, in declaring the patient incompetent, named the hospital director his guardian "to protect or sustain" his life.

Milwaukee County Judge Michael Sullivan, however, denied a Wisconsin hospital's attempt to rule a 77-year-old woman incompetent so surgeons could continue amputating her limbs. The woman suffered from hardening of the arteries and resultant gangrene; she refused to sign another surgical consent form. "There is absolutely no evidence of incompetence," Judge Sullivan ruled, "except that she is too weak to talk....We will leave her to depart in God's own peace."

Most religious organizations are receptive to passive euthanasia. Pope Paul VI told Catholic physicians last fall that prolonging life in the terminal stage could be "useless torture."

A Public-Private Issue

"But the core of the moral problem," argues Dr. Joseph Fletcher, an Episcopal minister and medical-ethics professor at the University of Virginia, "is still the freedom of people to choose, to be responsible, in every situation. How strange and contradictory it is that people should deliberately assume the responsibility to *initiate* a life, and to control its creation contraceptively, but still fail or refuse to *terminate* it no matter what the actual situation is."

"The core of the moral problem is still the freedom of people to choose, to be responsible, in every situation."

Last year a survey conducted by a University of Southern California sociologist showed that the overwhelming majority of elderly persons polled did not want their lives prolonged by medical "heroics."

But people change their minds, sometimes rapidly. Some psychiatric studies show that terminal patients may accept death calmly at one point, later becoming irrationally hopeful of cure. One problem with the living will, says Columbia's Dr. Kutscher, is that one might change his mind but be unable to change his will.

Above all, death is an individual matter, not easily amenable to collective solutions. In the end a doctor must decide when the art of prolonging life becomes the profanity of prolonging the act of dying.

Columbia's Chaplain Reeves sees two supreme challenges facing us all: to find an honorable equivalent to Spartan exposure on the rocks at the beginning of life, and an honorable equivalent to the Eskimo hole in the ice at the end of life.

"To choose one's own time to die," Reeves notes, "has been an honorable thing to do. But our culture brands it suicide. We regard death as the ultimate enemy. Almost all other cultures have regarded death as the ultimate friend. They knew that generations pass. We try to make believe this isn't so."

Lawrence Mosher, a journalist, is the author of this essay which is distributed by the Euthanasia Educational Fund, Inc.

"The patient is still conscious and competent, but meets a death that is quite different than he had bargained for."

Refusing Treatment Does Not Ensure Good Death

M. Pabst Battin

In recent years "right-to-die" movements have brought into the public consciousness something most physicians have long known: that in some hopeless medical conditions, heroic efforts to extend life may no longer be humane, and the physician must be prepared to allow the patient to die. Physician responses to patients' requests for "natural death" or "death with dignity" have been, in general, sensitive and compassionate. But the successes of the right-to-die movement have had a bitterly ironic result: institutional and legal protections for "natural death" have, in some cases, actually made it more painful to die.

There is just one legally protected mechanism for achieving natural death: refusal of medical treatment. It is available to both competent and incompetent patients. In the United States, the competent patient is legally entitled to refuse medical treatment of any sort on any personal or religious grounds, except perhaps where the interests of minor children are involved. A number of court cases, including *Quinlan*, *Saikewicz*, *Spring* and *Eichner*, have established precedent in the treatment of an incompetent patient for a proxy refusal by a family member or guardian. In addition, eleven states now have specific legislation protecting the physician from legal action for failure to render treatment when a competent patient has executed a directive to be followed after he is no longer competent. A durable power of attorney, executed by the competent patient in favor of a trusted relative or friend, is also used to determine treatment choices after incompetence occurs.

In the face of irreversible, terminal illness, a patient may wish to die sooner but "naturally," without artificial prolongation of any kind. By doing so, the patient may believe he is choosing a death that is, as a contributor to the *New England Journal of Medicine* has put it, "comfortable, decent, and peaceful." "Natural death," the patient may assume, means a death that is easier than a medically prolonged one. That is why he is willing to undergo death earlier and that is why, he assumes, natural death is legally protected. But the patient may conceive of "natural death" as more than pain-free; he may assume that it will allow time for reviewing life and saying farewell to family and loved ones, for last rites or final words, for passing on hopes, wisdom, confessions, and blessings to the next generation. These ideas are of course heavily stereotyped; they are the product of literary and cultural traditions associated with conventional death-bed scenes, reinforced by movies, books, and news stories, religious models, and just plain wishful thinking. Even the very term "natural" may have stereotyped connotations for the patient: something close to nature, uncontrived, and appropriate. As a result of these notions, the patient often takes "natural death" to be a painless, conscious, dignified, culminative slipping-away.

Earlier but Not Easier Death

Now consider what sorts of death actually occur under the rubric of "natural death." A patient suffers a cardiac arrest and is not resuscitated. Result: sudden unconsciousness, without pain, and death within a number of seconds. Or a patient has an infection that is not treated. Result: the unrestrained multiplication of micro-organisms, the production of toxins, interference with organ function, hypotension, and death. On the way there may be fever, delirium, rigor or shaking, and light-headedness; death usually takes one or two days, depending on the organism involved. If the kidneys fail and dialysis or transplant is not undertaken, the patient is generally more conscious, but experiences nausea, vomiting, gastrointestinal hemorrhage (evident in vomiting

M. Pabst Battin, "The Least Worst Death," *The Hastings Center Report,* April 1983. Reproduced with permission of *The Hastings Center Report,* © Institute of Society, Ethics and the Life Sciences, 360 Broadway, Hastings-on-Hudson, NY 10706.

blood), inability to concentrate, neuromuscular irritability or twitching, and eventually convulsions. Dying may take from days to weeks, unless such circumstances as high potassium levels intervene. Refusal of amputation, although painless, is characterized by fever, chills, and foul-smelling tissues. Hypotension, characteristic of dehydration and many other states, is not painful but also not pleasant: the patient cannot sit up or get out of bed, has a dry mouth and thick tongue, and may find it difficult to talk. An untreated respiratory death involves conscious air hunger. This means gasping, an increased breathing rate, a panicked feeling of inability to get air in or out. Respiratory deaths may take only minutes; on the other hand, they may last for hours. If the patient refuses intravenous fluids, he may become dehydrated. If he refuses surgery for cancer, an organ may rupture. Refusal of treatment does not simply bring about death in a vacuum, so to speak; death always occurs from some specific cause.

Dignified Death

Many patients who are dying in these ways are either comatose or heavily sedated. Such deaths do not allow for a period of conscious reflection at the end of life, nor do they permit farewell-saying, last rites, final words, or other features of the stereotypically "dignified" death.

"An untreated respiratory death involves conscious air hunger."

Even less likely to match the patient's conception of natural death are those cases in which the patient is still conscious and competent, but meets a death that is quite different than he had bargained for. Consider the bowel cancer patient with widespread metastases and a very poor prognosis who—perhaps partly out of consideration for the emotional and financial resources of his family—refuses surgery to reduce or bypass the tumor. How, exactly, will he die? This patient is clearly within his legal rights in refusing surgery, but the physician knows what the outcome is very likely to be: obstruction of the intestinal tract will occur, the bowel wall will perforate, the abdomen will become distended, there will be intractible vomiting (perhaps with a fecal character to the emesis), and the tumor will erode into adjacent areas, causing increased pain, hemorrhage, and sepsis. Narcotic sedation and companion drugs may be partially effective in controlling pain, nausea, and vomiting, but this patient will *not* get the kind of death he thought he had bargained for. Yet, he was willing to shorten his life, to use the single legally protected mechanism—

refusal of treatment—to achieve that "natural" death. Small wonder that many physicians are skeptical of the "gains" made by the popular movements supporting the right to die.

Right to Die Goes Wrong

Several distinct factors contribute to the backfiring of the right-to-die cause. First, and perhaps the most obvious, the patient may misjudge his own situation in refusing treatment or in executing a natural-death directive: his refusal may be precipitous and ill informed, based more on fear than on a settled desire to die. Second, the physician's response to the patient's request for "death with dignity" may be insensitive, rigid, or even punitive (though in my experience most physicians respond with compassion and wisdom). Legal constraints may also make natural death more difficult than might be hoped: safeguards often render natural-death requests and directives cumbersome to execute, and in any case, in a litigation-conscious society, the physician will often take the most cautious route.

But most important in the apparent backfiring of the right-to-die movement is the underlying ambiguity in the very concept of "natural death." Patients tend to think of the character of the experience they expect to undergo—a death that is "comfortable, decent, peaceful"—but all the law protects is the refusal of medical procedures. Even lawmakers sometimes confuse the two. The California and Kansas natural-death laws claim to protect what they romantically describe as "the natural process of dying." North Carolina's statute says it protects the right to a "peaceful and natural" death. But since these laws actually protect only refusal of treatment, they can hardly guarantee a peaceful, easy death. Thus, we see a widening gulf between the intent of the law to protect the patient's final desires, and the outcomes if the law is actually followed. The physician is caught in between: he recognizes his patient's right to die peacefully, naturally, and with whatever dignity is possible, but foresees the unfortunate results that may come about when the patient exercises this right as the law permits.

Unbearable Pain

Of course, if the symptoms or pain become unbearable the patient may change his mind. The patient who earlier wished not to be "hooked up on tubes" now begins to experience difficulty in breathing or swallowing, and finds that a tracheotomy will relieve his distress. The bowel cancer patient experiences severe discomfort from obstruction, and gives permission for decompression or reductive surgery after all. In some cases, the family may engineer the change of heart because they find dying too hard to watch. Health care personnel may view these reversals with satisfaction:

"See," they may say, "he really wants to live after all." But such reversals cannot always be interpreted as a triumph of the will to live; they may also be an indication that refusing treatment makes dying too hard.

How can the physician honor the dying patient's wish for a peaceful, conscious, and culminative death? There is more than one option.

Options for an Easier Death

Such a death can come about whenever the patient is conscious and pain-free; he can reflect and, if family, clergy, or friends are summoned at the time, he will be able to communicate as he wishes. Given these conditions, death can be brought on in various ways. For instance, the physician can administer a lethal quantity of an appropriate drug. Or the patient on severe dietary restrictions can violate his diet: the kidney failure patient, for instance, for whom high potassium levels are fatal, can simply overeat on avocados. These ways of producing death are, of course, active euthanasia, or assisted or unassisted suicide. For many patients, such a death would count as "natural" and would satisfy the expectations under which they had chosen to die rather than to continue an intolerable existence. But for many patients (and for many physicians as well) a death that involves deliberate killing is morally wrong. Such a patient could never assent to an actively caused death, and even though it might be physically calm, it could hardly be emotionally or psychologically peaceful. This is not to say that active euthanasia or assisted suicide are morally wrong, but rather that the force of some patients' moral views about them precludes using such practices to achieve the kind of death they want. Furthermore, many physicians are unwilling to shoulder the legal risk such practices may seem to involve.

But active killing aside, the physician can do much to grant the dying patient the humane death he has chosen by using the sole legally protected mechanism that safeguards the right to die: refusal of treatment. This mechanism need not always backfire. For in almost any terminal condition, death can occur in various ways, and there are many possible outcomes of the patient's present condition. The patient who is dying of emphysema could die of respiratory failure, but could also die of cardiac arrest or untreated pulmonary infection. The patient who is suffering from bowel cancer could die of peritonitis following rupture of the bowel, but could also die of dehydration, of pulmonary infection, of acid-base imbalance, of electrolyte deficiency, or of an arrhythmia.

Physician as Strategist

As the poet Rilke observes, we have a tendency to associate a certain sort of end with a specific disease: it is the "official death" for that sort of illness. But there are many other ways of dying than the official death, and the physician can take advantage of these. Infection and cancer, for instance, are old friends; there is increased frequency of infection in the immunocompromised host. Other secondary conditions, like dehydration or metabolic derangement, may set in. Of course certain conditions typically occur a little earlier, others a little later, in the ordinary course of a terminal disease, and some are a matter of chance. The crucial point is that certain conditions will produce a death that is more comfortable, more decent, more predictable, and more permitting of conscious and peaceful experience than others. Some are better, if the patient has to die at all, and some are worse. Which mode of death claims the patient depends in part on circumstance and in part on the physician's response to conditions that occur. What the patient who rejects active euthanasia or assisted suicide may realistically hope for is this: the least worst death among those that could naturally occur. Not all unavoidable surrenders need involve rout; in the face of inevitable death, the physician becomes strategist, the deviser of plans for how to meet death most favorably.

"Refusal of treatment does not simply bring about death in a vacuum."

He does so, of course, at the request of the patient, or, if the patient is not competent, the patient's guardian or kin. Patient autonomy is crucial in the notion of natural death. The physician could of course produce death by simply failing to offer a particular treatment to the patient. But to fail to *offer* treatment that might prolong life, at least when this does not compromise limited or very expensive resources to which other patients have claims, would violate the most fundamental principles of medical practice; some patients do not want "natural death," regardless of the physical suffering or dependency that prolongation of life may entail.

Legal Refusal of Treatment

A scenario in which natural death is accomplished by the patient's selective refusal of treatment has one major advantage over active euthanasia and assisted suicide: refusal of treatment is clearly permitted and protected by law. Unfortunately, however, most patients do not have the specialized medical knowledge to use this self-protective mechanism intelligently. Few are aware that some kinds of refusal of treatment will better serve their desires for a "natural death" than others. And few patients realize that refusal of treatment can be selective. Although many patients with life-threatening illness are receiving multiple kinds of therapy, from surgery to nutritional support, most assume that it is only the major procedures (like surgery) that can be refused. (This misconception is perhaps perpetuated by the standard practice of obtaining specific consent for major procedures, like surgery, but not for minor, ongoing ones.) Then, too, patients may be unable to distinguish therapeutic from palliative procedures. And they may not understand the interaction between one therapy and another. In short, most patients do not have enough medical knowledge to foresee the consequences of refusing treatment on a selective basis; it is this that the physician must supply.

"It sometimes occurs that physicians disclose the dismal probable consequences of refusing treatment in order to coerce patients into accepting the treatment they propose."

It is already morally and legally recognized that informed consent to a procedure involves explicit disclosure, both about the risks and outcomes of the proposed procedure and about the risks and outcomes of alternative possible procedures. Some courts, as in *Quackenbush,* have also recognized the patient's right to explicit disclosure about the outcomes of refusing the proposed treatment. But though it is crucial in making a genuinely informed decision, the patient's right to information about the risks and outcomes of alternative kinds of refusal has not yet been recognized. So, for instance, in order to make a genuinely informed choice, the bowel cancer patient with concomitant infection will need to know about the outcomes of each of the principal options: accepting both bowel surgery and antibiotics; accepting antibiotics but not surgery; accepting surgery but no antibiotics; or accepting neither. The case may of course be more complex, but the principle remains: To recognize the patient's right to autonomous choice in matters concerning the treatment of his own body, the physician must provide information about all the legal options open to him, not just information sufficient to choose between accepting or rejecting a single proposed procedure.

Dismal Problem

One caveat: It sometimes occurs that physicians disclose the dismal probable consequences of refusing treatment in order to coerce patients into accepting the treatment they propose. This may be particularly common in surgery that will result in ostomy of the bowel. The patient is given a graphic description of the impending abdominal catastrophe—impaction, rupture, distention, hemorrhage, sepsis, and death.

He thus consents readily to the surgery proposed. The paternalistic physician may find this maneuver appropriate, particularly since ostomy surgery is often refused out of vanity, depression, or on fatalistic grounds. But the physician who frightens a patient into accepting a procedure by describing the awful consequences of refusal is not honoring the patient's right to informed, autonomous choice: he has not described the various choices the patient could make, but only the worst.

Supplying the knowledge a patient needs in order to choose the least worst death need not require enormous amounts of additional energy or time on the part of the physician; it can be incorporated into the usual informed consent disclosures. If the patient is unable to accommodate the medical details, or instructs the physician to do what he thinks is best, the physician may use his own judgment in ordering and refraining from ordering treatment. If the patient clearly prefers to accept less life in hopes of an easy death, the physician should act in a way that will allow the least worst death to occur. In principle, however, the competent patient, and the proxy deciders for an incompetent patient, are entitled to explicit disclosure about all the alternatives for medical care. Physicians in burn units are already experienced in telling patients with very severe burns, where survival is unprecedented, what the outcome is likely to be if aggressive treatment is undertaken or if it is not—death in both cases, but under quite different conditions. Their expertise in these delicate matters might be most useful here. Informed refusal is just as much the patient's right as informed consent.

Humane Guidance

The role of the physician as strategist of natural death may be even more crucial in longer-term degenerative illnesses, where both physician and patient have far more advance warning that the patient's condition will deteriorate, and far more opportunity to work together in determining the conditions of the ultimate death. Of course, the first interest of both physician and patient will be strategies for maximizing the good life left. Nevertheless, any patients with long-term, eventually terminal illnesses, like multiple sclerosis, Huntington's chorea, diabetes, or chronic renal failure, may educate themselves considerably about the expected courses of their illnesses, and may display a good deal of anxiety about the end stages. This is particularly true in hereditary conditions where the patient may have watched a parent or relative die of the disease. But it is precisely in these conditions that the physician's opportunity may be greatest for humane guidance in the unavoidable matter of dying. He can help the patient to understand what the long-term options are in refusing treatment while he is competent, or help him to execute a natural-death directive or durable power of attorney that spells out the particulars of treatment refusal after he becomes incompetent.

Of course, some diseases are complex, and not easy to explain. Patients are not always capable of listening very well, especially to unattractive possibilities concerning their own ends. And physicians are sometimes reluctant to acknowledge that their efforts to sustain life will eventually fail. Providing such information may also seem to undermine whatever hope the physician can nourish in the patient. But the very fact that the patient's demise is still far in the future makes it possible for the physician to describe various scenarios of how that death could occur, and at the same time give the *patient* control over which of them will actually happen. Not all patients will choose the same strategies of ending, nor is there any reason that they should. What may count as the "least worst" death to one person may be the most feared form of death to another. The physician may be able to increase the patient's psychological comfort immensely by giving him a way of meeting an unavoidable death on his own terms.

"The key to good strategy is in considering all the possibilities at hand."

In both acute and long-term terminal illnesses, the key to good strategy is flexibility in considering *all* the possibilities at hand. These alternatives need not include active euthanasia or suicide measures of any kind, direct or indirect. To take advantage of the best of the naturally occurring alternatives is not to cause the patient's death, which will happen anyway, but to guide him away from the usual, frequently worst, end.

In the current enthusiasm for "natural death" it is not patient autonomy that dismays physicians. What does dismay them is the way in which respect for patient autonomy can lead to cruel results. The cure for that dismay lies in the realization that the physician can contribute to the *genuine* honoring of the patient's autonomy and rights, assuring him of "natural death" in the way in which the patient understands it, and still remain within the confines of good medical practice and the law.

M. Pabst Battin, Ph.D., is associate professor of philosophy at the University of Utah. She is the author of several essays on topics in classical philosophy and aesthetics and a book, Suicide.

Euthanasia Should Be a Doctor's Decision

Walter C. Alvarez

In 1905, I became an intern in the huge San Francisco City and County Hospital, and for the next year and a half I took care of hundreds of old people, many of them suffering from some hopeless disease, who had come in to die. I was soon impressed with the fact that most of these people had nothing more to hope for in life. Many of them said to me, "What would there be for me if you *could* cure my cancer—or my tuberculosis? I am too old ever to get a job, and I have no place to go; I have no relatives left who might possibly take me into their home, so why should I want to get well? That would only mean I would go from here to the poorhouse, and I would hate that."

A few of my patients were children with their bodies or brains so botched by nature that the only thing life could bring them was suffering. I remember one such child, an idiot with part of his brain sticking out of a big hole in the back of his skull; he had another bad defect in the lower part of his spine, and as a result his legs were paralyzed and he had little chance of ever being able to control his bowel or his urinary bladder. I was glad when I heard my chief, a fine kindly old doctor, say to the nurses and to us interns, "Don't make any effort to keep him alive." I was glad also when later the child did die, and the mental suffering of his parents was lessened.

Easy Death

Naturally, I became interested in euthanasia, and I have been interested in it ever since. While many people I have talked to have the idea that "euthanasia" means "mercy killing," in Greek it really means only "an easy or painless death." In my long life in medicine, I have never met any physician who wanted to take a patient's life, even if begged to

do so. I have, however, heard many physicians discussing the problem often met with today, which comes up when a person with, let us say, a big stroke, has had so much of his brain damaged that he has lost consciousness and has not regained it after weeks or months. The doctors have no hope for the man's recovery; but he is fed with an intravenous or stomach tube. Meanwhile, the huge costs may have financially ruined his family. Also, the hospital bed is badly needed by patients with illnesses that can be cured.

Often every doctor on the staff of a hospital will agree it is stupid to go on struggling to keep a stroke patient half alive. But two distressing questions arise: One is: "Who is going to pull out the tubes through which the patient is getting the food and medicine that is keeping him alive?"; and the other, "When should the tubes be pulled out?" The next of kin may not be willing to accept the responsibility of giving permission; further, their lawyer may advise them not to give it. The doctors in charge may not want to give the order, and their lawyer in turn might say, "No, you had better not. The law on that is not clear." As we improve our ability to keep alive half-dead people who cannot recover, these problems of when to pull out the tubes and who should pull them keep distressing many physicians.

I imagine that some day soon a law will have to be passed saying that the question of when to pull out the tubes must be left in the hands of the patient's physician or physicians. Such a law might save the country a few billion dollars a year.

Extending a Useless Life

When I was an intern, I had an experience that caused me to do much thinking. Still today, after some 66 years, I can see the bed in my big ward in which for some six months there lay, coughing often, an old German tailor, suffering terribly from a tuberculosis which had caused ulceration in his

Walter C. Alvarez, "Death with Dignity." This article first appeared in *The Humanist*, issue of September/October 1971, and is reprinted by permission.

larynx. As a result of this ulceration, every cough caused pain. I came to like the old fellow so much that one night when at last I saw he was dying, I gave him a big dose of codeine to relieve his suffering. This had such a good effect that the man slept most of the night. In the morning he was most grateful to me, but later in the day he said, "Doctor, I know you meant well when you gave me that calming medicine. You wanted to make my dying easier for me, and for that I am grateful. But now I am wishing you had let me finish my dying, because now I have to die all over again, and I dread the process." I have never forgotten that man's statement, and I think it was a good one.

"This problem of voluntary or obviously logical euthanasia can and should be left in the hands of us physicians."

A few years later, after I had begun practice as a family doctor, I came to like a fine intelligent engineer, aged 60, who was dying with a terrible cancer in his esophagus (gullet). When I first saw him, the cancer was inoperable, because it had scattered. It was eating into a number of very sensitive spots in his spine and chest, and as a result, he was suffering terribly—so terribly I could not relieve him with the amount of morphine that I dared give. Then one day, he got his very unpleasant wife out of the room and said, "Doctor, I just said good-bye to my son, who came 2,000 miles to see me; as you can see, my wife is not kind to me, so I have no reason for living any longer. Why should I go on with this dying for perhaps two or three more horrible months? Why not get my dying over with soon? You have been very kind to me, so I am asking you to get me a bottle with enough tablets of morphine in it so that one of these nights I can take a fatal dose. And with that I will be done with this agony of pain."

A Fatal Dose

I promptly got the man the morphine he wanted, but that evening his wife found the bottle under his pillow and angrily threw it out. Then the man begged me so piteously for another bottleful that I went out and got it for him.

The next evening, as his wife and the nurse were eating dinner, he got out of bed and went to his bureau where he had hidden the morphine. Unfortunately, as he started to swallow the tablets, because of his great weakness he fell to the floor; the wife came running in and again confiscated the medicine.

Then she telephoned me and asked, "Did you get that medicine for my husband?" I said, "Yes. He begged me for it." She said she was going to have me

arrested and jailed for attempted murder. I asked my lawyer about this, and he said, "Yes, if the district attorney wants to, I think he can make things hot for you." Fortunately, the woman did not carry out her threat.

The Right to Commit Suicide

I still think that that poor man, with his terrible pain, should have had a legal right to commit suicide, and that I should have had a right to get him the drug for which he had begged. I doubt that we doctors can help people like this, however, until our right to do so is established by law.

Because of my experiences I have read everything I could find in several libraries, trying to find out why for ages in some countries suicide has been looked upon as a sin and a crime. This was due largely to St. Augustine of Hippo, who taught that suicide was one of the greatest of crimes. A hundred years or more ago in England, if a man committed suicide, the government confiscated all of his estate. Eventually, it occurred to the lawmakers that they were severely punishing not the person who committed suicide, but whatever family he may have had, and they abrogated the old law.

Some people in Europe and America in the past thought suicide was a sin, a form of murder. Some felt it was a cowardly act; others said it deprived the local lord of a citizen. Curiously, in some countries, and in certain situations, suicide is highly condoned. In Japan, when a man "loses face" in some way, or is humiliated or disgraced, the finest thing he can do is to take a sword and disembowel himself. A prominent writer in Japan did that recently. For years, in India, when a man died and was cremated, his wife was expected to jump into the fire and die with him. That was thought the honorable thing to do. Now the law forbids it.

Brave Suicide

Sometimes, here in the United States, I have heard of a type of suicide that I thought was brave and very commendable. Thus, I can still see in my mind's eye the woman of 55 or so who came into my office years ago with an operable cancer of one breast. When I asked her if she wanted the operation, she said, "No, I will not go to such a terrible expense right now, because if I do, my son, who is beginning his senior year in college, may not be able to go on and get his degree." I greatly admired that devoted mother, and I am happy to say that when nine months later she returned, a surgeon found that the cancer, with its very low grade of malignancy, could still be removed.

Several other elderly people told me that they would like to commit suicide in order to free their grown children from the great expense of caring for them. I remember one fine mother who did commit suicide so that her daughter could be free to marry her restless fiance.

Right now I know of a woman who is not insane enough to be put in a hospital. Instead, she will live for some months with a married sister, and as a result her brother-in-law generally must leave the house and go to his club, where he remains until the half-insane woman is transferred to the home of another sister. If this psychotic person were to ask for voluntary suicide, I would be granting her the right, because she is mildly insane and for no useful reason she is almost ruining the lives of others.

Several able students of suicide have emphasized the fact that a high percentage of such deaths cannot be regarded as criminal or cowardly, because the person was definitely depressed or otherwise psychotic when he took his life. Incidentally, it should be noted that experts say that many deaths which look like automobile accidents are really suicides. Questioning of the family frequently reveals the fact that a man who, at high speed, drove his car into a bridge abutment had been under the care of a psychiatrist; he had been depressed, and he had talked of ending his life, which had become almost unbearable to him. Perhaps he once had had a month in a mental hospital. I feel that we physicians, and everyone, including the lawyers, should realize that so long as experts tell us that suicidal persons in most cases did what they did because they were suffering from a mild psychosis, we cannot be critical of them.

In many cases no one can ever be certain whether an apparently accidental death was a suicide or not. So long as suicide is frowned on, and so long as it invalidates life insurance policies, thousands of suicidal persons will figure out some way of making their exit from this world look like an accident.

Hospitals as Mausoleums

A while ago I was delighted and encouraged to find that that great and eminent theologian, Dr. Joseph Fletcher, Payne Professor of Ethics and Moral Theology at the Episcopal Theologic School at Cambridge, backs up those of us physicians who do not wish to keep struggling to preserve a "human vegetable." When a professor of ethics backs us up, I am sure we physicians can go ahead, as many of us want to do, letting hopeless old invalids die in peace. As Dr. Fletcher has asked, "May we morally omit to do some of the ingenious things we could do to prolong a patient's suffering....Unless we face up to the facts with hope and sturdiness, our hospitals and nursing homes will become mausoleums where the inmates will exist in a living death."

Recently, Dr. Maurice Visscher put in my hands a report from the *Proceedings of the Royal Society of Medicine* (October 11, 1969), telling of efforts in the British House of Lords to pass a law in favor of voluntary euthanasia. It nearly passed, but one lord blocked it by saying that it was badly drawn.

From what I read in the account, it appears that any man who now helps a dying man commit suicide can be prosecuted, perhaps at the request of an angry relative. In support of the present law against euthanasia, the argument came up that some families might otherwise put pressure on an old relative to commit suicide in order to save them from expense and annoyance. In 66 years of practice, however, I have never heard of such a case. The able Lord Platt suspected that physicians sometimes do help dying patients get out of this world more quickly and with less pain. But the point is that the people who are likely to need euthanasia are those who have been unconscious for days or weeks or years. One man I knew was kept alive but unconscious for seven years, and a wealthy woman was kept alive but unconscious for 10 years.

"Only we doctors should decide how much pain-relieving drugs a patient needs."

An interesting argument, and a valid one, was made to the effect that thousands of persons who attempt suicide and are rescued then go on living contentedly. But these people are not living unconsciously, with much of their brain destroyed. Other debaters said that an aphasic patient could not *say* that he wanted to die. And a few men raised the objection that a few people who in the late 1920s were facing death from diabetes were suddenly saved by the discovery of insulin. True; moreover, in the past two-and-a-half years, with a little oxycodone, I have been able to give back a comfortable and hence useful life to several persons who had been thrown out of work by disabling pain that their physicians had been too reluctant to treat effectively. But we cannot hope for recovery when a child is born without much of a brain or when a big stroke or tumor has destroyed so much of the brain that the patient has become a human vegetable.

Some day, of course, many people with cancer may suddenly be saved by a newly discovered treatment, but, obviously, when that day comes, we can forget the law and cure many of our patients.

Tube Feeding

Finally, I do not sympathize with the idea that if we doctors decide to quit giving artificial respiration to a man whose brain was smashed in an auto accident, we must have a court order and we must have the family and a priest present. As I must keep saying, I feel that this problem of voluntary or obviously logical euthanasia can and should be left in the hands of us physicians. Too often today the tendency is to keep up the artificial respiration and tube feeding of a brainless man. We do not have to be urged to do that.

But similarly, too many physicians, often afraid that they may run afoul of the narcotics people in Washington, are so reluctant to give pain relievers that they are letting thousands of sufferers go without relief. I think that only we doctors should decide how much pain-relieving drugs a patient needs; we must not leave that decision to the policeman on the corner.

Every so often I find an elderly person who for a few years, perhaps after a severe accident or stroke, has been so knocked out from pain that he has had to remain on a couch. By giving him enough of some pain reliever, in a few days I might have him up and about, and soon back at his old job. I maintain that we physicians should be doing this sort of thing more often, and no politician should tell us what we must not do.

Walter C. Alvarez, M.D., was emeritus professor of medicine at the Mayo Graduate School of Medicine, University of Minnesota, and for 25 years was a senior consultant in medicine at the Mayo Clinic. Retired in 1951, he wrote a widely read syndicated newspaper column and was the author of over 1000 articles and editorials.

"If the physicians have different ethical principles. . .about what benefits the patient, it creates a terrible dilemma."

Euthanasia Should Not Be a Doctor's Decision

Robert M. Veatch

Lucy Morgan is a 94-year old patient being maintained in a nursing home. Some years ago she suffered a severe cerebral hemorrhage. She is blind, largely deaf, and often in a semiconscious state. Mrs. Morgan is an educated woman, the wife of the former president of Antioch College. About four years ago she wrote an essay, entitled, "On Drinking the Hemlock," in which she pleaded for a dignified and simple way to choose to die. Now she, like thousands of other patients in hospitals, rest homes, and bedrooms throughout the world, is having her dying prolonged. What, before the biological revolution with its technological gadgetry, would have been a short and peaceful exit is now often drawn out for months or years by the unmitigated and sometimes merciless intervention of penicillin, pacemakers, polygraphs, tubes, tetracycline and transplantation.

Technology's new possibilities have created chaos in the care of the dying. What happens to Mrs. Morgan and others like her depends upon the medical and nursing staffs of the institutions in which these patients are confined. One patient may be mercilessly probed and primed with infusions so that dying is prolonged endlessly, while another in a similar condition may have heroic treatment stopped so that the process of dying may proceed uninterrupted, whether or not permission for the withdrawal has been given. A third patient may, with or without his consent, have an air embolism injected into a vein.

The Issues at Stake

Before examining some of the policies being proposed, we should get the issues straight. Lawyers and moralists make three distinctions in discussing euthanasia and the choice not to prolong dying. First, there may be legal and moral differences between directly killing the terminal patient and allowing him to die. In one study, 59% of the physicians in two West Coast hospitals said that they would practice what was called "negative euthanasia" if it were legal, while 27% said that they would practice positive euthanasia.

Euthanasia has become a terribly confused term in the discussion. In some cases, it is taken literally to mean simply a good death; in others it is limited to the more narrow direct or positive killing of the terminal patient. In light of this confusion, it seems wise to ban the term from the debate entirely.

The legality of directly ending a patient's life is highly questionable, to say the least. Legal cases are very rare. The one decision which is particularly relevant is in the case of Dr. Hermann N. Sander, a New Hampshire physician who entered into the chart of a cancer patient that he had injected air into the patient's blood stream. He admitted that his purpose was to end suffering and pain and the jury returned a verdict for the defendant. But the critical factor in the case was the pathologist's testimony that he could not establish the cause of death with certainty. Thus the jury was not condoning "mercy killing." According to Curran and Shapiro in *Law, Medicine amd Forensic Science*, "The general rule in the United States is that one who either kills one suffering from a fatal or incurable disease, even with the consent of that party, or who provides that party with the means of suicide, is guilty of either murder or manslaughter." It is safe to say that no lawyer would advise his medical clients that they would not be prosecuted if they practiced positive euthanasia.

On the other hand, the cessation of treatment may be a different matter, morally if not legally. It is well known that a competent patient has the right to refuse even lifesaving treatment. To my knowledge, there are no cases in which a physician has been

Robert M. Veatch, "Choosing Not to Prolong Dying," *Medical Dimensions*, December 1972. Reprinted with permission of the author.

brought to trial for stopping the treatment of a terminal patient. It seems most unlikely that he would be guilty of either moral or legal offense if a competent patient had ordered the treatment ended. If he had done so without the patient's instructions, however, the charge, presumably, would be abandonment. The legal status of ceasing to treat or omitting treatment is very much in doubt especially when a competent patient has not specifically refused treatment.

Mere Semantic Distinction?

At the moral level, some recognize the difference between killing and omitting or ceasing treatment. Others insist that this kind of distinction is mere semantics, because in either case the result is that the patient dies. Yet, if we were given the choice of turning off a respirator to allow a terminal patient to die or actively injecting an embolism, almost all of us would choose the first act, at least barring some extenuating circumstances which changed the moral calculations, such as the presence of extreme intractable pain and suffering.

"Half of the physicians in one study would exercise the choice not to prolong life if it were made legal."

There are two kinds of cases in which the distinction would make an actual difference. The first is when the prognosis had been in error and merely ceasing certain treatment could result in continued living, while active killing would result in death. The second involves the possibility of actual abuse. In any case, the physician should not be put in a position to dispose of unwanted patients. It is argued that for practical, if not moral, reasons, we need to separate active killing from cessation and omission of treatment, recognizing that many physicians favor the latter but not the former. It becomes expedient, then, to adopt a policy which would cover virtually all cases, minimize the chances for error, and be acceptable to a broader public.

It is a sad commentary on the tradition of medical ethics that the question of euthanasia is almost always raised in terms of what the medical professional should decide to do for a terminal patient: Should *he* treat; should *he* omit treatment; should *he* stop treatment; should *he* inject the embolism? Yet, there is another perspective: that of the patient. While the legal and moral status of killing and allowing a patient to die may be dubious, the principle of the right to refuse treatment is well recognized. It is morally and legally sound to emphasize the role of the patient as decision-maker when he is legally competent. Of course, this still

leaves open cases when the patient is not legally competent, but at least we have a moral and legal foundation from which to form a policy. The next step would be to decide upon an appropriate agent for the legally incompetent patient.

Patient Advocate

First priority should go to an agent whom the patient, while competent, would be permitted to appoint expressly for this purpose. When this has not been done, the next of kin should have both the rights and responsibilities to determine what is in the patient's interest. While the potential for abuse exists, the next of kin is in the best position to know the patient's personal values and beliefs upon which treatment-refusing decisions must be based. There would still be the established possibility of going to court to overturn the judgment of the next of kin in case he was acting maliciously or choosing not to prolong the patient's living rather than his dying. But the choice to refuse some death-prolonging treatment should not, in and of itself, be taken as evidence of immoral or illegal activity. In that rare case where no relatives are available, a court-appointed guardian might provide the best safeguard of the patient's interests.

A second distinction that must be clarified in a policy permitting the choice not to prolong dying is the difference between ordinary and extraordinary means. These terms have three meanings: usual vs. unusual treatment, useful vs. useless treatment, and simply imperative vs. elective treatment. The Catholic tradition as summarized by Pope Pius XII is: "Normally one is held to use only ordinary means—according to circumstances of persons, places, times, and culture—that is to say, means that do not involve any grave burden for oneself or another." Clearly, defining what is ordinary according to the circumstances named will make the distinction a difficult one. We can circumvent this entire quagmire simply by focusing on the moral principle of the right to refuse treatment as a basis for policy. This does not mean that it will always be moral to refuse treatment, but if patient freedom and dignity are to be central to policy decision, we may have to recognize that patients are entitled to make their own decisions and, therefore, to refuse even those treatments which are thought to be usual or useful. This might be the case when, for instance, a patient faces a lifetime hemodialysis regimen for chronic nephritis. Recently, such a patient decided that the thought of being attached by tubes for 16 to 24 hours a week for the rest of his life was an unbearable and dehumanizing possibility. He chose, we think morally and legally, to cease the dialysis treatment.

Third, it is important to distinguish between the choice not to prolong dying and the choice not to prolong living. Two closely related cases, which I have encountered recently reveal the difference. In the first, a baby was born with trisomy-18 and severe respiratory distress as well as gross CNS anomalies. He would not live no matter what heroic procedures were attempted. A second case was that of a mongoloid infant who had been born with esophageal atresia. The choice of the parents to refuse corrective surgery for the atresia was, in fact, the choice that the quality of life as a mongoloid would not be satisfactory either for the infant or his parents. On the other hand, the choice to cease respiration for the trisomy-18 baby was made when there was nothing that man could do to save the infant's life.

Any policy, which is adopted must come to terms with these distinctions, for it may be morally and legally acceptable to reject an unusually heroic and probably useless procedure but wrong, at least morally, to refuse a simple IV when it would lead relatively painlessly to many years of normal healthy life. It may be wrong to decide that someone else's life is not worth living but acceptable to recognize that even the forces of modern science are not able to cope with some diseases.

Some authorities say that we cannot adopt a systematic policy which would permit the choice not to prolong dying. The physician's duty, they feel, is to preserve life. When some treatment can be offered, even for a patient who is almost certainly going to die, that treatment *must* be offered. Even if this view is correct, it is utopian and one which few clinicians would be able to accept if taken literally as a practical way of dealing with death. We must stop the heroic procedures at some point. If the only course available for a patient in his last days is to fly him and the medical team around the country to try some newly devised experimental surgery, at least some will say that morally we are not required to proceed or, in fact, that it would be wrong to proceed. At some time, the decision must be made that the dying process has been tampered with long enough and that there is nothing more that man can or should do.

Physician *Ad Hoc* Decision-Making

Four policy alternatives are currently being debated. The first is the defense of the status quo: We should have no policy at all. In fact, right now we do have a policy—the individual physician decides, on an *ad hoc* basis at the moment when the patient is in a terminal condition, if and when treatment should be given. This is sometimes done in consultation with other members of the medical team, members of the family, and the clergyman, but, for the most part, the real decision rests in the doctor's hands.

A strong case can be made for the present policy. At least ideally, if not in practice, the physician knows the patient's condition and is committed to his best interest. Every doctor is aware that each medical case is unique, and to develop more systematic

decision-making procedures could be very dangerous. Nevertheless, it seems to me that the present policy is the second worst of all possible alternatives. We have aleady seen that about half of the physicians in one study would exercise the choice not to prolong life if it were clearly made legal. There is also a difference of opinion among patients. A random pairing of patient and physician views would mean that if the physician is making the decision, in many cases the patient who would not want the dying prolonged will have this done against his wishes; another patient who desperately desires the last heroic operation will not receive it.

"This living will. . .frees the physician from having to guess what the patient's wishes might be."

It may be even worse. There may be systematic differences between the medical professionals and the laymen. Many physicians claim that their special ethical duty is to preserve life. If the physicians have different ethical principles or even if they merely have different ethical judgments about what benefits the patient, it creates a terrible dilemma.

Even if physician and patient would reach the identical conclusion, the patient's freedom and dignity in matters most directly affecting his own living and dying would still be infringed upon. All of these objections have led to the search for other methods of decision-making.

The Professional Committee

In an attempt to take the burden off the shoulders of the individual physician, a growing number of hospitals now use committees of physicians to decide who should receive the last bed in the intensive care unit or the scarce and expensive hemodialysis treatment. The committee eliminates some of the random biases which an individual physician might have either in favor of excessively heroic intervention or inadequate treatment. Yet, is it right that a patient whose position is at one extreme or the other should have his own views moderated? Particularly if there are systematic differences between the professional and lay communities? Even the committee structure would impose upon many patients views which they find unacceptable.

This serious drawback to the committee must be added to the more obvious problem—that with the committee-making structure one loses the primary advantage of decision-making by the individual physician. While, hopefully, he would know some details of the patient's life and values, we cannot hope that this would hold true for the committee. Even more significantly, the committee mechanism perpetuates the view that the medical professional by his training has somehow acquired expertise in making the moral judgment about when it is no longer appropriate to prolong dying. If the committee structure is the alternative, perhaps we should stay with the status quo and let the individual physician make the choice unhindered and unguided.

Personal Letters

Other alternatives are beginning to appear. The Euthanasia Educational Fund has drafted a letter which an individual might address to his family physician, clergyman or lawyer. It directs that ''if the time comes when I can no longer take part in decisions for my own future, [and] if there is no reasonable expectation of my recovery from physical or mental disability, I request that I be allowed to die and not be kept alive by artificial means or heroic measures.'' This ''living will'' makes no pretense of being legally binding. It merely gives guidance to the physician and others concerned. It also frees the physician from having to guess what the patient's wishes might be.

"It is important to distinguish between the choice not to prolong dying and the choice not to prolong living."

The instructions are extremely vague, however, and while useful for general guidance, do not go very far in removing the difficulties of earlier proposals. For example, ''reasonable expectation'' and ''artificial means or heroic measures'' beg for clarification, and it is the reader of the will who will have to interpret. For this reason, we know of two physicians who have drafted very specific letters as instruction for their own terminal care. One instructs ''in the event of a cerebral accident other than a subarachnoid hemorrhage, I want no treatment of any kind until it is clear that I will be able to think effectively.... In the event of a subarachnoid hemorrhage, use your own judgment in the acute state....'' The other directs that there be no artificial respiration ''to prolong my life if I had lost the ability to breathe for more than two or three (not five or six) minutes.'' While possibily more specific than the ''living will,'' these instructions may not be of much help to the layman. He simply does not have the technical knowledge to be so precise.

In either case, the idea of a letter pre-addressed to one's personal physician assumes that one has a personal physician. This, unfortunately, is not always the case. Also required is that one be dying in the care of the physician to whom the letter is sent. Carrying the letter in a wallet might help, but certainly will not do much to relieve the anxiety of the potentially dying patient. Even if one assumes that a personal physician will be caring for the dying patient, the letter still requires trust and understanding. This can no longer be assumed, but if such a relationship does exist, the need for the letter decreases in proportion.

Legislation Needed

All of these problems have instigated legislative proposals which would give clearer procedures for the decision not to prolong dying. In 1969 a bill patterned after the British euthanasia legislative proposal was introduced into the Idaho legislature. It explicitly included both ''positive'' and ''negative'' actions and received very little support in this country. Rep. Walter Sackett, himself a physician, has placed several proposals before the Florida legislature. One bill, which was introduced in 1970 but did not pass, would have permitted an individual to execute a document specifying that ''his life shall not be prolonged beyond the point of a meaningful existence.'' If the patient himself cannot execute the document, the bill provided that the person of the next degree of kinship could. While this bill would have eliminated some of the problems of other proposals, the vagueness of the term ''meaningful existence'' is its critical flaw. The physician on the case presumably would be forced to determine whether or not the patient's life could ever again be meaningful.

A third type of legislation, to be based on the already existing right of the patient to refuse treatment, is worthy of consideration as a public policy. In cases where the patient is not competent, some agent must make the decision on the patient's behalf—that is an unpleasant reality of life. It seems to me that an agent appointed by the patient while competent should have first priority, then the next of kin, and finally, in the rare case where the patient has no relatives, a court-appointed agent.

The physician would thus be protected from having to make a non-medical, moral judgment about what is right for the patient. At the same time, the patient and his family would be able to fulfill their rights and obligations to look after the patient's welfare. Anything short of this will deprive the patient of life, liberty and probably happiness as well.

These four types of policy proposals will be receiving much more attention in the next few months. None of them is a panacea; each raises serious moral and public policy questions. But the chaos generated by biomedical technology's assault on death demands new policy clarification. That new policy will be forthcoming soon. It must be.

Robert M. Veatch, Ph.D., is a professor of medical ethics at the Kennedy Institute of Ethics in Washington, D.C.

"Nutrition and hydration are neither ordinary nor extraordinary medical treatments, for they are aspects of normal care and are basic necessities of life."

Intravenous Feedings Should Be Mandatory

Robert Barry

Because of two court cases in recent months, there is good reason to believe that this country has drawn quite a bit closer to the legalization of euthanasia.... Final action in both of these cases is still pending, but concern is especially justified because if the second of these cases turns out wrong, then principles could be established that would put the bedridden, senile, retarded and mentally ill at risk. The legalization of passive euthanasia in these cases could open the door to legal endorsement of practices that we cannot now imagine.

A few months ago, a California Court of Appeals held that the removal of intravenously administered fluids and nutrition from a man who was diagnosed by a board-certified neurologist to be unconscious, but not terminally ill, irreversibly unconscious or brain dead was done in accord with what the court considered to be current accepted standards of medical practice, and the physicians who withheld care from the man could not be prosecuted.

Dim Hope of Recovery

Clarence Herbert, a 55-year-old race track guard, entered Kaiser-Permanente Hospital in Los Angeles for routine surgery; he lapsed into unconsciousness in the recovery room after the operation. Medical records indicated that less than three days after Herbert fell into unconsciousness his two physicians obtained consent from his family to remove the respirator. He continued to breathe normally when the respirator was withdrawn. Familial consent was obtained later to remove what the physicians described to be medical treatments, and six days after he lapsed into unconsciousness, an intravenous feeding tube was disconnected. Six days after its removal, Herbert succumbed to dehydration.

Robert Barry, "Euthanasia and the Church," *Catholicism in Crisis*, February 1984. Reprinted with permission.

Remarkably, the medical records indicated that the neurologist summoned in the hospital to the case originally diagnosed Herbert's prospects for recovery to full neurological functioning to be only dim, but not hopeless. Only two days before he died did the neurologist change his diagnosis from a dim prospect of recovery to a hopeless one because the patient had been without fluids and nutrition for so long. But had Herbert been given fluids and nutrition, he would have been brain damaged, and for that reason, he had to die.

When Clarence Herbert was dehydrated to death, he had an 8 to 12% chance of recovery to full neurological functioning. One particularly important study of patients similar to Herbert found that at the end of one month after insult to the brain, 57% had died, 11% were irreversibly unconscious, 20% were severely disabled, 4% were moderately disabled and 8% had recovered fully. In short, if Herbert had survived another two and a half weeks, his chances for being either irreversibly unconscious or normal would have been about equal. And on the day on which the respirator was abruptly removed, he was in a category of patients that had a 35% chance of good recovery.

Never Acceptable

The principle endorsed by the appeals court in this case is remarkable, for Herbert was denied food and water when sound professional judgment declared him to be unconscious, but not brain dead or terminally ill. The action of the doctors went far beyond what the guidelines for treatment withdrawal issued by the Judicial Council of the American Medical Association would allow, for they only allow fluids and nutrition to be removed from patients who have been diagnosed as brain dead or irreversibly unconscious. What the physicians did in this case is clearly opposed to Church teachings, for the *Declaration on Euthanasia* issued by the Sacred

Congregation for the Doctrine of the Faith holds that normal care, which include food and water, are to be given even to terminally ill patients. And in spite of what the appeals court declared, it has never been an accepted standard of medical practice to dehydrate to death one who is merely unconscious.

The appeals court decision in the Herbert case is quite important for two reasons. First, it could very well establish, at least in California, a standard of practice that would allow physicians to remove nutrition and fluids from patients who are unconscious. Despite the guidelines approved by the Judicial Council, the American Medical Association did not object to what the physicians did, but only suggested that they acted precipitously. Second, before this opinion, prosecutors could intervene in cases where food and water were withdrawn from patients under the assumption that an act of this nature could only be done with a malicious intent. But the holding of the court that the removal of fluids and nutrition from a patient who was only unconscious was lawful, effectively prohibits prosecutors from intervening under the assumption that this act was done maliciously.

Too Much Attention to Ethics

An extremely important role in this decision was played by Fr. John Paris who testified at length that what the physicians did was fully in accord with the teachings of the Church. Fr. Paris has done extensive consultative work for the American Medical Association, and this past summer he moderated the Ethics Committee conference for the *Concern for Dying* Education Council, the successor of the Euthanasia Education Council of America, one of the oldest euthanasia propoganda organizations in the nation. Without this priest's testimony, the verdict on the Herbert case might well have been different, for the trial judge was later criticized for paying too much attention to ethics and not enough to the law.

"It has never been an accepted standard of medical practice to dehydrate to death one who is merely unconscious."

The appeals court decision in the Herbert case has significantly advanced the legalization of the practice of euthanasia, and the other case mentioned earlier could take this approach even further. Recently, the Supreme Court of New Jersey agreed to review a case involving the removal of a nasogastric feeding tube from an elderly woman who was not terminally ill, irreversibly unconscious, brain dead, in intractable pain, *or even unconscious.* Claire Conroy was merely a sick 84 year-old woman who suffered from diabetes and ulcers on her feet that turned gangrenous. She

was admitted to Claire Maas Memorial Hospital in Newark when the gangrene developed, and she was then placed on a nasogastric feeding tube because she had lost her ability to swallow. The feeding tube was all that she needed to survive, and she received no other medical treatments. Even though sometimes confused, she could move her hands, arms and head, was aware of other people and often smiled when people massaged her.

A Burdensome Life

Her nephew, who earlier refused to consent to treating the ulcers on her feet, petitioned the court to remove the nasogastric tube, and the trial judge agreed on the grounds that she had permanently lost her ability to swallow and because he believed that her life had supposedly become "impossibly burdensome" to her. However, before the tube could be removed, she succumbed to other causes. The trial judge's decision was appealed and a three-judge panel reversed the trial judge's decision. They held that the tube should not have been removed because it was only a minor intrusion which did not outweigh the compelling interest of the state in the protection of human life. The appeals court found that Miss Conroy was not different from thousands of other senile, retarded, mentally ill or bed-ridden patients who need only a feeding tube to survive.

The New Jersey Supreme Court agreed to review this case and settle the issue once and for all. If the trial judge's opinion should be upheld, a major victory for those promoting euthanasia would be won. Such a holding would allow physicians, at least in New Jersey, to starve or dehydrate people to death on the theory that their lives are "impossibly burdensome." A further consequence of such a judgment might be that the authority of the *Quinlan* decision could be replaced and overcome. The *Quinlan* case set something of a national standard of medical practice, and if it was effectively overturned by allowing food and water to be removed when life has been declared to be "impossibly burdensome" then a new nationwide standard of practice could develop from it.

Nutrition Is Not a Treatment

The appeals court in the Conroy case contended that nutrition and hydration were not medical treatments, but were only aspects of basic care that were not to be withdrawn if so doing would cause death. Food and water are not known to be therapies for any known pathological conditions. No medical school teaches that hunger and thirst are pathological conditions in and of themselves, even though extended deprivation of either of these can cause serious medical conditions. Administration of nutrition and fluids intravenously or nasogastrically does not make them medical treatments, for if the mode of administration constituted something as a medical treatment, then taking pills would not be a medical treatment because they are taken in the same way that peanuts and popcorn are taken. Medical treatments remedy diseases and pathological conditions, and conditions of hunger and thirst have never been diagnosed as diseases, even though prolonged lack of these can radically weaken one's resistance to a large number of diseases. . . .

Nutrition and hydration are neither ordinary nor extraordinary medical treatments, for they are aspects of normal care and are basic necessities of life that are to be given whenever they can achieve their proper objectives.

From the viewpoint of Catholics, these two cases are interesting because the testimony of Catholic moralists was critical in the decisions to remove fluids and nutrition from Herbert and Conroy. For in the Conroy case, the trial judge was greatly impressed by the testimony of Fr. Joseph Kukura who testified that the feeding tube should have been removed. And Fr. John Paris testified that what the two physicians did to Herbert was fully in accord with Church teachings. Why is it that, all of a sudden, Catholic priests who favor certain moral viewpoints, are being summoned to testify in court and are having such extraordinary influence on the practice of medicine? For years, the medical professional has appeared to care little for what Catholic ethicists have said, and yet now they are becoming very important and influential. There are hundreds of philosophers who have as much expertise in these areas as do Catholic clergy, and one has to wonder why Catholic clergy are being called on to play such important roles at this time. It is even more curious because nothing like this happened in the abortion cases of the past decade. The answer to these questions seems to lie in the fact that Roman Catholic ethical principles pose the strongest and most coherent opposition to the legalization of euthanasia in all of its forms. If euthanasia is to be legalized, its advocates must show that there is a social consensus in favor of it, and at the present time the most serious opposition comes from the Church. If proponents of euthanasia can show courts that Catholic teachings either do not object to or support various practices of euthanasia, they can then argue that there is a social consensus on the issue, and the courts will then probably allow the practice. To show that there is a social consensus, euthanasia activists only have to silence the opposition of the Church. But if they can get influential Catholic moralists to support their views, then they will have won an even greater victory.

Euthanasia Is Unacceptable

Many in our country now believe that withdrawing fluids and nutrition from the unconscious, bedridden, mentally retarded and disabled is a humane, compassionate, caring and even Christian thing to do.

But to gain full legal endorsement for some of these practices, euthanasia proponents must show that it is also a "Catholic" practice. Up until the present time, we owed a debt to Adolf Hitler and the Nazis, for they gave euthanasia such a terrible name that no one seriously thought of it as being socially acceptable. But it now seems that their influence has waned and that there are some who view these practices as humane, compassionate, caring, Christian and even Catholic.

"Normal care, which include food and water, are to be given even to terminally ill patients."

If the Church does not remain silent on this issue, it will be difficult for the courts of this nation to endorse practices of euthanasia on the grounds that there is a social consensus that favors it. It is therefore imperative that the objections of the Church to these practices continue to be voiced. Removing food and water from those who are bedridden, unconscious, mentally retarded or handicapped or merely infirm is not an act of love but is the moral equivalent of denying a cup of water or a morsel of food to one who is in need.

Father Robert Barry is with the Dominican community in St. Louis, Missouri.

"Nutrition and hydration by medical means need not always be provided."

Intravenous Feedings Should Be Optional

Joanne Lynn and James F. Childress

Many people die from the lack of food or water. For some, this lack is the result of poverty or famine, but for others it is the result of disease or deliberate decision. In the past, malnutrition and dehydration must have accompanied nearly every death that followed an illness of more than a few days. Most dying patients do not eat much on their own, and nothing could be done for them until the first flexible tubing for instilling food or other liquid into the stomach was developed about a hundred years ago. Even then, the procedure was so scarce, so costly in physician and nursing time, and so poorly tolerated that it was used only for patients who clearly could benefit. With the advent of more reliable and efficient procedures in the past few decades, these conditions can be corrected or ameliorated in nearly every patient who would otherwise be malnourished or dehydrated. In fact, intravenous lines and nasogastric tubes have become common images of hospital care.

Providing adequate nutrition and fluids is a high priority for most patients, both because they suffer directly from inadequacies and because these deficiencies hinder their ability to overcome other diseases. But are there some patients who need not receive these treatments? This question has become a prominent public policy issue in a number of recent cases. In May 1981, in Danville, Illinois, the parents and the physician of newborn conjoined twins with shared abdominal organs decided not to feed these children. Feeding and other treatments were given after court intervention, though a grand jury refused to indict the parents. Later that year, two physicians in Los Angeles discontinued intravenous nutrition to a patient who had severe brain damage after an episode involving loss of oxygen following routine surgery. Murder charges were brought, but the hearing judge dismissed the charges at a preliminary hearing. On appeal, the charges were reinstated and remanded for trial.

Denying Fluids to an Infant

In April 1982, a Bloomington, Indiana, infant who had tracheoesophageal fistula and Down syndrome was not treated or fed, and he died after two courts ruled that the decision was proper but before all appeals could be heard. When the federal government then moved to ensure that such infants would be fed in the future, the Surgeon General, Dr. C. Everett Koop, initially stated that there is never adequate reason to deny nutrition and fluids to a newborn infant.

While these cases were before the public, the nephew of Claire Conroy, an elderly incompetent woman with several serious medical problems, petitioned a New Jersey court for authority to discontinue her nasogastric tube feedings. Although the intermediate appeals court has reversed the ruling, the trial court held that he had this authority since the evidence indicated that the patient would not have wanted such treatment and that its value to her was doubtful.

In all these dramatic cases and in many more that go unnoticed, the decision is made to deliberately withhold food or fluid known to be necessary for the life of the patient. Such decisions are unsettling. There is now widespread consensus that sometimes a patient is best served by not undertaking or continuing certain treatments that would sustain life, especially if these entail substantial suffering. . . .

The Medical Procedures

There is no reason to apply a different standard to feeding and hydration. Surely, when one inserts a feeding tube, or creates a gastrostomy opening, or inserts a needle into a vein, one intends to benefit the

Joanne Lynn and James F. Childress, ''Must Patients Always Be Given Food and Water?'' *The Hastings Center Report,* October 1983. Reproduced with permission of *The Hastings Center Report,* (c) Institute of Society, Ethics and the Life Sciences, 360 Broadway, Hastings-on-Hudson, MY 10706.

patient. Ideally, one should provide what the patient believes to be of benefit, but at least the effect should be beneficial in the opinions of surrogates and caregivers.

Thus, the question becomes: is it ever in the patient's interest to become malnourished and dehydrated, rather than to receive treatment? Posing the question so starkly points to our need to know what is entailed in treating these conditions and what benefits the treatments offer.

Nasogastric Tube

The medical interventions that provide food and fluids are of two basic types. First, liquids can be delivered by a tube that is inserted into a functioning gastrointestinal tract, most commonly through the nose and esophagus into the stomach or through a surgical incision in the abdominal wall and directly into the stomach. The liquids used can be specially prepared solutions of nutrients or a blenderized version of an ordinary diet. The nasogastric tube is cheap; it may lead to pneumonia and often annoys the patient and family, sometimes even requiring that the patient be restrained to prevent its removal.

Creating a gastrostomy is usually a simple surgical procedure, and, once the wound is healed, care is very simple. Since it is out of sight, it is aesthetically more acceptable and restraints are needed less often. Also, the gastrostomy creates no additional risk of pneumonia. However, while elimination of a nasogastric tube requires only removing the tube, a gastrostomy is fairly permanent, and can be closed only by surgery.

The Peripheral IV

The second type of medical intervention is intravenous feeding and hydration, which also has two major forms. The ordinary hospital or peripheral IV, in which fluid is delivered directly to the bloodstream through a small needle, is useful only for temporary efforts to improve hydration and electrolyte concentrations. One cannot provide a balanced diet through the veins in the limbs: to do that requires a central line, or a special catheter placed into one of the major veins in the chest. The latter procedure is much more risky and vulnerable to infections and technical errors, and it is much more costly than any of the other procedures. Both forms of intravenous nutrition and hydration commonly require restraining the patient, cause minor infections and other ill effects, and are costly, especially since they ordinarily require the patient to be in a hospital.

None of these procedures, then, is ideal; each entails some distress, some medical limitations, and some costs. When may a procedure be foregone that might improve nutrition and hydration for a given patient? Only when the procedure and the resulting improvement in nutrition and hydration do not offer the patient a net benefit over what he or she would otherwise have faced.

Are there such circumstances? We believe that there are; but they are few and limited to the following three kinds of situations: 1. The procedures that would be required are so unlikely to achieve improved nutritional and fluid levels that they could be correctly considered futile; 2. The improvement in nutritional and fluid balance, though achievable, could be of no benefit to the patient; 3. The burdens of receiving the treatment may outweigh the benefit.

Futile Treatment

Sometimes even providing "food and water" to a patient becomes a monumental task. Consider a patient with a severe clotting deficiency and a nearly total body burn. Gaining access to the central veins is likely to cause hemorrhage or infection, nasogastric tube placement may be quite painful, and there may be no skin to which to suture the stomach for a gastrostomy tube. Or consider a patient with severe congestive heart failure who develops cancer of the stomach with a fistula that delivers food from the stomach to the colon without passing through the intestine and being absorbed. Feeding the patient may be possible, but little is absorbed. Intravenous feeding cannot be tolerated because the fluid would be too much for the weakened heart. Or consider the infant with infarction of all but a short segment of bowel. Again, the infant can be fed, but little if anything is absorbed. Intravenous methods can be used, but only for a short time (weeks or months) until their complications, including thrombosis, hemorrhage, infections, and malnutrition, cause death.

"Efforts to provide nutrition and hydration may well directly cause suffering that offers no counterbalancing benefit for the patient."

In these circumstances, the patient is going to die soon, no matter what is done. The ineffective efforts to provide nutrition and hydration may well directly cause suffering that offers no counterbalancing benefit for the patient. Although the procedures might be tried, especially if the competent patient wanted them or the incompetent patient's surrogate had reason to believe that this incompetent patient would have wanted them, they cannot be considered obligatory. To hold that a patient must be subjected to this predictably futile sort of intervention just because protein balance is negative or the blood serum is concentrated is to lose sight of the moral warrant for medical care and to reduce the patient to an array of measurable variables.

Some patients can be reliably diagnosed to have permanently lost consciousness. This unusual group of patients includes those with anencephaly, persistent vegetative state, and some preterminal comas. In these cases, it is very difficult to discern how any medical intervention can benefit or harm the patient. These patients cannot and never will be able to experience any of the events occurring in the world or in their bodies. When the diagnosis is exceedingly clear, we sustain their lives vigorously mainly for their loved ones and the community at large.

"The patient will be served best by not using medical procedures to provide food and fluids."

While these considerations probably indicate that continued artificial feeding is best in most cases, there may be some cases in which the family and the caregivers are convinced that artificial feeding is offensive and unreasonable. In such cases, there seems to be no adequate reason to claim that withholding food and water violates any obligations that these parties or the general society have with regard to permanently unconscious patients. Thus, if the parents of an anencephalic infant or of a patient like Karen Quinlan in a persistent vegetative state feel strongly that no medical procedures should be applied to provide nutrition and hydration, and the caregivers are willing to comply, there should be no barrier in law or public policy to thwart the plan.

Disproportionate Burden

The most difficult cases are those in which normal nutritional status or fluid balance could be restored, but only with a severe burden for the patient. In these cases, the treatment is futile in a broader sense—the patient will not actually benefit from the improved nutrition and hydration. A patient who is competent can decide the relative merits of the treatment being provided, knowing the probable consequences, and weighing the merits of life under various sets of strained circumstances. But a surrogate decision maker for a patient who is incompetent to decide will have a difficult task. When the situation is irremediably ambiguous, erring on the side of continued life and improved nutrition and hydration seems the less grievous error. But are there situations that would warrant a determination that this patient, whose nutrition and hydration could surely be improved, is not thereby well served?

Though they are rare, we believe there are such cases. The treatments entailed are not benign. Their effects are far short of ideal. Furthermore, many of the patients most likely to have inadequate food and fluid intake are also likely to suffer the most serious side effects of these therapies.

Dying Comfortably

Patients who are allowed to die without artificial hydration and nutrition may well die more comfortably than patients who receive conventional amounts of intravenous hydration. Terminal pulmonary edema, nausea, and mental confusion are more likely when patients have been treated to maintain fluid and nutrition until close to the time of death.

Thus, those patients whose "need" for artificial nutrition and hydration arises only near the time of death may be harmed by its provision. It is not at all clear that they receive any benefit in having a slightly prolonged life, and it does seem reasonable to allow a surrogate to decide that, for this patient at this time, slight prolongation of life is not warranted if it involves measures that will probably increase the patient's suffering as he or she dies.

Even patients who might live much longer might not be well served by artificial means to provide fluid and food. Such patients might include those with fairly severe dementia for whom the restraints required could be a constant source of fear, discomfort, and struggle. For such a patient, sedation to tolerate the feeding mechanisms might preclude any of the pleasant experiences that might otherwise have been available. Thus, a decision not to intervene, except perhaps briefly to ascertain that there are no treatable causes, might allow such a patient to live out a shorter life with fair freedom of movement and freedom from fear, while a decision to maintain artificial nutrition and hydration might consign the patient to end his or her life in unremitting anguish. If this were the case a surrogate decision maker would seem to be well justified in refusing the treatment. . . .

Obligation to Provide "Ordinary" Care

Debates about appropriate medical treatment are often couched in terms of "ordinary" and "extraordinary" means of treatment. Historically, this distinction emerged in the Roman Catholic tradition to differentiate optional treatment from treatment that was obligatory for medical professionals to offer and for patients to accept. These terms also appear in many secular contexts, such as court decisions and medical codes. The recent debates about ordinary and extraordinary means of treatment have been interminable and often unfruitful, in part because of a lack of clarity about what the terms mean. Do they represent the premises of an argument or the conclusion, and what features of a situation are relevant to the categorization as "ordinary" or "extraordinary"?

Several criteria have been implicit in debates about

ordinary and extraordinary means of treatment; some of them may be relevant to determining whether and which treatments are obligatory and which are optional. Treatments have been distinguished according to their simplicity (simple/complex), their naturalness (natural/artificial), their customariness (usual/unusual), their invasiveness (noninvasive/invasive), their chance of success (reasonable chance/futile), their balance of benefits and burdens (proportionate/disproportionate), and their expense (inexpensive/costly). Each set of paired terms or phrases in the parentheses suggests a continuum: as the treatment moves from the first of the paired terms to the second, it is said to become less obligatory and more optional.

However, when these various criteria, widely used in discussions about medical treatment, are carefully examined, most of them are not morally relevant in distinguishing optional from obligatory medical treatments. For example, if a rare, complex, artificial, and invasive treatment offers a patient a reasonable chance of nearly painless cure, then one would have to offer a substantial justification not to provide that treatment to an incompetent patient.

Worthwhile Benefits

What matters, then, in determining whether to provide a treatment to an incompetent patient is not a prior determination that this treatment is "ordinary" per se, but rather a determination that this treatment is likely to provide this patient benefits that are sufficient to make it worthwhile to endure the burdens that accompany the treatment. To this end, some of the considerations listed above are relevant: whether a treatment is likely to succeed is an obvious example. But such considerations taken in isolation are not conclusive. Rather, the surrogate decision maker is obliged to assess the desirability to this patient of each of the options presented, including nontreatment. For most people at most times, this assessment would lead to a clear obligation to provide food and fluids.

But sometimes, as we have indicated, providing food and fluids through medical interventions may fail to benefit and may even harm some patients. Then the treatment cannot be said to be obligatory, no matter how usual and simple its provision may be. If "ordinary" and "extraordinary" are used to convey the conclusion about the obligation to treat, providing nutrition and fluids would have become, in these cases, "extraordinary." Since this phrasing is misleading, it is probably better to use "proportionate" and "disproportionate" as the Vatican now suggests, or "obligatory" and "optional."

Obviously, providing nutrition and hydration may sometimes be necessary to keep patients comfortable while they are dying even though it may temporarily prolong their dying. In such cases, food and fluids constitute warranted palliative care. But in other cases, such as a patient in a deep and irreversible coma, nutrition and hydration do not appear to be needed or helpful, except perhaps to comfort the staff and family. And sometimes the interventions needed for nutrition and hydration are so burdensome that they are harmful and best not utilized.

Obligation to Continue Treatment

Once having started a mode of treatment, many caregivers find it very difficult to discontinue it. While this strongly felt difference between the ease of withholding a treatment and the difficulty of withdrawing it provides a psychological explanation of certain actions, it does not justify them. It sometimes even leads to a thoroughly irrational decision process. For example, in caring for a dying, comatose patient, many physicians apparently find it harder to stop a functioning peripheral IV than not to restart one that has infiltrated (that is, has broken through the blood vessel and is leaking fluid into surrounding tissue), especially if the only way to re-establish an IV would be to insert a central line into the heart or to do a cutdown (make an incision to gain access to the deep large blood vessels). . . .

"A decision to maintain artificial nutrition and hydration might consign the patient to end his or her life in unremitting anguish."

We do not have enough information to be able to determine with clarity and conviction whether withholding or withdrawing nutrition and hydration was justified in the cases that have occasioned public concern, though it seems likely that the Danville and Bloomington babies should have been fed and that Claire Conroy should not.

It is never sufficient to rule out "starvation" categorically. The question is whether the obligation to act in the patient's best interests was discharged by withholding or withdrawing particular medical treatments. All we have claimed is that nutrition and hydration by medical means need not always be provided. Sometimes they may not be in accord with the patient's wishes or interests. Medical nutrition and hydration do not appear to be distinguishable in any morally relevant way from other life-sustaining medical treatments that may on occasion be withheld or withdrawn.

Joanne Lynn, M.D., is on the staff of the division of geriatric medicine at George Washington University. She was an assistant director of the President's Commission for the Study of Ethical Problems in Medicine. James F. Childress, Ph.D., is commonwealth professor of religious studies and medical education at the University of Virginia.

"The question as to whether a person has the right to cope with the pain in his world by killing himself can be answered without hesitation. He does have that right."

viewpoint **33**

Suicide Is an Individual's Right

Jerome A. Motto

To speak as a psychiatrist may suggest to some that psychiatrists have a certain way of looking at things. This would be a misconception, though a common one. I know of no professional group with more diverse approaches to those matters concerning it than the American psychiatric community. All physicians, however, including psychiatrists, share a tradition of commitment to both the preservation and the quality of human life. With this one reservation, I speak as a psychiatrist strictly in the singular sense.

The emergence of thoughts or impulses to bring an end to life is a phenomenon observed in persons experiencing severe pain, whether that pain stems from physical or emotional sources. Thus physicians, to whom persons are inclined to turn for relief from suffering, frequently encounter suicidal ideas and impulses in their patients. Those who look and listen do, at least.

From a psychiatric point of view, the question as to whether a person has the right to cope with the pain in his world by killing himself can be answered without hesitation. He does have that right. With a few geographical exceptions the same can be said from the legal and social point of view as well. It is only when philosophical or theological questions are raised that one can find room for argument about the right to suicide, as only in these areas can restrictions on behavior be institutionalized without requiring social or legal support.

The problem we struggle with is not whether the individual *has* the right to suicide; rather, we face a twofold dilemma stemming from the fact that he does have it. Firstly, what is the extent to which the exercise of that right should be subject to limitations? Secondly, when the right is exercised, how can we eliminate the social stigma now attached to it?

Jerome A. Motto, "The Right to Suicide," *Life Threatening Behavior*, Vol. 2, No. 3, Fall 1972. Copyright © 1972 by Human Sciences Press, Inc., 72 Fifth Avenue, New York, NY 10011. Reprinted with permission.

Limitations on the Individual's Right

Putting limitations on rights is certainly not a new idea, since essentially every right we exercise has its specified restrictions. It is generally taken for granted that certain limitations must be observed. In spite of this, it is inevitable that some will take the position that unless the right is unconditional it is not "really" granted.

I use two psychological criteria as grounds for limiting a person's exercise of his right to suicide: *(a)* the act must be based on a realistic assessment of his life situation, and *(b)* the degree of ambivalence regarding the act must be minimal. Both of these criteria clearly raise a host of new questions.

Realistic Assessment of Life Situation

What is reality? Who determines whether a realistic assessment has been made? Every person's perception is reality to *him,* and the degree of pain experienced by one can never be fully appreciated by another, no matter how empathetic he is. Differences in capacity to *tolerate* pain add still another crucial yet unmeasurable element.

As formidable as this sounds, the psychiatrist is obliged to accept this task as his primary day-to-day professional responsibility, whether or not the issue of suicide is involved. With an acute awareness of how emotions can--like lenses--distort perceptions which in turn shape one's thoughts and actions, and with experience in understanding and dealing with this underlying substrate of emotion, he is constantly working with his patients on the process of differentiating between what is realistic and what is distorted. The former must be dealt with on a rational level; the latter must be explored and modified till the distortion is reduced at least to the point where it is not of handicapping severity. He is aware of the nature and extent of his own tendency to distort ("Physician, heal thyself"), and realizes that the entire issue is one of degree. Yet he must use his own perception of reality as a standard, shortcomings notwithstanding, realizing full well how much information must be carefully considered in view of the frailty of the human perceptual and reality-testing apparatus.

Some persons have a view of reality so different from mine that I do not hesitate to interfere with their right to suicide. Others' perceptions are so like mine that I cannot intercede. The big problem is that large group in between.

The Need For Quick Decisions

In the final analysis, then, when a decision has to be made, what a psychiatrist calls "realistic" is whatever looks realistic to *him*. At the moment of truth, that is all any person can offer. This inherent human limitation in itself is a reality that accounts for a great deal of inevitable chaos in the world; it is an article of faith that not to make such an effort would create even greater chaos. On a day-to-day operational level, one contemporary behavioral scientist expressed it this way: "No doubt the daily business of helping troubled individuals including suicides, gives little time for the massive contemplative and investigative efforts which alone can lead to surer knowledge. And the helpers are not thereby to be disparaged. They cannot wait for the best answers conceivable. They must do only the best they can *now*."

"Our most difficult problem is more with the person whose pain is emotional in origin and whose physical health is good."

Thus if I am working with a person in psychotherapy, one limitation I would put on his right to suicide would be that his assessment of his life situation be realistic as *I* see it.

A related concept is that of "rational suicide," which has enjoyed a certain vogue since at least the seventeenth century, when the "Rationalist Era" saw sharp inroads being made into the domination of the church in determining ethical and social values. According to one contemporary philosopher, "the degree of rationality of the [suicidal] act would depend on the degree of rationality of the philosophy which was guiding the person's deliberations." Rationality is defined as a means of problem solving, using "methods such as logical, mathematical, or experimental procedures which have gained men's confidence as reliable tools for guiding instrumental actions." The rationality of one's philosophy is determined by the degree to which it is free of mysticism. Further, "A person who is considering how to act in an intensely conflicting situation cannot

be regarded as making the most rational decision, unless he has been as critical as possible of the philosophy that is guiding his decision. If the philosophy is institutionalized as a political ideology or a religious creed, he must think critically about the institution in order to acquire maximum rationality of judgment. This principle is clear enough, even if in practice it is enormously difficult to fulfill."

Rational Suicide and Realism

The idea of "rational suicide" is a related yet distinctly different issue from the "realistic assessment of one's life situation" referred to above. Making this assessment involves assembling and understanding all the facts clearly, while the idea of a "rational suicide" can only be entertained after this assessment is done and the question is "what to do" in the light of those facts.

The role of the psychiatrist and the thinking of the rationalist tend to merge, at one point, however. In the process of marshaling all the facts and exploring their meaning to the person, the psychiatrist must ensure that the patient does indeed critically examine not only his perception of reality but his own philosophy. This often entails making that philosophy explicit for the first time (without ever using the term "philosophy"), and clarifying how it has influenced his living experience. The implication is clear that modification of the person's view of his world, with corresponding changes in behavior, may lead to a more satisfying life.

The rationalist concedes that where one's philosophy is simply an "intellectual channeling of emotional forces," rational guidelines have severe limitations, since intense emotional conflicts cut off rational guidance. These circumstances would characterize "irrational" grounds for suicide and would identify those persons whose suicide should be prevented....

Problems with Suicide in Healthy People

Our most difficult problem is more with the person whose pain is emotional in origin and whose physical health is good, or at most constitutes a minor impairment. For these persons, the discussion about regarding "rational" and "irrational" distinctions seems rather alien to the clinical situation. This is primarily due to the rationalist's emphasis on intellectual processes, when it is so clear (at least to the psychiatrist) that it is feelings of worthiness of love, of relatedness, of belonging, that have the strongest stabilizing influence on the suicidal person.

I rarely hear a patient say, "I've never looked at it that way," yet no response is more frequently encountered than, "Yes, I understand, but I don't feel any differently." It is after a continuing therapeutic effort during which feelings of acceptance and worthiness are generated that emotional pain is reduced and suicidal manifestations become less intense. Either exploring the philosophy by which one lives or carefully assessing the realities of one's life can provide an excellent means of accomplishing this, but it is rarely the influence of the philosophy or the perception of the realities per se that brings it about. Rather, it is through the influence of the therapeutic relationship that the modified philosophy or perception develops, and can then be applied to the person's life situation.

Manifestations of Ambivalence

The second criterion to be used as the basis for limiting a person's exercise of his right to suicide is minimal ambivalence about ending his life. I make the assumption that if a person has no ambivalence about suicide he will not be in my office, nor write to me about it, nor call me on the telephone. I interpret, rightly or wrongly, a person's calling my attention to his suicidal impulses as a request to intercede that I cannot ignore.

At times this call will inevitably be misread, and my assumption will lead me astray. However, such an error on my part can be corrected at a later time; meanwhile, I must be prepared to take responsibility for having prolonged what may be a truly unendurable existence. If the error is made in the other direction, no opportunity for correction may be possible.

This same principle regarding ambivalence applies to a suicide prevention center, minister, social agency, or a hospital emergency room. The response of the helping agency may be far from fulfilling the needs of the person involved, but in my view, the ambivalence expressed is a clear indication for it to limit the exercise of his right to suicide.

Reducing the Stigma of Suicide

The second horn of our dilemma about the right to suicide is the fact that the suicidal act is not considered respectable in our society. It can be maintained that granting a right but stigmatizing the exercise of that right is tantamount to not having granted it in the first place. In order to develop a realistic approach to this problem it is necessary to reduce the negative social implications attached to it.

The first step is to talk about it freely–with each other, with doctors, ministers, patients, and families. Just as with past taboos—TB, cancer, sex (especially homosexuality), drug addiction, abortion—it will gradually lose the emotional charge of the forbidden. The second step is the continued institutionalization of supportive and treatment services for suicidal persons, through local, state, and federal support.

News media should be responsible for reporting suicidal deaths with dignity and simplicity, without attempting either to cover up or sensationalize pertinent information. In an economically competitive field this would be a reasonable expectation unless it were made part of an accepted ethical code.

Instruction regarding this problem should be provided as a matter of course in the education and training for all health care personnel, emergency services (police, firemen), behavioral sciences (psychology, sociology, anthropology), and those to whom troubled people most often turn, such as ministers, teachers, and counselors, In short, every person who completes the equivalent of a high school education would be provided with an orientation toward the problem of suicide, and those responsible for responding to others in stressful circumstances should be prepared to assist in providing—or at least locating—help when needed.

A question has been raised whether incorporating concern for suicide into our social institutions might depersonalize man to some extent. I would anticipate the contrary. The more our social institutions reflect awareness of and concern for man's inner life and provide means for improving it, the greater is the implied respect for that life–even if this takes the form of providing a dignified means of relinquishing it.

Establishing Procedures

It seems inevitable to me that we must eventually establish procedures for the voluntary cessation of life, with the time, place, and manner largely controlled by the person concerned. It will necessarily involve a series of deliberate steps providing assurance that appropriate criteria are met, such as those proposed above, as we now observe specific criteria when a life is terminated by abortion or by capital punishment.

"News media should be responsible for reporting suicidal deaths with dignity and simplicity."

The critical word is "control." I would anticipate a decrease in the actual number of suicides when this procedure is established, due to the psychological power of this issue. If I know something is available to me and will remain available till I am moved to seize it, the chances of my seizing it now are thereby much reduced. It is only by holding off that I maintain the option of changing my mind. During this period of delay the opportunity for therapeutic effort—and the therapy of time itself—may be used to advantage.

Finally, we have to make sure we are not speaking only to the strong. It is too easy to formulate a way of dealing with a troublesome problem in such a manner, that if the person in question could approach it as we suggest, he would not be a person who would have the problem in the first place.

When we discuss—in the abstract—the right to suicide, we tend to gloss over the intricacies of words like ''freedom,'' quality of life,'' ''choice,'' or even ''help,'' to say nothing of ''rational'' and ''realistic.'' Each of these concepts deserves a full inquiry in itself, though in practice we use them on the tacit assumption that general agreement exists as to their meaning.

Therefore it is we who, in trying to be of service to someone else, have the task of determining what is rational for us, and what our perception of reality is. And we must recognize that in the final analysis it will be not only the suicidal person but we who have exercised a choice, by doing what we do to resolve our feelings about this difficult human problem.

Jerome A. Motto, M.D., is a professor of psychiatry at the University of California School of Medicine at San Francisco and an associate director of its Psychiatric Consultation-Liaison Service. He has had special interest in depressive and suicidal states.

"Few people who attempt suicide simply want to die. What they want is not to live if living means continued suffering."

Suicide Must Always Be Prevented

Ari Kiev

Every year, tens of thousands of Americans take their own lives.

Estimates of the incidence of suicide vary because many suicides are not reported as suicides and it is difficult to ascertain whether certain deaths are accidental or self-inflicted. The most reliable figures, however, place the number of suicides in the United States at between 25,000 and 50,000 per year—with the number constantly on the rise. The number of *attempted* suicides, moreover, may run as high as 250,000 per year! Obviously, suicide has become a public health problem of major gravity.

What kinds of people kill themselves?

When we think of someone taking his or her own life, we commonly imagine a thoroughly isolated individual—a morose, friendless soul with "nothing to live for" and no reason left to keep trying. While this image may fairly accurately describe many suicides, it by no means gives a picture of the range and diversity of suicidal individuals. Suicide is a contemplated or realized option in every stratum of our society, among people in every age group, ethnic cluster, and religion.

People with serious emotional difficulties, alcoholics, and drug-dependent individuals are, not suprisingly, among the most common suicides. But there are also several other classes of people to whom suicide seems especially attractive. These include, ironically, both the very old and the very young.

Suicide Among the Elderly and Young

In a nation where youth is exalted and age is conspicuously ignored, it's not unexpected that the neglected elderly should have high suicide rates. But, so the figures suggest, the dream of youth has provided little comfort to the young; suicide,

shockingly, is the third most common cause of death, after accidents and homicides, among American adolescents. Approximately 5,000 people between the ages of fifteen and twenty-four will kill themselves in this country in this year alone.

In the past twenty years, the incidence of suicide among the young has increased to epidemic proportions. The suicide rates for teenagers (ages fourteen to nineteen) *doubled* between 1960 and 1970—as did the rates for males in their twenties. Among females in their twenties, the rates *quadrupled.* Among American Indian youths and young urban black women, suicide ranks *first* among causes of death.

Why this shocking rise in self-destruction? And what, if anything, can be done about it?

Suicide has only recently come out of the closet, so to speak, to become a possible topic of conversation. Since our research on the subject is still in the early stages, we still face many unanswered questions.

Causes of Suicide

Is suicide, for example, caused by unhappy experiences in life or by a genetic mental imbalance? Is it an act of desperation or one of courage? Is it a radical response to distressing circumstances, or only a cry for attention? Most important, how can the people suffering from the kind of depression that commonly triggers suicide be helped to choose an alternative way of dealing with their unhappy situations?

From considerable scientific investigation over the past two decades, we now know much more about suicidal behavior. We know, for example, that few people who attempt suicide simply want to die. What they want is not to live *if* living means continued suffering.

We also know that depressive illness, which accounts for the vast majority of suicide attempts, is limited in duration and that it is a treatable condition. Yet despite such knowledge, and despite the availability of effective medications and a variety of psychotherapeutic and community mental health programs, the suicide rate in the United States has not declined.

There are complex sociological reasons for America's suicide problem. Mentioned among the causes have been the availability of lethal weapons, the effects of the "drug culture," and the general effects of such recent catastrophic events as the Vietnam War and the Kennedy and Martin Luther King assassinations.

Society's Contribution to Suicide

Such examples of social malaise and disruption may indeed contribute to the prevalence of depression—as, of course, does the economic and political climate in general. A recent report of the National Institute of Mental Health, for example, noted a link between unstable economic conditions and a sharp rise in the treatment of mental illness, particularly depression.

But these economic, social, and political stresses do not *cause* depressions and suicide. They merely *intensify the underlying conditions* in a depressed individual's life, and may aggravate them to the point where he or she "cannot take it anymore."

The real causes of suicide are personal, and the problem is really one of recognizing them before treatment is indicated. We must learn, for example, to differentiate symptoms of depression from normal reactions to everyday life stresses. We must learn to recognize how the many factors involved in an individual's depression—including the attitudes of friends and relatives, the presence of external life stresses, and the unwillingness to accept treatment—can all contribute to suicidal drives.

"For many potential suicides, the suicide crisis is a positive turning point."

In this [article] I examine the specific personal factors that can push an individual to the brink of desperation. Understanding these personal factors can enable a potential suicide to change direction, renew courage, and find new meaning and purpose in life.

In the past fifteen years I have evaluated and treated some 2,000 depressed and suicidal patients in my own private practice, at the crisis intervention clinic I established at New York Hospital and at the Social Psychiatry Research Institute in New York, which focuses on the development of new social and biological treatments for depression. In the course of this work I have found that, even when overwhelmed by seemingly insurmountable problems

and obsessed by the desire to die, such patients *could* be reached. Once patients realize that there is a way to master distressing symptoms, through psychological counseling and drug therapy, many of them develop the initiative to solve their "unsolvable" problems and begin their lives anew.

Suicide Crisis Is Positive

In fact, for many potential suicides, the suicide crisis is a positive turning point. Once it is passed, they find that they can redirect their self-destructive impulses toward positive, self-renewing activities. The suicide attempt sometimes seems to break the depressive cycle, to push the patient not over the edge but into a clearer, more productive reflection.

It is my hope that this [article] will enlighten those who suffer or know someone who suffers from depression and that it will help retard the rising rate of self-destructive behavior in general, and suicide in particular. A suicide attempt is not the end of the line. Often, it can be the first step on a widening, healthier journey. Depression may be a principal public health problem, but it *is* curable. Perhaps public policy cannot easily eliminate all the aggravating factors in suicide. But we can identify the immediate, personal factors and provide effective therapeutic help.

Helplessness, apathy, and despair are feelings we have all experienced. Do people who commit suicide, or attempt to do so, experience such feelings with greater intensity for longer periods of time than other people? Do they reach a point within despair where it begins to seem unalterable and permanent? Do they at that point see themselves as utterly powerless, unable in any way to make the choices that can influence the direction of their lives?

While it seems reasonable to suppose that the answers to these questions would be yes, in fact the situation is not quite so simple as that. It's often assumed that someone who takes his or her own life has drifted into the final act in a kind of mindless fog; suicide becomes, for such an individual, the only thing left, something he or she falls into rather than consciously chooses. The cliche is that the suicide simply "gives up."

Misleading Views of Suicide

This view of the suicide as someone who has forfeited all options is misleading, for in fact the person who tries to kill himself or herself must make a very clear choice, must initiate a critical decision over the direction of his or her life.

It is important to keep this in mind, for by recognizing that a suicide attempt requires energy, direction, and choice, we will be better able to counsel both patients and their families to deal with a dangerous crisis. Suicides are not will-less, floating casualties. Indeed, suicide often requires considerable courage and determination. It involves marshaling energies toward a specific goal, and this implies that the suicide has, far from giving up on choice, actually made a definite choice—albeit a self-destructive one.

It is the therapist's task, therefore, to redirect energies, to show the potential or "failed" suicide that the choice of self-destruction is not the only choice—and certainly not the best one.

I have often said to patients referred to me after a suicide attempt, "If you have the courage to attempt to kill yourself, why not apply that courage to living your life as you want to live it? Pursue your *own* interests for a change. Stop giving in to the demands and pressures of others."

"What the suicidal person must be urged to understand is that anyone with the courage to end his or her life can also develop the courage to begin it."

If you have the courage to die as you choose, you should have the courage to live as you choose....

Aspects of Treatment

I will discuss what I believe to be a sensible approach to this most severe type of self-destructiveness. Treatment, I believe, should involve three essential aspects:

1. The use of antidepressant medication, which alleviates the symptoms impairing normal functioning, and reduces suicidal thoughts and drives.

2. A program of psychotherapy, preferably involving the family as well as the patient. Here, the goal is to improve the individual's life-style, bringing all of his or her resources to bear in overcoming those small acts of self-destruction that feed the depression.

3. A plan for crisis intervention in order to cope with external pressures that may push a patient back to the brink of despair.

In dealing with suicide, the four key tasks of psychotherapy are:

1. *The search for the reasons behind the patient's problem.* This means investigating ostensibly innocent pressures experienced by the patient at home and on the job. Often such pressures can appear so benign that the patient doesn't recognize them as stress-creating, and as a result internalizes the stress, making demands on an already overwrought psyche. The first task of therapy, then, is to help the individual to recognize what it is he or she does *not* want to do—so much so that the patient would rather die than do it—and second, what the person really likes and *wants* to do.

2. *The mobilization of energy.* The recognition of pressures and the reduction of burdensome responsibilities liberates considerable time and energy. The seond task then becomes an attempt to discover meaningful personal direction for the liberated energy.

3. *The involvement of the immediate family.* This can be of great value if the family members can learn to lessen their demands—both spoken and unspoken—on the patient.

4. *Strengthening the patient's will.* In addition to helping the patient to say no to those demands of others that do not serve his or her best interests, the therapist must finally be able to direct the liberated energy of the patient into an area that the individual can identify as important and self-renewing. Ideally, the end of this process is a situation in which the patient discovers within something he or she had missed before, and is animated by the discovery to a new appreciation of the possibilities of his or her life.

No one has ever lost everything. In moments of "ultimate" disaster, something remains. It is the goal of the therapist, and of the suicidal person, to uncover that something and nurture it into the foundation of new energies, new possibilities, new choices.

What the suicidal person must be urged to understand is that anyone with the courage to end his or her life can also develop the courage to begin it.

Ari Kiev, M.D., is the author of eight books, including A Strategy for Daily Living *which grew out of his work at the Suicide Prevention Clinic. A practicing psychiatrist, Director of the Social Psychiatry Research Institute in New York, originator of the Life Strategy Workshops, and a pioneer in crisis intervention techniques and chemotherapy at Cornell University's Suicide Prevention Center, Dr. Kiev is one of the best known psychiatrists in America today.*

*"I regard my suicide planning as a
durable asset, a resource upon which I
can draw should the occasion arise."*

viewpoint **35**

Rational Suicide
Is Possible

Edward M. Brecher

No doubt, many people who face a lingering
death—from cancer, say, or some other
disease—contemplate suicide. But by the time they
are ready to take action, it is often already too late.
Closely monitored by family and caretakers, they
lack access to any effective means of suicide. They
may also be physically or mentally incapacitated.
Their last-minute, improvised suicide attempts are
quite likely to end in failure, humiliation and,
perhaps, additional pain. This is the case history of a
patient who firmly believes in advance planning. I
am that patient.

I received a diagnosis of cancer of the colon, and a
recommendation for prompt surgery, on June 17,
1983, shortly before my 67th birthday. As every
prudent person should, I had given some thought
during the preceding years to the advisability of
suicide in such a contingency, and I thought further
about it following my cancer diagnosis. As matters
turned out, suicide proved unnecessary in my case,
but I regard my suicide planning as a durable asset, a
resource upon which I can draw should the occasion
arise in the future.

I first began to think about the problem in October
1961. My wife and I and our 15-year-old son were
hiking through New England's glorious autumnal
foliage near our home when our aged German
shepherd, Rufty, suffered a heart attack and lay
writhing in the leaves, clearly in great pain. I hurried
home and phoned a veterinarian, who arrived quite
promptly. We found Rufty cradled in my son's arms.

"As soon as this convulsion is over," the
veterinarian said, "I'll put Rufty out of her pain."

"No, don't wait," my son replied. "Do it right
now."

The veterinarian extracted a syringe from his black

Edward M. Brecher, "Opting for Suicide," *The New York Times Magazine,*
March 18, 1979. Copyright 1979 by The New York Times Company.
Reprinted by permisison.

bag, inserted it in a vein, and pushed the plunger.
Rufty relaxed, and a moment later it was over. That
moment was fraught with emotion. I looked straight at
my son and blurted out what was in my heart:

"I hope someone will be as kind to me when my
turn comes."

A few years later, the father of a friend of mine
received the same kindness. The old man lay
terminally ill on his sickbed late one night,
surrounded by half a dozen members of his family.
The 75-year-old physician who had attended them all,
and had delivered several of them, was sent for. He
arrived, examined the patient briefly, then filled his
syringe and gave an injection.

"Is that to ease the pain?" someone asked.

"No, that was to ease the passing," the physician
said.

My friend likes to tell the story as an example of
how fortunate his New England village was to have a
horse-and-buggy doctor as recently as the 1960's.

The Decision for Suicide

My late wife, Ruth Brecher, who was also my
collaborator as a writer, developed inoperable cancer
in 1965 and died after a 19-month illness. Her care
was managed at home, in accordance with her
personal wishes, including adequate doses of
morphine and sedatives as often as she requested
them. I was deeply grateful to the physician who
abided by her desires—but I resolved to follow a
different course if I myself were ever in a similar
situation.

I was vividly reminded of these earlier matters in
1975, when the newspapers carried accounts of the
deaths of Dr. and Mrs. Henry P. Van Dusen. Dr. Van
Dusen, an eminent theologian, was for many years
president of the Union Theological Seminary in New
York. Years before their death, he and his wife had
entered into a suicide pact, resolving to depart from
life—voluntarily and together—at an appropriate time.

When Dr. Van Dusen was 77 and his wife 80, they agreed that the time had come. Together they swallowed what they assumed were adequate doses of sleeping medication. Mrs. Van Dusen died the next day; but Dr. Van Dusen was taken to a nursing home where he lived on for 15 days. He had failed in what was probably the most important action of his entire life.

Even so, the Van Dusens were fortunate. Many of those who attempt suicide are discovered, rushed by ambulance to the nearest hospital, and subjected to stomach pumping or other demeaning and painful emergency procedures. Those are often, alas, successful.

Among those moved by the Van Dusen episode, and by even more harrowing accounts of botched suicides and successful resuscitations, was a California psychiatrist. He wrote a letter to the editor of *Psychiatric News* proposing a "Hemlock Society" that would "dedicate itself to providing information and personal counseling to those giving serious consideration to suicide." I promptly wrote him requesting membership in the society, but it was never formed.

"A feasible alternative to surgery must be available....to enjoy life to the full as long as possible and then to terminate it in your own way at a moment of your own choosing."

"I regret to say that my own interest in this project waned," the psychiatrist subsequently wrote me. "It immediately became apparent to me that, if I pursued the matter in this community, I would be identified as 'the prosuicide psychiatrist,' or something equally controversial....Also, the local district attorney's office...advised me that I and all persons in a 'Hemlock Society' would be subject to prosecution if we were seen in any way as 'aiding and abetting a suicide.' Consequently, I had to move other projects higher on the priority system.

"I continue to believe that there are a large number of thoughtful and concerned people who would support such a movement if certain others provided the leadership."

The basic principle of such an organization, it seems to me, can be simply and clearly stated: Nobody who doesn't want to die of cancer, or of any other disease, should have to die of that disease. Alternative modes of death should be available.

Determining to Enjoy Life

I had more important business than suicide planning, however, during the period immediately following my own cancer diagnosis. My first need, as I saw it, was to determine whether I could continue to enjoy life—or whether a cancer diagnosis in itself was enough to sour the weeks and months ahead. Accordingly, two days after the diagnosis I took off (as previously scheduled) for a human-sexuality workshop on Cape Breton Island in Nova Scotia.

My two weeks there were among the richest and most rewarding of my life, in a dramatic setting, surrounded by exciting people, dealing with fascinating subject matter, and even including what I have always considered the ultimate of life's enjoyments—a full-fledged falling-in-love experience. Far from souring life, the cancer in my colon added a unique zest to those two weeks.

On my return home, I consulted with my three grown sons, all of whom were nearby. They, like me, vividly remembered their mother's last 19 months.

"Whatever happens," I assured each of them, "I am not going to die of cancer." All three fully understood my meaning, and were unreservedly supportive.

The question of whether to accept or refuse cancer surgery came next in my thinking. This is perhaps the most important decision cancer patients must make; yet few of them give it even a moment's consideration. They simply do what they are told to do. I think the medical profession is at fault in this respect. The surgical option is too often presented to the patient as if it were not an option at all but a foregone conclusion. Many patients, indeed, are "given the rush act" so they won't have time to think things through. Thus, at the very beginning of their careers as patients, cancer victims are deprived of an invaluable privilege of the human condition: the opportunity to plot their own course. Once they let others make that crucial decision for them, they are already reduced to a dependent status.

When a cancer patient does weigh the options, however, it immediately becomes apparent that refusing surgery is utterly irrational if the only alternative is to let nature take its course and to die miserably after a protracted period of suffering. A feasible alternative to surgery must be available if the choice is to have any meaning. That feasible alternative, I believe, is to enjoy life to the full as long as possible and then to terminate it in your own way at a moment of your own choosing. Accordingly, before I could decide whether or not to accept surgery, I had to make sure that suicide was an available option. I devoted my next two weeks to "suicide shopping."

Since guns, knives, dangling from ropes and jumping from high places are not my style, I soon narrowed my alternatives to three: an overdose of sleeping medication, intravenous injection of a rapid poison such as cyanide or nicotine, and carbon monoxide (automobile exhaust).

I was doubtful about carbon monoxide because of the Federal air-pollution regulations designed to curb automobile exhaust gases; but an engineer friend of mine assured me that there is still plenty of carbon monoxide in the exhaust from even a 1978-model car. It just takes a bit longer to be effective.

A physician friend of mine was also helpful. He offered to write a prescription for a month's sleeping medication, cautioning me that it should be taken under circumstances which would prevent my being discovered while still alive and having my stomach pumped.

The offer of sleeping medication is a traditional ploy used by some physicians to retain control of suicide-prone patients. The offer makes it almost certain that the patient will return for the prescription before taking action—and the physician, instead of supplying the medication, can then institute appropriate antisuicide measures. I was confident, however, that in my case the offer was made in good faith.

Discussing the Plans

It was at about this point that I made a most welcome discovery about attitudes toward suicide. In all, I discussed my plans very frankly with nine women and men. Eight of them, including my three sons, were fully supportive. The ninth, while not in agreement, made no effort to dissuade me. Attitudes toward suicide among civilized people, I concluded, are rapidly changing, although the change has not yet been publicly noted.

Another welcome discovery followed. I had always thought of suicide as an inevitably lonely experience—best performed, perhaps, deep in the woods near my home or in some distant motel room. I was therefore deeply moved when a young registered nurse who was very close to me said: ''Let me be with you and give you the injection. I love you and I'd consider it a privilege.''

''It is unfortunate that each patient must do his own suicide shopping without even the most rudimentary guidelines from the medical profession.''

A woman my own age made a similar suggestion—that I come to her island in the Caribbean, where I would be surrounded by affection.

I was even more moved when one of my sons approached me with another suggestion. He reminded me that many years earlier, when his mother and I used to read out loud to the children each night after dinner, we had read them Plato's account of the death of Socrates, describing Socrates surrounded by his intimate friends and enjoying their company to the full until the moment came for him to drink the hemlock.

''I have two requests,'' my son continued.

''First, I don't want you just to disappear. I want to be able to say goodbye. Don't go off to a meeting somewhere and not come back.

''Second, when you are considering alternatives, I wish you'd consider the Socratic alternatives—inviting in the friends you really want to be with for a last evening or even a weekend.''

My first reaction was one of shocked amusement. How could I possibly decide whom to invite to such an occasion? And think of the distress of those who were not invited! Surely that would be the ultimate snub. I reached no decision then on whether or not to follow the Socratic precedent, and I still have not, but I have decided I will not be alone.

By the end of my two-week suicide shopping period, I felt confident that I could rely on any of the three courses mentioned above, and that I could count on the support of those near and dear to me. I was ready for the decision about surgery. I chose to accept it. Actually, I chose a modified form of conservative surgery and found a surgeon who agreed. The hospital consent form was altered to eliminate the patient's traditional consent to ''any procedures which may prove necessary.'' But that is another story. Fortunately, the surgery was successful, and I now expect to die of a heart attack like any other self-respecting, cigarette-smoking, beef-eating, 67-year-old American male.

Accepting Help in Suicide

I have given some thought also to the ethical problem of accepting the help of others or of involving others in my planning—since aiding and abetting a suicide might result in their being prosecuted for murder.

Quite simply, the risk of being charged with murder would certainly not deter me from aiding someone I love if I deemed it appropriate. I would want to be sure, of course, that this was a considered decision rather than a momentary whim on the part of the person seeking my help. And the circumstances would have to be such that I understood and approved the decision. My decision to help would be easier to reach if I felt in addition that I would behave similarly in like circumstances. Since I am prepared to help others close to me despite the risk to me, I see no ethical objection to my accepting the help of others, despite the risk to them.

As a practical matter, the risk of prosecution is small if plans are prudently laid and skillfully executed. This is particularly true in terminal cases; for even if by mischance the facts become known, only an exceptionally strict prosecutor would willingly prosecute for murder someone whose only offense was helping a dying friend in dire need. Such prosecutors, I trust, will sooner or later—let us hope sooner—vanish from our society. Until then, prudence and caution should of course be exercised, both by those planning suicide and by those assisting them.

Even when prosecutors do intrude, juries have a way of demonstrating their sympathy and human concern. Among many cases, I need only cite that of George Zygmaniak of Monmouth County, N.J., who broke his neck in a motorcycle accident in 1973. Paralyzed from the neck down, he begged his brother to help him die. Four days after the accident, George's brother killed him with a shotgun. Following a widely publicized trial for murder, the brother was acquitted by a jury. Acquittal in a murder trial, it should be remembered, can be handed down only by a unanimous jury of 12 individuals.

My own plans, incidentally, took some account of the possibility that I might at some point—following a stroke, for example—be unable to give consent or take action myself. Those close to me agreed that, in that event, my present request for help would be taken as a continuing request.

It is unfortunate that each patient must do his own suicide shopping without even the most rudimentary guidelines from the medical profession. Most practicing physicians are themselves poorly versed in the advantages and disadvantages of various forms of voluntary life-termination available to laymen. Thus, all of us, quite unnecessarily, run the risk of suffering the fate of Dr. Van Dusen, or even worse.

As a modest first step, I suggest the preparation and widespread distribution of a pamphlet for laymen entitled "How Not to Commit Suicide," designed to warn against inadequate and inappropriate measures. If readers learn incidentally about some of the preferable ways, so much the better. I would like to write such a pamphlet, but I have not found a physician knowledgeable in such matters who is prepared to collaborate. A recent book—*Common Sense Suicide* by Doris Portwood, published by Dodd, Mead—is clear-eyed and honest, but is not a "how-to" guide.

I think it is high time that those who think as I do about suicide "come out of the closet." I am confident that even a modest band of women and men prepared to speak out frankly on the suicide issue can have a healthy impact on suicide law and on public attitudes toward suicide. My own experience indicates that coming out of the suicide closet can be a rewarding rather than a harrowing venture.

The suicide routes available and acceptable to me depended, obviously, on my personal tastes and preferences and on the particular people who are close to me. Others must lay their plans in the light of their own circumstances and resources. Many people, moreover, have deep religious, ethical or emotional objections to suicide by any means at all. But for a large and, I believe, growing portion of society who deem suicide vastly preferable to prolonged and unnecessary suffering, I strongly recommend advance planning. And the planning should be done years in advance of the occasion, so that the available alternatives can be unhurriedly explored and prudently weighed.

Edward M. Brecher is a long-time writer on science and medicine.

"Philosophical arguments in favor of rational suicide...provide little safeguard against irrational suicide."

Suicide Is Never Rational

David J. Mayo

Many contemporary philosophers argue that under certain conditions suicide would be a moral and rational act. But to espouse this view is to wield a double-edged sword for it is going to encourage suicide among those for whom it would be a tragic, irrational mistake. My concern in this paper will be to look briefly at some of the dangers lurking there.

Brandt, one of the most articulate spokespersons for rational suicide, is particularly concerned to warn against the ways in which people "in a state of despair" are apt to go astray when they undertake to make a rational decision on the basis of future consequences of their actions. Such persons, he notes, are particularly apt to overlook certain possible courses of action which might lead them from their present despair. Further, they are apt to assign unrealistically low probabilities to the likelihood that their actions will produce desirable consequences. Finally, they may well deny the possibility of experiencing happiness in the future, because they fail to project themselves beyond their present despair and inability to find happiness in certain kinds of experiences now—rather like the man who goes to the market just after he has eaten a huge meal, only to find there is nothing he thinks he'll enjoy eating tomorrow. Brandt spells out these pitfalls because he feels they are not trivial and must be guarded against; I agree. Nevertheless one is left with the impression that Brandt feels that awareness of them is apt to be adequate safeguard against them. Whether this is the case I leave for the reader to decide—preferably during a moment when he is not "in a state of despair."

Rational Attempts

The case considered by Brandt and others examining the issue of rational suicide is that of a person who is trying to be rational but who fails because his judgment is in some way clouded. My primary concern is with a different case, namely that of the person in such a state of despair that he simply abandons any serious commitment to making rational decisions. I concede most of us normally manifest such a commitment: we are usually moved to reconsider a situation, for instance, if someone we respect accuses us of being irrational. But I wish to argue that this is by no means universally the case. I suggest that an integral feature of acute despair is often that such a commitment is totally lacking. The person in such a condition is one of the most obvious examples of someone for whom being reasonable may have no appeal whatsoever. Worse yet is the fact that there seem to be situations which do not merely incline people to be unreasonable, but virtually require it.

The sorts of situations I have in mind involve human commitments, which may require some kind of irrationality if they are to be respected. Loyalty may involve such commitments; so may love, in its various manifestations. Consider, for instance, the familiar case of the mother who believes that her young child is exceptionally bright. Rather than viewing this belief as deplorable because it is irrational (which it almost always is), most of us are inclined to see it as commendable because it is evidence of the depth of the mother's love and devotion.

Again, imagine the case of someone mourning the loss of a love. The grieving-mourning process has more than a psychological dimension; it has an intentional one as well. That is, it may also be viewed as a final expression of a commitment to the lost one, which contains irrational cognitive components. This process strikes us as entirely appropriate, even though it may involve a refusal to accept certain facts which will be obvious to any outside observer. For instance, the intense feelings of loss which the mourner is

David J. Mayo, "Irrational Suicide," in *Suicide: The Philosophical Issues,* edited by M. Pabst Battin and David J. Mayo. Copyright © 1980 by M. Pabst Battin and David J. Mayo. New York: St. Martin's Press, Inc. Reprinted by permission.

experiencing will subside, cease to preoccupy him, and perhaps disappear entirely. Yet while it is probably true that someone who has just lost a spouse after thirty years of happy marriage will feel quite a bit better in a few weeks, be going to baseball games and laughing with friends again in a month, and perhaps even be looking for a new spouse within a year or so, it would be a gross impropriety to confront the mourner with such claims, and for him it would be an unthinkable display of "bad faith" with the lost love to find comfort in assenting to them.

Respecting Grief

By the same token the sixteen-year-old who is shattered when his first love leaves him for someone else is not disposed to listen to (true) claims about how this happens to most of us when we lose our first love, how he's certain to get over it and probably forget all about her, and how the chances are excellent that he'll find another about whom he'll feel just as strong and with whom he'll laugh someday over memories of his present distress. Indeed, from his point of view, to accept the assimilation of his case to a universal pattern, or to entertain seriously the possibility of forgetting all about his unrequited love and finding someone else, would constitute a profound betrayal of the very feelings for the first girl which are causing him so much anguish—again, "bad faith." The fact that this must happen eventually if he is to get on with his life does not negate the fact that we respect, and indeed expect, a period of mourning of which irrational pessimism is to be an integral part.

"My primary concern is with...the person in such a state of despair that he simply abandons any serious commitment to making rational decisions."

The ubiquity of such situations suggests that philosophical arguments in favor of rational suicide, even if they are accompanied by warnings of the ways in which reason may go astray, provide little safeguard against irrational suicide: the propensity to irrationality, especially in the kinds of interpersonal relationships which often occasion suicide, appears after all to be something we respect, even when it serves as a basis for action.

Do these considerations give reason for withdrawing philosophical arguments favoring the possibility of rational suicide and instead arguing against all suicide whatsoever, so as to prevent increases in irrational suicide? Perhaps those who argue for widespread accceptance of rational suicide—Barrington, for instance—should ask themselves whether the benefits

they see resulting from such a change in public attitude mightn't be outweighed in the long run by the costs which might accrue by way of an increased number of irrational suicides. Or perhaps the doctrine of rational suicide manifests the same paradoxical feature which is often attributed to the thesis of ethical egoism, namely that for those who believe it, it becomes a matter of moral obligation to keep it dark.

David J. Mayo was educated at Reed College and the University of Pittsburgh. He is now a member of the department of philosophy at the University of Minnesota-Duluth. His interests include value theory and medical ethics. He has published a paper on brain death.

"The suicide rate among young people in the United States has increased by about 300 percent while the rates among other age groups have not changed."

Teen Suicide in America: An Overview

Jane E. Brody

Several suicides by teen-agers in affluent suburban New York communities over the last few weeks have drawn attention to a phenomenon that is both frightening and baffling.

The four deaths in Westchester County and one in neighboring Putnam County are reminiscent of seven suicides in the well-to-do boom town of Plano, Tex., last year and a similar group of suicides in the prosperous suburbs north of Chicago in the late 1970's.

Is suicide "contagious"? Does publicity of one or two such deaths prompt other troubled teen-agers to follow suit? What causes young people, especially those with above average abilities and opportunities to take their own lives? Are those from affluent families especially at risk? What role do drugs and alcohol play?

While scientific research provides some clues, experts rely mainly on case histories and their clinical experience, which provide some correlations between suicides and social changes.

One fact is certain: Since the 1950's, the suicide rate among young people in the United States has increased by about 300 percent while the rates among other age groups have not changed markedly. Suicide is the second leading cause of death, after accidents, among teenagers. For every successful adolescent suicide, there are reported to be at least 50 and probably as many as 200 suicide attempts.

Suicide Rate Leveling Off

Nevertheless, the suicide rate among teen-agers has been leveling off. Provisional data for the early 1980's indicate there has been no increase since 1979. And although studies have shown that a large percentage of teen-agers entertain thoughts of suicide, the vast majority of young people weather the storms of adolescence without serious problems. Still, with about 12.5 recorded suicides among every 100,000 people aged 15 through 24, and perhaps twice that number that go into the record books as accidental deaths, there remains the haunting question of who is at risk and why. The suicide rate at all ages is highest among white males, followed by black males, white females and black females, in that order. It is lowest of all among Hispanic people, both male and female, despite the high incidence of poverty in that ethnic group. Experts say suicide occurs no more often in wealthy families than in very poor families. But when a well-off teen-ager takes his life, the death gets more publicity, in part because people view the act as especially tragic and unexplainable. Throughout the century, Dr. Paul C. Holinger, a psychiatric researcher of the University of Chicago, has shown the rate of teen-age suicides has risen whenever there was a large percentage of adolescents relative to the rest of the population. This suggests that competition—in school, sports and jobs—may be a suicide trigger for some young people who don't make the grade.

The increase in adolescent suicides has coincided with a dramatic increase in divorces and geographic mobility, says Dr. Eva Deykin, suicide epidemiologist at the Harvard School of Public Health.

Changing Schools Affects Teen Suicide

Judie Smith, program director of the Suicide and Crisis Center in Dallas, says that when teen-agers are up-rooted and change schools and communities, "they lose their extended family, friends and even familiar neighborhood merchants. Their loss is very similar emotionally to the grief reaction following a death or divorce."

New styles of child rearing that give youngsters the freedom to do whatever they want and the "benign neglect" of children in upper-class and two-career upwardly mobile families also seem to play a role.

According to Dr. Michael L. Peck, a psychologist and consultant to the Los Angeles Suicide Prevention Center, "a close, involved, loving family is the overall best suicide prevention factor." That is why, he believes, suicide is so uncommon among Hispanic children. "A lot of parents are afraid of their children, afraid to set rules and enforce them," he said. "A feeling that they can do anything they want is terrifying to kids. They fear a loss of control."

The rising use of alcohol and drugs by teen-agers has also coincided with the increase in suicide, but experts say these only aggravate rather than cause a potentially suicidal problem, such as depression or loss of self-esteem. Between 50 and 65 percent of adolescent suicides and suicide attempts are associated with alcohol, studies indicate.

> "Girls make many more suicide attempts than boys do, but they use methods... that leave more room for rescue."

The availability of firearms was shown in two studies to correlate with the increase in teen-age suicides. One reason for the disproportionately high suicide rate among boys is that, unlike girls, they tend to choose methods—such as shooting, hanging and gassing—that are reliably and rapidly lethal, Dr. Deykin said. In her review of all adolescent suicides in Massachusetts, she found that 80 percent of the deaths involved one of these three methods. Girls make many more suicide attempts than boys do, but they use methods, such as drug overdoses, that leave more room for rescue.

As for the role of the press, Mrs. Smith said, "Someone doesn't pick up a newspaper and commit suicide because they read about someone else who did. But if that person is already at risk of suicide, the media reports may inadvertently convey the message that it's O.K. to kill yourself, that suicide is an acceptable solution to your problems." Dr. Peck agreed that "contagion factors exist, but they are not dominant."

Jane E. Brody is a journalist for The New York Times. *Her articles are primarily in the field of science and health. The increase in adolescent suicides prompted her to write on causes of this phenomenon.*

"If all of us become aware of the clues to suicide...there will be more young people contributing positively toward making our world a better place to live."

viewpoint **38**

Recognizing the Warning Signs Can Prevent Teen Suicide

Nancy H. Allen and Michael L. Peck

In most countries throughout the world, suicide in adolescence has doubled over the past ten years and now ranks between second and third among the leading causes of death during teenage to young adult years. To some degree, this increase may be due to better and more accurate reporting on the part of coroners on death certificates. But better record keeping by no means accounts for the over 100 percent reported increase in suicides in young people. Many suicidologists feel that even more adolescent suicides are not reported as suicides but as accidental or undetermined deaths because of stigma to the family.

The extent to which the adolescent lives in a continuous state of turmoil has long been recognized. Developmental psychologists have pointed out that the internal pressures in adolescents are perhaps greater than in any other period of human development.

Today, we recognize that young people live under a great variety of pressures, including the stresses that result from the phenomena of adolescence, from the high expentancies of early adulthood and from those strains of competition and achievement that are unique to young people.

Only in recent years has the seriousness of the problem of suicides in youth begun to appear in the professional literature. The studies of suicidal behavior on the college campus, for example, have led to the conclusion that suicide is a serious public health problem and, in the college setting, ranks as the second or third leading cause of death.

Suicide at any age is always an enormously tragic event for the survivors. Grief, guilt and shame are feelings commonly experienced among the survivors who lament the needless waste and unfulfilled promise. When the self-inflicted death occurs in a

young person, all these reactions are understandably accentuated. The obvious question is: Why should a youth approaching his prime of life wish to terminate his life?...

Suicidal Intent is Temporary

It is important to recognize that this is a temporary state of mind and that the crisis will pass. Because adolescents are impulsive and may react impulsively, they must be taken seriously when a suicidal intention is expressed. Clues can be divided into three major categories: (1) verbal, (2) behavioral and (3) situational. Verbal clues can be direct or indirect—"I'm going to kill myself" or "You won't have to worry about me much longer." Any major changes in behavior can be regarded as a possible suicide indication. The person may become more of a loner and isolate himself more than usual, academic performance may decrease, there may be sleeplessness or sleeping all the time, loss of appetite or excessive eating. The young person's life situation might change where a loved one is lost, compounded by failures or disgrace at school.

In the Peck and Litman study of adolescent suicides, it was learned that nearly half of the suicidal youngsters were involved in some form of drug or alcohol abuse shortly before their suicidal death. This does not necessarily imply that it was the substance abused that led to the death. Rather, the same factors that made them unhappy enough to commit suicide probably contributed to their abuse of drugs. Many other factors were encountered that seemed, in one way or another, to contribute to the overall suicidality of these people. For example, nearly two-thirds were reported to have been on poor terms with their families, and nearly 90 percent felt that their families did not understand them. Not being appreciated or understood by their families seems to be the most common factor in the continuing chaos and unhappiness in the youth's life.

Nancy H. Allen and Michael L. Peck, *Suicide in Young People.* Pamphlet prepared by the American Association of Suicidology and published by Merck Sharp & Dohme. Reprinted with permisssion.

A surprisingly large number of this group (42 percent) was reported to have been in physical fights with other persons and an equally large number reported to have engaged in physical fights with persons in their own families. It was also reported that there was a considerable amount of physical and assaultive behavior among family members.

Nearly two-thirds of this group had had some form of psychotherapy or counseling and one-third had, at one time or another, been hospitalized for mental or emotional problems. The most common diagnostic category mentioned in relation to this sample was depression, although it is clear from the fighting and the drug and alcohol abuse that many changes in behavior were present.

"Suicidal youth...all have one thing in common: a nagging lack of optimism, lack of hope about their future and an enormous sense of unhappiness."

It should be pointed out that suicidal youth, regardless of the specific trigger factor, all have one thing in common: a nagging lack of optimism, lack of hope about their future and an enormous sense of unhappiness.

Determining Suicide Risk

Obviously, a person's current suicide plan is a significant aspect of his suicide risk. That is, what he thinks and plans about his own death and how he would accomplish it is an important item that needs to be assessed by anyone who would attempt to evaluate and help him. If a mental health professional is to determine the suicide risk that exists in an individual, he must assess the specific details of the suicide plan in order to determine the suicide risk. Highly lethal methods, such as gunshot or hanging, tend to increase the risk compared with slower methods, such as wrist cutting or a drug overdose. All methods can be lethal. In most areas of the country barbiturate overdose and gunshot wounds account for about 70 percent of committed suicides. In addition to the seriousness of the method, the specificity and timing of the plan have to be considered. The patient who talks of a specific plan, with well worked out details and timing, is a very high suicide risk. Contrary to popular belief, most suicidal persons honestly and openly discuss these issues once they are brought up.

Studies of committed suicides reveal an individual history of prior repeated suicide attempts or threats. Of special concern are those persons who have experienced suicidal episodes during which they nearly died. Anxiety, depression, confusion, and so on—form other components of suicide risk. The more intensive and extensive the symptoms, the greater the suicide danger. Depression, in the wide variety of ways in which it is expressed, is a major factor. The presence of a good friend, caring and loving family members, or involvement with helping professionals, can all lower suicide risk.

Learning the Clues

We all can do something about preventing suicides. Much is being done already—but not enough. The average person needs to learn the clues to suicide just mentioned so he can take action if he suspects someone to be suicidal. What he has to do is to tell someone—doctor, professional, clergyman, psychologist, parent—but someone.

Among young people, the first helping person they may encounter is either a friend, school teacher or school counselor, maybe even the family doctor, clergyman or hotline worker. All these persons can be helpful in encouraging the youth to talk about life's dilemmas and problems, thus enabling that person to obtain professional help.

The most effective way to do this is usually through a series of concerned, yet supportive, questions.

The helper may begin with a statement such as, "You sure don't seem to have been yourself lately." "You appear to be kind of down." "Is something bothering you?" An affirmative answer to any of these might lead to another question, such as, "Are you feeling kind of depressed?" An affirmative answer here might result in a question such as, "I guess sometimes it seems as though it's not worth it to go on struggling and fighting when so many things happen to you." An affirmative answer to that question might lead to, "Do you sometimes wake up in the morning and wish you didn't have to wake up, wish you were dead?" A "yes" might lead to, "Have you been thinking about killing yourself? Has suicide been on your mind?" What started to be an innocuous series of questions that any person might ask any other person can lead to a probing examination of the person's suicidal intent. Once the helping person has been taken into the confidence of the other party, he may then begin talking about where professional help can be obtained.

Death Classes

Suicide and death classes are being offered in many high schools and colleges throughout the United States. Educators and students are learning the complexities of suicidology and the fact that community resources can help the suicidal person. For example, they learn there are now nearly 200 Suicide Prevention Centers in the United States and just as many "Hot Lines" that receive calls primarily from the young who are counseled by trained peers.

The professional is becoming more sensitive and

better trained to recognize suicidal youth and to help. More attention is being given to the education of physicians, nurses, social workers and clergy in their basic curricula or through continuing education programs.

One common experience shared by suicide prevention centers is that most of the young people who call can be helped and later are grateful that they are still alive.

If all of us become aware of the clues to suicide and the actions that can be taken to assist those in a suicidal crisis there will be more young people contributing positively toward making our world a better place to live.

Nancy H. Allen, M.P.H., is senior administrative analyst and an adjunct lecturer in the department of neuropsychiatry at UCLA. Michael L. Peck, Ph.D., is a psychologist and consultant to the Los Angeles Suicide Prevention Center.

"The overriding principle is that an adolescent should have some adult outlet, some authority figure with whom he can comfortably share his concerns."

viewpoint **39**

Parents Can Prevent Teen Suicide

Peter Giovacchini

Perhaps the most common problem confronting parents in dealing with troubled adolescents is the refusal to admit that one's child is having difficulties that go beyond the boundaries of the "normal teenage problems."

Parents do not have any monopoly on denial. There is hardly a person on earth who does not find some aspect of his life so painful that he deals with it by putting it out of his mind entirely. The small investor who cannot admit that the stock that contains his life savings is going to continue to decline, a newlywed who senses her husband is "staying late at the office" because he is conducting his first extra-marital affair but cannot bring herself to confront him about it, the middle-aged son who refuses to see the deterioration of his elderly father because the imminence of his death is too painful—all these people use denial to avoid facing the reality of their situations.

Parents of troubled adolescents may say to themselves that their children will outgrow their current difficulties, that they have been raised properly so that nothing could possibly be wrong with them, and that anyhow adolescents must learn to work out their problems as their elders had to. That is all part of growing up.

Admitting a Child's Suffering

It is terribly painful to admit that one's child suffers, let alone that he or she may be disturbed.

No one wants to see his child in pain. Furthermore, many people cannot help but feel that the way a child turns out is a direct reflection on the parenting he received. No one likes to be told that he is unattractive or incompetent on the job. How much more magnified are the feelings when they concern one's parenting?

It is still true that the vast majority of people do not equate physical injuries with emotional ones. If a person accidentally closed a door on a child's finger, he would not deny that it took place because it was a direct reflection on him. Nor would he consider his child's injury a figment of the child's imagination, something he would outgrow. For that matter, he would not worry about what other people thought of him as a parent if they found out he had to take his child to the hospital emergency room to repair the injury. The reverse is normally true when it comes to accidental emotional injuries. In some cases, unfortunately, denial results in an emotional injury that never heals properly....

We need to underscore how important it is to take an adolescent's turmoil seriously. It is a common and very serious mistake for parents to feel that an adolescent's problems are not as "real" as an adult's. In some ways, in fact, an adolescent's problems may be more serious simply because he has not yet had the experience in coping with large problems.

Dismissing Teenage Crisis

An adult, for example, may look at a teenage boy depressed about losing a race for class president and dismiss the magnitude of his suffering because it does not have the same serious consequences as his father's highly mixed employee evaluation submitted last month. The student lost a meaningless election, the reasoning runs, but his father lost a raise needed to support his family and he may lose his job altogether. Unfortunately, that kind of reasoning fails to take into consideration that the son, perhaps suffering from low self-esteem in the first place, has just endured a mass rejection, something akin (in his mind anyhow) to everyone he knows standing up and saying that they think he is unattractive and that they like somebody else much better. Depending on the person, the adolescent may be humiliated and devastated enough by the election results to attempt to end his life.

His father, by contrast, would probably be capable of enduring the trauma if the very worst occurred, and after a few months of turmoil seeking a new job, he would be able to put it all behind him.

Acknowledging Teen Conflicts

None of this is to say that one should hover over a child relentlessly wringing one's hands over every disappointment. The principle involved here is to be able to acknowledge how important such matters are to an adolescent. For all his defiance and insistence that no one understands him, an adolescent gains enormous relief from seeing that a parent takes his identity problems seriously (a theme I will be expanding upon in our conclusion). However insensitive one's son may claim his parent is, he is usually very hungry for a parent to treat him and his crisis as worthy of adult respect. It conveys a sense of dignity to the adolescent, a sense that he is on the road to being a legitimate adult with legitimate concerns, rather than an ineffectual and useless person whose pain is not to be taken seriously. It is best to let our children know we take their problems as seriously as we take our own.

"A child who somehow senses that his mother cannot tolerate the threat of his independence can easily grow up feeling that he is totally responsible for his mother's mental balance."

One of the rewards for this attitude is that one can build upon it while being in better touch with one's child. One of the inadvertent penalties a person may pay for a lack of this appreciation is a breakdown in communication and resentments that may lead to a very poor relationship when the adolescent reaches adulthood. If the denial and the lack of appreciation are too severe and the adolescent feels increasingly alienated and lost in an overwhelmingly painful world, the result can be suicide. . . .

Teen Independence Upsetting

The prospect of a child's growing up and leaving home . . . is often the basis for the most explosive, destructive unconscious feelings some parents can harbor toward their offspring. The reasons for this are complex. The intensity of feelings can cover a broad spectrum. It can compel parents to attempt to block a child's romantic efforts. At its most destructive it can result in unconsciously murderous feelings toward one's own child.

Parents who are afflicted with these kinds of feelings are victims of an unhealthy need for a child's

dependency and admiration. They do not experience the inevitable growing-up process as a personal achievement. A son's growing autonomy is felt to be a rejection, that he is somehow abandoning them. . . .

Adult Inadequacy

It is important to keep in mind that destructive feelings toward an adolescent can be the outcome of one's own sense of inadequacy rather than of overtly brutal acts.

Some parents with low self-esteem need constant reassurance that they are worthwhile. Unfortunately, since fundamentally they are afflicted with the conviction that they are no good, the reassurance, once given, rarely has any effect.

A father, for example, who does not consider himself lovable may find it impossible to feel secure in his relationship with his son. If he does not hear from him because the son is busy with exams and other activities at a distant school, he may interpret this as a sign of rejection and neglect. When he does receive a call, he is likely to complain that his son is ungrateful, self-centered, and indifferent. He may add that the only way to prove him wrong is for the son to drop everything and come visit now. The message is clear. The father, having no confidence in the relationship or in his own attractiveness, instinctively relies upon guilt to acquire what he does not think he can get in any other way. Unfortunately, by doing so, the father creates his own vicious circle. He wants a command performance and that is exactly what he gets. As his son grows older and more resistant to such manipulation, he naturally finds ways of avoiding his father. He resents and flees from the source of unreasonable guilt. In the meantime the father has the opportunity to complain, with great accuracy, that his son calls him only out of obligation, not love.

Mothers Dependent on Children

Some mothers, whose self-esteem depends upon receiving constant reassurance, unconsciously use their children in order to feel comfortable with themselves. They need to feel important (as we all do) and they try to receive that feeling through their offsprings' accomplishments.

From all outward appearances, these unfortunate, insecure parents often appear indistinguishable from healthy, doting parents. They treat their children as prize ornaments. Everything their child may do, from infancy on up, must be celebrated exhaustively. But at the bottom these parents are desperately trying to celebrate a *positive reflection of themselves.*

The distinction I am drawing here is a very subtle one. It is normal and healthy to take pride in a child's accomplishments. Doing so is a first step toward helping a child learn that doing well for his own sake is perfectly acceptable. It threatens no one in the household. It is one basis upon which a child learns to feel competent and good about himself. Through a parent's healthy pride in his child's accomplishments, the offspring learns that he is loved for who he is, whether or not he achieves great academic and professional success.

Pride Can Be Disastrous

Contrast this with the attitudes of the insecure mother I have been discussing; the results of her kind of "pride" can be disastrous. Anyone who has, as a child, come home with a report card one grade short of straight A's only to be hounded by the words "Why not an A in penmanship?" probably went to sleep that night, and many nights thereafter, feeling like a complete failure. Such a mother has inadvertently telegraphed her own feelings of inadequacy and her fear of failure to her children.

One might well ask, But doesn't this kind of mother give her children something to strive for? Perhaps. More likely though, these types of expectations amount to considering perfection a minimum requirement. It is as unrealistic to require perfection of children as it is of parents. The secure and supportive parent places the main emphasis on the achievements the child has demonstrated.

Insecure parents, without realizing it, respond to their children with attitudes based upon their own insecurities rather than on their offsprings' inadequacies. These children sometimes become adolescents who are convinced that nothing they do is good enough. They may not rebel. They are driven, but unable to take pleasure in the accomplishments they do achieve. Needless to say, they tend to experience their parents as taskmasters or sources of guilt rather than of love and understanding.

Such children, unfortunately, often have had traumatic early childhoods. Again, from a distance their mothers seem to be anticipating their offspring's every need even before the child can express it. In reality the child often experiences the overabundance of attention as unbearably suffocating and assaultive.

Smothering Also Damaging

Being fed when they are already sated, being entertained and jostled when they are weary and want to sleep or simply to enjoy a few moments of solitude can produce feelings of fear and frustration just as intense as those of children who are deprived of even minimum amounts of attention.

A child who somehow senses that his mother cannot tolerate the threat of his independence can easily grow up feeling that he is totally responsible for his mother's mental balance and that only by his remaining dependent can his parent survive. When this kind of message is relayed from virtually the moment of birth, it becomes so ingrained that it is next to impossible to step outside the situation, and realize that being cared for is not synonymous with being needed to live. To be under someone's

dominance is equated, in the child's mind, with being loved.

If such children are gifted they often protect themselves from these kinds of parental onslaughts by cultivating their precociousness. As adolescents, they may appear self-assured to the point of smugness. They can be aggressive and successfully enterprising.

However, those traits often are skin deep. They conceal deep feelings of underlying helplessness and vulnerability. When these children find themselves in situations where their arrogance is not tolerated, as they inevitably will, their true fragility comes to the fore and they cease functioning smoothly.

Parental Influence

Analysts see many of this type of potentially suicidal adolescent. They invariably feel themselves to be nothing more than a reflection of their parents. They have neither a sense of being autonomous nor of having the inner wherewithal to evolve that feeling. As a result, they do not feel any purpose to their life.

Still other adolescents who have endured intrusive upbringings become high school students who are obsessively on guard against attack. This, in fact, is a reflection of how they see the world. They are often fanatical about preparing for the next day's schoolwork, not out of a hunger to excel but to overcome an overwhelming fear of being devastated and humiliated by not knowing the answer to questions.

"A mother who hates herself can have a destructive effect upon her children."

Analysis is most effective when a patient allows the seemingly random flow of thoughts to proceed without deliberation, thereby helping painful buried emotional problems to be expressed. These adolescents, by contrast, often find that process threatening and try instead to prepare everything they are going to say in advance.

Questions by a teacher are invariably interpreted as a challenge or an assault. Young men who have this type of conflict often develop a fascination for the martial arts, such as karate or judo. Being able to defend themselves against all comers with their bare hands, without the assistance of weapons, is crucial to them.

Familiar Household Patterns

Clinical experience over the past few decades has made us aware that there are familiar patterns that develop in certain troubled households. In a family where the mother is acting in a suffocating and destructive way, the husband is often a passive and ineffectual man who is unable either to recognize the problem or intervene to correct it.

Clinical experience has also shown that a mother often cannot help but convey her feelings about herself to her children, so that they come to see themselves as their mother sees herself. The secure and self-confident mother (or father for that matter) often implants those traits in a son or daughter. On the other hand, a mother who hates herself can have a destructive effect upon her children. Indeed, parents who hate themselves often fall victim to hating their children as well. Often it comes as an unconscious equation that runs something like this: "Nothing connected with me is any good, and since my children are indisputably flesh of my flesh they cannot be any good either."...

"Talking about suicide is a way of asking, crying out, for help."

These are the adolescents who do not believe there is any reason why anyone should like them, the ones who suffer the tortures of the damned around members of the opposite sex, the ones who believe they are naturally inferior and inadequate and therefore can look forward to a life consisting primarily of failures.

Self-hatred and a peculiar sense of revolt against an assaultive parent sometimes combine in an adolescent, with the result that the child, most frequently a female, contracts a psychosomatic illness that can end in death. I refer to a condition called anorexia nervosa, in which the sufferer may give up eating, sometimes claiming that she is far too overweight. This particular disturbance, as many readers may know, has been receiving increasing attention from the general public and medical community alike.

Research into this illness actively continues. It is not a well-understood entity. Its symptoms are showing up more and more frequently among adolescents. In its most severe forms, the sufferer loses up to 40 percent of her normal body weight. She ceases menstruating and, unless she receives medical help, may starve herself to death. No matter how thin, how emaciated she becomes, she often maintains, at least to herself, that she is overweight.

An anorectic's refusal to admit what she is really doing in the face of her parents' protests should not be surprising. The first, and often the most difficult, step for an institutionalized adolescent to take is becoming fully conscious that she is in a mental institution. Once she can openly admit that she is there because she is emotionally disturbed, she has, in effect, permitted the healthy part of her psyche to

get the upper hand and confront the problem directly. The same admission usually is the first step toward recovery for an anorectic, who frequently has to be institutionalized.

Primitive Part of Mind

It is my conviction that anorectics are being overwhelmed by the very primitive parts of their mind. On some fundamental level the sufferer typically resents her dependence upon the world, or rather the most basic source of nourishment, food. Since everyone's very first source of nourishment is mother's milk, the food normally stands in the child's mind for the mother. To refuse to eat is to be free of any dependence upon one's mother. The more a mother protests her child's refusal of nourishment, the more upset the mother becomes at the rejection of her meals. For the child, there is a feeling of gloating and revenge at a mother's helplessness and frenzy. This feeling is not so very different, one might add, from that of the young man we met earlier whose ultimate fantasy had him sitting on a sheet of ice, immune from the attempts of others to break through to him and to apprehend him.

Nor is the refusal to menstruate without meaning. It is simultaneously a way to keep from growing up and a way to remain free of sexual feelings, which so often propel us beyond our rational control into unfamiliar situations.

It is important to note that just as some of us get depressed from time to time without being what an analyst would diagnose as clinically depressed, so too can an adolescent girl refuse to eat temporarily and even miss a menstrual cycle without being considered an anorectic. Anyone who is concerned about an adolescent who may suffer from anorexia nervosa should consult a mental health professional immediately.

Having discussed self-hatred, we can now turn to another major emotional conflict that can drive adolescents to suicide—guilt over one's competitive urges.

As mentioned earlier, everyone's early urge to "replace" the parent of one's own sex in order to have the other one all to oneself ultimately becomes transformed into a desire to be like that parent and then to be "better than" him or her. In the unconscious mind of the adolescent this can present a conflict. For it seems a very ungrateful thing to do, "destroying" the person who has been the model for a sexual identity and who has in fact conceived and raised him. Besting or demolishing one's very first and most important "rival" would also mean (unconsciously) destroying the person that one is almost totally dependent upon for love and survival.

Since most of us naturally expect every "wrong" action to bring about an equal and opposite reaction or punishment, it would seem that the penalty for destroying someone else, or symbolically doing so by outcompeting them, would be death. . . .

How can a concerned adult recognize the most typical warning signs of a suicide attempt? What informal and practical steps can an adult take to assist a troubled youth? . . .

In trying to understand adolescent suicide and prevent it before it happens, we should keep in mind that the majority of those who attempt suicide do not truly want to die.

Like a convoluted and intricate cat's cradle, the suicide attempt represents a challenge for the adult who can, hopefully, be able to help an adolescent rework a destructive way of life.

The Seriousness of Suicide

In the past, much has been made of the distinction between those who are and those who are not serious about ending their lives. It is true that in most every instance someone who is fanatically committed to ending his life will find a sure means to do so. There are indeed those who fall into this category and who were discovered by what seemed to be accidental circumstances before it was too late. In those cases, they are institutionalized for extensive periods of time. They suffer from what mental health professionals call severe deficits, which means simply that their personalities are so fragile and that they have entered adolescence with such gaps in their emotional resiliency that they may be clinically unable to function on their own.

There are others who do not have these absolute deficits, who may be potentially suicidal, but who are capable of going on to very gratifying adult lives.

Unrealistic Distinctions

This does not mean, however, that we should simply dismiss those who are not serious. It might comfort us to draw a line separating the truly suicidal from the acting suicidal into two neat groups, but it really cannot be done. People do almost everything for a variety of motives, and attempting to take one's life usually carries with it a mixture of meanings. A small part of the determined person's mind may secretly wish that someone would intervene or that the circumstances driving him to a fatal act would arbitrarily change for the better. Just as important, those who are basically involved in life have enough of a truly self-destructive drive to do something that could potentially kill them. Anyone who tries to kill himself puts himself in a position where he may likely succeed. Even if he does not, in the sense that the means he chooses do not appear overwhelmingly lethal, he has developed a way of relating to the people and the events in his life that is dangerous. While other people deal with their problems in a constructive and assertive way in order to find the peace of mind resolution brings, the suicidal adolescent tries to resolve his problems by killing himself.

For that reason alone we should never minimize and belittle the seriousness of the act itself. By so doing we not only ignore the facts but we run the risk that an adolescent may someday be driven to actually kill himself to prove how seriously troubled he really was.

Warning Signs of Suicide

Are there any warning signs that give us clues that a young life is in danger?

The first dictum to destroy is the prevailing myth that anyone who talks about taking his life will not do so. Talking about suicide is a way of asking, crying out, for help. If that cry is ignored, under the illusion that as long as someone just talks about it he is sufficiently venting steam, a self-destructive act may well follow. There are reasons why people who are considering suicide do not talk about wanting to. The reason other people do talk about it is often that they are desperately hoping for someone mature and concerned to become involved in their lives before the despairing part within them proves overwhelming.

Observations have also shown that many adolescents who have attempted to kill themselves experienced a wild and drastic mood swing shortly before the act was committed. Puzzling as it sounds, the swing was often from dismal despair to exhilaration. In the past they had been apathetic, morose, withdrawn, and depressed. Suddenly, they became active, interested, and hopeful about the future. Relatives and friends were lulled into a false sense of optimism perhaps because they were not truly in touch with what was going on within the adolescent and therefore were just happy enough to see whatever it was that made the child miserable disappear. . . .

"Our relationship with them can become the most certain method we have of averting the irreparable and needless loss of life."

A friend may move away and no one else may realize how much the adolescent depended upon such an intimate relationship for solace, advice, and empathy. No one, in fact, may even be aware that the friendship existed, let alone that it provided an indispensable link to coping in the larger world. The loss of a friend may be just as desolating, emotionally, as the loss of a lover and evoke the same sense of being all alone in the world, uncared for and unnoticed.

Separation crisis can also be provoked, as we have seen by the loss of a steady boyfriend or girl friend.

One's whole world and much of one's self-esteem can revolve around the feeling of being loved and needed, the sense that one can be attractive to those outside the family circle, who in an adolescent's mind may love him because "they have to." Studies have found that the most traumatic emotional loss people of all ages endure is the loss of a loved one.

The loss or separation of a close family member through death or divorce can also have a devastating effect upon an adolescent.

"The hostility with which a parent or teacher treats an infatuation with a fad...may leave some vulnerable adolescents feeling foolish and 'unworthy' of adult consideration."

The loss of a familiar environment also represents a separation that is often a highly disturbing event. It can come in the form of a graduation from elementary or high school. In these cases an adolescent may not have been totally happy in the old milieu, but he at least knew how to fit into it adequately. Leaving one of these institutions sometimes involves involuntarily severing a relationship with a deeply trusted and beloved teacher or counselor. For adolescents who have a history of being vulnerable and depressed and who have a great deal of difficulty either adapting to unfamiliar situations or making new friends, the move can be traumatic. A child can feel just as alone and helpless as if his family had all perished suddenly, even though the beloved teacher may live in the neighborhood and the institution the child now attends is only a mile or two away from the old one.

Hero Figures and Disillusionment

Adolescents have a tremendous need to embrace ideals and worship authority figures that give them a solid system of values to cling to. The more passionately they believe in a particular system or person, the more tenuous their inner security may well be. When Larry's self-created environment broke down, the low self-image he had seeped through and overwhelmed him. When an adolescent cult follower discovers that his beliefs, and by extension his adherence to them, are false, the structure on which he based his existence has also collapsed. The same can be said of a hero who has proven to be all too mortal or venal.

Any adult who has seen everything he believed in turn to ashes knows how devastating this can be. Newspapers routinely carry stories describing the suicides of wealthy middle-aged people who abruptly endured the evaporation of their fortunes or the bankruptcy of the companies they built from scratch in their youth.

Parents and teachers, therefore, who may well recognize the fatuousness or the insipidity of an adolescent's devotion to a particular cause or leader, make a great mistake when they ridicule the infatuation itself. The adolescent is better served by the adult's focusing on the child's need to idolize and trying to understand the wellsprings, which is to say the emotional uncertainty, that drive him. No adult enjoys hearing his political opinions, his clothes style, or the manner in which he lives belittled, even if it comes from an adolescent "wet behind the ears." An adolescent, however, is often desperately unsure of his judgment no matter how smug he appears. The belittlement by authority figures is often interpreted as a crushing rejection of the person who holds the beliefs and not the ideology itself.

When the idealized belief or leader is reduced to dust, adolescents also experience it as the loss of something in themselves, something about themselves that was once valuable, perhaps the only thing about themselves they thought was worthwhile. In the past perhaps they were able to keep themselves emotionally together by identifying with the strength and the virtue of the religion or movement.

Adult Insensitivity

There is no one thing in and of itself that causes someone to end his life. A particular incident serves more like a straw that breaks the camel's back. With all the conflicts and pressures adolescents normally face in trying to create an independent adult identity, the camel's back metaphor is unusually apt.

Parents or teachers who make light of the distress an adolescent feels about a rejection, the loss of a friend, a poor grade report, or the sudden fascination with an ideology may accomplish nothing more than making him feel totally cut off from the world. Such a response may serve to accentuate the terribly painful feelings of being odd or different. It may well dam up the turmoil, permitting the pressure to build and build within the child until he explodes in a destructive act.

The hostility with which a parent or teacher treats an infatuation with a fad, even something as trivial as a new kind of popular music, may leave some vulnerable adolescents feeling foolish and "unworthy" of adult consideration. This does not mean that one must adore every trend an adolescent endorses simply because he has developed a momentary taste for it. Rather, a respect for the adolescent's right to his own tastes and the bare-minimum credit one might offer a stranger with interests at variance with one's own permit the child to feel more secure about himself. He may, in fact, rush home and offer to play a particularly jarring piece of insipid music. To ignore the opportunity to become closer to the adolescent, by permitting him to share something very precious, simply because one prefers Vivaldi or Telemann, can be terribly hurtful to a child.

No Perfect Childhood

It is unrealistic to see oneself as absolutely empathetic or totally insensitive. Like the emotional turmoil an adolescent may be vulnerable to, these traits are all a matter of degree. An adult who attempts to be "perfect" in his relationship to an adolescent is being as unfair to himself as is a teenager who expects that he must be the perfect child.

It is impossible to see directly into the heart and the mind of another human being. It is difficult enough being able to see unflinchingly into one's own psyche. It is reasonable, however, to aim for a fairly comprehensive overall understanding of what an adolescent's ideals and aspirations are.

If a parent knows nothing about these things, this in itself may be an ominous sign. To some degree adolescents may be taciturn and secretive. Adolescents often feel conflicted over "being grown up" and "living at home like a kid." They may feel embarrassed about their dependence and therefore keep their ambitions to themselves as a way of compensating, as a means of feeling that they are independent souls.

Nevertheless, an adolescent who shares so little of himself that no one in the family has any idea of what is going on in his mind may actually be acting that way because he is threatened by his parents. That is, he may be afraid of their disapproval or belittlement. All the more so if a major part of his own mind is unsure about the efficacy of his plans. Without realizing it, an adolescent may be unconsciously afraid that inner revelations will bring a parental reaction that confirms his own darkest fears about himself. Without realizing it, he may even go so far as to put his parents into the position of censor by interpreting a chance remark as vicious condemnation.

Cutting Off Family Support

The danger in this is obvious. For if an adolescent feels that the people who are closest to him are officers of an inquisition, he may cut himself off from the two most important sources of support and love he has. Similarly, parents and teachers who demonstrate no perceptible interest in a child's enthusiasms may also have a destructive effect.

It sometimes happens that an adolescent cannot help but feel his parents are unacceptable as confidants. He may feel that his mother, no matter how concerned, "makes him feel like a baby" if she asks him how he is and what he plans to do with himself. On the other hand, almost all of us have some painful memory of our father sitting us down to

ask "what your plans are." In retrospect we can probably now see that his intentions were good and responsible. At the time it could well have seemed that we were being put on the spot, as though the Judgment Day gavel was waiting to fall if our answer failed to "measure up" or our uncertainty seemed too vast.

Here the overriding principle is that an adolescent should have some adult outlet, some authority figure with whom he can comfortably share his concerns. A parent may not be the sole source of comfort and solace, but as long as the adolescent is receiving that kind of empathy from an equivalent figure (such as an aunt or a guidance counselor), the adolescent is assured some type of healthy outlet and by extension a way of staying in touch with the world around him. If a parent is concerned about an adolescent's close-mouthed behavior it is a sign of empathy, not defeat, to ask if he would like to talk to some other adult on an on-going basis. Such a suggestion in fact may well make it easier for an adolescent to seek counsel. With an overly withdrawn adolescent one must be empathic and make certain that the most immediate emotional need is addressed.

Teenage Well-Being

There are other questions an adult can profitably ask in trying to gauge an adolescent's emotional well-being. Does the teenager look forward to new social and intellectual experiences? Does he have enough confidence in himself and enough of an appetite for life to meet it enthusiastically? Again, we are dealing not with absolutes but with overall patterns. If an adolescent cannot bring himself to go out on a date, to attend a school social event of any kind, to place himself in new situations, he may have seriously emotional insecurities.

"It is impossible to see directly into the heart and mind of another human being."

Adolescence, after all, is a time in which one is supposed to be testing out the ability to conquer new challenges. It is by racking up some modest series of successes that one gains the self-confidence to tackle the ever greater ones of adulthood.

Those who have a strong urge to live are people who have generally clear notions of what they want from life. They are able to define relatively realistic goals. They are able to establish expectations and needs that can reasonably be fulfilled.

Adolescents often have the wildest possible expectations of life and of each other. They base these feelings not so much on experience as upon their ideals and their fantasies (being short of experience and long on ideals). Adolescents often have considerable difficulty reconciling how they want to live and what their goals ought to be with the very solid limitations of the real world. It is not easy to come to the realization that no one human being can make anybody totally and perpetually content. As adults we have all had to learn this the hard way, and very few people can completely give up the wish that it were possible.

A Supportive Buffer

To a degree, every person has to go through the various kinds of reality training life imposes on its own. An adult should be aware of what an adolescent's expectations from life are and be able, with empathy, to act as a supportive buffer through the difficult moments. At the very least, an adult should have some sense of when an adolescent is placing a dangerous amount of expectation of future happiness on a situation that cannot possibly provide it. . . .

"[Adolescents] need to draw upon our strength, our patience, our resilience, and our compassion."

The struggle to live and the struggle for independence are parallel processes. Adolescence is a time in which a child is transformed into an adult, a time in which dependency is exchanged for autonomy. We are all mixtures of self-reliance and autonomy.

Some philosophers maintain that the universe is a duality that consists of creative and destructive elements, of life and death. Adolescents plagued by suicidal thoughts and experiences also represent a profound and very moving duality. To explore with them the sources of the wasteland they sense within and around them is also a way of discovering the altruism and the high hopes that have often made their despair so overwhelming in the first place.

Judging Worth

It is adolescence, perhaps more than any other age group, that is obsessed with trying to find out what is worthless and false and what is meaningful and worthwhile. Most of us to one degree or another set our sights on survival, trying to enjoy what gratifications we can in passing. Survival is challenging enough, and we often carve out the most secure niche we can for ourselves and settle for that.

Adolescents, for all their vulnerability, strive for more than that. Like Icarus', their fall often comes from flying too near the sun.

They need to draw upon our strength, our patience, our resilience, and our compassion. Our rela-

tionship with them can become the most certain method we have of averting the irreparable and needless loss of young life. It is also the best means to test and reevaluate our values and our way of life. When we help adolescents achieve adulthood they can challenge us to acquire greater maturity, integrity, and insight into the meaning of our own lives.

Peter Giovacchini is a psychoanalyst and Clinical Professor of Psychiatry at the University of Illinois at Chicago. He is nationally known for his work with adolescents and their problems.

"Courts have found the right to reject life-saving medical care to be part of the fundamental constitutional right of privacy."

The Right to Die Is Determined by Law

John A. Robertson

The situation of critical illness most often dealt with by the courts, concerns competent adults who refuse medical treatment necessary to keep them alive. Until recently, most of these cases involved religious objectors such as Jehovah's Witnesses or Christian Scientists. With the development of life-prolonging medical technology, such groups as the elderly, the terminally ill, and the severely disabled also wish to avoid the burdens of medical treatment.

Typically, the patient refuses a medical procedure that could prolong his life. He may object because of the nature of the medical intervention, or the life-situation in which successful treatment will leave him. His family or doctors or officials of the state disagree with the choice and think the patient should live. They may find his choice to be misguided, irrational, uninformed, or even immoral. In some cases they may try to have him treated against his will.

The courts are now drawing upon the Anglo-American tradition of individual autonomy and self-determination, and constitutional rights of privacy, to resolve these conflicts. This chapter discusses the right of a competent adult patient to refuse treatment.

Question: May a competent adult refuse medical care necessary to keep him alive?

Answer: In general, yes. The right of self-determination and autonomy central to American law is now recognized and includes the right of a competent adult to reject life-saving medical care. This right is an application of the rule of informed consent to medical treatment. Under this rule, no doctor may treat a competent patient without his free, knowing consent. While the United States Supreme Court has not yet addressed the question, influential state courts have found the right to reject

From John A. Robertson's *The Rights of the Critically Ill.* Copyright 1983, American Civil Liberties Union. Reprinted with permission from Ballinger Publishing Company.

life-saving medical care to be part of the fundamental constitutional right of privacy. As a constitutional right, the state must show very strong reasons for intervening with an individual's exercise of the right.

Question: May a terminally ill person refuse medical treatment that would keep her alive?

Answer: Yes. If the patient is terminally ill, her right to refuse treatment will be recognized. The courts would find no compelling state interest served by prolonging the dying process of such a person.

The reasoning behind this position is clearly seen in a Massachusetts case that upheld the right of an incurable cancer patient to decline care when "the disease clearly indicates that life will soon, and inevitably be extinguished." The court stated:

> The interest of the State in prolonging a life must be reconciled with the interest of an individual to reject the traumatic cost of that prolongation. There is substantial distinction in the State's insistence that human life be saved where the affliction is curable, as opposed to the State interest, where, as here, the issue is not whether but when, for how long, and at what cost to the individual that life may be briefly extended. . . . The constitutional right to privacy . . . is an expression of the sanctity of individual choice and self-determination as fundamental constituents of life. The value of life as so perceived is lessened not by a decision to refuse treatment, but by the failure to allow a competent human being the right of choice.

The New Jersey Supreme Court adopted a similar position in the famous *Quinlan* case when it discussed the right of an irreversibly comatose patient to refuse treatment. It stated that while the courts might require treatment in a situation where the patient is "salvable to long life and vibrant health," they would not intervene where the patient is "terminally ill, riddled by cancer and suffering great pain," or is irreversibly doomed "to vegetate a few measurable months with no realistic possibility of returning to any semblance of cognitive or sapient life." In the court's view, the state's interest [in preserving life] . . . weakens and the individual's right to privacy grows as the degree of bodily invasion increases and the prognosis dims. Ultimately there comes a point at which the individual's right overcomes State interest.

The right of a terminally ill person to refuse necessary medical care is also well illustrated in the *Perlmutter* case. Joseph Perlmutter, a seventy-three-year-old former taxi driver and athlete, came down with amyotrophic lateral sclerosis (Lou Gerhig's disease), a degenerative terminal disease that left him respirator dependent. He did not wish to continue to live in this state, and pulled out the breathing tube, but the doctors, out of fear of legal liability, reinserted it. A lawyer brought his case to court. The judge ruled that his constitutional right of privacy and self-determination gave him the right to stay off the respirator, even if it meant that he would die, and ordered the doctors to stop the respirator.

Question: May a competent patient who is not terminally ill, refuse necessary medical treatment?

Answer: Yes. The right to refuse medical treatment is a right held by all competent adults, not just those who are terminally ill. However, like all rights, it is not absolute and can be restricted to serve important or compelling state interests, such as preserving life, protecting minors, protecting innocent third parties, preventing suicide, and maintaining the ethical integrity of the medical profession. (The right of prison inmates to refuse necessary medical treatment may be more limited because of the effect of such refusals on prison discipline).

"The courts will be most inclined to override the patient's choice when children are involved."

When the person is not terminally ill, doctors will be more reluctant to honor the patient's refusal, and courts are more likely to find the state's interests compelling. If the medical treatment necessary to keep the patient alive is not highly intrusive or painful, and the patient will be restored to a healthful condition, the courts are more likely to find that these interests outweigh the patient's interest in self-determination.

For example, the state's interest in preserving life may justify overriding the patient's refusal, because there would be no burden on the patient beyond the failure to follow his wishes. Thus, courts in Jehovah's Witness cases will generally order blood transfusions as long as the patient does not believe he will be damned forever if he receives it. The court order violates the patient's choice, but does not impose any other suffering on the patient.

On the other hand, if intrusive, painful, or prolonged medical procedures are necessary, or the patient will end up in a severely disabled or debilitated state, it is unlikely that courts would order treatment. Such cases could arise with severely burned patients, paraplegics or quadraplegics, persons facing amputation for gangrene, cancer patients in need of radiation and chemotherapy, or Jehovah's Witnesses who believe that blood transfusions will damn them forever. Forcing treatment in such situations would lessen the value of life rather than preserve it, and the courts are unlikely to order it.

Several cases illustrating this point have arisen with patients who refuse amputation. The *Quackenbush* case is typical. A seventy-two-year-old man living alone in a trailer, was brought to the hospital emergency room and found to be suffering from severe gangrene caused by advanced arterio-sclerosis. The doctors predicted that unless both legs were amputated, he would die within three weeks. When he refused, the hospital asked the courts to find him incompetent and to appoint a guardian to consent to the life-saving surgery. The court found that he was competent and had the right to refuse the amputation, despite the fact that he was not terminally ill and could live indefinitely if the operation were done. The state's interest in the preservation of life was not sufficient to outweigh his right of privacy. The operation would be highly invasive—amputation of both legs above the knee and possibly the thigh. He would probably be confined to a wheelchair for the rest of his life and be forced to move to a nursing home. The court upheld his refusal; forcing a person who is ready to accept death to undergo major surgery and amputation, and live as an invalid in a nursing home, would lessen, rather than enhance, the value of life, and thus not constitute a compelling state interest.

Question: May a competent adult with children refuse necessary medical treatment?

Answer: Yes and no. The courts frequently cite protection of children as a reason for overriding a competent patient's refusal of treatment, a situation most likely to arise with Jehovah's Witness parents who refuse blood transfusions. But no court has ever ordered a clearly competent patient to be treated against her wishes, solely to protect minor children. In the famous *Georgetown Hospital* case often cited as an authority for this position, a blood transfusion was ordered for a twenty-three-year-old mother of a three-year-old injured in an automobile accident, despite her apparent religious objections. However, the transfusion probably would have been ordered even if there were no child, since the patient was incompetent at the time; it was an emergency; and her true wishes, including her beliefs about compelled transfusions, could not be ascertained. In another case, a blood transfusion was ordered for a Jehovah's Witness woman in order to protect the fetus; she was eight months pregnant. However, this case arose before *Roe* v. *Wade* gave the mother the right to terminate a pregnancy for any reason, in the first six months.

In other cases, the courts have refused to order treatment over the objections of a parent of minor children. In the *Osborne* case, a thirty-four-year-old Jehovah's Witness with two young children, needed blood transfusions to save his life after a tree fell on him. He refused treatment, and his wife agreed. The court upheld his refusal, despite the grief it might cause the children.

The exact extent to which the existence of minor children will override the parents' refusal thus remains unclear. The courts will be most inclined to override the patient's choice when children are involved. But a close scrutiny of the competing interests will often show that the harmful effects of forcing treatment on the patient is greater than the burdens on a child whose parent dies by a conscientious refusal of medical treatment.

"The state's interest in preserving life may justify overriding the patient's refusal."

The strongest case for ordering treatment for the sake of children, would be where the child's life depended on it, as is shown by a decision of the Georgia Supreme Court in *Jefferson* v. *Griffin-Spaulding County Hospital Authority*. A woman who was thirty-nine weeks pregnant had placenta previa, a condition which, unless a Caesarean section were done, was very likely to cause a stillbirth and the mother's death as well. The mother refused. A court hearing was held to protect the interests of the unborn child and resulted in the decision that the Caesarean section be done. Where the child's life is not directly threatened, the case for imposing medical treatment against a person's wishes is much weaker.

Question: May the spouse or other family members who disagree with the competent patient's refusal of treatment, force treatment against his will?

Answer: No. The family does not have the right to control the health care given a competent adult—only the adult himself has this right. The right of autonomy and self-determination in health care is a right against interference by the family, as well as by doctors and the state. Doctors who treated at the family's behest would be violating the patient's rights and could be sued. They should never do so without first obtaining court approval for overriding the

patient's refusal, which is unlikely to be granted unless the patient has minor children or other factors justifying a limitation on the right to refuse treatment exist.

Question: What if the doctors disagree with the patient's choice to refuse medical care?

Answer: Doctors have sometimes asserted a right to save a life by treating an unwilling patient in order to fulfill professional or ethical obligations. Courts often recognize this concern. It was a significant factor in the *Heston* case which involved a twenty-two-year-old married women who ruptured her spleen in an automobile accident and needed a blood transfusion. She was a Jehovah's Witness, and appeared incompetent at the time, even though her mother insisted that she would not accept blood and refused to consent on her behalf. The judge called at 1:30 A.M. to hear the question, appointed a guardian to consent to the transfusion. The operation was performed and the woman survived. She then sought to vacate the order, but the judge's order was upheld by the New Jersey Supreme Court, which relied, in part, on the medical profession's standards:

> When the hospital and staff are thus involuntary hosts and their interests are pitted against the belief of the patient, we think it reasonable to resolve the problem by permitting the hospital and its staff to pursue their functions according to their professional standards.

While such concerns are likely to be recognized in emergency situations where the patient's competency and wishes may not be clearly established, in nonemergencies, the doctor's interest in preserving life ordinarily will not outweigh the patient's interest. A Massachusetts case, for example, recognized that the right to bodily integrity and self-determination contained in doctrines of informed consent and privacy, are "superior to the institutional considerations" of hospitals and the medical profession. Otherwise, doctors could always ignore patient wishes and thus eliminate self-determination in medical care.

Question: Has the person who dies because he has rejected medical care committed suicide?

Answer: Probably not, though the courts have not directly faced the question. Suicide means the intentional termination of one's life. Usually this occurs by active means, but the concept is broad enough to include such suicidal methods as starving oneself, or refusing medical care.

For legal purposes, the question of whether a death, caused by the refusal of necessary medical care is a suicide, may depend upon the legal context, or reason for asking the question. Classifying a death as suicide could affect (a) the cause of death listed on the death certificate, (b) the life insurance benefits, (c) the criminal liability of persons who assist the patient in avoiding medical care, and (d) the patient's right to refuse medical treatment.

The death certificate is completed by the doctor who determines that death has occurred. While there is no uniform practice among doctors, it is likely that persons who die from refusing care, would not be considered suicides. A doctor's statement that such a death is from natural causes, is not likely to be challenged by a coroner, who has the power to hold inquests and determine the cause of death.

Life Insurance

Most states now require that life insurance benefits be paid for deaths by suicide, usually after the policy has been in effect for a minimum period, such as two years, although this wasn't so in the past. Where the exclusion of suicide is applicable, the question of benefits for death from refusal of medical care has not yet been decided by the courts. It is unlikely that the courts would consider death from the refusal of treatment as suicide, where the patient was terminally ill, or wanted to live but could not accept certain treatments, such as blood transfusions. Indeed, states with living will laws usually provide that withholding care in accordance with the patient's directive does not constitute suicide or affect life insurance benefits.

Assisting Suicidal Patients

People who remove respirators or feeding tubes, would probably not be criminally liable. In the *Perlmutter* case the Florida court held that the removal of a seventy-three-year-old man with Lou Gerhig's disease from a respirator essential to keep him alive, was not self-murder, and that people who assist him could not be prosecuted for assisting a suicide.

Right to Refuse Treatment

Whether refusal is suicide is also important, because some courts have stated that the state's interest in preventing suicide may override the patient's refusal of treatment. However, if the patient is terminally ill or severely disabled, the refusal of treatment would probably not be considered suicide because the state's interest

> ...lies in the prevention of irrational self-destruction. What we consider here is a competent, rational decision to refuse treatment when death is inevitable and the treatment offers no hope of cure or preservation of life. There is no connection between the conduct here in issue and any State concern to prevent suicide.

If the patient is not terminally ill, courts may distinguish the patient's refusal from suicide on the ground that the patient did not set the death-producing agent in motion, or does not have a specific intent to die, but for religious or other reasons cannot accept medical treatment. If the patient's decision seems truly irrational and not understandable within his own religious or philosophical belief system, the courts could treat it

as a suicide attempt and override the patient's refusal, or more likely find the patient to be incompetent with no right to refuse treatment.

Question: When is a patient competent to refuse medical care?

Answer: A patient is competent if she can understand the nature of a proposed treatment and the consequences if it is not given, and is capable of exercising choice. The patient need not understand the medical theory behind a course of treatment, as long as she understands the nature and consequences of the choice. Also, she can be competent to make decisions about medical care without also being competent to manage her property, make a will, or do other legal acts.

Competency may also be independent of whether or not a person is mentally ill. Thus, persons committed to mental institutions have been found competent to decide about their medical care, because their mental illness was not found to interfere with their ability to understand the nature and consequences of proposed treatment. In the *Yetter* case, a woman in a mental institution was considered competent enough to refuse a biopsy for suspected breast cancer because the court was convinced that she understood the nature of the procedure and the consequences of refusing. She later died of breast cancer.

"Though her refusal seemed irrational to her doctors, it did not mean she was incompetent in the legal sense."

The meaning of competency—and the difficulties the determination sometimes involves—may be illustrated by two cases involving elderly women who refused the amputation of their gangrenous feet that had developed due to advancing arteriosclerosis. In *Lane* v. *Candura* a lower court had granted a petition appointing the daughter of a diabetic seventy-seven-year-old widow to be her mother's guardian for purposes of consenting to this operation. This decision was reversed and Mrs. Candura's right to refuse the amputation was upheld because the appeals court found ample evidence that she was aware of the consequences of refusing the operation, even though her sense of time was distorted, her train of thought sometimes wandered or was confused, and she often was defensive or combative in responses to questions. She did not want the operation because

> she has been unhappy since the death of her husband; she does not wish to be a burden on her children; she does not believe that the operation will cure her; she does not wish to live as an invalid or in a nursing home; and she does not fear death but welcomes it.

Though her refusal seemed irrational to her doctors, it did not mean she was incompetent in the legal sense, for her forgetfulness and confusion did not impair "her ability to understand that in rejecting the amputation, she is, in fact, choosing death over life."

In the Matter of Northern, by contrast, an appeals court upheld a finding that a seventy-two-year-old woman was incompetent to refuse the amputation of her gangrenous feet because of evidence suggesting that she did not fully appreciate the consequences of the decision. Though she was generally lucid and of sound mind,

> on the subjects of death and amputation of her feet her comprehension is blocked, blinded or dimmed to the extent that she is incapable of recognizing facts which would be obvious to a person of normal perception.
>
> For example, in the presence of this Court, the patient looked at her feet and refused to recognize the obvious fact that the flesh was dead, black, shriveled, rotting and stinking.
>
> The record also discloses that the patient refuses to consider the eventuality of death which is or ought to be obvious in the face of such dire bodily deterioration.

While this case may be criticized for not allowing persons who deny the existence of their medical situation to be found competent, it shows that persons who do understand the alternatives will be found competent.

Question: Must a competent patient's refusal of treatment be followed if he later becomes incompetent?

Answer: Probably, though courts have not squarely answered the question. The implication of *Lane* v. *Candura, Quackenbush,* and other cases that have found persons to be competent to decide against necessary treatment, is that their choices are to be followed, even if they later become so confused and disoriented that they no longer can understand the nature and consequences of the treatment they are rejecting. Similarly, courts have upheld, though not invariably, the right of adult Jehovah's Witnesses not to have blood transfusions administered even if they are incompetent to decide at the time that the blood is needed, as long as their objections were clearly made while competent. This principle was recognized by a trial judge in a New York case when a 41-year-old diabetic who had become blind and had both legs amputated wanted to stop the dialysis treatment keeping him alive. He was found competent by two psychiatrists, but the hospital sought a judicial order to keep treating him. Before a court hearing could be held, he lapsed into a coma. The court eventually upheld the refusal of treatment, even though the patient was now incompetent, because he had been competent when he refused treatment.

There are two reasons why the courts are likely to follow the competent person's wishes against medical care when they become incompetent. One is a policy interest in allowing competent persons to control medical interactions that occur when one becomes incompetent. The second is that treatment and the prolonged life that it provides, will not be in the interests of the person who becomes incompetent anymore than when he was competent. Mrs. Candura and Mr. Quackenbush wished to avoid suffering by refusing amputation; their decision would be upheld if they became incompetent. However, there may be situations in which an incompetent person, if now able to communicate his preferences, would no longer wish his prior refusal of treatment to be honored. In ascertaining an incompetent person's choice, this possibility has to be kept in mind. The mere fact of incompetency, however, does not mean that choices expressed while competent can be ignored.

Question: Can a patient be considered competent if she has intermittent periods of lucidity or is under medication?

Answer: Yes, though it will depend on the facts of each case. Senility, medication, diabetes, liver problems, and other conditions in which the patient has intermittent periods of lucidity, might make it very difficult to tell whether the patient is competent to refuse treatment. Choices made in a period of lucidity should be honored, even if he had earlier been, or later becomes, incompetent.

"A patient with a lawyer or family or friends to help him can also go to court to order the doctor to stop treatment."

An interesting example of how a person can be found competent to reject necessary treatment despite earlier periods of incompetency, occurred in the *Quackenbush* case. The hospital believed that the seventy-two-year-old man who refused amputation of his gangrenous legs was incompetent and asked the courts to appoint a guardian to consent to the operation. At the hearing, a psychiatrist testified that the patient was disoriented as to time and place and not aware that he was in a hospital or talking to a doctor or nurse and was suffering from visual hallucinations. He diagnosed the condition as an organic brain syndrome and stated that the patient was not competent to make an informed decision about the operation. Another psychiatrist who examined the patient five days later, found that the patient had no hallucinations, understood that he had gangrene and could die without the amputation, and thus was competent. The judge talked with the patient one day later and also found him competent to make an informed choice about the operation:

> He did not hallucinate, his answers to my questions were responsive and he seemed reasonably alert. His conversation did wander occasionally but to no greater

extent than would be expected of a seventy-two-year-old man in his circumstances. He spoke somewhat philosophically about his circumstances and desires. He hopes for a miracle but realizes that there is no great likelihood of its occurrence. He indicates a desire . . . to return to his trailer and live out his life. He is not experiencing any pain and indicates that if he does he would change his mind about having the operation.

Question: Who determines competency?

Answer: Legally a person is presumed to be competent unless declared otherwise by a court. As a practical matter, the doctor treating the patient will determine first of all, whether there are such doubts about a person's competency that the patient's decisions for medical care need not be followed. He may consult nurses, family members, and the patient, or call in other doctors or psychiatrists. If he believes that the patient is incompetent, he should ask the courts to have the patient declared incompetent and a guardian appointed to consent to medical care.

"Legally a person is presumed to be competent unless declared otherwise by a court."

In many cases, however, doctors may simply decide that the patient is incompetent and get the consent of the next of kin. There may often be no legal consequences from handling the matter in this way, particularly if the patient is benefited and the kin could have been appointed guardian. However, doctors who make such decisions on their own, may erroneously conclude that a patient is incompetent and thus deny the patient the right to make his own choice. To avoid such errors and possible suits for damages, they should seek an official determination of competency and, if necessary, the appointment of a guardian.

Question: Can a patient be found incompetent merely because he refuses medical care that the doctors want to give?

Answer: Not legally. Doctors will generally not question the competency of patients who consent to treatments that the doctor recommends. However, when the patient refuses, the doctor may suspect his mental competency and seek to have a guardian appointed in order to be able to treat him. This is more likely to occur when the doctor's personal beliefs are different than the patient's, and the doctor is not able to separate out his moral and personal views from his medical judgment. In *Lane* v. *Candura* the doctors regarded Mrs. Candura as competent to consent to medical care until she changed her mind and withdrew consent to the amputation. In their view she was making an irrational choice because she gave life a lower priority than they would. But the

refusal of medical care alone—despite the feeling of many doctors—is not proof that a person does not understand the nature and consequences of a proposed treatment and thus is incompetent. To protect their right to refuse care, patients should explain to the doctor their reasons for refusal and that they fully understand the choice. They should also inform their family or friends who might aid them if doctors seek to have them declared incompetent when they refuse or disagree about the care offered.

Question: What should families and doctors who are uncertain about the patient's competency do when he refuses treatment?

Answer: Since a competent adult patient, particularly one who is terminally ill, has a right to decline necessary medical care, doctors and families are obligated to honor this wish. (A court could order them to pay damages or stop treatment if this is done without the patient's consent.) On the other hand, doctors would have a legal duty to treat incompetent patients as long as treatment is in their interests. Doctors could be liable for manslaughter or wrongful death if they negligently conclude that a patient is competent and accept his refusal of treatment.

If there are doubts about a person's competency, the doctors should obtain psychiatric consultation. If the consultant advises that the patient is competent, the doctor may legally honor his refusal of treatment (indeed, would be obligated to). To be certain, however, as might be desirable if the patient's refusal of care could lead to death, the doctor might request a judicial determination of competency. In such a proceeding a guardian *ad litem* and attorney should be appointed to represent the patient.

If consultations suggest that the patient is incompetent, a guardian should be appointed to make decisions about medical care. A judicial decision will give the parties some certainty about the legality of their actions, and may prevent the abuse of a patient who is helpless to protect his right to have care withheld.

Question: What can happen to a doctor who treats a competent patient against his will, in order to keep him alive?

Answer: Doctors sometimes treat competent patients against their will because they believe the patient's decision is unwise or morally wrong, because the family wants treatment, or because the doctor fears legal liability if she fails to do everything possible to save the patient.

Such a doctor can be sued for damages for battery, false imprisonment, or lack of informed consent, and may be responsible for the cost of medical care. The patient or his family would need legal services to bring the suit, and would have to prove that the doctor knew, or should have known, that the patient was competent to refuse care. Such suits have been rare, and might not result in large damage awards, if the patient were claiming a right to die.

There have also been suits to protect the right of the patient not to be treated over his wishes, or to prevent unwanted treatment in the future. For example, Jehovah's Witnesses who have been treated against their will have gone to court to enjoin such interventions in the future, or to have court orders for blood transfusions vacated.

A patient with a lawyer or family or friends to help him, can also go to court to order the doctor to stop treatment. In the *Perlmutter* case when the doctors refused to allow the patient to turn off his respirator himself, he got a court to rule that he had a right to determine his own care and to order the doctors to allow him to leave the hospital. A doctor who then refused would be in contempt of court.

Question: Can a competent patient exercise her right to refuse treatment before the need for treatment arises?

Answer: Yes. It is clear in states with living will laws, and probably in states without them, that a competent patient can arrange that necessary care—respirators, drugs, surgery, and so forth—be withheld at some future time when the patient is no longer competent to decide. In some states doctors and families can be obligated to withhold treatment on this basis. In other states, directives made while competent, may protect doctors who follow them from liability for withholding care, but do not obligate doctors to do so.

"There is a growing recognition that death may be more easily accepted when it occurs in the supportive setting of one's home."

In several cases, courts have given effect to the prior expressed wishes of Jehovah's Witnesses who reject blood transfusions, even if the patient is presently incompetent, though this has not always been the case. In another case, a Christian Scientist whose beliefs against medical care were well-known, could not be forced to receive psychotropic medication in a mental institution when she became mentally ill and incompetent. The reasoning of these cases is likely to be extended to other decisions to reject medical care made while the patient is competent and to take effect when the patient becomes incompetent.

Question: Does a competent patient have a right to die at home?

Answer: Yes. If a competent person is critically ill, he has a right to refuse further care, including hospital care, and cannot be put in a hospital against his will. No law requires that a person die in a hospital or under a doctor's care, or prohibits dying at home.

Although eighty percent of deaths now occur in hospitals, there is a growing recognition that death may be more easily accepted when it occurs in the supportive setting of one's home. The hospice movement has facilitated dying at home, and the number of people choosing this option is likely to increase. As a practical matter, however, if family members object, they may be able to prevent a critically ill person from carrying out a desire to die at home. Disputes with family members on this question are not likely to reach the courts.

John A. Robertson is a professor of law in the law school and of medical ethics in the medical school at the University of Wisconsin. He is the editor of Rights of the Critically Ill, *an American Civil Liberties Union handbook.*

The Right to Die Is Determined by Doctors

Mark Siegler

Mr. D, a previously healthy sixty-six-year-old black man, came to a university hospital emergency room with his wife and described a three-day history of sore throat, muscle aches, fevers, chills, cough, sputum production, and blood in his urine. The patient was acutely ill with a high fever, shortness of breath, and a limited attention span. A chest X-ray demonstrated a generalized pneumonia in both lungs. The clinical impression was that Mr. D was critically ill, that the cause of his lung disease was obscure, and that a low platelet count and blood in the urine were ominous signs. He was treated aggressively with three antibiotics in an effort to cure his pneumonia.

The next day his condition worsened. After reviewing the available clinical and laboratory data, the physicians caring for this man recommended that two uncomfortable but relatively routine diagnostic procedures be performed: a bronchial brushing to obtain a small sampling of lung tissue to determine the cause of the pneumonia and a bone marrow examination to determine whether an infection or cancer was invading the bone marrow. The patient refused these diagnostic procedures. Separately, and together, the intern, resident, attending physician, and chaplain explained that these diagnostic tests were necessary to help the physicians formulate rational treatment plans. Mr. D became angry and agitated by this prolonged pressure, and subsequently began refusing even routine blood tests and X-rays.

A psychiatrist who evaluated Mr. D concluded that although he was obviously ill and had a degree of mental impairment manifested by poor memory, he was not mentally incompetent. The psychiatrist thought that the patient understood the severity of his illness and the reasons the physicians were

recommending certain tests, but that he was still making a rational choice in refusing the tests.

The patient's condition deteriorated further and twenty-four hours later he appeared near death. I was the attending physician, and it was my opinion that the only treatment left was to place Mr. D on a respirator as a stopgap measure that might sustain him for another day or two, during which time the antibiotics and antituberculosis drugs might become effective. Mr. D refused.

A Rational Decision

The physicians expressed considerable disagreement on whether Mr. D was sufficiently rational to refuse a potentially life-saving treatment. In an effort to resolve this controversy, I spent two forty-five minute periods at his bedside and explained as clearly as I could the reasons for our recommendations. I said that if he survived this crisis he would be able to return to a normal life and would not be an invalid or require chronic supportive care. During these two sessions, Mr. D was breathing rapidly and shallowly, and had trouble talking. But everything he said convinced me that he understood the gravity of his situation. For example, when I told him he was dying, he replied: "Everyone has to die. If I die now, I am ready." When I asked him if he came to the hospital to be helped, he stated: "I want to be helped. I want you to treat me with whatever medicine you think I need. I don't want any more tests and I don't want the breathing machine."

I gradually became convinced that despite the severity of his illness and his high fever, he was making a conscious, rational decision to selectively refuse a particular kind of treatment. In view of the frankness of our discussion, I then asked him whether he would want us to resuscitate him if he had a cardio-respiratory arrest. He turned away and said: "We've been through this before; now leave me alone." I left the bedside.

Mark Siegler, ''Critical Illness: The Limits of Autonomy,'' *The Hastings Center Report*, October 1977. Reproduced with permission of *The Hastings Center Report*, © Institute of Society, Ethics and the Life Sciences, 360 Broadway, Hastings-on-Hudson, NY 10706.

Throughout this day, despite vigorous attempts by social workers and neighbors, neither his wife nor children could be located.

Mr. D soon became semi-conscious and had a cardio-respiratory arrest. Despite the objections of the houseofficers, I did not attempt to resuscitate him, and he died.

Mr. D's case raised the following questions:

1. Would this critically ill man be permitted to establish diagnostic and therapeutic limits on the care he wished to receive from a health care team in a large university hospital?

2. What were the medically and morally relevant factors that would encourage or permit physicians to respect his wishes? Or, alternatively, on what ground would physicians usurp the patient's presumed rights to liberty, autonomy, and self-determination?

Rules of Conduct

One solution to moral-ethical dilemmas is to establish categorical rules of conduct which obviate the necessity for making agonizing choices in difficult situations. For example, in his writings Robert Veatch has consistently emphasized a commitment to individual freedom and self-determination, and the concomitant need to limit the power and authority of the medical profession. In discussing a patient's right to refuse treatment, Veatch makes the claim that "no competent patients have ever been forced to undergo any medical treatment for their own good no matter how misguided their refusal may have appeared." Veatch concludes that an adult may refuse any treatment as long as he is competent, and the principal determination to be made (in Veatch's view by the courts rather than by physicians) is whether the patient is competent.

"In the face of acute illness, the physician does not have sufficient time to assess the patient's motives."

In a recent paper entitled "The Function of Medicine," Eric Cassell describes an alternative attitude, and one equally familiar to clinicians. Cassell notes that in cases of acute illness (using pneumococcal meningitis as his example) "...it would be a rare hospital where such a patient would not be treated (even) against his will." In such a case, Cassell defends the decision to override a patient's wishes on the grounds that the refusal of treatment in acute illness is tantamount to suicide, that the physician has responsibilities to treat that cannot be relieved by the patient's refusal to accept treatment, that the patient is morally constrained not to prevent the physician from carrying out his responsibilities to treat him, and that in the face of acute illness, the

physician does not have sufficient time to assess the patient's motives.

The Veatch and Cassell positions appear not to take into account the medically and morally relevant factors that physicians assess when determining whether to respect the wishes of critically ill patients. Clinical ethics is premised on the particularities of clinical circumstances, and workable clinical guidelines must necessarily take into account and reflect the extraordinary complexity of the medical model.

Influencing Factors

1. *The patient's ability to make (rational) choices about his care.* Either every critically ill patient in the hospital is incompetent to make choices concerning his care or each case must be assessed separately to determine if there are limits within which the critically ill patient retains some intellectual judgment and is capable of making choices. In the case of Mr. D, as in other critical care cases, the issue confronting conscientious physicians was not simply whether to respect a patient's wishes, but whether it was morally justifiable to accept at face value a critically ill patient's statement of his wishes.

Mr. D's case illustrates the practical difficulties in adhering to any rigid rule (either to defend "radical autonomy" for competent adults or to accept the "doctor's burden to heal" viewpoint) in critical care situations. Mr. D's wishes were forcefully stated and clear. He wished to be helped and to be relieved of his discomfort and pain, and to this end he would permit physicians to treat him with intravenous fluids, oxygen, antibiotics, and other medications. But he was also firm in establishing absolute limits on the diagnostic studies he would permit and in refusing to accept a respirator as a form of treatment. Thus, the perplexing questions which continued to trouble his physicians was whether Mr. D was intellectually capable of exercising such a degree of discrimination and choice. Although there was a considerable difference of opinion among the physicians caring for Mr. D—some believed that his illness impaired his thought processes and rendered him incapable of making choices—in my capacity as the attending physician responsible for his care, I decided otherwise and elected to respect Mr. D's wishes. This decision was based upon my subjective clinical judgment that despite the intensity of his illness, Mr. D retained sufficient intellect and rationality to make choices.

Nature of the Patient

2. *The nature of the person making the choice.* Rather than assessing the rationality of a particular choice, one can ask an alternative question, whether Mr. D's decision were consonant with his nature as a person. Who was Mr. D? What were his values? And did his choices in the hospital reflect those he might have

made were he not ill? Was the patient acting autonomously—that is, with authenticity and independence? Alternatively, another question to be asked is: in the face of critical illness and within the narrow time-space frame characteristic of acute illness, is it ever possible to determine whether a patient's choices truly reflect his normal personality?

Obviously, if a patient and physician had previously established an ongoing relationship, the physician would be better acquainted with the personality, character, ideas, and beliefs of his patient. Another indicator to assess the validity of a patient's choice is whether it reflects a commitment expressed through time, such as the adherence to a particular religious belief (like a Jehovah's Witness refusing blood transfusions), or the signing and updating of a "living will," or the establishment of certain attitudes and behavior patterns in the course of a chronic illness. In Mr. D's case none of this information was available.

Another valuable insight into the patient as a person might be provided by the family as they describe the personality, character, and beliefs of the patient before the onset of this acute illness. The family could also be asked to offer an opinion on whether a patient is acting as he would normally act, or whether his behavior strikes them as aberrant and unusual. The family then would not be making choices for the patient, but would be indicating to physicians the probable validity of the patient's own choices. In Mr. D's case the family was not available and thus could not provide evidence one way or the other.

Rights Are Not Absolute

Many people believe that the rights of individuals are not absolute, but must always be weighed against their responsibilities to social groups like the family or to the community at large. Unfortunately, in Mr. D's case, the absence of family input effectively limited the grounds upon which physicians would accept or reject Mr. D's wishes.

In most clinical circumstances it is possible either from previous knowledge of a patient or from the contributions of his family to assess accurately whether a particular choice made by an ill patient is consistent with his previous behavior and values. In this respect, Mr. D's case represents an extreme example, since none of this background material was available.

In the absence of supporting data, the physician must rely upon his basic skills of communication with the patient and must assess the patient's verbal and non-verbal messages. So much of clinical judgment and clinical decision-making involves the gathering of primary data through talking with patients, that this situation should be seen as an extreme variant of the basic clinical model. Further, much of clinical judgment involves "life and death"

decisions, and thus this situation is not different in intensity from many others. I assessed Mr. D's personality as intelligent, proud, independent, wary of outsiders, and particularly suspicious of physicians and their motives. It seemed to me that the choices he was making were entirely consistent with his basic personality.

"Young physicians strive diligently to not harm the patients, but when their concept of harm remains obscure, 'do no harm' often means 'do everything.'"

Of anecdotal interest, since it did not influence my decision, was some information that became available only after Mr. D's death which indicated that ten years earlier he had left the hospital "against medical advice" after first refusing to have a bone marrow examination!

Age of the Patient

3. *Age.* Mr. D's age made a difference in my decision. Had he been twenty-six years old, the factors I would use to decide whether to override his wishes would probably have remained essentially the same—competence; the conformity of his choices to his personality, and the medical diagnosis and prognosis—but the standards I would apply to assess these might change. For example, I would have demanded a more perfect "mental status examination" and would have scrupulously checked a younger patient for evidence of a "toxic delirium" or an acute depression. My obvious wavering on this point may have something to do with the notion that wisdom and aging are associated, but more likely has to do with a concept of "natural death." The closer a patient gets to a "normal" life span, the more he has lived, and the more ready I am to let "nature take its course." Even though I appreciate the ambiguities and inconsistencies of taking age into account, I believe that I might have acted differently with a younger patient.

Nature of Illness

4. *Nature of the illness.* In this context, critical illness refers to an acute life-threatening illness. Several subdivisions of critical illness are necessary because physician behavior is premised on (a) whether the illness can be diagnosed or alternatively, whether it is obscure and refractory to diagnosis, and (b) what the prognosis is, whether or not the physician is able to make a diagnosis.

The most straightforward situation is one in which the physician can make a diagnosis that permits him to state with certainty that the prognosis of a particular disease is uniformly fatal if untreated, whereas with appropriate treatment complete recovery is possible. In addition to the infectious diseases such as pneumococcal meningitis which conform to this model, other medical emergencies such as acute respiratory failure, acute pulmonary edema, and diabetic ketoacidosis are also easily diagnosed and treated. It is precisely in such cases where diagnostic uncertainty is at a minimum and where the physician is confident about the probability of success with treatment, and the probability of death without treatment, that the physician will be most likely to usurp an ill patient's desires and treat him even against his wishes. In all other cases, however, the physician will be more inclined but not certain to respect the patient's wishes not to be treated. For example, certain diagnoses, in particular metastatic solid tumors or degenerative neurologic diseases, seem to generate a minimalist approach on the part of physicians and on occasion discourage physicians from aggressively treating patients with such diseases who may develop easily reversible acute conditions such as pneumonia.

The problem of uncertainty of diagnosis or uncertainty of prognosis is particularly disturbing. The absence of a diagnosis is a potential threat to the whole disease-oriented medical system, and generates a very aggressive, no-holds-barred approach to diagnostic testing. Mr. D's refusal to submit to certain routine but uncomfortable diagnostic procedures effectively blocked the efforts of his physicians to name his disease and surely contributed to their frustration. In cases of uncertainty, where the physician and patient are in agreement on pursuing diagnostic and therapeutic procedures, physicians will generally err on the side of diagnostic aggressiveness in an effort not to overlook a potentially reversible disease process. However, in cases of uncertainty where physicians and patients are in disagreement about diagnostic and therapeutic approaches, physician anxiety is maximized and the need for a moral-clinical decision is most urgent. In such cases, and Mr. D's case is a classic example, physicians must again rely upon their clinical judgment to assess the likelihood that a particular diagnostic study will yield a result that may permit a particular therapy which can change the outcome of the case. As the probability of a successful intervention decreases, most physicians can more easily, but not very easily conform to the patient's wishes.

Constrained by Law

In some cases, however, even if a particular intervention will guarantee success, the physician may still not usurp a patient's wishes. A frequent example of this latter situation arises in Jehovah's Witness cases where a simple blood transfusion could forestall a life-threatening emergency, but in which the physician is constrained by consistent legal precedents not to override a patient's wishes.

In the case of Mr. D, it soon became clear to me that whatever the diagnosis of his obscure illness was, it was fulminant and aggressive and would probably lead to his death. Even if we had been able to make a diagnosis from the bone marrow and bronchial brushing examinations, it was likely that no additional therapy would change his outcome. Even if he had consented to a respirator, his rapidly progressive deterioration suggested that he was not going to survive. I readily admit that my clinical judgment that the disease was rapidly progressive and almost certainly fatal further influenced me.

Attitude of Physician

5. *The attitudes and values of the physician responsible for the decision.* At every point in the decision making, the responsible physician has resorted to value judgment. The judgments of whether the patient was rational, of what his baseline personality was, of what importance to ascribe to his age, and of whether his disease was potentially treatable and reversible are all determinations that involve subjective value judgments based upon limited objective data.

"Although the attending physician may ultimately be responsible for decisions, he does not care for patients in isolation."

Further, although physicians as a profession may share some general values and biases, they are not homogeneous in their basic value orientation. They differ in moral and religious background, in age, in experience, and in specialty training, to mention just a few factors. Specifically, what is a particular physician's attitude toward life and death? Does a physician view the death of a patient as a personal defeat, an unavoidable tragedy? What is his concept of the role of the physician in the physician-patient relationship, that of a technician-scientist, or an advisor, or a friend, or a party to a contract? If the responsible physician invokes the doctrine of "do no harm," is his concept of harm that of omission or commission?

If all other factors were identical in arriving at a decision to support or override a patient's wishes not to be treated, we might discover that two physicians—one who believed in the primacy of life and another who believed in "death with dignity"— would reach entirely opposite conclusions. In Mr. D's case, my belief in the rights of individuals to determine their own destinies further encouraged me to support the patient's choices.

6. *The clinical setting.* Mr. D's case reflects some of the special problems of practicing medicine in a large, institutional, teaching setting. If a physician-patient encounter similar to the one described here had occurred in a patient's home, or in a nursing home, or even in many community hospitals (particularly one without housestaff), there would be little question about acceding to the patient's wishes. There are at least two reasons. First, the kind of technology and expertise necessary to do many of these procedures is best represented in the large teaching hospital.

"The intellectual and emotional strength necessary to resist the powers of the medical system. . .must have been enormous."

The second reason is more complex. It involves the nature of a teaching hospital in which authority and responsibility are diffused among the "health care team." Although the attending physician may ultimately be responsible for decisions, he does not care for patients in isolation. Indeed, most of the caring is performed by housestaff, students, nurses, and other health care personnel. The housestaff are very close to their patients and have very strong feelings about how best to care for them. Despite the housestaff's general lack of clinical experience, their views are often very accurate and persuasive. Further, housestaff are particularly skilled in the care of acutely ill patients. These young physicians strive diligently to not harm the patients, but when their concept of harm remains obscure, "do no harm" often means "do everything."

Houseofficers' Resistance

One interesting sidelight of this case was the houseofficers' wish to resuscitate this man after he died. They argued that at no time did the patient state he wanted to die; he did not offer a definitive "no" when asked whether he wished to be resuscitated; and clearly, after his heart and lungs stopped, he was no longer rational and decisions could then be made for him.

One final observation: this man was extremely strong and dignified in his last days. Despite his illness and fever, he resisted the onslaught of many physicians and consultants and the power of the hospital institution. He established limits for the health care team and would not permit those limits to be transgressed. The intellectual and emotional strength necessary to resist the powers of the medical system to persuade and force him to accept what they wanted to offer must have been enormous. He

died a dignified death, and attempts at resuscitation would have violated the position he held while alive. It is unfortunate, and I am sadly moved, that he had to expend his last measures of intellectual and physical energy to engage in ongoing debate with his physicians. But perhaps that is the price the medical system sometimes exacts from those who would assert their independence and preserve their autonomy while suffering from critical illness.

Mark Siegler, M.D., is a member of the Department of Medicine, division of the Biological Sciences and Pritzker School of Medicine, University of Chicago.

The Plea to Die Is a Plea for Help

Michael Platt

At the center of *Case 228* described by Dr. Robert S. White in the June *Report* is the plea, "let me die" uttered by a severely burnt young man. Dr. White found this man perfectly sane and yet, as he writes, "None of us who were responsible for his care could bring ourselves to say, 'You're discharged; go home and die.'" Dr. White does not specify the reasons which led him and his colleagues to do as they did. Since he also reports the happy ending of the case, we are tempted to judge the case in the light of its ending; but we should not, and we need not, for Dr. White videotaped a conversation with the burnt young man before he withdrew his plea "let me die."

The beginning of the videotape is abrupt, wordless, and disturbing. For about four minutes (it seems much longer) we see nothing but the burnt body of this man, first bandaged, then being unbandaged, then lowered into the Hubbard tank. We hear nothing from him; he neither speaks nor gestures. Instead we hear the noises he hears: metal on metal (from instruments banging against the tub), the squeak of gears hoisting him up and lowering him by jerks into the tub, the murmur of the attendants (or physicians?), and throughout, the chatter, pop music, and pushy advertising of a local radio station. Throughout these opening moments, this burnt man says nothing and no one says anything to him. Here and later during the conversation between Dr. White and this man, the camera keeps our eye on his burnt body. We are compelled to look at this body, almost to dwell inside it, at any rate to think about what it would feel like to be this man.

Patient's Point of View

I realize this man wants us, his anonymous viewers, to consider his situation from his point of view, but there is also something curious about

Michael Platt, "Commentary: On Asking to Die," *The Hastings Center Report*, December 1975. Reproduced with permission of *The Hastings Center Report*, © Institute of Society, Ethics and the Life Sciences, 360 Broadway, Hastings-on-Hudson, NY 10706.

meeting him in the way we do. Commonly in life the people we meet are clothed, and intimacy is a gradual thing. Precisely the exception to this rule is the case of medical treatment where, for good reason, we allow others (who may be utter strangers) to decide about intimacy and its usual markers, clothes. In this videotape the camera abruptly dispenses with intimacy and from then on it roves over his burnt naked body, placing us as close to him as friend is to friend at lunch and sometimes much closer. By doing this the camera imitates modern medicine and by so doing it reminds us of the personal space which, again for good reason, a man loses when he turns into a patient, when he exchanges a home for a hospital, his old clothes for new and commonplace pajamas.

Rehearsed Interview

Most of the tape is devoted to the interview itself. After the silence of the first four minutes, I was much relieved to hear him speak. Hearing him speak answered a question roused in my mind by looking so long at his silent body: Is there someone still there? But again the camera roams. Ordinarily in a conversation eyes meet. The speaker and the listener keep contact with their eyes; a silent anonymous eavesdropper like ourselves (the whole videotape casts us in this role) attends to the speaking faces. Not so here. The camera roams, like a person who does not pay full attention. Sometimes this roaming seems occasioned by what the burnt man is saying. When, at the doctor's request, he raises his stiff arm, the camera zooms in for a closeup. When he speaks of the activities he most enjoyed, the camera shows us pictures of him playing football or riding a bronco. At other times the camera just shows us more of the Hubbard tank treatment.

It is the rehearsed character of the interview which dictates this busy and distracted camera work. The doctor and the burnt man are going over old ground;

both know it is all being taped. Indeed, the conversation takes place for the sake of the tape.

"Correct me if I get the sequence mixed up," says Dr. White as he starts to narrate the man's recent history. Gradually control of the conversation passes to the burnt man himself; the past tense gives way to present tense. From asking, "How *did* you feel?" Dr. White moves on to asking, "How *do* you feel now?" Instead of nodding agreement to the doctor's version of events the burnt man begins to respond at length. Still, even when he and the doctor participate equally, the conversation is guided by a tacit agenda. Only at the end is the spell of rehearsal broken; the burnt man asks his first question and pushes it home.

> The way I see it, who is a doctor to decide whether a person lives or dies?. . . I had to undergo this painful treatment regardless of my feelings. If I'm not willing to go to the Hubbard tank, I'm picked up out of bed and just bodily placed on the stretcher and taken anyway, even if I have to be tied down to it.

The doctor's response terminates the conversation: "Well, that poses an important issue of course for you, for the physicians, and for the attorney."

Lame Answer

The doctor seems to feel the lameness of this answer for he adds, "Let's talk about it some further again soon." Perhaps the doctor saw the allotted video time ticking away. The burnt man nods with resignation; I suspect he wanted the conversation to continue. His own wish, to make the tape, interfered with his other wish, to talk with someone. We can only conclude that it is hard to have a satisfying conversation when the interlocutors converse for the sake of being overheard.

"Is it really true that he cannot kill himself? Couldn't he refuse to eat?"

Though helpless, the burnt young man is sane. He has suffered much pain and will suffer more in the course of continued treatment. His prospects for regaining the active life he loves are nil. Other less active lives seem unattractive. He wishes to go home and kill himself, but he cannot. He is too helpless to commit suicide. His commands to cease treatment are not heeded by the physicians. Nevertheless, the very same videotape which compels me to agree to the reasonableness of his demand causes me to think that the physicians were right not to cease treating this burnt man. I am persuaded that it is not in the common interest of all of us to ask doctors to perform euthanasia, active or passive; but it is not for this reason that I think the doctors were right to continue treatment. I think that if one looks and listens carefully to what is said in this interview one will conclude that the plea or command "let me die"

means more than it says and that it may mean the opposite of what it says.

As I listen to this burnt man speaking I do not hear despair, or self-pity, or lassitude. I hear resolution accented by indignation. His indignation is neither shrill nor hasty. He has reached his views in the course of thoughtful deliberation; his will is active, though thwarted. The suicide he desired is the antique and active kind, not a sinking or melting, and the death he speaks of helps us to understand what he finds intolerable in his present condition. He does not like the pain he has endured or the pain he may expect to endure but he tells us at one point that it would be endurable if there were more hope of regaining the active sporting life he so much enjoyed. Pain is not the worst thing. Even the loss of sports is not the worst thing, for as the conversation proceeds we hear more. Late in the conversation Dr. White says:

> Well, of course, you're so completely helpless, that is, unable to get out of bed even by yourself, that you're pretty much at the mercy of all the people around you now, as to whether you stay or leave. How do you feel about that?

(This seems to me one of those moments in the conversation which entirely dispels the atmosphere of rehearsal.) And the burnt man replies:

> It's a really sinking feeling. I've always been really independent, and I like to do things for myself. I've had my way of doing things. And I've pretty much, you know, done as I wished. Up to this point. And now I have to rely on someone else to feed me. . . . all my private functions I need help with.

Helpless Condition

It seems clear that what is worst about his condition is his helplessness and the prospect of more of the same.

This is underlined by another exchange midway through the interview; Dr. White and he come to the subject of his wish to die. Yes, he still wishes to die. He wants to go home. Why does he want to go home? He knows he would die of infection outside of the hospital, but that is not what he has in mind. "Actually, I just want a brief visit to home. I don't intend to die from the infection. . . I would use some other means." What if we asked him at this point: "By what other means?" (I think Dr. White refrains, and rightly refrains, from asking this question for the answer is obvious and painful.) The means this burnt man desires are entirely unavailable to him. He is quite helpless. He cannot pull a trigger. He cannot hang himself. He cannot grasp a knife. He cannot take a pill, turn on a gas stove, or light a fire. This question "by what means?" suggests another question equally pertinent to understanding this man's intentions and speeches. Is it really true that he cannot kill himself? Couldn't he refuse to eat? Couldn't he make a nuisance of himself and goad the staff into ignoring him? Couldn't he "turn his face to the wall''? Could intravenous feeding really keep him alive? Nothing in the videotape or in Dr. White's account in the *Report* suggests that he acted so as to die in these ways. These were not the ''means'' he wanted because they are all supine means. He did not wish to die supinely but deliberately and willfully.

Protest Against Helplessness

His plea to cease treatment expresses a protest against the helplessness of his condition; it also expresses a protest against the treatment which makes him helpless. He knows, of course, that the doctors are there to help, but he also knows what doctors may sometimes forget, that the medicine which brings great help also renders its beneficiaries greatly helpless. Understandably, they do not like it, and understandably this burnt man finds some measure of the autonomy he desires in carrying forward his demand to die towards a court decision. So, just after he has said in the passage I quoted above: ''all my private functions I need help with,'' he turns immediately to the question which astounds him, how a doctor can keep treating him when he doesn't want to be treated. By asking such questions, by asking for a lawyer, and by making this videotape, this burnt man seems already to be gaining some of the autonomy he desires. What modern medicine did not seem to be providing (and may necessarily have been actively depriving him of) seems to have been provided by these ''other means.''

My observations, I know, lead me and those who might share them into difficulty. Had the law or a court decision been present from the beginning the man might be dead. Of course, having the immediate right to command cessation of treatment might have changed his mind. Saying ''let me die'' when you know they will let you differs from saying ''let me die'' when you know they won't. On the one side there is the clarity which written law desires (and for which we desire it) and on the other there is the ambiguity of the burnt man's words. He means what he says but he also means both more than he says and something opposite from what he says. The law hears a man say he wants no more treatment, but a sensitive and caring observer may hear pleas to be relieved of helplessness and, in his protests against the doctors, find evidence of a preference for life. In this case the difficulty was overcome by what in other circumstances we protest as ''the law's delay.''

In American public life and in present discussion of American medical practice there is a disposition to believe that legislation is the best or the only solution to the things which trouble and afflict us. (There is a similar disposition to believe that modern medicine is such a solution.) If we must have legislation or court interpretations to cover such cases as that of this burnt man, let them be ones which prefer slowness to haste and which give a wide scope for human

judgment to determine such things as what a man means when he says he wants to die; it will be good for such legislation to designate for punishment only the clear and obvious abuses of duty. It is a difficult matter to decide when someone means something more or something different from what he says and a weighty and final matter when what he says is ''let me die,'' and it is wise for us to frame laws that recognize that the place of judgment in human affairs should not be usurped by legislation.

Lack of Sensitivity

This burnt man was telling the doctors treating him that he preferred death to more treatment, and Dr. White perceived that the caring response to this dilemma is not a quick move to the law but an attempt to find a better treatment. The very success of modern medicine visits a certain suffering upon the persons in the bodies it treats. Consider the present case. The refined and adroit techniques which preserve the man's life from infection and promote his slow recovery are the very ones which render him so helpless. Whatever helps a man renders him more helpless, and so the more modern medicine ''saves'' bodies the more it will impart a feeling of helplessness to the persons in those bodies.

''Saying, 'let me die' when you know they will let you differs from saying 'let me die' when you know they won't.''

It would seem that its success imposes the duty to relieve that sense of helplessness where it can (though I do wonder why the pain-killing or pain-relieving drug the burnt man speaks of was not administered earlier). What can be done? In the first four minutes of the videotape, the burnt man lies there. No one talks to him. In the final minute of the tape we hear him crying, ''Oh, easy. Oh, easy. Hey, easy on the back of my leg.'' No one responds with word or gesture. They go on working in silence. The noise which fills the first four minutes of the tapes is perhaps worse than silence. Have they asked this burnt man whether he wants that radio on? As we look at his burnt body and consider its appearance the radio hawks ''Royal Crown Hairdressing.'' Did we need to be reminded of cosmetics and appearance at a time like this? Did we or he need to be reminded how much we are judged by appearances or how much we are what we appear to others? The specious and annoying presence of the radio makes us ask: Will no one be present with this man? Does anyone talk to him? When is the last time he had a good conversation? I address these questions to those charged with the care of such men but not only to such men. The attempt to ignore misfortune by ignoring those whom it strikes is not confined to the hospital. When I mentioned this videotape to Professor Marvin Kohl (State University of New York at Fredonia), he reported that when he showed it to his class they were indignant, not at something it showed, but at him for showing it to them. They discussed, with much heat, not the question it raises but the morality of his showing it to them.

Education is a slow and difficult remedy but it is the proper remedy for what in human situations is not amenable to comparatively simple and easy solutions, like law and medicine. The hand of man performs wonders; without our hands we would have no arts like modern medicine, but sometimes when we are wretched we just want someone to hold our hand. The strength to suffer with those we see suffer is not a technique and it cannot be enforced by written law. It can only be promoted by education and example, and Dr. White deserves both our praise and our thanks for setting such an example.

Michael Platt, Ph.D., is an associate professor of English at the University of Dallas. He was a post-doctoral fellow of the Hastings Institute in 1975 when he wrote this viewpoint.

*"I didn't intend to die from infection,
but intended to commit suicide...I was
burned bad enough I didn't want to
live."*

viewpoint **43**

The Plea to Die
Is Usually Sincere

Margaret Engel

Ten years ago, the life of Dax Cowart, 35, of Henderson, Texas, changed completely. A former air force pilot, high-school athlete, golfer, surfer and rodeo rider, Cowart was working in his father's real-estate business that July day. A freak propane gas leak on a property he and his father were appraising caused an explosion. The blast killed his father. It left Cowart blind, with his hearing impaired, and with limited use of his arms. His burns have disfigured his once-handsome face and only one joint of one thumb remains on his hands.

Cowart spent the 14 months after the explosion in excruciating pain, caused particularly by daily immersions to sterilize his burns.

From his first communication with ambulance paramedics to doctors, ministers, nurses, as well as lawyers he hired against his family's wishes, Cowart repeatedly insisted that he be allowed to leave the hospital and die.

Nightmares and Pain

"I didn't intend to die from infection, but intended to commit suicide," Cowart said. "The nightmares and pain involved in the first few months were so bad, I can barely remember it myself. I couldn't tell what was really happening and what was a dream. I was convinced one of the interns was using me as one of his guinea pigs. I was burned bad enough I didn't want to live."

The American Medical Association in 1973 had endorsed the right of a competent patient to decide whether to continue life-prolonging treatment, but Cowart's wish was never granted.

Since his hospital discharge, Cowart has taken some graduate courses in law and business construction, but was forced to drop out because of

Margaret Engel, "After 10 Years, Burn Victim Still Wishes He'd Been Allowed to Die," *The Washington Post,* July 31, 1983. Reprinted with permission.

his physical limitations. He married a high-school acquaintance in February, now runs a seasonal small business and directs a local Chamber of Commerce committee.

Despite his re-entry into society, he still insists that he should have been allowed to die:

Question: Why didn't you commit suicide as soon as you were released?

Answer: I was watched practically every minute. I did not have very much use of my hands. I could not see to get things that I needed, especially being watched as much as I was.

Doctors' Prisoner

Question: You said you felt a virtual prisoner of some of the doctors. Why do you think they ignored your request to refuse treatment?

Answer: The doctors knew that I would not die from the injuries. I had a chance of being able to walk again. Their thinking, I'm sure, was that if they forced me to receive treatment, at some point I would want to live. I would change my mind after I had an opportunity to adjust. They felt it would be best for me in the long run.

Question: Why were those motives wrong?

Answer: The motives weren't wrong. What was wrong was the actual forcing of me to undertake the treatment. I had full use of my mind. I demonstrated that I could think. That I could reason. That I had given it some thought. I knew I was burned bad enough, I didn't want to live. There's no way I wanted to go on as blind and a cripple. When a patient is forced to undergo this treatment against his or her will, they are really forced to accept whatever treatment the doctors want. The person is completely at the mercy of the doctors on how much attention is given to pain control. The vast majority of people do not know what freedoms they can lose when they become physically incapacitated. Once you're inside a hospital's walls, things are different. With all the emphasis on civil rights, regardless of my feelings, if I wasn't willing to go to the tank, I was picked up bodily anyway and put on the stretcher. Why is it right to be subjected to painful treatment against someone's wishes, especially if he's demonstrated an ability to reason?

Doctors' Power

Question: Why do you think helpless patients are put in this position?

Answer: It's just a result of the doctors having the power. The doctors' interest has been to preserve life and also to benefit the patient. But they're trying to benefit the patient on their own terms rather than the patient's. My case was an example of where the two are not the same.

Question: How many operations did you go through?

Answer: I couldn't even count. I don't remember.

Question: Why did you want to die?

Answer: Because of the extreme amount of pain. I had to undergo many painful procedures day after day after day. Every day seemed like a year. The passage of time was so slow. Also, I simply did not feel that the quality of life that I would have upon recovering would be such that I would want to continue.

Question: How do you feel about that now?

Answer: In terms of how happy I am now, I have a very good quality of life. There's many things that have happened every day that are just extremely frustrating. Things that you take for granted (that I can't)—putting on clothes or going to the restroom or getting in the car or walking down to the store. Reading your mail. Reading the newspaper. It's a really sinking feeling. I've always been real independent. Now I have to rely on someone else to feed me—for all my private functions. Things like that are very frustrating.

Ends Do Not Justify Means

Question: Frustration, however, is different from not being able to do it at all. Do you still wish you had been allowed to die?

Answer: I don't know how anyone can say—at least I can't—that it's worth it. The best way I know how to answer that question is that I have had some very, very good experiences and happy experiences that I of course would not have had if I had died. My contention is that I should have been the one to make that choice at that time. And if I had made that choice I would have refused treatment. To me it's saying that the ends justify the means and I just don't happen to believe that way.

Question: Are you trying to make the point that nothing in your later life can be traded off with what you went through?

Answer: Yea. If it happened again tomorrow, would I still do the same thing? I know that definitely

the answer is yes. If I were burned again today? Had to go through this again but at the end of the road 10 years from now, I know it's going to be worth it? Knowing that, would I make a different decision? The answer is no.

Question: You would still opt to die?

Answer: Yes. I have a life that I did not have then. I might not make the decision as readily. I might be able to endure more pain and push myself to the outer edge. But I still do not want to be forced. I still want to remain in control. I want it to be my decision and not someone else's.

Question: Is your wife ever insulted when you say that you wish you had been allowed to die?

Answer: I don't think she's insulted. Someone might think that it casts a reflection on her, but it's not. I am happy now. I think what you're thinking is what many people say—well, doesn't the fact that I am happy now and I am enjoying life, doesn't that mean that the doctors did the right thing in forcing me to receive treatment?

"The vast majority of people do not know what freedoms they can lose when they become physically incapacitated."

Question: And how do you answer that?
Answer: Well, it's not.

Question: Do you hold any malice toward those doctors and nurses?

Answer: I don't really hold malice. Even with some of the individuals with whom I was the angriest. I'd be the last one to say that they're just bad individuals and I'm still just totally hostile. There are things that I'd still be outraged about if it were happening to me again. Nurses taking food out of the patients' refrigerator and eating it. A little boy that was burned from electrical shock and had both arms amputated—nurses that set his food down next to him, walked off without feeding him. Just leaving it there. Telling him to do it himself. Then there were nurses that would stay 30 minutes—sometimes an hour—after their shift was over, just sit and talk.

Wanting Control

Question: One of the medical articles about you said that you didn't really want to die, you simply wanted control. You wanted to assert your rights. What do you think about that theory?

Answer: He was right on the second assumption, wrong on the first. I wanted both. I wanted the right to control, like I always have wanted the right to control everything in my life possible, ever since I was born. But I also wanted to die. I wanted to be free from the pain. It wasn't just one or the other. It was both.

Question: Why didn't your doctors heed your instructions?

Answer: While I was adamantly opposed to the treatment, my mother was just as adamantly opposed to their stopping.

Question: How does she feel about it now?

Answer: She knows the amount of pain I went through. I have not asked her, but knowing everything that she knows now, she would probably make the same decision she made.

Question: Did you ever try to take your life?

Answer: Once about two years after I was released from the hospital I took a large overdose of tranquilizers and sleeping medications, anything I could find. Slashing my wrists, taking aspirin beforehand. Unsuccessful with that, too.

Question: Do you think that you would try to take your life in the future?

Answer: No, I don't think so.

Question: What's the change?

Answer: If I were in the state of people that I know right now—who are in a nursing home completely paralyzed in a fetal position with their fingers curled backwards and cannot move anything but open their eyes—I would certainly want to die. If things ever return to the point that I could just not function such as the point where I could not sleep—I just put so much effort into trying to achieve something. Then it all came tumbling down—if that were to happen—I don't expect it to, at least for the foreseeable future—I might possibly.

"What we're doing is not preserving life, we're really just drawing out the dying process."

Question: You've spent long hours reflecting on your fate and your life. Do you have a vision of what constitutes a human life? Has it changed your views on abortion? Has it changed your views on death?

No Quality of Life

Answer: People who are terminally ill, today it is insane for anyone to require that person to undergo cancer chemotherapy or whatever if that is not what that person wishes. What we're doing is not preserving life, we're really just drawing out the dying process. If any given patient wants to receive whatever treatment's available, I think that every effort should be made to accommodate him or her. But if we force people to undergo treatment, what we're doing is putting the individual at the mercy of whatever medical and scientific technology comes into being in the future. We may preserve, if you put it in quotes, "life," but what is left of the patient may be only the shell. No quality of life left. No ability to function—even think. If you define life as just the fact that the individual is not decaying, it's not any life that anyone I know would have an interest in maintaining.

Question: Do you think that medical technology should stop that quest to prolong life?

Answer: So many of the things that are done to preserve or prolong life can, in many cases, be beneficial. So I don't think the quest should be stopped. But it's something that should be chosen by the patient and not forced upon him or her. One thing I feel that is absolutely wrong, is when we maintain (terminal) individuals in an intensive-care unit, in a nursing home, at expense to the public, while we're denying funds that could be saving children that may need certain surgery to preserve their lives. We're not a bottomless pit when it comes to financial resources in our country. I think it's wrong to deny people medical attention while shelling out millions and millions of dollars to keep people in that kind of state alive. And those individuals often have no interest in continuing.

Question: When did you get to the point of deciding not to take your life?

Answer: In 1980, when I was able to get some sleep and function on a day-to-day basis, at least partially.

Question: What was your name?

Answer: My given name was Don.

Question: Why did you change that (to Dax)?

Answer: The primary reason was that I was constantly answering to someone that was not addressing me. I do not hear well, especially if there's a little bit of background noise. They can say John or Ron or anything close and I respond. I was trying to think of some way of handling that problem. It was happening all the time. I came up with changing my name to something that would not be confused with someone else.

Question: It's a very distinguished Texas name. It sounds like something that Carson McCullers would use for her main character.

Answer: Well, to be more precise it was in Harold Robbins' *The Adventurers.*

Question: What has this experience taught you about your personal strength?

Answer: I think that I had a lot of strength before the accident. I'm very calm by nature. Very analytical. Look at things and try to solve the problems and not get excited or hyper while in an emergency. But I feel without a doubt I have more mental strength than I did before. How much of it is a result of being 10 years older and more mature and how much is a result of the accident I don't know.

Margaret Engel is a journalist for the Washington Post.

"What the manipulator does is alter his victim's immediate and/or long-range circumstances in such a way that the victim himself chooses death as preferable to continued life."

The Elderly's Right to Die Is Manipulated by Society

M. Pabst Battin

Resuscitating an issue once quite widely explored by the Greeks, many contemporary bioethicists are now reexamining the notion of *rational* suicide, and are suggesting that death can, in some unfortunate cases (for instance, painful terminal illness), be a choice that is as reasonable, or more reasonable, than remaining alive. This often accompanied by a call for more than merely intellectual assent and a demand for its recognition in religion, custom, medicine, psychiatry, and law. Indeed, a relaxation of traditional impermissive attitudes about suicide is already—albeit—slowly beginning to take place.

Reservations about the notion of rational suicide may be based on the dangers of erroneous choice: the risk that acceptance of rational suicide might on some occasions encourage impulsive or irrational suicide among those whose choices are not reasoned or clear. However, this risk, it may be argued, is countered by the moral imperative of allowing individuals to exercise what is clearly their right to die. On this view, the moral issue in suicide centers on a weighing of the interests of two groups: the "irrational" suicides, who are now thwarted in their attempts, but in the absence of social, legal, and psychological barriers to suicide might succeed at something they do not really want, and the "rational" suicides, who, by these same barriers, are dissuaded from that to which they have a right.

Benefits in Mind

The benefits which most advocates of rational suicide have in mind seem to be based on a scenario something like this. Consider the cancer victim who suffers his illness in a society (like ours) which rejects suicide on religious, legal, social, and psychological grounds: he is, in effect, forced to endure the disease

until it kills him, watching it rob his family of financial security and emotional health, rather than perform an act which he and his family are led to believe would make him a coward, a sociopath, a deviant, a lunatic, and an apostate. "Hang on a little longer," he and they urge each other, for to do otherwise would on all counts be wrong.

But the same individual, suffering the same disease in a society that offers no barriers to self-administered death in the face of terminal illness, will be very much more able to choose suicide, since if he does he, and his family, may take him to be acting decently and rationally, to be making a socially responsible choice, and to be doing what is sane, moral, and devout. To make such choices possible, and to give them social support, it is held, would be a great gain for human welfare, by allowing us to forgo suffering for ouselves and ruin for others when they can in no other way be avoided. As David Hume once put this point:

> . . . both prudence and courage should engage us to rid ourselves at once of existence when it becomes a burden. This is the only way that we can then be useful to society, by setting an example which, if imitated, would preserve to every one his chance for happiness in life, and would effectually free him from all danger or misery.

But this is not the only outcome we might expect from the adoption of the notion of rational suicide. For, as I shall try to show, I think this notion— seemingly paradoxically—first gives rise to the possibility of large-scale manipulation of suicide, and the maneuvering of persons into choosing suicide when they would not otherwise have done so. This is the other, darker side of the future coin.

Circumstantial Manipulation

Let us try to describe manipulation into suicide by sorting out its cases; I think we can distinguish two principal mechanisms at work.

1. Circumstantial manipulation. The rationality or

irrationality of a given choice of suicide is in part a function of the individual's circumstances: his health, his living conditions, the degree of comfort or discomfort his daily life involves, his political environment, his opportunities for enjoyable or fulfilling activities and work, and so forth. Thus, when a person's circumstances change, so does the rationality or irrationality of his committing suicide: what may have been an unsound choice becomes, in the face of permanently worsened circumstances (say, a confirmed diagnosis of painful and incurable deteriorative illness) a reasonable one. But it is just this feature of suicide—that its rationality may change with changing circumstances—that makes one form of manipulation possible. What the manipulator does is alter his victim's immediate and/or long-range circumstances in such a way that the victim himself chooses death as preferable to continued life.

"Manipulation of this sort may happen in a glaring way. . . we call it coercion, and count it as a form of murder."

Manipulation of this sort may happen in a glaring way, as for instance in sustained toture; where blatant circumstantial manipulation of this sort is intended to result in suicide, we call it coercion, and count it as a form of murder. No doubt much more frequent, however, is the small, not very visible, often even inadvertent kind of manipulation that occurs in domestic situations, where what the manipulator does is to "arrange things" so that suicide becomes—given the other alternatives—the reasonable, even attractive choice for his victim. For instance, negligent family members may fail to change the bed sheets of an incontinent bedridden patient, and in other ways provide poor or hostile nursing care; abusive parents may so thoroughly restrict and distort the circumstances of an adolescent child that suicide seems the only sensible way out. Perhaps only because it is so often invisible, we do not always recognize this kind of "domestic" manipulation as coercion and thus do not always call it murder.

Circumstances change

Of course, suicide will not be the rational choice in such circumstances if these circumstances are likely to change or if they can be altered in some way. Where adverse circumstances are the result of coercion or manipulation by some other person or group, the obvious *rational* response would be to resist or attack the perpetrator in an effort to stop the manipulation and improve the circumstances. Thus, the incontinent bedridden patient's rational move is to complain to friends or authorities that his bed

sheets are unchanged and that the care he is given is cruel; the beleaguered adolescent's may be to fight back or to run away.

In some cases, however, resistance may not be possible: the victim may be unable to elude his torturers, and suicide may *in fact* be the only way of escape. Perhaps such cases are rare. But if we recognize the notion of rational suicide, we must also recognize that in such cases, suicide may be the only rational choice for the victim, whether he is coerced and whether his circumstances have been deliberately worsened or not. Where the victim can identify the perpetrator and retaliate in some effective way, to do so is clearly the more rational choice, but manipulation is not always easy to detect, and even when it is, its perpetrators are not always easy to stop.

Ideological Manipulation

2. Ideological manipulation. The rationality of suicide is also in part a function of one's beliefs and values, and these, like circumstances, can also change. Suicide can be said to be irrational not only if it is chosen in a hasty, unthinking way, or on the basis of inadequate information, but also if it violates one's fundamental beliefs and values. For instance, suicide can be said to be an irrational choice for someone who believes that it will bring unwanted, eternal damnation, or for someone who believes that active, this-world caring for another is his primary goal.

But, of course, suicide may also be in accord with one's most fundamental beliefs and values. For instance, Stoic thinkers held slavery to be a condition so degrading that death was to be preferred to it, and those who took their lives to avoid slavery (Cato, for instance) regarded themselves and were regarded by others as having made a fully rational choice. These fundamental beliefs, of course, vary from one society and era to another: though loss of virginity and chastity was a basis for rational suicide in early medieval times, the contemporary rape victim does not typically consider sexual assault reason to kill herself, even though it may cause very severe emotional distress. Nor does contemporary Western society countenance suicide in bereavement, for honor, or to avoid poverty, insanity, or disgrace, although all these have been recognized in various cultures at earlier times.

Once we see that the beliefs and values on which the rationality of suicide in part depends can vary from one individual or historical era to another, we also recognize that such ideology can change. Ideological change may occur as part of the natural evolution of a culture; however, such changes can also be engineered. The contemporary world is already well familiar with deliberate attitude and values manipulation, from the gentle impress of advertising to the intensive programming and conditioning associated with various religious and political groups. If our attitudes and values in other areas can be deliberately changed, it is not at all unreasonable to think that our conceptions of the conditions under which suicide would be the rational choice can be changed too.

Choosing Suicide

If we look at contemporary society, we can already see considerable evidence of change in areas relevant to the practice of rational suicide. To detect such change, of course, is not to find evidence of deliberate manipulation; but it is to show the kinds of change in association with which we might expect manipulation—deliberate or otherwise—to occur. These changes are all of a sort in which someone might be brought to choose suicide who would not otherwise have done so.

In the first place, we may note various kinds of circumstantial change relevant to the practice of rational suicide. Some are changes that might work to decrease the incidence of suicide: the development of more effective methods of pain relief, for instance, or institutions like Hospice. But others tend on the whole to worsen the conditions of certain individuals or groups: here one might cite our increasing tendency to confine elderly persons in nursing homes, the increasing expense of such institutional care, the loss of social roles for the elderly, and the increasingly difficult financial circumstances of those living on marginal or fixed incomes. One might also mention increasing loss of autonomy in the seriously ill, as "heroic" practices in medicine become increasingly mechanized; new abilities to maintain seriously injured or birth-defective persons in marginal states, and so forth. Gerontologists and patients' rights advocates have been pointing to the inhumane consequences of such circumstantial changes for some time, and such observations are hardly new; what is new, however, is alertness to their role with respect to rational suicide. Increasingly poor conditions, in a society which is coming to accept a notion of rational suicide, may mean an increasing likelihood that suicide will be the individual's choice.

Ideological Changes

Second, we can also diagnose in contemporary society several significant ideological changes. For instance, we may notice a profusion of recent literary accounts favorable to suicide and assisted suicide in terminal-illness cases—real-life stories of one partner assisting the other in obtaining and taking a lethal drug to avoid the ravages of cancer. We observe increasingly frequent court decisions favoring patients' rights to refuse medical treatment, even when refusal will mean death. We notice public accounts of suicides conceived of and conducted as rational: the Henry and Elizabeth Van Dusen, Wallace Proctor, and Jo Roman cases, to mention a

few. And we observe that some religious groups have begun to devote attention to the issue of whether suicide may be, in certain kinds of terminal circumstances, an act of religious conscience, even though Western Christianity has in general not allowed it since Augustine, for the past fifteen hundred years. Almost all these cases involve suicide in the face of painful terminal illness, and that illness is very often cancer. If we were to diagnose our own ideological changes with regard to suicide, we would probably say that they involve a very recent move— by no means universal, but already clearly and widely evident—from the recently predominant view that there is *no* good reason for suicide (and hence that all suicide is irrational or insane) to the view that there is after all one adequate reason for suicide: extreme and irremediable pain in terminal illness.

Reasons to Justify

Except for pain, none of these considerations is now generally recognized as a reason for *suicide*. But they are already recognized as reasons which may justify the killing of others and the nonprolongation of one's own life, and it is highly plausible to expect that they will soon be recognized as relevant in suicide decisions too.

"Increasing displacement of the elderly...operate to make the conditions of those who are faced with dying increasingly difficult."

The kinds of alterations in the ideology and circumstances of rational suicide we have diagnosed as now in progress all involve medical and quasi-medical situations. They would begin to allow what we might call euthanatic suicide, or a choice of death in preference to prolonged and painful death. As the circumstantial changes mentioned earlier—increasing displacement of the elderly and increasing loss of autonomy for the ill—operate to make the conditions of those who are faced with dying increasingly difficult, there is reason to think the attractiveness of euthanatic suicide as an alternative will increase. But there are no *a priori* checks on the breadth of such extensions of the concept of rational suicide and no reason why future extensions must be limited to euthanatic medical situations. As we've said, such conditions as dishonor, slavery, and loss of chastity have been considered suicide-warranting conditions in Western culture in the past; widowhood and public dishonor have assumed such roles in the East, and it seems merely naive to assume that these conditions, or others we now find equally implausible reasons for suicide, could not come to be regarded so in the future. This is particularly obvious if we keep in mind the possibility of circumstantial manipulation and of both inadvertent and deliberate ideological engineering. The motivation for such manipulation and engineering, in a society confronted with scarcities and fearful of an increasingly large "nonproductive" population, may be very strong. Old age, insanity, poverty, and criminality have also been regarded as grounds for rational suicide in the past; given a society afraid of demands from increasingly large geriatric, ghetto, and institutional populations, we can see how interest in producing circumstantial and ideological changes, in order to encourage such people to choose the "reasonable" way out, might be very strong.

Paternalistic Manipulation

Not all manipulation into suicide need be malevolent or self-interested on the part of the manipulator. Manipulation into suicide can also be paternalistic, where one pleads with a victim to "consider yourself" and end a life the paternalist perceives as hopelessly burdensome. And, of course, such pressures may be both paternalistic and other-interested at once: one imagines a counselor advising an old or ill person to spare both himself and his family the agony of an extended decline, even though this person would not have considered or attempted suicide on his own and would have been willing to suffer the physical distress. Can he resist such pressures? Not, perhaps, in a climate in which suicide is "the rational thing to do" in circumstances such as these. To resist, indeed, might earn him the epithets now applied to the individual who does choose suicide: coward, sociopath, deviant, lunatic, apostate. He has, after all, refused to do what is rational and what is believed to be not only in his own interests but in those of people he loves.

"One imagines a counselor advising an old or ill person to spare both himself and his family the agony of an extended decline."

It is important to understand that such choices of suicide can be manipulated only under a prevailing notion of *rational* suicide. Manipulation of this sort does not involve driving one's victims into insanity or torturing them into irrationality; rather, it consists in providing a basis for the making of a *reasonable* decision about the ending of one's life and in providing the criteria upon which that decision is to be made. The choice remains crucially and essentially voluntary, and the decision between alternatives free. Furthermore, in a suicide-permissive society, the choice of suicide would be protected by law, religion, and custom and would be recognized as evidence of sound mental health. But the circumstances of the choice have been restructured so that choosing now involves weighing not only one's own interest but those of others. Where, on balance, the costs of death will be less for oneself and for others than the costs of remaining alive, suicide will be the rational—and socially favored—choice. Indeed, perhaps the choice is not so free after all.

Euthanatic Suicide

As we've said, there is no reason to think that such questions must remain confined to medical situations or what we might call euthanatic suicide. Not only do these considerations apply to nonterminal- as well as terminal-illness cases (consider, for instance, the pain, dependence, expense, impact on the family, and use of scarce medical resources in connection with nonterminal conditions like renal failure, guadriplegia, or severe arthritis), but they will also apply to conditions where there is no *illness* as such at all: retardation, genetic deficiency, abnormal personality, and old age. One can even imagine that continuing ideological redefinition might invite us to regard life as not worth living and the interests of others as critical in a much wider variety of nonmedical situations: chronic unemployment, widowhood, poverty, social isolation, criminal conviction, and so forth. Such claims may seem hysterical. But all these conditions have been promoted as suicide-warranting at some time in the past, and they are all also very often associated with social dependence. After Hitler, we are, I trust, beyond extermination of unwanted or dependent groups. But we may not be beyond encouraging *as rational* the self elimination of those whom we perceive to constitute a burden to themselves and to others, and I think that this is where the risk in manipulated suicide lies.

But there is a problem. Manipulated suicide is morally repugnant, and we recognize that families, social groups, and societies ought to encourage loving care for their ill or disadvantaged members instead. But suicide may be both manipulated and rational, *and* herein lies the philosophical problem. Once we grant that it may be rational for an individual to choose death rather than to live in circumstances which for him are unacceptably or intolerably painful, physically or emotionally, or which are destructive of his most deeply held values, then we cannot object to his choice of death—even though he may be choosing to die because his circumstances have been deliberately or inadvertently worsened, because he has been brought to see his life as worthless, or because he believes he has an obligation to benefit his family by doing so. Certainly we can object to the manipulation of a person's circumstances or the distortion of his ideology. And we can attempt to point out to the victim what has happened. But we cannot object to his choice of suicide, if that remains his choice. To insist that we could not allow suicide which results from manipulation would be to insist that the victim remain alive in what to him have become intolerable circumstances or with his values destroyed; this would be to inflict a double misery—precisely what the notion of rational suicide is intended to prevent. Yet we must see that the very concept which allows this person escape is what first makes possible manipulation of these kinds, since it is the very notion of *rational* suicide which stipulates that under certain conditions one may reasonably seek to end one's life.

"Manipulated suicide is morally repugnant. . .societies ought to encourage loving care for their ill or disadvantaged members instead."

If we refuse to adopt the notion of rational suicide, we fail to honor the moral imperative of allowing individuals in intolerable and irremediable circumstances their fundamental right to die. If we do adopt it, we fail to honor a moral imperative of a different kind: protecting vulnerable individuals from manipulation into choices they otherwise might not make. Perhaps this second imperative is not so strong as the first, and a rational person may be willing to accept the possibility of manipulation which is engendered by the notion of rational suicide, in exchange for the social freedom to control one's own dying as one wishes—even knowing that he may eventually also succumb to that risk, and be "encouraged" to choose death sooner than might otherwise have been the case. Most of us, after all, will grow ill or old or both, and so become candidates for manipulation of this kind. But the alternative—to maintain or reestablish rigid suicide prohibitions—is not attractive either, and is particularly cruel to precisely those people for whom death is or may become the rational choice—that is, those persons in the most unfortunate circumstances of us all. I myself believe that on moral grounds we must accept, not reject, the notion of rational suicide. But I think we must do so with a clear-sighted view of the moral quicksand into which this notion threatens to lead us; perhaps then we may discover a path around.

M. Pabst Battin, Ph.D., is associate professor of philosophy at the University of Utah. She is the author of several essays on topics in classical philosophy and aesthetics and a book, Suicide.

viewpoint **45**

The Elderly's Right to Die Is a Rational Choice

Doris Portwood

An elderly woman, once an editor and writer, who built up to her suicide over a number of years, described in a letter left for friends the progress of her thinking and the criteria she used in judging the proper time. One of the friends was John Fischer who told her story in his *Easy Chair* page in *Harper's* in February 1973. "I want to go while I can still enjoy my friends who are so good to me and who I know can still enjoy me," she wrote, "while I can still feel a not too unfavorable balance between happiness and competence and interest and even limited usefulness of my days—and the difficulties and discomforts and pain and expense involved in trying first to maintain that balance and then later merely to prolong life."

This balance, whose weights on either side must differ with each individual, has been recognized as a factor in seemingly logical suicides. A German psychiatrist, Alfred Hoche, gave them a name in 1919 with the term "Bilanz-Selbstmord" or balance-sheet suicide. The label recognized that it was possible for a sane person, thinking logically, to set off the unacceptable or intolerable aspects of his or her life against the chances for betterment and find the result weighted on the side of death.

Although there can be no statistics on such suicides, one guesses their numbers are increasing. It must be added that no researcher has been anxious to look for such common-sense suicides. Because the whole weight of sociological research is on factors to enhance prevention, there is little impetus to find or explain successful or "justified" cases. Again, the sin-and-crime associations seem to frighten investigators away from those cases that defy classification as abnormal. It must also be said that common-sense suicides, like other successes, leave no defeated victims behind to be interviewed.

From Doris Portwood, *Common-Sense Suicide,* The Hemlock Society, P.O. Box 66218, Los Angeles, CA 90066. Copyright © 1983 The Hemlock Society, Reprinted with permission.

Balance-sheet suicide inevitably involves a factor of age unless there is severe disability or incurable disease. Young people can, and constantly do, believe that death is dictated because of failed exams, a disappointing love affair, some financial loss or career setback. They do not draw up a balance sheet. If they think they do, the entries they make one day are susceptible to radical change the next.

The elderly have an easier task. If there is one thing we learn in growing old, it is the rarity of reversals. Reversals of a sort are not impossible: a 76-year-old woman finds a man interested in her and she blooms—briefly. A woman near retirement age who fears being fired is instead promoted to a better job; she is invigorated. When the circumstances change—in a year, or five, or ten—these women will be like the majority of their contemporaries who did not have the brief and pleasant experience of a reversal of aging. Generally the process is dependable: failing vision does not brighten; wrinkles do not tighten; joint pains may come and go, but they don't go for long.

We all have variations in our way of aging, each with different levels of tolerance for the process. One person's balance sheet will tip in favor of death much earlier than another's. For many, the tipping point will never come. A woman who has had a hard life and innumerable tests of her endurance may be able to face more of the same with an equanimity unavailable to one with less conditioning.

Sense of Competence

The importance of a "sense of competence" in elderly suicide decisions is recognized. Maurice L. Farber (author of *Theory of Suicide* and many other writings on the subject) mentions that the mother of a Danish friend, "a matriarch of apparently strong character, committed suicide without having any acute difficulties but suffering only from a decline in her formidable powers." The contrast between what one is and was, or the difference between the goals once cherished and the recognized impossibility of attaining them—all go into the balance sheet.

Such factors will be subject to frequent change and revision. The death of friends can be important. ("Only a year ago the four of us got together for Marie's birthday. Now I'm the only one left.") Or family changes—the separation of a son and his wife and the removal of grandchildren to some distant point.

"The importance of a sense of competence in elderly suicide decisions is recognized."

Even the trivial can become of scale-tipping importance on occasion. "I never order a green salad when I eat out any more," a 70-year-old woman confided to a friend. "I don't find my mouth properly with a forkful of greens and the dressing drips on my chin. It's embarrassing. A few more of these things and I've had it. You feel such changes...."

"I want to go before I get into the food-hiding act," a cheerfully plump woman told her bridge-table friends.

"Oh-oh. Grandma's at it again? What was it this time?"

"Pancake syrup—in a drawer of lingerie. A loose top of course, I have to leave them loose or she can't open them. Well, you wouldn't *believe* the mess." She laughed, but added, "I *mean* it—I hope I'm gone by 70. No, make that 65. I'm sure I'm the food-hiding type."

"Oh, Helen, you get so specific," one of the companions said. "I can remember when you were determined to die by age 35. Let's get on with the game."

General laughter greeted this gem from the past. They all picked up their cards. Helen looked thoughtful and briefly unhappy. "I'd forgotten that, if I really said it...."

"You said it. Come on now. What's your bid?"

Failing Memory

Failing memory scares a lot of us. "Yes, that would be a big thing in my balance sheet," a late-60's woman who still works in an executive position says. She adds with a half smile, "That is, if I could remember to enter it." So long as she can joke about it, the failing of memory may not be too close. But she is aware of the danger and probably tries to plan what to do about it. "I write myself a dozen notes a day," she says, with another smile. Then she abruptly changes the subject.

I am glad she does, for her words have called up a picture of a relative who had a lovely sturdy yellow-

buff tom cat that had been in the family for years. Finally only she and Tiger, the tom, were left in the big frame house in the small town. She clung to the house and to her independence while her memory failed. The rooms of the house began to be plastered with notes—and one out of five would say something like "feed cat," "get cat food," "look for cat food." Only now and then, in a particularly clear moment, one assumes, did she remember Tiger's name and then a note might say "Tiger likes kidney—order some." In the end it was a half-starved Tiger who alerted a neighbor by climbing up the draperies of a sunny dining room window where uncared-for plants were dying in their pots. The neighbor called the local minister and they investigated. The badly undernourished woman was taken to a nursing home; Tiger was put to sleep, as the saying goes. Lucky Tiger.

Health entries, both physical and mental, would come first and carry a big part of the weight in the average balance sheet. Family and friends might come next, and economic factors after that. Economic factors, with many, would come second regardless of the presence or absence of family and friends.

Health and Solvency

Those who spend their time with the elderly report two overwhelming preoccupations among them: health and solvency. The two are inextricably tied. Inflation has dissolved into quicksand the foundations under the most careful and cautious economic plans of the retired. Even Medicare and Medicaid, which are unbelievably generous in terms of what many present senior citizens might ever have expected, still do not assure sufficient care, nor do they allow much element of choice to those who still feel competent to manage their own lives. A prolonged illness now can bankrupt even a wealthy person. For the elderly poor, the fear of such an illness is an ever-present terror.

The average ailing older person who has a pension, an annuity, a trust fund, investments, savings, real property—any or all of these—must face a time when a frying-pan or fire choice has to be made. If there is no family situation into which the person can fit, with reasonable financial justice for all, then a type of security must be bought with whatever assets remain. This often means turning over property and assigning social security and pension payments to a retirement home that, in turn, undertakes to see its clients through to the end. If available assets are too limited, many of the same institutions accept residents who, when their funds run out, will have to depend on Medicaid. Medicaid-bolstered institutions vary from excellent to horrible. In urban centers, particularly, they can be places of incredible inhumanity. Those institutions with a reasonably good reputation, often associated with religious or fraternal orders, may have long waiting lists.

Whether the specific retirement home is good or bad, its doors close with equal finality on a client's assets. Alternative arrangements, where the elderly hire private care within their own homes, often are equally expensive and equally unsatisfactory. Private-arrangement care also is less permanent—an interim solution that gives way to institutional care later on. In whatever way the change of life style may be handled, through one big step or a series of changes, the golden years for the less-than-healthy older person effectively consume the gold that might have gone in quite another direction.

Two men overheard in conversation on a commuter bus discussed their mothers. "It'll be two years tomorrow she's been in that home," one of them said. "And poor mom thinks she's still got those twelve hundred shares of AT&T."

"Her mind's okay, then?"

"No, no. Her mind's half gone. But she remembers AT&T—doesn't remember selling it, just having it. I guess it gave her comfort for so long she still leans on it. Real financial security." He laughed, briefly and half-bitterly.

"Yeah. Well, maybe it's better that way," his companion said. "My wife's mother still has all her buttons and she worries about every dime that's going down the drain. She was going to help Jeff through law school—and she remembers that. It's terrible to see her feel guilty about it."

"Sure. That's even worse."

Medical Bills

Statistics on individual cases of medical care in which bills have amounted to hundreds of thousands of dollars for a comatose, hopeless, long-living invalid are common enough. One such situation, going on for almost eight years, cost close to $300,000. Another reference cites almost $29,000 for the final 16 days of the life of a heart transplant patient, plus another $7000 worth of blood. Yet another citation refers to an accident victim—with irrecoverable injuries and $160,000 worth of care before she died. Sylvia Porter said, in a 1976 column, that hospital bills of $70,000 are "commonplace" these days.

Worse than the tremendous individual bill is the sum of those that are only relentlessly average. A middle-aged aide whose duties were mainly with eight patients on one corridor of a suburban nursing home became familiar with their situations. Three of the women had no relatives in the area. Two of these had been career women who used up their resources and were on Medicaid except for their social security. They suffered from crippling arthritis and a heart condition. The third, mildly senile, had a niece in another state who had power-of-attorney and made payments from available funds. She came twice (during the aide's time on the job) to see the aunt. "She was dressed like money—maybe they can afford it. And she was nice. Too bad her aunt didn't know

who she was."

Three of the other five—one in a wheelchair with a broken hip, one with advanced emphysema, one senile—had relatives who visited "fairly often" and among these visitors one couple appeared financially well off. Another, a daughter of a patient, looked "weak and sick and sometimes she cries." This daughter got particularly upset if there was need for any special attention that would entail an additional charge. "She must be the one who pays," because none of these three were on public funding so far.

Long-Term Cases

The other two women were on Medicaid funds and were long-term cases although neither was senile. One was partially paralyzed; the other had a bone disease that would not respond to treatment. Both had some family but no regular visitors. "I think they're good enough people," the aide defended them. "But they're hard up. They work—and it's not easy to come out here from the city. A little girl came and danced at a Christmas program. Great granddaughter I'd guess. The old lady was real proud of her—told everybody."

"Those who spend their time with the elderly report two overwhelming preoccupations among them: health and solvency."

That was the only comment about any kind of enjoyment of life in this eight-bed corridor. The sum of pain, confusion and discontent was evident. ("She has some bad nights. Sometimes the medicines help and then they wear off and before they have her on something else she might have nightmares or get afraid of something. . . ." And of the woman whose niece "dressed like money": "Sometimes she thinks guests are going to spend the night—like this whole place was her house or something. She won't want to go to bed because she says she's given this room to a guest and she plans to sleep somewhere else. Whoever's on that night may have to take her for a little walk so she forgets it, and then bring her back to her own bed.") If no one has time for "a little walk," or if during that walk some of the other seven charges of one attendant have special needs, the care of course must be rationed. In this particular place, one felt, the ration probably was well above average.

The sum of the fees for such an eight-bed corridor can be computed at about $3000 a week. The time-span for occupancy by each of these eight women was open-ended. Ten such corridors make up an average nursing home ($30,000). Fifteen thousand homes stretch across our land ($450 million). A year of $450-million-dollar weeks is a $23-billion-dollar year. What do we get for this $23-billion price tag? One thing we *don't* get is a green light at the end of the corridor.

Circumventing the Rules

Those of us who end up disabled and in our right minds may feel forced to make a moral choice between obeying or circumventing some of the rules of institutional retirement. If we have family members who need and depend on some help from us, it often is necessary to plan ahead, anticipate the worst, and arrange a transfer of funds and property titles within the legal limits. Such maneuvering, which allows us to approach the institution more or less emptyhanded, is common practice. It also is distasteful to the people of whom it is most likely to be required. It does not apply to the very rich or the very poor, but to the big middle class of people who budget and save and who could sincerely believe, at one time, in their ability to take care of themselves and to be thriftily generous with others close to them.

"The golden years for the less-than-healthy older person effectively consume the gold that might have gone in quite another direction."

Whether we turn early or late to public aid, however, the majority of us will draw down a sizable amount from Medicare and Medicaid on our way to the receding nearest exit. Medicare, the health insurance scheme that is part of the Social Security Administration, is primarily for the 65-up group of Americans. (The under-65 disabled beneficiaries of the program numbered only 2.1 million persons in mid-1975 out of a Medicare total of 24.6 million.) The program was inaugurated in the mid-1960s and the annual payout by 1971-1972 was $6.1 billion; by 1975-1976 the figures had risen to $12.4 billion. An assurance that the figures will continue to rise, and at a steeper rate, is contained not only in anticipated inflation but also in the fact that at least a thousand people are added to the 65-up population *every day.* About 4000 enter this golden-age area of our population daily; about 3000 depart. The net daily gain of one thousand, looked on statistically as aging bodies qualified for Medicare, is hardly a cause for fiscal celebration. Older Americans required a per capita health-care expenditure of $1360 in 1975 against one-third of that amount for younger people. Two-thirds of the $1360 was paid through public programs.

Medicaid, the program of health care for all needy persons regardless of age, with both federal and state

funding, also spends billions annually on the older population. Long-term nursing home residence, except for the relatively well-to-do, usually depends on Medicaid (nursing home time under Medicare is strictly limited). About 80% of nursing home patients receive Medicaid funds and the average stay in a nursing home is three years.

Whether these final years are paid for in private or public dollars, the bill must be paid. If the patient is mentally confused, the nursing-home stay can be, at best, a foggy and meaningless experience. At worst, of course, it can be torture. For the mentally alert, it is (quite apart from all other discomforts) a time when one must watch the rapid outflow of funds while being aware of all the things one would prefer to see the money applied to.

A decade ago, at a West Coast seminar on the subject of suicide, one of the informed speakers estimated that the saving of three persons from self-destruction would be worth one hundred thousand dollars to the community. This estimate was based on the assumption that the saved person would be an earner and a taxpayer; the figure was modest. The suicide of a nonproductive person with failing health is an entry for the other side of this public balance sheet. Her, or his, departure can hardly fail to be an asset to the community. If the suicide was a solvent taxpayer, taxes will be levied on the estate; if indigent, the government is spared further expense on a life basically finished. For the just-solvent in-betweens, the younger members of the family may benefit in a modest way, either through inheritance or by being spared the burden of further expense. The biggest dividends—which cannot be calculated mathematically—come in the curtailment of human misery.

Costs to Workers

One figure no aging person can afford to ignore is the ever-rising cost to each productive worker for his share of the burden of the elderly. ("Burden" is used more and more candidly in this connection; the press appears to find it no longer offensive.) Our expanded programs, with or without the expensive abuses that make them an even greater luxury, have to be paid for by the earning segment of our society. Our earners are, in theory, willing to share our total national product with the unproductive old because they understand that they themselves will grow old and require benefits. Nevertheless, a society aging as fast as ours is likely to impose a greater burden than some younger people will blandly accept. Already, the FICA (Social Security) deductions on many wage-earners' pay checks are far larger than income tax deductions. The FICA payments are unavoidable, applying to minimum wages as well as to the first specific few thousands ($16,500 in 1977) of a corporate executive's or TV star's high pay. Even so, the Social Security system operates at a deficit and faces long-term insolvency unless it is overhauled. In the overhauling, some basic decisions on how much the productive sector can afford to share with the unproductive will have to be made.

A well-known management consultant, speaking to a group of top business executives at a 1976 symposium sponsored by New York University's graduate school of business administration, stated that the "central concern" of economic planners in all developed nations from now on will have to be the growing burden of support for people who are past working age.

In the history of suicide, the shift from self-destruction as an aspect of individual morality to self-destruction as a social phenomenon coincided with the industrial revolution. In a way, the suicide became at that point a soulless early statistic in a readjusting economic society. Today, the needs of the individual and those of the social community appear to merge, in an economic sense, on the question of old-age suicide. A planned departure that serves oneself, one's family and also the state surely is worthy of decent consideration.

A Punctual Death

A Frenchman who was a retired railway worker planned his suicide four years in advance and pro-rated his assets of four million francs through those years. He had good friends and good hobbies (fishing and cooking) and was a locally noted raconteur who told adventure stories of his past experience in the Cameroons. He was busy, well-liked, apparently happy in the environment of his village. The four years ended with the man in obvious good health—and with a skeptical attitude evident on the part of his friends about the seriousness of his intent. But he meant it. The note he left, after taking an overdose of sleeping pills, said, "I am punctual. I think I've lived better than others. I die content."

"One figure no aging person can afford to ignore is the ever-rising cost to each productive worker for his share of the burden of the elderly."

This man was only 60—having opted at age 56 for more of the "good life" in less years than he might normally anticipate. Although there is nothing typical about his circumstances, his story indicates that there are some who prefer to go too early rather than too late.

Most of us will have more serious worries than how to preserve a bit of the good life with dwindling resources. Those worries would be relieved to some extent if we knew that, after careful planning and putting things in order, we could tote up our balance sheet, interpret the result and act on our own decision.

Psychiatrists can tell us various things about the personality of suicides. One opinion is that the suicide often is a person who likes to be in control. In the ferment of today's society, people who prefer being in control—which means self-control in the case of suicide—are assets.

There are going to be more than thirty million American senior citizens by the year 2000. More than two million of them will be in nursing homes—perhaps double the current number. Those who have the will to opt out may not (yet) get a public vote of thanks. But who can dare say that they will be missed?

This viewpoint is taken from a chapter in the book Common-Sense Suicide, *published by the Hemlock Society which supports the individual's right to choose death. Doris Portwood, the author, lives in New York.*

"The harder they struggle to avoid the inevitable death,...the more difficult it will be for them to reach this final stage of acceptance."

viewpoint **46**

Elisabeth Kübler-Ross on Coping with Death

Elisabeth Kübler-Ross

I remember as a child the death of a farmer. He fell from a tree and was not expected to live. He asked simply to die at home, a wish that was granted without questioning. He called his daughters into the bedroom and spoke with each one of them alone for a few moments. He arranged his affairs quietly, though he was in great pain, and distributed his belongings and his land, none of which was to be split until his wife should follow him in death. He also asked each of his children to share in the work, duties, and tasks that he had carried on until the time of the accident. He asked his friends to visit him once more, to bid good-bye to them. Although I was a small child at the time, he did not exclude me or my siblings. We were allowed to share in the preparations of the family just as we were permitted to grieve with them until he died. When he did die, he was left at home, in his own beloved home which he had built, and among his friends and neighbors who went to take a last look at him where he lay in the midst of flowers in the place he had lived in and loved so much. In that country today there is still no make-believe slumber room, no embalming, no false makeup to pretend sleep. Only the signs of very disfiguring illnesses are covered up with bandages and only infectious cases are removed from the home prior to the burial.

Why do I describe such "old-fashioned" customs? I think they are an indication of our acceptance of a fatal outcome, and they help the dying patient as well as his family to accept the loss of a loved one. If a patient is allowed to terminate his life in the familiar and beloved environment, it requires less adjustment for him. His own family knows him well enough to replace a sedative with a glass of his favorite wine; or the smell of a home-cooked soup may give him the

appetite to sip a few spoons of fluid which I think is still more enjoyable than an infusion. I will not minimize the need for sedatives and infusions and realize full well from my own experiences as a country doctor that they are sometimes life-saving and often unavoidable. But I also know that patience and familiar people and foods could replace many a bottle of intravenous fluids given for the simple reason that it fulfills the physiological need without involving too many people and/or individual nursing care.

Shared Mourning

The fact that children are allowed to stay at home where a fatality has stricken and are included in the talk, discussions, and fears gives them the feeling that they are not alone in the grief and gives them the comfort of shared responsibility and shared mourning. It prepares them gradually and helps them view death as part of life, an experience which may help them grow and mature.

This is in great contrast to a society in which death is viewed as taboo, discussion of it is regarded as morbid, and children are excluded with the presumption and pretext that it would be "too much" for them. They are then sent off to relatives, often accompanied with some unconvincing lies of "Mother has gone on a long trip" or other unbelievable stories. The child senses that something is wrong, and his distrust in adults will only multiply if other relatives add new variations of the story, avoid his questions or suspicions, shower him with gifts as a meager substitute for a loss he is not permitted to deal with. Sooner or later the child will become aware of the changed family situation and, depending on the age and personality of the child, will have an unresolved grief and regard this incident as a frightening, mysterious, in any case very traumatic experience with untrustworthy grownups, which he has no way to cope with.

It is equally unwise to tell a little child who lost her brother that God loved little boys so much that he took little Johnny to heaven. When this little girl grew up to be a woman she never solved her anger at God, which resulted in a psychotic depression when she lost her own little son three decades later.

Great Emancipation

We would think that our great emancipation, our knowledge of science and of man, has given us better ways and means to prepare ourselves and our families for this inevitable happening. Instead the days are gone when a man was allowed to die in peace and dignity in his own home.

The more we are making advancements in science, the more we seem to fear and deny the reality of death. How is this possible?

"Finally, we may achieve peace... by facing and accepting the reality of our own death."

We use euphemisms, we make the dead look as if they were asleep, we ship the children off to protect them from the anxiety and turmoil around the house if the patient is fortunate enough to die at home, we don't allow children to visit their dying parents in the hospital, we have long and controversial discussions about whether patients should be told the truth—a question that rarely arises when the dying person is tended by the family physician who has known him from delivery to death and who knows the weaknesses and strengths of each member of the family.

Flight Away from Death

I think there are many reasons for this flight away from facing death calmly. One of the most important facts is that dying nowadays is more gruesome in many ways, namely, more lonely, mechanical, and dehumanized; at times it is even difficult to determine technically when the time of death has occurred.

Dying becomes lonely and impersonal because the patient is often taken out of his familiar environment and rushed to an emergency room. Whoever has been very sick and has required rest and comfort especially may recall his experience of being put on a stretcher and enduring the noise of the ambulance siren and hectic rush until the hospital gates open. Only those who have lived through this may appreciate the discomfort and cold necessity of such transportation which is only the beginning of a long ordeal—hard to endure when you are well, difficult to express in words when noise, light, pumps, and voices are all too much to put up with. It may well be

that we might consider more the patient under the sheets and blankets and perhaps stop our well-meant efficiency and rush in order to hold the patient's hand, to smile, or to listen to a question. I include the trip to the hospital as the first episode in dying, as it is for many. I am putting it exaggeratedly in contrast to the sick man who is left at home—not to say that lives should not be saved if they can be saved by a hospitalization but to keep the focus on the patient's experience, his needs and his reactions.

The Sick Have Feelings

When a patient is severely ill, he is often treated like a person with no right to an opinion. It is often someone else who makes the decision if and when and where a patient should be hospitalized. It would take so little to remember that the sick person too has feelings, has wishes and opinions, and has—most important of all—the right to be heard.

Well, our presumed patient has now reached the emergency room. He will be surrounded by busy nurses, orderlies, interns, residents, a lab technician perhaps who will take some blood, an electrocardiogram technician who takes the cardiogram. He may be moved to X-ray and he will overhear opinions of his condition and discussions and questions to members of the family. He slowly but surely is beginning to be treated like a thing. He is no longer a person. Decisions are made often without his opinion. If he tries to rebel he will be sedated and after hours of waiting and wondering whether he has the strength, he will be wheeled into the operating room or intensive treatment unit and become an object of great concern and great financial investment.

He may cry for rest, peace, and dignity, but he will get infusions, transfusions, a heart machine, or tracheostomy if necessary. He may want one single person to stop for one single minute so that he can ask one single question—but he will get a dozen people around the clock, all busily preoccupied with his heart rate, pulse, electrocardiogram or pulmonary functions, his secretions or excretions but not with him as a human being. He may wish to fight it all but it is going to be a useless fight since all this is done in the fight for his life, and if they can save his life they can consider the person afterwards. Those who consider the person first may lose precious time to save his life! At least this seems to be the rationale or justification behind all this—or is it? Is the reason for this increasingly mechanical, depersonalized approach our own defensiveness? Is this approach our own way to cope with and repress the anxieties that a terminally or critically ill patient evokes in us? Is our concentration on equipment, on blood pressure our desperate attempt to deny the impending death which is so frightening and discomforting to us that we displace all our knowledge onto machines, since they are less close to us than the suffering face of another human being which would remind us once more of our lack of omnipotence, our own limits and failures, and last but not least perhaps our own mortality?...

Society's Defensiveness

Until now we have looked at the individual human reaction to death and dying. If we now take a look at our society, we may want to ask ourselves what happens to man in a society bent on ignoring or avoiding death. What factors, if any, contribute to an increasing anxiety in relation to death? What happens in a changing field of medicine, where we have to ask ourselves whether medicine is to remain a humanitarian and respected profession or a new but depersonalized science in the service of prolonging life rather than diminishing human suffering? Where the medical students have a choice of dozens of lectures on RNA and DNA but less experience in the simple doctor-patient relationship that used to be the alphabet for every successful family physician? What happens in a society that puts more emphasis on IQ and class-standing then on simple matters of tact, sensitivity, perceptiveness, and good taste in the management of the suffering? In a professional society where the young medical student is admired for his research and laboratory work during the first years of medical school while he is at a loss for words when a patient asks him a simple question? If we could combine the teaching of the new scientific and technical achievements with equal emphasis on interpersonal human relationships we would indeed make progress, but not if the new knowledge is conveyed to the student at the price of less and less interpersonal contact. What is going to become of a society which puts the emphasis on numbers and masses, rather than on the individual—where medical schools hope to enlarge their classes, where the trend is away from the teacher-student contact, which is replaced by closed-circuit television teaching, recordings, and movies, all of which can teach a greater number of students in a more depersonalized manner?

Invisible Enemy

This change of focus from the individual to the masses has been more dramatic in other areas of human interaction. If we take a look at the changes that have taken place in the last decades, we can notice it everywhere. In the old days a man was able to face his enemy eye to eye. He had a fair chance in a personal encounter with a visible enemy. Now the soldier as well as the civilian has to anticipate weapons of mass destruction which offer no one a reasonable chance, often not even an awareness of their approach. Destruction can strike out of the blue skies and destroy thousands like the bomb at Hiroshima; it may come in the form of gases or other means of chemical warfare—invisible, crippling, killing. It is no longer the man who fights for his

rights, his convictions, or the safety or honor of his family, it is the nation including its women and children who are in the war, affected directly or indirectly without a chance of survival. This is how science and technology have contributed to an ever increasing fear of destruction and therefore fear of death.

Is it surprising, then, that man has to defend himself more? If his ability to defend himself physically is getting smaller and smaller, his psychological defenses have to increase manifoldly. He cannot maintain denial forever. He cannot continuously and successfully pretend that he is safe. If we cannot deny death we may attempt to master it. We may join the race on the highways, we may read the death toll over national holidays and shudder, but also rejoice—"It was the other guy, not me. I made it."

Need to Face Death

Groups of people, from street gangs to nations, may use their group identity to express their fear of being destroyed by attacking and destroying others. Is war perhaps nothing else but a need to face death, to conquer and master it, to come out of it alive—a peculiar form of denial of our own mortality? One of our patients dying of leukemia said in utter disbelief: "It is impossible for me to die now. It cannot be God's will, since he let me survive when I was hit by bullets just a few feet away during World War II."

"I favor talking about death and dying with patients long before it actually happens."

Another woman expressed her shock and sense of incredulity when she described the "unfair death" of a young man who was on leave from Vietnam and met his death in a car accident, as if his survival on the battlefield was supposed to have guaranteed immunity from death back home.

Chance for Peace

A chance for peace may thus be found in studying the attitudes toward death in the leaders of the nations, in those who make the final decisions of war and peace between nations. If all of us would make an all-out effort to contemplate our own death, to deal with our anxieties surrounding the concept of our death, and to help others familiarize themselves with these thoughts, perhaps there could be less destructiveness around us.

News agencies may be able to contribute their share in helping people face the reality of death by avoiding such depersonalized terms as the "solution of the Jewish question" to tell of the murder of millions of men, women, and children; or to use a more recent issue, the recovery of a hill in Vietnam through elimination of a machine gun nest and heavy loss of VC could be described in terms of human tragedies and loss of human beings on both sides. There are so many examples in all newspapers and other news media that it is unnecessary to add more here.

"The third stage, the stage of bargaining, is less well-known but equally helpful to the patient."

In summary, then, I think that with rapid technical advancement and new scientific achievements men have been able to develop not only new skills but also new weapons of mass destruction which increase the fear of a violent, catastrophic death. Man has to defend himself psychologically in many ways against this increased fear of death and increased inability to foresee and protect himself against it. Psychologically he can deny the reality of his own death for a while. Since in our unconscious we cannot perceive our own death and do believe in our own immortality, but can conceive our neighbor's death, news of numbers of people killed in battle, in wars, on the highways only support our unconscious belief in our own immortality and allow us—in the privacy and secrecy of our unconscious mind—to rejoice that it is "the next guy, not me."...

Postponing the Inevitable

Though every man will attempt in his own way to postpone such questions and issues until he is forced to face them, he will only be able to change things if he can start to conceive of his own death. This cannot be done on a mass level. This cannot be done by computers. This has to be done by every human being alone. Each one of us has the need to avoid this issue, yet each one of us has to face it sooner or later. If all of us could make a start by contemplating the possibility of our own personal death, we may effect many things, most important of all the welfare of our patients, our families, and finally perhaps our nation.

If we could teach our students the value of science and technology simultaneously with the art and science of inter-human relationships, of human and total patient-care, it would be real progress. If science and technology are not to be misused to increase destructiveness, prolonging life rather than making it more human, if they could go hand in hand with freeing more rather than less for individual person-to-person contacts, then we could really speak of a great society.

Finally, we may achieve peace—our own inner peace as well as peace between nations—by facing and accepting the reality of our own death....

Among the over two hundred dying patients we have interviewed, most reacted to the awareness of a terminal illness at first with the statement, "No, not me, it cannot be true." This *initial* denial was as true for those patients who were told outright at the beginning of their illness as it was true for those who were not told explicitly and who came to this conclusion on their own a bit later on. One of our patients described a long and expensive ritual, as she called it, to support her denial. She was convinced that the X-rays were "mixed up"; she asked for reassurance that her pathology report could not possibly be back so soon and that another patient's report must have been marked with her name. When none of this could be confirmed, she quickly asked to leave the hospital, looking for another physician in the vain hope "to get a better explanation for my troubles." This patient went "shopping around" for many doctors, some of whom gave her reassuring answers, others of whom confirmed the previous suspicion. Whether confirmed or not, she reacted in the same manner; she asked for examination and reexamination, partially knowing that the original diagnosis was correct, but also seeking further evaluations in the hope that the first conclusion was indeed an error, at the same time keeping in contact with a physician in order to have help available "at all times" as she said.

This anxious denial following the presentation of a diagnosis is more typical of the patient who is informed prematurely or abruptly by someone who does not know the patient well or does it quickly "to get it over with" without taking the patient's readiness into consideration. Denial, at least partial denial, is used by almost all patients, not only during the first stages of illness or following confrontation, but also later on from time to time. Who was it who said, "We cannot look at the sun all the time, we cannot face death all the time"? These patients can consider the possibility of their own death for a while but then have to put this consideration away in order to pursue life.

Denial Is a Buffer

I emphasize this strongly since I regard it a healthy way of dealing with the uncomfortable and painful situation with which some of these patients have to live for a long time. Denial functions as a buffer after unexpected shocking news, allows the patient to collect himself and, with time, mobilize other, less radical defenses. This does not mean, however, that the same patient later on will not be willing or even happy and relieved if he can sit and talk with someone about his impending death. Such a dialogue will and must take place at the convenience of the patient, when he (not the listener!) is ready to face it. The dialogue also has to be terminated when the patient can no longer face the facts and resumes his previous denial. It is irrelevant when this dialogue takes place. We are often accused of talking with very sick patients about death when the doctor feels—very rightly so—that they are not dying. I favor talking about death and dying with patients long before it actually happens if the patient indicates that he wants to. A healthier, stronger individual can deal with it better and is less frightened by oncoming death when it is still "miles away" than when it "is right in front of the door," as one of our patients put it so appropriately. It is also easier for the family to discuss such matters in times of relative health and well-being and arrange for financial security for the children and others while the head of the household is still functioning. To postpone such talks is often not in the service of the patient but serves our own defensiveness....

Second Stage: Anger

If our first reaction to catastrophic news is, "No it's not true, no, it cannot involve me," this has to give way to a new reaction, when it finally dawns on us: "Oh, yes, it is me, it was not a mistake." Fortunately or unfortunately very few patients are able to maintain a make-believe world in which they are healthy and well until they die.

When the first stage of denial cannot be maintained any longer, it is replaced by feelings of anger, rage, envy, and resentment. The logical next question becomes: "Why me?" As one of our patients, Dr. G., puts it, "I suppose most anybody in my position would look at somebody else and say, 'Well, why couldn't it have been him?' and this has crossed my mind several times....An old man whom I have known ever since I was a little kid came down the street. He was eighty-two years old, and he is of no earthly use as far as we mortals can tell. He's rheumatic, he's a cripple, he's dirty, just not the type of person you would like to be. And the thought hit me strongly, now why couldn't it have been old George instead of me?"

Difficult for Family

In contrast to the stage of denial, this stage of anger is very difficult to cope with from the point of view of family and staff. The reason for this is the fact that this anger is displaced in all directions and projected onto the environment at times almost at random. The doctors are just no good, they don't know what tests to require and what diet to prescribe. They keep the patients too long in the hospital or don't respect their wishes in regards to special privileges. They allow a miserably sick roommate to be brought into their room when they pay so much money for some privacy and rest, etc. The nurses are even more often a target of their anger. Whatever they touch is not right. The moment they have left the room, the bell rings. The light is on the very minute they start their report for the next shift of nurses. When they do shake the pillows and straighten out the bed, they are blamed for never leaving the patients alone. When they do leave the patients alone, the light goes on with the request to have the bed arranged more comfortably. The visiting family is received with little cheerfulness and anticipation, which makes the encounter a painful event. They then either respond with grief and tears, guilt or shame, or avoid future visits, which only increases the patient's discomfort and anger.

"The depression is a tool to prepare for the impending loss of all the love objects."

The problem here is that few people place themselves in the patient's position and wonder where this anger might come from. Maybe we too would be angry if all our life activities were interrupted so prematurely; if all the buildings we started were to go unfinished, to be completed by someone else; if we had put some hard-earned money aside to enjoy a few years of rest and enjoyment, for travel and pursuing hobbies, only to be confronted with the fact that "this is not for me." What else would we do with our anger, but let it out on the people who are most likely to enjoy all these things? People who rush busily around only to remind us that we cannot even stand on our two feet anymore. People who order unpleasant tests and prolonged hospitalization with all its limitations, restrictions, and costs, while at the end of the day they can go home and enjoy life. People who tell us to lie still so that the infusion or transfusion does not have to be restarted, when we feel like jumping out of our skin to be doing something in order to know that we are still functioning on some level!

Everything Is Irritating

Wherever the patient looks at this time, he will find grievances. He may put the television on only to find a group of young jolly people doing some of the modern dances which irritates him when every move of his is painful or limited. He may see a movie western in which people are shot in cold blood with indifferent onlookers continuing to drink their beer. He will compare them with his family or the attending staff. He may listen to the news full of reports of destruction, war, fires, and tragedies—far away from him, unconcerned about the fight and plight of an individual who will soon be forgotten. So this patient makes sure that he is not forgotten. He will raise his voice, he will make demands, he will complain and ask to be given attention, perhaps as the last loud cry, "I am alive, don't forget that. You can hear my voice, I am not dead yet!"

A patient who is respected and understood, who is given attention and a little time, will soon lower his voice and reduce his angry demands. He will know that he is a valuable human being, cared for, allowed to function at the highest possible level as long as he can. He will be listened to without the need for a temper tantrum, he will be visited without ringing the bell every so often because dropping in on him is not a necessary duty but a pleasure.

"The patient should not be encouraged to look at the sunny side of things, as this would mean he should not contemplate his impending death."

The tragedy is perhaps that we do not think of the reasons for patients' anger and take it personally, when it has originally nothing or little to do with the people who become the target of the anger. As the staff or family reacts personally to this anger, however, they respond with increasing anger on their part, only feeding into the patient's hostile behavior. They may use avoidance and shorten the visits or the rounds or they may get into unnecessary arguments by defending their stand, not knowing that the issue is often totally irrelevant. . . .

Third Stage: Bargaining

The third stage, the stage of bargaining, is less well known but equally helpful to the patient, though only for brief periods of time. If we have been unable to face the sad facts in the first period and have been angry at people and God in the second phase, maybe we can succeed in entering into some sort of an agreement which may postpone the inevitable happening: "If God has decided to take us from this earth and he did not respond to my angry pleas, he may be more favorable if I ask nicely." We are all familiar with this reaction when we observe our children first demanding, then asking for a favor. They may not accept our "No" when they want to spend a night in a friend's house. They may be angry and stamp their foot. They may lock themselves in their bedroom and temporarily express their anger by rejecting us. But they will also have second thoughts. They may consider another approach. They will come out eventually, volunteer to do some tasks around the house, which under normal circumstances we never succeeded in getting them to do, and then tell us, "If I am very good all week and wash the dishes every evening, then will you let me go?" There is a slight chance naturally that we will accept the bargain and the child will get what was previously denied.

The terminally ill patient uses the same maneuvers.

He knows, from past experiences, that there is a slim chance that he may be rewarded for good behavior and be granted a wish for special services. His wish is most always an extension of life, followed by the wish for a few days without pain or physical discomfort. A patient who was an opera singer, with a distorting malignancy of her jaw and face who could no longer perform on the stage, asked "to perform just one more time." When she became aware that this was impossible, she gave the most touching performance perhaps of her lifetime. She asked to come to the seminar and to speak in front of the audience, not behind a one-way mirror. She unfolded her life story, her success, and her tragedy in front of the class until a telephone call summoned her to return to her room. Doctor and dentist were ready to pull all her teeth in order to proceed with the radiation treatment. She had asked to sing once more—to us—before she had to hide her face forever.

Attempt to Postpone

Another patient was in utmost pain and discomfort, unable to go home because of her dependence on injections for pain relief. She had a son who proceeded with his plans to get married, as the patient had wished. She was very sad to think that she would be unable to attend this big day, for he was her oldest and favorite child. With combined efforts, we were able to teach her self-hypnosis which enabled her to be quite comfortable for several hours. She had made all sorts of promises if she could only live long enough to attend this marriage. The day preceding the wedding she left the hospital as an elegant lady. Nobody would have believed her real condition. She was "the happiest person in the whole world" and looked radiant. I wondered what her reaction would be when the time was up for which she had bargained.

I will never forget the moment when she returned to the hospital. She looked tired and somewhat exhausted and—before I could say hello—said, "Now don't forget I have another son!"

The bargaining is really an attempt to postpone; it has to include a prize offered "for good behavior," it also sets a self-imposed "deadline" (e.g., one more performance, the son's wedding), and it includes an implicit promise that the patient will not ask for more if this one postponement is granted. None of our patients have "kept their promise"; in other words, they are like children who say, "I will never fight my sister again if you let me go." Needless to add, the little boy will fight his sister again, just as the opera singer will try to perform once more. She could not live without further performances and left the hospital before her teeth were extracted. The patient just described was unwilling to face us again unless we acknowledged the fact that she had another son whose wedding she also wanted to witness.

Most bargains are made with God and are usually

kept a secret or mentioned between the lines or in a chaplain's private office. In our individual interviews without an audience we have been impressed by the number of patients who promise "a life dedicated to God" or "a life in the service of the church" in exchange for some additional time. Many of our patients also promised to give parts of or their whole body "to science" (if the doctors use their knowledge of science to extend their life)....

Fourth Stage: Depression

When the terminally ill patient can no longer deny his illness, when he is forced to undergo more surgery or hospitalization, when he begins to have more symptoms or becomes weaker and thinner, he cannot smile it off anymore. His numbness or stoicism, his anger and rage will soon be replaced with a sense of great loss. This loss may have many facets: a woman with a breast cancer may react to the loss of her figure; a woman with a cancer of the uterus may feel that she is no longer a woman. Our opera singer responded to the required surgery of her face and the removal of her teeth with shock, dismay, and the deepest depression. But this is only one of the many losses that such a patient has to endure.

"There are a few patients who...keep a hope that makes it almost impossible to reach this stage of acceptance."

With the extensive treatment and hospitalization, financial burdens are added; little luxuries at first and necessities later on may not be afforded anymore. The immense sums that such treatments and hospitalizations cost in recent years have forced many patients to sell the only possessions they had; they were unable to keep a house which they built for their old age, unable to send a child through college, and unable perhaps to make many dreams come true.

Inability to Function

There may be the added loss of a job due to many absences or the inability to function, and mothers and wives may have to become the breadwinners, thus depriving the children of the attention they previously had. When mothers are sick, the little ones may have to be boarded out, adding to the sadness and guilt of the patient.

All these reasons for depressions are well known to everybody who deals with patients. What we often tend to forget, however, is the preparatory grief that the terminally ill patient has to undergo in order to prepare himself for his final separation from this world. If I were to attempt to differentiate these two

kinds of depressions, I would regard the first one a reactive depression, the second one a preparatory depression. The first one is different in nature and should be dealt with quite differently from the latter.

When the depression is a tool to prepare for the impending loss of all the love objects, in order to facilitate the state of acceptance, then encouragements and reassurances are not as meaningful. The patient should not be encouraged to look at the sunny side of things, as this would mean he should not contemplate his impending death. It would be contraindicated to tell him not to be sad, since all of us are tremendously sad when we lose one beloved person. The patient is in the process of losing everything and everybody he loves. If he is allowed to express his sorrow he will find a final acceptance much easier, and he will be grateful to those who can sit with him during this state of depression without constantly telling him not to be sad. This second type of depression is usually a silent one in contrast to the first type, during which the patient has much to share and requires many verbal interactions and often active interventions on the part of people in many disciplines. In the preparatory grief there is no or little need for words. It is much more a feeling that can be mutually expressed and is often done better with a touch of a hand, a stroking of the hair, or just a silent sitting together....

Fifth Stage: Acceptance

If a patient has had enough time (i.e., not a sudden, unexpected death) and has been given some help in working through the previously described stages, he will reach a stage during which he is neither depressed nor angry about his "fate." He will have been able to express his previous feelings, his envy for the living and the healthy, his anger at those who do not have to face their end so soon. He will have mourned the impending loss of so many meaningful people and places and he will contemplate his coming end with a certain degree of quiet expectation. He will be tired and, in most cases, quite weak. He will also have a need to doze off to sleep often and in brief intervals, which is different from the need to sleep during the times of depression. This is not a sleep of avoidance or a period of rest to get relief from pain, discomfort, or itching. It is a gradually increasing need to extend the hours of sleep very similar to that of the newborn child but in reverse order. It is not a resigned and hopeless "giving up," a sense of "what's the use" or "I just cannot fight it any longer," though we hear such statements too. (They also indicate the beginning of the end of the struggle, but the latter are not indications of acceptance.)

Acceptance should not be mistaken for a happy stage. It is almost void of feelings. It is as if the pain had gone, the struggle is over, and there comes a time for "the final rest before the long journey" as one patient phrased it. This is also the time during which the family needs usually more help, understanding, and support than the patient himself. While the dying patient has found some peace and acceptance, his circle of interest diminishes. He wishes to be left alone or at least not stirred up by news and problems of the outside world. Visitors are often not desired and if they come, the patient is no longer in a talkative mood. He often requests limitation on the number of people and prefers short visits. This is the time when the television is off. Our communications then become more nonverbal than verbal. The patient may just make a gesture of the hand to invite us to sit down for a while. He may just hold our hand and ask us to sit in silence. Such moments of silence may be the most meaningful communications for people who are not uncomfortable in the presence of a dying person. We may together listen to the song of a bird from the outside.

"It takes just a little time but it is comforting for the patient to know that he is not forgotten when nothing else can be done for him."

Our presence may just confirm that we are going to be around until the end. We may just let him know that it is all right to say nothing when the important things are taken care of and it is only a question of time until he can close his eyes forever. It may reassure him that he is not left alone when he is no longer talking and a pressure of the hand, a look, a leaning back in the pillows may say more than many "noisy" words.

Evening Visits

A visit in the evening may lend itself best to such an encounter as it is the end of the day both for the visitor and the patient. It is the time when the hospital's page system does not interrupt such a moment, when the nurse does not come in to take the temperature, and the cleaning woman is not mopping the floor—it is this little private moment that can complete the day at the end of the rounds for the physician, when he is not interrupted by anyone. It takes just a little time but it is comforting for the patient to know that he is not forgotten when nothing else can be done for him. It is gratifying for the visitor as well, as it will show him that dying is not such a frightening, horrible thing that so many want to avoid.

There are a few patients who fight to the end, who struggle and keep a hope that makes it almost impossible to reach this stage of acceptance. They are the ones who will say one day, "I just cannot make it anymore," the day they stop fighting, the fight is over. In other words, the harder they struggle to avoid the inevitable death, the more they try to deny it, the more difficult it will be for them to reach this final stage of acceptance with peace and dignity.

Elisabeth Kübler-Ross is a psychiatrist and world-renowned authority on death and dying. She is the author of the best-selling book On Death and Dying *which not only influenced professional and private attitudes toward death but spawned a whole new science of thanatology.*

"Ordering of those stages implicitly serves a behavior control function for the busy American death professional."

A Critique of Elisabeth Kübler-Ross

Ron Rosenbaum

The curious tale of the Queen of Death and the lustful "entities" of Escondido is one of those little disturbances of man you may have missed if you haven't been tuned in to developments in the fast-growing "death awareness" movement. The scandal that developed over the erotic escapades of the "entities" represented a serious image crisis for the movement. Defenders of death awareness feel that the incident is merely an aberration being used unfairly by the medical establishment and its pawns in the press—servile minions of the "cure-oriented," "interventionist," "high-technology life-prolonging" old regime—to discredit the work of the dedicated devotees of death and dying. But a case can be made that intercourse with entities—okay, let's call it sex with the dead—is not an aberration but a summation, a consummation, of the whole misbegotten love affair with death that the movement has been promoting.

The Queen of Death, of course, is Dr. Elisabeth Kubler-Ross, who reigns over a mountaintop "Death-and-Dying-Center" in Escondido, California, whose work single-handedly created the death-and-dying movement, and who, until now, endowed it with respectability.

Author of *On Death and Dying, Living With Death and Dying, Questions and Answers on Death and Dying,* and *Death: The Final Stage of Growth,* recipient of twenty honorary degrees, Kubler-Ross is now taught, in her estimation, in 125,000 death-and-dying courses in colleges, seminaries, medical schools, hospitals, and social-work institutions. She has come to be regarded as the last word on death. Not only do "death professionals"—hospital and hospice workers, clergymen, and psychiatrists—get their basic training from Kubler-Ross in order to counsel the dying, but her books are so widespread that most people who

die these days are familiar with her "five stages of dying."

Kubler-Ross's thought has given birth to whole new academic industries—"thanatology" and "dolorology"—helped create the hospice movement, "Conscious Dying Centers," and, more recently, an increasingly cultlike exaltation, sentimentalization, and even worship of death.

Out of Hand

In the past, like most sensible people, I've been content to leave strenuous thinking about death in the capable hands of others. Somehow I assumed from all the acclaim from varied quarters that Kubler-Ross couldn't be *too* foolish, assumed that she embodied the typical post-Enlightenment secular consensus on the subject: awareness of death giving an urgency and intensity to life, etc. Probably sensible, caring and boring. But I have a feeling that the rest of you must have been averting your eyes from what Kubler-Ross was saying all this time, and that we're beginning to see the consequences. Because something's gone awry with the death-and-dying movement Kubler-Ross helped create. Things have gotten out of hand: Kubler-Ross herself has become the guru to a nationwide network of death 'n' dying centers called "Shanti Nilaya"; the "Conscious Dying movement" urges us to devote our life to death awareness and also opens up a "Dying Center"; a video artist kills herself on public television and calls it "artistic suicide"; the EXIT society publishes a handy, do-it-yourself Home Suicide guide that can take its place next to other recent Home Dying and Home Burial Guides; a pop science cult emerges around the "near death experience," which makes dying sound like a lovely acid trip (turn on, tune in, drop dead); attempts at two-way traffic with the afterlife abound, including a courier service to the dead using dying patients and even phone calls *from* the dead; belief in

Ron Rosenbaum, "Turn on, Tune in, Drop Dead," *Harper's,* July 1982. Copyright © 1982 by Ron Rosenbaum. Reprinted with permission.

reincarnation resurfaces as "past lives therapy."...

While this billing and cooing about death did not originate with Kubler-Ross—the cult of "the Beautiful Death" is a recurrent one in stagnant societies—she did come up with one concept that single-handedly revolutionized and *restructured* the worship of death in America and gave it an up-to-date "scientific" foundation: the five stages of dying.

Stage One

Dividing dying into stages was a stroke of genius. Kubler-Ross brought forth her five stages at just about the time when people were dividing life into "passages," stages, predictable crises. Getting dying properly staged would bring every last second of existence under the reign of reason. As every student of elementary thanatology soon learns, the famous five stages of dying are: denial, anger, bargaining, depression, acceptance.

"Something's gone awry with the death-and-dying movement Kübler-Ross helped create."

What's been lost in the general approbation of Kubler-Ross's five stages is the way her ordering of those stages implicitly serves a *behavior control* function for the busy American death professional. The movement from denial and anger to depression and acceptance is seen as a kind of spiritual *progress,* as if quiet acceptance is the most mature, the highest stage to strive for.

What Kubler-Ross calls bargaining, others might call a genuine search for reasons to live, to fight for life. But she has no patience with dilly-dallying by the dying. She disparages "bargaining" that goes on too long, describes patients who don't resign themselves to death after they've gotten the extra time they bargained for as "children" who don't "keep their promises" to die.

Yet by "acceptance," Kubler-Ross means the infantilization of the dying: "It is perhaps best compared with what Bettelheim describes about early infancy," she says. "A time of passivity, an age of primary narcissism in which...we are going back to the stage we started out with and the circle of life is closed."

More Manageable Patient

Certainly this passivity makes for a quieter, more manageable hospice. Crotchety hospice guests who quixotically refuse to accept, who persist in anger or hope, will be looked on as recalcitrant, treated as retarded in their dying process, stuck in an "immature" early stage, and made to feel that it's high time they moved on to the less troublesome

stages of depression and acceptance.

Now let's look at the practical effect of this premium on passivity on an actual encounter between a dying person and a "death professional." Let's look at a little hand-printed pamphlet entitled *It's Been a Delightful Dance:* the story of Ellen Clark as told in a sermon by Dr. Richard Turner.

This is an account of the therapeutic relationship between Turner and Clark, who was dying of cancer when she approached the Cancer Project of "Life Force," Turner's therapy organization, for counseling.

"Cancering"

The California-based Life Force was one of several holistically oriented therapy groups that specialize in what has come to be called "cancering." Turner charged forty-five dollars an hour for such counseling.

I came across Turner and his group in 1980, in the Grand Ballroom of the Ambassador Hotel in Los Angeles, at a convention of the Cancer Control Society, a national organization that supports scores of "unorthodox" and forbidden cancer "cures"— everything from apricot kernels and coffee enemas to secret-formula serums and salves. I was somewhat puzzled to find someone like Turner speaking here, since the acceptance-oriented death-and-dying rhetoric in his speech contrasted with the feverish never-say-die, last-minute, miracle-seeking emphasis of the unorthodox-cancer-cure movement. "With certain patients I've counseled it becomes clear that at some level they are ready to die," Turner told me, when I questioned him after his talk. "They've made their choice, they feel they've lived their life. There was one patient of mine who'd done the holistic cures. But as I counseled her on her dying experience, it was as if this was what she wanted, it was as if she was releasing all her barriers and becoming fully human for the first time. She turned into a living, beautiful person so that by the time she died she'd done all her life's work in her last few weeks. Her name was Ellen Clark. In fact I wrote up my experience with her in a sermon I delivered. It's in our literature."

Idealizing Dying

Reading Turner's description of the progress of his therapy with the late Ellen Clark, it's impossible not to notice the influence of Kubler-Ross in the way he idealizes the progressive infantilization of the dying.

The big breakthrough that Ellen Clark achieves as she's wasting away with cancer is, according to Turner's sermon, that she "develops a childlike transparency." How does Turner deal with this in his counseling sessions? He's eager to encourage it, eager to "reinforce those feelings that we were like children in kindergarten." His technique for reinforcing this? He responds completely only to Ellen's "childlike," "magical" looks; even when she's trying to tell him something in adult sentences he makes sure that "only part of my attention went back to what she was saying. . . . The result was that heavy subject matter such as life and death and problem-solving progressively lost its dominance and an air of lightness pervaded our meetings."

A Compliant Child

No wonder. Dealing with an adult who's been turned into a happily compliant dying child is much more fun for friends and family than facing the complexities presented by a stubborn adult who's frantically fighting to live.

As in other tales in the contemporary Beautiful Death literature, an element of parasitism seems to creep into the stories told by the selfless survivors. Turner tells us that after Ellen became the "transparent child," *he* really started getting off on the sessions. He reports feeling "light and alive" after each session. "I was gaining as much from our meetings as her." (Maybe he should have been paying *her* $45 an hour for the privilege.) Ellen's friends also "reported quite consistently being touched and healed in her presence." Touched and healed: the magical powers of the dying are frequent causes for amazement in the literature.

By turning herself into an agreeable, transparent, loving child with Turner's encouragement, by refusing crankily to seek out some new cure or make a desperate gamble for her life, Ellen made it easy for people to be around her and feel loving. The message for dying patients in that sermon is, to revise Dylan Thomas, "*Do* go gentle into that good night."

Dance of Death

And then the climax of the *Delightful Dance* sermon: "The morning after I heard about Ellen's death I went out for my daily jog," Turner tells us. "A beautiful orange butterfly landed in front of my foot. I immediately felt *as if I knew this butterfly,* and apparently it had this same connection with me. . . . The butterfly and I were doing a get-acquainted dance. . . . I felt I was doing a get-acquainted dance with the butterfly within me. I feel I am ready to let go of being the caterpillar. . . . I am more ready to dance with my life. . . ."

And so, according to Turner, Ellen's pretty little death turned out to be a plus for everyone: Ellen got to be a butterfly and he got to dance during his daily jog. The whole thing sounded like a dance of death to me.

This is only the beginning, this reverence for the life-giving holiness of the compliantly childlike death object. It's a long way from there to going to bed with the dead, but the route is direct, and after reading the recent profusion of death-and-dying literature, I've divided it—in homage to Kubler-Ross—into five stages:

Stage 1: worship of the dying;
Stage 2: longing to *be* dying;
Stage 3: playing dead;
Stage 4: playing *with* the dead;
Stage 5: going to bed with the dead.

Stage Two

We've already seen Stage 1, with its reverence for the wisdom of the terminally ill. In Stage 2, death 'n' dying is seen to be an attractive option for healthy people. Why let the dying get all the benefits of facing death? To maximize the high of the dying experience when it comes, healthy people are urged by Stage 2 literature to devote their life to preparing for a beautiful death. Stage 2 advocates range from the Conscious Dying movement and its subsidiaries, the Dying Project and the Dying Center in New Mexico, to the "rational suicide" advocates. The London-based EXIT group is only one of several that put out practical do-it-yourself guides to painless suicide; other books tell you how to arrange the particulars of your death or burial at home. The late Jo Roman, evangelist of "creative suicide," went one step further—she did it on TV.

"What Kübler-Ross calls bargaining, others might call a genuine search for reasons to live, to fight for life."

Stage 2 advocates tend to be the nags of the death-and-dying movement. Since we are not fortunate enough to be terminally ill, they tell us, we must make strenuous efforts to overcome our handicap by concentrating our lives on death and suicide.

It is never too early to start. "Should schoolchildren be asked to write essays on 'How I Would Feel if I Had to Die at Midnight' or compositions envisaging why and in what circumstances they propose to end their lives?" asks Mary Rose Barrington, past chairman of EXIT. "The answer may well be that they should," says Mary Rose, who, oddly enough, is also "Honorary Secretary of the Animal Rights Group." (Do they favor the right to suicide for parakeets?)

Tomorrow May Be Too Late

Missing out on early-childhood death education is no excuse to avoid the subject now. And that means today. Tomorrow may be too late if you believe the nagging of Steven Levine, director of the Dying Project. "Tomorrow," he points out, "could be the first day of thirty years of quadriplegia. What preparations have you made to open to an inner life so full that whatever happens can be used as a means of enriching your focus?" The first day of thirty years of quadriplegia. It's a particularly ironic formulation of the challenge because Levine and the Dying Project, and the Dying Center (where people check in to check out are spiritual descendants of ex-Harvard professor and psychedelic pioneer Richard Alpert (now Ram Dass), and thus of a brand of spiritualism that expressed its incurable optimism with the slogan "Today is the first day of the rest of your life." Sure, but tomorrow the wheelchair and the catheter. Such a shift says something about this branch of the Pro-Death movement—either they've run out of good acid and have been dipping into the melancholy Hospice Mix, or, as they grow older, they're suddenly scared of death and afraid to admit it.

"Dealing with an adult who's been turned into a happily compliant dying child is much more fun for friends and family."

If you read Levine's testament, *Who Dies,* a bible for the Conscious Dying movement, you begin to suspect he's trying to smother his fear of death in protestations of his devotion to it. He's constantly hectoring the reader for having failed to do his death homework: "If you should die in extreme pain how will you have prepared to keep your mind soft and open?" he scolds. "What have you done to keep your mind present, so that you don't block precious opportunity with a concept, with some idea of what's happening, open to experience the suchness, the living truth, of the next unknown moment?"

Inauthentic Dying

You could dismiss this scolding as mere school-teacherish sanctimony, or life-insurance-salesman scare tactics (buy my theory of dying now or you'll be condemned to die inauthentically), but there's something more frightened and frightening in this prose. I think it comes out in the Dying Project co-director's description of the ideal Conscious Dying movement-approved death:

> *I've been with people as they approached their death and seen how much clarity and open-heartedness it takes to stay soft with the distraction in the mind and body, to stay with the fear that arises uninvited, to keep so open that when fear comes up they can say, 'Yes, that's fear all right.' But the spaciousness from which they say it is not frightened. Because the separate "I" is not the predominant experience, there's little for that fear to stick to. Clearly a useful practice would be to cultivate an openness to what is unpleasant, to acknowledge resistance and fear, to soften and open around it, to let it float free, to let it go. If you wrote down a list of your resistances and holdings, it would nearly be a sketch of your personality. If you identify with that personality as you are, you amplify the fear of death; the imagined loss of imagined individuality.*

This is metaphysical heroin, a Brompton's Cocktail of the mind, the same basic anodyne for the tears of things that all Eastern cults offer: if you detach yourself and experience all passion at one numb remove, in the context of the infinitude of being, nothing hurts as much. If you go the whole route and cease being a person—that "imagined individual" Levine disparages—then you won't even die because there won't be a you to die. You'll never be a person afraid of death because you won't be a person. You'll be, instead, "the spaciousness" that is not frightened. Nonbeings can't cease being. If you make life as spacious and empty as death, you won't notice any transition between living and dying; you might as well be dead.

Which is exactly what the "creative suicide" people say. Or they might call it "CREATING ON MY OWN TERMS THE FINAL STROKE OF MY LIFE'S CANVAS," as video death artist Jo Roman wrote in her last letter to friends. ("By the time you read these lines I WILL HAVE GENTLY ENDED MY LIFE on the date of this letter's postmark," she announces with typical gentleness.)

Roman's trend-setting originality, of course, was not in her committing the act or justifying it on artistic grounds. It was in doing it so publicly. Suicide-proud self-murderers have in the past been content to have their feverish last thoughts and justifications publicized. But Jo Roman insisted on making a federal case of the act itself and the whole tearful "dying process," summoning friends and forcing them to grovel at the altar of her honesty while the videotape cameras rolled. She made the additional breakthrough of claiming for suicides the status of an oppressed *lifestyle* group in need of televised validation: "I want to share it with others in order to raise consciousness. Also, and importantly, because I am averse to demeaning myself by closeting an act which I believe deserves respect."

Of course, creative suicide is not the exclusive province of sick and exhibitionistic video artists. There were the healthy young teenagers in Seattle, a boy and a girl, who, inspired by the transcendent optimism about the indestructibility of the soul in *Jonathan Livingston Seagull,* proceeded to get into a Pontiac and drive it at eighty miles per hour flat out into a stone wall, in order to ensure they spent eternity together.

Suicide and suicide pacts are a predictable enough consequence of the death 'n' dying movement. By romanticizing dying, by making death more "authentic" than life, suicide is made to seem an attractive, artistic, even heroic choice.

Stage Three

Another way of promoting the attractiveness and allure of death is through the creation of an inviting, reassuring, sugarcoated vision of the afterlife. Which brings us to Stage 3 in the development of contemporary death worship: the romance of the Near Death Experience (NDE), or playing dead.

At first the NDE seemed to be a freak, based on a few isolated reports. People who had been pronounced "clinically dead," people who "died" on the operating table, in the ambulance, or the intensive care ward, whose heart and vital functions ceased for ten, twenty minutes, would sometimes, after miraculous "resurrections," tell tales of leaving the body and traveling through a remarkable, otherworldly realm.

Aside from the *National Enquirer* ('DEAD MAN' SPEAKS!), no one paid much attention to these isolated reports until a philosophy professor named Raymond Moody compiled 150 of them into a book called *Life After Life,* which was published in 1975 with an endorsement by none other than Elisabeth Kubler-Ross, who claimed that she had been doing exactly the same kind of research and that Moody's findings duplicated hers.

Afterlife Vision

The "NDE" became the semi-official afterlife vision for the death-and-dying religion. It was appealing because it made death seem like something to look forward to. The "undiscovered country from whose bourn no traveller returns," whose mysteries had long terrified the human imagination, now seemed, from the reports of Raymond Moody's travelers, to be about as frightening as a day trip to the Jersey shore.

Let's look at Moody's "theoretically complete model" of the life-after-life experience, which I have here divided into seven easy-to-follow steps.

1. *A streetcar named death:* Our traveler hears himself pronounced dead. Next he hears "a loud ringing or buzzing and at the same time feels himself moving very rapidly through a long dark tunnel."

2. *The fly on the wall:* "He suddenly finds himself outside of his own physical body.... He watches the resuscitation attempt from this unusual vantage point...in a state of emotional upheavel."

3. *Family reunion:* "He glimpses the spirits of relatives and friends who have already died."

4. *The heavenly customs inspector:* He meets "a loving warm spirit of a kind he has never encountered before—a being of light....This being asks him a question, nonverbally, to make him evaluate his life...."

5. *The highlights film:* The "being of light" helps him along by "showing him a panoramic instantaneous playback of the major events of his life."

6. *Heaven can wait:* "He finds himself approaching some sort of barrier or border apparently representing the limit between earthly life and the next life. Yet, he finds that he must go back to the earth, that the time for his death has not yet come."

7. *Deportation:* "He is taken up with his experiences in the afterlife and does not want to return. He is overwhelmed by intense feelings of joy, love, and peace. Despite his attitude," though, he's forced to rejoin the unpleasant world of the living.

Riddle of Existence

Of course, it's possible that this pallid panorama of sweetness and light may actually *be* the afterlife and the ultimate riddle of existence has been solved. There are certainly millions of people who would like to believe its reassuring, nondenominational, downy-soft delights: Moody's book and his sequel *Reflections on Life After Life,* and its paperback rackmates *Life Before* and *Reliving Past Lives,* have all become big dime-store and drugstore best sellers, creating a popular NDE-based cult.

"To maximize the high of the dying experience when it comes, healthy people are urged by Stage 2 literature to devote their life to preparing for a beautiful death."

The only stumbling block that prevents the NDE from becoming the center of a new popular religion for the living has been that the actual ecstatic death trip experience seemed to be restricted to those privileged few whose heart, breathing, and vital functions had ceased for a certain period, or who were fortunate enough to be survivors of a plane crash, car wreck, or other near death trauma.

Enter the ever helpful Elisabeth Kubler-Ross, who not only endorsed Moody's NDE but took the NDE cult a crucial step further by staking out that bright landscape and its loving beings of light for routine visits by the living—those among the living who learned the correct way of *playing dead.*

Out-of-Body Experience

She discovered this pastime from her own travels in that realm of bright beings, she says. Her first "out-of-body experience" came at a time when she was, if not near death, at least by her account, dead tired from several years of exhausting nonstop travel, lectures, seminars, and workshops promoting death 'n' dying awareness. Drifting off into a trance-like sleep, she says, "I saw myself lifted out of my physical body....It was as if a whole lot of loving beings were taking all the tired parts out of me, similar to car mechanics in a car repair shop....I experienced a great sense of peace and serenity, a feeling of literally being taken care of, of having no worry in the world. I had also an incredible sense that once all the parts were replaced I would be as young and fresh and energetic as I had been prior to this rather exhausting, draining workshop.

...Naturally I associated this immediately with the stories of dying patients who shared with me their near death experiences....Little did we know then that that was the beginning of an enormous amount of new research, which ultimately led to the understanding of death and life after death."

While this first experience was involuntary, she discovered, after hooking up with some out-of-body occultists in Virginia, that she could learn to repeat it at will. She could play dead. Whenever her bodily vehicle needed a tune-up, whenever she wanted to set back the old odometer, rejuvenate the spark plugs, she could take a revitalizing dip into death, that refreshing fountain of youth.

Stage Four

But Kubler-Ross did not stop there. She sailed right on into Stage 4: playing with the dead.

Remember that benevolent "being of light" who greets you when you alight from the streetcar named death? Well, he has friends up there. Plenty of them. Spirit guides. Guardian angels. The enlightened "afterlife entities."

"By romanticizing dying, by making death more 'authentic' than life, suicide is made to seem an attractive, artistic, even heroic choice."

The way Kubler-Ross describes it now, all the while she was garnering her honorary degrees, her acclaim from clergy, shrinks, and academics for working with the dying, she was spending an ever increasing amount of her time playing with the dead. She made her own decisions only in consultation with her guardian angels and spirit guides. She counseled the living to make their decisions based on the guidance of entities from the Other Side.

Dead Are Wiser

In Stage 4, the implications of the previous stages become explicit: *death is much more wonderful than life,* the dead are much wiser, and, since two-way communication with the Other Side is now possible, it's better to consult with them about the tiresome business of getting through life. By Stage 4, the dead are not really "dead" at all. They're more alive than we, the living, can hope to be. They're not even called "dead" anymore. For Stage 4 death worshipers they are "afterlife entities"; by the time we reach Stage 4 there is no such thing as death.

This was another Kubler-Ross discovery, I learned from her "media person" in Escondido. "Elisabeth doesn't like the term 'near death experience,'" he explained to me, "because she doesn't believe that death exists."

Doesn't believe in death?

"No such thing," he said. "She believes there are just...transitions. So it's not a near death experience because it's available to normal living people every day if they tune in to it."

Turn on, tune in, drop dead.

National Pastime

Playing with the dead has become a rapidly expanding national pastime. Spirit guides and guardian angels are becoming for many adults the comforting imaginary playmates they had to abandon as children, the perfect loving parents they never had. This two-way traffic takes some curious forms. According to a *Washington Post* story (apparently not a hoax), a California company has hired a number of terminally ill patients who will, for a fee, act as couriers, memorizing messages to be delivered to the dead as soon as they arrive on the Other Side. A whole new category of spiritualist phenomena is chronicled in the book *Phone Calls from the Dead,* which cites reports that phones all over America are practically ringing off the hook as chatterbox "entities" from the Other Side pester their friends and relatives among the living.

Stage Five

Considering this feverish eagerness to be in touch with entities one way or another, it's not surprising that some death 'n' dying cultists have carried worship of the dead to Stage 5: going to bed with the dead.

It seems as if there has always been a subtext of eroticism in the growth of the death 'n' dying movement. Take the story behind Kubler-Ross's first big break into the national awareness.

"She was doing her seminars with dying patients virtually unnoticed in Chicago," her media person told me over the phone. "But then *Life* magazine heard about her and was going to send someone to see if there was a story in her work. There was this elderly man dying who was going to be the subject of the seminar when *Life* was there, but the old man died the night before."

There followed a hasty search for an understudy dying patient, and what happened next was in the best Broadway tradition: "They found a beautiful young girl to replace the old man." She was twenty-four or twenty-six, the media person told me. "And then *Life* knew they had a story. A real heart-throbber." It was this dying-heartthrob story in *Life,* he said, that made Kubler-Ross a sudden national sensation and enshrined her as Queen of Death.

If the dying can be heartthrobs, if the afterlife entities can be warm and loving and intimate with the living, why would anyone hesitate to go to bed with the dead?

By the time the sexual scandal broke in 1980,

Kubler-Ross seems to have been bewitched into buying every last spiritualist trick in the book. She had no less than four personal entities—she called them "Mario," "Anka," "Salem," and "Willie"— attending her. She now believed in reincarnation and claimed to have memories of being alive in the time of Jesus. Where once her seminars had helped the dying, their friends, and their relatives live with despair, she now offered them a grab bag of Big Rock Candy Mountain fantasies of "life after life" to escape from life. And, finally, she'd allied her personal organization with a local sect that called itself the Church of the Facet of Divinity, hailing its minister, faith healer, and medium Jay Barham as "the greatest healer in the world."...

Franchising Death

For a year after the affair of the erotic entities, she defended Barham and continued to work with him, franchising death, dying, and entity-encounter sessions throughout the country. She now insists, however, that she was no fool, that nobody had pulled the wool over her eyes, that unbeknownst to everyone "I have been conducting my own first-person investigation of...Barham." This investigation, which she must have pursued with all the stealth of Richard Nixon's personal "investigation" of the Watergate cover-up, finally uncovered unspecified conduct by Barham that "did not meet the standards...of Shanti Nilaya."

"It's not surprising that some death 'n' dying cultists have carried worship of the dead to Stage 5."

None of this substandard behavior, she insisted, took place on her premises or involved her workshops. The clincher in her investigation, Kubler-Ross told a writer, was her decision to have a doctor "measure" Barham's faith-healing power. This test, whose exact nature she did not disclose, revealed to her that his healing skills had declined measurably and that the decline was proof of his misuse of his powers.

"There are those who might say this has damaged my credibility," she conceded. "But it's not important whether people believe what I say....I'm a doctor and a scientist, who simply reports what she sees, hears, and experiences."

Although Kubler-Ross has consistently stone-walled all inquiries about her reported presence at the scene of the assignations with the aroused afterlife entities, there is every indication that her disillusion with Barham has not diminished her swooning worship of death.

Ron Rosenbaum is writing a novel about cancer cures.

"A number of studies have shown. . . that 80 percent of doctors oppose telling dying patients the truth, while 80 percent of their patients want to be told."

viewpoint 48

Patients Should Be Told They Are Dying

Thomas Powers

On November 8, 1970, Barbara B., a woman in her middle sixties, was admitted to New York Hospital with an unexplained intestinal blockage. Because it was a Sunday and her own doctor was unavailable, the doctor of a friend took over. He had never met Mrs. B. and knew nothing of her medical history. When he asked what was wrong she described her symptoms during the preceding few days but volunteered nothing else. Dr. C. began making arrangements for an exploratory operation in the next day or two if the situation did not correct itself.

A friend had accompanied Mrs. B. to the hospital. Later that day her daughter and son-in-law came up to see her. Mrs. B. was in considerable pain so there was not much conversation. When they did talk, it was about matters of little consequence. Not knowing exactly what Mrs. B.'s condition was they all hoped that an operation would not be necessary, but they did not speculate as to what might have caused the blockage. Each of the four had a pretty good idea of the cause: none of them mentioned it that first day.

On Monday Dr. C. contacted Mrs. B.'s regular doctor and was told she had had a cancerous breast removed in the summer of 1968, that malignant skin nodules had reappeared in the summer of 1970, and that laboratory tests showed spreading cancer. It was obvious to Dr. C. that Mrs. B.'s cancer had reached her abdomen and that she did not have long to live. When he spoke to Mrs. B.'s family, however, he was somewhat more tentative. He said he was not sure (which was true; he was not *absolutely certain)* what was causing the blockage, that the blockage might disappear, that he advised waiting for a few days to see how things developed. He admitted, in response to direct questions, that Mrs. B. was suffering from a serious case of cancer and that serious in her case probably meant fatal. He muted only the probably (but not yet *certain)* fact that Mrs. B. had already begun to die.

Continual Discomfort

During the following few days Mrs. B. was in continual discomfort but nevertheless remained the same person her family had always known: witty, unsentimental, interested in gossip, a passionate reader, a stern critic of everything about President Nixon except the good looks of his daughters, in all things a woman determined to be strong. When friends or family came to visit she talked about politics, life on Tenth Street, what she was reading, and so on. Everyone asked how she was feeling. She always answered, "Oh, all right," with a look of disgust. Once or twice she said she hoped she would not need an operation. A kind of unspoken agreement was in effect: cancer was not to be mentioned. The reasons for the agreement varied. Mrs. B. felt it was weak to discuss bodily ills, and wanted to spare her daughter. Her daughter wanted to spare her mother. Mrs. B. and her family all knew her cancer had reappeared, but discussion of the possible operation was based on the unstated assumption that the cancer and the intestinal blockage were two entirely separate conditions. In other words, everyone knew the end was coming, but resisted the notion that it was coming *now.*

When the blockage persisted into the middle of the next week, however, it became increasingly difficult to ignore the seriousness of Mrs. B.'s condition. Mrs. B. had nothing but contempt for people who complained and was inclined to think that any mention of her own condition was a kind of complaining. In spite of this, she began to refer to it elliptically.

One evening, as her son-in-law was just leaving, she abruptly mentioned a Kingsley Amis novel she had once read in which a character visits a hospitalized friend who is dying with cancer (Mrs. B.

winced at the word) of the stomach. In the novel, the dying friend makes little pretense of interest in the conversation; he is simply trying to hold on until his next pain shot.

Living for Pain Shot

"I'm beginning to feel that way myself," Mrs. B. said with a bitter smile, apologizing for her failure to keep up her end of the conversation and ashamed of herself for bringing it up. "When something really hurts, all you live for is that pain shot."

A couple of days later Mrs. B.'s son-in-law arrived just as Mrs. B.'s roommate was coming out of anesthesia following an operation to determine if she had breast cancer. The son-in-law asked what the verdict had been. "She had two tumors but neither was malignant," Mrs. B. said. "Some people have all the luck."

"Dying is not a subject to which doctors have traditionally paid much attention."

Mrs. B. refrained from talking about her feelings directly on all but one or two occasions. Once she told her daughter, "I've got so little to look forward to," but then regained her composure. "Sometimes I can't help feeling blue," she explained. There were other slips, but generally she refused to talk about what she was going through, or to let anyone else talk about it. Neither she nor anyone else had yet admitted fully what was now the one great fact in her life: she was dying.

Death Is Uncommon Topic

Dying is not a subject to which doctors have traditionally paid much attention. Their first purpose is to preserve life, and once life can no longer be decently extended they tend to lose interest. Until fairly recently, the medical professional reacted to death as if the subject were adequately covered by the children's old skip-rope song:

Doctor, doctor, will I die?
Yes, my child, and so will I.

Since death was inevitable, discussion was restricted to secondary matters, centering on three main questions. The first was how to determine when the patient was really dead. Before the twentieth century, people were occasionally buried while still alive, and wills sometimes included a stipulation that the deceased remain above ground until his body actually began to smell. The second question, still much discussed, was whether or not to tell the patient he was dying. The third question, of more interest to doctors of divinity than of medicine, concerned the individual after the process of dying was complete: specifically, did the soul survive, and if so, in what form? All three questions are still

open to dispute, and the first has attracted considerable scientific attention since the advent of organ transplants. Laws that require embalming before burial preclude the possibility of being buried alive, but there is still plenty of contention about identifying the precise moment in which a patient becomes sufficiently dead to justify the removal of vital organs.

The question of dying itself has been ignored. In 1912 a Boston doctor, Roswell Park, suggested that nothing was known about the subject and coined a word for its study—thanatology. No one remembered the word or undertook the study. With the exception of books on death as a religious event, almost nothing was published on the subject. The few books that were often had a cultist flavor, like *Death, Its Causes and Phenomena,* also published in 1912, which included a chapter on "Photographing and Weighing the Soul." Medical scientists acted as if Woodrow Wilson had adequately described death and dying in his last words before slipping into unconsciousness: "I am a broken machine. I am ready to go." Scientists were interested in the machine during, not after, its breakdown. They described dying exclusively in terms of the specific diseases or conditions which accompanied it, almost as if dying would not occur if there were no disease.

Expanding Thanatology

Since the second world war the subject has begun to receive some attention. In 1956, the American Psychological Association held a major symposium on death at its annual convention. In 1965, Dr. Elisabeth Kubler-Ross began a prolonged study of dying patients at the University of Chicago's Billings Hospital. Other organizations, institutes, and centers, usually with a highly specialized focus, have been established in Cleveland, Boston, Durham, North Carolina, and elsewhere. In 1967, a number of doctors in New York created the Foundation of Thanatology (the coincidental use of Dr. Park's word was not discovered until later) to encourage the study of death and dying from a broad perspective. They chose the word thanatology to make it easier to raise funds, figuring that philanthropists, like others, would find the word death so disturbing they would prefer to have nothing to do with it. La Rochefoucauld, the seventeenth-century French writer, said, "One can no more look steadily at death than at the sun." The Foundation of Thanatology has found that the attention span of those they approach for funds is generally just long enough to say no. Independent researchers have experienced similar difficulties and disappointments, including outright hostility on the part of doctors, nurses, and hospital administrators. Nevertheless, some important work has been done, and dying as a biological and psychological event is beginning to be understood.

The biological aspects of death have received the

most attention. In most, but not all, cases an autopsy will reveal exactly how an individual died, by which doctors now usually mean what caused his brain to cease functioning. Since respirators and other machines can keep the heart beating and other organs functioning virtually indefinitely, doctors have begun to accept "brain death" as adequate confirmation that the patient is actually "dead." The brain is considered to be dead when an electroencephalogram (EEG) is flat, which means that it detects no electromagnetic activity within the brain. It is a useful definition, compromised to some degree by the fact that patients have, if only rarely, recovered completely following two or even three days with absolutely flat EEG. Brain death is generally (but not always) caused by a lack of oxygen, which is generally (but not always) caused by failure of the heart or lungs. The number of exact ways in which a human can die are, however, vast. Medical scientists are successful in describing how the body breaks down, not quite so successful in explaining why it breaks down; they admit that in a significant number of cases death occurs for no apparent medical reason whatever.

Fear of Death

Dying as a psychological event, as an experience, is even more elusive. The principal obstacle to its study has been the fear of death on the part of patients, relatives, doctors, nurses, and the dispensers of funds for research. Since no one can say convincingly what death is, it is not easy to say why people fear it. In general, the fear of death has been broken down into the specific fears of pain, loneliness, abandonment, mutilation, and, somewhat more difficult to define, fear of the loss of self. This is not just another way of saying fear of death, but a kind of disassociation of the self as a conscious entity (the sense of *me*-ness one feels) from the self as a particular individual, with his particular history in the everyday world. That individual is one's closest associate and one fears his loss.

The fear of death also has a primitive, nonrational dimension, like fear of the dark and fear of the unknown. Conscious effort can bring such fear under control but cannot suppress it entirely. One doctor in New York uses complaints about the food in hospitals as a rule of thumb for gauging the fear of death: the more passionate and unreasonable the complaint, he has found, the greater the fear of dying. Everyone apparently experiences the fear of death in some degree, but reacts to it in his own way. People tend to die as they have lived, as suggested in the saying "Death is terrible to Cicero, desirable to Cato, and indifferent to Socrates."

The experience of death is obviously related to its immediate cause. Heart disease and stroke are the conditions most likely to grant the widespread wish for death to occur in sleep. Heart patients who have been saved by modern techniques report they felt only a sudden pain and the beginning of mingled alarm and surprise. In earlier times, those sensations would have been death (as they presumably still are for those not saved). Patients who have suffered severe heart attacks often regain consciousness in some hospital's intensive-care unit with the words, "I'm dying, I'm dying," suggesting that awareness of death can be almost, but not quite, instantaneous. Nurses then find themselves in the awkward position of having to explain that the patient is not dying, without making clear the fact he still might at any moment. Diseases which do not attack vital centers directly and massively, and especially the forms of breakdown associated with old age, allow considerable warning before death actually arrives.

Suffering from Fear

When an individual begins to die, much of what he suffers is the result of the fear of death on his own part and on the part of those around him. He reminds people that they, too, are going to die, which they naturally are not eager to consider. As a result, the first problem faced by the dying individual is to discover the truth about his condition.

"The first problem faced by the dying individual is to discover the truth about his condition."

In some rare instances doctors make a practice of telling patients the truth immediately, but in most cases the patient has to find out by himself. In their book, *Awareness of Dying*, Barney G. Glaser and Anselm L. Strauss describe a struggle for the truth which is sometimes Byzantine in its complexity, with patients trying to pick up clues while doctors, nurses, and relatives join in a conspiracy to conceal the patient's actual condition. The reason for withholding the truth, doctors say, is that the patient would find it too upsetting, that he needs hope in order to keep on fighting for life, that one can never be absolutely certain of a diagnosis, that patients really do not want to know.

Doctors View Death as Defeat

A number of studies have shown, however, that 80 per cent (more or less, depending on the study) of doctors oppose telling dying patients the truth, while 80 per cent of their patients want to be told. Doctors apparently shy from the subject because death represents a defeat and because, like everybody else, they find death upsetting to talk about. The psychological stratagems of medical students confronting death for the first time are notorious. The atmosphere of autopsy rooms is one of macabre humor, a degree or two short of hysteria. Doctors generally end by suppressing awareness of death so thoroughly some researchers speculate that that is why they are drawn to medicine in the first place.

Even while doctors and nurses do everything in their power to withhold the truth, resorting with a smile to outright lies, they customarily believe that the majority of their patients know the truth anyway. Relatives of the dying have the same mixture of feelings, trying to suppress the truth and yet assuming that eventually the patient will realize what is happening. Husbands and wives, each knowing the truth, often tell a third party that *they* know, but not to let the *other* know because he (or she) "couldn't stand it." The pretense naturally grows harder to sustain as the dying patient approaches a final decline. Nevertheless, the pretense is often maintained by sheer will until the end, even when all parties know the truth, and know the others know it too.

"Dr. Kübler-Ross has found. . .that the grieving patient will often come out of his depression and face the prospect of death more calmly."

In rare instances patients refuse to recognize the truth, ignoring the most obvious clues (such as the visit of a relative who lives thousands of miles away) and insisting up until the end that they will be better in no time. For such patients almost any explanation will suffice. One woman dying of cancer, for example, believed (or pretended to believe) that she was only the victim of a slightly new strain of flu. Dr. Kubler-Ross describes a woman Christian Scientist who insisted until the end that faith in God was sufficient physic for an open cancer which was clearly killing her. As the woman declined she put on ever more garish makeup, until finally she was painting her white and withered cheeks a deep red, suppressing the distinctive smell of cancer with perfume and using false eyelashes and deep green eye shadow to insist she was still alive and even attractive. In most cases, however, patients eventually sense they are not getting better and either ask their doctors directly (by no means always getting an honest answer) or set verbal traps for nurses, relatives, and other patients, checking their responses for every discrepancy. One woman fatally ill with a rare disease discovered her condition when she casually ran across an article in *Newsweek* which described every symptom in exact detail. Nurses believe that "way deep down" patients sense when they are dying, and there is some evidence this is true. Patients who know they are dying will often tell

a nurse, "I'm going to die tonight," and then do so. Occasionally, however, patients feel they are going to die when, in fact, they are going to live. Persuading such a patient he's going to recover can be a frustrating experience, particularly when he has watched doctors and nurses deliberately deceive other patients who really were dying.

Pattern of Behavior

When patients finally do realize they are dying, a pattern of behavior often follows which was first described in detail by Dr. Kubler-Ross. Based on interviews with hundreds of dying patients over the past five years, she divides the reaction to knowledge of impending death into five distinctive stages.

The first stage is one of denial, even when a patient has suspected the worst and fought to determine the truth. All his life he has casually accepted the fact that "we all have to go." He is stunned to realize that now *he* has to go. After the discovery, patients often retreat into a self-imposed isolation, remaining silent with friends or relatives or even refusing to see them, while they get used to the fact that no mistake has been made, that they are *now* in the process of dying. Dr. Kubler-Ross believes that the dying never completely lose hope that a cure for their disease will be discovered at the last minute or that an outright miracle will occur ("the Scripture says that nothing is impossible with God"). This hope remains a deep-seated thing, and for practical purposes, such as writing wills and settling their affairs, the dying generally accept the fact they are dying once they have been told, directly or indirectly, that it is truly so.

The second stage is one of anger, especially when the dying individual is young. The anger can be released in any direction: at the doctors for doing nothing, at relatives because they are going to live, at other patients for not being quite so ill, at nurses for being young and healthy, at God for being unjust. In 1603, when Queen Elizabeth was told by her physician, Sir Robert Cecil, that she was seriously ill and must go to bed, she flared back, *"Must!* Is *must* a word to be addressed to princes? Little man, little man! Thy father, were he alive, durst not have used that word."* Her mood quickly shifted to gloomy self-pity. "Thou art so presumptuous," she said, "because thou knowest that I shall die."

Eventually the anger subsides and the dying patient enters a curious stage in which he tries to bargain for his life. He begins to talk about all the things he has failed to do but will undertake if he recovers. He laments the fact he spent so much time earning a living and so little with his family, promising to alter his priorities if he gets home again. The most explicit bargains, generally proposed to God, are usually kept a secret. They are often legally precise, offering regular chuch attendance and sincere belief in return for a few more years. The bargains tend to be selfless, for the dying person knows he is about to lose himself altogether. Bargains can be offered for almost anything, for the chance to attend a son's wedding or to see another spring, but they all have one element in common: they are *never* kept. If the dying person actually does live until spring he immediately proposes another bargain.

Bargaining with God

Religious individuals often insist they submit themselves happily to God's pleasure ("Thy will be done") but are prepared to propose a reasonable compromise. St. Anselm, the Archbishop of Canterbury, dying in 1109, told fellow clerics gathered about his deathbed, "I shall gladly obey His call. Yet I should also feel grateful if He would grant me a little longer time with you, and if I could be permitted to solve a question—the origin of the soul." God did not accept the offer, and St. Anselm shortly died, but if He had, Dr. Kubler-Ross suggests that Anselm would quickly have proposed another bargain.

The fourth stage is one of altogether reasonable depression, part of the process doctors refer to as "anticipatory grief." In effect, the dying patient is grieving for himself before the fact of death, since he is about to lose everything he loves. It is this grieving which is probably most feared by doctors and relatives. It is painful to witness a death, and doubly painful when the dying person reacts in a fearful or hysterical manner. This is exceedingly rare, and yet doctors and relatives, perhaps unsure what their own reactions would be, fear the possibility so greatly that they put off discussion of death as long as possible and sometimes, as mentioned above, deny the truth until the end. In every other circumstance of life, no matter how bleak, some consolation can be genuinely offered; with those who know they are dying, there is nothing to say. Dr. Kubler-Ross has found, however, that the grieving patient will often come out of his depression and face the prospect of death more calmly for having been through it.

The final stage, not always reached, is one of acceptance.

Refraining from Tears

When Mrs. B. woke up one afternoon following a nap, she saw her daughter standing by her bed with tears streaming down her cheeks. "Now, we're not going to have any tears," Mrs. B. said.

Nevertheless, she, too, had recognized the seriousness of her condition. During the first week she was in the hospital she made a point of telling her daily visitors they really didn't have to come so often. Now she admitted to looking forward to every visit. "It's nice to wake up and find somebody there," she confessed. Her last roommate had remained only a day before moving into a single room, so Mrs. B. was entirely alone between visits.

The roommate, a woman in her forties who had also had a cancerous breast removed, had been shifted by her husband when he learned of Mrs. B.'s medical history. He said he wanted to protect the feelings of his wife, but she was acutely embarrassed by the move and came to see Mrs. B. every day. When the woman left the hospital she stopped by to say goodbye and suggested that she and Mrs. B. meet in New York for lunch someday. "Or," she said, "we have a place near you in the country. Maybe we can get together next spring." Mrs. B. said that would be fine and then added, "Good luck."

Weighing Alternatives

By the second week it was obvious Mrs. B.'s intestinal blockage was not going to clear by itself. Her doctors told her family the cancer had reached her liver and had probably affected her entire abdominal area. The sole remaining question was how long it would take Mrs. B. to die and whether or not she would be able to go home again in the time remaining. The only way she could leave the hospital, the doctors said, would be to undergo an operation in order to remove whatever was obstructing her intestine. They warned that she was in a weakened condition and might die during the operation, or that cancer might have affected so much of her intestine that nothing could be done. The alternatives were also presented to Mrs. B., although in less detail and more tentatively. Both she and her family decided it would be better to go ahead.

"After the discovery, patients often retreat into a self-imposed isolation... while they get used to the fact."

Mrs. B.'s eldest daughter, living in California, already had made plans to come East for Thanksgiving, knowing it would probably be her last chance to see her mother. When she was told about the operation she asked over the phone, "Shall I wait until next week or should I come now?"

"I think you'd better come now," her brother-in-law said. She arranged for someone to take care of her three children and made a plane reservation for the day after the operation. Mrs. B.'s two brothers were also called, but they decided to wait until after the operation before coming to New York. "If I came now it would scare her to death," said the brother who lived in Washington.

A Week to Live

The operation was scheduled for the morning of Thursday, November 19. Her family remained by the phone throughout the day. At 6 P.M. the surgeon finally called and said Mrs. B.'s intestine was blocked by cancer every two or three inches. There was nothing he could do. He was asked how long Mrs. B. might live. "Perhaps a week," he said.

Later that evening Mrs. B.'s family visted her briefly after she came up from the recovery room. She was pale and drawn and barely able to speak. The operation had obviously been an ordeal. "Never again," she whispered. "Never again."

"The abandonment which dying patients fear can be as much emotional as literal."

The next day Mrs. B.'s eldest daughter flew to New York and went to see her mother, already beginning to regain her strength after the operation. Before the family went to see her on Saturday they tried to decide what to say if she should ask about her condition. The hard thing was finding out what Mrs. B. already had been told by her doctors. Until they reached Dr. C., they decided, they would tell Mrs. B. everyone was worried but didn't yet know the full results of the operation. They feared she would press them, and they knew that if she asked directly whether or not the cancer had been cut out, the only possible answers would be the truth or an outright lie. They did not want to lie, knowing how much Mrs. B. would hate being lied to, but they dreaded equally talking about the true situation. They could not have explained why.

Unusual Questioning

As things turned out they need not have worried. Mrs. B. had cross-examined her doctors on a number of occasions since Thursday night, when she had found the strength to say, "It was my cancer, wasn't it?" Dr. C. later explained that Mrs. B. kept after him until she had the truth. His practice was to answer all questions truthfully, leaving it up to the patient to decide which questions to ask. Some patients asked nothing. Others stopped as soon as Dr. C. indicated their condition was serious. Mrs. B. had been unusual, he said, in questioning him precisely about her condition.

On Sunday Mrs. B. began to weaken again. When her son-in-law arrived about 11 A.M., she shooed the nurse out of the room. "I want to be alone with my son-in-law," she said. As soon as the door was closed she said, "I'm dying. There's no use kidding ourselves."

She told her son-in-law where all her papers were and what was in her will, asking him to make sure his mother got the red leather box which Mrs. B. had bought for her in Czechoslovakia the previous summer, and then had liked so much she kept it.

"I've been feeling guilty about that," she said.

She also asked her son-in-law to get her lawyer on the phone so she could give him "a pep talk." When she reached him she said, "Now listen, you take care of the kids and try and keep the government from getting it all." She gave her best to his wife and said goodbye.

Finally Mrs. B. asked her son-in-law to make sure her eyes went to the eye bank and that her body was given to "science." (Mrs. B.'s surgeon told her son-in-law he wanted to do an autopsy, but that cancer had destroyed her body's usefulness as far as "science" was concerned. Mrs. B.'s second choice had been cremation without any service, and that wish was carried out.)

After Mrs. B. had straightened out her affairs to her own satisfaction, she relaxed and began to chat and even joke about her situation. A few minutes later she suddenly weakened and seemed to doze off. After awhile she started awake, staring intently at the ceiling. "Is there anything up there, right over my bed?" she asked her son-in-law. He said there was not. A look of resigned disgust came over Mrs. B.'s face. "I'm afraid I'm going to have hallucinations," she said.

During the following days her decline was obvious to herself and her family. She spent more time dozing, was coherent for shorter periods which came farther apart. During one such moment she told her daughter, "I hadn't believed it would happen so fast."

Clouded by Drugs

In most American hospitals the experience of death is clouded by drugs. When drugs are necessary to relieve pain there is no alternative, but heavy sedatives, tranquilizers, and pain-killing drugs are also used for purposes of "patient management." In the final stages of dying the greatest fear of patients is abandonment, with good reason. When possible, hospitals will try to send patients home to die. Doctors often cut back their visits, overworked nurses save most of their attention for "those who can be helped," and even the families of the dying frequently begin to detach themselves. The belief that life must go on can be carried to brutal limits, with relatives and even husbands or wives acting as if the dying individual were already dead. When dying patients pester the nursing staff for attention, they are often simply trying to alleviate their loneliness; if the pestering becomes irksome there is a tendency to respond with drugs.

The abandonment which dying patients fear can be as much emotional as literal. Nurses say they do not become hardened to death and often dream about the death of their patients. As a result they attempt to distance themselves from the dying by thinking of them as no longer quite there, referring to the care of unconscious patients, for example, as "watering the vegetables.'' The terrible moment which demands that life-sustaining equipment be turned off is emotionally masked by the phrase, ''pulling the plug.''

The impulse to abandon the dying can become overwhelming. It is policy in most hospitals to move dying patients into single rooms as death approaches. Doctors, nurses, and even relatives tend to find good reasons to stay out of the dying patient's room. The pretense is that no one wants to ''disturb'' the dying person while he is ''resting,'' but nurses say they have seen too many clusters of relatives outside hospital rooms at the moment of death to consider it a coincidence.

A Shrinking World

As death approaches, the world of the dying gradually shrinks. They talk less of their disease and more about their exact symptoms, how they feel, what they plan to do tomorrow, or this afternoon, or in the next hour. Hope generally remains until the final moments, but its focus tends to shift. The Rev. Robert Reeves, Jr., the chaplain of Columbia-Presbyterian Hospital in New York, tells of one middle-aged man who hoped to get back to his business up until five weeks before his death. During the first week after that he talked about getting home for Thanksgiving. During the second week he hoped to be able to get out of bed again. In the third week he hoped to regain the ability to swallow food. At the beginning of his final week of life he hoped for a good night's sleep. A day later he hoped his pain medicine would work. The day before he died he hoped he would die in his sleep. He was denied every hope except the last, and yet each had eased his way toward death.

When the layman speaks of death he is referring to *somatic* death, or the death of the entire organism. The traditional signs of somatic death are *rigor mortis* (the stiffening of certain muscles), *algor mortis* (the cooling of the body) and *liver mortis* (the purplish-red discoloration of the skin caused by the settling of the blood). Somatic death includes the death of all bodily tissues, but an individual is commonly said to be ''dead'' long before all his tissues have died. The death of the ''person,'' then, is only one stage in what an increasing number of doctors tend to think of as a distinct physiological process.

One doctor likens the process of death to menopause, which has long been known to include profound biological changes in women going far beyond the simple cessation of ovulation. The fact of putrefaction can also be cited as evidence that dying is a coherent biological event, and not simply the exact condition which precipitates death (heart failure, say, or kidney shutdown). When the body dies, organisms escape the gastrointestinal tract and begin the process of general decomposition by which the body is returned to Biblical ashes and dust. Built

into the body, in other words, is the biological mechanism of its own dissolution, a fact which hardly can be dismissed as a coincidence. In arguing for an expanded notion of death, doctors also mention the characteristic return of the dying to infancy. Gradually they sleep longer each day, until they wake for only minutes at a time. Emotionally, the dying become increasingly dependent. Waking in the night they may cry if they discover they are alone, or sink back to sleep if someone is there.

Seeking a Peaceful Death

Given a choice, the vast majority of people would prefer to die in their sleep. The next best, they say, would be a ''peaceful'' death, a consummation largely under the control of doctors. ''Dear gentlemen,'' said the eighteenth-century English doctor, Sir Samuel Garth, to physicians whispering together at the foot of his bed, ''let me die a natural death.'' The ability of doctors to extend the process of dying, if not life, is incomparably greater now. Medical ''heroics'' can keep the heart beating, the lungs breathing, the kidneys functioning, the brain flickering long after death would normally have arrived. The deterioration of the body from disease, and especially from cancer, proceeds further than it would without medical intervention. The result is that patients often lose consciousness long before they die because doctors, or relatives, refuse to give up when the body does. One nurse with years of experience in an intensive-care unit says she finds it increasingly difficult to tell when a patient has died, since machines sustain his vital signs.

''The crisis for the dying patient characteristically arrives when he stops 'fighting' to live.''

Once the process of dying has begun, death can arrive at any time. Some patients die quickly; some linger for months with conditions that ought to have been quickly fatal. Doctors are still exceedingly cautious about predicting when someone will die, since they are so often surprised. Thomas Lupton, a sixteenth-century English writer, made the following attempt to list sure signs of imminent death:

> If the forehead of the sick wax red, and his brows fall down, and his nose wax sharp and cold, and his left eye becomes little, and the corner of his eye runs, if he turn to the wall, if his ears be cold, or if he may suffer no brightness, and if his womb fall, if he pulls straws or the clothes of his bed, or if he pick often his nostrils with his fingers, and if he wake much, these are almost certain tokens of death.

Signs which modern nurses look for are dilated nostrils, sagging of the tongue to one side of the mouth, and a tendency for the thumbs to tuck in toward the palms of the dying patient's hands. Just as dying people frequently sense the imminence of their own death and predict it accurately, nurses develop a sense which tells them (but not always correctly) when a patient is going to die.

Early Stages of Dying

In the early stages of dying, the patient remains essentially himself, afflicted only by the knowledge of impending death and the effect of that knowledge on himself and those around him. In the final stages, consciousness in the dying sometimes undergoes qualitative changes. This experience is the least well understood of all, since the nearer a patient approaches to death, the less he can describe what he feels. The crisis for the dying patient characteristically arrives when he stops "fighting" to live. Doctors cannot say just how patients "fight", but they are unanimous in saying that patients do so, and that "fighting" can make all the difference in situations which can go either way. A man fighting to stay alive apparently duplicates the experience of a man fighting to stay awake, i.e., alternating flashes of lucidity and delirium. Patients often signal the approach of death by simply saying, "I can't fight any longer." The period that follows is unlike any other experienced in life.

"History and modern research agree that, for unknown reasons, the dying do not find it hard to die."

Until the twentieth century, this final period was often called "the dying hour," although it can last considerably longer than an hour. Physicians described it as being a peaceful period in which the dying person, accepting the lost struggle and the inevitable end, is relaxed and ready to depart. The patient may gradually distance himself from life, actually turning away close friends and relatives, literally turning to the wall (as suggested by Lupton) as he prepares himself to die. Accepting the fact of their own death, the dying frequently turn their attention to those who will live, who are sometimes aggrieved by the readiness of the dying to leave them behind. At the end it is often the dying who comfort the living. Even so self-centered a figure as Louis XIV said to those around his deathbed, "Why weep ye? Did you think I should live forever?" After a pause he reflected with equanimity, "I thought dying had been harder."

Just a Little Dreamy Anxiety

Dying patients who remain fully conscious, or nearly so, say they are tired, feel a growing calm, are ready to go, are perhaps even happy. When Stephen

Crane died of tuberculosis in England in 1900, only twenty-nine years old, he tried to describe the sensation to a friend: "Robert—when you come to the hedge—that we must all go over. It isn't so bad. You feel sleepy—and you don't care. Just a little dreamy anxiety—which world you're really in—that's all."

Dr. Austin Kutscher, one of the creators of the Foundation of Thanatology, has been studying death and related questions since the death of his wife in 1966. He emphasizes that in some ways the living tyrannize over the dying, studying the experience of the latter for the sake of those who remain. An example is the effort of medical scientists to narrow the definition of death in order to allow the organs of the dying to be used for transplants. The decision to accept brain death as death itself may be valid, Kutscher says, but it can hardly be argued that the definition was framed for the benefit of the dying. As a result of this natural bias on the part of the living, the study of death and dying has tended to ignore the nature of the event, and of its experience.

"Isn't there something rather magical about life that defies measurement by a piece of apparatus?" Dr. Kutscher says. "We are begging the issue by trying to define death when we can't even define life."

The scientific study of dying is relatively recent, but there exists a vast literature, amounting to case studies, of the approach of death. The final moments of great men have always been minutely recorded, these accounts ranging from those in the *Lives of the Saints,* which tend to a dull predictability, to the moment-by-moment narratives of death as experienced by generals, poets, and kings. Again and again the last words of the dying concede their readiness to depart; an unfeigned peace seems to ease the final flickering out. History and modern research agree that, for unknown reasons, the dying do not find it hard to die.

Last Moments Are Least Accessible

The very last moments are, of course, the least accessible. Some doctors have found evidence that the experience of patients still conscious has an element of the mystical. The doctors are quick to say that they are not talking about God and religion and parapsychological cultism; also they admit that such experiences might be the result of anoxia, or oxygen starvation in the brain. Nevertheless, they say, there is reason to believe the dying can experience a sense of surrender which borders on ecstasy. In a secular age, as practitioners of a science which tends toward mechanism, doctors reluctantly speak of "soul" or "spirit." But, in the safety of anonymity, they return again and again to the puzzle of what it is that dies when the body ceases to function. One doctor, attempting to describe the mystery he had sensed in dying patients, quoted the dying words attributed to the ancient philosopher Plotinus: "I am making my last effort to return that which is divine in me to that which is divine in the universe."

During her final five days of life, Mrs. B. was rarely conscious. The hospital left the second bed in her room empty. Her doctors and family decided not to attempt extreme efforts which could only prolong her dying, but Mrs. B. continued to receive intravenous feeding and was regularly turned by the nurses as a precaution against pneumonia.

On two occasions, Mrs. B. started violently awake and insisted, "Something is terribly wrong." She did not know her daughters and believed her doctors were conspiring against her. She was given heavy sedation, and her daughters felt that, in effect, she had already died. Nevertheless, on a few last occasions she regained consciousness and knew her family, if only briefly. Two days before she died, as her surgeon was examining her, she suddenly asked, "Why don't I die?"

"Because you're tough," the surgeon said.

"I don't want to be tough that way," Mrs. B. said.

"I'm Gone"

Because one test of a patient's grip on life is the ability to respond, the doctors and nurses would call her name loudly from time to time to ask if she wanted anything. "Mrs. B.?" one of the nurses nearly shouted one night. "Mrs. B.?"

"I'm gone," said Mrs. B. in a faint whisper.

"No, you're still with us," the nurse said.

"So long expected, death had arrived unnoticed."

Mrs. B. grew steadily weaker. Her kidneys began to fail. She began to breathe rapidly and heavily, then stopped altogether, and after a moment began again. A nurse called this "Cheyne-Stokes breathing" and said it was probably a sign that the end was approaching. Some of the nurses thought Mrs. B. was completely unconscious; others felt she had only lost the ability to respond. Not knowing who was right, her family spoke as if she could hear and understand everything said in the room.

When Mrs. B.'s youngest daughter arrived about 11 A.M. the morning of Thanksgiving Day, November 26, she found her mother breathing slowly and regularly. Her body was completely relaxed over onto one side. It was a bright sunlit day. Mrs. B.'s daughter sat down by the large bank of windows overlooking Manhattan to the south and tried to read, but found herself thinking of her mother. After a while she looked up and saw that her mother had stopped breathing. So long expected, death had arrived unnoticed. For eighteen days Mrs. B.'s daughter had restrained her tears. Now, finally, when

her mother was no longer there to comfort or be comforted, she began to cry.

Thomas Powers is a graduate of Yale and has worked as a journalist in Rome, London, and New York. He is the author of Diana: The Making of a Terrorist.

*"There is cause to believe that...
elements in his own psychological
makeup may cause the physician to be
singularly ill-equipped to be the bearer
of bad tidings."*

Patients Should Not Always Be Told They Are Dying

Bernard C. Meyer

Among the reminiscences of his Alsatian boyhood, my father related the story of the local functionary who was berated for the crude and blunt manner in which he went from house to house announcing to wives and mothers news of battle casualties befalling men from the village. On the next occasion, mindful of the injunctions to be more tactful and to soften the impact of his doleful message, he rapped gently on the door, and, when it opened, inquired, "Is the widow Schmidt at home?"

Insofar as this essay is concerned with the subject of truth it is only proper to add that when I told this story to a colleague, he already knew it and claimed that it concerned a woman named Braun who lived in a small town in Austria. By this time it would not surprise me to learn that the episode is a well-known vignette in the folklore of Tennessee where it is attributed to a woman named Smith or Brown whose husband was killed at the battle of Shiloh. Ultimately, we may find that all three versions are plagiarized accounts of an occurrence during the Trojan War.

Physician-Patient Communication

Apocryphal or not, the story illustrates a few of the vexing aspects of the problem of conveying unpalatable news, notably the difficulty of doing so in a manner that causes a minimum amount of pain, and also the realization that not everyone is capable of learning how to do it. Both aspects find their application in the field of medicine where the imparting of the grim facts of diagnosis and prognosis is a constant and recurring issue. Nor does it seem likely that for all our learning we doctors are particularly endowed with superior talents and techniques for coping with these problems. On the contrary, for reasons to be given later, there is cause

to believe that in not a few instances, elements in his own psychological makeup may cause the physician to be singularly ill-equipped to be the bearer of bad tidings. It should be observed, moreover, that until comparatively recent times, the subject of communication between physician and patient received little attention in medical curriculum and medical literature.

Within the past decade or so, coincident with an expanded recognition of the significance of emotional factors in all medical practice, an impressive number of books and articles by physicians, paramedical personnel, and others have been published, attesting to both the growing awareness of the importance of the subject and an apparent willingness to face it. An especially noteworthy example of this trend was provided by a three-day meeting in February 1967, sponsored by the New York Academy of Sciences, on the subject of *The Care of Patients with Fatal Illness.* The problem of communicating with such patients and their families was a recurring theme in most of the papers presented.

Both at this conference and in the literature, particular emphasis has been focused on the patient with cancer, which is hardly surprising in light of its frequency and of the extraordinary emotional reactions that it unleashes not only in the patient and in his kinsmen but in the physician himself. At the same time, it should be noted that the accent on the cancer patient or the dying patient may foster the impression that in less grave conditions this dialogue between patient and physician hardly warrants much concern or discussion. Such a view is unfounded, however, and could only be espoused by someone who has had the good fortune to escape the experience of being ill and hospitalized. Those less fortunate will recall the emotional stresses induced by hospitalization, even when the condition requiring it is relatively banal.

A striking example of such stress may sometimes

be seen when the patient who is hospitalized, say, for repair of an inguinal hernia, happens to be a physician. All the usual anxieties confronting a prospective surgical subject tend to become greatly amplified and garnished with a generous sprinkling of hypochondriasis in physician-turned-patient. Wavering unsteadily between two roles, he conjures up visions of all the complications of anesthesia, of wound dehiscence or infection, of embolization, cardiac arrest, and whatnot that he has ever heard or read about. To him, lying between hospital sheets, clad in impersonal hospital clothes, divested of his watch and the keys to his car, the hospital suddenly takes on a different appearance from the place he may have known in a professional capacity. Even his colleagues—the anesthetist who will put him to sleep or cause a temporary motor and sensory paralysis of the lower half of his body, and the surgeon who will incise it—appear different. He would like to have a little talk with them, a very professional talk to be sure, although in his heart he may know that the talk will also be different. And if they are in tune with the situation, they too know that it will be different, that beneath the restrained tones of sober and factual conversation is the thumping anxiety of a man who seeks words of reassurance. With some embarrassment he may introduce his anxieties with the phrase, "I suppose this is going to seem a little silly but...''; and from this point on he may sound like any other individual confronted by the ordeal of surgical experience. Indeed, it would appear that under these circumstances, to say nothing of more ominous ones, most people, regardless of their experience, knowledge, maturity or sophistication, are assailed by more or less similar psychological pressures, from which they seek relief not through pharmacological sedation, but through the more calming influence of the spoken word.

"The doctor seeking to communicate with his patient.... may find himself too troubled to use words wisely."

Seen in this light the question of what to tell the patient about his illness is but one facet of the practice of medicine as an art, a particular example of that spoken and mute dialogue between patient and physician which has always been and will always be an indispensable ingredient in the therapeutic process. How to carry on this dialogue, what to say and when to say it, and what not to say, are questions not unlike those posed by an awkward suitor; like him, those not naturally versed in this art may find themselves discomfited and needful of the promptings of some Cyrano who will whisper those words and phrases that ultimately will wing their

way to soothe an anguished heart.

The difficulties besetting the physician under these circumstances, however, cannot be ascribed simply to his mere lack of experience or innate eloquence. For like the stammering suitor, the doctor seeking to communicate with his patient may have an emotional state in his message. When that message contains an ominous significance, he may find himself too troubled to use words wisely, too ridden with anxiety to be kind, and too depressed to convey hope. An understanding of such reactions touches upon a recognition of some of the several psychological motivations that have led some individuals to choose a medical career. There is evidence that at times that choice has been dictated by what might be viewed as counterphobic forces. Having in childhood experienced recurring brushes with illness and having encountered a deep and abiding fear of death and dying, such persons may embrace a medical career as if it will confer upon them a magical immunity from a repetition of those dreaded eventualities; for them the letters M.D. constitute a talisman bestowing upon the wearer a sense of invulnerability and a pass of safe conduct through the perilous frontiers of life. There are others for whom the choice of a career dedicated to helping and healing appears to have arisen as a reaction formation against earlier impulses to wound and to destroy. For still others among us, the practice of medicine serves as the professional enactment of a long-standing rescue fantasy.

Emotional Reactions of Physicians

It is readily apparent in these examples (which by no means exhaust the catalogue of motives leading to the choice of a medical career) that confrontation by the failure of one's efforts and by the need to announce it may unloose a variety of inner psychological disturbances: faced by the gravely ill or dying patient the "counterphobic" doctor may feel personally vulnerable again; the "reaction-formation" doctor, evil and guilty; and the "rescuer," worthless and impotent. For such as these, words cannot come readily in their discourse with the seriously or perilously ill. Indeed, they may curtail their communications; and, what is no less meaningful to their patients, withdraw their physical presence. Thus the patient with inoperable cancer and his family may discover that the physician, who at a more hopeful moment in the course of the illness had been both articulate and supportive, has become remote both in his speech and in his behavior. Nor is the patient uncomprehending of the significance of the change in his doctor's attitude. Observers have recorded the verbal expressions of patients who sensed the feelings of futility and depression in their physicians. Seeking to account for their own reluctance to ask questions (a reluctance based partly upon their own disinclination to face a grim reality), one such patient said, "He looked so tired." Another stated, "I don't want to upset him because he has tried so hard to help me"; and another, "I know he feels so badly already and is doing his best." To paraphrase a celebrated utterance, one might suppose that these remarks were dictated by the maxim: "Ask not what your doctor can do for you; ask what you can do for your doctor."

Adherence to a Formula

In the dilemma created both by a natural disinclination to be a bearer of bad news and by those other considerations already cited, many a physician is tempted to abandon personal judgment and authorship in his discourse with his patients, and to rely instead upon a set formula which he employs with dogged and indiscriminate consistency. Thus, in determining what to say to patients with cancer, there are exponents of standard policies that are applied routinely in seeming disregard of the overall clinical picture and of the personality or psychological makeup of the patient. In general, two such schools of thought prevail; i.e., those that always tell and those that never do. Each of these is amply supplied with statistical anecdotal evidence providing the correctness of the policy. Yet even if the figures were accurate—and not infrequently they are obtained via a questionnaire, itself a rather opaque window to the human mind—all they demonstrate is that more rather than less of a given proportion of the cancer population profited by the policy employed. This would provide small comfort, one might suppose, to the patients and their families that constitute the minority of the sample.

Truth as Abstract Principle

At times adherence to such a rigid formula is dressed upon in the vestments of slick and facile morality. Thus a theologian has insisted that the physician has a moral obligation to tell the truth and that his withholding it constitutes a deprivation of the patient's right; therefore it is "theft, therefore unjust, therefore immoral." "Can it be," he asks, "that doctors who practice professional deception would, if the roles were reversed, want to be coddled or deceived?" To which, as many physicians can assert, the answer is distinctly *yes*. Indeed so adamant is this writer upon the right of the patient to know the facts of his illness that in the event he refuses to hear what the doctor is trying to say, the latter should "ask leave to withdraw from the case, urging that another physician be called in his place." (Once there were three boy scouts who were sent away from a campfire and told not to return until each had done his good turn for the day. In 20 minutes all three had returned, and curiously each one reported that he had helped a little old lady to cross a street. The scoutmaster's surprise was even greater when he learned that in each case it was the same little old

lady, prompting him to inquire why it took the three of them to perform this one simple good deed. "Well sir," replied one of the boys, "you see she really didn't want to cross the street at all.")

"To insist that a patient is hopelessly ill may at times be worse than a crime; it may be a mistake."

In this casuistry wherein so much attention is focused upon abstract principle and so little upon humanity, one is reminded of the no less specious arguments of those who assert that the thwarting of suicide and the involuntary hospitalization of the mentally deranged constitute violations of personal freedom and human right. It is surely irregular for a fire engine to travel in the wrong direction on a one-way street, but if one is not averse to putting out fires and saving lives, the traffic violation looms as a conspicuous irrelevancy. No less irrelevant is the obsessional concern with meticulous definitions of truth in an enterprise where kindness, charity, and the relief of human suffering are the essential verities. "The letter killeth," say the Scriptures, "but the spirit giveth life."

Role of Secrecy in Creating Anxiety

Another common error is the assumption that until someone has been formally told the truth he doesn't know it. Such self-deception is often present when parents feel moved to supply their pubertal children with the sexual facts of life. With much embarrassment and a good deal of backing and filling on the subjects of eggs, bees, and babies, sexual information is imparted to a child who often not only already knows it but is uncomfortable in hearing it from that particular source. There is indeed a general tendency to underestimate the perceptiveness of children not only about such matters but where graver issues, notably illness and death, are concerned. As a consequence, attitudes of secrecy and overprotection designed to shield children from painful realities may result paradoxically in creating an atmosphere that is saturated with suspicion, distrust, perplexity, and intolerable anxiety. Caught between trust in their own intuitive perceptions and the deceptions practiced by the adults about them, such children may suffer greatly from a lack of opportunity of coming to terms emotionally with some of the vicissitudes of existence that in the end are inescapable. A refreshing contrast to this approach has been presented in a paper entitled "Who's Afraid of Death on a Leukemia Ward" [Joel Vernick and Myron Karon, *American Journal of Diseases of Children*, May 1965]. Recognizing that most of the children afflicted with this disease had some knowledge of its seriousness, and that all were worried about it, the hospital staff abandoned the traditional custom of protection and secrecy, providing instead an atmosphere in which the children could feel free to express their fears and their concerns and could openly acknowledge the act of death when one of the group passed away. The result of this measure was immensely salutary.

Similar miscalculations of the accuracy of inner perceptions may be noted in dealing with adults. Thus, in a study entitled "Mongolism: When Should Parents Be Told?" [C. M. Drillien, *British Medical Journal 2,* 1964], it was found that in nearly half the cases the mothers declared they had realized before being told that something was seriously wrong with the child's development, a figure which obviously excludes the mothers who refused consciously to acknowledge their suspicions. On the basis of their findings the authors concluded that a full explanation given in the early months, coupled with regular support thereafter, appeared to facilitate the mother's acceptance of and adjustment to her child's handicap.

"Still another misconception is the belief that if it is certain that the truth is known it is all right to discuss it."

A pointless and sometimes deleterious withholding of truth is a common practice in dealing with elderly people. "Don't tell Mother" often seems to be an almost reflex maxim among some adults in the face of any misfortune, large or small. Here, too, elaborate efforts at camouflage may backfire, for, sensing that he is being shielded from some ostensibly intolerable secret, not only is the elderly one deprived of the opportunity of reacting appropriately to it, but he is being tacitly encouraged to conjure up something in his imagination that may be infinitely worse.

Problem of Definition

Nor should it be forgotten that in the healing arts, the matter of truth is not always susceptible to easy definition. Consider for a moment the question of the hopeless diagnosis. It was not so long ago that such a designation was appropriate to subacute bacterial endocarditis, pneumococcal meningitis, pernicious anemia, and a number of other conditions which today are no longer incurable, while those diseases which today are deemed hopeless may cease to be so by tomorrow. Experience has proved, too, the unreliability of obdurate opinions concerning prognosis even in those conditions where all the clinical evidence and the known behavior of a given disease should leave no room for doubt. To paraphrase Clemenceau, to insist that a patient is hopelessly ill may at times be worse than a crime; it may be a mistake.

There are other pitfalls, moreover, that complicate the problem of telling patients the truth about their illness. There is the naive notion, for example, that when the patient asserts that what he is seeking is the plain truth he means just that. But as more than one observer has noted, this is sometimes the last thing the patient really wants. Such assertions may be voiced with particular emphasis by patients who happen to be physicians and who strive to display a professional or scientifically objective attitude toward their own condition. Yet to accept such assertions at their face value may sometimes lead to tragic consequences, as in the following incident.

> A distinguished urological surgeon was hospitalized for a hypernephroma, which diagnosis had been withheld from him. One day he summoned the intern into his room, and after appealing to the latter on the basis of we're-both-doctors-and-grown-up-men, succeeded in getting the unwary younger man to divulge the facts. Not long afterward, while the nurse was momentarily absent from the room, the patient opened a window and leaped to his death.

Still another misconception is the belief that if it is certain that the truth is known it is all right to discuss it. How mistaken such an assumption may be was illustrated by the violent rage which a recent widow continued to harbor toward a friend for having alluded to cancer in the presence of her late husband. Hearing her outburst one would have concluded that until the ominous word had been uttered, her husband had been ignorant of the nature of his condition. The facts, however, were different, as the unhappy woman knew, for it had been her husband who originally had told the friend what the diagnosis was.

Denial and Repression

The psychological devices that make such seeming inconsistencies of thought and knowledge possible are the mechanisms of repression and denial. It is indeed the remarkable capacity to bury or conceal more or less transparent truth that makes the problem of telling it so sticky and difficult a matter, and one that is so unsusceptible to simple rule-of-thumb formulas. For while in some instances the maintenance of denial may lead to severe emotional distress, in others it may serve as a merciful shield. For example,

> A physician with a reputation for considerable diagnostic acumen developed a painless jaundice. When, not surprisingly, a laparotomy revealed a carcinoma of the head of the pancreas, the surgeon relocated the biliary outflow so that postoperatively the jaundice subsided. This seeming improvement was consistent with the surgeon's explanation to the patient that the operation had revealed a hepatitis. Immensely relieved, the patient chided himself for not having anticipated the "correct" diagnosis. "What a fool I was!" he declared, obviously alluding to an earlier, albeit unspoken, fear of cancer.

Among less sophisticated persons the play of denial

may assume a more primitive expression. Thus a woman who had ignored the growth of a breast cancer to a point where it had produced spinal metastases and paraplegia, attributed the latter to "arthritis" and asked whether the breast would grow back again. The same mental mechanism allowed another woman to ignore dangerous rectal bleeding by ascribing it to menstruation, although she was well beyond the menopause.

In contrast to these examples is a case reported by [C. Winkelstein and R. Blacher in a personal communication, 1967] of a man who, awaiting the report of a cervical node biopsy, asserted that if it showed cancer he wouldn't want to live, and that if it didn't he wouldn't believe it. Yet despite this seemingly unambiguous willingness to deal with raw reality, when the chips were down, as will be described later, this man too was able to protect himself through the use of denial.

From the foregoing it should be self-evident that what is imparted to a patient about his illness should be planned with the same care and executed with the same skills that are demanded by any potentially therapeutic measure. Like the transfusion of blood, the dispensing of certain information must be distinctly indicated, the amount given consonant with the needs of the recipient, and the type chosen with the view of avoiding untoward reactions. This means that only in selected instances is there any justification for telling a patient the precise figures of his blood pressure, and that the question of revealing interesting but asymptomatic congenital anomalies should be considered in light of the possibility of evoking either hypochondriacal ruminations or narcissistic gratification.

Therapeutic Approach

Under graver circumstances the choices confronting the physician rest upon more crucial psychological issues. In principle, we should strive to make the patient sufficiently aware of the facts of his condition to facilitate his participation in the treatment without at the same time giving him cause to believe that such participation is futile. "The indispensable ingredient of this therapeutic approach," write [J. S. Stehlin and K. A. Beach in the *Journal of the American Medical Association,* July 1966], "is free communication between [physician] and patient, in which the latter is sustained by hope within a framework of reality." What this may mean in many instances is neither outright truth nor outright falsehood but a carefully modulated formulation that neither overtaxes human credulity nor invites despair. Thus a sophisticated woman might be expected to reject with complete disbelief the notion that she has had to undergo mastectomy for a benign cyst, but she may at the same time accept postoperative radiation as a prophylactic measure rather than as evidence of metastasis.

A doctor's wife was found to have ovarian carcinoma with widespread metastases. Although the surgeon was convinced she would not survive for more than three or four months, he wished to try the effects of radiotherapy and chemotherapy. After some discussion of the problem with a psychiatrist, he addressed himself to the patient as follows: to his surprise, when examined under the microscope the tumor in her abdomen proved to be cancerous; he fully believed he had removed it entirely; to feel perfectly safe, however, he intended to give her radiation and chemical therapies over an indeterminate period of time. The patient was highly gratified by his frankness and proceeded to live for nearly three more years, during which time she enjoyed an active and productive life.

A rather similar approach was utilized in the case of Winkelstein and Blacher previously mentioned.

In the presence of his wife the patient was told by the resident surgeon, upon the advice of the psychiatrist, that the biopsy of the cervical node showed cancer; that he had a cancerous growth in the abdomen; that it was the type of cancer that responds well to chemotherapy; that if the latter produced any discomfort he would receive medication for its relief; and finally that the doctors were very hopeful for a successful outcome. The patient, who, it will be recalled, had declared he wouldn't want to live if the doctors found cancer, was obviously gratified. Immediately he telephoned members of his family to tell them the news, gratuitously adding that the tumor was of low-grade malignancy. That night he slept well for the first time since entering the hospital and he continued to do so during the balance of his stay. Just before leaving he confessed that he had known all along about the existence of the abdominal mass but that he had concealed his knowledge to see what the doctors would tell him. Upon arriving home he wrote a warm letter of thanks and admiration to the resident surgeon.

"Communication between the physician and his patient. . .demands an ear that is sensitive to both what is said and what is not said."

It should be emphasized that although in both of these instances the advice of a psychiatrist was instrumental in formulating the discussion of the facts of the illness, it was the surgeon, not the psychiatrist, who did the talking. The importance of this point cannot be exaggerated, for since it is the surgeon who plays the central and crucial role in such cases, it is to him, and not to some substitute mouthpiece, that the patient looks for enlightenment and for hope. As noted earlier, it is not every surgeon who can bring himself to speak in this fashion to his patient; and for some there may be a strong temptation to take refuge in a stereotyped formula, or to pass the buck altogether. The surgical resident, in the last case cited, for example, was both appalled and distressed when he was advised what to do. Yet he steeled himself, looked the patient straight in the eye, and spoke with conviction. When he saw the result, he was both relieved and gratified. Indeed, he emerged from the experience a far wiser man and a better physician.

The Dying Patient

The general point of view expressed in the foregoing pages has been espoused by others in considering the problem of communicating with the dying patient. [R. C.] Aldrich stresses the importance of providing such persons with an appropriately timed opportunity of selecting acceptance or denial of the truth in their efforts to cope with their plight. [Avery D.] Weisman and [Thomas] Hackett believe that for the majority of patients it is likely that there is neither complete acceptance nor total repudiation of the imminence of death. "To deny this 'middle knowledge' of approaching death," they assert, "...is to deny the responsiveness of the mind to both internal perceptions and external information. There is always a psychological stream; fever, weakness, anorexia, weight loss, and pain are subjective counterparts of homeostatis alteration....If to this are added changes in those close to the patient, the knowledge of approaching death is confirmed."

"There is a hierarchy of morality, and. . .ours is a profession which traditionally has been guided by a precept that transcends the virtue of uttering truth for truth's sake."

Other observers agree that a patient who is sick enough to die often knows it without being told, and that what he seeks from his physician are not longer statements concerning diagnosis and prognosis, but earnest manifestations of his unwavering concern and devotion. As noted earlier, it is at such times that for reason of their own psychological makeup some physicians become deeply troubled and are most prone to drift away, thereby adding to the dying patient's physical suffering, the suffering that is caused by a sense of abandonment, isolation, and emotional deprivation.

In contrast, it should be stressed that no less potent than morphine nor less effective than an array of tranquilizers is the steadfast and serious concern of the physician for those often numerous and relatively minor complaints of the dying patient. To this beneficent manifestation of psychological denial, which may at times attain hypochondriacal proportions, the physician ideally should respond in

kind, shifting his gaze from the lethal process he is now helpless to arrest to the living being whose discomfort and distress he is still able to assuage. In these, the final measures of the dance of life, it may then appear as if both partners had reached a tacit and a mutual understanding, an unspoken pledge to ignore the dark shadow of impending death and to resume those turns and rhythms that were familiar figures in a more felicitous past. If in this he is possessed of enough grace and elegance to play his part the doctor may well succeed in fulfilling the assertion of Oliver Wendell Holmes that if one of the functions of the physician is to assist at the coming in, another is to assist at the going out.

If what has been set down here should prove uncongenial to some strict moralists, one can only observe that there is a hierarchy of morality, and that ours is a profession which traditionally has been guided by a precept that transcends the virtue of uttering truth for truth's sake; that is, "So far as possible, do no harm." Where it concerns the communication between the physician and his patient, the attainment of this goal demands an ear that is sensitive to both what is said and what is not said, a mind that is capable of understanding what has been heard, and a heart that can respond to what has been understood. Here, as in many difficult human enterprises, it may prove easier to learn the words than to sing the tune.

Bernard C. Meyer, M.D., is a practicing psychoanalyst and emeritus professor of psychiatry at the Mount Sinai School of Medicine in New York. He is the author of psychoanalytical biographies of Houdini and Joseph Conrad.

"The time came...when I had to accept that the real question was not, 'Is God responsible?' but, 'How should I react now that this terrible thing has happened to me?'"

Death Must Be Accepted

Wightman Weese

I arrived as pastor just a few weeks before Bob Farrow had to stop coming to church. The small Conservative Baptist church was fighting to stay alive, and I learned that Bob was one of the main reasons it kept going.

Dozens of kids swarmed around their Sunday school superintendent when he walked in each Sunday. When Bob passed the collection plate, smiling and winking at his special people, heartbroken mothers and discouraged husbands and wives said they suddenly felt the love of God.

Bob was a furniture salesman—a good one. He was the father of five children, and a good one. He ministered love and encouragement everywhere he went. Waitresses competed to serve him when he went for coffee each morning.

Teenagers found him easy to talk to. When a man in the community contemplated suicide, he called Bob.

Fighting for Life

I soon learned that Bob, like the tiny church he urged on month after month, was also fighting for his life. Cancer wasted his body.

I remember how loosely his clothes hung on him when he spoke to the Wednesday night prayer meeting one of his last times at church. I couldn't get his talk off my mind.

Each time I visited his home to minister to him, I came away ministered to. Finally, I asked if he had kept the notes from the prayer meeting talk. He directed me to the desk across the room.

As I read, I heard his words come alive as they had that cold Wednesday night last winter. Those words had to be shared with others.

Writhing in pain, he gave me consent to try to share his story.

Wightman Weese, "The Man Who Taught Me to Die," *Moody Monthly*, March 1981. Reprinted with permission.

In his talk, Bob had told how helpless he used to feel around other people in great pain. When they asked, "Why me?" he didn't know what to tell them. And what he did say always seemed so foolish.

Then he told of the many who had come to his hospital room in previous months. He knew they all meant well.

But several of their statements confused things more than helped:

"God is surely trying to teach you something," some would say. They implied that he harbored some sin or disobedience, or that he had stepped out of God's will.

"What is God telling you?" they asked.

He really didn't know, he said, but he surely wanted to find out so the pain could stop.

Some tried to cheer him up, ignoring the problem. They entered his hospital room, bubbling with joy, attempting to drive out the suffering with cheer.

He appreciated that; but after the visitors left, he was alone again to suffer. They hadn't helped the pain.

"I was watching so-and-so (some faith healer) on television the other night," others told him. Sickness, to these visitors, was not God's will.

"Truly believe that you'll be healed and God will answer that belief," they counseled.

Bob said he had faith. He knew God *could* heal if He wanted to. For a while, he wondered what it would take to convince God that he believed enough to be healed. He didn't know how to muster up any more faith.

"You must praise God for everything," others told him, urging him to come to the place where he could say, "God, I love you for making me suffer like this."

He tried that. Knowing God was good, he knew God was working out this pain for good; and he really wanted to be thankful for that. But that didn't remove the suffering.

"You are having the privilege of participating in

Christ's suffering," others told him. "You have been appointed to suffer for Him and He will reward you."

When the pain really got bad, he found himself asking the same questions others had asked him: "Why me?" And he still didn't know the answer.

Plenty of Christians seemed stronger than he was. Why couldn't God have chosen some of them?

"I have felt led to pray for complete healing for you." He reminded his visitors that he had already been praying for healing, and so far nothing had happened.

Problems of Dying

As Bob talked that night, some of us heard ourselves. We began to realize that a dying man had enough problems without his friends trying to persuade him to ignore the obvious.

Bob had come a long way to find peace about his coming death. But we hadn't come along with him.

Our confusing statements at his bedside, denying the truth, were making it impossible for him to be honest with us about his pain. Our attempts at comfort were out of touch with reality. Rather than encouraging, we were actually pushing him farther into loneliness.

"When we suffer, we should look ahead to what God can make of seeming tragedy."

"The time came," Bob said, "when I had to accept that the real question was not, 'Is God responsible?' but, 'How should I react now that this terrible thing has happened to me?'

"James wrote: 'Consider it pure joy, my brothers, whenever you face trials of many kinds, because you know that the testing of your faith develops perseverance. Perseverance must finish its work so that you may be mature and complete, not lacking anything.'

"Peter wrote: 'Dear friends, do not be surprised at the painful trials you are suffering, as though something strange were happening to you. But rejoice that you participate in the sufferings of Christ, so that you may be overjoyed when His glory is revealed.'

"I know my pain was not a direct result of persecution, as Peter was talking about. But if God permitted my suffering, then I could say that in a sense I was suffering for His sake.

"The Bible spotlights the end result of things," Bob went on. "When we suffer, we should look ahead to what God can make of seeming tragedy.

"At the time, it isn't clear to us how suffering or evil can be transformed into a cause for celebration. But that is what we are asked to believe, and we should allow God to help us do it.

Bob told us of the many people he knew who had turned away from the Lord because they didn't understand his suffering.

Some of his closest friends found it hard to talk to him because they were saying, "How could anyone believe in a God who would allow someone to suffer like that?" That especially grieved him.

"Every morning I awake, I am grateful for what God has given me: grace to meet every moment, a wonderful peace, and a hope for the future when I'll be with Him for eternity."

In the following months, Bob's health began to wane. Almost every visit with him I could see him go down a bit. At first, I visited every week; later, several times a week; and, finally, several times a day.

He often pointed to a plaque on the bedroom wall: "Help it all make sense, Lord!"

He pleaded to be left at home rather than go to the hospital at the end. Minutes before he died, I sat and held his hand and told him again how much I had come to love him during those last months.

His smile was the answer.

Moments later, as he held his daughter's hand, Bob's spirit slipped away from a tired, diseased body.

"Why him?"

I still couldn't answer.

Who would wink at discouraged people and hug children coming to Sunday school? Certainly God didn't take Bob because he—or we—didn't love Him.

The church in which he had worked so hard was filled for his funeral. More than half stood to dedicate their lives to Christ.

Bob taught me a bit more of how to face the end of life on earth. The next time a friend is dying, I will be better prepared to help him face those moments victoriously and honestly.

I won't tell a dying person that he isn't dying when he knows he is.

I won't make a dying person play-act for my benefit. I'll just say, "You're really hurting today, aren't you, friend? I sure wish I could bear it for you a while."

I won't ask his wife how he is feeling if he can talk for himself.

I won't whisper outside his door.

And I won't be afraid to laugh—or to cry—in front of him.

If Jesus could weep when His friend died, certainly I can too when I see someone I love hurting.

Enough of the shallow Christianity that cannot reconcile genuine trust in God with genuine emotions.

Many dear friends have taught me how to live. But I will always be grateful to a friend who taught me how to die.

Wightman Weese is a book editor for Tyndale House Publishers, Wheaton, Illinois.

"We should. . .consider resistance the highest form of a meaningful death."

Death Must Not Be Accepted

H. Paul Santmire

And I will show that nothing can happen more beautiful than death.

Walt Whitman

The death and dying movement is well established. Throughout the country, mental-health professionals, physicians and nurses, educators, youth workers, members of the clergy and other community leaders have adopted the popular testament of Elisabeth Kubler-Ross, *On Death and Dying* (Macmillan, 1970), as their Bible. In a culture which has been reputed to deny death and dying with a passion—this was one of the celebrated conclusions of Jessica Mitford's *The American Way of Death* (Simon & Schuster, 1963)— "thanatology" has now become, 13 years after the Kubler-Ross book first appeared, a household word for thousands of people in the helping professions. As a result, concerns such as caring for the terminally ill and ministering to the bereaved, and the charged issues of euthanasia and the right to death with dignity, have become common topics of conversation.

Few will disagree that the older American habit of dealing with death by denial was itself moribund. Still, the death and dying movement merits careful scrutiny. Ironically, perhaps, this movement seems to be symptomatic of a pervasive pathology in our whole culture, with roots deep in our national past.

In the Old World, America had been idealized as the land of the peaceable kingdom, where the lamb would lie down with the lion in an untainted garden. The early settlers quickly discovered that the wilderness was a harsh world, full of death and destruction. That perception of an alien wilderness was still very much alive in the first half of the 19th century in writers such as Henry David Thoreau. Although Thoreau found a certain heavenly quiet in

Walden, he self-consciously viewed that soothing, spiritual home as a middle ground between the decadence of society and the ravages of the uncultivated wilderness.

Later in the 19th century, however, as nature came to be more and more tamed and as people's daily experience tended to be increasingly remote from actual contact with the wilderness, alienation from the ravages of nature began to be less typical of the American mind. In its place, a domesticated perception of the peaceable kingdom began again to come to the fore. By the end of the century nature had become a convenient place of repose for affluent city-dwellers, a place to pursue their avocations of bird-watching and moralizing.

Spirit of Idealization

Funeral and burial practices in the 19th century seem to have followed a parallel course. They moved from a mood of alienation to a spirit of idealization or beautification. For a long time cemeteries in America were unkempt, even ugly places, full of weeds. But as the nation carved out its life in the new land, and wealth and social stability came to be taken for granted, a trend toward a certain unalienated appreciation of death began to appear. Symbolically, the cemetery came to be a kind of peaceable kingdom, and the dead themselves were less and less regarded as aliens and strangers, but instead as fellow travelers in an idealized world of peace and bliss in nature.

The founders of the rural cemetery movement in America would probably have been delighted with Walt Whitman's confession that "nothing can happen more beautiful than death." Among the first of these great institutions was Mt. Auburn Cemetery in Cambridge, Massachusetts, dedicated in 1831. Its hallmark was a carefully designed rolling landscape of variegated beauty, which it retains to this day.

In the second half of the century, a new emphasis

H. Paul Santmire, "Nothing More Beautiful than Death?" Copyright 1984 Christian Century Foundation. Reprinted by permission from the December 14, 1983 issue of *The Christian Century*.

emerged, as protective embalming and cosmetic treatment of the dead became increasingly popular. Stylized displays of grief in public were still common, yet there was a tendency to emphasize the gracious and the beautiful rather than the somber and the frightful.

State of the Dead

In a sense, the state of the dead itself was domesticated through the spiritualist movements that peaked in the 1850s and 1870s. The implication of communication with the dead seemed to be that passing on was merely a change of status, rather than some terrible moment of destruction with an uncertain outcome. This motif was confirmed in the popular writings of the era, especially in the works of the widely read novelist Elizabeth Stuart Phelps. "Casting off the traditional images of heaven," historian Charles O. Jackson explains, "her detailed depiction of the afterlife reduced the once awesome mystery of the spiritual world into a state much like a splendid, though quite familiar, middle-class American community."

Now, this is by no means to suggest that death as a brutal, destructive power was unknown in 19th century America. After all, this was the century during which thousands of native people were gradually driven into a state of cultural and physical marginality, or slaughtered outright. It was the century in which a burgeoning national economy was created with the indispensable help of the death-wielding violence of slavery. It was the century during which the ruling masters of the land, having eliminated the Indians and trod down the Africans, then turned viciously on each other, North and South. It was the century, in its waning years, which witnessed the emergence of an industrial economy which featured oppressive institutions such as child labor, which consigned countless workers to early deaths, and which began a rape of the land itself which still has not subsided. The century that came to beautify death was the century that also waged death on an enormous scale.

Attitudes toward death in our time show a remarkable continuity with those 19th century trends, with the same kind of cultural schizophrenia very much in evidence. And still more ominous trends seem to have emerged. The pathology of our culture seems to be deepening rather than moving in some remedial direction.

Daily Experience

On the one hand, we see the affluent classes in America compulsively at work in our great urban-technological centers, aspiring to the life of elegance symbolized by the watering places they frequent at the top of the World Trade Center and in other pinnacles of the modern industrial spirit. But most of their daily work—the bulk of their time, in fact—is

lived in the trenches, dedicated to the economic realities of productivity, efficiency and financial success, and predicated on an ethic of survival of the fittest. This daily experience is understandably debilitating. Thus, it is no surprise to see the same people focusing much of their spiritual energies on the prospect of escape: to the green belts around the city where they bed down, to romantic mountain ski retreats, or to the sensual allurements of the Bahamas. In these escape fantasies, the beleaguered servants of our industrial civilization think of themselves as children of nature, sometimes with self-conscious reference to Thoreau's Walden.

"Questions can also be raised concerning Kübler-Ross's normative image of the dying person as one who should increasingly be allowed to be alone."

However, the actual workings of this affluent civilization are vast, dominating bureaucracies and powerful, globe-circling corporate structures. In this mass society the individual has become increasingly isolated and enervated, with little or no viable access to "mediating institutions" which would offer protection and an effective voice, together with a sense of cultural and personal significance.

Psychic Numbing

The most fearsome aspect of the mass society as we know it today is undoubtedly its perceived potential for unleashing instant thermonuclear holocaust on the whole world. A coming day of mass annihilation now seems inevitable to many in the United States. Psychologist Robert Jay Lifton has described this kind of trauma as "psychic numbing," an expression he first employed to refer to the psychic state of the Hiroshima survivors. Numbing, it seems, is the final step of withdrawal that the isolated individual takes in the continued process of disengagement from the anonymous, person-obliterating institutions of the mass society.

It is no wonder, then, that individuals should become more and more attracted, subconsciously if not consciously, by the prospect of suicide. The suicide rate among today's youth, in particular, is strikingly high.

What becomes of funeral and burial practices in such a world? On the one hand, we met some of the same practices we noted in the 19th century, various expressions of the beautification of death: rooms overflowing with memorial flowers, the often incredibly lifelike corpses in funeral parlors, burials in settings of great natural beauty, such as Mt. Auburn Cemetery. But on the other hand, the beautification of death has more and more become the etherealization of death, or the reduction of death to next to nothing of significance. This seems to be one social expression of the psychic numbing Lifton has described.

Perpetual Care

Witness the emergence of "memorial parks," which offer "perpetual care," thereby ensuring that the bereaved will never have to visit the grave again. Witness the removal of the dying from their own family environments (if they have any) to hospitals, where they are invisible as far as their own family is concerned (the hospice movement is attempting to reverse this trend). Even the increased popularity of cremation seems to point in this direction. Gone are the times of pilgrimage of family, friends, and neighbors to the graveside where the body was laid. Now the body is turned to ashes, which are "deposited" somewhere. In the same spirit of isolation, the familiar social gatherings for the bereaved and their friends following the burial appear to be increasingly infrequent. Most people go right back to work, as if nothing unusual had happened that would require any special kind of human bonding.

"The validity of this stage theory has been challenged."

Although death is either beautified or etherealized in these ways, the social significance of dying is reduced to almost nothing, and the individual is left very much alone to bear his or her grief in private when a loved one dies. It is nevertheless striking to note how much the daily business of U.S. society has to do with death or the prospect of death—reminiscent of trends in 19th century America. This is the nation that gave the world Hiroshima, Nagasaki and Dresden, with scarcely a ripple of troubled national conscience. This is the nation whose best and brightest sent enormous arsenals of death to Vietnam, and that drinks up the world's petroleum resources gluttonously, while the vast majority of the world's people need those resources for irrigation pumps and for fertilizer, lest they face starvation. This is the nation that exports billions of dollars' worth of arms to the world, including nuclear technology. This is a society in which millions of black teen-agers are unemployed, with no hope for tomorrow, experiencing a kind of rape of their selfhood every day as they stand around doing nothing, feeling worthless and unwanted. At the apex of all these programs and prospects of death stands the most fearsome specter of all, global nuclear catastrophe—at which, until very recently, the great

majority of our citizens have simply blinked, as if it were not there at all.

This schizoid American approach to death—its domestication and the reduction of its significance on the one hand, and the waging or the threat of deadly violence on an immense scale on the other hand—is not a desirable psychosocial pattern. Our society would be much better off if most Americans were able to confront death as something less than beautiful and more than ethereal. Then we would begin to curtail the nation's systematic, if often unknowing, allegiance to the principalities and powers of death all over the globe.

The development of the death and dying movement in this country during the past two decades would therefore appear to be an event of major positive cultural significance. It would seem to offer American society a remedy for a deeply seated pathological condition. But, on close analysis, that movement seems to be more an expression of the pathology than a cure. Perhaps the best way to illuminate this situation is to turn to the aforementioned study by Kubler-Ross, *On Death and Dying*. This enormously popular work has come to function as the Holy Writ, as it were, of the death and dying movement.

Rooted in impressive clinical concerns, Kubler-Ross's efforts also emerge out of a more global set of interests. At the outset she refers to the mass destruction of our era, to the bomb at Hiroshima and to wars in general. Taking a cue from Freud, she asks: "Is war perhaps nothing else but a need to face death, to conquer and master it, to come out of it alive—a peculiar form of denial of our own mortality?" She then suggests that if all of us would make an all-out effort to contemplate our own deaths, to deal with our attendant anxieties, and to familiarize others with our discoveries, "perhaps there could be less destruction among us."

The bulk of her study focuses on the now familiar idea of five stages of grieving through which, she believes, dying patients typically pass: denial, anger, bargaining, depression and acceptance. The validity of this stage theory has been challenged. In response, Kubler-Ross has argued that by stages of experience she means *types* of experience, that her analysis is intended not to be prescriptive, but descriptive. It seems, nevertheless, that she does want to be on both sides of the question at the same time, as the normative nuances of the word "stage" suggest.

Advocating Acceptance

Roy Branson of the Kennedy Institute for the Study of Human Reproduction and Bioethics at Georgetown University has argued convincingly that Kubler-Ross does in fact advocate acceptance as the normative resolution of our anxieties about death. This, in other words, is where our feelings about death *should* come to rest, if they are allowed or encouraged to unfold naturally, and not inhibited or blocked by immature needs of the dying person or those who are close to or seeking to help that person. Kubler-Ross is not distressed, Branson points out, if a dying patient moves back and forth from one emotional response to another, from one stage to another, *except* in the case in which the patient has reached acceptance. She thinks of the one who leaves the stage of acceptance as regressing. Acceptance, indeed, as she says often in so many ways, is the resolution of the grieving process. Most patients would reach this stage, she suggests repeatedly, if only the health professionals or the family of the dying would not hang on so long.

What is this final stage like? According to Kubler-Ross, it is a state of peace and tranquillity, "almost void of feelings." It is a time of sleep and a need to withdraw. The patient's circle of interests diminishes, she explains. "He wishes to be left alone....Visitors are not often desired, and if they come, the patient is no longer in a talkative mood....Moments of silence may be the most meaningful communication."

End Is Like Beginning

Thus the end of life is like the beginning. Death is like birth, a natural event in the life cycle, the primary narcissism of the infant's experience, when the self is experienced as encompassing everything, is recapitulated in the experience of the dying person. As death draws near, according to Kubler-Ross, the eternal rhythms of nature now speak their quietly beautiful truth. "Watching a peaceful death of a human being," she writes, "reminds us of a falling star; one of the million lights in a vast sky that flares up for a brief moment only to disappear into the endless night forever."

One can sympathize with Kubler-Ross's motives and welcome her attempt to humanize the experience of dying. Nevertheless we are obligated to evaluate her work critically, since it deals with such an enormously significant subject, with such wide-ranging implications, as she herself recognizes.

Ironically, perhaps, whatever Kubler-Ross's intentions might be, some of her themes are uncannily familiar. It is not far, for example, from the external peace and tranquillity of a Mt. Auburn Cemetery to the internal peace of acceptance as Kubler-Ross depicts it. Is she presenting us, then, with a spiritual beautification of death? Her references to the eternal rhythms of nature are reminiscent of 19th century themes. Her more recent interest in the survival-world after death is also reminiscent of the 19th century interest in spiritualism, and its attempt to integrate the world of the dead into the world of ordinary experience.

Image of Acceptance

Similarly, Kubler-Ross's image of acceptance as the ideal and her picture of the accepting person as one who withdraws, leaving significant ties behind, might be taken as an indirect expression of the contem-porary American trend to privatize death. She wants professionals and relatives to be supportive of the dying, but for her that support is ideally rendered not by holding on to relationships with the dying person, but by letting go at the very end, so that the dying person can be truly alone with his or her death experience.

Is acceptance the highest response to death? Is it not dangerous, indeed, to champion such an idea in a historical situation in which people already have been socially programmed to think of death as something with little or no significance, the same people who systematically blink at, or otherwise avoid seeing, the death-wielding powers of our mass society?

"We all might better join together in resisting the principalities and powers of death, to our last human breath."

It might be said that Kubler-Ross is dealing only with the terminally ill in hospitals, and that in this context acceptance is surely an appropriate response to be encouraged. But what if the patient who has cancer is one of the people who grew up next to Love Canal? Is not anger a much more appropriate response to his or her impending death than acceptance? Does not anger affirm such a person's human worth in a way that acceptance never could?

Kubler-Ross observes that the last two stages of the grieving process are depression and acceptance. Could it not be that depression is a sign of repressed anger, and should be dealt with as such? Could it not also be that acceptance—*however peaceful it looks to the attending friend or counselor*—might in fact be a sign of internal resignation to meaninglessness, a kind of entry into a state of psychic numbness, and that it should be treated as such?

Dying Alone

Questions can also be raised concerning Kubler-Ross's normative image of the dying person as one who should increasingly be allowed to be alone, so that he or she can be in solitude with the immediate prospect of dying. In given situations, one can readily imagine that this strategy would be appropriate. But as a general principle, as a guideline for practice, can we really accept the idea of letting go of the dying and still hold on to our common humanity? Are not human beings existentially constituted, as Martin Buber, Karl Barth and others have maintained, not as isolated individuals but as selves in relation to others? Therefore it is a deeply legitimate human instinct to hold on to that world of relationships which constitute our identity. To do otherwise would be to suffer a diminishment of our humanity.

If we consider the stages of the maturation process depicted by Erik Erikson, the last three stages—intimacy, generativity and integrity—all require relationships with others. Should we encourage the dying to let go of the solidarity of human companionship, to jettison, as it were, half of one's identity? Is the infantile, undifferentiating, oceanic feeling Freud spoke of to be the final expression of human growth? Or is some communal reality, such as that suggested by the biblical image of the New Jerusalem, more appropriate as a goal for the end of life? Perhaps the traditional scene of the dying one calling others to his or her bedside for the deathwatch should be cherished as the kind of metaphor we need as we think about death and dying. It seems far more adequate than the image of a narcissistic infant drifting off to sleep in a blissful state of unversalized egoism.

"It will not be sufficient for us to focus our efforts mainly on the problem of training professionals to be more understanding of death and dying."

In terms of our essential "co-humanity" (Barth), we should instead consider *resistance* the highest form of a meaningful death. This motif cannot be allowed to stand alone; if it were, it might lead to futile and dehumanizing attempts to prolong biological existence, an occurrence well documented by those interested in death with dignity. The metaphor of resistance also would be problematic were it to be taken abstractly, apart from the matrix of human interconnectedness. To resist death in a humanly authentic way, one must always think and act in the name of human wholeness and human solidarity.

Suggesting Resistance

To suggest resistance in this way is not to encourage the denial of death. On the contrary, it may well signal the most radical kind of facing up to death and its destructive powers. Indeed, the person who wills to give his or her life in love for a brother or sister, or for the sake of many, is resisting death in the highest way—by accepting it. In this sense, resistance may be viewed as the most authentic form of acceptance.

All these considerations point us toward a much more social construct of death, and away from the quasi-biological idea that death is natural. Therefore it will not be sufficient for us to focus our efforts mainly on the problem of training professionals to be more understanding of death and dying. Particularly in view of our isolation as individuals, facing the gargantuan, often destructive powers of the mass

society, we will have to focus large amounts of creative energy on the challenge of inventing new communal structures: in hospitals, religious institutions, neighborhoods, unions, professional associations, universities, civic organizations, geopolitical regions—everywhere. We will have to invest new rituals that will help us to express our solidarity with each other and with the dying, so that we all might better join together in resisting the principalities and powers of death, to our last human breath.

A few years ago, C.F. Shatan published a study in the *American Journal of Orthopsychiatry* concerning the grief work of Vietnam Veterans Against the War. These were his conclusions:

> To men who have been steeped in death and evil beyond imagination, a "talking cure" alone is worthless. And merely sharing their grief and outrage with comrades in the same dilemma is similarly unsatisfying. Active participation in the public arena, active opposition to the very war policies they helped to carry out, was essential. By throwing onto the steps of Congress the medals with which they were rewarded for murder in a war they had come to abhor, the veterans symbolically shed some of their guilt. In addition to their dramatic political impact, these demonstrations have profound therapeutic meaning. Instead of acting under orders, the vets originated actions on their own behalf to regain control over events—over their lives—that was wrested from them in Vietnam.

This is a much more fruitful model for the kind of response to death that we need in America today, given the dehumanizing fragmentation and atomization of our culture, than the model of a single individual on a journey alone, looking ahead toward the time when he or she can drift blissfully off to another world, like a sleeping baby.

Joining Together Against Death

The fast developing nuclear freeze movement seems to offer numerous psychosocial possibilities for overcoming the schizoid approach to death which has been so dominant in the past two centuries in our culture—many more possibilities, indeed, than the more privatized and professionalized death and dying movement. People who are committed to the freeze—including many from the helping professions, it should be noted—are rising up in the village square, as it were, to resist the principalities and powers of death. They are not simply bowing down before them and going to the beyond as quietly and as painlessly as possible. They are joining together on behalf of life, against death. They are not disengaging themselves from the body politic, in favor of some private experience of resignation to the inevitable.

The Markan and the Matthean Christ struggled with death. For Mark and Matthew, the cross was an absolute ending, a *finis*. So the Crucified Christ cries in anguish, in these Gospels: "My God, my God, why hast thou forsaken me?" (Mark 15:34, Matt. 27:46).

From this angle of vision, only the resurrected Lord offers the final fulfillment, the *telos* of human life, as *Christus Victor*. The Lukan and the Johannine Christ, in contrast, is finally at peace with death. Death appears to be both the *finis* and, in some measure, the *telos* of his life. Accordingly, he says on the cross: "Father, into thy hands I commit my spirit" (Luke 23:46), and "It is finished" (John 19:30).

"Peace in the death experience. . .comes only through trust in the faithfulness of the God who has power over death, not through any direct contemplation of death itself."

The mystery of death as it is portrayed in the New Testament requires us to hold on to both images, the struggle and the peace. We are not permitted by the New Testament witness to take some kind of romantic, sentimental or stoic detour around the anguish of death in order to arrive, by whatever stages, at the moment of final peace in this world. The New Testament will not have us beautifying or etherealizing death at any stage. Death always remains "the last enemy" in the life, as Paul says (I Cor. 15:26). Peace in the death experience, according to the New Testament, comes only through trust in the faithfulness of the God who has power over death, not through any direct contemplation of death itself.

Given our cultural situation today, deeply rooted in our nation's past, it would seem that we are obligated to struggle against death perhaps more than ever before, and to reject any hint of the pacification of death in this world. Self-conscious struggle with death, resistance against death in the name of human solidarity, would seem to be much more beautiful to behold than death itself.

H. Paul Santmire is pastor of Grace Lutheran Church in Hartford, Connecticut.

"Grief takes time and effort. It doesn't just happen; it is something people must let happen."

A Four-Stage Process Resolves Grief

David Hitch

"Good-bye son...I love you."

Emotion overwhelmed Donald Murphy as he buried his face on the chest of Joshua, his 3-year-old son. Loud sobbing filled the cramped room of the intensive-care unit. Donald gently kissed Josh's forehead. He paused a moment to stroke lightly the ruffled, blond hair, and through tear-filled eyes muffled a final good-bye. Reluctantly he turned to leave the bedside of his only son.

"I don't understand," he said. "I've prayed and prayed. So many people have told us how they are praying for Josh, but it doesn't seem to do any good. I thought that God would hear our prayers and answer them."

Nothing can be more traumatic than the death of a husband or wife, a parent, a child, a brother or sister, or a grandparent. None of us likes to think of the death of someone in our family, and yet that death is something we all must encounter. The reaction of human beings to the death of someone close to them has often been recorded in literature. The reaction is grief. What is it like to grieve?

Grief Is Like Fear

"No one ever told me that grief felt so like fear," C.S. Lewis wrote after the death of his wife.

Grief is the process of making the fact of a death real and learning to live with it. Grief does not take place once-for-all, but over a period of time which is a period of mourning.

Grief takes time and effort. It doesn't just happen; it is something people must let happen. Because grief is so frightening and painful, most people tend to avoid and postpone its expression. Grief hurts....

Human beings express themselves through their emotions. The emotion of grief is the human way of expressing sadness—sadness over a loss. Grief is the price to pay for loving. Grief is the price to pay for being human....

There are four typical phases in the grief process: shock and numbness, sadness and yearning for the deceased, apathy and loss of interest and reorganization.

Shock and Numbness

"Why doesn't he cry?" I wondered as I sat with 36-year-old Gary Blaine. For the past two weeks his 13-year-old daughter had lain in a coma while doctors puzzled over her condition. All this time I had not seen him cry.

"I just can't believe it. It doesn't seem real. I know what they said, but I don't feel anything," Gary finally said to me.

The attending physician had just informed him that Deborah was dead. Her heart had stopped and they were unable to revive her.

Gary Blaine was in a phase of shock and numbness. The death of his daughter had not registered emotionally. The whole experience did not seem real. For the past two weeks he and his wife, in spite of the cautions relayed by the medical team, had not allowed themselves to think that Deborah might die. It is not surprising then that Gary's initial reaction was disbelief.

The phase of shock and numbness usually does not last very long—a few hours to a few days. Even when the death is expected, it is common to experience a sense of shock and disbelief. The disbelief usually passes as the bereaved person is continually confronted with the reality of the death. There is a sense, however, in which disbelief continues for years after the death. It is not uncommon to hear someone say, "After all these years, there are times when I still don't believe he's dead."

"What was Deborah like?" I gently asked Gary after the doctors had left. "What are some of the

From "How to Live with a Death in the Family" by Father David Hitch, published by Claretian Publications, 221 W. Madison St., Chicago, IL 60606. Reprinted with permission.

things she liked to do? Do you have a picture of her in your wallet? What are you going to miss about her?''

Such probings might seem harsh and cruel on the surface. After all, Gary had just been informed that his daughter was dead.

Sadness and Yearning

Then it came. A sudden rush of emotion. Quickly Gary covered his face with his hands and buried them on his knees. Deep sobs and wailings broke the stillness and tension that had filled the room. Painful and intense grief had found expression. He was beginning to yearn and pine for his dead daughter.

The Blaines were slowly moving from their state of disbelief to the gradual realization that Deborah was dead. Such a realization takes place in many ways. Sometimes seeing and touching the body begins the gradual process. This phase of mourning, which may last for months, has several characteristics.

The first of these is an intense feeling of sadness, accompanied by crying. This is the time when a sudden memory brings tears quickly to the eyes. The picture on the mantle, the dusty bicycle in the garage, or the empty place at the breakfast table brings a sudden flood of tears.

Sometimes Panic

Anxiety and fear are other characteristics of this phase of sadness. This feeling sometimes borders on panic as persons realize that something awful has taken place.

This phase is also marked by a kind of searching, a yearning for the deceased. It is not unusual for the bereaved to hear sounds or to see sights that momentarily convince them that the beloved is present. Often a widow is convinced that she has heard the door slam at the time her husband usually arrived home. Or the mother is certain she heard ''Hi, Mom!'' at the time her child usually got home from school.

This is also the time when the bereaved begin to question the death, often directing questions to God. ''It isn't fair!'' or ''He worked so hard all his life; why is this happening now?'' Such questions are typical as the bereaved person searches and pines for the deceased.

''I have no reason to get up in the morning. I have nothing to do. My whole life has changed. I don't cry much anymore. But my life . . . it seems so bland.''

Apathy Phase

As the weeks turn to months, the sudden weeping comes less frequently. But as the tears dry, the bereaved find that life itself seems to slow down and lose its zest. They have little energy and, worse yet, little desire to do anything. They find themselves going through the motions, but the feeling isn't there. They have passed into the phase of apathy and loss of interest.

It is as though they have given up the search for the dead person and realized that they will not find the deceased after all. A sense of emptiness occupies their lives. Their struggle is over, and with it their hope of recovery. They are left drained.

It is during this phase that other people can seem so insensitive. In our society mourners are expected to bounce back in a short period of time. After all, didn't they have three days off for the funeral? The deep reality of the loss is just beginning to sink in, but people around the bereaved are already expecting more and more from them. A friend of the mother of a 7-year-old girl who died of a congenital heart defect wrote of the mother's feelings months after the funeral: ''She said she felt people were pushing her to put all this behind her. She was rather angry and kept telling me, 'People are so cruel.'''

Final Phase

''We're going to have a baby!'' Mary announced to the family gathered around the dinner table.

The announcement was received with joy, but tempered by memories of the child who was not with them. It had been over a year since 5-year-old Bobby had died of a mysterious infection.

''There are four typical phases in the grief process.''

The previous year had been a terrible one for the Tucker family. Bobby's absence was acutely felt. Only recently—some 13 months later—had a semblance of energy returned to the family.

The final phase of mourning is reorganization. It can go on for a long time. In this phase the mourner comes to the gradual realization that ''I can make it.'' The mourners recognize their survival of the death— the death that months previously they never thought they would manage.

In this phase life begins to have some color again. Feelings return to fill the space that had been empty for some time. Sunrises regain their beauty. Apple pie tastes good again. It is important to recognize that life is not the same again—people do not return to the way it was—rather they find again a life that is enjoyable, enriched, and worth living.

Slowly the mourner becomes interested in people again. New relationships are formed and enjoyed. Families begin thinking about having a baby. Children can enjoy the games they play with their schoolmates. Memories of the deceased remain—as they should—but life goes on, as it should.

Grief takes time. Much longer than people would like. The tendency is to rush it and not give grief its due. But people proceed through grief only by grieving. There are no shortcuts. Grieving is something that is to be done. In doing it persons pass through and arrive on the other side.

There are four features of the grief process that need to be highlighted: anger, guilt, sadness, and relief. Because they can impede or postpone a person's reaction to death, they need a closer look.

Ordinarily people don't like to talk about or even acknowledge the presence of these four features in their reaction to death. In this society people feel that it's wrong to get angry, or to feel guilt or relief at the death of a loved person. And they tend to consider it a weakness to be sad. And yet, these reactions are very normal features of grieving.

Angry Feelings

What do people do about angry feelings? Anger is a very difficult emotion. The explosiveness of anger is frightening. I'm convinced, however, that anger is a predominant feeling through the grief process—anger at oneself, at others, including the deceased, and even at God.

"Damn it," Nancy shouted. "Damn, damn, damn!" With her hand she slapped her thigh sharply. The sound rang through the waiting room. In her other arm she carefully cradled the dead body of her first-born baby. Nancy was angry at the outrage that was taking place.

When the death of a family member occurs, it is difficult to know at whom to be angry. Doctors, nurses, and relatives are often ready targets for the angry feelings we have at what has happened.

There is often anger toward the person who died. This may be the hardest kind of anger to acknowledge. Yet many people feel anger toward the deceased. Recently my aunt told me, "It isn't fair that he left me so suddenly without saying good-bye." She was referring to her husband, who had died suddenly in his sleep. How can the parent not feel anger at the child who got hit by a car in the street? Many times anger is directed toward God: "I was so angry at God for what had happened that I had no desire to go to Mass or pray. I hated him!"

What God could not be moved by this honest expression of rage by a suffering mother? My hope is that those around her could at least allow her this expression of grief. Too often Christians want to come to God's defense and forbid others to blame him.

Guilt Feelings

Feelings of guilt are another normal part of the grief process. They are often revealed in such phrases as: "If only I had . . ." or "We should have gone to the doctor earlier." Often these feelings are unrealistic, but they are real to the mourner. Usually people have done all that they could be expected to do.

Children are especially vulnerable to unwarranted

feelings of guilt. Time must be taken to explain to children, usually several times, that they were not the cause of the death.

Let It Out

Another form which feelings of guilt may take refers to the life of the survivors. What grandparent has not wished: "It should have been me. I've lived my life. She was so young, only 2 years old." Spouses often feel guilt at enjoying life when their mate has died. They wonder why they should still be living. It is normal to have such feelings.

"Grief does not take place once-for-all, but over a period of time."

The important thing with guilt, as with all feelings, is to become aware of what one is feeling and to acknowledge that that is how one feels. Then it is good to talk with someone who understands and who will allow you to express your feelings. The Christian heritage provides people with rich resources of forgiveness. Real guilt can be forgiven. God forgives; but can people forgive themselves? Often talking with a concerned listener helps one to realize that irrational feelings of guilt are just that.

I have been present with a woman, herself struggling with leukemia, when she learned of the sudden death of her adult son. Her sobs came from deep within and carried the pain and suffering that only a mother can know. Her tears flowed freely and unashamedly. A part of herself had died.

Tears Can Be Gift

If you can cry and feel like crying, cry. Tears can be a gift from God to express sadness felt at the time of a death. The crying and tears will return many, many times in the days to come.

And yet, embarrassment and apology often accompany this display of grief. People often say, "I'm sorry," or "I don't know what is the matter with me!" when they burst into tears. I want to say, "How could you help crying? Someone you love and miss very much is dead."

The feeling of relief is a very common reaction after the death and funeral of a loved person. It's most common when the death has involved a long illness.

Relief and Pride

Mixed with the feeling of relief may often be a strange sense of accomplishment, almost like pride. We can feel good that we "made it" through what months ago seemed an impossibility. We feel a sense of satisfaction at having stood by during a difficult ordeal. It is all right for the young couple to recall with satisfaction the countless hours they sat at the bedside of their dying son attending to his needs. They can also be glad that it is over—for him and for themselves.

"Do you want to hold my baby?" Nancy said, through reddened and tear-stained eyes, to her mother and grandmother.

Hesitantly, they nodded.

Nancy's dead, 2-day-old baby son, bundled in a brand-new blue blanket, was passed from the arms of his mother, to his grandmother, and in turn to his great grandmother. This was the only time they would hold this descendant of their family line. Tears flowed as they felt the lifeless body in their arms pressed against their breasts. The generations of this family were literally embracing their loss.

Make It Real

Embrace your loss. Make it real. Acknowledge that it happened; it happened to you.

Do you want to hold my baby? No, not really, to be honest. Who wants to hold a dead baby? Nancy was extending an invitation to feel her grief with her and a challenge to make their own feelings of pain and suffering real.

Christians have a model in Mary for embracing their loss. Michelangelo, in his Pieta, captured in stone Mary embracing the dead body of her son. It is an example of how all could embrace their loss.

Do not be afraid of emotion. Express your feelings. Let the tears come.

"People proceed through grief only by grieving. There are no shortcuts."

How unfortunate that our society does not encourage the display of grief! We refer to it as "breaking down." Tears are hurriedly wiped away. We are ashamed to allow others to see our humanness. Men are especially prone to this kind of thinking. Christians seem to have forgotten that grieving is a Beautitude: "Happy those who mourn: They shall be comforted."

Talk About Loss

Talk about your loss. "Give sorrow words. The grief that does not speak knits up the o'erwrought heart and bids it break," says a character in a Shakespeare play. You will need to go over and over your story of grief. Talking with a sympathetic friend can help you keep things in perspective, and you will thus feel less alone in your journey through grief.

Grieve with others. Unfortunately many people do their grieving alone. It is not uncommon to hear a spouse say, "I don't want to upset her." It's even more common to hear a parent say, "We must be strong for the children." Even while their "hearts are nearly breaking," people distance themselves from their family at a time when they most need a shoulder to lean on.

It is difficult to be around a bereaved family. People feel ill-at-ease. They don't know what to say. What does one say to the 6-year-old whose mother has died? Friends feel helpless, and often in their helplessness they avoid the family. This avoidance makes the mourning more difficult for the family. It deprives them of the very thing they most need—the supporting, caring presence of relatives and friends.

Ways to Be Helpful

But there are ways that one can be helpful. *Be present* to the bereaved family. Do not avoid them. Do not let your own anxiety prevent you from being with them. There is not a whole lot you can say, but a reassuring "I'm sorry," accompanied by a firm handshake or a gentle touch on the arm, will convey your concern.

Avoid cliches. In our anxiety people are tempted to use platitudes such as "I know how you feel" or "It'll be better tomorrow." Such comments often hurt more than they help. They are premature and offer little reassurance.

Be patient. As mentioned earlier, grief takes time—a long time. Usually it takes a lot longer than other people are prepared to grant to the mourners. It is important not to rush people through the grieving process.

Be available for continued support, especially during the first three months and at important anniversaries. In the days after the funeral the bereaved family are often forgotten. This is the time when they need an understanding listener, someone who will allow them to tell their story over and over. This talking makes real the loss. It is important.

Be aware of your own feelings. Exposure to the grief of others will remind everyone of their own mortality. Feelings will be aroused by the death of others. Don't be afraid to reveal your feelings. To tell the bereaved family honestly, "I don't know what to say" or "I feel so helpless and sad for you" shows them that you are not ashamed of having these feelings. Then you become a model for the griever.

To walk with others through their grief is a rich and rewarding experience. Those who do that with others are rehearsing their own journey through grief. The journey need not be depressing; on the contrary, it may be filled with growth and possibility. The reminder of one's own mortality gives one's present days an added significance. Life becomes more precious.

David Hitch is a Roman Catholic priest who works with bereaved parents in the Davenport, Iowa, diocese.

"The phone is exquisite in its immediacy. . . . If you close your eyes, it's just you and that person."

A "Hot Line" for the Dying Resolves Grief

Daniel Goleman

When the "hot line" telephone rings at the home of Stephen and Ondrea Levine in Taos, New Mexico, callers may hear this taped message: "Hello. This is the Dying Project consultation phone for the terminally ill and those sharing in the death of another . . . In the heart lies the deathless. Have a good day." When they are free, the Levines call back. They rarely hear good news.

The father of an 8-year-old girl who has been struck and killed by a car calls. He and his wife are devastated: alternately enraged and bereft. What troubles him most is the insistent thought that the one thing a parent should do is protect his child from such a terrible fate. He feels overwhelming guilt.

A woman dying of cancer has decided to stop all treatment. Chemotherapy and radiation have not worked and she has accepted the fact that she will die soon. Her daughters are her dilemma. She feels close to one, who lives at home with her. But another daughter, with whom she doesn't get along, and who has been on her own for six years, now wants to come home to live with her while she's dying. The dying woman wants to know how to tell this daughter 'no' without hurting her feelings.

A young man is still full of remorse about his brother's death eight years before. The brother underwent intense pain toward the end. Even so, the young man urged his brother to "hold on." He now feels that the last two weeks of his brother's life were a pain-racked hell, needlessly endured because of his own pleas.

The Levines, co-directors of the Dying Project, listen calmly to each story, and try to help the callers explore their grief, guilt, pain, or anguish. Their advice, in general, is to be open to whatever feelings arise, to accept them as a natural part of the process of dying.

Counseling the terminally ill and those close to them is hardly new. When I was a graduate student in psychology at Harvard, in the late 1960s, Edwin Shneidman (now at UCLA) taught a course on death and dying. At the same time, Richard Kalish taught a similar course at the School of Public Health at UCLA, and cofounded *Omega,* a journal about death and dying. Elisabeth Kubler-Ross brought death out of the closet and onto the best-seller lists in 1969 with her book, *On Death and Dying.* In the 1970s, the hospice movement encouraged families to take the dying out of the often impersonal world of the hospital, and bring them into the warmth of the home or to a place specially designed for dignified death. Today, courses and books on death and dying are proliferating.

The Dying Project has made the Levines prominent spokesmen for what has become known as the "conscious dying" movement, which tells people to face their deaths fully aware of the physical and emotional process they are going through, and to spend their remaining days living as well as dying. But like many prominent thanatologists today, Stephen Levine now denies the fashionable notion that there is such a thing as a fitting or "correct" death, and takes issue with his mentor, Kubler-Ross, who proposed that there are five distinct stages in which the dying person comes to terms emotionally with his inescapable end. Levine doesn't think that death can be reduced to a formula. As Avery Weisman, a psychoanalyst at the Harvard Medical School, has written, "Kubler-Ross's magnetic personality and dedication have imprinted these stages indelibly, if inaccurately, on the minds of the present generation."

The Levines give dozens of lectures and workshops each year, attended by hospital and hospice staffs, psychiatrists, psychologists, and social workers. Those who attend may have cancer or some other serious disease, or have just lost a close friend or relative, or are thinking of "taking Grandma home to die." Stephen Levine's recently published book, *Who Dies?*, is being used in college courses on death and dying and as a training manual for hospice staffs.

Growing Prominence

The Levines' growing prominence brings hundreds of letters and about 300 calls each month from people who learn about the hot line from friends or from the Levines' writing and public appearances. Many of the callers have been referred by their therapists or physicians, and an increasing number of calls come from the therapists and physicians themselves, who may be troubled by the death of a patient.

How did Stephen Levine come to be such an expert on death and dying? He has no academic credentials or professional training in psychology or counseling; his background is in Buddhism and meditation. But, as he writes in *Who Dies?*, he had an early and profound experience with death:

When I was 7, my best friend died. . . Eric had leukemia. When we met we instantly tuned into each other. Our play had a joy I had never known, a camaraderie and equality I had not experienced. He was my first real friend. . . . My heart was wide open; we loved each other. We could hardly wait to get together after school. Then one day he wasn't in class. After school I ran the two blocks to his home only to be met at the door by his weary mother, who told me Eric was too ill to play. He died two weeks later. I was torn apart, bewildered, disbelieving, angry. It couldn't be so! I had at last a close friend, but where had he gone? Who could I turn to? No one understood. . . .

Now, as I think back to that time, tears still come, and I feel Eric still in my 7-year old heart. And though I somehow still miss him, I sense that his death was a kind of initiation for me. What I felt seems never to have quite left. Each dying friend I am with reminds me to let my heart be torn open, that love never dies.

Early Books

Levine's early books reflect both his spiritual bent and his interest in death and dying. In his 20s and 30s he was a poet, writer, and editor. In 1972, he edited a book called *Death Row*, a collection of autobiographical portraits of prison inmates sentenced to death. In *A Gradual Awakening*, he presented a Buddhist interpretation of psychology. During this time he became increasingly interested in meditation, and began teaching the technique to small groups in California.

In 1977, Elisabeth Kubler-Ross invited Levine to teach meditation at her workshops on death and dying, which launched him in his current profession. He worked with her for about two years. But by 1978, after Kubler-Ross had become involved with an occult group in Southern California, she and Levine came to a friendly parting of the ways, and he began teaching workshops on his own.

Stephen Levine's wife, Ondrea, met him when she attended one of his workshops three years ago, after two battles with cancer. Her own work with the dying had begun in her teens, when she worked in convalescent homes.

"In working with the elderly," she says, "you can't help but work with the dying. Every place I went I would volunteer to work with people who were terminally ill. Soon word got around, and people started to call up because their sister's boyfriend had just died in an accident, or their grandmother had had a heart attack. Then the local doctor began sending me people and one thing just led to another."

Hot Line

Soon after they were married, the Levines started their Dying Project hot line, which is now supported by fees from the couple's lectures, workshops, tapes, and writing. Attendance at their weekend or five-day workshops ranges from 75 to 200; fees run from $25 per day up to $180 for the five-day affairs.

I visited the Levines recently at their home outside Taos, which looks out over an unbroken sweep of the Sangre de Cristo mountains. In a cluttered 6-by-10 foot office off the kitchen, they spend up to 10 hours a day on the phone.

"Levine doesn't think that death can be reduced to a formula."

Calls come in at the rate of 10 per day. Some are urgent: a cancer patient in such intense pain that he can hardly speak through his groans; a suicidal woman holding in her hand the poison she plans to take. Many calls are spurred by loss or grief unrelated to death, such as the mother who has just learned that her newborn child has Down's syndrome. Others seem minor, although the feelings they arouse in the caller are major, like the lonely young man whose dog had just died. The Levines return all the calls; their conversations generally run 30 to 45 minutes.

The Levines rarely initiate contact themselves, says Stephen Levine. "If someone calls us and says, 'My sister-in-law's dying and doesn't want to talk about death—would you call her?' our answer is 'No, that's unkind. If she wants to call us great. Otherwise, no.'

"We'll speak to many of the people just once. But then there are those we'll be talking to for months and months. For instance, a young woman called from North Carolina saying that she had just been diagnosed as having leukemia. When I asked what her feelings were, she said, 'Fear and confusion.'

" 'Those feelings are natural; just let them be,' I told her. 'Be open to the process as it unfolds. There's no one right way to go through this. Just trust yourself and take it easy.'

"Two days later she called to say that she was feeling differently. Lots of anger. 'Stay with that,' I told her. It may go on for months, until one afternoon she calls to thank us, or to say goodbye, or just to report another change. We may never meet her, but our calls with her will be the most intimate contact we're having for that time."

"Sometimes we'll get a call and the voice will be distorted with pain. They can barely gasp, 'Help me.'"

One of those who called was Karen Hope, whose 12-year-old son was brutally murdered in their Denver home last fall. "I didn't know who the Levines were," she says, "but a week or two after Eric's death a friend of mine called them and put me on the phone. My initial reaction was, 'What am I going to say to someone I don't know?' The first thing Stephen asked was, 'What are you feeling in your body?' Not what emotions was I going through, or 'Isn't this horrible?' He wasn't reacting like people around me, who were totally off-balance. It was very striking for me—he was able to cut through all the hysteria. I felt he knew what was happening to me. I was in an incredible state of shock, but I immediately felt I could talk to him.

Someone to Help

"Everyone around me was relieved that there was someone who could help. No one else knew what to do or say. Stephen said to me, 'Your life will never be the same again, will it?' And at first I said, 'Oh no, it's no different'—and then I stopped. What he said was the truth. It's been seven months now, and it has not been the same. His saying that was a pivotal point in my dealing with Eric's death."

"The phone is exquisite in its immediacy," says Stephen Levine. "When you meet someone in person, there is all the delay and confusion of the body language, setting up roles, the ritual interchanges. On the phone you can cut through all that. You are just a voice floating in space, and if you close your eyes, it's just you and that person.

"Sometimes we'll get a call and the voice will be distorted with pain. They can barely gasp, 'Help me.' We'll start right in: 'I understand your pain,' I'll say. 'I don't need to know your name. Just listen.' And we'll go right into a guided meditation on dealing with pain. You could never be that direct if you were sitting across a room from a stranger.

"Because we travel so much, people will come up to us at a workshop and say, 'I'm Fred. You've been talking to me for three months on the phone.' Or,

'I'm Fred's wife. Fred died the day before yesterday. He hoped to get here, but he said goodbye to you.'"

They once got a call from a mother whose 13-year-old daughter had just died in her arms. "We talked to her twice the next day," says Stephen Levine. "Since it was local, we went over to see her and her husband at their house. Then, two days later, the school called. They wanted us to come over and talk to her classmates. So we went over and talked to the whole school.

"Some of the 11- and 12-year-olds were going through a lot of guilt because they had fought with her the day before she died. Some other girls in her class were very upset because she'd been very popular in school and they had been jealous. We just encouraged them to feel whatever they had to, and to express it. Mostly we talked about it being all right to be sad, okay to cry. 'She's the teacher now,' we said. 'This is the most powerful thing you're going to learn this whole school year.' The teachers were crying and the kids were crying. Afterward, they came up to us and hugged us and said, 'I could never talk to my parents about this. Thank you.' "

Finishing Business

The need that brings many people to call the Levines is what they call "finishing business"—anger or hurts unexpressed, words unsaid, confidences never shared. In his book, Stephen Levine suggests:

Imagine that you are lying in an emergency room, critically injured, unable to speak or move, the concerned faces of loved ones floating above you, the pain beginning to dull from the morphine just injected. You wish to tell them something, to finish your business, to say goodbye, to cut through years of partial communication.

What would you say? Think of what has remained unsaid and share that each day with those you love. Don't hesitate. Tomorrow is just a dream.

Finishing business does not necessarily mean you clear up all the particulars of a lifetime of incomplete trust and fractured communication. Many think of finishing business as a totaling of accounts, coming to bottom-line-zero, balancing out the predicaments of the past in a long talking through of events. In my experience there is often not enough time or trust or self-confidence or simply not enough energy to deal with such old holdings and resentments, fears, doubts.

Feelings in a Letter

Levine once tried to help a 15-year-old finish her business with her mother, who was dying of cancer. The mother didn't want to discuss her disease or death, but her daughter was brimming over with feelings. The girl's aunt called Levine for advice. "I said to tell the girl that she can write everything she wants to say to her mother in a letter and leave it with her, saying, 'Mom, this is what I want to say to you.' The mother is free to read it at her own pace. Maybe she'll have a moment of openness at 4 in the morning when she's in pain and lonely. She can read it then, if she wants, or stop at any point. That way the daughter can speak her heart, and the mother can read what she can handle.''

Many of those who call the Levines do so because they are in physical or mental pain, or are close to someone who is suffering.

"It's uncomfortable just to be around someone in pain,'' says Stephen Levine. "One woman with spinal cancer had incredible pain. She said, 'You know there are two groups of people that come into the room. One group comes in and says, "Oh, how good you look today, how wonderful.'' And they can't look you in the eye. They fidget while they're sitting there, and they can't wait to get out. They have no room for my pain, because they have no room for their own. Another group comes in and they know there's nothing they can do to help me. They're helpless, but they have room for my pain. That's enough for me. I'm happy just to have them be with me.'

When Fear Meets Pain

"When fear meets pain, that's pity,'' Levine continues. "Pity is a selfish feeling. But when love meets pain, that's compassion. It's all right that they're in pain, even if there's nothing you can do to relieve it. But you can stay with them; you can look them in the eye. You don't close your heart.

"People call us to ask how they can get out of their pain. We tell them not to try to escape it, but to investigate it. What *is* pain? They'll say it's awful, or it's unbearable. But that's their response—not the pain itself. Most of what people call pain is actually resistance. The reflex is to see pain as the enemy, as something to be eradicated under any circumstances. But we get people to look at it in detail. Is it steady? Does it move? Does it vibrate? Is it hot? Burning? Cold? Does it have tendrils? The idea is not to get rid of the pain, but just to see what it is. When people look directly at their pain, they can see how their resistance is like an amplifier, magnifying the pain.''

Some of the calls to the hot line come from people familiar with but confused by the five "stages of dying'' popularized by Kubler-Ross: denial, anger, bargaining, depression, and acceptance. Levine feels that these concepts of his former mentor have become formulistic gospel among those who work with the dying, and that they may have outlived their usefulness. To Levine, there is no specific progression through which people must go as they face death, no necessary pilgrimage through psychological way stations.

Definite Stages

"It's not as easy or neat as A to Z, or one, two, three, four, five,'' he writes. "Even the idea of definite stages is confusing because it makes solid something that is actually flux and flow. How many

times at nursing stations have I heard, 'He's in denial' or 'He's in the anger stage'? People are not stages.''

"We often get calls from nurses or therapists who are confused because their patients don't seem to be dying in the orderly way the books say they should,'' says Ondrea Levine. "They've read or learned in their training that people should go from denial to this, that, and the other stage. But Elisabeth offered those stages as a generalized insight into the feelings that surround death. People try to codify the stages, to use them as a way to keep from having to be open to whatever feelings a patient is having at a given moment. It's an ongoing moment-to-moment unfolding.

"People call us to ask how to escape their pain. . . .We tell them not to try to escape it, but to explore it."

"One day a woman called and said, 'My grandmother's a brat; she won't die the way I want her to. I want her to die consciously.' People are hearing lots these days about the so-called 'right way' to die—they should at least get to the stage of acceptance. This woman was helping her dying grandmother and trying to make this elderly woman die acknowledging the love between them, how meaningful it was, and so on. The granddaughter was getting frustrated because her grandmother wouldn't cooperate by fitting this model of how you are 'supposed' to die.''

"A hospice worker called,'' Stephen Levine says, "and said she was working with a woman who was in denial. She wanted to know how she could get this woman to move through the stages. 'First of all,' I said to her, 'why do you want her to move through the stages?' She had just taken it for granted that she should. I said, 'Trust that this woman will do exactly what she needs for herself, feel just what she has to, on her own.' ''

Levine's Methods

Stephen Levine's methods, and his penchant for Buddhist concepts and for phrases reminiscent of the human-potential movement (like "the okayness of death''), have made him a target of critics of the "dying movement,'' which certainly has its less reputable adherents and advocates. Kubler-Ross herself was recently involved in a scandal with a spiritualist minister who conducted seances in which people contacted (and had sex with) "afterlife entities.'' And then there's the California company that supposedly hires the terminally ill to carry messages to the dead from their friends and relatives.

In a recent article in *Harper's* magazine on the

follies of what he calls the "cult of the beautiful death," Ron Rosenbaum lumped Levine with the movement's most eccentric elements, and dismissed his message as "metaphysical heroin." Certainly the influence of Eastern religious thought, along with smatterings of humanistic psychology, make his techniques seem somewhat odd to people trained in traditional psychology. But having read transcripts of the Levines' calls, and having listened to some, I find their work skillful and sensitive. They don't foist their views on callers. Instead, they are good listeners who are more familiar than most of us are with the emotional territory that surrounds death.

"Despite the recent surge of frankness about dying, our culture continues to be uncomfortable with the facts of death."

For another view of the Levines' work, I called psychologist Edwin Shneidman, professor of thanatology in the Department of Psychiatry at the UCLA Medical School. Shneidman, a co-founder in the 1950s of a Los Angeles suicide prevention center, understands the dangers—and the advantages—of telephone counseling, and purposely did not engage in it. "The *sine qua non* of such a service is careful selection, comprehensive training, and continuous supervision," he says. "I'm skeptical of people who have not gone through these steps. The impulse to do good should be defended against—those too eager to help can be harmful" if they lack adequate preparation.

Intuition and Sensitivity

The Levines have no academic credentials or professional training, but these things may not be all that relevant for counseling the dying. Death raises questions that are beyond the scope of psychology. Psychology has been claiming its place in helping people cope with dying, but that territory was the province of religious counselors long before modern psychology developed. The essential skills in such work are intuition and sensitivity—not virtues that professional training or academic credentials can guarantee.

"The Levine's work," says Shneidman, who is unfamiliar with their hot line, "will be only as good as they are. A call between strangers can be as awkward as a blind date. Further, most serious clinicians believe that you simply can't do in a few minutes what should take hours to handle. But someone who calls asking for advice is willing to hear it. What the counselor gives is nurturance; what the caller gets is succor. Just listening and giving permission for feelings can be enough. Besides, there's no trademark on these skills. Alcoholics Anonymous puts many therapists to shame. Likewise, the presence of good neighbors helping informally is the greatest source of solace in our culture. Still, once people organize these efforts, they need some professional standards."

Richard Kalish, a clinical professor in the Department of Psychiatry at the University of New Mexico, is familiar with Levine and his Dying Project. Says Kalish, "People in the field who know about Levine's work are never neutral: the humanistic types are uniformly delighted with Levine; many of the more traditional types see him as somewhat flaky, although they recognize that the program may be helpful. He doesn't have much connection with mainstream thanatology."

My own reading of the Levines' message and service is that it fills an essential need in American life. Despite the recent surge of frankness about dying, our culture continues to be uncomfortable with the facts of death; its frightening intrusions leave many of us at a loss for a suitable response. We can turn for solace to family, friends, clergy, or therapists. But in our rootless society, there are many who have no one to turn to, and many who have exhausted their alternatives. Stephen and Ondrea Levine provide one more alternative.

Daniel Goleman is senior editor of Psychology Today.

"Bereavement . . . can be prepared for, and not only when a lifetime partner becomes ill in a threatening way."

Rehearsing Bereavement Resolves Grief

Alex Comfort

Ernest Hemingway wrote that "there is no happy ending to a genuine love affair." At the same time an ending is inevitable, in view of human mortality. In a sense, bereavement in later life is "no different" from bereavement when we are younger, and could be less of a bombshell because it is expected, or at least seen as a contingency to be thought about. On the other hand, late in life most couples resemble two beams propped against each other, and if one is pulled out a whole life pattern, which was in viable equilibrium, collapses.

There is no way of *dealing* with bereavement so as to make it painless. Neither the British technique of pretending death didn't happen nor the American mortician-promoted technique of cosmetics, rip-offs and open caskets work. Both tend only to limit the overt expression of normal emotions of grief, rage and despair, which then surface a bit later as depression or illness. Bereaved people tend to be quite unexpectedly boycotted by friends who don't know how to handle death—and stay away.

Bereavement, when it comes, can only be lived through. On the other hand, it can be prepared for, and not only when a lifetime partner becomes ill in a threatening way. Thinking through each other's possible deaths at least once—economically, practically, emotionally—isn't ghoulish or bad luck. It is loving, because each partner is considering the preservation of the other. There is nothing loving in asserting that if X dies you will die of grief. You won't, and you do X no honor by promising to live in a state of misery.

Mutually Agreed Plan

You normally take out insurance for a surviving partner. Take out survivor insurance by having a mutually agreed plan of reaction which will go into

operation automatically if death should occur. First you need to allow time—eight weeks is average—for mourning, confusion and the state of being "shut down." In planning from then on, remember that all relict spouses at all ages are more vulnerable in health for a year after bereavement. Set up a program which can take over from your own willpower until it recovers. Arrange machinery so that financial business and other transactions operate without you or operate automatically during the mourning period, but not so that you can't immerse yourself in them if you find that helpful.

Insurance Against Shock

Having a schedule like that of the astronauts' space reentry, which removes the need to improvise, is the best insurance against the shock, emptiness and strangeness which follow loss. Long-term improvisations can come later, in response to circumstances then obtaining, but the time for your fire drill is early in life, with regular updates on all arrangements. You may feel queasy the first time, but remember that fire drills don't cause fires.

Often the unspoken aspects of bereavement do the most damage. One of these is relief. *All* long-term partners, however loving, have a perfectly comprehensible sense of relief mingled with desolation at losing a companion, and many react to this component (which is especially strong when there has been a long, trying illness), not by recognition, but by guilt at their lack of proper emotion and by idealizing the dead person. This is a major contributor to "widower's impotency" at remarriage.

People vary in their handling of actual grief. Some are helped by keeping everything as it was, as if the dead person were on holiday, others by turning out every vestige of the lost person and rearranging the house. Don't be guilty about this strategy either, if you select it. You are not destroying their memory, only

Reprinted from A GOOD AGE by Alex Comfort. Copyright © 1976 by Mitchell Beazley. Used by permission of Crown Publishers, Inc.

death/dying **263**

asserting that you must now embark on a new life trajectory.

Rehearsal by Discussion

Rehearsal by discussion, when you are both present and well, may limit some of the strong, irrational reactions you will have in the event. Financial as well as emotional rehearsal is essential (so you know where all the keys, papers, etc., are). You may like to carry out this exercise with help (from an attorney or from a counselor). Oddly enough, you will not find it depressing in fact, although it sounds a downer in prospect. Women in particular, who, because of longer life and the fact they are often younger than their husbands, face a high chance of being widows, are often deeply relieved once it has been done.

Facing Deep Emotions

The point of having expert help is that deep and unfaced emotions are involved. Handled properly a death rehearsal can open up a marriage, but you don't want to do this with a crowbar or you may have trouble getting it back together. One recalls the French king whose wife on her deathbed told him lovingly that he must remarry. "No! No!" blubbered the king, "I'd rather have mistresses!" Spouses have to be able, ideally, to accept the idea that "their" person can and will if necessary go on without them, and even find new resources in the experience. They need also to accept that they themselves can and will if necessary go on without their partner and find new resources there, too, which does not preclude grief at loss, gratitude for what has been and loyalty to a relationship now discharged to the full. If these things are indeed faced, and the relationship is deepened by facing them, bereavement is not painless. Grief will and should be felt and expressed, but it will lack the elements of guilt, self-deception and role playing which contribute far more than genuine love to making bereavement destructive to the survivor.

"Thinking through each other's possible deaths at least once—economically, practically, emotionally—isn't ghoulish or bad luck."

In old age it is less these interpersonal forces than the collapse of mutual support and the disruption of a stable way of life, between people who didn't realize how much they supplemented each other, which are destructive, and resources are also less then to face such problems. Here help will be needed from family, friends and the senior community. If you can plan some structure of fallback for yourself, or for others who don't plan it for themselves, this is

worthwhile and can bring some peace and comfort to a survivor that would otherwise be lacking. The kindest thing you can do for a bereaved person of any age is to be there, listen, support and show yourself open to his or her emotions. Do not hide because you don't know what to say. Saying should be avoided.

Alex Comfort, M.D., Ph.D., is known world-wide for his books The Joy of Sex *and* The Biology of Senescence. *His life work is human biology with special reference to aging.*

"I visited him three times and never said what I wanted to say. So there were no last words. And there was no benediction."

Consoling the Dying Resolves Grief

Anthony Brandt

It is the seventh anniversary of my father's death. I don't feel any great sorrow. I don't visit his grave on this date, or on any other, nor do I shed tears; the tears were all shed when he died. What I do feel is a persistent, almost nagging regret. Before his death, my father lay for four days in the intensive-care unit of the local hospital. He was fully conscious the whole time and not in severe pain. I knew, intuitively but certainly, that he wouldn't live for long. He knew it, too; he had said as much to my mother, and the knowledge was plain in his face and eyes. It was my last chance, then, to say what I wanted to say to this man. But the words stopped in my mouth. Instead I made only those inane hopeful statements people use in such situations: "You'll be all right, Dad. The doctors say you'll be up in a week or so," and "When you get out of here we'll get you on a proper diet, better for your heart." Things like that. All lies. I visited him three times and never said what I wanted to say. So there were no last words. And there was no benediction.

Yet when I reflect on what it was I wanted to say to him, I find it hard to formulate any clear statement. That I loved him went without saying. He was a Swede and bore many of the attributes the world thinks typical of Swedes: He talked little, kept his own counsel, was undemonstrative physically, and seemingly not very emotional. But he buried a lot beneath his benignly phlegmatic exterior—an unquestioning devotion to my brother and myself; a capacity for long, intense anger; a great fear of dying. We returned his devotion with as little outward display and as much intensity as he himself showed. During those last four days my brother bent the entire force of his will to keeping my father alive; when he died my brother tried to put his fist through

a wall. As for myself, the younger, subtler brother, my father knew well enough how I felt. He was satisfied with us both, so that neither of us, at the end, needed to say a word to him about love.

Fear of Dying

It was the fear in him, I think, that I wanted to speak to, the fear of dying. I was offering cliched messages of hope while all the time wanting to say *goodbye, Father, don't be afraid, don't be afraid, don't be afraid.* Not that I had any particular reason that he shouldn't. It is now common for people who survive accidents, heart attacks, or whatever, to come back and recount to us the blessings of the afterlife, the great peace and the unimaginably bright but somehow not blinding light that comes to them. I didn't have that in mind. I had come to my intellectual majority in a tradition that eschewed such easy comforts, that suggested, indeed, that there were no comforts at all and that the way of a brave man was to live without security, in no certain knowledge of anything, without hope or expectation of a more meaningful life, much less a future one. My father was no intellectual, but he lived out the same belief, or lack of it. He never attended church, never prayed, did not profess to believe in God or anything else. It wasn't that he was an atheist; he just took no interest in such things. Religion was irrelevant to his life. He cared most about his wife and children, then his house, then his garden. I don't think his thoughts extended much beyond that. That was his life— beyond it, he had nothing to say.

Delving into the Past

He did, to be sure, have a past, which he talked about when someone asked him. His father came to this country in the early 1890s to look (without success) for a brother who had arrived some years earlier and disappeared. His mother, my grandmother, also Swedish, came a little later.

Anthony Brandt, "Last Words for My Father," *Psychology Today,* April 1982. Reprinted with permission of author.

Grandfather and Grandmother were married here, settling in a small Swedish community in Plainfield, New Jersey. I remember attending their 50th wedding anniversary, celebrated at a Lutheran church in Plainfield, and being amazed at how many Swedes there were in the world. At the time I was perhaps 8 years old.

My father was born in 1899. Like me, he was the younger of two brothers. He played baseball, not professionally but well, and when he was in his late 20s his nose was broken by a grounder that took a bad bounce. Mine was broken by a fly ball when I was 13. My father had acne through adolescence; I had it into my 20s. I inherited his wide, almost womanish hips, his ability to sit reading for long periods of time, and his long silences.

Waste of Intellect

The silences naturally intrigued us all. If he was thinking, he never said so or explained what he was thinking about. For a long time I attributed to him more depth than he probably had. He did not know a great deal; he could finish *The New York Times* Sunday crossword puzzle, and sometimes the more difficult double-crostic, without looking anything up. It was more information than knowledge, however, a lot of facts with no presiding intellectual interest or discernible philosophy to integrate them. He had never gone to college, never formally studied philosophy, history, literature. What he knew he had picked up over the course of his life, in bits and pieces. It seemed to me a prodigious waste of intellect and talent. He had a clear, powerful singing voice but no occasion to use it. He had artistic talent: When I was struggling once to draw a dock, being preoccupied with sailboats at the time, he took the sketch away from me and produced a precise, carefully shadowed drawing that astonished me with its grace. I never saw him draw at any other time. My mother, on the other hand, painted a great deal, but had nothing like his talent. In my youthful presumption, in the years after I graduated from college (an opportunity made possible by considerable self-sacrifice on his part), I used to want to urge him to develop his talents before it was too late. But then, too, I failed to say the words. Some stubbornness or indifference in him stopped me. He was a man trapped by sociology, so to speak, suspended between two kinds of lives, his working-class immigrant father's and his upwardly mobile sons'. His fate was sealed, he could not escape, and I think he knew that and accepted it; I instinctively did well not to disturb the placid surface, which concealed a certain amount of defeat.

My mother felt no such compunctions. She wanted him to be more aggressive at the office, and while she did not hound him, she was often critical. He worked as an underwriter for what was then the Railroad Insurance Association in New York, rising over a period of more than 30 years, in a small office, no higher than assistant manager. He never made more than $10,000 a year. My mother's father had himself been the manager before he died; they met when she was working as her father's secretary. She clearly wanted a man as successful as her father had been; it always bothered her that he wasn't. No one knows whether it bothered him. He didn't like bosses, a trait his two sons share, and may not have wanted to be one. His friends in the office were people like himself, from the ranks. His work apparently didn't interest him much, and he was delighted when it came time to retire. Much of what he did was routine. I visited him several times at work and remember most clearly the columns of figures he wrote and added in his head, without the benefit of an adding machine. They were so neat that they might have come from the hand of some Victorian clerk who had spent years learning penmanship. I remember that, and also his great sociability at work, which surprised me in a man so quiet at home. He liked to chat and gossip, it seemed, and he could be very funny. He may not have liked the work, but he liked the job, liked being there. He was rarely sick and rarely missed work. He was never in a hospital, in fact, until those last four days.

"If I could have pulled his fear into the open, . . . perhaps he might have risen to the occasion and exorcised it."

"In my end is my beginning," wrote T.S. Eliot. The beginning of the end came for my father a few months before he was to retire. He blacked out in his office during a meeting. A vascular spasm in the brain, the doctor said. It wasn't too serious, he added, but it frightened my father, a man who had had little experience with the ills that flesh is heir to. He struggled to be brave about it but was not. The Railroad Insurance Association let him retire right away. For the next 10 years he stayed home, carefully nursing his health, not overexerting himself, letting his garden go, visibly winding down. All this time, I think, he lived in fear: of the angina pectoris that occasionally plagued him; of going blind (but he refused to have the cataracts that were developing in one eye removed, being more frightened of an operation than of blindness); of dying. He did not want to die. It wasn't that he particularly wanted to live, that he had some project to finish or some mission to perform. He simply did not want to die. He saw no kind of beginning in his end.

It's hard to think of your father as being afraid. Fathers are supposed to be slightly bigger than life, not subject to the weaknesses of children. It was confusing during those last four days, as if there had been a reversal of roles and I was the father, not he. That's a common experience, to be sure; the old have lost their authority somehow, and grown children have increasingly taken on the role of guardian to their elderly parents. America is full of King Lears. But that's not what I mean. For in spite of the fear that I saw in him during the last 10 years of his life, he still commanded my respect. He was afraid, but not a coward. He avoided pain, but when it came he accepted it stoically. He did his best to keep his feelings inside, and he did that well. The fear was there, but you had to sense it, see it, intuitively understand it; he never spoke of it directly.

At the End

That's why, at the end, it seemed so important to say something. *Don't be afraid, Father oh Father.* If I could have pulled his fear into the open, I tell myself now, got it out there where we could all look at it, perhaps he might have risen to the occasion and exorcised it. My mother rose to her occasion. "Well," she said, leaning over and kissing him, "we've had a good marriage." It was her way of saying goodbye. I could not rise. "How are you feeling now, Dad?" I asked him. "You'll be out of here in no time." Banal and insincere. I knew that he was dying, and I, the writer, the subtler son, specialist in saying things, couldn't find the appropriate, meaningful words that might have eased him out of life.

Don't be afraid. How does one comfort the dying without feeling comfortable with death oneself? In my bravest moments I believe in nothing but what is, seeing myself, my precious self, as an insignificant and transitory processor of experience, part of an unimaginably complex pattern of events that is being moved forward into nonbeing—colonizing it, and feeling that it doesn't matter to be finished, that that particular piece of work has been done, that the wave has passed over one and it is enough to have been part of the whole. That's in my bravest moments. Most of the time, of course, one isn't brave; most of the time it is decidedly not enough to be anything less than alive. Thoughts like these are cold comfort in any case. I couldn't have made such a speech. It sounds, and is, too much like philosophy, and he needed not a discourse on the meaning of life, but courage.

"The doctor says you're looking better, Dad." He wasn't looking better, he was moving on. The spirit, whatever that is, passes through and leaves, and we stand there helplessly. I was in a car when he died, driving home, the radio playing a Beatles song: "Get back, get back, get back to where you once belonged." I got back the next day. My mother, my brother, and I chose a grave site and consulted with the funeral director. My mother said that my father wanted a closed coffin. He didn't want people staring at his dead body; he thought that was obscene. I agreed. I didn't want to see him dead, whom I had not been

able to speak to while alive. I didn't want to face him. I felt that I had failed him and failed myself. And I was afraid, too, that he might have known all along what I was struggling with, had known and had lain there waiting, and is waiting still, always in vain, for me to speak.

Sometimes, when I am least brave, most like a child, there's no comfort of any kind. In my beginning, my bloody biological beginning, is only my end.

"He might have known all along what I was struggling with, had known and had lain there waiting, and is waiting still, always in vain, for me to speak."

Don't be afraid. It has taken me seven years to understand that it was my own fear I wanted to speak to. The day we buried him my daughter hugged me tight and wouldn't let go. It was obvious what she was thinking: He'll be next. There was now no father to go before me; indeed, I will be next. I'm almost certain now that he saw what was happening to me those last four days, how I was struggling to find the words, not for him but for me. He must have seen and, with his bleak Nordic self-control, kept still and waited for me to say the unsayable. With what feelings, what mixture of contempt, pity, and love I do not want to contemplate, he waited to see if I would break through. *Take comfort, Father, I will be coming after you. When I am as ready as you are.*

Not ready yet, I could not say the words. He kept still and died in silence.

Anthony Brandt, a journalist, is working on a book about the American Dream.

"One of the worst things you can do is to isolate yourself. Get out among people."

A Full Social Life Resolves Grief

Vernon Pizer

The last of the mourners had left and yet he lingered, numbed with overwhelming sorrow, bewildered by the awful finality of the moment, unwilling to turn away from the newly dug grave. Later, recalling that moment, he said, "I could not accept the fact that it was my wife who had been lowered into the earth. Why her? How could I come to terms with that? After the years with her to share the good times and to ease the bad, how could I face a future that did not include her? Her life had ended and mine had shattered and I did not know how to pick up the pieces."

The sad truth is that most of us will one day have to ask ourselves those same doleful questions. Finding the answers—the right answers—is vital. In a unique way they will constitute the final expression of compassion and love between the one who has died and the one who must go on living.

Though we try to close our minds to it, we recognize and reluctantly accept that death is the inevitable, natural progression from birth, but our awareness is always in the context of an older generation—grandparents, parents, uncles, aunts. We are unprepared for the death of a contemporary, especially a wife or husband, the sole person to whom we are related not by biological caprice but by conscious choice, the person whom we have vowed to cleave to, forsaking all others. So the trauma of "marital survivorship" is devastating. How can we deal with it? How can we overcome it? How can we fashion a new life for ourselves?

Marital Survivorship

A popular TV commercial depicts a busy throng freezing into rigidly immobile eavesdroppers when one says to another, "My broker is E.F. Hutton and

Vernon Pizer, "Till Death Do Us Part," *The American Legion,* April 1982. Copyright 1982, the American Legion Magazine. Reprinted by special permission.

Hutton says. . . ." That script, with only minor alteration, could apply to Dr. Donald R. Bardill, dean of Florida State University's School of Social Work. Sociologist, clinical psychologist and marital counselor, when Bardill speaks his professional peers listen attentively. This is what he has to say about marital bereavement: "It isn't a fun subject and because it isn't, for too long there has been a tendency to shy away from it. But looking the other way doesn't make it disappear; it only makes matters worse. Fortunately, the situation is changing today. The complex question of marital survivorship is coming out of the closet and is being discussed openly. Professionals in a number of different disciplines are studying the subject and all of its implications. Their findings are helping the survivors to cope with the tragedy and then move ahead on the pathway toward resumption of a normal life."

From the moment his wife died, friends and family of the bereaved husband rallied around him in a conspiracy of kindness designed to cushion the blow. Making sure that he was not left alone with the misery wracking him, they tried to divert his attention toward "safe" areas, to steer conversations into directions leading away from the death, arranged activities intended as distractions, threw up a screen around tangible reminders of his dead mate. In all of this, according to the experts, they were doing precisely the wrong thing.

Tears Need to Be Shed

"Grief is a crucial part of the recovery process," says Dr. Benjamin Fabrikant, professor of psychology at New Jersey's Fairleigh Dickinson University. "The survivor must be allowed to grieve, to express and experience the deep emotion within. Men, particularly, often find it difficult to express their overwhelming sorrow openly, somehow feeling it is unmanly to shed tears, yet those tears need to be shed."

Rabbi Jacob Goldberg, director of the inter-faith

Commission on Pastoral Bereavement Counseling, puts it this way: "'Good grief!' is more than an exclamation; it is a necessity. The mourner needs to mourn, needs to articulate his emotions, thoughts, worries and fantasies. It's necessary therapy for him or for her."

To bottle up grief in some inner recess is to court disaster. "That way," says Dr. Bardill, "it becomes an internal time bomb ticking away while you exist in a kind of emotional limbo. Eventually, sometimes years later, the bomb goes off with devastating effect. Grief is normal, natural, cleansing, and its prompt expression must not be denied."

Coping Begins with Understanding

There is agreement among the experts that coping begins with understanding the nature of the grief that a marital survivor experiences. Explains Bardill, "It is a special kind of wrenching sorrow that creates its own peculiar effects. One effect is what I call 'spouse imagery,' a sensation that the dead partner is present—sitting in the accustomed place at the dining table, nestling close in bed, doing familiar chores around the house. Patients of mine who undergo spouse imagery often tell me that they fear they are cracking up mentally, but those fears are groundless. It is a common reaction that usually disappears promptly."

A young woman, recently widowed, describes her encounter with spouse imagery: "For the first few weeks after his death I had the strange feeling that he was still with me, not visible but somehow there within reach. At night, especially, I felt his presence there in the bedroom. One night I awoke because I thought I felt a warm hand touching my shoulder. Gradually, the sensation of his presence grew dimmer and then disappeared entirely."

Another frequent reaction is a feeling of guilt—guilt over things unsaid or undone while the partner was still alive, over promises unkept, over hopes and plans unrealized. Guilt over past unkindnesses or acts of inconsideration, fancied or real. Even guilt, sometimes, over the very fact of survival. If the death was preceded by illness there are often guilty self-doubts over whether great enough or prompt enough efforts were made to obtain the very best medical care. Grief-stricken and confused, the mourner finds it difficult initially to place these self-recriminations into proper perspective within a framework of objectivity and logic. In some instances, of course, there may be a measure of justification for a stirring of guilt but, reports Dr. Fabrikant, "most often it is unreal and unjustified by the facts and the survivor needs to realize that."

Survival Withdrawal

Even certainty that the finest care has been obtained for a terminally ill husband or wife does not always bar a feeling of guilt. This is because of what the experts term "survivor withdrawal"—recognition

that death is approaching and preparation for it by beginning to detach oneself mentally from the failing partner. Even though psychologists point out that withdrawal is a perfectly normal reaction it does not prevent pangs of conscience. There is, however, a beneficial aspect of withdrawal, as Dr. Judith Newman of Pennsylvania State University makes clear. It is this: during the illness the surviving mate is able to begin grieving in an anticipatory way so that after the death the sorrow is less intense and less prolonged.

"The best, most effective way to begin reweaving the torn tapestry of your life is not to flee but to resume normal activities and interests."

No marriage is ever completely free of an occasional dispute between husband and wife. But when one leaves—whether for work, an errand or an extended trip—following an unresolved argument and while absent suffers a sudden death, the guilt engendered by knowledge that the last words uttered were in anger is wrenching for the one who remains. "This is needless, preventable anguish," Dr. Bardill says. "My wife and I vowed 25 years ago that we would never part angry. Never since then has one of us left the house or gone to sleep after a dispute without first kissing and making up." He adds, with an engaging smile, "All other considerations aside, a policy of immediate kiss and make up has its own sweet rewards."

Acute Grief

The human mind and spirit are resilient. The tears dry. Unreasonable self-recrimination becomes purged by logic. The memories do not become erased; the void, the loss, the sadness are still there. But the period of acute grief comes to an end, usually in a matter of a few weeks. "If it persists beyond about six weeks, professional counseling should be sought," Dr. Bardill advises, "preferably with a counselor who is accredited by the American Association for Marriage and Family Therapy."

Having come to terms with the tragedy, what now? How do you make a fresh start, a new life?

All knowledgeable sources agree that you should not hastily adopt any major decisions involving a significant alteration in your way of life. Judgments reached quickly in the aftermath of burying a mate are too often faulty. Dr. Newman suggests it is wise to delay major decisions for as much as a year. "You should certainly wait at least three months before undertaking any radical changes," Dr. Bardill says. "Even then it should be only after talking the proposals over thoroughly with competent advisors. Enough profound change has come into your life without quickly taking on more. That doesn't mean you shouldn't plan for the future—you should—but give those plans an opportunity to stand the test of time; in six or seven months your views may be entirely different."

"My first thought was that I must get away from everything that could remind me of the terrible ordeal I had just passed through," a widow recalls, "so as soon as possible after my husband's death I gave up my job and my apartment and moved to another city. It was a mistake. I missed everything that had been familiar and comforting to me. In turning my back on reminders of my sorrow I had also turned my back on all the things that had brought me happiness, the things that gave me stability and a sense of belonging."

Resume Activities

The best, most effective way to begin reweaving the torn tapestry of your life is not to flee but to resume normal activities and interests. Dr. Fabrikant encourages "a return to work and other usual activities and a resumption of a full social life as soon as possible." Dr. Bardill emphasizes and enlarges upon the same advice. "One of the worst things you can do is to isolate yourself. Get out among people.

"Dr. Fabrikant encourages a return to work and other usual activities and a resumption of a full social life."

Because the pattern of your earlier social life probably fell into a 'couples' format, broaden your circle by making new friends among whom a 'singles' format is common. But in seeking new friends bear in mind that where you go determines the kind of people you meet. If you make the bar scene you wind up with bar-type people and for most of us that isn't what we want. There are too many more rewarding places than a bar stool—satisfying, productive alternatives like church clubs, cultural organizations of all kinds, sports and recreational groups, evening college classes geared to mature students, travel clubs, square dance groups, and so on. I know of several warm friendships that developed in such unlikely places as Weight Watchers, jogging trails and little theater groups. The point is that man is a social animal and you can't be social in a vacuum. You have to go where the people are."

Inevitably, in striking out for yourself in an enlarged social setting, you confront the question of dating the opposite sex. If I go out on a date, you ask yourself, am I breaking faith with my dead mate, am I being disloyal? No, say all of the experts

emphatically. It is unnatural, unrealistic and harmful to shun the company of the opposite sex, they agree. Dr. Fabrikant cautions against dedicating oneself to the memory of the lost mate, to enshrining her or him, and to resisting getting back into the "real world of other people, both male and female."

Testimonial to Spouse

Eventually, for many marital survivors, the matter of remarriage comes to the fore and it is now that the feeling of disloyalty to the former partner is likely to be strongest. "This is illogical and, in fact, it even does a disservice to the memory of the dead mate," according to Dr. Bardill. "When one remarries it is really a testimonial to the former spouse. It says that that marriage was so happy, so fulfilling, that you want once again to be married."

Three years ago widespread public attention was focused on the courageous efforts of Marvella Bayh—wife of the then senator from Indiana—to cope with the cancer that was taking her life. Because he is a prominent figure whose words carry weight and because the events are fresh in his mind, I asked Senator Birch Bayh to share with readers of *The American Legion* magazine his experiences in coming to grips with the tragedy. "My wife and I were extremely close," he says. "She was my right arm, my heart and my soul, so losing her was the ultimate loss. Three factors helped me to cope.

"First, our deep faith prepared us to accept the Lord's will. I must confess as a mere mortal I could not understand why one so full of life and so occupied with helping others should be taken prematurely, but I accept that the Almighty knew better. Second, since my wife during her life had done so much good I tried to dwell on the fact that her good works were continuing even after she went on. Third, my son Evan was a tremendous comfort to me. Not only were we able to console one another, but Evan provided living proof that his mother lived on through him.

"We have to grieve and we have to cry—there is nothing unmanly about tears. We have to take solace from the positive aspects of the one who has gone on. And we have to go on living, trying to make our lives count for something." Recently, he remarried. Dr. Bardill would call it a testimonial to the great happiness he had found in marriage to Marvella.

Perhaps Thornton Wilder summed it up best when he wrote, "The highest tribute to the dead is not grief but gratitude."

Vernon Pizer, a retiree in Valdosa, Georgia, is a free-lance writer.

"To surrender to one's own grief and to become actively engaged in it require tremendous courage."

Surrendering to Emotions Resolves Grief

Alla Bozarth-Campbell

Grieving is a normal, healthy, healing activity. Grieving is an experience that we all encounter sooner or later as part of the human condition on this planet. Grieving is something that human beings must do in order to survive losses.

Grieving is hard. It need not be hellish. What often makes grieving hellish are all the messages we get about it—especially the messages that tell us that sad feelings, expressed or unexpressed, are inappropriate, awkward, and often selfish.

Where do the messages about grief come from? What influences our conscious and unconscious attitudes about grieving?

I believe that the strongest influences are important cultural attitudes against the expression of feelings and the value of painstaking process. These attitudes are communicated to us in blatant and subtle ways—often in our families, in school, in the marketplace.

Cultural Influences

An opposite point of view—much more limited in its influence—comes out of some of the "pop" psychologies, with their emphasis on the theatrics of self-expression, whether related to genuine feeling or not.

Then there are the influences of more moderate psychologies, which call upon us to become "integrated" or "whole" persons, an expectation which may seem unrealistic in the face of intense grief.

After a brief examination of these influences which add to unwritten laws against honest grieving, we can consider an alternative, a new unspoken permission allowing the feeling activity of authentic grief. We can learn to "grieve well."

Certainly not *all* feelings are looked on as bad or disgraceful. The message is that "good" feelings of happiness and well-being ought to be expressed. People should behave in a way that makes everyone else around them feel comfortable.

Telephone commercials on television always show people calling their loved ones long distance to express some happy feeling to them across the miles. This is well and good. But what is not shown is that people also need to reach across the miles to one another for love and support in·times of emotional pain and crisis. No one ever falls apart seriously in the ideal world of the TV commercial. Why? Because it's unpleasant to see someone in emotional pain. Emotional pain, unlike physical pain, is not acceptable in our culture. Unlike the seemingly acceptable violence of television, it makes the viewer feel responsible and guilty in some vague, discomfiting way.

Grief is taboo.

The Jackie Kennedy Syndrome

The strongest communication of the grief-is-taboo idea in our culture came to American families through their television sets in the early sixties. We all watched the impressive funeral proceedings for John F. Kennedy. Days earlier we were struck with the horror of President Kennedy's assassination, the immediate anguished response of Jackie Kennedy, her pink suit splattered with blood, crawling over the back of the car, shrieking for help. What a striking and disconcerting contrast the funeral rite was—subdued, in order, according to form. Even the widow's tears were subject to public protocol. Behind her thin black veil we saw that same face, not contorted in pain, but mask-like, frozen, still. No human emotion intruded from Jackie's countenance into the controlled arena of grief-according-to-regulation.

I was disturbed by the self-restraint in Jackie Kennedy's bearing, by the way she had managed to bring her emotions under such severe control in so short a time. Now, years later, I see that what was disturbing about the experience for me was that her image at the funeral, walking stiffly beside her dead husband's cortege, was being put across to the American people as *an example of how we ought to behave in grief*. To be fair, she may have been in shock, but this was not the general interpretation of her behavior. I remember being puzzled by British commentators' reactions during a BBC interview. One of them called her "Queen Jackie" because of the "majesty" of her public bearing. Another praised her because she never let herself be seen with a tear or grimace on her face. To equate the apparent smothering of feelings with royal style seemed to me a marked instance of inhumanity. What human queen would not feel profound pain at the loss of a loved one? And why should she not show her pain and her love openly, assuring us of her humanity and our own? I have no doubt that my first image of Jackie Kennedy, wailing her despair spontaneously at the moment of disaster, was the truer of the two images given to the world.

Stoicism and Pain

Three hundred years before Christ, the Greek philosopher Zeno founded the school of Stoicism, which taught that all events were pre-ordained by divine will, and therefore human passions, joy as well as grief, were superfluous and should be avoided. The contemporary version of Stoicism leaves out the first part of this belief system and creates a caricaturized distortion of the original Stoics' ideals. Their ideal of serenity was based on trust and was far from the artificial calm of suppressed emotions that modern people so often suffer. Stoicism had as its goal the abolition of suffering. Modern social form merely denies it and so makes it worse, and more damaging to the sufferer. Instead of truly entrusting ourselves and our pain to a benevolent and all-wise God, we too often ignore the pain and cultivate emotional dishonesty as a virtue. Pain has a stubborn habit of not going away just because we deny it exists. In fact, the more pain is denied, the deeper it tends to go inside our bodies and souls, and the harder it is to identify and deal with and ultimately grow beyond.

The Search for Silver Lining

Pain is an essential part of any growth process—the process of growing up, growing old, growing beyond grief. However, in our fast-paced world we have come to expect fast results. We expect to find the cloud with the silver lining without having to spend time looking for it. We have become impatient of processes.

How easy it is to avoid the real issue of suffering by looking immediately for ways to "grow" because of it. How many times have I sabotaged myself by leaping ahead of my own healing process, trying so

desperately to "feel better" that I make myself feel even worse because I have added to my primary pain the new complication of failure! In cheating myself of the necessary time to feel bad I have cheated myself of the only process that could really heal me.

Ultimately, the only way to get through something is to get *through* it—not over, under, or around it, but all the way through it. And it has to take as long as it takes.

"What often makes grieving hellish are all the messages. . .that tell us that sad feelings, expressed or unexpressed, are inappropriate."

A bad situation is often just that, a bad situation; with nothing—at least at the time—to redeem it. The Christian Good Friday is good only in retrospect. At the time it happened it was only bad. Horrible Friday. The end of the line. And if it had been less bad and horrible, Easter would not mean so much.

To pretend that real distress and real despair never happen is also to reject the possibility for redemption. Only what is really lost can be redeemed. Only what is truly dead can be brought back to life.

In the long run, pain that is met head-on is always assimilated, but only if we truly meet it and take it for what it is.

A False Comfort

People fool themselves in many ways. We give ourselves false comfort when we by-pass the genuine sorrow of a deep loss or disappointment and tell ourselves some cheerful platitude. We lie to ourselves about our real feelings because it is sometimes easier to live a comforting lie than to work hard at the truth.

People with religious backgrounds may dismiss the pain of a situation with a shrug and a forced smile and say, "Oh well. It's God's will." God never wills pain, though pain truly faced may lead to untapped sources of grace. The important emphasis is on *truly facing* the total reality of the situation—the outer circumstances and one's full inner responses to it.

Those who have gone before us on their own grief journeys can reassure us that the needed strength is already there, within ourselves. Others who care about us can help us find access to it, so we can allow ourselves to take the time we need to go all the way through our own grief process.

Comfort and hope are words we often hear associated with grief.

The word "comfort" comes from two Latin words meaning "with strength." To be comforted truly is to be given the strength to meet a situation, to face it fully.

Hope is precious, but it does not wipe out pain. Pain becomes bearable when we are able to trust that it won't last forever, not when we pretend that it doesn't exist. We may be able to paint the clouds silver, but our dreams will show them more starkly grey than ever; dreams tell only the truth and can be tormenting if we deny the truth when we are awake.

A kind psychiatrist once told a friend of mine who was struggling to find something "good" in a bad situation, "A scar is really a scar, and it's no good trying to make it into a beauty mark." Scars may have their own value, and in time some of them may become transformed into beauty marks on their own. Some remain deformities as a reminder of the human condition we all share in pain and imperfection; some make us stronger than before, because scar tissue is very tough; some add a mystery of distinction to us which can either distance others or draw them to us; and some scars have no particular value at all.

"Pain becomes bearable when we are able to trust that it won't last forever, not when we pretend that it doesn't exist."

Whatever the transforming nature of wounds which become scars in time, they are part of what makes each of us unique. We can learn to bear them with dignity as signs of what life has taught us, for we carry their meaning and lessons with us all our lives.

A Stressful Society

We all know what stress is: the feeling of being alternately or simultaneously closed in and pulled apart by the pressures and tensions of daily life. When life includes an experience of painful loss, stress sometimes becomes nearly unbearable.

Healthy ways to deal with stress involve recognizing our feeling responses to the bad situation which is causing the stress, and expressing those responses in safe ways.

The fine art of expressing feelings creatively is seldom learned at home or in school, and each generation grows up with a backlog of unexpressed feelings, or worse yet, feelings which sometimes are expressed in destructive, anti-social behavior.

A Place for Emotionalism

In the adult world, men and women are given messages that "emotionalism" in response to deep personal grief has no place in their business or professional lives. As there continues to be professional pressure to "stifle yourself" (Archie Bunker's prescription to combat Edith's expressiveness)—or at least to leave emotions at home—working men and women become victims of frozen feelings in their personal lives as well.

The burden to suppress emotions and to function solely by reason is heaviest upon men—and upon women who are succeeding in traditionally male jobs. Even when their lives are falling to pieces, career persons are expected to preserve their on-the-job image of being totally together. Dedication to the company or the craft is expected to conquer any tendency toward self-indulgence in private grief. The effects can be devastating! Those who deny themselves necessary grieving time merely put off the process, which often emerges years later in the form of neurosis, or even psychosis. . . .

Countercultural Influences

One obvious result of an extremely suppressive culture is the emergence of an extremely expressive counterculture. Popular psychologies of the past decade reflect the movement away from a thinking or analytical approach to therapy and towards methods which acknowledge the psyche and deal with feelings. These modes may not be authentically intuitive, integrative, or holistic. Often in the hands of unskilled or ungifted therapists, faddish therapies become nothing more than emoting sessions. Instead of psychic synthesis or integration through self-expression, destructive forms of psychological anarchy or emotional mayhem may occur.

Primal therapy and Scream therapy often put tremendous pressure on individuals to produce the Ultimate Emotion and then to emote it. Told how bad holding feelings in can be for people, the person who submits to Primal or Scream therapy can fairly easily come up with the desired results and work up a powerful case of the screams or the sobs. The problem is that forcing feelings to well up and to push them out does very little long-range good if these aren't connected with the whole context of a person's life. Anyone who is exhibitionist enough can scream on command, but no one is guaranteed good psychological health because of that ability. Fake feelings, like empty rituals, can be worse than no feelings or no rituals at all. They often leave one with the feeling of "being had," being promised something wonderful and then being left with an emptiness or a slightly rancid taste in the mouth of the soul.

To rebel against emotional inhibitions, either external or internal, simply for the sake of rebellion may be fun for the moment, like making mud pies. But in real life mud dries and hardens and cakes on our hands and becomes very uncomfortable unless we let the rain wash it off in time. The activity of working in the soil, digging weeds and planting seeds, may not always be as much fun as mud-pie-making and may be somewhat harder and more frustrating. But the results will be longer-lasting and will have the bonus of providing nourishment for one's self and for others as well.

In a similar way, genuine grieving—digging, weeding, growing—is not only a healthy activity, it is a worthwhile and necessary process. Forced sorrow is no substitute for the real grief process that may include anger, fear, guilt, or any complex interweaving of spontaneous feelings. A person who has experienced loss will not benefit from forcing out feeling responses any more than from denying feelings altogether. What is needed to grieve well is to discover the nature of the losses and their meanings and the impact of the feelings within ourselves, and then to find appropriate ways of responding. There are no short cuts. Therapies more sophisticated than the Primal or Scream sort can create more sophisticated pressures. In the mainstream of humanistic psychology, perhaps the most pervasive concept is that of integration. The existential therapies encourage us subtly but steadily to integrate all of our experiences into a beautiful wholeness. There is no heavy push to express strong emotion, but there is a quiet, often guilt-producing expectation that we work to "become whole," to "be centered." Sometimes the underlying assumption is that any state other than wholeness, integration, or centeredness is, if not sinful, at least not so good.

Those of us who have read Eric Fromm or Abraham Maslow or Frederick Perls may unconsciously begin to judge ourselves in the light of successful self-actualization, or self-acceptance, or creative love, or other-directedness, or total communication. We may judge ourselves as failing miserably, and blame ourselves because we *should* be doing better since we know so much about it. Insight *should* be enough, just as love *should* be enough, but it isn't. We should be "integrating" those bad feelings, or "converting" our tendencies to deny reality and pain. We should be "open." With all these "shoulds" in our heads, we haven't got a chance.

Frankly Unglued

There are times in life when each of us, no matter how mature and well, is frankly unglued. We need to find a way to integrate the real disintegration within us—in other words, to release ourselves from the moral expectations of psychological growth, and simply allow ourselves the clumsiness and awkwardness of being hurt and untogether.

Each Thing in Its Own Time

The only comforting thing about being hurt and untogether is that it won't last forever.

Once when I was going through an excruciating grief process and had actually lost the ability to imagine I would ever feel better, the most important words I heard were *it won't last forever.* I didn't believe the words, but I trusted the person who kept ⌐ving them to me, and knowing that *she* believed ⌐ got me through.

I have worked with persons coping with loss at intense levels of feeling and discovery through differing situations: divorce or other kinds of death in relationships; retirement grief; unemployment; the grief of poverty; of emotional, physical, or spiritual sterility; of aging; of pregnancy, birth; of crises in parenting; the grief of sickness, and even the odd grief for loss of healthy striving that comes with success.

I myself have had occasion to grieve over the loss of one thing or another for the past nine years. I want to share with you what I have learned about the human process of grieving from observation and from experience. I want to offer you the assurance that it is possible and necessary to allow oneself to fall apart in order to be able to come together and that no part of the process can be safely ignored.

Spectacular Spring

Sometimes in my own experience I have wondered, "Will it ever end?" It seems that I am never without a loss to face, some little death I have to die in order to become reborn once again. But again and again? One wearies of so much growth! A little rest in between—that's all I ask. But no, in reality life continues to be cyclic, not a steady, dependable straight line in one direction. It is not cyclic in that we never get anywhere, but like the rest of nature, human life has its regular seasons which extend the length of a lifetime and are repeated over and over again. The encouraging part of this realization is that if I can survive winter, I will be rewarded with a proportionately spectacular spring. As Shelley wrote so truly, "If winter comes can spring be far behind?" Well, it can seem far, but it will follow eventually, and usually just as we think we've reached our limit for enduring the deprivation, misery, or just plain tedium of winter.

"To equate the apparent smothering of feelings with royal style seemed to me a marked instance of inhumanity."

Lately I have been helped by a metaphor from science. Astronomers are speaking and writing a great deal these days about Black Holes in space— invisible spots of such astounding density that an entire star or solar system may be sucked into one and promptly annihilated by its incredible compression and pressure. A terrifying possibility. No one really knows how this happens, but to complete the theory, the White Hole has been postulated. We are asked to imagine the Black Hole as an unimaginably vast and dense pressure chamber that is funnel shaped, the point of entry being the wide end of the funnel. What destruction, condensation, or transformation goes on inside the funnel is impossible to account for. What is observable is that beings and systems literally disappear. At some point, however, in the highly concentrated, invisible power chamber, activity mounts at the narrow end of the funnel and—surprise! A whole new universe explodes out the small side! The White Hole—the small end of the funnel—is the birth canal for new creations in space. The processes by which things fall into Black Holes and are transformed and pushed out the other side through White Holes, turning up as new beings in new worlds, are unfathomed as yet. But scientists believe they happen. Just so, I believe that within human experience there are spiritual counterparts to Black and White Holes.

"I'm not suggesting that one needs to 'lose control' blindly in order to grieve well."

Only by recognizing that we have somehow fallen into the annihilating space of a dense, high-powered Black Hole, and by experiencing the impact of it, can we hope eventually to be pushed out the other side into new life. This is a space-age metaphor for the age-old wisdom that only by losing yourself can you find yourself, only by dying can you be reborn.

The Validity of Control

I am not suggesting that one needs to "lose control" blindly in order to grieve well. Control is a very valuable trait. We learn self-control and control of the environment as very young children. The abilities to control ourselves and to manipulate our environment are absolutely necessary for survival and self-protection. Babies are helpless and dependent before they acquire these skills. Control becomes a problem or a barrier only when we fail to discriminate between situations in which we need to control our expressiveness and those in which to do so would not only be unnecessary, but harmful. Defenses are essential, but when we use them when they are not needed, they can hurt us.

There is a time in intense sorrow or rage when self-control can protect us from our own overwhelming feelings. And there is a time when we need to experience fully the feelings, to be controlled by them for a while, in order to become free of their destructive power in our lives and to incorporate them creatively into ourselves. In grief, there is a time when pain seems to be in control. Then there is a turning point and a time following when pain may still be there, but we are once again in charge of our lives.

To surrender to one's own grief and to become actively engaged in it require tremendous courage.

This courage is vastly different from putting up a good front, showing a cheerful face to our friends when we are really hurting. That is mere pretense, hollow bravado, and serves no good purpose, for we seldom fool our friends any more than we fool ourselves.

Real courage is owning up to the fact that we face a terrifying task, admitting that we are appropriately frightened, identifying sources of help and strength outside and within ourselves, and then going ahead and doing what needs to be done.

Grief is a passion, something that happens to us, something to endure. People can be stricken with it, victims of it, stuck in it. Or they can meet it, get through it, and become quiet victors through the honest and courageous process of grieving. The difference between being grief-stricken and grieving is the difference between remaining a passive victim and actively making use of a situation. Grief is a passion to endure, but with courage to grieve, you make it an action. Grieving is something you do.

Alla Bozarth-Campbell, Ph.D., is an Episcopal priest and therapist.

"Home care rather than a hospital or a nursing home is always possible when there is a support system available."

Dying at Home Benefits Patients and Families

Elisabeth Kübler-Ross

After five years at the University Hospital in Chicago, where I attended to dying patients and taught medical students, hospital chaplains, nurses, and social workers about the needs of dying patients—about their loneliness and about their ability to communicate if only they had a listening ear—it became clear that I had to leave. I had to leave so that others would have the courage to continue to serve and to listen to these patients, rather than to call on me for consultation. Yet only after I left the hospital did I realize that patients would continue to call, and that I was unable to visit them in hospitals where I no longer had hospital privileges.

I started to reflect on the need for loving care, with adequate pain relief, in a positive and fear-free environment. Many of my patients and their families began to realize that they actually had a choice. Very few families had considered taking their patients home to die. Rather, it was the norm to send patients to the hospital when they were close to dying. Not only was this the norm throughout society, but it was almost expected; it implied that the family had done everything possible, that nobody was to blame, that the best specialists and the best equipment were nearby when their next of kin was close to the transition. It was a different thought and a different philosophy when they were confronted with our opposite approach, namely: Take them to the hospital only as long as appropriate treatment is available, as long as more chemotherapy and radiotherapy are needed, but take them home whenever treatment has failed to bring about positive results.

We naturally used the same approach with children who had brain tumors, after other treatments, including experimental drugs, had been used. There

was a time when children themselves gave us the cues that they had had enough of all the shots, of all the bone marrow tests, of all the treatments. They wanted to go home. We were able to convey these wishes to the parents, who, often because of their own fears and their own anxieties, were unable to hear it. We showed it through the children's drawings, through their symbolic language communications. And many, many parents were able to hear the pleas of their little ones. Many a wife was able to take her husband home and many a husband was willing to take a wife home, as long as they had a support system, as long as they were able to call up somebody when they became frantic, anxious, or panicky because of some unexpected behavior or symptoms unfamiliar to the caregivers.

Supportive Challenge

We were quite aware that very few physicians make house calls. And due to my extensive traveling, it was also clear that I could not be everywhere at one time, since my patients were located anywhere from San Francisco to New York. We simply challenged the families to consider the choice of taking their dying family members home, made ourselves available, and told them on which dates I would be able to contact them either by telephone or with a private house call. We would challenge them to do it; we confronted them with their own fears and we encouraged them to mobilize their courage to try it.

The beauty of these consultations was that they required very little time. Often within half an hour the families contemplated alternatives, became aware of the possibilities of taking a patient home. They began to appreciate the advantages of a familiar environment and also far less expensive care to their loved ones, the possibility of their physical, constant presence, and the most important fact that they— family and patient—actually had a choice.

After we discussed the matter with the terminally ill, many patients and families were willing to take a chance and discussed the matter with the treating physician. They often mobilized friends and neighbors to help them with the move back to their houses, with the changing experience, with the supply of an oxygen tent or a suction machine or a bed that is easily movable with a rubber ring. They found the help they needed to turn any living room into a comfortable sickroom.

The children in a household were perhaps most affected by this change, as many of the children had not seen their terminally ill Mommies and Daddies for weeks when they were away at hospitals. The joy was overwhelming when they realized that "Mommy is coming home once more." They were prepared for the fact that Mommy looked a little different, that Mommy was not able to do things for them anymore, or walk around. They were taught not to make too much noise, not to slam doors, and not to watch television unless they asked Mommy for permission first. But these little shortcomings and adjustments that the children had to make were more than compensated by the presence of their Mommy, who was still able to stroke their hair, who was still able to wave to them, to touch them and hold their hands and smile at them, able sometimes to shed a tear.

"It is important that family members continue to live, that they not wean themselves from all other relationships."

Many children were held in Mommy's arms and again and again said, "Mommy, I'm so happy you're home." The most important thing, no matter how ill a parent is, is for a child to be near his or her mother or father, to have them physically close and not isolated and away at a hospital where children can never visit.

Children will even become cooks and servants and nursemaids. Little Rusty became a medical technician for his little sister, Jamie, and was able to take care of the suction machine and the oxygen tent. Contributing to the care of a little sister and also relieving the mother can give a child a tremendous sense of achievement. It became important to emphasize this to families and to make them realize that one person alone can never take care of a terminally ill patient, that it takes a minimum of two people in order for life to continue as naturally and as normally as possible.

The wife of a terminally ill man was encouraged to continue to go to the hairdresser once a week if she did that before the illness. A man was encouraged to go bowling with his friends once a week if that's what he did prior to his wife's illness. It is important

that family members continue to live, that they do not wean themselves from all other relationships, since the loss would be enormous and that would make the restarting (after a death had occurred) far more difficult. Children should be allowed to bring friends home, even though they may have to play quietly in another room. We have encouraged them to talk with the patients, whether they are siblings, parents, or grandparents, about anything they want to talk about, including the impending death or funeral arrangements. They have discussed these things with their dying Mommies and Daddies, with their brothers and sisters, and sometimes even with grandmas and grandpas, who seemed to be more reluctant to talk about them.

Children often finish the unfinished business for parents. Such a situation occurred in the house of a terminally ill mother. Her husband was no longer able to tolerate the situation and in an expression of impotent rage and anguish, he hollered at her that he was sorry he had ever married her, that he would put the children into foster homes and that he would think about it twice before he married again. He left his 28-year-old wife in tears and agony in the hospital, totally despondent and feeling unable to do anything for her children, one and five years old. A girl friend who visited her became aware of this disaster, pleaded with the physician to discharge this young dying woman, and called me for a consultation. I prepared the husband to take his young wife home in order to finish their unfinished business. He was more than appreciative, and he cooperated. I then sat with the one-year-old and the five-year-old at the kitchen table asking the five-year-old to draw a picture and to tell me all about Mommy's illness and her dying.

On the second evening after the patient's return home, I made another house call and we decided also to invite the patient's parents, who had a bad relationship with their daughter and who had their own private problems not related to their young daughter's impending death. The mother was a hypochondriac and the father had been an alcoholic for 15 years, almost incommunicative with wife and daughter and rejected by the family, all of whom were alienated from him. Their idea was that they were too "weak" and unable to stand the stress of watching their daughter's death. I was of a different opinion. I believed that they had the right to be with their one and only daughter, and that it might give them the strength to overcome their own weaknesses.

Chance to Repair Relationships

As it turned out, we were able to put the patient under the living room window in a comfortable bed. I was sitting with the one-year-old and the five-year-old on my lap in front of her, her husband on my left, and her mother on my right. Automatically and without thinking, her mother reached out and put her arm over her husband's shoulder. He was very touched and moved by this unexpected closeness; he reached out to his daughter, who was holding her husband's hand, and without planning or rehearsing anything, we suddenly became a circle of human beings surrounding this young woman at the time of her premature but beautiful and peaceful death.

A few hours before her death, she opened her eyes and looked smiling at her family and at us holding her children on our lap. It was at this moment that the five-year-old started to verbalize all the unspoken words that the grownups were unable to share. She looked at her Mommy and then at me and said suddenly, "Dr. Kubler-Ross, do you think it's all right if I pray to God tonight that he can take my Mommy?"

I told her it would be all right, that God would understand and listen to her prayers. After a moment of thought she turned around again and said, "I hope He doesn't mind if I add another prayer after that and tell Him to send her back again." I told her that she could say anything that she wanted to God, that He would hear and understand, but that she could be sure that she would see her Mommy again. But she also had to understand that in the place where Mommy was going time was very different from our time, and though she would certainly see her Mommy again, it would not be tomorrow or the day after tomorrow. After a few moments of reflection, this little girl looked again at Mommy and then said, "If this Mommy dies, does that mean that I'm going to get a foster mother?"

Silently the young mother touched her husband's hand, expressing her concern about their short and painful marriage to one another and encouraging him to go ahead and marry another woman if he should find one who truly loved him and who could bring him more happiness than they had in their short marriage together. By then, they all had tears in their eyes. The five-year-old continued, undisturbed by the turmoil of the grownups. She asked, "If all my Mommies die, who's going to cook for me?"

"Those children will never associate death with loneliness, isolation, playing games, and deceit."

I laughed and told her that I had a big kitchen and if all her Mommies should die, which was highly improbable, she could always move into my house and I would always love to cook for her. She put her warm, cuddly arms around me and gave me a big hug. A little while later we asked her to kiss her Mommy goodnight and we tucked the two children into bed shortly before ten o'clock. A neighbor

brought me home an hour later, and shortly before midnight I received a telephone call that the young mother had died peacefully in her sleep. Not only were we able to prevent a guilt-ridden, grief-stricken widower who would have had a hard time starting a new life and eventually getting remarried, but we were able to help two young children to be present at one of the most important moments in life, namely at the time of their mother's transition, shared with three generations.

Everyone's Opportunity

With her favorite music playing, with candlelight on the table, with the children near, and with flowers next to her picked by her own children, she died a very different kind of death than had she stayed in the hospital. Those children will never associate death with loneliness, isolation, playing games, and deceit. They will remember it as a time of togetherness with their parents, grandparents, and friends who cared and were able to acknowledge their own anxieties and their own fears, and together were able to overcome them.

After having witnessed a few deaths like this in a home, it became very clear that every person has such an opportunity. Home care rather than a hospital or a nursing home is always possible when there is a support system available. And it requires very little time on our part to be the facilitator and the catalyst of such a constructive, positive choice.

Elisabeth Kübler-Ross is a psychiatrist and world-renowned authority on death and dying. She is the author of the best-selling book On Death and Dying *which not only influenced professional and private attitudes toward death but spawned a whole new science of thanatology.*

"Hospice treatment...emphasizes relieving the physical and emotional suffering of the incurably ill and their families."

Home Hospice Care Allows Patient Independence

Milt Freudenheim

The hospice movement, just a decade old in America, is growing dramatically as a way to take care of the terminally ill.

The first American hospice began operating 10 years ago in New Haven. Today 600 hospice organizations are treating patients across the country; 700 more are in developmental or planning stages.

Hospice treatment, which emphasizes relieving the physical and emotional suffering of the incurably ill and their families, is administered at the patient's home rather than in a hospital, whenever possible. Hospices also arrange for household help, shopping trips, and visits from volunteers.

A week ago, after a demonstration project that began in 1980, hospices were officially added to the Federal Medicare system. Medicare money is expected to mean further expansion, but directors of many hospices are concerned that payment ceilings and other requirements may force changes that could undermine the concept.

'Closer to the Hearth'

The rapid growth in hospices reflects moral, social and material concerns. "Many Americans became aware of gaps in the health system in meeting humanistic as well as medical needs," said Louise Bracknell, executive director of the National Hospice Association. "They read articles about hospices and went out and organized them in their own communities. There has been a trend of wanting to get closer to the hearth in sickness and death, perhaps because the rest of life is so complicated."

Barbara McCann of the Joint Commission on Accreditation of Hospitals emphasized "the growing awareness within cancer care that there is a point at which palliation is the appropriate treatment."

Val J. Halamandaris, president of the National Association for Home Care, said Elisabeth Kubler-Ross's books on dealing with death were influential. "Moral and humane treatment of the elderly also became an issue after the New York nursing home scandals," he said. On the economic side, Blue Cross plans started several pilot hospice programs five years ago that pointed to major cost savings.

For a patient to qualify for Medicare hospice benefits, a physician must certify that life expectancy is no more than six months. Ninety percent of hospice patients have cancer.

"The whole basis is to help the patients to stay in their homes," said Mary A. Cooke, hospice director at Cabrini Medical Center, 227 East 19th Street in Manhattan. "They don't want to be institutionalized; they want to be at home. Our emphasis is on helping the family take care of the patient."

Volunteers Come to Chat

Fay Zaldin, a Cabrini hospice patient who is 74 years old, says she has had cancer for many years, which lately became life-threatening. Her husband died in September. "I didn't want to be a burden to anybody," Mrs. Zaldin said. "I looked around for a hospice."

Cabrini sends two volunteers to visit her in the comfortable Chelsea apartment where she has lived for 22 years. Ingrid Ganga Stone and Jane Bhadra Helsel, friends who work together in a midtown vegetarian restaurant, come to chat, shop for Mrs. Zaldin and arrange treats. "They took me out yesterday," she said. "We went by cab to see a movie. I haven't done anything like that in a long time."

A home health aide comes three hours a day to clean and cook. "She is learning to cook Jewish dishes," Mrs. Zaldin said. "I was pretty depressed for a while. That's the worst. I've gotten over that."

Miss Cooke, the hospice director, said that in line

with the emphasis on relieving pain, morphine is used in the great majority of cases. "It is very effective," she said, recalling that in her career as a nurse before the advent of hospice care, "we did not use it; it was not even discussed."

Families Treated as Well

Miss Bracknell said the hospice movement "sees the person not just as a physical being but as a social, spiritual and psychological being, with needs in all of those areas."

"We treat the patient and the family as a unit," she said. "At the most vulnerable time in the patient's life, we bring the health system to them. A happy consequence is that hospices are also cost-efficient."

A study published in September by the Case Western University School of Medicine and Blue Cross of Northeast Ohio reported that hospice care resulted in "relative savings of approximately 40 percent," largely because patients getting conventional cancer care were hospitalized more often.

To qualify for Federal certification and Medicare payment, hospice programs must provide in-patient beds, a requirement usually met in a hospital, but 80 percent of the patients, on average, must be at home. "The objective of in-patient acute care," Miss Cooke said, "is to help them to go back home, to stabilize their illness so the family can take over."

"The hospice movement 'sees the person not just as a physical being but as a social, spiritual and psychological being, with needs in all of those areas.'"

Medicare will pay $46.25 a day for routine home care, with adjustments for regional wage scales; $271 a day for in-patient care, and $358.67 for continuous home care for patients in acute phases of illness. A maximum of $6,500 may be spent per patient. The hospice remains responsible for a patient even if Medicare does not cover the bills. It must make up the difference from other sources, such as donations.

Problems in Inner City

The requirement of having 80 percent of the patients at home creates problems for Sister Patrice O'Connor, director of St. Luke's-Roosevelt Hospice, 419 West 114th Street, which serves 40 patients at a time, many of them in central Harlem.

"Many of our patients do not have a stable home environment or a stable family situation," she said. "For that reason and because of the $6,500 ceiling per patient, the program is discriminatory in an urban setting." The average cost per patient at St. Luke's has been $11,000. Hospices serving inner-city patients in Chicago and St. Louis are having the same sort of problems, according to Miss McCann of the accreditation commission.

She said 40 percent of the 1,300 hospices in operation or on the drawing boards were owned by hospitals, 18 percent were owned by home health agencies, 41 percent were independent and the rest were affiliated with nursing homes or county health departments.

"Most are small," she said. "Some in rural areas have as few as one or two patients at a time. When we surveyed them last year, nearly half reported annual budgets of less than $75,000." But some California hospices care for 70 patients at once.

New Haven's Was First

Connecticut Hospice in New Haven, one of the larger operations, was the first in the country. It opened in 1974 with the support of Yale medical faculty members who were impressed by the accomplishments of a British doctor, Cicely Saunders, at St. Christopher's Hospice in London. In 1980, the Connecticut Hospice opened its own specially designed 44-bed facility.

The administrator, Rosemary Johnson-Hurzeler, says home care is provided in 18 Connecticut cities and towns with a combined population of 500,000. Three-fourths of the costs are paid by insurers and the rest by donations, notably from the New Haven Foundation.

In Orange, Tex., 100 miles east of Houston, the Southeast Texas Hospice has a mixture of rural and small-city patients in five counties. It was started seven years ago by two nurses, Peggy McKenna and Al Brannick, the Rev. Bill Manger, pastor of St. Mary's Catholic Church, and Joan Lyons, a homemaker.

"People kept calling me to help with someone who wanted to stay at home and die," Mrs. McKenna recalled. "The major problem was poor pain control. People and families were suffering."

Mrs. McKenna's daughter Mary is the hospice administrator. The McKennas and six fellow workers are paid for only a portion of their time. A physician donates his services. There are 66 other volunteers.

Mary McKenna criticized the new Medicare payment rate of $46.25 for routine home care, a cut from the $53.17 the Reagan Administration announced in August. "I think the Administration has taken the heart out of hospice by reducing the home care rates," she said. "I really thought the Medicare law would pay for things we do so we could pay for the doctor."

More Contributions Needed

Carolyn Fitzpatrick, president of the National Hospice Association, runs the Good Samaritan Hospice in Battle Creek, Mich., which cared for more than 44 percent of the people who died of cancer in its area last year. She, too, criticized the new Medicare rates. "At $53 a day," she said, "we would have to go to the community to raise about 10 percent of our $530,000 budget for home care. At $46.25, we will have to raise $59,000 more, a total of nearly $1 for every person in our community."

In New York City, Barbara Ward, director of the extended-care program at the Visiting Nurse Service, is also concerned. "It is going to be very tight," she said, but she plans to apply for state and Federal certification and hospice benefits. Donations will have to make up the difference.

"Ten hospices in New York State are applying for Federal certification," Sister Patrice of Cabrini said. "At this point, we are not" because of the requirement that 80 percent of the patients be treated at home.

"People kept calling me to help with someone who wanted to stay at home and die."

Representative Leon E. Panetta, Democrat of California, a sponsor of the new hospice law, said, "These low payment rates may discourage participation, thus undermining the new hospice program." He and a co-sponsor, Representative Bill Gradison, Republican of Ohio, said they would consider legislation to raise the rates.

Margaret M. Heckler, the Secretary of Health and Human Services, said the Medicare payment rates were based on new information covering 4,000 patients that indicated the reduced amount would be adequate. Mr. Gradison said Mrs. Heckler had not made that data available and that he and Mr. Panetta wanted to review it.

Milt Freudenheim is a journalist for The New York Times.

"One of the unique features of hospice is that the focus of care is not on the patient alone, but the patient and her family."

viewpoint 60

Institutional Hospices Offer Comfort and Care

Laurence Cherry

Last June should have been a happy time for Lenore Todd (the name has been changed). Attractive and gifted, she eagerly looked forward to graduating from Columbia University Law School in New York and embarking on a promising career as a criminal lawyer. But what might have been the happiest of times became the most bitter when, a few months before her twenty-eighth birthday, Lenore was diagnosed as having incurable cancer.

At St. Luke's/Roosevelt Hospital Center she was far from the ideal patient. Sullen and angry, she gradually alienated almost all the members of the staff during her weeks in the hospital. Shunned and disliked even by fellow patients for her temperamental outbursts, she would likely have become increasingly isolated—if it had not been for St. Luke's Hospice Program, created in 1975 to specifically help the terminally ill.

"We realized it was quite natural for Lenore to be bitter at the world, at life, at everything," says Sister Patrice O'Connor, the program's coordinator. "Who of us wouldn't have been, in her place? Our goals were simply to make sure that she suffered as little pain as possible, and if we could, to help her deal with her anger." Eventually, members of the hospice team were able to achieve both aims. They visited Lenore daily, treating her without pity but with friendly openness, helping her to come to terms with her approaching death. At her request, telephone calls were made for her to distant relatives, letters written to friends, and, after several efforts, the team was able to alleviate the symptom that bothered her most: the odor from her cancerous leg. At an impromptu birthday party held for her in her room one day during the Memorial Day weekend, Lenore suddenly announced she had something to say to the

hospice team. "Somehow you've made me able to face the end," she said, as she held up a glass of champagne that one of the members had poured for her. "I want to thank you for putting up with me. I lift my glass to all of you." Three days later, Lenore slipped into a coma and died peacefully, surrounded by a few members of the hospice team whom she had come to think of as caring friends rather than mere professional attendants.

Change in Attitudes Toward the Dying

Only a short while ago, dying patients such as Lenore would likely have been discreetly installed in isolated hospital rooms, so that their deaths would not depress or "disturb" others around them. As terminal patients, they probably would have found that hospital staffs politely but quite unmistakably avoided them—since their illnesses, being incurable, would likely have seemed an implicit association of medical failure. "Until recently, dying was too often a nasty, painful and solitary business for all too many people," says Josefina Magno, M.D., the executive director of the National Hospice Organization, headquartered in McLean, Virginia. "Happily, that's beginning to change."

Death is a fact of life for all of us, no matter what our age. And most of us, while remaining healthy ourselves, are still affected by the deaths of our friends and relatives. For almost all of us, then, hospices are vitally important institutions.

The word itself derives from an old term for a way station for travelers, a place for replenishment and care during a long journey. In 1967, St. Christopher's, the first modern hospice for the dying, was opened in the outskirts of London. The (then) startling premise of St. Christopher's was that no dying person need remain in chronic pain; modern medicine has enough potent analgesics to abolish discomfort in the vast majority of patients, while allowing them to remain lucid almost until the day of death. As important, the goal at St. Christopher's was to make sure that the dying did not end their days in emotional pain. This was considered to be as important as ending their physical suffering.

Elisabeth Kübler Ross

At about the same time, a startling change in attitudes toward the dying was taking place in this country—largely thanks to the efforts of Swiss-born psychiatrist Elisabeth Kubler-Ross, M.D. Approached by a group of students who asked her help in conducting what was then a highly unique study about terminally ill patients, Dr. Kubler-Ross suggested a series of conversations with dying patients, who could simply be asked to discuss their thoughts and feelings. To her surprise, many of the doctors to whom she turned for help at the University of Chicago's Billings Hospital flatly refused her permission to see their patients. Talking about dying with people who were terminally ill would be useless and far too upsetting, they claimed. And yet, as Dr. Kubler-Ross soon discovered when a few physicians allowed her access to their patients, most of the dying were almost pathetically eager to talk. Isolated, frightened, many confided that they felt caught up in a useless charade, pretending to be ignorant about their true condition so that their families and hospital staff would not recoil from their despair. In 1969, Dr. Kubler-Ross published her now classic work, *On Death and Dying*, which soon became almost required reading for many medical experts around the country, and which clearly demonstrated the need for new approaches to handling the terminally ill.

"Somehow you've made me able to face the end."

But how to go about setting up an American hospice with a new attitude toward the dying, when so many physicians seemed opposed to such a "morbid" preoccupation? A small but stubborn group was determined to try, and in 1971 Hospice Inc., now The Connecticut Hospice, opened in New Haven. The new hospice soon began to have a striking impact on the lives—and deaths—of those who came to it for help. A year after he retired, for example, Bob Gery's sixty-four-year-old father was told that he had inoperable cancer of the pancreas. "He was bitter," Bob recalled. "He argued with my mother. He argued with me . . . with my wife, things that in normal health would be considered just small things. At first I kept saying, 'Dad, how can you treat Mom like this?'"

Admitted to the Hospice in New Haven, the dying man was soon able to emerge from the terrible depression into which the gloomy diagnosis had plunged him. The staff told him that "how he chose to die over the next several months depended on him and on what they could do for him, *if* he let them," reports Gery. Gradually, the man's attitude began to improve, relieving the enormous emotional burden his family had suffered. "Hospice gave us hope in a time of no hope," says Gery. "It allowed us to put ourselves together, all of us.. . . My Dad said things to me that he'd probably never have said before. He told me, 'I love you. I love your mother and brother and I want you to go on doing that too. I want you to tell them that because I've never had the chance.'" Reconciled to his fate, and without suffering, Gery's father died on May 11, 1976.

Cheerful Setting

In 1980, The Connecticut Hospice moved to a newly constructed building in Branford. Containing 44 beds, it seems closer to the cozy atmosphere of a home than a hospital. On a visit there not long ago, I saw hospice patients sunning themselves on the patio, while the brightly colored rooms were alive with cheerful conversation. Patients' families— including young children—are free to come and go at all hours, not needing to abide by the rigid visiting hours imposed by most hospitals. Fireplaces, pantries and washer-dryers were all in use, and patients and their relatives relaxed in greenhouse areas attached to their rooms, easily accessible even if the patients were in a bed or wheelchair.

Obviously, places such as The Connecticut Hospice can accommodate only a tiny number of the terminally ill (and in its case, primarily Connecticut residents). But fortunately, there are now many other hospices elsewhere (more than eight hundred) that can provide the same kind of considerate expert care, says Dr. Magno. A former cancer patient herself, the Philippine-born Dr. Magno had a mastectomy operation in 1972. After watching the agony of fellow cancer victims, Magno, the mother of seven children, decided to use whatever time she had left to work with the hospice movement.

Since then, she's discovered that to control pain in the dying, it's necessary to maintain a level of analgesics in the body that can control pain without clouding consciousness. "We want someone who's completely pain-free, but completely alert," she says. "That's the only way anyone can be meaningful to anyone, including herself. Physical suffering can destroy many people."

Not "Charnel Houses"

One unpleasant stereotype that hospices must still overcome is the idea that they're "charnel houses," places of death, from which return to normal life is impossible. Even some doctors share this view. "To be referred to a hospice is a death sentence," wrote Donald L. Sweet, M.D., of the University of Chicago

School of Medicine to the prestigious *New England Journal of Medicine* not long ago. However, others disagree. "If anything, hospices prolong life, by giving patients the best medical attention and by counteracting distressing symptoms," says Daniel C. Hadlock, M.D., former medical director of a New Jersey hospice and past-president of the National Hospice Organization, now with Hospice, Inc., in Miami. "According to most authorities, for example, an adult with acute leukemia should die within four months. The *shortest* survival time we saw in the New Jersey hospice was eight months." And although the official criterion for admission to most hospices is that the patient be expected to survive only six months, nearly one out of ten of the New Jersey hospice's patients were eventually discharged with their distress under control. "A hospice is definitely not the kind of place where you tell patients, 'Abandon hope, all ye who enter here,'" says Dr. Hadlock. "In my experience—and I'm hearing this from other hospice physicians all around the country—distress can kill just as effectively as disease. If you can get the distress under control, you can really work wonders."

Another common misconception is that all patients who come to hospices will be continually reminded that they are dying. This is a particular concern of families who've kept the prognosis of impending death from relatives whom they fear may not be able to cope with it. "But we're not trying to force anyone to face something he or she doesn't want to," says Dr. Hadlock. "We sound them out very carefully. If you have a sense that you're trespassing, that they don't want to know anything about their condition, of course you draw back."

But more often than not, nearly everyone underestimates the dying person's ability to confront the fact of her approaching death. "Most people are not afraid of death itself, but they *are* frightened of the process of dying," Dr. Hadlock told me. "They want to know what's going to happen to them along the way, to be assured they'll be listened to, cared for when they need it. And the other things that worry them most are very practical, down-to-earth problems: Who will support their wife, take care of their kids after they're gone? That's where the hospice team can really make a difference, by finding answers to those pressing concerns." For Mrs. Gregory (not her real name), a patient at the hospice, her main concern was about her only child, a daughter who had just given birth to an illegitimate child. The girl and her boyfriend were planning to marry, but Mrs. Gregory, realizing that she had only a short time to live, insisted the date be pushed up. "We sat down with the couple and said, 'Are you sure you're doing this for yourselves and not for her?'" Dr. Hadlock remembers. "The girl then had a wedding, and a christening for the child, and her

mother was able to attend. She saw people she hadn't spoken to in years. She got her affairs in order, and when the end came, it was very peaceful. She felt that her daughter and grandchild had somehow been taken care of."

A Concept, Not a Place

Perhaps because of the worldwide publicity that St. Christopher's has attracted, most people tend to think of hospices as institutions, separate buildings. "But actually, hospice is far more a concept of care than a place," says Dr. Magno. "And the concept can take many different forms." Both The Connecticut Hospice and St. Christopher's in England are "free-standing": separate institutions exclusively concerned with caring for the dying. Other hospice programs, such as the one at St. Luke's, are "scattered bed"—instead of a separate wing or floor. Hospice patients are scattered among the hospital's various departments, and the team makes daily rounds to visit them. "Hospice also means homecare, whenever appropriate," says Dr. Magno. "I think most people, if given the choice, would prefer to die in their own home surrounded by their family and possessions.

"If anything, hospices prolong life, by giving patients the best medical attention and by counteracting distressing symptoms."

We try to make that possible whenever we can. It may mean the team makes daily visits, or sometimes even sends in people to help out both day and night."

Not uncommonly, a family may simply not be able to provide that total care that a dying relative needs. "I think few people can imagine how exhausting that kind of care can be, both physically and emotionally," says Dr. Magno. "I've had family members tell me, 'Jo, I simply can't take it any more. It's become too much for me to handle.' And there's no reason in the world why they should feel guilty. But at that point you have to explore other options."

The family of twenty-five-year-old Jane Zorza reached such a point in 1978. Two years earlier, Jane had noticed an ugly, puffy, black-purple lump about the size of a coin just above her middle toe. Although diagnosed as melanoma, a particularly pernicious form of skin cancer, it was easily removed, and all seemed well. But then, a few months later, while working in Greece, Jane suddenly noticed a small white lump in her groin. Back in England, it was diagnosed as malignant. Silently but now unmistakably, the disease had spread through her body.

"It was as if the word 'cancer' was a hammer blow that had smashed the pattern of our lives into little pieces," write the Zorzas in their recent book, *A Way To Die*. "I don't want to die," Jane told them. In her diary, she revealed a fear so close to panic that, in a strangely paradoxical reaction, she seriously contemplated suicide. "I don't want to have cancer," she wrote. "I don't want pain. . . ."

Hellish Journey

From then on there followed a hellish journey through useless treatments, horrifying pain, family misery, until finally, by accident, Rosemary Zorza remembered an article she'd read about hospices. "It isn't a hospital or a nursing home, it's more like a real home," she told her daughter. "The article said they treated everyone like people, not just patients, and looked after them with love and compassion."

Jane's doctor helped arrange admission into a hospice, and once she was there, things suddenly seemed to fall into place. "We were at the hospice, we had been expected, and, it seemed, were welcome," say the Zorzas. "We still inhabited a world of pain, but we were no longer isolated in it." One of Jane's main fears was of being left alone—and the hospice team arranged that one member or one of her parents remain with her at all times. Very slowly, she began to discuss with the hospice team her fears of dying, and something of their own matter-of-fact, unflinching attitude toward death seemed to be transmitted to her. "For us, the memory is not pain and anguish, but of her calm smile and peace of mind," her parents say. "Jane was ready for what she knew must come, accepted it with a serenity that belied her early fears." Of course, by no means do all hospice patients achieve that calm, but when the Zorzas stood beside their daughter's bed and watched the last breath gently leave her body, they felt no devastating sorrow.

"More often than not, nearly everyone underestimates the dying person's ability to confront the fact of her approaching death."

One of the unique features of hospice is that the focus of care is not on the patient alone, but the patient *and* her family. "You find the families are full of unanswered questions," says Dr. Magno. "Doctors, nurses simply don't have time to handle them. So they're left to wonder: Will their relatives smother to death, will there be much bleeding or pain or disfigurement? That should all be explained to them. And we have to take the time to help them too, to find out what *their* needs are." Dr. Magno remembers a frantic call from a dying patient in the middle of the night. He was in agonizing pain: Could

she come to his home and do something to relieve it? She arrived a half-hour later, and after easing his pain, turned to his wife and asked, "How are *you?*" To her surprise, the woman burst into tears and said, "Doctor, that's the first time in all these horrible months that someone's asked how *I* am."

Treatment for Family

The strain shows on family members in many ways. "You find all kinds of stress-related problems cropping up," says Jane L. Hoskovec, administrator of the St. Mary's Hospital for Children in New York, which is developing the first hospice in the country for dying children under the age of sixteen. "Many patients' parents get divorced, many siblings develop emotional problems. That has to become one of the hospice team's concerns, too."

Most hospice programs maintain contact with families of dying patients for more than a year after their relative has died. "We usually contact the family the day the patient dies, at the end of the first week, and then during the third week of bereavement," says Sister Patrice O'Connor. "We follow them over the course of a year, helping them whenever we can, and the case stays open as long as the family needs us. Some of them visit us regularly, and, of course, we always make time for them."

Probably the most important reason for the success of hospices in both Britain and the U.S. is the very high caliber of most hospice team members. "We have to screen them very carefully," says Sister Patrice O'Connor. "We have a rule about not hiring anyone who's had a loss within the past year—and the loss can be anything from a death in the family to a divorce." Other hospice experts told me that they are careful not to include people who want to see themselves as "angels of mercy" or need, as Dr. Magno puts it, "to work out their own problems through the illnesses of others." The reason for a well-adjusted staff is obvious: The stress of caring for the dying can be enormous. At The Connecticut Hospice, there's a special sound-proofed "screaming room" where hospice members can go to release their pent-up anger, frustration or sorrow.

Reliance on Volunteers

Nearly every hospice program heavily relies on its volunteers, as important to the team as its doctors or nurses. "In a pediatric hospice like ours, you obviously need people who genuinely like children—which some people don't," says Jane Hoskovec. "And you need volunteers who genuinely enjoy helping other people." Sometimes that good will can be put to a severe test. "Some of our patients and their families are very demanding, and the volunteers have to be very dedicated to put up with it," says Dr. Magno. The helpers come from all social circles, from all walks of life. Dr. Magno remembers the time that the very demanding wife of a hospice patient who had just died decided to have a party for the mourners who would be arriving for the funeral. She preemptorily ordered the wife of famous Admiral Hyman Rickover, a hospice home-care volunteer, to clean up her very large house. "Mrs. Rickover rolled up her shirtsleeves and cleaned up the whole house without a word of protest," says Dr. Magno. "Our volunteers are wonderful people—they really will do everything that's needed."

"Obviously, with so many hospices now open, there are variations in the excellence of the care being provided."

Despite its obvious success in helping the dying, the hospice movement is still criticized by some physicians and some legislators. One objection is cost. "Some people say: Why take care of the dying, when money could be better spent on those who can be cured?" reports Dr. Hadlock. "After all, hospice teams are on call twenty-four hours a day, which means more money. We run support groups for families after their relatives die—which adds to the cost. Everybody's asking about expense, from medical insurance companies to politicians. And the statistics to justify what we do are only just coming in." One study in 1979 of the hospice program at George Washington University Medical Center in Washington, D.C., indicated it cost only $141 a day to care for a hospice patient compared with a hospitalization tab of $300 a day.

The attitude of many medical insurers is nevertheless wary and varies from place to place. Some hospices have contracts with major carriers that covers much of the cost of running the institution; other hospices do not. "Finally, this is something that is going to have to be straightened out, to be standardized," says one hospice expert.

About Living as Well as Dying

Yet another concern is about the quality of care patients receive. Obviously, with so many hospices now open, there are variations in the excellence of the care being provided. "I've seen one or two places where the attitude of the staff could have been better," one hospice expert told me privately. "Now that hospice care will be paid for by (insurance) carriers, the same people who brought us nursing homes will soon be in the hospice business," wrote one concerned physician to *The New England Journal of Medicine* not long ago. "There is no way to assure quality. Profit will become the motivation." Dr. Hadlock admits to his own worries. "I think people have a right to be cautious," he says. "There is a danger that this may just be another trendy fashion—and that profiteers will get involved. It's something

we have to watch." The National Hospice Organization has published standards and is developing accreditation documents. The Association of Hospice Physicians has also been established.

"One woman told me, 'I used to be afraid of dying—afraid that I'd be in pain, and be alone. But now that hospice is here I'm not afraid anymore,'" recalls Dr. Magno. Dr. Magno continues: "Can you imagine what that gives millions of people? It makes their lives so much easier. And that's really our main concern, our chief task. Hospice is really as much about living as it is about dying."

Laurence Cherry is a New York-based freelance writer.

Therapeutic Relationships Also Help the Therapist

Charles A. Garfield

Most would readily agree that from an experiential point of view that we, the living, know little of death or the process of dying. Yet, as health-care professionals who work with the terminally ill, we often collude in the belief that we are experts in the psychosocial issues surrounding life-threatening illness. This somewhat illusory expertise often translates in practice into an attempt at hyper-efficiency in biomedical duties, the use of heavy sedation to reduce severe pain but also to diminish the likelihood of having to relate to emotional needs expressed by the patient, and diminished contact with and withdrawal from the patient using the rationale "we've done all we can do." The basic and often unacknowledged premise is that dying is a biological process demanding biomedical intervention. As death approaches and treatment toward improved health is no longer a possibility, staff may initially adopt a more rigid, inaccessible posture especially with more assertive patients who express their emotional needs. The dying patient is clearly not a neutral element in the psychosocial field of the health-care professional. At times, the extreme anxiety of physician or nurse becomes the major issue in the relationship between staff member and patient. Dying is not solely a biological or even psychobiological set of events and experiences. The social or interpersonal concomitants of the dying process, which impact powerfully on patient and health-care professional alike, expose the fact that we are dealing with a sociopsychobiological process with extensions to the religious realm. However, we rarely consider the impact on the professional of intensive or extensive contact with the dying. What follows is a personal case history of my initial encounter with a dying patient. The data were journal notations written throughout the death trajectory and reexamined after 5 years of research and clinical work with dying individuals. These writings constitute as powerful an introspective exercise as I have ever done.

To Be with One Who Is Dying

All I could hear was my father singing "Sunrise, sunset, sunrise, sunset, swiftly go the years." Over and over this seemingly endless refrain pounded through my head as I left the hospital. Periodically, it mixed with the Tibetan mantrum "Om Mani Padme Hum," my fifth grade teacher singing "America the Beautiful," or Mick Jagger shrieking "I can't get no satisfaction." Larry had just died. This was the first time in my work with cancer patients that I was forced to confront the death of someone with whom I had shared many hours. I walked around the university campus the rest of that day wondering why no one else understood what had happened. It seemed outrageously bizarre that everyone else, in uniforms as diverse as professional-looking white coats and jeans a la Haight-Ashbury "street freakery," was not attending to the monumental event that had just occurred.

I had met Larry 2 months before, following a psychological consultant request from his physician. The request stated simply, "Patient having problems dealing with emotional aspects of malignancy." I imagine so! Since then I've received many similar requests and have always wondered how bizarre they seemed. For instance, what would be the reverse? "Patient having no problems dealing with emotional aspects of malignancy"? Then I might truly be concerned. It appears strange that anyone would even question the existence of strong feelings connected with so monumental a process as an advanced cancer. In work with both inpatients and outpatients I have rarely encountered an individual with cancer who did not at times manifest powerful

Charles A. Garfield, "Impact of Death on the Health-Care Professional," from *New Meanings of Death* edited by Herman Feifel. McGraw-Hill Book Company, copyright © 1977. Reprinted with permission.

and often painfully disorienting emotional reactions. What I have seen frequently are well-intentioned but overburdened medical and nursing personnel without the time or psychological expertise necessary to assess accurately the emotional status of their patients.

In some settings, when a psychiatric or psychological consultant is requested, a different drama unfolds. The mental health professional, encumbered by psychotherapeutic systems usually requiring extended therapeutic processes over time, may fail miserably with the patient who has a limited life span. With rapid changes in physiological status, body image, and mood resulting from both the disease and its treatment, interpersonal consistency tends to be the exception rather than the rule. To assess this as psychopathology is frequently nonsense, since it is often an appropriate response by the patient to an extreme stressor. To pretend that we, the professional staff, would not respond similarly, given the same diagnosis and contextual demands, is harmfully naive. What appears true, despite the reality of our time pressures and biomedical duties, is that we ourselves are not psychologically comfortable around the dying and may resort to extreme psychological defensive postures, i.e., denial, intellectualization at case conferences, etc., to avoid meaningful relationships with our patients.

Who Helps Whom?

I think my ability to work with people such as Larry is directly related to the degree to which I risk being emotionally accessible to them. This work continually forces me to confront fears about my own death and to realize that my primary data are secured by trusting the patient as an accurate source of information. The largest single impediment to providing effective emotional support to the dying is the powerful professional staff distinction between *us* and *them*. It is a deeply conditioned and tradition-bound assumption in the hospital context that *we* are the professionals and you are the patients, and *we* will help you out of our technological mastery and beneficence. This distinction is most unfortunate. With regard to emotional reactions to life-threatening illness, *we* are literally *they*. We use all our bio-medical and psychological sophistication to facilitate healing, but then what? For myself, it is to imagine "my" experience, feelings, thoughts, and emotional needs as patient in the same demanding situation; to share even if minimally the pain, confusion, and insight resulting from yet another human encounter with death. Whenever a professional colleague tells me, "I can't get emotionally involved," I think, "How unfortunate," and wonder to myself "How long has this horrid affliction persisted?" To identify emotionally with a person(s) under duress to the point of being dysfunctional is of little help to

anyone. However, to deny any emotional connection is violence. I understood Larry's plight as well as I did because I could imagine my own response in the same situation. When I was confused about how best to help him, I'd immediately confer with Larry. My skills as a clinical psychologist are, of course, a tremendous asset, but the issues revolve more around human authenticity than professional expertise. I've learned since my work with Larry that a primary assumption in working with seriously ill cancer patients is that there are always emotional issues and that people trained to be sensitive to these issues can be an enormous help. Patients with "emotional difficulties related to malignancy" are the norm, certainly not the exception.

"The largest single impediment to providing effective emotional support to the dying is the powerful professional staff distinction between us *and* them.*"*

My initial reaction to Larry was one of surprise. Here was a man sitting stripped to the waist with a muscular body and appearing at least as strong as I. The difference was that Larry had a presumed diagnosis of childhood leukemia. We spoke for some time, and I learned that Larry was an ex-Marine, 20 years old, who had spent a great deal of time distancing himself emotionally and psychologically from his family. He had been somewhat of a rebel all his life and had joined the Marines on a bet. Two of Larry's major problem areas were (1) the fact that although he had been told that there was a 75 percent cure rate for his form of childhood leukemia, he was not feeling well; although he was receiving positive feedback from his physician and the nursing staff concerning his medical condition, he did not feel the improvement, and (2) his relationship to his family. Channels for communication on an intimate level had never been established. Larry's life experience thus far had been based on an extended adolescent rebellion. Now, however, he was sick, frightened, and needed his family desperately but was without the interpersonal skills and the insight needed to establish communication. The reverse was also true. There was no one in Larry's nuclear family who could openly and honestly relate to him.

We spoke about both of these issues, and I decided that I could do something very concrete concerning (1). I would consult with Larry's physician and find out if he had any ideas. First, I decided to check Larry's chart. Much to my dismay, I discovered that 2 weeks before Larry's diagnosis had been changed to acute adult leukemia, and that his prognosis was now very poor. Larry had not been informed of this change in diagnosis. He was still operating on the old assumption that there was a 75 percent chance of cure for his form of "childhood leukemia," and that he would be up-and-around in several weeks. This seemed outrageously unfair, and when I mentioned this to Larry's physician, he responded, "I just started this rotation. It's not my responsibility to tell him. It should have been done by his previous physician." I was unable to accept this response, and in further discussion with the physician I volunteered to tell Larry about the change in his diagnosis. Larry's new physician was a young, sensitive, and intelligent man who identified strongly with Larry. He realized that Larry should know about the change in diagnosis but was tremendously afraid to break the news for fear of devastating Larry (and himself!). When he saw the strong feelings I and Larry had concerning concealment of such information and recognized I was correct, he broke down, and I spent an hour in supportive psychotherapy with the physician before he was able to go in and talk to Larry. This was one of the most moving situations in which I have ever been involved.

Early in my work I learned the difficulty inherent in the physician's role. Culturally defined as a *healer*, he may be forced to resort to an extreme psychological defensive posture to deny the reality of many of the situations in which he works. That is, with regard to many forms of cancer, medical tools toward care are minimal, and the physician must face the fact that the patient will die. For a culturally defined healer, death is tantamount to failure, and the emotional consequences for the physician are often severe. Little has yet been written on the emotional impact of patient death on the physician, and yet this appears to be a vital area of inquiry.

"We ourselves are not psychologically comfortable around the dying."

We went in to see Larry together, and for 10 minutes the physician did his best to break the news. Larry was painfully aware of the inconsistency of the situation; i.e., he had never before seen his physician and me together and knew something was wrong. His heart was pounding in the manner of people and animals responding to stark terror. After this brief visit his physician left hurriedly, and I remained to deal with the emotional aftermath. Larry experienced an enormous amount of emotional upheaval. He cried and raged about not having been told the truth and was furious at the Cosmos for this horrible turn of events. Finally, after much pain, he asked me to thank his doctor for attempting to carry out what must have been a very difficult task.

From then on the nature of our work changed.

Larry was extremely intent on establishing meaningful contact with each member of his family and I suggested that we meet as a group. On the scheduled day, I arrived a few minutes late, looked in, and saw each family member standing in an opposite corner of the room as far from Larry's bed as possible. The general tone of the situation was conflictual, and I felt I had walked into the middle of an argument. I apologized, saying that I'd wait outside until their discussion was completed. Larry's mother hurriedly said, "I'd like to come out and speak with you." As soon as we left the room, she broke into tears saying that she did not know how to talk to Larry anymore. She had always felt close to him but didn't understand what was happening with his illness. She was very unsure of what to say to Larry for fear of upsetting him.

Avoiding the Fact of Death

What had developed was the kind of conspiracy of silence that often engulfs and isolates the dying. Although the family knew what was going on medically and realized the gravity of the situation, and Larry similarly understood the severity of his condition, neither party was able to discuss this information openly for fear of upsetting the "emotional equilibrium" of the other. I decided to speak with the various members of the family, discussing their feelings about Larry, his deteriorating physical condition, and ways in which they thought they could assist him. I learned from Larry's mother that she wished to be close to her son and saw this as a long-desired opportunity to breach the communication gap that existed between Larry and the other family members.

Larry's father, with whom he had never shared anything more intimate than a slap on the back and a can of beer at a football game, revealed an enormous amount of previously unexpressed feeling about his son's plight. Although he wished to say much to his son, channels of communication on an emotional level had never been developed. Larry's father asked me to help him in "getting the two of us together." By his own admission, he cried for the first time in 30 years and explained that he couldn't let his son go to his death without some communication of love between them.

Larry's sister and brother followed closely the model of their parents. They were also interested in communicating with Larry about his illness and had a somewhat easier time doing so. By acting as a facilitator, friend, therapist, and participant, I was able to give the family permission to discuss all aspects of the situation freely and openly with Larry. It is important to remember that I had spent hours with Larry in advance of this meeting and knew very well what his feelings and preferences were with regard to such communication. Larry was extremely adamant about demanding as open a communicational context as possible. Within a short period of time, Larry's family was sitting on or near his bed, laughing, joking, crying, and sharing in a far more authentic manner, the essence of what was transpiring.

As with many dying adults, Larry was frightened and puzzled by those issues and feelings summarized by the phrase "How could I not be among you?" He wanted to explore the possibility of leaving something behind—a personally relevant extension of himself to those people for whom he cared. I helped him secure the tools for doing leather work, and Larry fashioned leather goods for his family: wallets for his father and brother and purses for his mother and sister. On each item he etched "with love always—from Larry." Sensing that part of him would survive, these items meant a great deal to Larry. Such self-extensive forms of expression have been important to many dying people and amount to personal symbols of (or "testimonials" to) one's incarnate existence.

Moments Beyond the Pain

My work with Larry continued to change form as we discussed many topics formerly inaccessible to consciousness. He asked whether I believed in a life-after-death, and if so, in what form. We spent hours discussing the purpose of his life (and mine); whether he (Larry) and I (Charlie) would ever meet again, in a recognizable form, in another time and place. We spoke of loving people, of relationships, of the pain inherent in confusing roles (such as patient, psychologist, or doctor) with people. It was no longer theoretical analysis or philosophical debate in the manner learned during my quarter century of "academic tutelage." Larry's limited life span gave the interchange an urgency and vitality absent elsewhere. We were two representatives of the somewhat odd and physically vulnerable species *Homo sapiens* struggling to understand why we were sitting (or lying) on an oblate spheroid whirling somewhere in the Milky Way. It was both frightening and exhilarating, and I'll not likely forget those shared "struggles." Perhaps the content didn't matter at all. Perhaps we were "only" defining our relationship while protecting each other from the void like children huddling together in the dark...
perhaps...perhaps...perhaps.

The Patient as Teacher

As his disease progressed, Larry grew weaker and his family, sensing the outcome, withdrew emotionally. This process, sometimes accurately called *anticipatory grief*, is a psychological reaction to impending death frequently experienced by family members and hospital staff. While helping to prepare the survivors psychologically, this reaction can easily be experienced by the patient as a painful abandonment. While I, too, was bracing myself for the worst, I remained with Larry, discussing those things that

were uppermost in his mind. He suggested that I take notes so that I might subsequently use his "story" in teaching health-care professionals. When I agreed, Larry seemed to know that his painful drama might positively affect the experiences of other seriously ill people.

"Neither party was able to discuss [the gravity of the situation] openly for fear of upsetting the 'emotional equilibrium' of the other."

I saw Larry on Friday before returning home, and we talked about pain, both emotional and physical, loneliness, and the fact that he felt his family withdrawing. He also felt the staff withdrawing and was enormously saddened by the fact that both his physician and favorite nurses were now visiting much less frequently. He repeatedly thanked me for being "the one person who was not afraid to share this awful pain," and asked if there was any way he could repay me. I assured him that I had been repaid many times over, but Larry insisted on giving me something. I asked him to be my teacher and translate his experiences for me. "When you're alone, Larry, what thoughts and feelings do you have?" "Specifically, what is it that makes you afraid?" "Teach me how best to help you." In a situation that I have since encountered many times, Larry faded in and out of waking consciousness. In lucid moments, he was extremely clear in responding to my questions, but then would drift into a sleeplike state. He taught me much during that period, and I know I was a support to him as well.

I learned how vital it is to remember that we are dealing not with a professional issue, but a human one. As health-care professionals we are trained as healers, and it is clear that death is an unacceptable outcome for many of us. To imagine that trained healers—i.e., doctors, nurses, and other biomedical personnel who experience themselves as adversaries of illness and death—can respond effectively to the dying patient is often an erroneous expectation. It is more often the case that the professional's anxiety and sense of impotence drives him away, leaving the patient emotionally and psychologically isolated and often physically abandoned. I learned the importance of training both professionals and lay people to relate effectively to the dying person. If we are ever to transcend our barbaric isolation of the terminally ill, we need to stop relating to dying people as lepers. We must realize that at our current level of scientific expertise, death is not always the result of a biomedical mistake or a mysterious virus, but may be seen as a natural winding down of the human psychobiological totality.

Shortly before I left that Friday, I sat watching Larry with his black and blue body, sunken eyes, and yellow skin. As he lay there with his intravenous "life supports," I thought of Auschwitz and Treblinka, my grandfather Aaron, and Vietnam. Suddenly, as if sensing my despair, Larry awoke, looked straight at me, and said, "I have something very important to say to the people who will read your book." I listened carefully, somewhat surprised by Larry's intensity. Finally, he said, "Dying alone is not easy."

"The professional's anxiety and sense of impotence drives him away, leaving the patient emotionally and psychologically isolated and often physically abandoned."

There was a calm and clear tone to Larry's message that was uncanny, and he smiled peacefully, adding to my uneasiness. His words haunted me for days. The following Monday I hurried to visit him again. When I arrived at the nurses' station, I was told that Larry had died. I was sad, angry, relieved, confused. Finally I was left with the feeling that somehow I should have known that what Larry was really saying on Friday was good-bye. Yet it didn't feel like good-bye. There was a tranquil and accepting look on Larry's face so remarkably discontinuous with those tormented, pain-wracked experiences I had witnessed previously. There was a powerful sense that Larry had transcended the somatic entrapment that bound him for so long. I believe that what Larry was communicating to me that Friday was "Dying alone is not easy, but the job is done, and I've reached a place of peace. . . . I appreciate and love you for what you've shared with me, and if by chance we meet again . . .

Charles A. Garfield, Ph.D., is a member of the clinical faculty of the school of Medicine at the University of California in San Francisco. He is the founder and director of the SHANTI Project, an international prototype for volunteer human services programs. A leader in the field of peak performance, he is the author of over six books on that subject.

"The changes that occur in cancer patients following psychedelic therapy are extremely varied, complex, and multidimensional."

viewpoint 62

Psychedelic Therapy Aids Death Acceptance

Stanislav Grof and Joan Halifax

The helping professions seem today to be keenly aware of the importance of the problems related to dying and of the need for far-reaching changes in current medical practices and procedures in this area. The number of articles and books on death and on the management of patients with incurable diseases is rapidly increasing, as are lectures, workshops, symposia, and conferences dealing with this topic. More and more research seems to be directed toward developing effective ways of helping the dying and gaining more insight into the psychological aspects of the processes of dying and death.

The research with LSD and other psychedelic drugs conducted over the last twenty-five years has opened up new possibilities for alleviating the emotional and physical suffering of patients dying of cancer and other chronic diseases, and has offered unexpected approaches to a deeper understanding of the experiences of dying and death. The spontaneous occurrence of chemically evoked experiences of death and rebirth in psychedelic sessions of normal subjects and psychiatric patients has made it possible to realize that the potential for such experiences is inherent in the human unconscious....

The Spring Grove Program

By 1974 more than one hundred persons dying of cancer were part of the Spring Grove program of psychedelic therapy. These individuals can be divided into four groups: the early patients, who received LSD psychotherapy in the period of pilot experimentation prior to the introduction of the rating system; those who volunteered for a systematic study of psychedelic therapy utilizing LSD; persons in whom dipropyltrytramine (DPT), a short-acting psychedelic substance, was used as an adjunct to

psychotherapy in lieu of LSD; and out-of-town patients, self-referred or referred by physicians from various parts of the country, who could not be included in the main LSD or DPT study because of unavailability for the follow-up team.

Most of the people in the LSD or DPT cancer study were in- and out-patients from Sinai Hospital in Baltimore. The psychiatrist-in-charge (Walter Pahnke and, later, Stanislav Grof) spent one day a week in the oncology unit at Sinai, participating in the examinations in the out-patient clinic, attending staff conferences, and making rounds on the oncology ward. During these procedures those dying individuals who might benefit from psychedelic psychotherapy were recommended for the experimental treatment program. The primary criteria for acceptance into the program were: some degree of physical pain, depression, tension, anxiety, or psychological isolation associated with the patient's malignancy; a life expectancy of at least three months (since we were interested not only in the immediate treatment outcome but also in the duration of the results); no major cardiovascular problems, such as cardiac failure, history of myocardial infarction, high degree of arteriosclerosis, or brain hemorrhage (not because of any direct pharmacological danger from psychedelic drugs, but because they elicit powerful emotions that can be extremely dangerous for such individuals); no gross psychopathology preceding the onset of malignancy or prepsychotic condition at the time psychedelic treatment was being considered. In the later stages of research we required that there be no evidence of brain metastases or serious organic brain disease. This was based on poor results with several people treated in the early years who had brain neoplasms. A history of epileptic seizures is generally considered to be another contraindication; in persons with epileptic disposition psychedelics can occasionally trigger a rapid sequence of seizures (status epilepticus) which are very difficult to control.

If the cancer patient met these criteria, the psychiatrist and the attending physician suggested that he or she consider participating in a program of psychedelic therapy. In a special interview we explained the nature of this treatment and discussed openly with the dying individual and family the benefits and risks inherent in this experimental form of psychotherapy. If we reached an agreement, the patient was asked to sign a consent form and was accepted into the program.

Three Phases of Therapy

After the dying person had the initial interviews, he or she was introduced to one of the therapists at the center and the therapeutic work began. The course of psychedelic therapy consisted of three phases. The first was the preparatory period; it involved a series of interactions in which we explored the patient's past history and present situation and established a relationship of trust with the dying individual and the family. The second phase was the drug session itself; during the treatment day the patient spent many hours in a special suite assisted by a therapist and a co-therapist, always a male-female dyad. The third phase involved several interviews in the postsession period, in order to facilitate the integration of the psychedelic experiences into the dying individual's life. . . .

"In no case was psychedelic therapy presented as a potential cure for cancer."

In no case was psychedelic therapy presented as a potential cure for cancer. If we were asked about this issue, we talked about the importance of psychological factors in determining the course of the pathological process and the ability of the organism to defend itself against the disease. On occasion we discussed some of the hypotheses implicating psychogenic factors in the etiology of cancer. This left open the possibility of exploring the psychosomatic aspects of cancer if these emerged in the sessions, but at the same time saved patients from disappointment in the event of limited success in their endeavors to heal themselves. . . .

Changed Perceptions

According to our observations, those individuals who have experienced death and rebirth in their sessions show specific changes in their perception of themselves and of the world, in their hierarchies of values, general behavior, and overall world-views. Those who prior to these experiences had various forms and degrees of emotional and psychosomatic discomfort usually feel greatly relieved. Depression

dissolves, anxiety and tension are reduced, guilt feelings are lifted, and self-image as well as self-acceptance improve considerably. Individuals talk about experiencing themselves as reborn and purified; a deep sense of being in tune with nature and the universe replaces their previous feelings of alienation. Profound serenity and joy can dominate their mental lives. This is usually accompanied by a general increase in zest and a sense of physical health and good physiological functioning.

Some of these persons report that the death-rebirth process seems to have removed a subtle film from their senses which previously prevented them from experiencing reality fully. Sensory input in this new state feels very fresh and intense, almost to the point of being overwhelming; individuals can feel that prior to the experience of rebirth they had never really seen colors, smelled the variety of fragrances and odors, tasted the infinite nuances in food, or experienced the sensual potential of their bodies. Sexual activities can become freer, and potency in men, as well as orgasmic ability in both sexes, is often greatly augmented. Many individuals become intensely interested in nature and find a capacity for ecstatic experiencing of natural beauty, frequently for the first time in their lives. The same is true for the perception of art, particularly music; it is not infrequent that as a result of psychedelic experiences of this kind nonmusical persons develop vivid interest in music and others discover entirely new ways of experiencing it. Aggressive feelings and impulses are usually strikingly reduced and interpersonal and philosophical tolerance increases considerably. Individuals experience a new sense of empathy and warmth toward other people and perceive the world as a fascinating and basically friendly place. Everything in the universe appears perfect, exactly as it should be.

Individuals almost always experience a definite reorientation regarding time. They ruminate less on the traumatic aspects of the past and show less anxious anticipation of or wishful clinging to the future; these are replaced by an enhanced emotional emphasis on the here and now. The relationship between situations and things considered trivial and those seen as all-important usually changes drastically. Individuals tend to discover meaning and beauty in ordinary objects in their everyday environments. The boundary between the miraculous and the banal disappears. Values that were previously pursued with unusual determination and investment of energy are perceived as irrelevant. Excessive striving for power, status, and material possessions appears as childish and symptomatic of spiritual blindness. The most profound wisdom is found in the simplicity of life. This reduction of unrealistic ambitions is frequently combined with an increased ability to accept one's own limitations as well as one's role in the world.

Another common occurrence following a complete and well-integrated death-rebirth experience is a great increase of interest in philosophy, religion, and mysticism. New spiritual feelings are usually of a cosmic or pantheistic nature; the individual can see many additional spiritual dimensions to human life and sense the presence of a spiritual creative force behind the phenomena of everyday reality. Many persons have also experienced an awakening of intense interest in Oriental or ancient religions and philosophies. For some these new interests took a purely intellectual form; for others they were associated with a deep commitment to systematic spiritual practice. In many instances individuals found a new ability to understand universal religious symbols, the metaphors of holy scriptures and other sacred texts, and the language of certain complicated philosophical essays. If the experience of death and rebirth is followed by feelings of cosmic unity, individuals usually see the world and themselves in terms of spiritual energy involved in a divine play and tend to perceive ordinary reality as essentially sacred.

These transformations are usually very pronounced for several days or weeks after a profound and well-resolved LSD session involving the death-rebirth experience. Changes are frequently so striking that LSD therapists refer to them in their clinical jargon as "psychedelic afterglow." Sooner or later they tend to decrease in intensity; under the influence of the demands and pressures of the social environment, many subjects more or less lose touch with their cosmic feelings. However, the new philosophical and spiritual insights into the nature of reality that the experient discovered tend to persist indefinitely. With discipline it is possible to use the profound knowledge acquired in the death-rebirth process as a guideline for restructuring one's entire life. Some individuals are thus capable of creating a situation for themselves in which not only the cognitive insights but also the new spiritual feelings are potentially available much of the time. . . .

the innermost significance of ancient mysteries, various spiritual practices, and rites of passage.

Rabbi Herschel Lymon, who volunteered for our LSD training program, described his unique insight into this dialectic relationship between life and death. During reentry from his LSD session, in which he experienced a shattering encounter with death and subsequent feelings of spiritual rebirth, he remembered a famous statement made five hundred years ago by Leonardo da Vinci. At the time when he was dying, Leonardo summarized his feelings about his right and productive life by saying: "I thought I was living; I was only preparing myself to die." Rabbi Lymon, describing the death-rebirth struggle in his LSD session, paraphrased Leonardo's words: "I thought I was dying; I was only preparing myself to live."

Stanislav Grof is a physician who has worked with and extensively written about therapy with psychedelic drugs. Joan Halifax is a medical anthropologist.

"Death and life, usually considered to be irreconcilable opposites, appear to actually be dialectically interrelated."

Death and life, usually considered to be irreconcilable opposites, appear to actually be dialectically interrelated. Living fully and with maximum awareness every moment of one's life leads to an accepting and reconciled attitude toward death. Conversely, such an approach to human existence requires that we come to terms with our mortality and the impermanence of existence. This seems to be

"The thanatology movement . . . has succeeded in sentimentalizing, trivializing, and leveling down death."

An Over-Emphasis on Death Therapy Trivializes Death

Francis Kane

A few decades ago we experienced in our popular culture what has been called (perhaps a bit presumptuously) a "sexual revolution." What that revolution promised was a liberation from the repressive Victorian taboos and inhibitions that surrounded sexual activity. Following on its heels has come another similar revolution—this one in the area of death, dying, and grief. Like its predecessor, the death and dying revolution attempts to liberate us from the irrational fears and repressive anxieties that surround the experience of death. Death has been brought out of doors, chronicled, discussed, even experimented with and, above all (to use Philip Rieff's phrase) therapeutically managed. Again, much like the sexual liberation that led to sexual education, the death and dying movement has spawned its own *paidea;* death and dying courses and films, death and dying nurses, therapists, and specialists. And, like all disciplines seeking respectability, it coined its own nomenclature; "thanatology." Eros and now thanatos have been liberated from the last bastions of Victorian prudery and opened to the managerial expertise of the therapist.

Undoubtedly, some of this new enlightenment has been and continues to be beneficial. But liberation, however exhilarating, can involve needless violation and garish light thrown in dark places can overexpose—rather than reveal—reality. Serious questions and challenges (not just from conservatives) have been put to the aims, intention, goals, and motives of the sexual movement. Perhaps because it is a newer phenomenon, such serious scrutiny of the thanatology movement has not occurred, although it has started. . . .

One of the methodological assumptions of the thanatology movement which would preempt any

reflective critique is what might be termed its "emotivism" or anti-theoretical bias. "Get in touch with your feelings" seems to be a prime imperative for death care practitioners as well as for the dying themselves. Now the raising of so-called "gut level" feelings to sacrosanct heights is hardly new or surprising and bears little consideration—except that, practically speaking, it is so often effectively utilized by experts in the field who wish to deflect any possible criticism.

Thoughtful reservations about interventions and techniques of death and dying care are often met with a patient, benign, and paternalistic pat on the head that goes something like this: "Ah, but you're rationalizing again!" The young movement has learned its lesson well from its parent, the sexual awareness movement. Yet, one need not deny the importance of feelings—though one wonders in today's world why we need be admonished to get in touch with them—without making the equally important point that "pure" feelings do not even exist and, even if they did, they certainly would be inarticulate without a consciousness that mediates and gives them meaning. Rather, what we may well need to be admonished about is "to think what we are doing"—to use Hannah Arendt's insightful phrase—if for no other reason than it might eliminate a great deal of gut level flatulence.

What is it, then, that strikes us when we think what we do even when that doing, in the case of dying, is our own un-doing? It is an almost commonplace truth nowadays to assert that death is an event which we cannot control. That truth is in danger of being misunderstood or trivialized unless it is recognized that death is not just one event among others peculiar only in that, unlike most, it stands impervious to our efforts at control; but rather death, my own death, reveals that at the very heart of existence I am not in control.

We are, each of us, beings who have been thrust

Francis Kane, "Therapeutic Death," *Commonweal,* February 24, 1984. Reprinted by permission of The Commonweal Foundation.

unwittingly into a world and who must quit that world whether we wish it or not. Death encroaches on us and compels us to admit our own finitude. Curiously enough, the death and dying movement seems to have little quarrel with an affirmation of the fragility of human existence; indeed, such an understanding is often utilized in their battles against the medical profession's often frenetic attempts to keep a patient alive at all costs. Nonetheless, there is a hint in the new practice of thanatology of a much more subtle but no less real effort at controlling death.

Grief Management

A particularly striking example of this new "will-to-control" is the activity usually described in the literature as "grief management." This notion, made popular by one of the guiding lights of the American Hospice movement, Marcia Lattanzi, certainly belies the old Shakespearean maxim: "Everyone can master a grief but he that has it." Instead the grief-stricken ones are now urged to "master" and "control" their grief, to "work through" the grieving process—the very words betraying a resolute if not desperate attempt to overcome our vulnerability. As one person, active in the movement, said about his own grief in tones of obvious self-congratulatory relish: "I was surprised how quickly I worked through it." Besides establishing a new battlefield for narcissistic self-enrichment (I will get to that later), such an attitude denies a fundamental truth about ourselves— that life exists not as a problem that needs solution but a mystery that continually thwarts our attempts even at understanding much less controlling it.

"Such self-conscious manipulation. . . is but an ingenious device for distancing ourselves from the very reality we seek to confront."

Grief, like any significant human experience, does have its pathological expression, but a criticism of that pathology would lie on grounds other than failure to "work it through." Indeed, what makes "grief management" itself almost pathological is its failure to suffer it through. To undergo grief, to let death be death—in its utter finality—would strike terror in our hearts, leaving us helpless and vulnerable. Yet, not unlike the sexologists who teach their clients how to manipulate their pleasures, the new thanatologists teach us how to get on top of and master our grief and dying.

Such self-conscious manipulation—this feverish anxiety by which we monitor our progress through the various stages—is but an ingenious device for

distancing ourselves from the very reality we seek to confront. And since this splitting of the self into two—the grieving or dying self and the transcendent solicitous self watching over the process—is no mean trick, we need the help of experts who alone can show us how to get it right. Management is the goal of these experts, so it is no surprise that the final stage of the process is always "acceptance." But it is an acceptance cheaply purchased whose chief end seems to be the transformation of the patient into a tractable subject. "Infantilization" is the term Rosenbaum uses and he rightly notes it amounts to a subtle form of behavior control.

"Infantilization" of Death

Transforming obstinate adults into docile, childlike patients certainly eases the burden of one's case load. An instructive contrast to these misplaced and hence ineffectual techniques of control might be the old blues singers who at least had the good sense to know that you cannot master, avoid, or dismiss life's troubles. You can only "sing the blues"—and that is not a technique for dealing with troubles but a way of suffering through them.

The attitude of the will-to-control leading, as it does, to the "infantilization" of death offers us a transition to the next presupposition of the movement —its narcissism or gospel of self-fulfillment. Certainly, infantilization implies narcissism for the will-to-control, which aims at self-mastery, easily fixates on the self. In his study of contemporary culture, Christopher Lasch nicely expresses the identity of the will-to-control and narcissism:

> The manager's view of the world . . . is that of the narcissist who sees the world as a mirror of himself and has no interest in external events except as they throw back a reflection of his own image (*The Culture of Narcissism*, p. 96).

Given the finality of death, however, it might seem that the thanatology and self-fulfillment movements would make for strange bedfellows. But the leap from the "good" orgasm to the "good" death is not all that hard, as David Guttman has observed (in Feifel, *New Meanings of Death*).

> Pop psychologists have reduced their productions of books on achieving the good orgasm; instead, they are now telling us how to compose an aesthetic decomposition—the graceful death.

He refers to a recent example, the book *Coming to Terms with Death,* and quotes from the publisher's blurb: "A do it yourself book on how to die gracefully . . . the perfect gift for Mom." Such a ludicrous advertisement could easily be dismissed or become grist for the comedian's mill—except that the attitude it betrays is so pervasive and its theoretical underpinnings cut deeper than it first appears. To return to our example of grief management, what is so striking is the total fixation on the self. Lattanzi expresses it quite well:

> Basically . . . people are mirrors in our lives. We spend

our lives getting close to people, and certain people reflect dimensions or parts of ourselves as we'd like to see ourselves. So when we lose someone who is important to us, it's like a piece of ourselves taken away. And the way we have seen ourselves is no longer the way we are now.

What is mind-boggling in this statement (in which the personal and possessive pronoun is repeated twelve times) is the complete forgetfulness of what occasioned the grief, the death of the other. The death of the unique and irreplaceable other becomes a fissure in ourselves that needs to be therapeutically repaired. The death of the other as an-other is repressed and, ironically, the very devil which the movement sought to expel returns with a vengeance. It is but a short step, then, to deny one's own death, to view it as illusion, or merely (in Kubler-Ross's quaintly reassuring phrase) "A transition." After all, how could this marvelously self-managed and self-developed person ever face a real break in its existence?

Exhibitionism

One of the most pernicious effects of the sexual revolution has been the complete blurring of the distinction between public and private. Love—which includes the intimate feelings, desires, and acts of lovers—has been exposed, even flaunted, under the garish light of the leering public eye. By denying love the dark and sheltering intimacy it needs, we have transformed it into something else, a mere exhibition complete with self-glorified exhibitors and an array of voyeuristic spectators. Such exhibitionism has now crept into the dying process so that the privacy of the bedroom where one loved and died has been totally violated.

Curiously, though perhaps not surprisingly, the violation often finds the dying victim cooperating, even inviting the display of his or her own demise. Film seems to be the medium of choice, and we are now inundated with *Cinema Verite* analysis of the last dying gasp of the cancer-ridden, the elderly, and even the suicidal. The narcissist, Lasch pointed out, "cannot live without an admiring audience" and so it is hardly surprising that the urge to self-display would be found here even though one might hope a sense of dignity and shame (now, perhaps, outdated) would inhibit the performance.

If cinema is the more dramatic expression of this "publicization" of the private, a less dramatic though more universal example is the almost continual and incessant stream of chatter about dying that the movement has fostered. A cardinal sin of the movement is not to verbalize how you feel about your dying. Thanatology trainees spend a good deal of their time learning how to elicit the appropriate responses. On a certain superficial level it's all a bit tiresome, reminding one of the old vaudeville routine where the "corpse" keeps rising out of the coffin for

one last admonition to the harried family until finally, out of exasperation, they just close the lid. Yet, on a deeper level, there seems to be a lack of realization that in the face of such an awesome event as death silence may well be the only appropriate response. In the *Book of Revelation*, "there was silence in heaven for about a half an hour" when the Lamb broke open the seventh seal. Such was the traditional wisdom, but in today's world death has become public and perhaps lost its awe-full character. Yet it is probably more the case that by making it public we have, like children insisting on their night light, simply repressed for a while the very real darkness that hovers over our beds.

"There is a hint in the new practice of thanatology of a much more subtle but no less real effort at controlling death."

The upshot of this progressive "publicization" of death is that it has given the movement professionals a rationalization for some highly intrusive methods. In one metropolitan hospital, the social workers were insisting that they be called immediately upon the death of the patient and, despite innocent intentions, one could not help but see one more professional cadre crowding around the bedside to get a piece of the action. Indeed, one fear, perhaps not all that remote or silly, is that these same professionals will soon seek to determine who is "qualified" enough to "deal with" the dying.

Loss of the Sacred

The argument of this essay has, by now, I trust, come into sharper focus. The thanatology movement—at least in some quarters—has succeeded in sentimentalizing, trivializing, and leveling down death until it has become but one more overexposed event in the life of "homo dominator." Death has lost its power and its sting, not because of the transcendent mystery that is faith, but because it has been stripped of its terror and transformed into an ordinary event subject to our will to control. In short, it has been secularized.

One need not be "religious" to sense that when every human event becomes so leveled down and equalized—grist for the managerial mill—then, as Bob Dylan put it, "there's nothing really sacred." Ironically, even some believers, whether wittingly or not, are not immune from such reductionistic tendencies. Yet, in one of the few perceptive articles on death and dying (in *Social Research* for Autumn, 1972), William May hammers home the distinction of the sacred from the profane and its implication for our will to control.

. . . The sacred is dintinguished from ordinary profane

power in that it does not appear as something that man can fully master and use toward his own appointed ends. It confounds the efforts of the practical man to control it and the contemplative man to know it. It is full of surprises and therefore it insists upon its own unfolding; refusing to submit to the normal procedures by which ordinary, profane, secular man handles his life.

To lose the sense of the sacred, what transcends us, overwhelms us, measures us, is to lose the sense of ourselves, our vulnerability, our shame, our finitude. Death is or ought to be a continual, albeit painful, reminder of that. Yet of such frailty the thanatology movement wants no reminder. Their muddled attack on the "obscenity of death" is particularly instructive. When they call death the "last obscenity" they seem to have in mind the refusal to speak about it and deal openly with it. Properly corrected, our attitude toward death will lose its obscene character and, like our sexual comportment, bask in open and liberated expression.

Publicness Not the Solution

The confusion here is two-fold. First of all, publicness could hardly be the remedy for the obscene since it is the public display of intimate acts that fuels our voyeuristic intents. Rather than harmful inhibitions, the covert and surreptitious glances that often accompany the viewing of obscene matters might well be indices of shame, recognizing that some things ought not be viewed—not at least without the sheltering commitment of love or, in the case of death, grief.

"Life exists not as a problem that needs solution but a mystery that continually thwarts our attempts even at understanding much less controlling it."

Secondly, it is not in the name of the sacred (as one might expect) that the obscenity of death is attacked but a rather more mundane effort to level the experience to more manageable proportions. Such naive leveling underestimates the power of the obscene to shock and violate. Yet one can only violate what was first held to be sacred. Obscenity is the sacred's counter-image. Contemporary culture seems hell-bent on liberating us from any sense of violation and thereby eliminating altogether the category of the obscene. Yet in a world where nothing is obscene, nothing can be saved. And so no longer exposed to the obscenity of death, we are now treated (by the new thanatology experts) to its utter banality.

The terror and the shame have been therapeutically excised from death, as evidenced in the droning boredom of film like *Joan Robinson: One Woman's Story* or the silly saccharine placebos of the spiritualist in *Poltergeist* or finally, the trendy proclamation by Kubler-Ross that we should no longer speak of death, only another "transition." Such therapeutic surgery is nothing more than an intellectual lobotomy that cuts us off from the terrifying experience of what lies beyond our control. Instead, we need to stand humble before this humbling event, suffer its indignity, and perhaps reverence what may lay beyond it. "There is nothing to be done toward the sacred," writes William May, "except to let it be what it is, permit it to run its course, and let one's own life be caught up in its force." Such an attitude would resist the temptation to reduce the strange to the familiar, the dreadful to the manageable, the careful to the ordinary. Again, in May's words, it would simply "let death be death."

Early on in this reflection I quoted Hannah Arendt's injunction that we "think what we do." I should like to close in a similar chord by invoking the memory of the poet John Keats whose verse represents an authentic encounter with death as death. One poem in particular, the "Ode to a Nightingale," is wrenched from his experience of ministering to his dying brother. Here is the real world of dying, the "fever and the fret...where youth grows pale, and spectre-thin and dies." He even speaks of the temptation to be "half in love with easeful Death" but resolutely bids it "adieu" realizing "the fancy cannot cheat so well as she is famed to do."

Like Arendt, Keats knew full well our task—only in a world of suffering and death it is a melancholy one—here "where but *to think* is to be full of sorrow and leaden-eyed despairs." What redeems such agony is not the faddish gimmicks of the thanatology movement but men and women of virtue who with humility and courage suffer the shame of death rather than manage it away. In such a crucible, what Keats called the "vale of soul making," and only in such a crucible might we then become emboldened to speak. But even then our speech would be the language of indirection, a poem (of the nightingale) a song (about the blues) or a story (from the Bible). As Homer long ago reminded us—"any sorrow can be borne if it is told in a story." Such an attitude which let death be death would ultimately redound to those who remain and then, perhaps, life might truly be life.

Francis Kane is an associate professor and chairman of the philosophy department at Salisbury State College in Maryland.

"Prepare your mind for life extension. The beliefs of the subconscious have a tremendous effect upon what we are able to do with our lives."

Delaying Death Should Be Our Ultimate Goal

Durk Pearson and Sandy Shaw

The slowing down and partial reversal of aging involves much more than knowledge of life extension techniques. Without the right attitude, you won't be able to implement that knowledge, no matter how much you know. You may be immobilized by a number of myths about aging that you believe without even realizing it. . . . Don't let obsolete assumptions and misconceptions drive you prematurely to your grave.

It takes action on your part to extend your life span. Nothing is free. You have to decide that you want to extend your life, then you must study various techniques for doing so, and finally you actually have to apply one or more of these methods. . . .

Prepare your mind for life extension. The beliefs of the subconscious have a tremendous effect upon what we are able to do with our lives. The slowing, prevention, and partial reversal of aging is a new phenomenon, one that we are not prepared for by the general culture around us. The following ideas may help you to alter your own attitudes toward life extension.

Some Facts About Life Extension

• The general population does not know the true nature of aging, which is usually considered a single, time-related process. Actually, aging refers to a naturally occurring progressive deterioration of various biochemical and cellular functions. There are several aging mechanisms that attack different functions of the body at different rates, leading to impaired health and a decreased probability of surviving as the years progress.

• The activities of the general population are not good indications of when and how you can extend your life and at what cost.

• An increased risk with age of degenerative diseases like cancer and heart disease for the general population does not have to mean that *you* are at risk for these conditions. You can lower your risks greatly by appropriate actions, regardless of whether most other people do so.

• It is wise to take advantage of life extension techniques now rather than waiting for some indefinite time in the future—when everyone is using such methods. Such a time may come, but don't bet your life on it. When more effective techniques come along, you will be better able to take advantage of them if you have kept yourself in good condition. Life extension methods can improve health now, not just in the distant future.

• Life extension does not happen without serious effort. It would be nice if it were free, but natural aging processes occur whether we like it or not unless we do something about them. Reducing the damage of aging processes requires your purposeful action. You'll have to decide what you want to do and how to do it.

• Your desire for life extension does not imply an ability to choose between no life extension and immortality. There are different degrees of action possible, and what you do depends upon your resources and values; for example, how much you wish to change your habits, and what you are willing to spend in time, effort, and money.

Plan Carefully

• You will not suddenly become immortal. At best, you will have to creep up on it, a step at a time, by inhibiting aging and the age-associated disorders of cancer and occlusive atherosclerosis. There is no final answer. You may never reach immortality, but you can live much longer and in far better health than you expected.

• Your present life expectancy is probably far from what you could achieve with your present resources and possible range of actions. Your approach to this optimum must be discovered by careful planning and investigation. You do not have automatic knowledge of this subject, and living the same life as that of the general populace will get you roughly the same life span.

• The Food and Drug Administration (FDA) does not approve drugs specifically for life extension, and the approval of a new drug for conventional anti-disease purposes takes eight to twelve years, on the average. The scientific information upon which the drugs have been based will generally be known many years before any practical applications may be offered in the American marketplace.

• Life extension does not begin by stopping all aging mechanisms at once; you start by slowing down one and then another, and so on.

"It is wise to take advantage of life extension techniques now rather than waiting for some indefinite time in the future."

• Anyone now attempting life extension is a pioneer. It will be many years before life extension intervention is a routine part of most people's lives. Before taking any life extension drugs, carefully read and reread our cautions. Remember that one description of a pioneer is a guy with an arrow in his back, so think before acting, and don't try to develop your own life extension program overnight. Life extension is a lifelong activity, so wade in prudently and gradually, rather than jumping in over your head....

Fears of Life Extension

A greatly extended human life span will bring about many changes in our society. It is wise to be prepared for these changes by anticipating as many as we can. The following explores some of the possible negative consequences of life extension which people have expressed to us.

• If people lived a lot longer, we would have a severe population explosion. The birth rate would be much higher than the death rate and remain that way, owing to constantly improving life extension technology. This would lead to a food and energy shortage of terrible proportions.

There would be an increase in population only if people reproduced at a higher rate than the reduced death rate. At the present time in the United States, the birth rate is below that required for replacement. Our birth rate is now lower than during the Great Depression, and the rapid growth of vocational opportunities for women is apt to keep it this way. In

addition, there is every reason to suppose that the future populations of this and other nations will not be limited only to the planet Earth. The practicability of large space colonies, capable of holding many billions of persons, has been demonstrated with calculations based on present principles of engineering. It seems likely that such colonies will be a reality within the next fifty years. Energy from thermonuclear fusion and space solar satellites holds the key to adequate power for a much larger population than lives now on earth, and these generators, too, are possible using near-term technological principles. Most important, people's lives will be extended in the productive part of life, not in the decrepit dependent part of life. Thus, most of the extended-life-span population will be increasing wealth, rather than merely consuming it. As with other food and energy crises throughout history, technological solutions can prevent disaster.

• Life extension will encourage selfishness.

Life extension encourages concern with oneself in much the same way as any type of self-improvement (memory and learning drugs, psychological self-exploration, or training for a new job). Selfishness is a necessary part of life. There is no guarantee that, now or in the future, individuals with an extended life span will show more wisdom in their actions than those living the traditional three score and ten years.

Life Extension and Population

• Widespread life extension will result in a large population of old people who are set in their ways and hence become obstacles to new thinking. Our society will stagnate.

This scenario would be a serious problem if life extension prolonged mainly the old-age part of life. However, life extension methods described in this book extend the vigorous productive part of life and can improve mental, as well as physical, functions. Life extension causes people to live longer because their bodies and brains are better able to repair and prevent aging damage. When a person's ability to cope with this damage reaches a minimal point, death becomes very likely. In life extension experiments on laboratory animals, the animals with extended life spans do not have prolonged periods of decline. In fact, in some experiments the animals are vigorous and, to all outward appearances, youthful until just a few hours before death, when they succumb suddenly. In our society, there may be a problem in those organizations where seniority is very important, such as corporations, unions, philanthropic organizations, and governments, allowing officeholders to hold power for many decades before dying. In industry, if the old life-extended executives do not adapt to new situations, their companies will eventually go out of business because of competition from young, innovative companies. In government, which allows no competition, the problem may well be more serious. The seniors on Capitol Hill may uphold older thinking, in opposition to younger constituencies. Structural reforms may alleviate the difficulties (such as less power for seniority and more frequent turnover of elected congressmen). Biochemical reform to increase the imagination and creativity of congressional seniors may also be possible. Or government as we now know it may simply become less important as a source of leadership—the most likely alternative, in our opinion.

Concerns About Society

• What about the survival of social institutions in a society of long-lived people? Can marriage still be meaningful when people are living two or three times longer than at present? What about family structure? Will great-great-great-great-great-great-grandparents still be concerned about their descendants?

These are difficult questions to answer, involving entirely novel situations. We can't perform experiments to let us know what will happen to these human institutions. It seems reasonable to suppose that family and marriage will continue to exist in varied and modified forms because they are basic parts of our genetic heritage. We can count on the development of new social institutions to replace older ones that no longer function well. People will continue to care about one another and to have social groups. A long-lived individual will still seek friends and other social relationships. People will certainly continue to want offspring, though the timing of childbearing may be altered.

• Life extension will destroy society because the people who extend their lives will be opposed by other people who disapprove of life extension.

In many science-fiction stories, life extension techniques were generally available only to a few rich, politically powerful, or genetically fortunate individuals, thus creating envy in the rest of the population. But today's life extension technology is available to all who have the desire to make use of it and the willingness to acquire the necessary knowledge. Neither power nor riches nor genetic luck are necessary in an effective life extension plan. Government programs which transfer wealth from young to old—particularly Social Security—have a very real potential for creating serious class friction, and irresponsible politicians often thrive on worsening class polarization.

• Life will become boring.

If you're bored now, you'll probably be bored in the future. But you'll have more time to find out how to stop being bored. If you're not bored now, there is no reason to suppose that you'll be bored later, especially since the rates of social, scientific, and technological change will continue to accelerate.

• If a person lives long enough, he or she will use up all the brain's memory storage capacity and be unable to absorb any new experiences.

This is a problem that may occur with regularity in the declining years of an ordinary life span. Neurochemicals required for memory and data processing decline in concentration in the brain of aging individuals, making it more and more difficult for these people to acquire new memories and to learn. However, biochemical therapies now exist for some of these problems. Memory may be improved by a variety of nutrients and other chemicals, and there are also a variety of creativity-increasing substances that have been developed (but these are not yet widely available, due to the Food and Drug Administration regulations).

Social Consequences

The consequences to ourselves and our society of greatly extended human life span are sure to be far reaching. An extended life span does not mean that we simply go on living as we have except that we go on a lot longer. The quality of our life changes as well as its length.

"The quality of our life changes as well as its length."

As with all rapid technological change, some people will find the pace or the type of change not to their liking. Many people do not want to live an indefinite life span. Some people may want to but lack the courage to try it and resent those who do. Other people want the power to determine when and by what means other people extend their lives. This includes power seekers within government and in the medical profession. For example, the Food and Drug Administration (FDA) and the Congress have been retarding some applications of life extension research by greatly hindering the introduction of new drugs into the marketplace. The FDA and the FTC (Federal Trade Commission) have prevented vitamin, nutrient, and pharmaceutical manufacturers from making scientifically valid health claims for their products. We surmise that the government's concern about where they will get funds to cover their welfare and funds-transfer programs for the aged underlies some of their reluctance to fund biological aging research. Dr. Alexander Leaf, former head of the President's Commission on Aging, has said that it would be irresponsible to spend resources on extending human life span until after funding is found to support the increased number of older people. As we mentioned before, only about 10 percent of the funds dispensed by the National Institute of Aging actually goes into basic research on biological aging. (And none of these funds are specifically aimed at extending human life span.) An extended human life span, if it happens "too fast," will create serious problems for the government's vast income-transfer schemes (from young to old) that include Social Security. The Social Security system is in trouble, life extension or no life extension. Life extension didn't create Social Security's problems, but it may accelerate Social Security's collapse. If people live 20 percent longer, for example, they might collect Social Security for twenty-two years instead of the present average of about eight years. This could require Social Security taxes to increase from 14 percent of pre-tax income to 40 percent, severely reducing your take-home pay.

The Life Extenders

Such problems, however, will not happen overnight. At present, only a relatively small percentage of the population is seriously involved in personal life extension, perhaps because most people do not feel adequate to decide how to go about it. We hope to help remedy this situation.

How will your life change? The most important change you will notice as you become more confident of your ability to extend your life span is a realization of how much more time there is to do the things you want to do. You can afford to spend more time learning new skills or enjoying leisure activities because there is more time available. At any moment in your life, you can expect that more time remains than you would have had in the absence of intervention. The reproductive period will take up a smaller percentage of most people's extended lifetimes, thus leaving more of their lives available for other activities. People will have time available as never before to explore different ways to enjoy life.

"People will have time available as never before to explore different ways to enjoy life."

The promise of increased time does not, of course, guarantee happiness. The use of the extra time is up to each person. Some will use it wisely, others won't. Because of the potential for a greatly increased life span, the planning that most people do today for their post-retirement life (assuming retirement at sixty-five and living for about an additional ten years) will be adequate. With life extension, planning should consider the possibility of living at least twenty or thirty years beyond retirement at age sixty-five.

Society will have to deal with the existence of a new class of persons—the life extenders—and reconcile this with the non-life extenders who (as in many science-fiction stories) may oppose or resent extended life spans for others as well as for themselves.

Durk Pearson, a futurology consultant to industry, graduated from MIT with a degree in physics. He started a scientific consulting business in aerospace, energy, and life extension research. Sandy Shaw has a degree in chemistry from UCLA. She is an independent scientific consultant to many large companies.

"I think that the risk of unforseeable catastrophe will probably be sufficient to turn us away from the research to extend life."

Delaying Death Should Not Be Our Ultimate Goal

Sir Peter Medawar

Over the past thirty years, research on aging has raised the serious possibility that life expectancy might someday be extended by as much as one fourth. Many different lines of research—on diet, metabolism, and the immune system, among other things—are being pursued. One of the most promising of these originated with Denham Harman, professor of medicine and biochemistry at the University of Nebraska, who proposed, in 1954, that the highly reactive molecular fragments known as "free radicals," which are especially damaging to biological microstructures, might to some extent be counteracted by the increased consumption of antioxidants. These chemical compounds, of which vitamin E is the best known, occur naturally in some foods and are added as preservatives to others—in most countries in tiny and strictly regulated proportions.

Harman and many others are of the opinion that, just as small amounts of antioxidants preserve foods, in larger amounts the compounds might preserve human tissue. Many antioxidants have since been tested for such an effect on laboratory animals, and the increased longevity observed was equivalent, in Harman's reckoning, to an extension of the average human life expectancy from seventy-three to ninety-five years.

If antioxidants can be ingested safely by human beings, the result is not expected to be an extra decade or two of zombie-like existence, in which people would be alive only in the purely technical sense (or alive enough, shall we say, to avoid becoming transplant donors). Not at all. What the researchers hope for is a prolonging of life such as would be achieved if the seven ages of man were marked off on a length of rubber and the rubber

were stretched. A seventy-year-old would have the address to life of a sixty-year-old, and an eighty-year-old that of a seventy-year-old.

Growing Old

How successful any treatment to prolong life might be is unclear. Growing old is a bad thing quite apart from the decline of bodily faculties and energies that it entails. Even if the process of senescence could be arrested temporarily, we would still suffer from the passage of years. Consider, for example, the likely consequences of extending a woman's reproductive life to the age of sixty, or beyond. The older a woman is at the age of reproduction, the longer her finite endowment of egg cells will have been exposed to influences that are inimical to it. Thus, even though a woman of sixty might be as physically fit as a woman of thirty, the likelihood of a chromosomal aberration, such as that which causes Down's syndrome, would have increased with her age. The etiology of cancer is a similar example. Researchers believe that a malignant tumor can start with the mutation of a chromosome following the body's exposure to ionizing radiation, a toxic chemical, or some other mutagen. Thus, the longer one lives, the longer one has to cross the path of such hazards, and the greater one's chances of contracting cancer.

Because it is not easy to see a remedy for these side effects of old age, I fear that the incorporation of antioxidants into our diet will have a more modest result than proponents of the theory expect. But there are people who say that such research ought not to proceed at all. Their opposition compels us to ask, Is the extension of the life-span a possibility that we should welcome or a temptation that we should resist?

The Bible

The case against efforts to increase longevity takes several forms. It is said, for example, that the

Peter Medawar, "When We Are Old," *The Atlantic Monthly,* March 1984. Reprinted with permission of the author.

prolonging of life runs counter to biblical teaching. Yet "threescore years and ten" *(Psalms 90:10)* has no authority other than the opinion of a psalmist. In fact, the phrase is something of a cliche in the Bible, standing for quite a number but less than a hundred. Thus we are told that there were threescore and ten palm trees in Elim *(Numbers 33:9)*; that when the house of Jacob entered Egypt, it comprised threescore and ten persons *(Deuteronomy 10:22)*; that Jerubbaal had threescore and ten sons *(Judges 9:2)*. It might be more in accord with the spirit of the Bible if the human life-span were construed to be that which, for better or worse, human beings cause it to be.

People say that extending life is a crime against nature. I consider this a despondent view, which rests on an implicit nostalgia for supposedly healthy, happy, exuberant, and yea-saying savages that Jean-Jacques Rousseau spoke for—creatures whose life expectancy did not exceed twenty-five or thirty years. This attitude echoes the literary propaganda of the Romantic revival, and it is surely wider of the mark than Thomas Hobbes's assertion that the life of man in a state of nature is "solitary, poor, nasty, brutish, and short."

Medical Advances

Human life has always been what human beings have made of it, and in many ways we have improved on nature. It cannot be too strongly emphasized that all advances in medicine increase life expectancy; their efficacy is measured by the degree to which they do so. I am referring not only to insulin, penicillin, and the other spectacular innovations of medical history but also to aspirin (which lowers fever and reduces inflammation, besides relieving pain), adhesive bandages, and washing one's hands before eating. These, too, have contributed years to our life-span.

The whole philosophy of the prevention of disease—and where prevention fails, the cure—represents a deep and long-standing moral commitment to life, and the research in question here is its logical development. Thus, one could argue that, our commitment to the preservation of life having already been made, it is too late for us to cease to be ambitious.

"The threat of gerontocracy—government by the aged and probably for the aged—is less easy to dismiss."

Other objections to prolonging old age have to do with population control and age distribution. For example, it is asked, Dare we propose to add to a burden that is almost insupportable now? Shall the resources of underprivileged nations be consumed at an even faster rate by the technologically more advanced peoples of the Northern Hemisphere and of the West generally—those who will be the first to take advantage of new medical procedures?

In partial extenuation, it can be said that the increase in population would not be exponential, because it is unlikely that older people would choose to add to their families. Admittedly, though, they would have mouths, and they would use energy and other raw materials at the high rate characteristic of people in the developed parts of the world.

One hears that the likely increase in population size would provoke wars, as if the linkage were an established truth. But it does not stand up to scrutiny. No one will challenge Europe's claim to the dunce's cap for political aggression and warmaking, yet war has been no more frequent in Europe over the past hundred years than it was in medieval times or in the fifteenth century or in the seventeenth, even though the population has grown steadily.

A Gerontocracy

The threat of gerontocracy—government by the aged and probably for the aged—is less easy to dismiss. Certainly old people require special attention, and their rising numbers would lay an extra burden on social-welfare services in a caring society. That burden would have to be shouldered by the young. A vigorous elderly generation would also probably hold on to jobs that otherwise would pass to the young, thereby exacerbating unemployment. Who knows? A gerontocracy might have the nerve to impose a special tax on jobholders below some minimum age, and at the same time reward older jobholders with generous concessions.

Without minimizing these last worries, I must point out that the political and sociological effects of a population shift would not be felt overnight. We should have between fifty and 200 years to adapt.

The process might completely overturn our present ideas about work and retirement, but in reality such a revolution has been in progress for the past 150 years, as the proportion of older people in the population has grown with advances in medicine and sanitary engineering. It is reasonable to assume we can solve the problems of the future, since they are not qualitatively new.

Past Attitudes

Jane Austen wrote her novels around the turn of the nineteenth century, and they are a mine of information about the manners and attitudes of her day. Consider, in particular, Austen's first published novel, *Sense and Sensibility.* The hero, Colonel Brandon, is rated at thirty-five an old man and quite past it—so much so that Marianne Dashwood, the eighteen-year-old girl whose hand he seeks, regards his suit as a kind of geriatric charade. In the book the question arises of laying down a sum to purchase a fifteen-year annuity for Marianne's mother, who is described as a healthy woman of forty. The man who would have to provide for the annuity protests, "Her life cannot be worth half that purchase." So Austen seems able to take for granted her readers' doubt that a woman of forty could live to be as old as fifty-five.

> *"My personal sympathies are with the daredevils who want to try out these new procedures."*

Suppose someone had told Austen's contemporaries that their life expectancy could be doubled. If they were to react as some people do today, they would have held up their hands in horror at the impiety of interfering with nature—at the very idea that a man of thirty-five would not have one foot in the grave and that a woman of forty would live another fifteen years! Yet the average life-span of a century or more ago seems pathetically short from the perspective of today. How can we be certain that a generation as close to us as we are to Jane Austen would not look upon our fears with pained condescension?

Some lines by the poet Walter Savage Landor, which have the cadences of a requiem, seem to rebuke the wish to delay death:

> Nature I loved; and next to Nature, Art.
> I warmed both hands before the fire of life;
> It sinks, and I am ready to depart.

Perhaps this declaration is a Christian acquiescence to an inevitable fate, but to me it sounds spiritless. A person who is loved and in good health has reason enough to want to live a few years longer than might seem to be his due: to learn, for example, how the grandchildren turn out, and whether the flux of history coroborates or refutes his expectations. A writer will want to complete his book, or even turn his thoughts to another, and no gardener will willingly surrender his hope of taking part in the wonder and joyous expectations of another spring. From the point of view of biology, the strength of our hold upon life has been the most important single factor in bringing us to our present ages and, indeed, in the fact that human beings have evolved at all.

Evils of Prolonged Life

Some of the evils that confront mankind—the havoc of war, for example—can be anticipated and guarded against. Others are more insidious. They are the outcomes of well-intentioned actions and could not have been predicted. I have in mind the deaths from cancer of the pioneers of x-radiography, who could not have known that x-rays are among the most potent cancer-causing agents.

Likewise, overpopulation is the consequence of a reduction of mortality, especially in childhood, through medicine and sanitary engineering, which has not been matched by a corresponding reduction in the birthrate.

All else being equal, I think that the risk of unforseeable catastrophe will probably be sufficient to turn us away from the research to extend life. But what I *hope* will happen is this: perhaps a dozen enthusiasts for the prolonging of life will go ahead and try to prolong their own lives. If they become wise and oracular nonagenarians or centenarians, they will be counted among the benefactors and pathfinders of mankind. If senile dementia is their fate, they will have warned us off, and that would be an equally useful service.

Sir Peter Medawar won the Nobel Prize for Medicine and Physiology in 1960. He is currently a member of the scientific staff of the Medical Research Council in Harrow, England.

"I completely forget for hours at a time that a kidney machine keeps me alive. And when I remember, the realization intensifies whatever I am doing."

Medical Advances Save Lives

Lee Foster

Last September my kidneys failed. As a consequence I am on a rigidly restricted diet and must limit my fluid intake. In addition, I am attached to an artificial kidney machine three days a week, five hours each day, undergoing a blood-cleansing process called hemodialysis. It is a regimen I will have to endure as long as I live or until I get a successful kidney transplant. When people ask me how it feels, I say, "Great—considering the alternative." The alternative is death.

My lifestyle has been radically altered. I love to cook and to eat, I have written about gastronomy and edited a cookbook, but now I am forbidden many of my favorite foods and denied all but small portions of others. I have always been a big drinker—I don't mean liquor—and now I have to think twice before I take a single sip of water, soup, coffee, wine, anything liquid. I am the Assistant Travel Editor of the *New York Times* but I have had to say goodbye to carefree trips. I can travel no farther than two days from a kidney machine; and to use one away from home, I have to make arrangements weeks in advance. Such is my life with failed kidneys. I also have osteoarthritis of both hips, cannot put on my own shoes without a long, specially made shoehorn and walk with a cane.

Is all this too terrible to be borne? No. I still put in a full work week, go out to lunch, play bridge, pursue my hobby of photography, attend Philharmonic concerts, see Broadway shows, visit museums and get out of town on occasional weekends.

These days—actually nights—I dialyze at home with a leased kidney machine. My wife, Leslie, assists me. The machine does two things: it rids my system of excess salt and edema-causing fluid and it cleanses

my blood of waste products formed by the body's metabolism. These waste products—urea, creatinine, phosphate, potassium, uric acid and others—are normally filtered out of the blood by the kidneys, sent to the bladder, and excreted in the urine. Since my kidneys are nonfunctioning, they no longer remove the waste products, which if allowed to accumulate in my body would in a short time turn me uremic and kill me.

My Routine

The machine I use looks something like an old-fashioned washing machine. I fill its stainless steel tub with twenty-five gallons of water to which I add a large bottle of concentrated dialysate, a sort of brine with many of the chemical properties of blood. To a hollow rod in the tub I attach a coil that consists of a cellophane-like membrane wound round and round inside a plastic holder. In this coil, when I am hooked up to the machine, the actual dialysis takes place, a process I will explain later. A circulating pump keeps the dialysate bath surging around the membrane inside the coil at a steady rate. A heating element keeps the bath at the correct temperature.

After I have filled the tub and tested the coil by pumping air into it to make sure the membrane won't leak or rupture under pressure, I rig the machine. This procedure involves stringing and connecting yards of complex plastic tubing and priming the tubing by pumping saline solution through it. Meanwhile Leslie lays out a tray of needles, syringes, alcohol wipes, heparin bottles, gauze squares, tape, clamps, and other supplies. Then, I get into pajamas to be comfortable and weigh myself to see how much fluid I have accumulated since my last dialysis. I bare and wash my right arm with a prepackaged, presoaped sterile scrub brush, sit down in a reclining lounge chair next to the machine, and take and record my blood pressure and pulse. Leslie inserts two thick hollow needles into a vein in my arm and

Lee Foster, "Man and Machine: Life Without Kidneys," *The Hastings Center Report*, June 1976. Reproduced with permission of the *Hastings Center Report* © Institute of Society, Ethics and the Life Sciences, 360 Broadway, Hastings-on-Hudson, NY 10706.

connects them by means of slender saline-filled tubes to the tubing already attached to the machine. Then she turns on the machine's blood pump, which starts the process of dialysis, and injects heparin into the tubing carrying my blood to prevent clotting.

After the machine is switched on, my blood flows from one of the needles through a tube to the coil that contains the membrane. The blood is on one side of the membrane, the dialysate bath on the other. Since the salt, urea, creatinine, potassium, uric acid, and other substances are in higher concentration in my blood than in the bath, they filter from the blood through the membrane into the bath by a process of osmosis. Thus my blood is cleansed as it passes by the membrane again and again during my five-hour session. Also, excess fluid that has accumulated in my tissues is forced out through the membrane. A second tube leads from the membrane back to me, continually returning my blood via the second needle. Before entering my body the blood passes through a chamber that traps air bubbles and another that traps blood clots, should any develop despite the heparin injection.

"The last year or so before I went on dialysis I was chronically anemic and could barely walk twenty steps without stopping to rest."

Connected to the main tubes are four subsidiary tubes. One runs to a gauge that indicates the pressure being built up by the machine. A second leads to a device that automatically turns off the blood pump if the pressure gets too high. A third is attached to a saline bag for the administration of saline solution should my blood pressure drop sharply as the result of excessive loss of fluid, causing dizziness and muscle cramps. A fourth permits Leslie to raise or lower the blood level in the chamber that traps air bubbles. On the face of the machine are switches and dials that I operate or monitor as dialysis proceeds. When I first began dialyzing, I felt like a flight engineer at the control panel of a Boeing 747.

Things *Can* Go Wrong

Things can go wrong during dialysis so even when I'm fully relaxed I can never be completely oblivious of the machine. Needles often need adjusting, connections can loosen, on rare occasions the tubing can split. Although it has not happened so far, the membrane can even rupture despite all precautions, which would cost me a pint of blood I can ill afford. I have to watch the pressure gauge and adjust the pressure, be certain the heating element is keeping the dialysate bath at the right temperature, and

observe the color of the bath by means of a mirror attached to the machine to make sure the membrane hasn't sprung a slow leak. I have to watch the air chamber for bubbles, which would indicate that a loose connection is allowing air to mix with the blood. I have to watch a small plastic chamber called the pillow; if it collapses, the pressure drops sharply and a needle has to be repositioned or a line unkinked. I also have to take my blood pressure and pulse every hour, sooner if I don't feel well, and give myself saline, lower the pressure and slow down the blood pump if I get faint, dizzy, or start getting muscle spasms.

But mostly things go well on dialysis. While on the machine I read and listen to music, or watch a little television, and even eat a simple dinner left-handed. (My right arm, with the needles in it, is largely immobilized during dialysis.) Yet sometimes when I'm feeling fine, and the machine is running perfectly, and I've enjoyed the dinner, and the music is good and the book I'm reading is interesting, and our cat is purring around my feet, and Leslie is smiling at me, a thought suddenly runs through my head: "How the hell did I get here?"

My Condition

My kidney disease is called chronic glomerulonephritis. The only good thing about it is that it took a long time to reach a critical stage. Which was fine with me because I was in no hurry.

Physicians say I was probably stricken with the disease as a child as the result of some illness or fever. For many years I didn't even know I had a potentially fatal kidney condition although albumin kept showing up in my urinalyses. In my mid-forties I developed high blood pressure. After a battery of tests, I got the bad news: my kidneys had degenerated and were continuing to degenerate, slowly but inexorably. Even so, they retained at least minimal function until I reached the age of fifty-three.

The last year or so before I went on dialysis I was chronically anemic and could barely walk twenty steps without stopping to rest. Agonizing muscle spasms cramped my fingers and toes and, even worse, my insteps, calves, and thighs. I would sometimes get as many as a dozen massive spasms a night, so agonizing that I would leap from bed kicking and thrashing, occasionally falling to the floor and more than once knocking over a heavy night table. I also had nosebleeds. All, I now know, were consequences of kidney failure.

Now that I am on dialysis my life is much improved. Like all chronic kidney patients I am still anemic, but dialysis, injections of testosterone, and iron pills have raised my red blood count considerably. My feeling of exhaustion is gone. My blood pressure is normal. I no longer get nosebleeds.

I started dialysis at Columbia Presbyterian Hospital in New York City as an in-patient. There a surgeon sewed an artery to a vein in my right arm to form a fistula. This increased the blood flow in the vein to such an extent that if you were to place the tips of your fingers lightly on my arm where the fistula scar is, you would feel the blood coursing through the vein as a sort of electrical tingle. Medically this tingling is known as a "thrill," a rather sexy term to apply to the end product of vascular surgery. The fistula not only increased the blood flow in the vein, it also gradually enlarged the vein. The object was to create permanent, easy access to my blood supply.

Exaggerated mood swings are a byproduct of kidney disease. At Columbia Presbyterian, when I learned that I would be a dialysis patient, attached to a kidney machine for three days out of every seven, I wept in my hospital bed in the dark of night and sometimes by the light of day. Having known for years that life on a kidney machine might some day be inevitable didn't cushion the shock. I was very depressed when I reported to the Rogosin Kidney Center at New York Hospital after being discharged from Columbia Presbyterian, which has only an in-patient dialysis unit. But to my amazement what I found at Rogosin was not just another hospital. The patients were in street clothes, sitting in reclining lounge chairs, reading, watching individual ceiling-mounted TV sets, chatting with one another, even taking tiny sips of coffee or tea from plastic cups or sucking chips of ice. It could have been a social club, except each of the patients had blood-filled tubing running from one arm into a kidney machine. In a short time I cheered up....

Home Training Unit

I chose to join a small group in the Home Training Unit. Upon completion of my training I would lease a machine and dialyze in my own apartment. Two factors influenced my decision. First, a nurse had told me that the patients who dialyzed at home seemed to do the best, next came those who performed their own dialyses at a kidney center, last those who simply lay back in a hospital bed and let the nurses and technicians do it all. Second and even more compelling was my desire to put in a full work week, which I would be able to do only if I dialyzed at home at night.

For approximately three months I went to the Rogosin Center every Tuesday, Thursday, and Saturday and to the *Times* every Monday, Wednesday, and Friday. My only free day was Sunday. Now I dialyze at home every Monday, Wednesday, and Friday night, go to work every weekday, and have weekends off. I go back to Rogosin only once a month for a check-up, laboratory work, and to have my dialysis records reviewed....

My five-hour kidney-machine sessions actually run to about eight hours because it takes an hour and a half at home to prepare for dialysis and a half-hour or so afterwards to strip and clean the machine. Even so, I do not find my dialysis sessions unduly confining. I feel hemmed in only when I get the urge to travel and think of all the arrangements I will have to make and the tight itinerary I will have to follow.

In some respects my regimen between dialysis sessions is more onerous than the hours I spend hooked up to the machine because of the restrictions on my fluid intake. Without functioning kidneys I do not excrete enough water in the form of urine, and if too much fluid collects in my tissues, because I have drunk too much or eaten too many foods with a high water content, I will get water-logged, short of breath, my ankles will swell and my blood pressure will rise, which can lead to a stroke or heart attack. Thus it is imperative that I take in no more fluid between dialysis sessions than I can take off during a dialysis. I generally take off between five and six pounds of fluid every time I am on the machine.

"My five-hour kidney machine sessions actually run to about eight hours.... Even so, I do not find my dialysis sessions unduly confining."

Besides limiting my intake of fluid, I cannot use salt or eat salty foods. I must even eat sparingly of most fruits and vegetables because they contain so much water.

Resisting fluid is not so easy. The Sunday of the last Super Bowl game, for example, was disastrous. We were invited to a houseparty in the country. There was a heaping buffet and a well-stocked bar. I lost all control, stuffed myself with forbidden salty foods, washed them down with martinis, developed a raging thirst and drank glasses of water, cider, and ginger ale. I gained eleven pounds.

Pains of Indulgence

I was still dialyzing at Rogosin at the time, and a special high ultrafiltration coil was installed on my machine to wring all that fluid out of me. In five hours I took off the eleven pounds but toward the end I nearly blacked out. I was dizzy and clammy with sweat and both my legs went into agonizing muscle spasms simultaneously, becoming as rigid as iron bars from my toes to my hips. As the nurses and technicians worked over me, giving me saline and massaging my legs, I panted through clenched teeth and hissed like a lizard. I had to wait hours before I was physically able to get home in a cab and I was weak and in pain for two days. Every time I got out of bed during those two day, the muscles in my abdomen and at the back of my neck knotted up in excruciating pain, I got woozy, and I felt I would pass out.

Besides being on a no-salt and fluid-restricted diet, I am also allowed very little protein because the breakdown of protein creates waste products in the blood. I can eat only one egg, one ounce of cheese, and six ounces of meat, fish, or poultry a day.

Enough of restrictions? Not quite. I am also on a low potassium diet because I can get rid of potassium only when dialyzing and too much potassium in the system does something unfortunate: It stops your heart. So goodbye to orange juice, bananas, melons, peaches, apricots, nuts, chocolate, dark green vegetables, dried fruits, split peas, beans, and a host of other foods. The amount of raw fruit of any kind I can eat is limited. Ditto salad greens and vegetables. And the vegetables I eat at home are cooked in lots of water and then drained to leach out some of the potassium. Salad greens and potatoes are soaked for days in a large container of water, which is changed periodically, for this also eliminates some potassium.

"I would give a year of my life to be able to chug-a-lug a huge schooner of cold, foaming draft beer."

Do I cheat on my diet? Of course I do, being only human. But I know how to cheat cautiously and creatively. Hardest of all to resist is taking a good long drink whenever I want to. I am tired of little sips of this and that. I would give a year of my life to be able to chug-a-lug a huge schooner of cold, foaming draft beer, to feel it rush down my parched throat like a flash flood through a desert ravine. I would give another year to slug down an ice cream soda in two huge gulps. And a third year for a whole pitcher of ice water, beaded with little drops of condensation on the outside, cool, crystal clear and a half-gallon deep within.

Ways to Cope

But life goes on and I am happy to be living it with all its restrictions. We have found ways to cope. Leslie freezes fruit drinks in the ice cube tray of the refrigerator and I suck the cubes. Each cube works out to about an ounce of fluid but it lasts a while. I save two ounces of my daily fluid allotment for an after-dinner liqueur that I can savor for an hour or more. Leslie and I have found a dozen foreign restaurants that prepare exotic dishes that I can eat. At home we find cooking a challenge because of my dietary limitations and thus more fun than ever as we adjust old recipes and devise new ones. I have, after six years of abstinence, taken to smoking a pipe again, and derive great satisfaction from it.

Far more important, I feel much more energetic. Even my mood swings have abated. Before my system adjusted to dialysis, I developed common, unpleasant symptoms—cramps, dizzy spells, intense itching, a feeling sometimes of being unable to catch my breath, even terrible searing heartburn and hiccups from my medication. (Dialysis patients take lots of pills; I gulp down eight every morning, five at lunch, five at dinner and three before I go to bed.) All those symptoms have now passed. . . .

My Future

What does the future hold? I could stay on dialysis for the rest of my life, however long that may be. The record for longevity on a kidney machine, the last time I checked, was fourteen years, and if I stay on dialysis I am to break the record. Or I could opt for a transplant. However, no one in my family is capable of donating a kidney to me, and the statistics on cadaver transplants are not too encouraging. Half reject within two years, about two-third within five. Some patients have had two or three transplants.

If I get a kidney transplant and my body rejects the new kidney, I would simply go back on dialysis again. But, of course, I would go back in poorer shape than before because I would have had one major operation to put the kidney in, another major operation to take it out, and all the while it was in me I would have been getting powerful drugs to uppress my body's rejection mechanism.

Meanwhile, new breakthroughs seem to be on the horizon for dialysis. Smaller, portable machines, for example. Even more exciting, some physicians are experimenting with sorbents, edible substances that, when eaten, would absorb waste products and bind them to the stool for excretion. Sorbents would decrease the number of times a week a kidney patient would have to dialyze.

So I'm going to make the best of things, and when the time comes my physician and I will decide whether I should have a transplant. Meanwhile, every day, when I am immersed in work or some leisure activity, I completely forget for hours at a time that a kidney machine keeps me alive. And when I remember, the realization intensifies whatever I am doing. It sharpens my senses and heightens my appreciation of even such a simple thing as a beautiful spring day. I savor all the golden moments. Most important, being a dialysis patient has brought my wife, always close to me, immeasurably closer. That's worth everything. Even that schooner of beer.

Lee Foster worked as assistant travel editor for The New York Times *up until the time of his death in April 1977.*

viewpoint 67

Medical Advances Provoke Suicide

Avery D. Weisman

[The following viewpoint is excerpted from a case illustration that uses initials rather then names to identify the speakers.]

ADW: Organ transplantation is one of the great achievements of modern medicine. However, with each medical advance there are new problems. The price of progress may be that people are saved from one fatal disease only to die of others. Certainly this is true with organ transplantation. In preventing tissue rejection, infections may be ignited, healing delayed, neoplasms initiated. Patients become exceedingly vulnerable—psychologically as well as physically—to what would ordinarily be minor injuries.

Only the kidney has been transplanted often enough to offer a feasible procedure for large groups within the population. Here, too, survival itself imposes many secondary problems. Extension of life does not necessarily restore the quality of life. Renal dialysis patients may choose to discontinue the program because they are so hampered by the narrow range of options available to them. In a sense, they elect death rather than unrelieved dependency. Kidney transplants that are technically successful may create emotional and social disasters, and when repeated transplants fail, patients may give up entirely. The case today will not settle anything, but it will show what happens to some people who undergo this procedure.

HSO: Kidney patients usually have a very extensive medical history. This man was no exception, so I will confine myself to a brief account of the major events. Then we'll hear from the head nurse and social worker on the Kidney Transplant Unit staff.

This man first developed progressive kidney disease at age nineteen, and finally succumbed at age forty-one—a span of time that consumed about half his lifetime. He was a fisherman, like the rest of his family. They all lived on a common tract of land in northern Maine. But they shared more than a common occupation and residence. He was the third youngest of twelve siblings, and learned from earliest childhood to share property and to maintain staunch family loyalty. During one of his few remissions, he started to build a fishing boat for the family. He relapsed again before it could be completed. The unfinished boat still stands on family property, a mute symbol of an unfinished life, but a life of devotion and loyalty to their common aim.

He was first admitted here ten years ago, when he was aged thirty-one. Six years ago, he had the first kidney transplant, with his brother as donor. It was rejected fourteen months later. Then a second transplant, with his sister as donor, was performed, but this, too, was rejected. A third transplant from an anonymous nine-year-old was carried out about a year ago. But let's hear from the social worker.

IP-1: I knew the patient and his wife very well, following them for a long time. He was a stolid and agreeable man, who always went along with family decisions. His wife said that she had seen him angry only once during their eighteen-year marriage. He was diligent, hardworking when his health allowed, and was very unhappy whenever he was away from home.

I'd like to concentrate on the events of the past year, after the third transplant. In addition to an endless series of medical complications, he lost his father through a heart attack, a brother, an aunt, and a sister. His mother died of diabetes twenty years ago. These losses evidently were contributing factors because when admitted to the hospital for a checkup, he was obviously depressed, and no longer the stoical

Avery D. Weisman, *The Realization of Death*, New York: Jason Aronson, Inc. 1974. Reprinted with permission.

man I had expected.

IP-2: I have been the head nurse on the unit, and know the patient, his wife, children, and some members of his family. When he returned after the third transplant, he was not only depressed, but complaining (he never complained very vociferously) of failing vision. This was attributed to diabetes, a complicating disease of therapy.

"Kidney transplants that are technically successful may create emotional and social disasters...patients may give up entirely."

Even during the years of dialysis, he was quietly optimistic, even though it was difficult for him to be away from home. It was a happy day for all when he was first selected for a transplant. In the months that followed, he returned regularly for checkups, always bringing up boxes of clams and lobsters. Then the rejection process commenced. He had to be hospitalized again and again in futile efforts to save the kidney. Later, he was again hospitalized for the second transplant. This lasted for a couple of years. About a year ago, however, he began to fail. Vision and diabetes worsened. He developed a testicular abscess which resisted antibiotics, and the testis finally had to be removed. There were numerous infections at various sites, which healed with great difficulty, if at all. I do remember one hospitalization in which both the patient and the entire staff were very depressed and discouraged. After he went home, I happened to be driving through his town and stopped to visit. He was remarkably improved in spirits, showing that just being at home helped.

We were all very pessimistic, but went ahead with a third transplant....

A Signal

HSO: In the early spring, when fishing industry flourishes, [our man] must return to the hospital once more. The testicle has been removed, but the abscess persists. Diabetes is difficult to control, and his vision diminishes.

One night he simply asks the nurse to remove the scissors from the room because he is afraid of what might happen. The following day he asks his wife not to let him be alone with the children. No reason is given because she assumes that he does not want his children to see him crying, as he had.

Several months later, he is admitted again, suffering with recurrent infections, pneumonia, and anginal attacks. It is the middle of the week, and the only unusual event is that he is to have a leave-of-absence

for the next weekend, so that he can stay with his wife and children in a small apartment they had rented near the hospital. He has an arteriovenous shunt in his arm. Earlier in the day, several sutures from his back were removed, but a furuncle persists, causing some pain. Nothing else is noted until that night, shortly after midnight. The nurse on duty makes her rounds, goes into his room and finds the patient engulfed in blood, his rubber shunt cleanly cut.

I saw him within two hours, but of course, emergency measures had started before that. He lost about five units of blood, and was sedated. When I was able to talk with him on the following morning, he was amnesic, but said that he must have cut the shunt, although he couldn't recall. His wife did report that he had said she'd be better off without him. Evidently, this was not an unusual statement because she didn't tell anyone.

What I want to ask this group is why *now* does he make a suicide attempt. He was desperate, discouraged, preterminal, I suppose, but still...twelve years of hospitalization, including ten years of repeated admissions here...why?

ADW: When we don't know how to answer a question, we usually turn it back on the questioner. What do you think?

HSO: Well...he was steadily getting worse, deteriorating in every respect. His quiet optimism was gone; mental problems and physical disabilities were multiplying. He was not only depressed, but intermittently confused. Even the mildest, most sedentary work was out of the question, due to his angina and his failing vision. He couldn't carry out any life-threatening behavior, because he always complied with what was expected of him. He did give a signal to the nurse and his wife about the scissors. I think that cutting the shunt was the only effort of which he was capable, and it meant severing his link to the hospital, as well. He didn't want his children to see him so depressed before, and with the forthcoming weekend, this could have been decisive so far as ending his life.

ADW: I don't suppose any of use could elaborate on that.

Some Reasons

HSO: You must realize that patients on the Kidney Unit usually enter with great expectations. Not only do they regard transplantation as a miraculous reprieve that just wasn't available a few years ago, but they have been selected. They are reprieved both from certain death and from the restrictions of a dialysis existence. Transplantation is a kind of miracle. It is not unreasonable for some patients to ignore the risks, failure, or rejection, and to anticipate returning to a full and effective life. For most patients—statistics bear me out—this will be a futile hope. They don't find their independence restored. Their survival may be stretched out, but at a price of more sickness than they ever imagined enduring. It is one thing to talk about hope, but something else to keep hope or even a little courage alive, when everything else is falling to pieces. For this man, only bitter fragments. I come back to the half-built boat which will never sail. He, too, will never fish, perhaps never see or walk by the sea again.

He had little to lose by suicide. He was also ashamed of his failures. By this I mean two kinds of failure: failure as a family member, husband, and father, and the failure of the two transplants. His brother and sister had forfeited their kidneys on his behalf and to no avail.

RSS: Were these donors the ones who died during the past year?

HSO: No, they were other siblings. But let's not get away from my question, why now?...

IP-2: I mentioned that all of us were very discouraged, and this might have been conveyed to him. And he did get a lot of drugs. He was in a kind of stupor much of the time. I agree that he, like others, expected miracles, but by now, he knew that this wasn't the place where miracles would be performed. He wanted to be home, not at the apartment.

LCJ: It sounds as if he felt he'd let everyone down, doctors and nurses, as well as his family. A lot had been invested.

JWW: I did some psychological tests with him after the attempt, not before, and the circumstances were far from ideal. His answers were brief. The TAT outcomes were either very tentative, or had no outcome at all. The word *probably* prefaced everything he said. It indicated a rather detached and impersonal approach, not a closely analytic qualification.

"He was diligent, hard working when his health allowed, and was very unhappy whenever he was away from home."

He would prefer being a dog, because they're taken care of and lead an easy life. But—this is strange—he couldn't think of any animal that he would prefer not being. It was as if any animal were better off than he. I found no sign of further suicidal ideation.

One week later, testing him with the POMS, his tension was high; he was scored as low on anger, but moderately high on depression and quite confused—not confused enough, however, because he did carry out the test, which is self-administered. He was ashamed of the suicide attempt, and didn't want to discuss it further.

ADW: What about the future for this man? He went home again, didn't he?

IP-1: We don't have to speculate. He did go home, didn't improve. Over the next seven months he had two heart attacks which were treated in a local hospital. I kept in telephone touch with his wife, and learned that he said very little. Maybe he was just too sick, but no further suicide attempts were made. He also had a lot of intestinal ulceration. He had been out of the hospital for about two weeks, and was sitting on their porch, doing nothing in particular. When his wife brought lunch out to him, she found him dead.

HSO: By our silence, I see that we all empathize with this man's sense of futility. We have nothing to say. Perhaps we can respect his right to call it quits, and not to endure further illness and pain. His life was already over when he went home. He had further heart attacks, probably recurrent angina, and pain from the ulcerated intestines. At least he was at home. He could await death passively. Suicide was no longer an imperative.

Avery D. Weisman, M.D., is a pioneer in thanatology, past president of the American Association of Suicidology, and Chairman of the Suicide Prevention Review Committee, National Institute of Mental Health. He is the author of the book The Realization of Death.

"Research produces knowledge; knowledge generates technology; and technology truly revolutionizes the way all of us live."

Technological Advances Should Have No Limits

John Glenn

In his State of the Union Address, President Reagan said that his Administration—and I quote—"is committed to keeping America the technological leader of the world now and into the 21st century."

The next day, scientists announced that they had verified the existence of a new sub-atomic particle—the so-called "W" particle—that brings us a giant step closer to understanding the forces of nature. Now, this discovery would have been newsworthy no matter when it happened. But it was all the more significant coming only one day after the President sought to assure us that America was still the world's pre-eminent technological power. Because the research that led to that discovery wasn't conducted in an American lab, but at the European Nuclear Research Center in Switzerland. The fact is that America has lost its position as the world leader in high energy physics. The tragedy is, we didn't have to. The discovery could have been made at the Fermi National Accelerator Laboratory in Batavia, Illinois. It could have, that is, had the research not been called off there for lack of money.

In my opinion, America today stands at a critical crossroad with respect to research and development. And like the traveller in Robert Frost's immortal poem, the road we choose will have an enormous impact on our future—and on that of our children as well. I've got some strong feelings on this subject—and I'd like to share them with you this afternoon.

Rx for America: Basic Research

Historically, research and development has been mankind's most fundamental tool for meeting and shaping the challenges of the future. But today, the cutting edge of that tool—basic research—is under sharp and unrelenting attack.

John Glenn, speech given before the High Technology Seminar of the National Journal in Washington DC, February 2, 1983.

Evidence of this hostility is all around us. You can see it in the shrinking number of scientists at our national laboratories, and it's evident in America's retreat from the frontiers of space.

Even in the halls of Congress, important, basic research is often cynically disparaged and presented with facetious awards implying that it is little more than a clever rip-off. For some people, inquiry into the unknown has become too costly, too visionary and too far removed from such "real world" problems as hunger, disease and poverty.

In reality, of course, the facts prove just the opposite. Research produces knowledge; knowledge generates technology; and technology truly revolutionizes the way all of us live.

Research Leads to New Potential

Even in an era of austerity, we must remember that research is not amenable to the rigors of cost-accounting. In fact, the one thing we know about research when we start it is that we don't know what we'll find when we finish it. Who could have predicted that Sir Alexander Fleming's experiment with green mold in 1929 would lead to the discovery of penicillin and the development of antibiotics? Or who foresaw that civilian spin-offs from the American space program would someday include digital watches, hand-held calculators and the burgeoning new field of microelectronics?

Those who condemn scientific undertakings as foolish, unnecessary or wasteful would do well to recall the famous exchange between Benjamin Disraeli and the English scientist Michael Faraday. Faraday had just invented the dynamo and expected the British Prime Minister to be excited by the news. But after Disraeli inspected this earliest of generators, he asked: "What good is this?" To which Faraday replied, "What good is a baby, Mr. Disraeli?"

Well, we all know that the good of a baby lies in its potential—and we *ought* to know that the potential of any new discovery is as difficult to determine as the potential of an infant.

In the past, we've always understood that our ability to reach national goals and realize our potential depends on our government's support for research and development. From the establishment of the first telegraph line to the invention of the transistor, from the invention of the laser through the development of high yield grains that helped feed a hungry world, publicly supported and privately developed research—along with the technology needed to exploit the fruits of that research—has made America the wealthiest, most productive and most technologically advanced nation in human history.

America Rates Second in Technology

Today, it is a different story. The loss of American leadership in high energy physics is not an isolated instance but a symptom of a much larger problem. If our current direction in the field of research is not reversed, America will become a second-rate technological power. It's just that simple.

"If our current direction in the field of research is not reversed, America will become a second-rate technological power."

Unfortunately, there is mounting evidence that we are intent on strangling the goose that laid the golden egg. Over the past 16 years, the proportion of America's GNP invested in research and development steadily declined—dropping more than 20 percent since 1967. In the first two years of this decade, our Federal investment in nondefense research dropped by over 16 percent in real dollars. And even though Congress increased our nondefense research investment by more than a billion dollars over the Administration's request for the fiscal year, that still represented a real increase of only two percent. And more to the point, it still leaves us with a research investment that is 10 percent less than it was two years ago.

But that's not all. Because while we mistakenly try to trim our growing budget deficits by taking a machete to our research commitments, our competitors are moving in the opposite direction. As a percentage of GNP, Japan will increase its research investment by almost a third in the next seven years—and they're doing it by upping their government's support for research and development by nearly 50 percent.

Japan is already challenging us for world leadership in the field of computers. But the Japanese have *also*

embarked on a series of national projects—including the National Superspeed Computer Project and the Fifth Generation Computer Project—to give them supremacy in the next generation of computers as well.

Deadly Implications

The implications are deadly serious. Because besides having application for the design of large-scale integrated circuits, geophysics, aerodynamics, automotive design, and a host of other civilian purposes, super computers are also vitally important for national defense. And whether we speak of America's military preparedness or her industrial strength, we simply cannot afford to become dependent on computers that are manufactured abroad. The competition in supercomputers is one race we dare not lose—and it points up a broader lesson we dare not forget. In the short run, we can't nourish our economy by cannibalizing our government research efforts. In the long run, no nation can remain prosperous simply by feeding off the research of others.

Today we're told that the private sector will fill whatever gaps are left by the government's flagging research commitment—and that if a project is worth doing, the private sector will.

In my opinion, that attitude not only ignores American history—and the histories of our agriculture, aerospace, communications, computer and nuclear industries—but it also ignores some fundamental facts of life in a capitalist economy.

Basic Research is Fact of Life

The first of these facts is that a large part of the research and development effort we need is *basic* research—and basic research is not always attractive to industry because it doesn't always result in a saleable end-product. Second, at a time when many firms cannot generate enough capital for new equipment and plant modernization, it is simply unrealistic to expect them to spend all that is needed for research. And third, most American firms—for good or for ill—must make investments that will yield a return within three to five years. As we all know, however, the dividends of basic research are often not apparent for ten or twenty years.

But you don't have to take my word for the importance of government-sponsored research. The facts speak for themselves. Last year, I conducted a survey of American Nobel Laureates in science between 1967 and 1981. The results were astounding. More than 80 percent of our Nobel Prize winners received substantial support—meaning at least half their funds—directly from the U.S. Government. Moreover, with only two exceptions, all those who received Federal support said that these funds were crucial to sustaining the work that led to their Nobel award. And let me say that that work has been vitally important. It led directly to today's biotechnology industry and to advances in microelectronics, lasers, pharmaceuticals and medicine.

Now, I am *not* suggesting that the government should either compete with or supplant the business community's research and development efforts. But I *am* suggesting that the government should work in *concert* with the private sector's research efforts wherever possible and be prepared to assume the lion's share of the burden whenever necessary.

Invest in People

I also believe that we should increase our investment in people. More specifically, we must start producing scientists, engineers and other highly skilled people necessary to meet the challenges of the coming decade.

In 1982, American colleges and universities granted 65,000 degrees in engineering. By contrast, the Soviet Union graduated about 300,000, and Japan—with roughly half our population—graduated 87,000.

What's worse, this intense demand for technically trained people has produced handsome salaries which are luring faculty and graduate students away from even our best universities. Right now, one out of every ten faculty positions in engineering is vacant. In computer sciences, the faculty shortage is 15 percent. As a result, one of every four faculty members hired last year in engineering was a foreign national—as were 41 percent of all engineering students. If we don't turn this around, who will teach our next generation of scientists and engineers?

Problems in Education

But the crisis in human capital does not begin or end with our universities. Our high schools aren't giving our young people the kind of background they need today—and part of the reason is a lack of qualified science and math teachers at the precollege level.

Last year, the Administration's response to all of this was frightening. First, they cut virtually all funds for science education from the budget of the National Science Foundation. Then they tried to dismantle the NSF's Science Education Division. And then they appointed a Commission on Precollege Science and Math Education to tell us what to do about the problem they exacerbated. That's almost like the child who murdered his parents—and then asked the court for mercy because he was an orphan.

Apparently, the Administration has finally realized they made a mistake. Just two days ago—months before their own commission will issue its final report—the Administration announced a 75 million dollar crash program to train science and math teachers. But as Werner Von Braun once observed:

> "(crash programs) fail because they are based on the theory that with nine women pregnant, you can produce a baby a month."

The simple fact is that we cannot turn our education and research systems on and off like water faucets. Any research program worthy of the name requires a long lead time—time to train people, to conduct experiments and to build facilities. Once this effort is disrupted, the effects can be severe and long-lasting. So while I welcome the Administration's new proposals as a solid step in the right direction, I hope they recognize that we must stay the course. Because where research and education are concerned false starts do *not* constitute a "new beginning."

Remove the Limits

In my opinion, there are at least six things we must do to recapture America's technological superiority.

First, we should restore funding for research programs which have potentially high payoffs but little short-term profit for the private sector. Government funding for basic research should be both stable and predictable—and we should make multiyear grants for projects that directly involve our national security or our national economic health.

"We must start producing more scientists, engineers and other highly skilled people necessary to meet the challenges of the coming decade."

Second, we must address the crisis in human capital. We should encourage our brightest students to go on to post-graduate training and compensate our scientists at a level commensurate with their abilities and contributions. We ought to encourage industry to endow university chairs and to allow industrial laboratory equipment to be used for graduate training and research.

Third, we ought to encourage a closer partnership between industry and our universities in both basic and applied research. Industry must recognize its responsibility to support the training of the next generation of scientists and engineers. For their part, universities must recognize that improved research means more economic growth and more economic growth means more support for our universities. At the same time, however, we must never allow the independence of our institutions or the integrity of our scholars to be compromised.

Fourth, we must recogize that the challenges of the future demand a scientifically and technologically literate population—and that means that we must improve science and math education at every level. As a first step, we should rebuild the National Science Foundation's Science Education Program. For the future, we must increase the supply of science and math teachers in our primary and secondary schools. This week, I introduced legislation to help us reach that goal.

Fifth, we must improve the climate for private sector research and development. Two years ago, I proposed—and Congress enacted—incentives for companies to conduct research here in the United States. I believe that ought to become a permanent part of our tax code. To encourage innovation and cooperative research ventures, I've also proposed changes in our antitrust and trade policies.

Sixth and finally, I believe we need a coherent national policy on science and technology. And if the White House Office of Science and Technology is too weak to give us one, then we ought to start thinking about creating a Cabinet level Department of Science and Technology. Just as war is too important to be left to the Generals, so national science policy is too important to be left only to lawyers and accountants.

Technology Crisis Challenges Everyone

Behind the six proposals I've just outlined is a common thread—and a common need. Since 1970, we've seen over two million jobs leave our shores for foreign countries. Products that once provided wages for our workers and profits for our businesspeople are now made overseas. Research that was once conducted by American scientists is now conducted by foreign scientists—in labs both here and abroad.

We can't stand by and allow these trends to continue. And while government can help, *everyone* will have to do their part.

"The simple fact is... where research and education are concerned, false starts do not constitute a 'new beginning.'"

Those of you in business must increase your research and development investment—and I supported several amendments to the 1981 Tax Act which gave you incentives to do so. Businesses should also attempt to form more organizations like the semiconductor research cooperative, to conduct joint research and development efforts with our universities.

For their part, universities will have to be more open to these joint research efforts and take a leading role in raising educational standards across the board.

Labor will have to cooperate as well, by working to increase productivity with technological improvements.

Now I know there are those who will say that America is no longer capable of this kind of partnership; that we have become too jaded and too selfish to come together for the common good. Well, I say those voices are wrong. I say we *will* rise to the challenge and again reach new horizons. Because of

this much I am sure: given the proper education, tools and incentives, we Americans can still outwork, outinvent, outproduce and outcompete anyone on the face of this planet....

Although we are now falling behind in that competition, it is not too late to improve our standing. For as Oliver Wendell Holmes once observed, the great thing in this world is not so much where we stand, as in what direction we are moving.

John Glenn is a senator from the state of Ohio. On February 20, 1962, he became the first American and the third person to be put into orbital space flight.

"We need not squander our resources on patchwork or bionic Mister Magoos....We can come to accept, with grace and dignity, death."

Technological Advances Need Limits

David Lygre

As our technology advances, and the average age of our population rises, we will find increasing numbers of people who would benefit from replacement parts. But where will those parts come from? For people needing a complex organ, the best solution will usually be a transplant. Animal organs will generally be used only as a last resort, so the recipients will have to depend on other people to furnish those organs. But that raises several ethical and legal problems.

First, let us consider the issues with live donors. Many people believe a person's body is a gift from God, and some interpret this to mean that no one may choose to be mutilated (as in donating an organ) except when it is for the welfare of his own body. Indeed, France has prohibited surgery that is not for the benefit of the patient, and this has had the effect of prohibiting transplants from live donors. On the other hand, surely the well-being of the total person, including his psychological and spiritual health, is more important than his physical health alone. Otherwise, it would be immoral for people to have vasectomies or cosmetic surgery, even though they considered it to be in their own best interests. And it would be immoral for anyone to endanger himself to help others—for example, trying to rescue a fallen mountain climber, protecting family members from attack—or donating an organ.

People should have the right to decide for themselves whether the benefits of donating an organ outweigh the risks. They must weigh the risks to their own health, such as the risk of dying from an operation to remove a kidney, or from being left with a single kidney. They must also consider the psychological effects. After surgery, some donors feel depressed; they resent the recipient and the people who encouraged them to donate. But those feelings usually disappear, and in the end most donors feel much better about themselves, even if the transplant fails.

The risks are real, nevertheless, so it is important that each donor truly give his voluntary and informed consent. This high, but necessary, standard would generally exclude minors, mental incompetents, and people such as prisoners who are under duress. It is also hard to ensure that a donor, regardless of age, truly gives his consent voluntarily when he is related to the recipient. For example, he may "volunteer" in order to avoid feelings of guilt or to demonstrate his loyalty and courage. Because of these problems, hospitals often use procedures such as the following: A psychological evaluation is given to assess, however imperfectly, whether the donor is mentally stable and whether he is being coerced; the evaluation is done before the recipient enters the hospital, and by people who are not involved with the care of the recipient; the donor is fully informed about the risks to himself, the chances for a successful transplant, and other medical options; he is given ample time to consider his decision; and he is told that if he decides not to donate, the physician will provide a technical excuse if necessary.

Finding Organs to Transplant

People do not always decide to donate. In 1978 a thirty-nine-year-old man dying of a rare disease (aplastic anemia) needed a bone marrow transplant. The only person who was suitably matched was his cousin, but he declined to donate. The patient went to court, asking that his cousin "aid a dying man (through) a medically safe, experimentally proven, minor procedure which will at most result in minor and temporary discomfort." The judge denied the request on the grounds that "it would defeat the sanctity of the individual." The man died two weeks later.

From the book *Life Manipulation: From Test Tube Babies to Aging* by David Lygre. (c) 1979 by David Lygre. Reprinted with permission by the publisher, Walker and Company.

The complications of using live donors are great, and the types of organs they can supply are limited, so we will have to look elsewhere for most of our replacement parts. Which brings us to the only other source of human organs—cadavers.

Our growing dependence on cadavers raises another set of problems. We might imagine, for example, new opportunities for grave robbers and body snatchers. But organs deteriorate so rapidly that the culprits would find a rather small market for their wares. Indeed, it is safe to assume that a "hardhearted person" will remain only a figure of speech. . . .

Deciding to Be a Donor

The Uniform Anatomical Gift Act, a piece of model legislation that has been substantially adopted by all fifty states, allows any mentally competent person of eighteen years or older to donate any or all of his cadaver to any hospital, accredited medical or dental school, university, organ storage facility, physician, or individual for use in scientific research, education, therapy, or transplantation. He can make the donation in his will, or by a signed, written statement in the presence of two witnesses. No one can overrule the donation. The law also allows the next of kin to authorize donations unless there is evidence that the decedent would have objected.

Despite this legislation, we still do not have enough organs for transplantation. Indeed, thousands of people in the United States alone are currently waiting for a suitable kidney. . . .

Choosing Recipients

Supplying replacement parts is only part of the problem; we also have to decide who will receive them. With natural organs in short supply, the task is fairly straightforward with transplants. First, patients become eligible if they meet certain medical criteria such as age (generally, sixty years or less) and health. They may also receive a psychological screening to assess whether they can deal with the possible problems—feelings of guilt toward a live donor, an impaired body image, an identity crisis. According to Denton Cooley: "Not everyone wants to live with someone else's heart inside him. It's an eerie thing." Then, from the pool of eligible candidates, the actual recipients are chosen simply on the basis of whoever happens to be the best match for an organ that is available. The selection is done by a computerized antigen-matching system.

With artificial organs, however, the decisions are not as clear-cut. For one thing, the psychological adjustments may be more difficult. Not everyone can accept a regimen of twenty to thirty hours every week connected to a dialysis machine, or the reality that his life and activities depend on a machine. And people with external devices, such as an artificial arm

or larynx, must cope with sometimes being considered less than a full person. Improved design will ease some of these problems, but this can only be part of the answer. For until we are able to interact comfortably with others who bear some mark of abnormality, their psychological problems will be compounded by ours.

"Not everyone wants to live with someone else's heart inside him. It's an eerie thing."

Even after medical and psychological criteria are applied, there are still situations where there are not enough artificial organs for the people who qualify. This problem has arisen with people who need kidney transplants; they are maintained on "artificial kidney" machines until a natural kidney becomes available. But that can take a long time, and there are a limited number of machines at a dialysis center, so sometimes a decision must be made on who will get to use a machine.

How do we make such life-and-death decisions? One method has been to assess "social worth." Some hospitals have used a committee of physicians and, perhaps, other community members to select the winning candidates. The committee members evaluate such factors as occupation, marital status, number and age of dependents, life expectancy, social standing, and contributions to society. Contributions to the hospital presumably don't count.

This approach has serious drawbacks. One is the suspicion (even if it is unjustified) that political factors influence the decisionmaking. Another is the basic belief that no one can validly judge the worth of another human being. These concerns have led to other, nonjudgmental methods. The most common is first come, first served; random selection is another. While it is not at all clear these methods are better, it is just as well they are being tried. For the "social worth" approach has produced an alarming decline in the number of philosophers.

Technology's Cost vs. Benefits

Since we do not have the resources to supply everyone with every replacement part, we must also weigh costs against benefits. For complex organs, transplants will usually be cheaper and more effective than mechanical devices; when only one part of an organ is damaged, or a body part is mostly mechanical, artificial substitutes will often be better. But the problem of cost is especially great with artificial parts. The Food and Drug Administration, which regulates medical devices, upholds high standards of safety, effectiveness, and quality control. This increases the cost of developing and testing new products, so companies often find that if the potential market is small, they have little chance of making a profit unless they receive a subsidy. Indeed, there is at least one instance where a private company declined to make a needed medical device because the cost of doing the necessary tests far outweighed the potential sales.

As our artificial parts become more intricate, we will reach a point of diminishing returns, where we decide certain features are just not worth the extra cost. We may have to set both minimum and maximum requirements for medical devices, and each ''extra'' will have to be justified on a cost-benefit basis.

''We will still reach a limit on how much we can spend...and we will have to choose our priorities within that budget.''

We also have to weigh the costs and benefits to society as a whole. Everyone may be morally entitled to be a six-million-dollar person, but we simply do not have the resources to do it. One physician even predicted: ''The pattern of advance of medical technology suggests that before too long we may have to decree that the various pumps, potions and prostheses which can keep a man alive beyond his natural span should be withdrawn when he reaches some statutory age.''...

We must also face the prospect of a shrinking proportion of young people having to support an increasing number of old people. One critical area will be medical services. People sixty-five and older already account for nearly one-third of the health costs in the United States, and this proportion will increase. Furthermore, as more people come to believe health care is a basic human right that should not depend on a person's ability to pay, we will commit increasing amounts of our public resources to health care. That money will have to come from somewhere: perhaps higher taxes, or less money for such areas as law enforcement, education, housing, national defense, and social services. But whatever we do, we will still reach a limit on how much we can spend on medical care, and we will have to choose our priorities within that budget.

Life and Death

Here we must acknowledge a harsh reality: As our physical and mental abilities dim, we become increasingly poor investments for those limited resources. George Pickering, professor of medicine at Oxford University, remarked: ''The present goal of medicine seems to be indefinite life, perhaps in the end with somebody else's liver, somebody else's

arteries but not with somebody else's brain. Should transplants succeed, those with senile brains will form an ever-increasing fraction of the inhabitants of the earth. I find this a terrifying prospect.''

That does not have to happen; we need not squander our resources on patchwork or bionic Mister Magoos. Fortunately we have a simpler and more satisfying answer, both for the individual and for society as a whole: We can come to accept, with grace and dignity, death.

One physician has written: ''Doctors can keep almost anyone alive artificially nowadays. That's the measure of medical progress in the second half of the 20th century.'' Indeed our hospitals now have an impressive array of hardware to keep us going. As temporary measures, respirators, heart assist devices, and other machines have helped us save many lives. But they also force us to make agonizing decisions about when to use them.

Prolonging Life

On the night of April 15, 1975, for reasons that were never fully determined, twenty-one-year-old Karen Ann Quinlan went into a coma. She was rushed to Newton (New Jersey) Memorial Hospital and placed on a respirator. Nine days later she was transferred to another hospital. As weeks and months passed by, she remained on the respirator unconscious. She had short periods of spontaneous breathing; her eyes and mouth occasionally opened; her eyes sometimes followed the source of sounds; and she had some brain activity. She did not meet the medical criteria for death, but no doctors held any hope that she would recover. Her body gradually curled into a rigid, twisted state, and her weight dropped.

After several months Karen's parents asked that the respirator be removed. The attending physician declined on the basis that such action would be illegal and contrary to the medical code. Then her parents asked the New Jersey State Court to designate the father as guardian so he could authorize that the respirator be removed. Their request was denied. But in March 1976 the New Jersey Supreme Court unanimously granted Joseph Quinlan the request under the condition that competent medical authorities agreed Karen had no reasonable chance of recovery. It was done; in May Karen was taken off the respirator. To almost everyone's surprise, she was able to breathe on her own....

Her case stirred people to think carefully about life-sustaining machines and the problems in setting limits on their use. The answers are not easy, and there are many factors to consider. Friends and relatives feel great distress while a loved one teeters indefinitely in the misty no-man's-land between life and death. Sometimes they are also drained financially. While Karen Quinlan was on the respirator, for example, her total expenses exceeded one hundred thousand dollars. But in her case, and many others, the expenses are borne primarily by the public. Now we could argue that, as a matter of public policy, the most productive use of our medical resources is to reserve them for patients who have a reasonable chance of recovery. Yet few people would go so far as to insist, in the name of the public good, that individuals may not cling to a thread of life, however slender.

Prolonging Death

One answer is to let the family decide. For example, the Medical Society of New Jersey has proposed that each hospital establish a committee capable of assessing whether borderline patients are likely to function again at a reasonable mental level. The committee would advise the family and, if the prognosis were negative, the family could choose whether to have the life-support system removed.

A physician may argue, however, that his first and foremost duty is to preserve his patient's life. But preserving life is not necessarily the same thing as prolonging dying. Furthermore, as one physician remarked: "The obligation of the physician is to do the best he can for the patient. And sometimes the best thing he can do is let the patient die." When a patient's mind is fading and his capacity for self-reflection and human relationships is lost irretrievably, according to competent medical judgement, insisting that his physical life go on may be more cruel than loving. There is a profound difference between living and existing.

Others may protest that life is a gift from God and, therefore, man has no moral right to terminate it. It does not necessarily follow, however, that we should use machines to prolong life, even when there is no reasonable chance of recovery. Over two decades ago, Pius XII said that "extraordinary" means were not required to prolong life. And the Church of England has stated that life-support machines may be withdrawn from a patient if doctors determine that his organs will never again function on their own. Nevertheless, some people believe that pulling the plug is immoral because it frustrates God's will for us to live. . . .

People on the verge of death, however, are not always competent to make binding decisions. So some people have signed "living wills," specifying in advance that extraordinary means should not be used to keep them alive. Those documents may not be legally binding except in states that have adopted a living-will statute. California was the first to do so (in 1976), and other states have followed suit. As Gordon Rattray Taylor, a science writer, remarked: "The attempt to die, despite the efforts of those who would keep one alive, might form the most macabre of dramas, and the right to die may one day need to be

defended as the most fundamental of human liberties."

It is about time. Living-will statutes will not set off a stampede of customers, or cause instant bankruptcy for life insurance companies. But they will encourage many of us to think realistically about death, and to develop some attitudes and answers we literally can live with. . . .

"If we truly respect human life, we cannot insist that everyone live as long as modern technology can keep his body sort of functioning."

We need not cringe at the prospect of death; it is a natural and necessary part of life. Although in the twentieth century we have largely removed death from the home to the hospital, we are coming again to realize that the most important need of a dying person is to be with his family and friends. One answer is the "hospice," a concept of care that enables the patient to live as normal a life as possible. Whether he is in his home, a hospital, or some other facility, the dying person receives whatever pain-killing and anxiety-relieving drugs he needs, and he is with people who care for his other needs—relatives, friends, and specially trained health personnel and social workers. He is free to talk about death, and to share his experience with those around him.

Indeed, we are learning a great deal from the terminally ill. The major pioneer has been Elisabeth Kubler-Ross, a Swiss-born psychiatrist who has encouraged thousands of dying patients to talk about their experiences. She has also interviewed people who have returned from the brink of death, and their experiences are comforting. . . .

If we truly respect human life, we cannot insist that everyone live as long as modern technology can keep his body sort of functioning. To the contrary. We should help people feel the rich fabric of life, but we also should respect their decisions to decline further treatment when life has become only a burdensome existence. We must learn how to make death a decent and humane experience, not something bitterly contested to the last gasp. Paul Ramsey has termed death "the ultimate indignity." Living will proponents often speak of "death with dignity." But the point of it all is to enhance human dignity, not particularly in death, but in life.

Dr. David Lygre, a professor of biochemistry, has been a postdoctoral fellow of the American Cancer Society at Case Western Reserve University in Cleveland and at the University of York in England. He is the author of Life Manipulation.

"As this explosion of knowledge continues, it will quickly become evident that we can indeed triumph over death in our time."

Medical Technology Can Conquer Death

Alvin Silverstein

We need not be the last generation to die—because we can conquer the diseases that kill. We can conquer death in our time.

Indeed we are well on our way to conquering death by expanding our understanding of the life processes. In 1976 a group of eminent men in biomedicine, members of the President's Biomedical Research Panel, reported to the nation that with the proper support, medical researchers could learn to control or prevent *all* human diseases—within several decades. . . .

What lies behind this confidence in the imminent cure of the major diseases? As a species, we have always been impelled by a desire to know more about the world, but in recent times our acquisition of information and knowledge has been growing explosively. Information is accumulating so rapidly that the total is doubling every five or six years. If we continue to amass facts at the present rate, in a hundred years we will know more than a million times as much about our world as we know today. Even scientists have difficulty appreciating the magnitude of the scientific revolution that is engulfing us, but as this explosion of knowledge continues, it will quickly become evident that we can indeed triumph over death in our time.

The Knowledge Explosion

What are the reasons for this explosive growth in the sciences and technologies? There are many. One of the most basic has been a shift in emphasis in our culture. In recent centuries we have become a technologically oriented society. A large fraction of our material and human resources is now being allocated to the sciences and technologies. Science has evolved from an avocation of the few to a vocation for the many. More than 90 percent of all the scientists who have ever lived are alive and working today. This army of ten million men and women, representing every nation in the world, is contributing to the current flood of scientific and technological advances.

New tools are constantly expanding the scope of human intellect and achievements. Modern electronic computers accomplish in seconds tasks that would take skilled mathematicians months or even years to perform. Powerful microscopes have revealed the invisible worlds of the ultrasmall.

New techniques are opening up areas that could not have been effectively explored before. One of the most exciting fields of biomedical research today, for example, is the study of the human genome—the complete set of hereditary information that shapes each of us. A comprehensive knowledge of our genes and how they work is crucial if we are to wipe out disease and death itself. With the techniques extant in 1974, we already had the capability of elucidating the entire human genome. But it would have required an enormous undertaking. An army of a thousand dedicated research teams would have had to toil for more than 100,000 years. But in the last few years, spectacular advances have been made in procedures for working out the human genome. Using these methods, such an army could now do the job in less than five years!

The Chemistry of Life

The new tools and techniques that are daily being developed and perfected are aiding us in our fight against disease and death. But just how do we die? We do not yet know, really. And that is the essence of the problem. We do not know precisely how bacteria kill. We do not entirely understand how viruses can destroy their host. We do not know why we age and wither away year by year. But these forms of disease, death, and decay have one thing in common: They all have a basis in chemistry. Indeed, virtually everything that occurs in the body is a result of chemical reactions. Each time a cell divides, each time we move or speak or even think, chemicals are reacting within us. . . .

In dozens of laboratories throughout the world, scientists are now reaching critical stages in the development of instruments and techniques that are bringing the needed light to the molecular world. A number of these laboratories have a common goal: to perfect a device capable of revealing the chemicals of life in clear detail—down to the very atoms that compose them. . . .

With a knowledge of the chemistry of life, can we then modify the chemical processes of living things to postpone or even eliminate death?

We have already modified our body chemistry countless times. Every time you take an aspirin you are intervening in your body chemistry. Virtually every drug works by modifying biochemical processes, and our ever-growing arsenal of drugs has already saved millions of lives.

"Our commitment to the conquest of death must not be half-hearted or lackadaisical."

Even an incomplete knowledge of the chemistry of life has already brought great power to life scientists in their constant struggle against disease and death. Aspirin was used for about seventy years before researchers learned how it worked. Even now, the mechanisms have not yet been completely worked out, but its uses are expanding. Aspirin is now being widely recommended by doctors to cut the incidence of death from heart disease and strokes. Meanwhile, the knowledge that has been gained has been used to produce effective aspirin substitutes. . . .

Achieving *Emortality*

Similar stories can be told in many areas of biomedical research. The theme is essentially the same: The acquisition of basic knowledge of body chemistry has led to the use of specific chemicals and drugs to influence these body reactions.

With more complete knowledge of the body we will be well on our way toward the conquest of death. Mystery after mystery can be solved. Disease after disease will give way.

Despite our best efforts, we will never truly be immortal. Unavoidable accidents and unforeseeable events will continue to take their toll in human lives.

Death may persist, but it will be rare. People may live for hundreds and even thousands of years and will possess vigorous youth and agile and active minds throughout their entire lives. In this golden age, we will have achieved what might be called

emortality—a condition in which "natural death" is no longer inevitable.

This will be a new era in human history. In the world of emortals, life will take on new meaning, and for the first time we will be genuinely concerned with the quality of life. We will strive to banish poverty and pain. There will be no more "old" people, for the knowledge that will permit the conquest of death will also bring eternal youth. . . .

Conquering Death

We are in a race against death. The conquest of death will come. Some of us will make it—some of us will be emortal. How many will depend upon our efforts.

Each day, each moment, new facts are flooding in from the laboratories, expanding our understanding of the living world, giving us new insights and new avenues to exploit these insights. Steadily the boundaries of our knowledge of life processes are being pushed back. We are learning the things we need to know to conquer death. . . .

We are engaged in a war against death. Our commitment to the conquest of death must not be half-hearted or lackadaisical. This effort must receive one of the highest priorities in the allocation of our resources of manpower, money, and materials. A victory over death will return far more in dividends than it costs in expenditures. . . .

The 1980s will be the Decade of the Scientific Payoffs. The impressive decline in the incidence and mortality of heart disease that has already begun to gather momentum will accelerate. Cancer deaths will dip and then plunge. Dramatic progress in aging will bring new youth for the millions. The close of the decade will bring a virtual end to disease and a welcome reduction of pain and suffering.

Most of those alive today who are under fifty will probably cheat death. A percentage of those over fifty will also live on. The size of this percentage will depend to a great degree on the effort—the number of dollars poured into the Emortality Program.

These odds are changing every year. The heart disease rate has been falling annually since the early fifties. The cancer death rate may have already turned down and will continue to do so at an accelerated pace in the years ahead. During the next decade, further advances will bring a striking improvement of the odds.

If you survive the next ten years, you will live on indefinitely in youth and vigor—you may become emortal.

Alvin Silverstein is a professor of biology. He is the author of Biological Sciences *and* The Genetics Explosion *and has collaborated with his wife Virginia B. Silverstein on over forty science books for children.*

"If you believe that the worst thing is to die of cancer, then we can try to change that for you...but then you will have to die of something else."

Medical Technology Cannot Conquer Death

Jane J. Stein

Death takes place today in an age of technology in which few limits are placed on efforts to extend life. From the treatment of half-formed babies with no ability to breathe independently to that of eighty-five-year-old senile terminal cancer patients, there is a seemingly endless list of medical wonders that can be used to postpone death.

But how much can death really be postponed? What if nobody died of cancer, the disease that 80 percent of Americans fear more than any other? What if the federal government's heralded War on Cancer, in which nearly $1 billion is spent annually to detect causes and cures of the disease, is won?

Then the 400,000 people dying each year of cancer would die of something else. Actuaries report that if cancer were eliminated as a cause of death, the average life expectancy would be increased by a mere 2.5 years for those under thirty-five-years of age. And for those sixty-five years old, the expectation of life would be increased by only 1.4 years.

"If you believe that the worst thing is to die of cancer," said surgeon Glenn Geelhoed at the George Washington University Medical Center in Washington, D.C., "then we can try to change that for you with surgery, chemotherapy, radiation, and immunotherapy. But then you will have to die of something else."

And if there is no disease to confound one's efforts to live on, each person will die, after all, of old age. "Old ones come to be dead," wrote Gertrude Stein in *The Making of Americans.* "Any one coming to be an old enough one comes to be a dead one." Pneumonia used to be the friend of the old ones, but now it no longer steals them away, as diseases are kept at bay with medical technologies that help maintain virtually every part of their bodies. More

sophisticated medical interventions will be developed to avert the aging process and to postpone death further—perhaps the reprogramming of genes through advances in genetic engineering, insertion of chemicals to promote longer-living cells, or replacement of poorly functioning hearts with implanted artificial ones.

Death is now a changing concept because of medical technological interventions. The way of dying, the time of dying, even the signs of dying have been altered. The classic indications that death has taken place—no breath on a mirror, no heartbeat or pulse—are no longer valid in some circumstances, since a respirator can keep a moribund person breathing indefinitely, and a heart-lung machine can provide respiratory and circulatory functions at least temporarily....

Age of Medical Technology

While the age of medical technology continues to flourish, there are more and more plugs to turn off and techniques to employ before all hope is given up. A man with liver problems follows simple medical treatments for years—for example, he takes bile salts to help absorb food and to clear up a mild jaundice condition—and ends his days with terminal liver failure, hooked up to a dialysislike liver perfusion machine. A woman with circulatory deficiencies takes digitalis to increase her cardiac output, which in turn improves the blood flow throughout her body. After fifteen years of drug therapy, her condition has deteriorated to the point where a heart-lung machine is the only way to keep her blood pumping. A totally implanted artificial heart, when it is perfected, could help prolong her life even further, but eventually she will die, and morticians will have to invade her body to remove the power source that keeps her heart beating.

There are technological interventions to forestall the time of death for virtually every life-threatening condition. Even the dead are willing to wait for technological advances. A California physician who was dying of lung cancer requested that his body be put in cold storage—and thawed out when a cure for his disease is found.

Dying isn't easy when technology intervenes.

A Case of Not Giving Up

Stanley Wilks was forty-four years old when he died in the summer of 1977—after nine months of being drastically ill, after nine months of radical efforts to save his life, and after nine months of intensive care, which cost nearly a quarter of a million dollars.

The cause of Mr. Wilks's illness eluded the medical staff at the George Washington University Medical Center, but they persisted in their efforts to save him because of their great faith in medical technology. "He did not have a malignant disease, and if we could have only found out what was wrong, he could have returned to the kind of life he had led before he got sick," commented Dr. Geelhoed, one of the physicians who treated him.

Wilks, a mathematician with the army, father of four children, and a man usually in good health, complained about pains of indigestion in the fall of 1976. Being a cautious man, he discussed this pain with his doctor and had an electrocardiogram, to make sure his heart was working properly—which it was. But the day before Hallowe'en, he had another series of bad chest pains and collapsed on the floor. His wife, Jocelyn, assumed he was having a heart attack.

"There are technological interventions to forestall the time of death for virtually every life-threatening condition."

But Stanley didn't have anything that simple to detect: he was diagnosed as having an inflammation of the pancreas, though doctors never found the cause of this flare-up.

What his doctors did discover early on was that Stanley Wilks was very, very sick. One lung was infected, and he had a pseudocyst on his pancreas, which meant that the pancreas was essentially eating itself up. The cyst blocked the normal flow of digestive enzymes from the pancreas, so the enzymes began digesting the pancreas itself and would soon spread out to "eat" nearby organs. The temporary solution was the insertion of several tubes to drain the excess juices from his pancreas. Surgery to remove the pancreas was too risky: it carries a 10 percent chance of death in otherwise healthy individuals, and surgeons reasoned that the chance of mortality would be much greater for someone in as

weak a condition as Wilks. A pancreatectomy posed additional problems: His surgeon, Dr. Geelhoed, explained, "Assuming his survival, which is why we would have wanted to operate, Wilks would have become a diabetic since insulin is produced in the pancreas. He also would have had trouble digesting foods without a pancreas."

Draining the cyst did not solve the problem, and Wilks continued to be very sick, with temperatures running more than 108° F. Placing him between ice blankets cooled his body, but could not control the cause of the recurring fevers. By Christmas he was losing so much weight and was so weak that it was hard for him to sit up. "Previously there was a limit to the amount of torture we put someone through," said Geelhoed. "If a patient lost fifteen percent of his total body weight, he would die. Now we can prevent patients from reaching that state by giving them a few bottles of 'food' a day—a special liquid diet of amino acids and sugar." Wilks, a six-footer, consumed more than 500 bottles of special hyperalimentation nutrition, and his weight fell only thirteen pounds—from 180 to 167.

Search for the Cause

What was wrong with Stanley Wilks still eluded his physicians, but they didn't stop seeking. On the theory that there was a pocket of infection in his body, hiding somewhere between his lungs and intestines, surgeons opened him up for investigation. They found a distended gallbladder, some gallstones, but no infection.

Before they could all agree where next to search for the cause of his illness, Wilks's body went into high gear. Temperatures of 108°, forty breaths per minute (healthy people usually take fifteen breaths per minute), and a high state of anxiety. In an effort to slow down his body so that it could have a chance to fight off the pancreatitis and the other unknown problems that were sure to kill him, doctors put him in a state of suspended animation for seventy-two days by injecting him with curare. This substance, used by South American tribes on their blowgun darts to paralyze or kill enemies, can serve as a relaxant. Wilks was relaxed, intentionally, to the point where he was paralyzed and barely conscious. He was unable to move a single muscle or breath without the aid of a respirator. But he was still able to get sicker: he hemorrhaged, went into shock, got infections, and developed toxic reactions to medicines.

"It was a blessing that he didn't know what was going on," recalled Jocelyn. "There were so many IVs and drains coming out that his bedside looked as if it were surrounded by spaghetti."

She shuddered, thinking about those days, but added that she had agreed to permit all of the procedures performed on her husband. "How could he have lived without them?" she asked incredulously. "The hospital staff told me that his major vital organs were compatible with life and were working well—if they could only get rid of the pancreatitis. If he were comatose and had lousy brain waves, major organ failure, and no hope—that would be one thing. But everyone had hope and was convinced that he could get better."

And Glenn Geelhoed remained optimistic. "Clinically speaking, there was no evidence of irreversibility of his condition, even though it might have taken him years to recuperate and regain muscle contraction and coordination. Doctors are usually the last to admit defeat, but even if we wanted to, we couldn't keep a person alive indefinitely. If a person has many problems going, some strengths are needed. And Stanley Wilks had those strengths."

The Will to Live

After the curare treatments were stopped, Wilks remained paralyzed for several weeks longer. He was fed by a tube running directly into his gastrointestinal tract, a ploy to give him more calories, which in turn might help him heal faster. And he was given large doses of steroids to treat internal swelling of his body's organs.

Stanley Wilks stopped hemorrhaging, began to cool off, and one day in early April he croaked out from behind his tracheotomy tube, which connected him to the respirator, "I want a chair."

"From nothing, he came awake and wanted to sit in a chair," remembered Jocelyn. "No one could believe that a person could be so ill and still living. And there he was, a few weeks later, sitting up in a chair—reading, laughing and joking."

The George Washington physicians were considering sending him home in late April, but he had a low-grade fever that he could not shake, and again they were not able to pinpoint its source. "He tried so hard to get well. He wanted to go home so badly," Jocelyn Wilks said. But he never got well. Again he started getting one medical problem after another. He developed blood clots in his legs and was treated with blood-thinner medication; he developed infections in his digestive system and had to go back to liquid feedings. For each problem, the hospital staff could only find a temporary solution.

Out of Control

Late in July he developed high fevers again, and an infection was detected in his blood that physicians could not get rid of, no matter what antibiotics were used. He had a CAT scan of his body, and something suspicious appeared on his lung. But before they could investigate what it was, Stanley Wilks was on a spiral—fevers, shock, back on the respirator. But this time, the spiral was getting out of control. All the systems that had worked before began to fail. There was too much acid accumulating in his blood, and he

needed a lot of fluids to combat it. But the fluids he was given went straight to his lungs. Diuretics, which normally leach out excess liquid, did not work because his kidneys were not functioning. And putting him on a dialysis machine would not help because his blood pressure was too low to get his blood moving around the dialysis coils.

"Previously, Stanley had different things fail sequentially. We could treat the one thing at a time. But now so many things were going wrong. We couldn't borrow time against his own body any longer," said Dr. Geelhoed, who admitted that he probably would not have treated Wilks so aggressively if, when he came in nine months earlier, he had been as sick as he was in his final days, with so many parts of his body not working.

"The cause of Mr. Wilks's illness eluded the medical staff...but they persisted in their efforts to save him because of their great faith in medical technology."

Two days later, Stanley Wilks finally succumbed, after nine months of lingering death. Ironically, the inflammation of the pancreas, the initial cause of all his problems, had healed. He died of an abscess on his lung.

"Stanley never gave up hope. His optimism kept him going for so long," said his wife, "but it just wasn't enough to sustain him this last time."

"Yet," added Geelhoed, "he almost made it. It's like making a hundred-yard dash and getting tripped at the ninety-third yard."

An Epitaph

Now he is dead: 170 days and $248,486 worth of health care paid for by a $500-a-year prepaid health-maintenance organization policy. The extraordinary cost of Wilks's care will be shared in part by members of his group insurance plan, who will add minimally to a scheduled increase in premiums.

How much health care is one person worth? How much effort should be expended to avoid dying? In Stanley Wilks's case, no one was willing to stop the effort. There was never a time in the nine month seige—until the last two days—when his case looked hopeless. Even a few weeks before he died, he was out on the hospital balcony with his family, watching the Fourth of July fireworks blasting over the Washington Monument. Was there anything else to do with a man like this except treat him?

"Was Wilks worth our care?" Geelhoed asked. "Was he worth displacing health-care delivery at the grassroots level? Probably not, but those are political decisions, and I do not have the capacity to deliver health to needy people in rural West Virginia. I have a concern for the total health economy, but I was responsible not for the good of the state but for one man. This [all the care] is what Stanley wanted. He never said it wasn't worth the effort. And remember that Stanley Wilks always had a life with potential beyond his stay at the hospital—if only he could have gotten out of it alive."...

The vast array of life-extending technologies that are available gives each one of us many choices about how to die, even when we die. Having a variety of choices implies that decisions will have to be made about which one to use—and when. Dying in a technological age has become a complicated affair.

Jane J. Stein is a Washington-based journalist who has covered science and medical news for several years. She is the author of Making Medical Choices *as well as articles for* Smithsonian *magazine,* The Washington Post, The Encyclopedia Britannica, *and many other publications.*

"There is one common enemy: Biological death. It must be avoided at all costs."

Cryonics Will Delay Death

Rita Mary Ippoliti

For the past decade or so, thanks to the continued interest of the news media, the general public has been made aware of the existence of a movement labeled as the "cryonics movement." For those few who have never heard of cryonics, a small explanation is in order. Cryonics, which is derived from the Greek *kryos* meaning "icy cold", is the science of low temperature preservation of human beings by a method known as cryonic suspension. Cryonic suspension is the complex procedure by which patients are preserved or frozen immediately after pronouncement of clinical death. Theoretically, those patients will await in their icy limbo until such a time when they can be revived and restored to active life, health, and youth.

The basic foundation upon which the cryonics movement rests is two-fold. It consists of a tremendous amount of optimism and sincere belief in the future of medical science and advanced scientific technology. Cryonicists, or people who are active in the cryonics movement, love life. The idea of growing old and eventually dying is one that they simply cannot cope with. By looking back over the years and examining the leaps and bounds by which science in general and medical science in particular have grown, it seems quite reasonable to expect that they will continue to grow at the same rate, if not faster, in the future. Therefore, it appears logical to assume that eventually the average life-span of human beings will be extended to untold lengths. Since medical science will operate on a more advanced level of capability, we will all enjoy a higher standard of health care which will in turn make us better able to enjoy living. Since most cryonicists love life now, it overwhelms them to imagine how great life will be in the future.

Rita Mary Ippoliti, "The Immortalists," *Progressive World*, November/December 1977. Reprinted with permission.

Therefore, cryonic suspension evolved as the necessary tool to be utilized to bring today's cryonicists to this wonderful world of the future. By making the necessary arrangements to have themselves frozen at death, cryonicists are able to plan today for their eventual reanimation and possible immortality.

By examining the methods which cryonicists use to extrapolate from the medical advances of the recent past and apply them in predicting the future, some people may be inclined to feel that these cryonicists are merely engaged in idle folly. But is this true? Don't business organizations use the very same methods to predict their own futures and determine their fiscal policies? Of course they do. It is called forecasting. A business enterprise will use its past performance and those economic conditions prevailing at the time in order to predict its future performance and resulting profits. It is quite a legitimate practice.

The one man who has probably been the most leading force behind the organization and popularization of the cryonics movement is Robert C.W. Ettinger. Ettinger, who is currently a physics professor in the state of Michigan, initially got the idea of freezing humans at death when he was convalescing in a state-side hospital from wounds received in World War II. It was while there that he read an account of the work performed by Professor Jean Rostand of France. Rostand had been experimenting with the freezing of frog sperm. It was during those experiments that he discovered the protective effect of a substance called glycerine. He found that glycerine acted as a cryoprotectant and minimized freezing damage to tissues when they were exposed to sub-zero temperatures. Ettinger then took Rostand's observations and applied them on a much broader scale. If Rostand could successfully preserve his frog sperm at sub-zero temperatures with a minimum of freezing damage, then why can't human beings be preserved in the same manner? After pronouncement of clinical death a person could be frozen and then stored to await for such a time when the particular affliction from which he died could be cured....

Ettinger's "New" Movement

Once [Ettinger's book] *The Prospect of Immortality* hit the bookstores, a wave of instantaneous publicity erupted. All of a sudden everyone became interested in this new "thing." Television and radio talk-show hosts invited Ettinger to appear on their programs and discuss his ideas along with the rationale behind them. Major newspapers in several cities serialized Ettinger's book and presented it daily to their readership. Magazines took it upon themselves to devote full-length feature articles to the discussion of Robert Ettinger's new "movement." In fact, it was during this wave of national publicity that cryonics officially received its name, which was coined from the existing cryogenics. While cryogenics referred to the study of extremely low temperatures in general, cryonics was to deal specifically with the freezing and storing of human organisms at those low temperatures.

> "A person could be frozen...to await such a time when the particular affliction from which he died could be cured."

During the years immediately following publication of Ettinger's book, dozens of interested persons across the U.S. and abroad banded together and formed several "cryonics societies." Most of these groups were non-profit organizations whose main purpose was to educate the general public about cryonics and related disciplines. These societies were established in such places as New York, California, South Florida, Kentucky, the San Francisco Bay Area, France, and even Australia. Robert Ettinger himself headed up his own group, The Cryonics Society of Michigan. Most of these organizations, along with the many others not mentioned, have received a fair amount of publicity over the years. As a result, many have withstood the test of time and are still in existence today.

"Never Say Die"

Once cryonics had been brought to the forefront of public attention, cryonicists became eager to prove that what they were contending to be possible could actually be executed. In 1967 they got their chance. James Bedford of Glendale, California became the first human being to be placed into cryonic

suspension. As a retired psychology professor, Bedford was not an extremely wealthy man. However, as he became exposed to the cryonics movement through the news media, he began to see that what the cryonics people were proposing was not really all that far-fetched. After obtaining the cooperation of his immediate family and completing the necessary legal and financial arrangements, Bedford set aside a special fund to be used for research in cryobiology and related sciences. Upon his death in 1967 this fund, consisting of more than $100,000, was used to establish the Bedford Foundation whose work may one day make it possible for Bedford and the many others like him to return to the ranks of the living.

One year after Bedford's entry into cryonic suspension, another highly publicized freezing was performed in New York. While Professor Bedford had lived a long, full life, this second patient was a mere child by comparison. Steven Jay Mandell had always been deeply fascinated by science. Anything new and futuristic held a unique interest for him. Being an avid science fiction fan, Mandell saw an ad placed by the Cryonic Society of New York in one of his science fiction publications. The ad, featuring the society's slogan "Never Say Die!" immediately sparked his interest. Steven, who was in fairly good health at the time, filed the required application forms and became enrolled as a member of the Cryonics Society of New York. Completing the C.S.N.Y. membership application, however, caused Steven to recall a boyhood memory of his father's death and burial. While standing in the cemetery looking down upon his father's grave, Steven had asked his mother to promise him that she would never allow them to bury him under the ground when he died. Mrs. Mandell immediately comforted her son and assured him if the time came, she would surely honor his wishes. However, his mother never really believed that she would see the day when she would have to fulfill that promise.

While in his early twenties Steven, who was then an aeronautical engineering major at New York University, was stricken down with a severe intestinal ailment. Shortly thereafter, he died. Immediately Mrs. Mandell contacted officials of the Cryonics Society of New York and the group mobilized into action at once in their efforts to get Steven's body frozen as quickly as possible. Steven Mandell was placed into cryonic suspension in July of 1968. Along with the freezing of Professor James Bedford, Steven's entry into cold storage received a tremendous amount of publicity. Both the print media and the electronic media alike sought to give the event maximum coverage. The leaders of the Cryonics Society of New York, attorney Curtis Henderson and editor Saul Kent, found themselves overwhelmed with requests for interviews. Probably best of all was the fact that most of this media coverage tended to be favorable and therefore it benefited the movement by bringing in new members to join with the existing ranks of the believers. But things would not always go so well for the cryonics people.

The Freezing Process

Cryonic suspension is a very complex and very expensive process. There are very few individuals or business firms around with the specialized facilities and capabilities to perform the procedure. TRANS TIME, Inc. is one of those few.... Art Quaife, TRANS TIME's president and chief executive officer, described the freezing procedure as a multi-stage process. "Immediately upon pronouncement of death by a licensed physician, the patient is placed on a heart-lung resuscitator to maintain the circulation of oxygenated blood. Next we begin cooling the body rapidly to about 32°F by use of ice packs externally and circulating chilled fluids internally. These measures will virtually eliminate neurological damage (brain damage), that would otherwise occur after circulation ceases. Next we begin introducing cryoprotective chemicals such as DMSO, (dimethyl sulfoxide), into the circulatory system. Such cryoprotectants will greatly reduce the freezing damage that would otherwise occur. After further cooling, the patient is wrapped in layers of plastic and aluminum foil, and placed within a large cryogenic storage capsule. These units are constructed of stainless steel and have vacuum jacket insulation. The capsule is then hoisted upright and filled with liquid nitrogen. This refrigerant reduces the patient's body temperature to a frigid -320°F (-196°C), where virtually no further deterioration or decay will take place."

Once the patient has been placed in cryonic suspension, there is still plenty of work remaining to be done. The huge cryogenic storage units, or "cryocapsules," which Art Quaife spoke of are housed with TRANS TIME's multi-purpose storage facility. This facility, located in the San Fancisco Bay Area, is equipped for both performing suspensions as well as providing storage and capsule maintenance services. The liquid nitrogen in the capsule gradually evaporates or "boils off." Therefore, it becomes necessary to replenish the nitrogen at least five times per year. However, Art Quaife states that "TRANS TIME refills its capsules on a much more frequent basis in order to safeguard its patients."

It is probably this maintenance aspect that causes cryonic suspension to be so expensive. In interviews with both Curtis Henderson of the Cryonics Society of New York and Art Quaife of TRANS TIME, I discovered that it costs at least $50,000 for a patient to be placed into suspension and maintained. The majority of this amount, or about $35,000 to $40,000, is used strictly for the maintenance purposes. In addition to liquid nitrogen costs, maintenance

expenses include facility rent and up-keep, utilities, salaries for the services of facility employees, and incidental expenses.

Cryonic Life Insurance

Since the cost of cryonic suspension is quoted so high, many people tend to reject cryonics solely on the basis of their feeling that they could never raise such a huge sum of money. Well, TRANS TIME, Inc. offers a rather simple solution to this dilemma. It is called cryonics life insurance. Jim Yount, Marketing Director for TRANS TIME, explains how easily cryonics life insurance can aid someone who wishes to be suspended at death:

"The ad, featuring the society's slogan, 'Never Say Die!' immediately sparked his interest."

"In order to participate in TRANS TIME's life extension program, one must provide the necessary funds for his own freezing and storage. Life insurance is one of the best ways to do this. Although TRANS TIME encourages its clients to take out substantially larger amounts of life insurance, we must insist on $50,000 worth as the absolute minimum. TRANS TIME has already organized its own team of "agents" who are authorized to sell cryonics life insurance policies for TRANS TIME. Many of these agents are also licensed to sell conventional life insurance as well. While just about any insurance company can write a policy usable for cryonic suspension purposes, our agents are especially trained to council the prospective client and advise him of the various options available at the time." Mr. Yount then informed me that if I wanted to prepare for my own eventual cryonic suspension, I could probably obtain a $50,000 whole-life policy for a mere $600.00 a year in premiums. Currently, I am twenty years old. If I would rather seek term insurance, the same size policy would run about $100.00 a year in premiums. Of course, with term insurance the premium amount escalates with age. When one looks at the cost of freezing and storage in this light, it really doesn't seem all that bad. Six hundred dollars a year for a shot at immortality. Worth it?

Once deciding to opt for cryonic suspension, how does one go about completing the multitude of arrangements? Jim Yount explains: "Besides allocating the required funds for suspension, an individual desiring to be frozen at death must meet other prerequisites. TRANS TIME, who principally extends its services to members of the Bay Area Cryonics Society, will usually require a potential donor to seek suspension membership in that organization. This is done by filling out a special packet of forms including the donor release which is required under the Uniform Anatomical Gift Act. Then of course, you have your application for suspension membership. This form is quite detailed and it seeks to give the donor several options relating to his own suspension. For instance, if his body was badly mutilated in an accident, under what conditions would he still wish to be suspended, and in what manner would he like his donor fund used if for some reason it would be impossible to suspend him? A source of funds statement is also completed by the donor. This form details the funds being allocated for the patient's eventual suspension and the sources from which they come. For instance, life insurance, bonds, savings, etc. Finally, we come to the suspension membership dues. Unfortunately, these may seem to be quite high to some people, but they aren't really that costly. For a lifetime suspension membership, BACS requires a fee of $1,000. Except for $30 per year membership renewal charge and a $40 per year retainer fee payable to TRANS TIME, this $1,000 charge is all that the donor will be asked to remit."...

"When one looks at the cost of freezing and storage,....it really doesn't seem all that bad."

There appears to be a true sense of brotherhood and friendship among the cryonicists. All members are pulling together for a common goal: The indefinite extension of their own lives. As a result, there is plenty of cooperation among existing societies and very little competition. When a member of one of the groups is struck down by death, his fellow members quickly mobilize to "rescue" him and place him in suspension as rapidly as possible. The intensity of their efforts and dedication resemble that of a modern CPR team. For in both cases there is one common enemy: Biological death. It is to be avoided at all costs....

A Utopian Future

For over twelve years, the cryonics movement has managed to survive and like most things, it has experienced both ups and downs in its efforts to gain public acceptance. The cryonicists, themselves, refuse to be discouraged in their efforts to achieve immortality. When asked the basis of their beliefs, they are quick to show the many scientific advances that have already been made in cryobiology and related fields. Art Quaife fights down the opposition by pointing out that animals have already been frozen and thawed successfully and although there are still a lot of problems to be worked out, a perfected freeze-thaw process may be developed in the foreseeable

future. Quaife also states that with our modern technology becoming so advanced, the future will really be something to behold. And it is right here, on this concept that the whole cryonics movement is centered.

Some people believe that the aim of cryonicists is simply to popularize the idea of freezing as an alternative to burial. But this is not so. Cryonicists want to live indefinitely, not die coldly. They only see the freezing of their bodies as a necessary means to achieve a worthwhile end. Saul Kent, who is currently a BACS member and the publicity advisor to TRANS TIME, has often been quoted as saying, "The only thing worse than being frozen is to die and not be frozen." Most cryonicists firmly believe in utopia. They believe that all of the world's problems can one day be solved. Cryonicists argue that immortal man will not harm the earth and waste its valuable resources. On the contrary, cryonicists will do everything in their power to build a better world since it is their plan to inhabit it for a very long time.

Cryonicists argue that cryonic suspension is not really very radical. It is only another life-preserving medical technique which seeks to prolong the human life-span. While several people attack cryonics on the basis of its attempts to "resurrect" the dead, the cryonics societies point out the fact that many people have already been brought back to life after having been in clinical death for as long as twenty minutes. Cryonics, therefore, can be thought of as simply another resuscitative technique which does not seek to "create" life, but merely prolongs it....

Thousands of people all across the world die and go into the grave annually. Certainly there isn't one dedicated cryonicist around who can see or understand the logic of this phenomenon. While they cannot comprehend needless burial, the cryonicists do believe that people have the right to choose their own fate in this, our democratic, society. As a result, many individuals will insist on what Robert Ettinger calls their "right to rot." And they will have it since the cryonics people refuse to shove their ideas down anyone's throat, but will simply cling to them as their own salvation. My own feelings about cryonics can be expressed quite simply. It is definitely one of the most interesting, challenging and rewarding things that has ever come into my life and I firmly believe that one day freezing the dead for eventual reanimation will become a standard practice in our society. But, from a member of the Bay Area Cryonics Society, what else could you expect?

Rita Mary Ippoliti is a member of the Bay Area Cryonics Society in San Francisco, California.

"Since human beings thus long frozen may have suffered irreversible brain damage, the question of whether people frozen to death should necessarily be revived arises."

Cryonics Is a Biological Time Bomb

Gordon Rattray Taylor

The fact is, in all probability ageing is not a 'clinical entity.' Like cancer or rheumatism, it is not just one disease but several which ordinarily get lumped together because the visible effects are much the same.

For example, there are almost certainly emotional factors in ageing, and even emotional reasons for death itself. Any doctor can tell you of patients who, learning they have an incurable disease, 'turn their faces to the wall' and give up hope. The British surgeon Sir Heneage Ogilvie once said that he could look around a table at a group of men in their 50's and tell from their faces which of them would die of cancer. Since we know that the secretion of hormones is under emotional control, there is nothing too surprising in this. Cases where one of a married couple dies and the other loses all zest for living and dies soon after are also not too uncommon.

If, then, there is an emotional factor in ageing, the prolongation of life may conceivably be effected by psychotherapy, euphoriant drugs or whatever new means of mental prophylaxis the future may develop. Conversely, if the general character of life in the society of the future becomes more stressful or less satisfying, the prolongation of life may be made more difficult....

The proposal that human beings could be preserved alive by freezing would, it is pointed out, offer the possibility to people suffering from an incurable disease of waiting around until a cure was discovered. And it is true that if a person who died of pneumonia in 1920, say, had been preserved until today, he could most certainly have been saved.

Social Problems

If the process proved free from risk, others might wish to store themselves for awhile, simply in order to see the world of the future, or to see how their own children turned out (though the latter might disappoint them by being frozen themselves!) or even because they were passionately interested to know the solution of some scientific problem. And if they did not like the world they found, they could presumably return to the freezer for a second period. The social consequences of any such proposition are obviously so fantastic and far-reaching that it is worth evaluating its practicability very carefully. Among the problems one can see arising are those of inheritance property. Children expecting to inherit would be irked at being balked of their inheritance, and if they managed the property during its owner's glacial period would not like turning out on the specified date of his return to normal life. The incentive to postpone reviving him on some excuse or other, would be, in many cases, overwhelming. A son who had taken over the management of a business owned by his frozen father and had expanded it, would not want to be ousted by the old man, and would have become dependent on the income it brought him, to say nothing of the prestige or social status.

Again, the Inland Revenue might suffer a considerable loss of revenue from a decline in death duties, and would perhaps attempt to discourage such ventures by a tax on absentee owners or their properties. One might ask too whether the law could insist on reviving a frozen individual required to give evidence in court, or one against whom a charge was to be preferred. And what damages might be brought against someone who revived a freezee against his will, if he died or was injured during his unwished-for visit to the land of the unfrozen?

The political situation remains somewhat obscure: would a freezee (someone is going to have to invent a name for them) have a vote? If so, could he leave it to a particular party indefinitely?

Apart from these individual problems, there would certainly be a fantastic economic problem, or set of problems, if ever the practice became popular. The maintenance of the hibernacula, freezatoria, or whatever they may be called, with all precautions against infection, periodic inspection by medical staff of the freezees, and so forth, cannot be cheap. A decreasing number of active people might find themselves saddled with the task of maintaining an ever-growing accumulation of hibernating ones. Though some financial provision may have to be made by the candidate for glaciation, somebody has to do the work, and money in the bank is not the same thing. Inflation could reduce or wipe out the sums set aside by a freezee for his maintenance, and presumably he would then have to be awakened whether he wished for it or not. However, the return to life of large numbers of people, unadapted to the society in which they find themselves, also presents problems. At the least, they will need retraining in the use of mechanical devices, which will have changed completely, and will also need bringing up to date on the legal position. (They may also be greeted by a considerable pile of unopened letters, bills, writs and other surprises.) At most they might completely unbalance the market, changing the pattern of demand and supply of labour in a manner hard to predict. They will, of course, require outfitting with new clothes, and countless gadgets equivalent to the fountain pens, electric razors and wrist-watches of our own day, but more numerous, more intricate and more costly.

Dead Serious

This prospect is being taken so seriously by some people that, in the United States, a number of societies have been founded to accelerate progress, notably the Life Extension Society of Washington, the Immortality Research and Compilation Association of California, and the Anabiosis and Prolongevity Institute of New York. Furthermore, a number of people have paid sums to ensure that, at death, their bodies will be preserved by freezing, in the belief that techniques whereby they can be revived will be shortly discovered.

Dr. James H. Bedford, a retired professor of psychology, set aside $4,200 for this purpose before his death of cancer, at the age of 73, in California last year. The Cryonics Society of California advised, and Dr. B. Renault Able performed the cryo-burial, if that is the word. The first step was the injection of an anti-clotting agent, heparin, after which the chest was opened and heart massage applied, so that the brain should be kept supplied with blood. As soon as possible Dr. Bedford was transferred to a heart-lung machine and the body temperature lowered by packing with ice to 8°C. At this point most of the blood was withdrawn and replaced with a solution of salts plus the 'wonder solvent' DMSO, which I mentioned earlier in connection with skin storage. The temperature of the body was then lowered to -79°C. and it was flown to Phoenix, Arizona, for storage at -190°C. in liquid nitrogen. It will cost about £ 100 a year to maintain it at this temperature.

Dr. Bedford did not imagine that no freezing damage would be caused, but believed that before too long scientists would find a way of repairing such damage, and reviving stored bodies. To aid in this, he left $200,000 to found the Bedford Foundation for Cryobiological Research. However, since DMSO has many adverse effects, not yet fully understood, his chances are slim, even apart from the problem of damage from the concentration of electrically charged fluids within his body cells. As Dr. Stanley W. Jacob, the Associate Professor of Surgery at Oregon University, commented at the time: 'The poor man's funds have been wasted as far as his own chances are concerned.'

Freezing Tissue

However, experts in the freezing of tissues are divided about the technical possibility of any such process. Possibly the world's leading expert is Dr. Audrey Smith, of Britain's National Institute of Medical Research at Mill Hill, near London, known for her work on freezing the cornea of the eye for storage. She sees some hope of storing organs—and has done work on the lung. . . .But there is a world of difference between storing inert tissues like the cornea, or skin, and storing actively metabolizing cells, especially for long periods of time. There is evidence that certain membranes in the cell are only maintained by a process of continual reconstruction, and may disintegrate when the cell is brought to a standstill.

"A decreasing number of active people might find themselves saddled with the task of maintaining an ever-growing accumulation of hibernating ones."

Early attempts to freeze organs and, still more, entire animals, were defeated by the formation of ice-crystals within the cells, which punctured the walls. The discovery that immersing the cell in a solvent such as glycerine and controlling the freezing rate very carefully could overcome this hazard led to the successful freezing of certain organs, as already described.

Certain cases where human beings have been frozen in natural circumstances give the impression that freezing of human beings is possible. Thus in 1960, a Russian tractor driver, Vladimir Kharin, who had become lost in a snowstorm, was found unconscious, stiff and blue, but without frostbite or putrefaction. It appeared that he had lain under the snow three hours, and it is thought he had been narcotized by the carbon dioxide in his own breath. Taken to a hospital, he recovered and eventually returned to work. In Tulsa, Oklahoma, a similar incident was reported: a negro woman, found frozen stiff on a cold winter's night, was revived, despite some frostbite to her extremities. It is certain that the body temperature of these people did not fall below zero. The lowest level to which human body temperature has ever been depressed, with subsequent survival, is 9°C. This was during surgery with hypothermia. Normally such surgery takes place at about 25°C, against the body's normal 37°C.

"Probably the candidate for freezing will have to undergo elaborate preliminary rejigging of his body chemistry."

Currently, the situation is that a mammal can be revived without ill effect after up to an hour's cold storage, by which time 50 percent of the water in the body has turned to ice. As the water freezes, the concentration of the salts in what remains increase, with destructive effects, particularly on the cell membranes; moreover, the various cellular processes are slowed by different amounts, so that biochemical anarchy ensues. Not only rats and mice but dogs and monkeys have been revived after an hour of sub-zero body temperature, but rarely longer. Insects and bacteria are a different matter. Professor H.E. Hinton, of Bristol University, has frozen the larvae of midges for ten years and thawed them out, while bacteria can survive indefinitely under such conditions. Some bats can withstand sub-zero temperatures—they are, of course, hibernators—for reasons which are not clear. Even cold-blooded animals do not tolerate extensive freezing.

Desaturation of body fats seems to help hibernators, and may therefore help other mammals, if a means of bringing it about can be devised. (Many oils can take up hydrogen, whereupon they become solid, as when margarine is made from vegetable oils: this process is known as saturation. Conversely, butter left to go rancid desaturates and becomes oily. In general, animal fats are normally saturated, vegetable fats are not.) Probably the candidate for freezing will have to undergo elaborate preliminary rejigging of his body chemistry.

It is worth pointing out that the animal whose heart beat and breathing have stopped is clinically dead, and hence that these experiments are experiments in the revival of the dead, medically speaking. The biologist escapes this paradox by jesuitically defining death as 'the state from which resuscitation of the body as a whole is impossible by any currently known means.' If it revives, it wasn't really dead. But since human beings thus long frozen may have suffered irreversible brain damage, the question of whether people frozen to death should necessarily be revived arises.

Russian workers claim to have pushed the process a little further, though not without the anticipated adverse effects on brain function.

The Russians started experimental work on this subject some twelve years ago, at the Laboratory of Experimental Physiology for Resuscitation, maintained by the Russian Academy of Medical Sciences, starting with dogs. They drained the animal's blood completely, and reanimated it after 5-6 minutes initially; subsequently the period was extended by stages to an hour.

Animal Experiments

More illuminating, I think, are the experiments performed on baboons at the Institute of Experimental Pathology and Therapy at Sukhumi in the Caucasus. The animals temperatures were first reduced to about 24°C, and their blood drained. Kefa was the name of one of these baboons. Four hours after resuscitation she opened her eyes. After six hours she was playful enough to seize a syringe and run round the operating theatre with it. Kefa retained her former food preferences, which argues that abstract memories were retained as well as skills. But not all the animals survived, and in some cases it took three months before the higher nervous system was restored to normal after 30 minutes of 'death'. This is progress of a sort, since animals which had been dead only 2-4 minutes, without cooling, took 7-9 months to return to normal. In later experiments, the temperature was lowered further to 10°C, and the period of 'death' extended to two hours. But after this experience, it took twenty hours to restore hearing, three days to restore sight and seven days for total recovery. There was also some heart fibrillation (an irregular fluttering due to disturbance of the electrical impulses which control the heart-beat), a sign of imminent heart failure.

While it is rather remarkable that the body can rebuild the connections which have broken down at all, considering the limited adaptability of neurones, the prospects of surviving a prolonged 'death' without major damage and impairment, by the techniques available at present, seem remote, and it will be a brave man who first risks the experience. Since the brain seems to be the vulnerable spot, it may be that we shall have to think in terms of removing the brain and storing it separately from the body in different conditions. At Kobe Medical College, Japanese workers led by Professor I. Suda have recently reported some success with this. After removing the brain — that of a cat — it was cooled in a bath of glycerol and stored for no less than seven months at −20° C. Prior to this, the blood had been replaced with a glycerol solution, while the animal was anaesthetized. After restoring to normal conditions, 'approximately normal' electrical activity restarted, and the brain cells looked 'almost normal' under the microscope.

So we need not lose hope.

Professor A.S. Parks declares: 'Science fiction notwithstanding, the prospect of suspending animation for indefinite periods in man by freezing him is remote.' But elsewhere he has given himself a saving clause: 'All this of course sounds fantastic, but we have learned to use the word "impossible" with caution. Ten years ago no normal mammalian cell had been frozen to temperatures compatible with long storage. Today this procedure is commonplace.'

Gordon Rattray Taylor is a scientific journalist and the author of The Biological Time Bomb.

"The standard is . . . that 'the person is dead if the brain is dead.'"

Brain Death: An Overview

Ellen Rudy

Many years ago the commonlaw understanding of death was "total stoppage of the circulation of the blood and a cessation of vital functions, such as respiration, pulsation, etc." In some cases quoted in court records, the actual flowing of blood was used as a criterion to show that circulation had not ceased, and therefore, death had not yet legally occurred. This detail may seem trivial, but in a court case where survivor rights are important, the question of who died first can be very important.

This common-law criterion of death was eventually made obsolete by medical progress. During the 1950s and 1960s, cardiopulmonary resuscitation became common practice in hospitals and frequently was carried out by resuscitation "teams," usually composed of physicians and nurses. By the 1960s it was recognized that if patients who presented the most risk of having a cardiac or respiratory arrest could be placed in the same setting with trained personnel, resuscitation procedures could be carried out more effectively and mortality rates reduced. However, resuscitation teams soon learned *not* to resuscitate patients if circulation and/or respiration had been absent long enough to have caused death to the brain. If brain recovery was not deemed possible, resuscitation was not attempted and the patient was simply declared dead. While not fully appreciated at the time, this decision was an early step in the recognition of the concept of brain death.

In the 1960s and on into the 70s, further advances in medicine, such as the use of respirators and improved cardiopulmonary resuscitation, resulted in the clinical problem of "respirator brain"—a condition perhaps best described as total loss of brain function accompanied by ongoing biologic functions in all other parts of the body maintained by

ventilatory support (respirators), cardiogenic drugs and other measures of intensive care. This unhappy clinical situation was often the result of the rule, "If in doubt, resuscitate."

In these cases, the need arose to judge "death" by other criteria than the common-law definition. Sophisticated medical judgment became necessary, where previously the physician's observation of cessation of heartbeat and breathing had merely confirmed what was already apparent to others. Medical management of this "respirator brain" syndrome resulted in recognition of "brain death" in the presence of continuing circulation and artificial respiration, and acceptance of this standard alone as a sufficient basis for considering the person to be dead, regardless of the status of circulation.

Harvard Committee Definition

In the landmark report by the Ad Hoc Committee of the Harvard Medical School to Examine the Definition of Death, the first widely accepted criteria to determine brain death were published in 1968. It was clearly the intent of this committee to define brain death in terms of the whole brain—that is as a state in which no discernible central nervous system activity exists. The committee also emphasized the necessity for ruling out the common causes of *reversible* coma, such as drug intoxication and hypothermia, before clinically determining brain death.

Along with biomedical advances of the 1960s, early recognition and acceptance of brain death was encouraged by advances in organ-transplant surgery, which focused attention on the necessity to declare a person dead as soon as it could be established that the brain was irreversibly damaged and all cerebral functions had ceased. The point, of course, was to allow for the retrieval of viable organs for transplant. With a widening acceptance of the concept of brain death, life can be declared extinct at a time when

Ellen Rudy, "Brain Death," *Dimensions of Critical Care Nursing,* May/June 1982. Reprinted with permission.

healthy organs are still adequately perfused and thus provide the potential for successful organ transplant.

The concept of cerebral death or brain death does not introduce a second type of death nor a second means of determining death. This point is of particular importance when such a discussion is presented to the public. It simply more clearly defines what has been recognized for years by nurses, doctors, and philosophers—that death occurs when there is irreversible absence of all brain function. The standard is, as the "Harvard criteria" concluded, that "the person is dead if the brain is dead." This conclusion has withstood all subsequent developments, both biomedical and philosophical.

Brain-Death Statutes

As the health-care profession began to accept the concept of brain death, the issue then became how to establish the legal recognition of brain death while avoiding the slow route of multiple court rulings. Although brain death can be established as a legal definition of death by case law—that is, by the decisions of courts in many individual cases—the resulting law is often fragmentary in provisions and applicability. The second, and more direct, route to legalizing the concept of brain death is through enactment of state statutes. At this writing twenty-eight states have a statutory definition of death. (As laws change frequently, check your state's present statutes.) These states, listed alphabetically with the date of ratification, are listed below:

•Alabama	(1979)
•Alaska	(1974)
•Arkansas	(1977)
•California	(1974)
•Connecticut	(1979)
•Florida	(1980)
•Georgia	(1975)
•Hawaii	(1978)
•Idaho	(1977)
•Illinois	(1975)
•Iowa	(1976)
•Kansas	(1970)
•Louisiana	(1976)
•Maryland	(1972)
•Michigan	(1975)
•Montana	(1977)
•Nevada	(1979)
•New Mexico	(1977)
•North Carolina	(1977)
•Ohio	(1982)
•Oklahoma	(1975)
•Oregon	(1975)
•Tennessee	(1976)
•Texas	(1979)
•Vermont	(1981)
•Virginia	(1973)
•West Virginia	(1973)
•Wyoming	(1979)

Among those states that have statutes recognizing brain death, there is variation in the laws. Some laws provide for alternative definitions of death, with one definition based on the absence of spontaneous respirations and cardiac functions and one based on brain death. Others allow for the determination of brain death only when the heart and lungs are artificially maintained. Another type of statute allows for the determination of death *only* by brain death, with no other provision for determination of death based on respiratory or cardiac cessation.

"At this writing twenty-eight states have a statutory definition of death."

It is interesting to note that the American Medical Association's statement in 1974 on death refers to brain death as but one of a number of criteria that may be used in the medical diagnosis of death. Further, it was the position of the AMA in 1974 that state statutes on the determination of death were "neither necessary nor desirable."

However, by 1977 the AMA House of Delegates adopted a resolution that withdrew its earlier opposition to any state statutes on criteria of death. The new position was not to encourage such statutes, but to urge that any such statute that recognized brain death criterion also recognized other criteria.

AMA Model Bill

Finally, in 1979, the AMA House of Delegates passed a model bill on the definition of death:

> An individual who has sustained either (a) irreversible cessation of circulatory and respiratory functions, or (b) irreversible cessation of all functions of the entire brain, should be considered dead. A determination of death shall be made in accordance with accepted medical standards.

For those states that have *not* enacted statutes defining death, there is a great variation in the approaches to defining and determining death. In general, the recognition of brain death is widespread even in those states without laws that give legal backing to the concept. As can be expected, adoption of this concept of brain death depends on the sophistication of the medical technology available to the medical staff, as well as the philosophy of the institution. Generally, in states without death statutes, the larger medical centers have adopted policies recognizing the concept of brain death and have established clinical criteria for determining it. The adoption of such criteria has been facilitated in institutions actively involved in organ transplant surgery. In smaller community hospitals, acceptance of the concept of brain death is often forced on the physician and staff by the occasional totally unresponsive patient sustained by mechanical ventilation and circulatory support. If death does not occur from cardiac arrest or other complications, the patient may be eventually removed from life-support machines and pronounced dead. Situations such as these are usually handled on an individual basis, without the aid of legal clinical criteria for death or established medical protocols.

These situations are particularly difficult for critical care nurses, who may be uncertain of what life-saving actions to take if physicians disagree on the brain death criteria, change their ethical position, or give only verbal orders, and who may also be placed in the dilemma of what to tell the bewildered family.

Criteria for Brain Death

Even after these legal and philosophical statements, the question remains, what is brain death? Both courts and legislatures have been careful to avoid identifying specific medical criteria for brain death, leaving these criteria to medical experts who determine "accepted medical practice." In this way, as criteria for brain death changes, so too will the determination of what constitutes brain death. For example, some believe that brain death can only occur if brain metabolism has ceased. However, so far we have no universally acceptable means of measuring cessation of brain metabolism, so it is not yet a useful criterion. Therefore, by not putting into law specific criteria for determining brain death, the courts are allowing for gradual changes in criteria as technology becomes more sophisticated and knowledge of brain physiology increases.

"The situation is further complicated by our sometimes imprecise technology in determining absence of brain activity."

Presently many different combinations of clinical criteria have been proposed for identifying brain death. This area is particularly difficult because the higher cognitive brain functions are guided by the cerebrum (cerebral hemispheres) while the respiratory and circulatory functions are guided by the brainstem. The situation is further complicated by our sometimes imprecise technology in determining absence of brain activity and by moral, ethical and religious considerations of what death is.

In brain death *all* functions of the brain have ceased. This includes both the higher centers of the cerebral hemisphere and the lower centers of the brain stem.

Cerebral Cortex Functioning

The cerebral hemispheres perform the cognitive and higher level mental-functions of the body. In a comatose patient any responsiveness to light, sound, motion or other such stimuli demonstrates some degree of cerebral function; that is, that the brain is capable of receiving and responding to stimuli. Any utterance of sounds or coordinated eye movemens also are obvious evidence of some degree of cerebral functioning. Therefore, the complete absence of the cognitive functioning of the brain can be determined by lack of verbal response, lack of spontaneous eye movement or coordinated eye movement, and total lack of any response to various stimuli such as light, sound, motion, or pain, including lack of muscle flexion or extension (decorticate and decerebrate activity).

Patients in a severe vegetative state may, in fact, have a total lack of cerebral cognitive functioning such as that described above. Such a state may be irreversible, but these patients are not declared dead until brain stem functions are also determined to be absent. Karen Quinlan is the prime example of a patient lacking any evidence of cerebral cognitive functioning, but who is not brain dead, by virtue of a functioning brain stem.

Brain-Stem Functioning

The brain stem is the route through which impulses travel from the brain to the spinal cord and to the peripheral nervous system. In addition, the brain stem houses the nuclei for 10 of the 12 cranial nerves and groups of neurons that have been referred to as "centers," the most important being the *respiratory center*. Most criteria for brain death rely on testing brain-stem functioning, although some critics believe the tests are too crude to accept as criteria for declaring a person as dead.

Ellen Rudy, R.N., Ph.D., is an associate professor of nursing at Kent State University, Kent, Ohio. She is also the program director at Kent State of the Graduate program in Nursing of the Adult.

The Harvard Committee Criteria for Determination of Death

The Ad Hoc Committee of the Harvard Medical School

Our primary purpose is to define irreversible coma as a new criterion for death. There are two reasons why there is a need for a definition: (1) Improvements in resuscitative and supportive measures have led to increased efforts to save those who are desperately injured. Sometimes these efforts have only a partial success so that the result is an individual whose heart continues to beat but whose brain is irreversibly damaged. The burden is great on patients who suffer permanent loss of intellect, on their families, on the hospitals, and on those in need of hospital beds already occupied by these comatose patients. (2) Obsolete criteria for the definition of death can lead to controversy in obtaining organs for transplantation.

Irreversible coma has many causes, but *we are concerned here only with those comatose individuals who have no discernible central nervous system activity.* If the characteristics can be defined in satisfactory terms, translatable in action—and we believe this is possible—then several problems will either disappear or will become more readily soluble.

More than medical problems are present. There are moral, ethical, religious, and legal issues. Adequate definition here will prepare the way for better insight into all of these matters as well as for better law than is currently applicable.

Characteristics of Irreversible Coma

An organ, brain or other, that no longer functions and has no possiblility of functioning again is for all practical purposes dead. Our first problem is to determine the characteristics of a *permanently* nonfunctioning brain.

A patient in this state appears to be in deep coma. The condition can be satisfactorily diagnosed by

"A Definition of Irreversible Coma: Report of the 'Ad Hoc' Committee of the Harvard Medical School, Under the Chairmanship of Henry K. Beecher, M.D., to Examine the Definition of Brain Death," *Journal of the American Medical Association,* August 1968, Vol. 205, pp. 85-88. Reprinted by permission.

points 1, 2, and 3 to follow. The electroencephalogram (point 4) provides confirmatory data, and when available it should be utilized. In situations where for one reason or another electroencephalographic monitoring is not available, the absence of cerebral functions has to be determined by purely clinical signs, to be described, or by absence of circulation as judged by standstill of blood in the retinal vessels, or by absence of cardiac activity.

1. *Unreceptivity and Unresponsitivity.* There is a total unawareness to externally applied stimuli and inner need and complete unresponsiveness—our definition of irreversible coma. Even the most intensely painful stimuli evoke no vocal or other response, not even a groan, withdrawal of a limb, or quickening of respiration.

2. *No Movement or Breathing.* Observations covering a period of at least one hour by physicians is adequate to satisfy the criteria of no spontaneous muscular movements or spontaneous respiration or response to stimuli such as pain, touch, sound, or light. After the patient is on a mechanical respirator, the total absence of spontaneous breathing may be established by turning off the respirator for three minutes and observing whether there is any effort on the part of the subject to breathe spontaneously. (The respirator may be turned off for this time provided that at the start of the trial period the patient's carbon dioxide tension is within the normal range, and provided also that the patient had been breathing room air for at least ten minutes prior to the trial.)

Absence of Reflexes

3. *No Reflexes.* Irreversible coma with abolition of central nervous system activity is evidenced in part by the absence of elicitable reflexes. The pupil will be fixed and dilated and will not respond to a direct source of bright light. Since the establishment of a fixed, dilated pupil is clear-cut in clinical practice, there should be no uncertainty as to its presence.

Ocular movement (to head turning and to irrigation of the ears with ice water) and blinking are absent. There is no evidence of postural activity (decerebrate or other). Swallowing, yawning, vocalization are in abeyance. Corneal and pharyngeal reflexes are absent.

As a rule the stretch of tendon reflexes cannot be elicited: i.e., tapping the tendons of the biceps, triceps, and pronator muscles, quadriceps and gastrocenemius muscles with the reflex hammer elicits no contraction of the respective muscles. Plantar or noxious stimulation gives no response.

4. *Flat Electroencephalogram.* Of great confirmatory value is the flat or isoelectric EEG. We must assume that the electrodes have been properly applied, that the apparatus is functioning normally, and that the personnel in charge is competent. We consider it prudent to have one channel of the apparatus used for an electrocardiogram. This channel will monitor the ECG so that, if it appears in the electroencephalographic leads because of high resistance, it can be readily identified. It also establishes the presence of the active heart in the absence of the EEG. We recommend that another channel be used for a noncephalic lead. This will pick up space-borne or vibration-borne artifacts and identify them. The simplest form of such a monitoring noncephalic electrode has two leads over the dorsum of the hand, perferably the right hand, so the ECG will be minimal or absent. Since one of the requirements of this state is that there be no muscle activity, these two dorsal hand electrodes will not be bothered by muscle artifact. The apparatus should be run at standard gains 10 v/mm, 50 v/mm. Also it should be isoelectric at double this standard gain which is 5 v/mm or 25 v/mm. At least ten full minutes of recording are desirable, but twice that would be better.

It is also suggested that the gains at some point be opened to their full amplitude for a brief period (5 to 100 seconds) to see what is going on. Usually in an intensive care unit artifacts will dominate the picture, but these are readily identifiable. There shall be no electroencephalographic response to noise or to pinch.

All of the above tests shall be repeated at least 24 hours later with no change.

The validity of such data as indications of irreversible cerebral damage depends on the exclusion of two conditions: hypothermia (temperature below 90° [32.2 °C]) or central nervous system depressants, such as barbiturates.

Other Procedures

The patient's condition can be determined only by a physician. When the patient is hopelessly damaged as defined above, the family and all colleagues who have participated in major decisions concerning the patient, and all nurses involved, should be so informed. Death is to be declared and *then* the respirator turned off. The decision to do this and the responsibility for it are to be taken by the physician-in-charge, in consultation with one or more physicians who have been directly involved in the case. It is unsound and undesirable to force the family to make the decision.

Legal Commentary

The legal system of the United States is greatly in need of the kind of analysis and recommendations for medical procedures in cases of irreversible brain damage as described. At present, the law of the United States, in all 50 states and in the federal courts, treats the question of human death as a question of fact to be decided in every case. When any doubt exists, the courts seek medical expert testimony concerning the time of death of the particular individual involved. However, the law makes the assumption that the medical criteria for determining death are settled and not in doubt among physicians. Furthermore, the law assumes that the traditional method among physicians for determination of death is to ascertain the absence of all vital signs. To this extent, *Blacks's Law Dictionary* (fourth edition, 1951) defines death as

> The cessation of life; the ceasing to exist; *defined by physicians* as a total stoppage of the circulation of the blood, and a cessation of the animal and vital functions consequent thereupon, such as respiration, pulsation, etc. (italics added).

In the few modern court decisions involving a definition of death, the courts have used the concept of the total cessation of all vital signs. Two cases are worthy of examination. Both involved the issue of which one of two persons died first.

"Our first problem is to determine the characterisitics of a permanently *nonfunctioning brain."*

In *Thomas vs. Anderson*, (96 Cal App 2d 371, 211 P 2d 478) a California District Court of Appeal in 1950 said, "In the instant case the question as to which of the two men died first was a question of fact for the determination of the trial court...."

The appellate court cited and quoted in full the definition of death from *Black's Law Dictionary* and concluded, "...death occurs precisely when life ceases and does not occur until the heart stops beating and respiration ends. Death is not a continuous event and is an event that takes place at a precise time."

The other case is *Smith vs. Smith* (299 Ark, 579, 317 SW 2d 275) decided in 1958 by the Supreme Court of Arkansas. In this case the two people were a husband

and wife involved in an auto accident. The husband was found dead at the scene of the accident. The wife was taken to the hospital unconscious. It is alleged that she "remained in coma due to brain injury" and died at the hospital seventeen days later. The petitioner in court tried to argue that the two people died simultaneously. The judge writing the opinion said the petition contained a "quite unusual and unique allegation." It was quoted as follows:

> That the said Hugh Smith and his wife, Lucy Coleman Smith, were in an automobile accident on the 19th day of April, 1957, said accident being instantly fatal to each of them at the same time, although the doctors maintained a vain hope and effort to revive and resuscitate said Lucy Coleman Smith until May 6th, 1957, when it was finally determined by the attending physicians that their hope of resuscitation and possible restoration of human life to the said Lucy Coleman Smith was entirely vain, and That as a matter of modern medical science, your petitioner alleges and states, and will offer the Court competent proof that the said Hugh Smith, deceased, and said Lucy Coleman Smith, deceased, lost their power to will at the same instant, and that their demise as earthly human beings occurred at the same time in said automobile accident, neither of them ever regaining any consciousness whatsoever.

The court dismissed the petition as a matter of law. The court quoted Black's definition of death and concluded:

> Admittedly, this condition did not exist, and as a matter of fact, it would be too much of a strain of credulity for us to believe any evidence offered to the effect that Mrs. Smith was dead, scientifically or otherwise, unless the conditions set out in the definition existed.

Later in the opinion the court said, "Likewise, we take judicial notice that one breathing, though unconscious, is not dead."

Responsible New Criteria

"Judicial notice" of this definition of death means that the court did not consider that definition open to serious controversy; it considered the question as settled in responsible scientific and medical circles. The judge thus makes proof of uncontroverted facts unnecessary so as to prevent prolonging the trial with unnecessary proof and also to prevent fraud being committed upon the court by quasi "scientists" being called into court to controvert settled scientific principles at a price. Here, the Arkansas Supreme Court considered the definition of death to be a settled, biological fact. It refused to consider the plaintiff's offer of evidence that "modern medical science" might say otherwise. In simplified form, the above is the state of the law in the United States, concerning the definition of death.

In this report, however, we suggest that responsible medical opinion is ready to adopt new criteria for pronouncing death to have occurred in an individual sustaining irreversible coma as a result of permanent brain damage. If this position is adopted by the

medical community, it can form the basis for change in the current legal concept of death. No statutory change in the law should be necessary since the law treats this question essentially as one of fact to be determined by physicians. The only circumstance in which it would be necessary that legislation be offered in the various states to define "death" by law would be in the event that great controversy were engendered surround the subject and physicians were unable to agree on the new medical criteria.

It is recommended as a part of these procedures that judgment of the existence of these criteria is solely a medical issue. It is suggested that the physician in charge of the patient consult with one or more other physicians directly involved in the case before the patient is declared dead on the basis of these criteria. In this way, the responsibility is shared over a wider range of medical opinion, thus providing an important degree of protection against later questions which might be raised about the particular case. It is further suggested that the decision to declare the person dead, and then to turn off the respirator, be made by physicians not involved in any later effort to transplant organs or tissue from the deceased individual. This is advisable in order to avoid any appearance of self-interest by the physicians involved.

"All of the above tests shall be repeated at least 24 hours later with no change."

It should be emphasized that we recommend the patient be declared dead before any effort is made to take him off a respirator, if he is then on a respirator. This declaration should not be delayed until he has been taken off the respirator and all artificially stimulated signs have ceased. The reason for this recommendation is that in our judgment it will provide a greater degree of legal protection to those involved. Otherwise, the physicians would be turning off the respirator on a person who is, under the present strict, technical application of law, still alive.

Comment

Irreversible coma can have various causes: cardiac arrest; asphyxia with respiratory arrest; massive brain damage; intracranial lesions, neoplastic or vascular. It can be produced by other encephalopathic states such as the metabolic derangements associated, for example, with uremia. Respiratory failure and impaired circulation underlie all of these conditions. They result in hypoxia and ischemia of the brain.

From ancient times down to the recent past it was clear that, when the respiration and heart stopped, the brain would die in a few minutes; so the obvious criterion of no heartbeat as synonymous with death was sufficiently accurate. In those times, the heart was considered to be the central organ of the body; it is not surprising that its failure marked the onset of death. This is no longer valid when modern resuscitative and supportive measures are used. These improved activities can now restore "life" as judged by the ancient standards of persistent respiration and continuing heart beat. This can be the case even when there is not the remotest possibility of an individual recovering consciousness following massive brain damage. In other situations "life" can be maintained only by means of artificial respiration and electrical stimulation of the heart beat, or in temporarily bypassing the heart, or, in conjunction with these things, reducing with cold the body's oxygen requirement.

"It is recommended. . .that judgment of the existence of these criteria is solely a medical issue."

In an address, "The Prolongation of Life" (1957), Pope Pius XII raised many questions; some conclusions stand out: (1) In a deeply unconscious individual vital functions may be maintained over a prolonged period only by extraordinary means. Verification of the moment of death can be determined, if at all, only by a physician. Some have suggested that the moment of death is the moment when irreparable and overwhelming brain damage occurs. Pius XII acknowledged that it is not "within the competence of the Church" to determine this. (2) It is incumbent on the physician to take all reasonable, ordinary means of restoring the spontaneous vital functions and consciousness, and to employ such extraordinary means as are available to him to this end. It is not obligatory, however, to continue to use extraordinary means indefinitely in hopeless cases. "But normally one is held to use only ordinary means—according to circumstances of persons, places, times, and cultures—that is to say, means that do not involve any grave burden for oneself or another." It is the church's view that a time comes when resuscitative efforts should stop and death be unopposed.

Summary

The neurological impairment to which the terms "brain death syndrome" and "irreversible coma" have become attached indicates diffuse disease. Function is abolished at cerebral, brain-stem, and often spinal levels. This should be evident in all cases from clinical examination alone. Cerebral, cortical, and thalamic involvement are indicated by a complete absence of receptivity of all forms of sensory stimulation and a lack of response to stimuli and to inner need. The term "coma" is used to designate this state of unreceptivity and unresponsivity. But there is always coincident paralysis of brain-stem and basal ganglionic mechanisms as manifested by an abolition of all postural reflexes, including induced decerebrate postures; a complete paralysis of respiration; widely dilated, fixed pupils; paralysis of ocular movements; swallowing; phonation; face and tongue muscles. Involvement of the spinal cord, which is less constant, is reflected usually in the loss of the tendon reflex and all flexor withdrawal or nocifensive reflexes. Of the brain-stem-spinal mechanism which are conserved for a time, the vasomotor reflexes are the most persistent, and they are responsible in part for the paradoxical state of retained cardiovascular function, which is to some extent independent of nervous control, in the face of widespread disorder of cerebrum, brain stem, and spinal cord.

Neurological assessment gains in reliability if the aforementioned neurological signs persist over a period of time, with the additional safeguards that there is no accompanying hypothermia or evidence of drug intoxication. If either of the latter two conditions exists, interpretation of the neurological state should await the return of body temperature to normal level and elimination of the intoxicating agent. Under any other circumstances, repeated examinations over a period of 24 hours or longer should be required in order to obtain evidence of the irreversibility of the condition.

In 1967, a committee of physicians and scholars from Harvard University, convinced of an increasing need for specific criteria for determining when a person is dead, prepared this statement, which remains a widely accepted standard.

The Uniform Determination of Death Act

Medical Consultants on the Diagnosis of Death

The advent of effective artificial cardiopulmonary support for severely brain-injured persons has created some confusion during the past several decades about the determination of death. Previously, loss of heart and lung functions was an easily observable and sufficient basis for diagnosing death, whether the initial failure occurred in the brain, the heart and lungs, or elsewhere in the body. Irreversible failure of either the heart and lungs or the brain precluded the continued functioning of the other. Now, however, circulation and respiration can be maintained by means of a mechanical respirator and other medical interventions, despite a loss of all brain functions. In these circumstances we recognize as dead an individual whose loss of brain functions is complete and irreversible.

To recognize reliably that death has occurred, accurate criteria must be available for physicians' use. These now fall into two groups, to be applied depending on the clinical situation. When respiration and circulation have irreversibly ceased, there is no need to assess brain functions directly. When cardiopulmonary functions are artificially maintained, neurologic criteria must be used to assess whether brain functions have irreversibly ceased.

More than half of the states now recognize, through statutes or judicial decisions, that death may be determined on the basis of irreversible cessation of all functions of the brain. Law in the remaining states has not yet departed from the older, common law view that death has not occurred until "all vital functions" (whether or not artificially maintained) have ceased. The language of the statutes has not been uniform from state to state, and the diversity of proposed and enacted laws has created substantial confusion. Consequently, the American Bar

Association, the American Medical Association, the National Conference of Commissioners on Uniform State Laws, and the President's Commission for the Study of Ethical Problems in Medicine and Biomedical and Behavioral Research have proposed the following model statute, intended for adoption in every jurisdiction:

Uniform Determination of Death Act

An individual who has sustained either (1) irreversible cessation of circulatory and respiratory functions, or (2) irreversible cessation of all functions of the entire brain, including the brain stem, is dead. A determination of death must be made in accordance with accepted medical standards.

This wording has also been endorsed by the American Academy of Neurology and the American Electroencephalographic Society.

The statute relies upon the existence of "accepted medical standards" for determining that death has occurred. The medical profession, based upon carefully conducted research and extensive clinical experience, has found that death can be reliably determined by either cardiopulmonary or neurologic criteria. The test used for determining cessation of brain functions have changed and will continue to do so with the advent of new research and technologies. The "Harvard criteria" (JAMA, 205:337, 1968) are widely accepted, but advances in recent years have led to the proposal of other criteria. As an aid to the implementation of the proposed uniform statute, we provide here one statement of currently accepted medical standards.

Introduction

The criteria that physicians use in determining that death has occurred should:

    (1) Eliminate errors in classifying a living individual as dead,

Medical Consultants on the Diagnosis of Death to the President's Commission for the Study of Ethical Problems in Medicine and Biomedical and Behavioral Research, "Guidelines for the Determination of Death," 1984.

(2) Allow as few errors as possible in classifying a dead body as alive,

(3) Allow a determination to be made without unreasonable delay,

(4) Be adaptable to a variety of clinical situations, and

(5) Be explicit and accessible to verification.

Because it would be undesirable for any guidelines to be mandated by legislation or regulation or to be inflexibly established in case law, the proposed Uniform Determination of Death Act appropriately specifies only "accepted medical standards." Local, state, and national institutions and professional organizations are encouraged to examine and publish their practices.

The following guidelines represent a distillation of current practice in regard to the determination of death. Only the most commonly available and verified tests have been included. The time of death recorded on a death certificate is at present a matter of local practice and is not covered in this document.

These guidelines are advisory. Their successful use requires a competent and judicious physician, experienced in clinical examination and the relevant procedures. All periods of observation listed in these guidelines require the patient to be under the care of a physician. Considering the responsibility entailed in the determination of death, consultation is recommended when appropriate.

The outline of the criteria is set forth below in capital letters. The indented text that follows each outline heading explains its meaning. In addition, the two sets of criteria (cardiopulmonary and neurologic) are followed by a presentation of the major complicating conditions: drug and metabolic intoxication, hypothermia, young age, and shock. It is of paramount importance that anyone referring to these guidelines be thoroughly familiar with the entire documents, including explanatory notes and complicating conditions.

The Criteria for Determination of Death

An individual presenting the findings in *either* section A (cardiopulmonary) *or* section B (neurologic) is dead. In either section, a diagnosis of death requires that *both cessation of functions*, as set forth in subsection 1, *and irreversibility*, as set forth in subsection 2, be demonstrated.

A. AN INDIVIDUAL WITH IRREVERSIBLE CESSATION OF CIRCULATORY AND RESPIRATORY FUNCTIONS IS DEAD.

1. CESSATION IS RECOGNIZED BY AN APPROPRIATE CLINICAL EXAMINATION.

Clinical examination will disclose at least the absence of responsiveness, heartbeat, and respiratory effort. Medical circumstances may require the use of confirmatory tests, such as an ECG.

2. *IRREVERSIBILITY* IS RECOGNIZED BY PERSISTENT CESSATION OF FUNCTIONS DURING AN APPROPRIATE PERIOD OF OBSERVATION AND/OR TRIAL OF THERAPY.

In clinical situations where death is expected, where the course has been gradual, and where irregular agonal respiration or heartbeat finally ceases, the period of observation following the cessation may be only the few minutes required to complete the examination. Similarly, if resuscitation is not undertaken and ventricular fibrillation and standstill develop in a monitored patient, the required period of observation thereafter may be as short as a few minutes. When a possible death is unobserved, unexpected, or sudden, the examination may need to be more detailed and repeated over a longer period, while appropriate resuscitative effort is maintained as a test of cardiovascular responsiveness. Diagnosis in individuals who are first observed with rigor mortis or putrefaction may require only the observation period necessary to establish that fact.

B. AN INDIVIDUAL WITH IRREVERSIBLE CESSATION OF ALL FUNCTIONS OF THE ENTIRE BRAIN, INCLUDING THE BRAINSTEM, IS DEAD.

The "functions of the entire brain" that are relevant to the diagnosis are those that are clinically ascertainable. Where indicated, the clinical diagnosis is subject to confirmation by laboratory tests as described below. Consultation with a physician experienced in this diagnosis is advisable.

1. CESSATION IS RECOGNIZED WHEN EVALUATION DISCLOSES FINDINGS OF a *AND* b:

a. CEREBRAL FUNCTIONS ARE ABSENT, AND . . .

There must be deep coma, that is, cerebral unreceptivity and unresponsivity. Medical circumstances may require the use of confirmatory studies such as EEG or blood flow study.

"To recognize reliably that death has occurred, accurate criteria must be available for physicians' use."

---

b. BRAINSTEM FUNCTIONS ARE ABSENT.

Reliable testing of brainstem reflexes requires a perceptive and experienced physician using adequate stimuli. Pupillary light, corneal, oculocephalic, oculovestibular, oropharyngeal, and respiratory (apnea) reflexes should be tested. When these reflexes cannot be adequately assessed, confirmatory tests are recommended.

Adequate testing for apnea is very important. An accepted method is ventilation with pure oxygen or an oxygen and carbon dioxide mixture for ten minutes before withdrawal of the ventilator, followed by passive flow of oxygen. (This procedure allows $PaCO_2$ to rise without hazardous hypoxia.) Hypercarbia adequately stimulates respiratory effort within thirty seconds when $PaCO_2$ is greater than 60 mmHg. A ten minute period of apnea is usually sufficient to attain this level of hypercarbia. Testing of arterial blood gases can be used to confirm this level. Spontaneous breathing efforts indicate that part of the brainstem is functioning.

Peripheral nervous system activity and spinal cord reflexes may persist after death. True decerebrate or decorticate posturing or seizures are inconsistent with the diagnosis of death.

2. *IRREVERSIBILITY* IS RECOGNIZED WHEN EVALUATION DISCLOSES FINDINGS OF a *AND* b *AND* c:

a. THE CAUSE OF COMA IS ESTABLISHED AND IS SUFFICIENT TO ACCOUNT FOR THE LOSS OF BRAIN FUNCTIONS, AND...

Most difficulties with the determination of death on the basis of neurologic criteria have resulted from inadequate attention to this basic diagnostic prerequisite. In addition to a careful clinical examination and investigation of history, relevant knowledge of causation may be acquired by computed tomographic scan, measurement of core temperature, drug screening, EEG, angiography, or other procedures.

b. THE POSSIBILITY OF RECOVERY OF ANY BRAIN FUNCTIONS IS EXCLUDED, AND...

The most important reversible conditions are sedation, hypothermia, neuromuscular blockade, and shock. In the unusual circumstances where a sufficient cause cannot be established, irreversibility can be reliably inferred only after extensive evaluation for drug intoxication, extended observation, and other testing. A determination that blood flow to the brain is absent can be used to demonstrate a sufficient and irreversible condition.

c. THE CESSATION OF ALL BRAIN FUNCTIONS PERSISTS FOR AN APPROPRIATE PERIOD OF OBSERVATION AND/OR TRIAL OF THERAPY.

Even when coma is known to have started at an earlier time, the absence of all brain functions must be established by an experienced physician at the initiation of the observation period. The duration of observation periods is a matter of clinical judgment, and some physicians recommend shorter or longer periods than those given here.

Except for patients with drug intoxication, hypothermia, young age, or shock, medical centers with substantial experience in diagnosing death neurologically report no cases of brain functions returning following a six hour cessation, documented by clinical examination and confirmatory EEG. In the absence of confirmatory tests, a period of observation of at least twelve hours is recommended when an irreversible condition is well established. For anoxic brain damage where the extent of damage is more difficult to ascertain, observation for twenty-four hours is generally desirable. In anoxic injury, the observation period may be reduced if a test shows cessation of cerebral blood flow or if an EEG shows electrocerebral silence in an adult patient without drug intoxication, hypothermia, or shock.

"Drug intoxication is the most serious problem in the determination of death."

Confirmation of clinical findings by EEG is desirable when objective documentation is needed to substantiate the clinical findings. Electrocerebral silence verifies irreversible loss of cortical functions, except in patients with drug intoxication or hypothermia. (Important technical details are provided in: American Electroencephalographic Society, *Guidelines in EEG 1980*, Section 4: "Minimum Technical Standards for EEG Recording in Suspected Cerebral Death," pp. 19-24, Atlanta, 1980.) When joined with the clinical findings of absent brainstem functions, electrocerebral silence confirms the diagnosis.

Complete cessation of circulation to the normothermic adult brain for more than ten minutes is incompatible with survival of brain tissue. Documentation of this circulatory failure is therefore evidence of death of the entire brain. Four-vessel intracranial angiography is definitive for diagnosing cessation of circulation to the entire brain (both cerebrum and posterior fossa) but entails substantial practical difficulties and risks. Tests are available that assess circulation only in the cerebral hemispheres, namely radioisotope bolus cerebral angiography and gamma camera imaging with radioisotope cerebral angiography. Without complicating conditions, absent cerebral blood flow as measured by these tests, in conjunction with the clinical determination of cessation of all brain functions for at least six hours, is diagnostic of death.

Complicating Conditions

A. Drug and Metabolic Intoxication

Drug intoxication is the most serious problem in the determination of death, especially when multiple drugs are used. Cessation of brain functions caused by the sedative and anesthetic drugs, such as barbiturates, benzodiazepines, meprobamate, methaqualone, and trichloroethylene, may be completely reversible even though they produce clinical cessation of brain functions and electrocerebral silence. In cases where there is any likelihood of sedative presence, toxicology screening for all likely drugs is required. If exogenous intoxication is found, death may not be declared until the intoxicant is metabolized or intracranial circulation is tested and found to have ceased.

Total paralysis may cause unresponsiveness, areflexia, and apnea that closely simulates death. Exposure to drugs such as neuromuscular blocking agents or aminoglycoside antibiotics, and diseases like myasthenia gravis are usually apparent by careful review of the history. Prolonged paralysis after use of succinylcholine chloride and related drugs requires evaluation for pseudo-cholinesterase deficiency. If there is any question, low-dose atropine stimulation, electromyogram, peripheral nerve stimulation, EEG, tests of intracranial circulation, or extended observation, as indicated, will make the diagnosis clear.

"The absence of all brain functions must be established by an experienced physician."

In drug-induced coma, EEG activity may return or persist while the patient remains unresponsive, and therefore the EEG may be an important evaluation along with extended observation. If the EEG shows electrocerebral silence, short latency auditory or somatosensory evoked potentials may be used to test brainstem functions, since these potential are unlikely to be affected by drugs.

Some severe illnesses (e.g., hepatic encephalopathy, hyperosmolar coma, and preterminal uremia) can cause deep coma. Before irreversible cessation of brain functions can be determined, metabolic abnormalities should be considered and, if possible,

corrected. Confirmatory tests of circulation or EEG may be necessary.

B. Hypothermia

Criteria for reliable recognition of death are not available in the presence of hypothermia (below 32.2 °C core temperature). The variables of cerebral circulation in hypothermic patients are not sufficiently well studied to know whether tests of absent or diminished circulation are confirmatory. Hypothermia can mimic brain death by ordinary clinical criteria and can protect against neurologic damage due to hypoxia. Further complications arise since hypothermia also usually precedes and follows death. If these complicating factors make it unclear whether an individual is alive, the only available measure to resolve the issue is to restore normothermia. Hypothermia is not a common cause of difficulty in the determination of death.

C. Children

The brains of infants and young children have increased resistance to damage and may recover substantial functions even after exhibiting unresponsiveness on neurological examination for longer periods than do adults. Physicians should be particularly cautious in applying neurologic criteria to determine death in children younger than five years.

D. Shock

Physicians should also be particularly cautious in applying neurologic criteria to determine death in patients in shock because the reduction of cerebral circulation can render clinical examination and laboratory tests unreliable.

The Medical Consultants on the Diagnosis of Death were a group of 56 physicians from a variety of practices who advised the President's Commission for the Study of Ethical Problems in Medicine and Biomedical and Behavioral Research. They wrote the above proposal as a model statute defining death. The statute was approved by several major medical and legal organizations. It was also recommended by the President's Commission as a model for the states to follow.

"When I was a medical student...I was taught very carefully by my clinical mentors how to tell when a patient had died."

viewpoint**77**

Traditional Clinical Signs Can Determine Death

Bernard Towers

The words *clinic* and *clinical* are derived from the Greek word for bed or couch. Traditionally that is where patients find themselves when they are sick; that is where clinical observations are made and where clinical care is rendered, in a hospital ward, outpatient clinic, or, more traditionally, by the bedside at home. Clinical observations and clinical care are made or given by professionals, a fact that accounts for a secondary dictionary meaning of clinical, namely, "objective" or "dispassionate." It is this component of professionalism that has led in turn to the somewhat unfortunate expression "coldly clinical." This more recent emphasis on the noncaring elements implied by the word itself is surely due to the enormous growth of scientific and technological aspects of medicine and often a concomitant loss of those essential human qualities that formed the cornerstone of the doctor-patient relationship in traditional medical practice.

The orginal meaning of the word clinical, that is, "at the bedside," has clearly undergone further loss and corruption in recent years. Medical schools have traditionally divided the curriculum into preclinical studies such as anatomy, physiology, biochemistry, and pathology and clinical studies carried out directly on patients in the teaching hospital or clinic. Recently some law schools have introduced what they call by analogy a "clinical component" into the law school curriculum. It does not necessarily have to do with medico-legal cases (as I thought when I first heard the term), or possibly with marriage and family law. It simply means the exposure of the budding lawyer to real life situations and to real life clients, where they can practice their "clinical" (by now "professional" or simply "practical") skills in ways not encouraged in the older theory-laden curriculum.

Professional observations made by a physician or nurse on the condition of a patient need no longer necessarily be made close to the bed or couch. They can be carried out by remote control. The clinical condition, for instance, of the cardiovascular system, is assessed today in terms of heart rate, blood pressure, electrocardiogram tracing, and physicochemical recordings of components of the blood. The observer-clinician sitting in front of a bank of TV controls may be far away from the patient and yet know much more about what is actually happening in the patient's body than a doctor or medical student standing literally at the bedside. As with all technical progress there are advantages and disadvantages in the developments we choose to exploit. It requires sound judgment to determine whether a new mode of behavior is in the patient's best interest. Thus, it is appropriate to discuss clinical care as it relates to changing concepts of death.

When I was a medical student and house officer in England in the early 1940s I was taught very carefully by my clinical mentors how to tell when a patient had died and to do it with enough certainty to feel confident about actually signing the death certificate. That required signature was and still is an awesome responsibility that society has placed on physicians. The pronouncement is final. Nothing can be the same again or even remotely like what it was, not for the individual concerned, not for the family, not for anybody who remains alive.

Clinical Signs and Symptoms

We were taught many clinical signs of dying and death. The recognition and correct interpretation of "clinical signs and symptoms" represented a major component of medical education in Britain, as indeed used to be the case in American medical schools, following the traditions of Sir William Osler, first chairman of medicine at Johns Hopkins University

Bernard Towers, "Changing Concepts of Death: Clinical Care." Reprinted by permission of the author.

death/dying 357

and subsequently Regius Professor at the University of Oxford. Clinical *symptoms* are what the patient tells you (in words or body language) about his or her physical and mental state. Clinical *signs* are what the examining physician can detect, at the bedside, concerning normal or abnormal functioning of the body's organ systems and the patient's overall well-being. Traditionally observations were made and clinical tests conducted with the use of the examiner's senses of sight and touch and of taste, hearing, and smell as appropriate to the situation. When such observations are combined with in-depth reflection on the complex syndromes revealed, the exercise as a whole represents a total involvement of the personality of the physician with that of the patient. One unfortunate result of the development of modern technological aids to observation is that analysis is often and sometimes more accurately pursued at some distance removed from the actual patient whose clinical signs are under review. One can picture the day when determinations as to appropriate measures to take in caring for the dying patient (including the decision to declare that death has indeed occurred) will be made in front of a set of television and computer terminals or even by those hardware units themselves; it would be possible to program the system so that when two or three certain objective signs appear (or, more probably, cease to appear or start to run at less than some preset figure) the system will in effect declare that death has occurred and will itself turn off the switch or pull the plug on which the patient's or ex-patient's continued functioning depends. It has not reached that point yet, and certainly during my own period of training in medical school the concepts of death and of the clinical care that should attend it were very different.

"Professional observations. . . need no longer necessarily be made close to the bed or couch. They can be carried out by remote control."

As I remarked above, we were taught many clinical signs of dying and death. We listened for a heart beat, we felt for a pulse, we checked for breathing with a mirror or a wisp of cotton wool placed before mouth and nose. We looked into the eyes, those windows of the soul. If anything moved then the patient was still alive. When nothing moved we folded the corpse's arms and pulled the sheet over the face. Movement has always been associated in the human psyche with living creatures, and lack of movement with the lifeless state. Something that moves by itself is to be looked at and looked after very carefully. This is probably why that literal self-

mover, the early automobile, as recently as the start of this century, was required to have someone walk in front of it as it journeyed down the thoroughfare. It helped dispel some of the fears engendered by a manufactured but apparently living (because moving) machine. Similar fears, about living and dying and being dead, are still at large and rightly so. But when we young doctors observed, long ago at the patient's bedside, that all movement had apparently ceased, we were ready to state that the patient was indeed dead and to sign the certificate that permitted appropriate disposition of the corpse.

Sometimes in the operating room a patient's heart would stop, and the surgeon would perform cardiac massage and save a life. Apart from such an extraordinary event we accepted the time-honored medical definition of death as "the consequence of total stoppage of the circulation of the blood and the cessation of vital functions consequent thereupon such as respiration, pulsation etc" (Black's Law Dictionary, 4th Edition, 1951).

Realistic Ethical Precepts

As physicians-in-training we inherited much medical lore and wisdom accumulated over the centuries. Three major ethical precepts to which we committed ourselves as professional healers were (a) to save life whenever possible; (b) to relieve pain and suffering; and (c) above all to do no harm to a patient. With these precepts we pursued our vocation with clear consciences, recognizing that the cure of illness might indeed sometimes involve infliction of distress, but only when necessary to preserve life or to avoid the greater distress caused by the illness itself. We were taught to be realistic about acknowledging that death was imminent and that further intervention would be useless. Then we prepared the members of the family for what was expected, and we waited and watched for the signs listed above. We were taught to be very careful before making the final pronouncement that death had indeed occurred. There are many stories of people coming to life in the morgue or in a coffin. The thought of being buried alive and waking up in total isolation and unable to do anything about it strikes terror in everyone. Edgar Allan Poe wrote one of his most successful tales of mystery and imagination on this theme, a story written in the first person of a man who was terrified of being buried alive and who woke in pitch darkness to feel wooden planks immediately above him, then beneath him, and then in mounting terror, to his side. It turns out that he is in a ship's bunk, but initially he is convinced he is in a coffin, six feet underground. History is replete with examples of people giving instructions that after presumed death and before burial arrangements to be made for a communication system to be incorporated in the death chamber; or that their veins be cut; or that they be chemically embalmed; or that they be cremated. But by and large society agreed that when the heart stopped and breathing ceased then the individual was dead.

If the old terror was of being buried alive while capable of becoming conscious again, the modern fear is of being irreversibly unconscious and yet maintained indefinitely in an intensive care unit, buried while questionably alive in a morass of electronic gadgets. One can ask the question, as Edward Albee did over a decade ago in his play *All Over*, are they (the electronic gadgets) keeping a corpse alive or is the corpse keeping them and their operators functional? Does the financial stability of the ICU depend in part on the newly dead keeping the whole apparatus in action?

Obsolete Criteria

Modern medical technology has made the older criteria of death obsolete, at least in certain circumstances. Techniques of cardiopulmonary resuscitation and of cardiopulmonary bypass surgery daily give extended life to many persons who would have been declared dead according to the older criteria. Death occurs in stages and by degrees and not necessarily in the same order for everyone. There is death of cells, of tissues, of individual organs of the body, of complex organ systems; and there is death or loss of the organizing principle that integrates the parts on behalf of the whole body. In higher vetebrates this integration requires the functional cooperation of the central nervous system and especially of its expanded portion encased within the skull, the brain.

The concept of brain death sounds simple enough at first glance. It might be thought to be merely an extension of the older cardiopulmonary definition; after all, cessation of heart beat and respiration deprives the brain of oxygen and leads to its inevitable death (except under special circumstances such as extreme cooling.) Loss of consciousness is an early sign of cerebral anoxia. We die, finally unaware of the fact. With death of the brain, integrating functions within the body's various systems cease and dissolution occurs.

But the concept of brain death is not so easy, in fact. The vertebrate brain is a composite of many component parts, and the human brain is the most complex of all. The evolution of the brain stretches back over a period of hundreds of millions of years; its embryological development follows a similar pattern (ontegeny recapitulating phylogency, as the saying goes) during nearly half a million minutes of intrauterine life and many more millions leading to maturity. The centers in the brain stem are the first to be formed and the last to go; the higher centers of midbrain and forebrain develop later in fetal life, are more complex in organization, and are more susceptible to oxygen deprivation than is the more robust area of the hindbrain, where reflex physiological centers can continue to function long after the disappearance of the thinking and feeling centers of the forebrain. The adult cerebral cortex can survive oxygen deprivation for only about four minutes. The younger, more primitive cortex of the fetus and newborn can survive (though not necessarily wholly intact) longer periods of oxygen deprivation: vital fetal organs such as heart and brain contain a great deal of glycogen, an energy source that can be used by the anaerobic (non-oxygen-consuming) metabolic pathways that represent an important survival mechanism for the newly born. The adult cerebral cortex, however, as we have said, can survive without oxygen for only a very few minutes. The adult brain stem, on the other hand, where many vegetative reflexes are located, can survive for 15 to 20 minutes. This represents again, a primitive evolutionary survival mechanism. The trouble today is that many "successful" resuscitations occur during that critical interval between 4 and 15 minutes following cardiac arrest.

Modern Problems

Modern technology therefore has permitted the survival of increasing number of "brain stem preparations" (people? living corpses?). Members of society, including members of the medical profession, simply do not know what to do about them. Medical writers have posed the problems in recent times in striking terms, for instance, Robin Cook in his novel and film *Coma,* and Willard Gaylin in a very perceptive essay entitled "Harvesting the Dead," which first appeared in *Harper's* in September 1974.

"Movement has always been associated in the human psyche with living creatures, and lack of movement with the lifeless state."

Ethical, legal, and medical problems abound for the attending physicians and nurses in determining what constitutes appropriate clinical care for patients who have sustained death of some part(s) but not of all of the brain. The President's Commission for the Study of Ethical Problems in Medicine and Biomedical and Behavioral Research has recommended that a person shall be (not may be) declared dead if he or she has sustained "irreversible cessation of all functions of the entire brain, including the brain stem" (p. 73).

Such total cessation of function is usually due to the development after brain trauma of increasing pressure inside the skull: when the intracranial pressure rises to a level higher than the blood pressure (that is, the pressure inside the arteries that drives the blood on to supply the brain tissue itself) then circulation ceases and brain cells everywhere die off very rapidly. The position on diagnosis of brain death adopted by the President's Commission, which requires demonstration of brain stem death before a death certificate can be signed, is a very conservative one and will be noncontroversial, it is hoped. At least it allows for and even requires the turning off of the machines even though the rest of the central nervous system (the spinal cord) may be intact, as also might be most or all other organs of the body. The question remains: Where does one draw the line between being alive and being dead? Is one alive if some parts of the medulla oblongata are still functioning but not if function is confined to the spinal cord? How much of medulla or pons or midbrain are needed for "personhood"? Or is it the case that what we really mean by "the brain" is that with which we think and feel and relate to our surroundings, in other words the forebrain? If that part is irretrievably destroyed, so that loss of consciousness is total and irreversible, then can we legitimately say that the patient as person is "gone" and should or must be declared to be dead?

"Modern medical technology has made the older criteria of death obsolete, at least in certain circumstances."

Only when these medical, ethical, theological, and legal questions are answered will we know how best to provide clinical care for our patients in ways that will not offend at least one of the three ethical precepts of medicine refered to earlier in this essay.

Physicians who are as humane and as caring as professional traditions demand are currently much exercised about what constitutes appropriate clinical care in light of changing concepts of death. Modern skills permit quality survival from a host of diseases that were previously incurable. Even if the quality of the extended life is less than optimal, most people would opt for it rather than for death. But grey zones abound. When we lay out the pros and cons of this or that action or reaction, we often find ourselves in a dilemma as to what is best or right to choose and what is best or right to advise the patient or the relatives. Such dilemmas are moral ones. We need the expertise of philosophers to help us resolve them. But the philosophers must first become fully conscious of the medical (biological and psychological) aspects of the clinical case histories before their ethical analyses can be of much help. What we need is much more transdisciplinary discussion.

Bernard Towers is a professor of anatomy and psychiatry at UCLA.

Determining Death Requires Consideration of Many Concepts

President's Commission

The enabling legislation for the President's Commission directs it to study "the ethical and legal implications of the matter of defining death, including the advisability of developing a uniform definition of death." In performing its mandate, the Commission has reached conclusions on a series of questions which are the subject of this Report. In summary, the central conclusions are:

1. That recent developments in medical treatment necessitate a restatement of the standards traditionally recognized for determining that death has occurred.

2. That such a restatement ought preferably to be a matter of statutory law.

3. That such a statute ought to remain a matter for state law, with federal action at this time being limited to areas under current federal jurisdiction.

4. That the statutory law ought to be uniform among the several states.

5. That the "definition" contained in the statute ought to address general physiological standards rather than medical criteria and tests, which will change with advances in biomedical knowledge and refinements in technique.

6. That death is a unitary phenomenon which can be accurately demonstrated either on the traditional grounds of irreversible cessation of heart and lung functions or on the basis of irreversible loss of all functions of the entire brain.

7. That any statutory "definition" should be kept separate and distinct from provisions governing the donation of cadaver organs and from any legal rules on decisions to terminate life-sustaining treatment.

To embody these conclusions in statutory form the Commission worked with the three organizations which had proposed model legislation on the subject,

the American Bar Association, the American Medical Association, and the National Conference of Commissioners on Uniform State Laws. These groups have now endorsed the following statute, in place of their previous proposals:

Uniform Determination of Death Act

An individual who has sustained either (1) irreversible cessation of circulatory and respiratory functions, or (2) irreversible cessation of all functions of the entire brain, including the brain stem, is dead. A determination of death must be made in accordance with accepted medical standards.

The Commission recommends the adoption of this statute in all jurisdictions in the United States.

The One Great Certainty

Death is the one great certainty. The subject of powerful social and religious rituals and moving literature, it is contemplated by philosophers, probed by biologists, and combatted by physicians. Death, taboo in some cultures, preoccupies others. In this Report the President's Commission explores only a small corner of this boundless topic. . . .

The diagnosis of death has, of course, significance beyond its role as a physiological concept. Therefore several different explanations of the "meaning" of human life and death are examined. Formulations based upon the functions of the whole brain include those that focus on the integrated functioning of brain, heart and lung and on the primacy of the brain among organs as the body's regulator. Some people have argued for a "higher brain" formulation, such as one which attempts to enumerate the characteristics essential to "personhood" or one that bases death on the loss of "personal identity," viewed here as a consequence of discontinuity in certain mental processes. Finally, several explanations of death not oriented to brain functions are also reviewed, such as those which hold death to occur when the soul leaves the body or which equate life with the flow of air and blood through the body.

The President's Commission for the Study of Ethical Problems in Medicine and Biomedical and Behavioral Research, *Defining Death: Medical, Legal and Ethical Issues in the Determination of Death,* 1981.

The Commission had some points of disagreement with all of the formulations. Nevertheless, without resolving all the conceptual issues, the Commission found that all the formulations, except perhaps the last, were consistent with the public policy recommendations of this Report....

Understanding the "Meaning" of Death

It now seems clear that a medical consensus about clinical practices and their scientific basis has emerged: certain states of brain activity and inactivity, together with their neurophysiological consequences, can be reliably detected and used to diagnose death. To the medical community, a sound basis exists for declaring death even in the presence of mechanically assisted "vital signs." Yet before recommending that public policy reflect this medical consensus, the Commission wished to know whether the scientific viewpoint was consistent with the concepts of "being dead" or "death" as they are commonly understood in our society. These questions have been addressed by philosophers and theologians, who have provided several formulations.

"It now seems clear that a medical consensus... has emerged: certain states of brain activity and inactivity... can be reliably detected and used to diagnose death."

The Commission believes that its policy conclusions, including the statute recommended, must accurately reflect the social meaning of death and not constitute a mere legal fiction. The Commission has not found it necessary to resolve all of the differences among the leading concepts of death because these views all yield interpretations consistent with the recommended statute.

Three major formulations of the meaning of death were presented to the Commission: one focused upon the functions of the whole brain, one upon the functions of the cerebral hemispheres, and one upon non-brain functions. Each of these formulations (and its variants) is presented and evaluated.

The "Whole Brain" Formulations

One characteristic of living things which is absent in the dead is the body's capacity to organize and regulate itself. In animals, the neural apparatus is the dominant locus of these functions. In higher animals and man, regulation of both maintenance of the internal environment (homeostasis) and interaction with the external environment occurs primarily within the cranium.

External threats, such as heat or infection, or internal ones, such as liver failure or endogenous lung disease, can stress the body enough to overwhelm its ability to maintain organization and regulation. If the stress passes a certain level, the organism as a whole is defeated and death occurs.

This process and its denouement are understood in two major ways. Although they are sometimes stated as alternative formulations of a "whole brain definition" of death, they are actually mirror images of each other. The Commission has found them to be complementary; together they enrich one's understanding of the "definition." The first focuses on the integrated functioning of the body's major organ systems, while recognizing the centrality of the whole brain, since it is neither revivable nor replaceable. The other identifies the functioning of the whole brain as the hallmark of life because the brain is the regulator of the body's integration. The two conceptions are subject to similar criticisms and have similar implications for policy.

Integrated Functioning

The functioning of many organs—such as the liver, kidneys, and skin—and their integration are "vital" to individual health in the sense that if any one ceases and that function is not restored or artificially replaced, the organism as a whole cannot long survive. All elements in the system are mutually interdependent, so that the loss of any part leads to the breakdown of the whole and, eventually, to the cessation of functions in every part.

Three organs—the heart, lungs and brain—assume special significance, however, because their interrelationship is very close and the irreversible cessation of any one very quickly stops the other two and consequently halts the integrated functioning of the organism as a whole. Because they were easily measured, circulation and respiration were traditionally the basic "vital signs." But breathing and heartbeat are not life itself. They are simply used as signs—as one window for viewing a deeper and more complex reality: a triangle of interrelated systems with the brain at its apex. As the biomedical scientists who appeared before the Commission made clear, the traditional means of diagnosing death actually detected an irreversible cessation of integrated functioning among the interdependent bodily systems. When artificial means of support mask this loss of integration as measured by the old methods, brain-oriented criteria and tests provide a new window on the same phenomenon.

On this view, death is that moment at which the body's physiological system ceases to constitute an integrated whole. Even if life continues in individual cells or organs, life of the organism as a whole requires complex integration, and without the latter, a person cannot properly be regarded as alive.

This distinction between systemic, integrated functioning and physiological activity in cells or individual organs is important for two reasons. First, a person is considered dead under this concept even if oxygenation and metabolism persist in some cells or organs. There would be no need to wait until all metabolism had ceased in every body part before recognizing that death has occurred.

More importantly, this concept would reduce the significance of continued respiration and heartbeat for the definition of death. This view holds that continued breathing and circulation are not in themselves tantamount to life. Since life is a matter of integrating the functioning of major organ systems, breathing and circulation are necessary but not sufficient to establish that an individual is alive. When an individual's breathing and circulation lack neurologic integration, he or she is dead.

Primary Organ View

The alternative "whole brain" explanation of death differs from the one just described primarily in the vigor of its insistence that the traditional "vital signs" of heartbeat and respiration were merely surrogate signs with no significance in themselves. On this view, the heart and lungs are not important as basic prerequisites to continued life but rather because the irreversible cessation of their functions shows that the brain had ceased functioning. Other signs customarily employed by physicians in diagnosing death, such as unresponsiveness and absence of pupillary light response, are also indicative of loss of the functions of the whole brain.

This view gives the brain primacy not merely as the sponsor of consciousness (since even unconscious persons may be alive), but also as the complex organizer and regulator of bodily functions. (Indeed, the "regulatory" role of the brain in the organism can be understood in terms of thermodynamics and information theory.) Only the brain can direct the entire organism. Artificial support for the heart and lungs, which is required only when the brain can no longer control them, cannot maintain the usual synchronized integration of the body. Now that other traditional indicators of cessation of brain functions (i.e., absence of breathing), can be obscured by medical interventions, one needs, according to this view, new standards for determining death—that is, more reliable tests for the complete cessation of brain functions.

Critique

Both of these "whole brain" formulations—the "integrated functions" and the "primary organ" views—are subject to several criticisms. Since both of these conceptions of death give an important place to the integrating or regulating capacity of the whole brain, it can be asked whether that characteristic is as distinctive as they would suggest. Other organ systems are also required for life to continue—for example, the skin to conserve fluid, the liver to detoxify the blood.

The view that the brain's functions are more central to "life" than those of the skin, the liver, and so on, is admittedly arbitrary in the sense of representing a choice. The view is not, however, arbitrary in the sense of lacking reasons. As discussed previously, the centrality accorded the brain reflects both its overarching role as "regulator" or "integrator" of other bodily systems and the immediate and devastating consequences of its loss for the organism as a whole. Furthermore, the Commission believes that this choice overwhelmingly reflects the views of experts and the lay public alike.

"Death is that moment at which the body's physiological system ceases to constitute an integrated whole."

A more significant criticism shares the view that life consists of the coordinated functioning of the various bodily systems, in which process the whole brain plays a crucial role. At the same time, it notes that in some adult patients lacking all brain functions it is possible through intensive support to achieve constant temperature, metabolism, waste disposal, blood pressure, and other conditions typical of living organisms and not found in dead ones. Even with extraordinary medical care, these functions cannot be sustained indefinitely—typically, no longer than several days—but it is argued that this shows only that patients with nonfunctional brains are dying, not that they are dead. In this view, the respirator, drugs, and other resources of the modern intensive-care unit collectively substitutes for the lower brain, just as a pump used in the cardiac surgery takes over the heart's function.

Startling Differences

This criticism rests, however, on a premise about the role of artificial support vis-a-vis the brainstem which the Commission believes is mistaken or at best incomplete. While the respirator and its associated medical techniques do substitute for the functions of the intercostal muscles and the diaphragm, which without neuronal stimulation from the brain cannot function spontaneously, they cannot replace the myriad functions of the brainstem or of the rest of the brain. The startling contrast between bodies lacking *all* brain functions and patients with intact brainstems (despite severe neocortical damage) manifests this. The former lie with fixed pupils, motionless except for the chest movements produced by their respirators. The latter can not only breathe, metabolize, maintain temperature and blood pressure, and so forth, *on their own* but also sigh, yawn, track light with their eyes, and react to pain or reflex stimulation.

It is not easy to discern precisely what it is about patients in this latter group that makes them alive while those in the other category are not. It is in part that in the case of the first category (i.e., absence of all brain functions) when the mask created by the artificial medical support is stripped away what remains is not an integrated organism but "merely a group of artificially maintain sub-systems." Sometimes, of course, an artificial substitute can forge the link that restores the organism as a whole to unified functioning. Heart or kidney transplants, kindney dialysis, or an iron lung used to replace physically-impaired breathing ability in a polio victim, for example, restore the integrated functioning of the organism as they replace the failed function of a part. Contrast such situtations, however, with the hypothetical of a decapitated body treated so as to prevent the outpouring of blood and to generate respiration: continuation of bodily functions in that case would not have restored the requisites of human life.

"'Personhood' consists of the complex of activities. . .such as thinking, reasoning, feeling. . .which make the human different from, or superior to, animals or things."

The living differ from the dead in many ways. The dead do not think, interact, autoregulate or maintain organic identity through time, for example. Not all the living can always do *all* of these activities, however; nor is there one single characteristic (e.g., breathing, yawning, etc.) the loss of which signifies death. Rather, what is missing in the dead is a cluster of attributes, all of which form part of an organism's responsiveness to its internal and external environment.

While it is valuable to test public policies against basic conceptions of death, philosophical refinement beyond a certain point may not be necessary. The task undertaken in this Report, as stated at the outset, is to provide and defend a statutory standard for determining that a human being has died. In setting forth the standards recommended in this Report, the Commission has used "whole brain" terms to clarify the understanding of death that enjoys near universal acceptance in our society. The Commission finds that the "whole brain" formulations give resonance and depth to the biomedical and epidemiological data. Further effort to search for a conceptual "definition" of death is not required for the purpose of public policy because, separately or together, the "whole brain" formulations provide a

theory that is sufficiently precise, concise and widely acceptable.

Those holding to the "whole' brain" view—and this view seems at least implicit in most of the testimony and writing reviewed by the Commission—believe that when respirators are in use, respiration and circulation lose significance for the diagnosis of death. In a body without a functioning brain these two functions, it is argued, become mere artifacts of the mechanical life supports. The lungs breathe and the heart circulates blood only because the respirator (and attendant medical interventions) cause them to do so, not because of any comprehensive integrated functioning. This is "breathing" and "circulation" only in an analogous sense: the function and its results are similar, but the source, cause, and purpose are different between those individuals with and those without functioning brains.

Policy Consequences

For patients who are not artificially maintained, breathing and heartbeat were, and are, reliable signs either of systemic integration and/or of continued brain functioning (depending on which approach one takes to the "whole brain" concept). To regard breathing and respiration as having diagnostic significance when the brain of a respirator-supported patient has ceased functioning, however, is to forget the basic reasoning behind their use in individuals who are not artificially maintained.

Although similar in most respects, the two approaches to "whole brain death" could have slightly different policy consequences. The "primary organ" view would be satisfied with a statute that contained only a single standard—the irreversible cessation of all functions of the entire brain. Nevertheless, as a practical matter, the view is also compatible with a statute establishing irreversible cessation of respiration and circulation as an alternative standard, since it is inherent in this view that the loss of spontaneous breathing and heartbeat are surrogates for the loss of brain functions.

The "integrated functions" view would lead one to a "definition" of death recognizing that collapse of the organism as a whole can be diagnosed through the loss of brain functions as well as through loss of cardiopulmonary functions. The latter functions would remain an explicit part of the policy statement because their irreversible loss will continue to provide an independent and wholly reliable basis for determining that death has occurred when respirators and related means of support are *not* employed.

The two "whole brain" formulations thus differ only modestly. And even conceptual disagreements have a context; the context of the present one is the need to clarify and update the "definition" of death in order to allow principled decisions to be made about the status of comatose respirator-supported patients. The explicit recognition of both standards—cardiopulmonary and whole brain—solves that problem fully. In addition, since it requires only a modest reformulation of the generally-accepted view, it accounts for the importance traditionally accorded to heartbeat and respiration, the "vital signs" which will continue to be the grounds for determining death in the overwhelming majority of cases for the foreseeable future. Hence the Commission, drawing on the aspects that the two formulations share and on the ways in which they each add to an understanding of the "meaning" of death, concludes that public policy should recognize both cardiopulmonary and brain-based standards for declaring death.

The "Higher Brain" Formulations

When all brain processes cease, the patient loses two important sets of functions. One set encompasses the intergrating and coordinating functions, carried out principally but not exclusively by the cerebellum and brainstem. The other set includes the psychological functions which make consciousness, thought, and feeling possible. These latter functions are located primarily but not exclusively in the cerebrum, especially the neocortex. The two "higher brain" formulations of brain-oriented definitions of death discussed here are premised on the fact that loss of cerebral functions strips the patient of his psychological capacities and properties.

A patient whose brain has permanently stopped functioning will, by definition, have lost those brain functions which sponsor consciousness, feeling, and thought. Thus the higher brain rationales support classifying as dead bodies which meet "whole brain" standards, as discussed in the preceding section. The converse is not true, however. If there are parts of the brain which have no role in sponsoring consciousness, the higher brain formulation would regard their continued functioning as compatible with death.

The Concepts

Philosophers and theologians have attempted to describe the attributes of a living being must have to be a person. "Personhood" consists of the complex of activities (or of capacities to engage in them) such as thinking, reasoning, feeling, human intercourse which make the human different from, or superior to, animals or things. One higher brain formulation would define death as the loss of what is essential to a person. Those advocating the personhood definition often relate these characteristics to brain functioning. Without brain activity, people are incapable of these essential activities. A breathing body, the argument goes, is not in itself a person; and, without functioning brains, patients are merely breathing bodies. Hence personhood ends when the brain suffers irreversible loss of function.

For other philosophers, a certain concept of

"personal identity" supports a brain-oriented definition of death. According to this argument, a patient literally ceases to exist as an individual when his or her brain ceases functioning, even if the patient's body is biologically alive. Actual decapitation creates a similar situation: the body might continue to function for a short time, but it would no longer be the "same" person. The persistent identity of a person as an individual from one moment to the next is taken to be dependent on the continuation of certain mental processes which arise from brain functioning. When the brain processes cease (whether due to decapitation or to "brain death") the person's identity also lapses. The mere continuation of biological activity in the body is irrelevant to the determination of death, it is argued, because after the brain has ceased functioning the body is no longer identical with the person.

Critique

Theoretical and practical objections to these arguments led the Commission to rely on them only as confirmatory of other views in formulating a definition of death. First, crucial to the personhood argument is acceptance of one particular concept of those things that are essential to being a person, while there is no general agreement on this very fundamental point among philosophers, much less physicians or the general public. Opinions about what is essential to personhood vary greatly from person to person in our society—to say nothing of intercultural variations.

"Determinations of death must be made in a consistent and evenhanded fashion."

The argument from personal identity does not rely on any particular conception of personhood, but it does require assent to a single solution to the philosophical problem of identity. Again, this problem has persisted for centuries despite the best attempts by philosophers to solve it. Regardless of the scholarly merits of the various philosophical solutions, their abstract technicality makes them less useful to public policy.

Further, applying either of these arguments in practice would give rise to additional important problems. Severely senile patients, for example, might not clearly be persons, let alone ones with continuing personal identities; the same might be true of the severely retarded. Any argument that classified these individuals as dead would not meet with public acceptance.

Equally problematic for the "higher brain" formulations, patients in whom only the neocortex or subcortical areas have been damaged may retain or regain spontaneous respiration and circulation. Karen Quinlan is a well-known example of a person who apparently suffered permanent damage to the higher centers of the brain but whose lower brain continues to function. Five years after being removed from the respirator that supported her breathing for nearly a year, she remains in a persistent vegetative state but with heart and lungs that function without mechanical assistance. Yet the implication of the personhood and personal identity arguments is that Karen Quinlan, who retains brainstem function and breathes spontaneously, is just as dead as a corpse in the traditional sense. The Commission rejects this conclusion and the further implication that such patients could be buried or otherwise treated as dead persons.

Policy Clarification

In order to be incorporated in public policy, a conceptual formulation of death has to be amenable to clear articulation. At present, neither basic neurophysiology nor medical technique suffices to translate the ''higher brain'' formulation into policy. First, it is not known which portions of the brain are responsible for cognition and consciousness; what little is known points to substantial interconnections among the brainstem, subcortical structures and the neocortex. Thus, the ''higher brain'' may well exist only as a metaphorical concept, not in reality. Second, even when the sites of certain aspects of consciousness can be found, their cessation often cannot be assessed with the certainty that would be required in applying a statutory definition.

"The implication of the personhood and personal identity arguments is that Karen Quinlan. . . is just as dead as a corpse in the traditional sense."

Even were these difficulties to be overcome, the adoption of a higher brain ''definition'' would depart radically from the traditional standards. As already observed, the new standard would assign no significance to spontaneous breathing and heartbeat. Indeed, it would imply that the existing cardiopulmonary definition had been in error all along, even before the advent of respirators and other life-sustaining technology.

In contrast, the position taken by the Commission is deliberately conservative. The statutory proposal offers legal recognition for new diagnostic measures of death, but does not ask for acceptance of a wholly new concept of death. On a matter so fundamental to a society's sense of itself—touching deeply held

personal and religious beliefs—and so final for the individuals involved, one would desire much greater consensus than now exists before taking the major step of radically revising the concept of death.

Finally, patients declared dead pursuant to the statute recommended by the Commission would be also considered dead by those who believe that a body without higher brain functions is dead. Thus, all the arguments reviewed thus far are in agreement that irreversible cessation of *all* brain functioning is sufficient to determine death of the organism.

The Non-Brain Formulations

The various physiological concepts of death so far discussed rely in some fashion on brain functioning. By contrast, a literal reading of the traditional cardiopulmonary criteria would require cessation of the flow of bodily ''fluids,'' including air and blood, for death to be declared. This standard is meant to apply whether or not these flows coincide with any other bodily processes, neurological or otherwise. Its support derives from interpretations of religious literature and cultural practices of certain religious and ethnic groups, including some Orthodox Jews and Native Americans.

Another theological formulation of death is, by contrast, not necessarily related to any physiologic phenomenon. The view is traditional in many faiths that death occurs the moment the soul leaves the body. Whether this happens when the patient loses psychological capacities, loses all brain functions, or at some other point, varies according to the teachings of each faith and according to particular interpretations of the scriptures recognized as authoritative.

Critique

The conclusions of the ''bodily fluids'' view lack a physiologic basis in modern biomedicine. While this view accords with the traditional criteria of death, as noted above, it does not necessarily carry over to the new conditions of the intensive care unit—which are what prompts the reexamination of the definition of death. The flow of bodily fluids could conceivably be maintained by machines in the absence of almost all other life processes; the result would be viewed by most as a perfused corpse, totally unresponsive to its environment.

Although the argument concerning the soul could be interpreted as providing a standard for secular action, those who adhere to the concept today apparently acknowledge the need for a more public and verifiable standard of death. Indeed, a statute incorporating a brain-based standard is accepted by theologians of all backgrounds.

The Commission does not regard itself as a competent or appropriate forum for theological interpretation. Nevertheless it has sought to propose policies consistent with as many as possible of the diverse religious tenets and practices in our society.

The [recommended] statute does not appear to conflict with the view that the soul leaves the body at death. It provides standards by which death can be determined to have occurred, but it does not prevent a person from believing on religious grounds that the soul leaves the body at a point other than that established as marking death for legal and medical purposes.

> *"For patients who are not artificially maintained, breathing and heartbeat . . . are reliable signs either of systemic integration and/or of continued brain functioning."*

The concept of death based upon the flow of bodily fluids cannot be completely reconciled with the proposed statute. The statute is partially consistent with the "fluids" formulation in that both would regard as dead a body with no respiration and circulation. As noted previously, the overwhelming majority of patients, now and for the foreseeable future, will be diagnosed on such basis. Under the statute, however, physicians would declare dead those bodies in which respiration and circulation continued *solely* as a result of artificial maintenance, in the absence of all brain functions. Nonetheless, people who believe that the continued flow of fluids in such patients means they are alive would not be forced by statute to abandon those beliefs nor to change their religious conduct. While the recommended statute may cause changes in medical and legal behavior, the Commission urges those acting under the statute to apply it with sensitivity to the emotional and religious needs of those for whom the new standards mark a departure from traditional practice. Determinations of death must be made in a consistent and evenhanded fashion, but the statute does not preclude flexibility in responding to individual circumstances after determination has been made.

The President's Commission for the Study of Ethical Problems in Medicine and Biomedical and Behavioral Research began meeting in January 1980 to determine whether a federal statute defining death was necessary and to formulate such a statute if need was determined. In July 1981 the Commission submitted its report, from which this viewpoint is excerpted.

"We [neurologists] are probably the best equipped to teach...the subtle distinctions between death and dying,...and between a fatal prognosis and a persistent vegetative state."

Neurologists Should Determine Death

Gaetano F. Molinari

About a year ago a BBC telecast contrasted for the British public the system used to pronounce "brain death" in the United Kingdom with criteria used in the United States, Norway, and other countries. Superficially, it seemed that the major variable was the amount of technology used to guarantee the accuracy of the diagnosis in each country. The TV program attributed the high organ donation rate in Norway to public confidence in their technology-rich criteria, which include both an EEG and four-vessel cerebral angiography.

Reaction to the broadcast from both the British medical profession and the public was swift, sustained, and emotional. While the British public seemed to be tearing up donor cards, the medical profession produced its own data base and other data to vindicate the position that nobody ever survived who met the critera for "brain death" used in that country.

Closer scrutiny of the apparent conflict reveals, however, that the criteria used in three jurisdictions each accurately describes three fundamentally different concepts of "brain death." Black pointed out [in the *New England Journal of Medicine,* 1978] that in the United States "brain death" was defined physiologically as the permanent nonfunctional state of the brain. This idea was enhanced by American clinical neurophysiologists who advocated the use of the EEG as a sophisticated and sensitive confirmatory indicator of the nonfunctioning state. However, in Europe and elsewhere, the understanding of the term was influenced by neuropathologists to mean total brain destruction, or more precisely, infarction caused by lack of cerebral circulation. The physiologic definition was given preeminence by the Harvard Committee in its "Definition of Irreversible Coma."

Gaetano F. Molinari, "Brain Death, Irreversible Coma, and Words Doctors Use," *Neurology* 1982; 32(4):400-402 (April 1982). Reprinted by permission of the author.

Subsequently, an ambitious American study tried to collate the essential clinical, physiologic and pathologic features of "brain death" to expedite the cost-effective use of intensive care beds and ensure the viability of donated cadaver organs. That study required prospective standardized neurologic observations in a large series of comatose and apneic patients, including all brainstem and spinal reflexes described in the Harvard criteria, and EEGs obtained at about the time of each examination, all collated with gross and microscopic features of the brain specimens obtained at autopsy in fatal cases.

Patients were to be followed to outcome without intervention by the investigators. By the time the study was designed, some already suspected that the 24-hour period recommended by the Harvard Committee to ensure permanence of the state might be overly restrictive, because many people died of spontaneous cardiac arrest during that interval and potentially viable organs were lost.

Before that study ended, Mohandas and Chou reported [in the *Journal of Neurosurgery,* 1971] clinicopathologic correlations, showing that less restrictive criteria invariably predicted a fatal outcome after only 12 hours, without the need for an EEG. In 1976 a British group published a detailed document based on the belief that the cerebral changes leading to "brain death" proceed in a rostrocaudal direction and that the permanent functional death of the brainstem is responsible for "brain death." Both papers concluded that in cases of known structural pathology in the brain, once the clinical findings indicated absent function of the brainstem, artificial support only prolongs the dying process and treatment should be withdrawn.

Definitions of Death

It was not until later, however, that these criteria were recommended for use by physicians as the definition of death itself, which permits removal of cadaveric organs either simultaneous with, or shortly before, the termination of artificial means of "life support." In his reaction to the BBC telecast, C. Pallis defined brain death: "The British criteria seek to identify a clinical syndrome of brainstem death and to equate it (given essential prerequisites already referred to) with a clearly stated prognosis: 'classical death' within a very short period."

There are now three alternative interpretations of the term "brain death":

1. A permanent pathophysiologic state of a nonfunctioning brain in which organs may be kept functional for prolonged or even indefinite periods of time; persistence of the nonfunctional state of the brain for some arbitrary time (e.g., 24 hours) provides the proof of irreversibility.

2. Destruction or infarction of the entire brain, as inferred by clinical demonstration that there is no cerebral circulation for a brief period, measured in minutes or hours rather than days.

3. A nonfunctional state of the brainstem that predicts death of the rest of the body within a short but unspecified time.

The American Collaborative Study of 503 cases could not identify a subset of clinical criteria or a specific time for persistence of the totally nonfunctional state that invariably correlated with pathologic evidence of a totally destroyed brain. Although there was generally excellent correlation between clinical finds such as the absence of cephalic reflexes, electrocerebral silence by EEG, and findings of a "respirator brain" at autopsy, there were numerous exceptions.

Incidental Findings

Two incidental findings of that collaborative study require particular attention. First, clinical history alone was unreliable in excluding drug intoxication as at least a contributing factor to the overall clinical picture. Of 503 deeply comatose and apneic patients, 36 were recognized initially as cases of self-inflicted drug intoxication. In 313 patients, blood samples were taken promptly to measure the content of barbiturates, and 61 contained measurable amounts of these drugs. Initial screening revealed another 25 cases involving drugs among the "brain death" suspects with other diagnosed structural lesions. Split sample analysis, using a more comprehensive screening procedure, raised the number of cases involving depressant drugs to 87. Therefore, the number of cases involving drugs increased dramatically with the sensitivity and thoroughness of the testing procedure.

Second, Allen et al reported three men with brainstem hemorrhages, who had coexistent coma, apnea, and absent cephalic reflexes in one or more of the required examinations. In all three cases there was persistent EEG activity despite clinical signs suggesting "brainsteam death." In one man

respirations returned in the final 24-hour period of survival. All three patients ultimately died of cardiac arrest. Therefore, the signs of "brainstem death" do not always evolve in a rostrocaudal direction.

In the United States, largely because the prospective study showed that unresponsive coma, absent cephalic reflexes, and electrocerebral silence may all be present for up to a week or more before spontaneous cardiac arrest occurs, it has been concluded that brain death and irreversible coma are not one and the same.

Confusing Lack of Definition Agreement

The lack of conformity underlying the conceptualization of "brain death" causes confusion among physicians, and this uncertainty is transmitted to families either explicitly or implicitly. If "brain death" is to mean a syndrome of eventual death or even imminent death, the public may rightly object to the removal of viable organs from moribund relatives. On the other hand, it is not necessary to pronounce "brain death" before withdrawing treatment in hopeless cases, particularly if the wishes of the patient are known to the family. The individual, through the family, has the right to participate in deciding how much therapy is desirable when the disease is known and the outcome invariably fatal, but the family cannot help doctors decide when death occurs. The term "brain death" should now be abandoned, because it perpetuates professional and public confusion. It implies a degree or kind of deadness!

"It has been concluded that brain death and irreversible coma are not one and the same."

The diagnosis of death must be separated from the issue of organ donation, and it does not involve the patient's or the family's wishes or beliefs. The definition of death has not changed; only the way in which the diagnosis is made has been broadened. The new methods must convey the same degree of medical certainty to both the medical profession and the public as traditional criteria once did.

In the "Code of Practice" distributed to every practicing member of the National Health Service to assist in making the diagnosis of brain death, the British Working Party stated: "It is now widely accepted that electroencephalography is not necessary for the diagnosis of brain death," and that "it is only necessary to consult the neurologist or neurosurgeon when the primary diagnosis is in doubt. A pronouncement of brain death should not normally require a specialist's advice."

In the BBC broadcast it was suggested that

increased technology is used in the United States because of the litigious atmosphere in which medicine is practiced. In the United States, it is not unreasonable to obtain an EEG, because that service is available in virtually every hospital and the method eliminates the possibility of residual cerebral function that might be masked by a primary or secondary brainstem lesion. Similarly, whenever depressant drugs are identified in the blood or used in the clinical management of the patient and there is any doubt about the irreversibility of the clinical state, the physician always has the option of delaying the diagnosis of irreversibility until there is reasonable medical certainty.

"The term 'brain death' should now be abandoned, because it perpetuates professional and public confusion. It implies a degree or kind of deadness!"

Once death is pronounced unequivocally, the family knows exactly what to do only if there is an organ donor card. In cases of sudden devastating neurologic disease in young people, when organ procurement is most desirable, the grief-stricken relatives can rarely be introduced to the concept of "brain death" for the first time.

Uniform Determination of Death Act

The President's Commission for the Study of Ethical Problems in Medicine and Biomedical and Behavioral Research recently proposed the Uniform Determination of Death Act: "An individual who has sustained either (1) irreversible cessation of circulatory and respiratory functions or (2) irreversible cessation of all functions of the entire brain, including the brainstem, is dead. The determination of death must be made in accordance with the accepted medical standards."

The statement does not use the term "brain death," nor does it list what the criteria are or should be. In other words, death may be diagnosed by either traditional criteria or neurologically. Who better than a neurologist is qualified to use neurologic criteria to confirm that death has occurred, with or without confirmatory technology? Wherever transplantation is within the technical capability of the medical community, neurologic consultation should certainly be within the standard of medical practice. Although we in neurology are sometimes perceived by our medical colleagues as thinking too much and doing too little, we are probably the best equipped to teach those same colleagues and the public at large the subtle distinctions between death and dying, between "brain death" and irreversible coma, and between a fatal prognosis and a persistent vegetative state.

We are also best able to interpret the new legislative definition of death and to explain the advantages and limitations of "living wills" and organ donations to our communities. If we abrogate our traditional teaching responsibilities, life-death distinctions may be made by others who are not so fussy in their use of words.

Gaetano F. Molinari, M.D., is a professor and chairman of the department of neurology in the School of Medicine and Health Sciences at George Washington University.

"There are all sorts of intermediate stages between life in the full sense and death in the full sense, and we are faced with the problem of where to draw the line."

Death Is Difficult to Define

John Ladd

There is a rapidly growing literature concerned with the definition of death, i.e. with establishing criteria for determining whether a person is alive or dead as well as for determining the moment of death. Before the advent of modern medical technology, the stoppage of respiration and the circulation of the blood were universally accepted as sufficient signs of death. However, the new technology has made it possible to reverse these stoppages and to "bring a person back to life," e.g. after cardiac arrest. We now have to cope with the fact that some vital functions can be sustained even though others have ceased. There are all sorts of intermediate stages between life in the full sense and death in the full sense, and we are faced with the problem of where to draw the line. Strictly speaking, however, the problem is not one simply of drawing a line; rather it is a problem of deciding which particular functions or set of functions are essential to human life and what signs shall be taken as indicating the presence or absence of these functions.

There are, of course, practical exigencies that make the question of determining the occurrence of death of more than purely academic interest. The dramatic development of techniques of organ transplantation has made this question peculiarly urgent, because if one waits too long after death before removing an organ, the organ will begin to deteriorate. There are also a number of legal issues that hang on the definition of death, e.g. issues relating to such things as inheritance or culpability for murder.

Nevertheless, even though there has been a great deal of writing on the definition of death and the problem of defining death is an urgent practical problem, little attention has been given by those concerned with the subject to the notion of definition

itself, despite the fact that there is a considerable philosophical literature on the subject of definition going back to Plato and Aristotle and continuing down to the present. This neglect of the philosophical literature on definition is especially unfortunate because in recent years philosophers have devoted special attention to the distinctive properties of the kinds of definitions that are used in ethics, law and science.

If we wish to proceed philosophically in the matter of defining death, we need to ask a number of preliminary questions. What kind of definition is being sought? What will the definition be used for? What standards of propriety should be used for deciding whether or not a proposed definition is the correct one or whether it is the best definition? And, finally, is there any reason to assume that there is only one definition of death? May there not be a number of correct definitions valid respectively for the different contexts in which they are used?

Requirements of Definition

A few preliminary observations in regard to these questions about definitions will be helpful. First, it is obvious that since a definition of death will be used for important practical purposes, the kind of definition that is required cannot be an arbitrary stipulative definition, as are some mathematical and scientific definitions. Therefore, any definition of death that is proposed needs to be defended by arguments that will show it not to be arbitrary. Moreover, as a practical definition with practical import a definition of death will, of necessity, be value-laden; in Stevenson's terms, it will be a "persuasive definition," since anyone proposing a definition of death will *ipso facto* be advocating certain courses of action or nonaction. Hence, some sort of ethical justification of the definition is required. Finally, inasmuch as any defintion of death is likely to be controversial, if discussion is to be rational, argumentation is required. Thus, for a number of reasons, a definition of death requires a full-fledged rational vindication; appeals to intuition, to medical practice or to authority are not enough.

Second, following Wittgenstein and other recent authors, we must assume that not only is it possible, but it is highly likely that the concept of death is not definable at all in the strict sense. Many of our concepts, as Wittgenstein pointed out, are not univocal but are "family-resemblance" concepts, open-textured; and for that reason are incapable of definition in terms of necessary and sufficient conditions. Achinstein has argued that even scientific concepts like copper or acid are not definable in this sense; that is, it is not possible to specify all those properties that are logically necessary and sufficient to justify classifying a thing in a certain way. Such concepts are often called "cluster-concepts"; that is, they refer to a cluster of properties such that the possession of a number of them is sufficient to justify classifying a thing as a certain kind of thing, but no single one of these properties is of itself necessary or sufficient for this purpose. The properties in a cluster are generally called *criteria*.

"It is highly likely that the concept of death is not definable at all in the strict sense."

Considerations such as those just mentioned suggest that we might well ask whether we are dealing with a single, univocal concept of death or with a family-resemblance concept. It is conceivable that there might be a biological, a medical, a legal, a moral, a theological and a metaphysical concept of death, none of which are the same except in a family-resemblance sense. (I shall return to this point later.)

Medical Definitions

Finally, a few observations should be made about "medical" definitions of death. One of the chief difficulties in finding a medical definition of death that will be specific enough to pinpoint the moment of death comes from the physiological fact that dying is a process, and different parts of the body, different functional systems and organs, cease functioning at different times. The fact is not simply that dying is a continuous process but that it is also a multiple process, so that theoretically at least there are a number of different processes the termination of any one of which could be used as a definition of death. For obvious reasons, the kinds of processes that are the most plausible ones to use in a definition of death are brain processes of some kind, since stoppage of circulation or of respiration, if not reversed, will lead quickly to death of the brain. There have been a

number of definitions of death based on the concept of brain death orginally formulated by the Ad Hoc Committee of the Harvard Medical School to Explore the Definition of Brain Death. The criteria set forth in this document consist of: (1) unreceptivity and unresponsivity, (2) no movements or breathing, (3) no reflexes, and (4) flat electroencephalogram. All tests are to be repeated after twenty-four hours. (These criteria are slightly modified in more recent versions.)

In regard to medical definitions of death, two points are worth noting. First, the only requirement for a definition of death that is generally agreed upon to be absolutely necessary is that the condition designated by the definition be *irreversible*. Indeed, medical discussions of the definition of death focus almost exclusively on irreversibility as the test of the correctness of a definition and virtually the only consideration advanced for or against a particular definition in the medical literature relates to the reversibility or irreversibility of the processes in question.

It goes without saying that irreversibility is not sufficient, for we must be able to specify which particular function has been lost irreversibly. The emphasis in the medical literature on irreversibility is easy to understand, because the determination that a certain function has been destroyed irreversibly is a scientific matter, a question on which medical scientists are the experts, whereas other questions about the definition of death, e.g. which particular function must be destroyed irreversibly, may also be questions for philosophers, theologians, or lawyers. I shall presently try to explain why irreversibility is such an important element in the concept of death.

Signs and Criteria

Second, in considering definitions of death it is important to distinguish between clinical *signs* (or indicators) of death and *criteria* (or determinants) of death. Following current philosophical usage, I shall use the term "criteria" to stand for those properties that pertain to the meaning of "death." "Signs" will be used to stand for clinical evidence that the criteria have been fulfilled. Thus on certain accounts, electrocerebral silence, apnea (absence of spontaneous respiration), and deep coma (unresponsivity) would be signs of brain death. Brain death, in turn, would be a criterion of death, for to be brain dead would be part of the meaning of "being dead," if that is the definition in question. Signs are directly observable and as such are called "clinical signs of death." The conditions inferred from them are the criteria of death. (They may reflect what Achinstein calls the "underlying structure.") The distinction between signs and criteria is a logical one representing the distinction between contingent connections that are established empirically and connections that are logical and necessary. Thus, for example, the connection between a clinical sign such as a flat EEG and what it signifies, e.g. brain death, is an empirical connection founded on observation. Whether or not the total destruction of the brain is a necessary condition of death, or a criterion of death, is not an empirical question at all: it is a question of meaning or of conceptual analysis.

The distinction that I have just drawn between signs and criteria suggests an interesting philosophical question, namely, whether the clinically observed factors in a given definition of death, e.g. unresponsivity, are simply signs of an irreversible physiological condition that constitutes death, e.g. brain death, or whether these factors are themselves criteria of death, i.e. constitutive of death in the sense that they are part of what we mean by being dead. In other words, if unresponsiveness plus a number of other observable conditions are manifestations of brain death, do we want to say that the person in question is dead because his brain is dead, or do we want to say that he is dead because he makes no responses? Which represents death, the cause or the effect? The problem suggests that sooner or later we may be forced to choose between a behavioristic and a physiological definition of death. Or must we settle for a cluster concept?

Behind this general problem of signs versus criteria, or of clinical observations versus inferred conditions, lies the more general issue concerning what it is that we are trying to determine when we ask whether someone is dead. Death has traditionally been defined as the departure of the soul from the body. Contemporary philosophers prefer to say that death is the ceasing to exist of a person. Are we to assume that when the brain (or part of the brain) ceases to function that the soul has departed or that the person ceases to exist? Is irreversible coma sufficient to say that this event has occurred? How could such questions be settled?

Demythologizing Death

It is difficult for us not to picture dying as the soul leaving the body, just as a person leaves his house. This creates a mythological concept of death. We feel that if a person can no longer make certain responses or if his brain is dead, then the soul must have left. But we will not get anywhere with the problem of defining death, until we divest ourselves of this picture. The first thing we have to do is to demythologize the concept of death, for if we fail to do so we will look for realities in places where they do not exist and we will not see them where they do exist. We will, for example, picture the soul quietly resting in the body of a comatose person, waiting to be released when the brain stem ceases to function! The picture forces on us a mythology that there is still something in the body as long as any part of the brain continues to function.

It appears that we are working with two quite different conceptions of death, a mythological conception and a medical conception; the first views death as an event, like leaving the house, and the second views it as a process, like a house burning down. But the picture theory of concepts is not only misleading, it generates false dichotomies. The only way out of the apparent impasse between these two conceptions is to take a cue from Wittgenstein and think of concepts, like the concept of death, as tools, tools that we use for various purposes in our social discourse and transactions with one another. Different concepts, according to Wittgenstein, operate in different ways; their functions are as diverse as the functions of the handles in the cabin of a locomotive. The concept of death might be likened to a handle that turns things off. But like a handle in a locomotive, the concept of death can only be understood by showing its relation to other concepts that we use in practical life. In order to show this we must return to the notion of definition.

Definition's Purpose

The criterion of a good definition is that it serves its purpose well, for definitions, like concepts in general, are tools. Hence, our first task in seeking a definition is to ask what the definition will be used for. Definitions in general may be regarded as rules for connecting the term (or concept) to be defined, generally called the *definiendum*, with the terms (or concepts) that define it, generally called the *definiens*. Very roughly speaking, a definition of death is supposed to connect death in its ordinary meaning (the definiendum) with certain physiological facts, functions or processes. Just how this is to be done depends on the prior logical properties of the definiendum; in particular, what the concept of death is to be used for. (It might be used, for example, for an ethical, legal, or theological purpose.)

"Are we to assume that when the brain . . . ceases to function that the soul has departed or that the person ceases to exist?"

It is presumed that here we are concerned with ethical issues, so that we can answer this question about the use of the concept of death from the ethical point of view. If our ethics is Kantian, as mine is, that would mean that we are interested in death as it relates to treating persons as ends and not merely as means. If our purposes are legal, on the other hand, the concept might be used to settle certain kinds of conflicts of interest, say, with regard to an inheritance.

In general, then, the kind of definition that we are

looking for in a definition of death is a practical definition; that is, one that takes into account how the concept functions while at the same time providing criteria for applying the concept to particular kinds of processes or events.

The difference in purposes explains why the definition of the death of, say, a tree differs from the definition of the death of a person.

"Paradoxically. . .a person would be dead only if we turn off the respirator, but we can turn off the respirator only if that person is dead."

The two sides of a definition may become clearer by relating them to what Kovesi calls the *formal* and the *material* elements of a concept. The formal elements, according to Kovesi, are connected with what the concept is used for; that is, they pertain to the point of calling something a so-and-so; the material elements, on the other hand, consist of what are often called the "criteria" for the application of the concept. As Kovesi points out, most concepts of a practical nature are opentextured, since the material elements or criteria will change as conditions change. The formal element, in contrast, is fairly constant, for it is what enables us to bring a thing under a rule: "without the formal element, we cannot follow a rule in using a term." For example, it is the formal element in a concept like the concept of murder that allows us to bring a certain act under a rule, e.g. against murder; whereas the material element in the concept of murder determines what is to count as murder. As Kovesi points out, the material elements cannot be enumerated in a final list, as is required in a definition in the strict sense. For the same reasons, it might be argued that concepts like the concept of death cannot, strictly speaking, be defined in the sense of providing a definitive list of the necessary and sufficient conditions for applying them. The open texture of concepts such as these is what makes them cluster concepts.

Uses of Death Concept

Let us see what light Kovesi's distinction between the formal and the material elements of a concept can shed on the controversy surrounding the definition of death. We may begin with the formal aspect of the concept of death and ask: What is the point of saying that someone is dead or, to be more specific, of saying that a person died at a certain time?

There are, of course, a number of different answers to this question. In general terms, it is obvious that when a person dies certain readjustments— psychological, social and legal—are required on the part of other individuals and on the part of society. Let us ignore wider metaphysical, theological, phenomenological and psychological functions of the concept of death and focus on some obvious practical reasons why we need to know that a person has died and the time of his death.

First, we need to know that a person has died, and the time of his death, for a variety of specific legal purposes; such as the determination of inheritance or taxes, or the remarriage of the spouse.

Second, we need to know that a person is dead in order to know when and when not to apply criminal statutes, e.g. statutes concerning murder or homicide: if a man is already dead, you cannot kill him.

Third, if we know that a person has died, we are free to terminate treatment: turn off the respirator, cease feeding, cease administering drugs.

Finally, if a person is dead we can do various things with the body: perform an autopsy on it, remove organs from it for transplantation, bury it.

Formal Requirements

Every one of the points mentioned involves a rule of one sort or another such that the ascription of death to a person brings the rule into operation. In order to determine whether or not any of these rules is operative, a moment of death must be specified. For certain purposes the time designation may be given in very general terms, but in any case, death must be categorized as a dateable event. Death must also be taken to happen to a person as an integral unit; that is, it is the person as a whole that dies the death and not just some part of him. In that regard his personhood is simple and indivisible, not separable into parts or distinguishable into degrees. Finally, death must be irreversible, for the actions they permit have effects that cannot be undone. In sum, for all the purposes mentioned in our list, death must be thought of as *momentary, holistic* and *irreversible*. These, then, are the formal requirements of the concept of death by virtue of which it can be used as a practical, moral, and legal concept.

Let us now turn to the material aspects of the concept of death, i.e. the criteria to be used for determining what counts as being alive or dead for purposes of the kinds of rules that I have mentioned. It is obvious that physiological processes can never exactly match the formal requirements of these practical rules. Formerly, it was possible to use the breakdown of general bodily systems as a criterion of death, e.g. the cessation of respiration or of heartbeat. But now these roughly matching criteria will not do, since we have artificial means for continuing the processes in question. Thus, even if at one time there were criteria that were approximately momentary, holistic and irreversible, now, in certain cases at least, the required kind of criteria are no longer available. We should not be surprised at this, however, since the material elements in almost any concept change as conditions change.

Of course, it might be argued that the Harvard criteria effectively satisfy these requirements. The trouble with the Harvard criteria is that they are too stringent; in some cases, they make possible the indefinite prolongation of life-support, and in other cases some of the procedures required seem to be unnecessary. Perhaps more important for us is the real likelihood that future advances in neurology will make it possible to resuscitate parts of the brain artificially. So that even if criteria like the Harvard criteria work today, they may be out-of-date tomorrow, if they are not already.

But even granted that the Harvard criteria or other criteria of brain death provide sufficient conditions of death, they certainly do not establish the necessary conditions of death. Yet, for purposes of definition we need all of the necessary conditions as well as a sufficient condition of death; there are lots of sufficient conditions of being dead that are of little help practically. For example, having been born in A.D. 1000, or having been decapitated or cremated are sufficient conditions of being dead, but they are obviously not necessary. A necessary condition of death is, of course, logically equivalent to the absence of a sufficient condition of life—and who is to say what that is?

Sometimes, indeed, it is even difficult to specify an unexceptional, sufficient medical condition or set of conditions of death. If we consider the criteria customarily applied by physicians, including such things as absence of respiration or heart beat, or flat EEG for a certain time, it is evident that under normal conditions they are sufficient conditions of death, but under abnormal conditions they are not; for example, the test of flat EEG does not apply under hypothermia or when drugs have been used.

Considerations such as these, as well as the constant development of new tests, go to show that as has already been suggested, the material element in the concept of death is open-textured and subject to change. In this sense, death cannot be defined at all in the sense of providing a complete set of necessary conditions that are jointly sufficient for the occurence of death. But as we shall see presently, the quest for a definition of death runs into even greater difficulties, difficulties of a logical nature that arise as a result of trying to define death under conditions created by modern medical technology.

Problems of Technology

For the time being, let us leave aside the large proportion of death determinations that create no new problems and focus on the new kind of case that medical technology has created for us. The critical fact is that the new technology has given us the power to control dying; that is, to control the timing and manner of death. We may not be able to reverse the deterioration of most life-sustaining functions, but

we can continue at will some of the processes that we used to refer to as signs of "life," i.e. processes the termination of which formerly served as criteria of death. Since some of these functional changes can now be reversed, e.g. cardiac arrest, they can no longer be used as criteria of death—in a simple-minded way, at least.

"One can imagine situations where the timing of death might be manipulated for . . . insidious purposes."

The result of these new developments is not simply that we are confused because things have become more complicated, but that by acquiring the power to control such things as the time of death we have created a paradox. For *this new power undermines the practical functions that the concept of death is designed to perform;* the formal element in the concept of death presupposes that the moment of death is not subject to manipulation, i.e. that death is irreversible, while the material elements that determine what is to count as death have now become subject to manipulation through the advance of medical technology, i.e. they are reversible. Paradoxically, if we can postpone death by keeping a person on a respirator, then we cannot use the occurrence of death to justify turning off the respirator. A person would be dead only if we turn off the respirator, but we can turn off the respirator only if that person is dead.

It is unnecessary to examine other paradoxes resulting from our new power to manage death. All of them are due to the fact that we are now able to select at will the time at which the rules mentioned in the list above will come into operation. With sufficient cunning this kind of manipulation can be used for all sorts of purposes. It is clear that Generalissimo Franco's death was managed by the politicians for their own special purposes. So far in the United States the manipulation of death has been governed chiefly by the interests of institutional medicine, lawyers and the suppliers of health care equipment and materials; but one can imagine situations where the timing of death might be manipulated for even more insidious purposes.

To summarize this part of the chapter: a presupposition of death in its formal aspect is its being beyond human control, i.e. its irreversibility. This presupposition no longer holds true in a number of cases. That means that the point of calling a person dead or alive at a certain time has been undermined —under some circumstances, at least. We can, of course, stipulate a definition of death for particular purposes, but a general all-purpose definition of the old-fashioned sort is probably no longer possible.

In the final analysis, the question we have to face is

whether to change the criteria (the material element) or to change the rules that employ the concept of death as a category. In any case, it is clear that we need new categories and new rules; either different categories of death, or new rules concerning what can or cannot be done. In fact, of course, we have already moved in the direction of changing both the criteria and the rules; for example, what is happening in practice with regard to the latter is that issues concerning the determination that death has occurred are now simply bypassed when decisions need to be made concerning the continuation or termination of treatment. Perhaps that is all to the good. As far as the law is concerned, a revamping of legal concepts and rules relating to death will probably soon be necessary for the same sorts of reason. For, although traditionally law has devised many ways for coping with situations in which a person's death has been deliberately hastened (e.g. by murder), it has not yet had to cope with situations in which death is deliberately delayed to suit the interests of other parties, e.g. to secure an inheritance, to avoid being convicted of murder, or to provide organs for transplantation.

John Ladd is a professor of philosophy and the author of several books including The Structure of a Moral Code. *He has been actively involved in the Committee on Philosophy and Medicine of the American Philosophical Association and the American Society for Political and Legal Philosophy.*

"We use the term death to mean the loss of what is essentially significant to an entity—in the case of man, the loss of humanness."

Death Can Be Defined on Four Different Levels

Robert M. Veatch

It seems strange to ask what death means. Throughout history men have had a good enough idea to transact the business of society—to cover the corpse, bury the dead, transmit authority. But now that technology permits us to treat the body organ by organ, cell by cell, we are forced to develop a more precise understanding of what it means to call a person dead. There is a complex interaction between the technical aspects of deciding a person is dead—all the business involving stethoscopes, electro-encephalograms, and intricately determined medical diagnoses and prognoses—and the more fundamental philosophical considerations which underlie the judgment that a person in a particular condition should be called dead.

On May 24, 1968, a black laborer named Bruce Tucker fell and suffered a massive head injury. He was rushed by ambulance to the emergency room of the Medical College of Virginia Hospital, where he was found to have a skull fracture, a subdural hematoma, and a brain-stem contusion. At eleven o'clock that evening an operation was performed (described as "a right temporoparietal craniotomy and right parietal bur hole" in a later court record of the case), opening the skull to relieve the strain on the brain. A tracheotomy was also done to help his labored breathing. By the next morning Tucker was being fed intravenously, had been given medication, and was attached to a respirator. According to the court record, he was "mechanically alive"; the treating physician noted, his "prognosis for recovery is nil and death imminent."

In cases like Tucker's, the patient has frequently stopped breathing by the time he arrives at the hospital, and his heart may have gone into fibrillation. However, the rapid application of an electrical shock can cajole the heart back into a normal rhythm, while a respirator forces the breath of life from the tube of the machine into the tube of the patient's trachea. Thus technology can arrest the process of dying.

The Medical College of Virginia, where Tucker was taken, is the hospital of David M. Hume who, until his own recent accidental death, headed one of the eminent heart transplant teams of the world. At the time Tucker was brought in, there was a patient on the ward named Joseph Klett who was an ideal recipient. Bruce Tucker, with irreversible loss of brain function from a period of oxygen starvation in the brain and an otherwise healthy body, was an ideal heart donor.

Tucker's EEG

Early in the afternoon a neurologist obtained an electroencephalogram (EEG) to determine the state of Tucker's brain activity. He saw that the electrical tracing was a flat line "with occasional artifact." Assuming the artifacts were the kind normally found from extraneous causes, this meant there was no evidence of cortical activity at that time. If the flat line on the EEG is not caused by drug overdose or low body temperature and is found again in repeated tests over several hours, most neurologists would take it to mean that consciousness would never return. Nevertheless, the respirator continued pumping oxygen into Tucker's lungs and, according to the judge's later summary, "his body temperature, pulse, and blood pressure were all normal for a patient in his condition."

In August of the same year a prestigious committee from the Harvard Medical School published more rigorous criteria for irreversible coma. Drafts of the report were circulating among professionals early in the year, but there is no evidence that the physicians in Virginia had access to it. Their use of their own judgment about criteria for diagnosing irreversible

Robert M. Veatch, *Death, Dying, and the Biological Revolution.* Yale University Press, copyright © 1976. Reprinted by permission.

coma is still the subject of controversy.

At 2:45 that afternoon Tucker was taken back into the operating room to be prepared for the removal of his heart and both kidneys. Oxygen was given to preserve the viability of these organs. According to the court record, "he maintained, for the most part, normal body temperature, normal blood pressure and normal rate of respiration," but, in spite of the presence of these vital signs, at 3:30 the respirator was cut off. Five minutes later the patient was pronounced dead and the mechanical support was resumed to preserve the organs, and his heart was removed and transplanted to Joseph Klett. According to the record, Tucker's vital signs continued to be normal until 4:30, soon before the heart was removed.

"Four separate levels in the definition of death debate must be distinguished."

The heart was removed although it had continued functioning while the respirator continued to pump. It was removed without any attempt to get the permission of relatives, although Tucker's wallet contained his brother's business card with a phone number and an address only fifteen blocks away. The brother was in his place of business that day, and a close friend had made unsuccessful inquiries at three information desks in the hospital. The heart was removed although Virginia law, according to the interpretation of the judge in the subsequent trial, defines death as total cessation of all body functions.

Suit Upholds Brain Death

William Tucker, the "donor's" brother, brought suit against the surgical team for wrongfully ending Bruce Tucker's life. During the trial, physicians testified that Tucker was "neurologically dead" several hours before the transplant and that his heart and respiratory system were being kept viable by mechanical means. To this William Tucker responded, "There's nothing they can say to make me believe they didn't kill him." Commenting on the decision in favor of the surgeons, Dr. Hume said, "This simply brings the law in line with medical opinion."

The *New York Times* headline read, "Virginia Jury Rules That Death Occurs When Brain Dies." Victor Cohn's *Washington Post* story announced, "'Brain Death' Upheld in Heart Transplant." The medical news services were equally quick to treat this unquestioningly as a brain-death case. The *Internal Medicine News* claimed, "'Brain Death' Held Proof of Demise in Va. Jury Decision." Even a law review article considered the judgment to affirm that cessation of brain activity can be used in

determining the time of death. There has been some outcry, especially in the black community, over the hasty removal of a man's heart without permission from the next of kin, but the general public seemed undisturbed by the decision. The medical community felt that one of their outstanding members had been exonerated.

Although the press, public, and some legal opinion treat this case as crucial in establishing the legitimacy of the use of brain criteria for death (thus bringing the law in line with "medical opinion"), more issues than that are at stake. The case raises basic questions about the definition of death.

The debate has become increasingly heated in the past decade, because fundamental moral and religious issues are at stake. The very meaning of the word *definition* is ambiguous. Some of the issues are indeed matters of neurobiological fact and as such are appropriate for interpretation by medical opinion. But judgments about facts made by scientists with expertise in a particular and relevant field can be called *definitions* only in an operational sense. The debate over the definition of death also takes place at philosophical, religious, and ethical levels, probing into the meaning of life and its ending. The more practical, empirical problems are an important part of the debate, but they must be separated from the philosophical issues. The philosophical question is, What is lost at the point of death that is essential to human nature? We can avoid the serious philosophical errors committed in the Virginia trial only by carefully separating the levels of the debate.

Four Levels of Definition

Four separate levels in the definition of death debate must be distinguished. First, there is the purely formal analysis of the term *death*, an analysis that gives the structure and specifies the framework that must be filled in with content. Second, the *concept* of death is considered, attempting to fill the content of the formal definition. At this level the question is, What is so essentially significant about life that its loss is termed *death*? Third, there is the question of the locus of death: where in the organism ought one to look to determine whether death has occurred? Fourth, one must ask the question of the criteria of death: what technical tests must be applied at the locus to determine if an individual is living or dead?

Serious mistakes have been made in slipping from one level of the debate to another and in presuming that expertise on one level necessarily implies expertise on another. For instance, the Report of the Ad Hoc Committee of the Harvard Medical School to Examine the Definition of Brain Death is titled "A Definition of Irreversible Coma." The report makes clear that the committee members are simply reporting empirical measures which are criteria for predicting an irreversible coma. (I shall explore later the possibility that they made an important mistake even at this level.) Yet the name of the committee seems to point more to the question of locus, where to look for measurement of death. The committee was established to examine the death of the brain. The implication is that the empirical indications of irreversible coma are also indications of "brain death." But by the first sentence of the report the committee claims that "Our primary purpose is to define irreversible coma as a new criterion for death." They have now shifted so that they are interested in "death." They must be presuming a philosophical concept of death—that a person in irreversible coma should be considered dead—but they nowhere argue this or even state it as a presumption.

Even the composition of the Harvard committee membership signals some uncertainty of purpose. If empirical criteria were their concern, the inclusion of nonscientists on the panel was strange. If the philosophical concept of death was their concern, medically trained people were over-represented. As it happened, the committee did not deal at all with conceptual matters. The committee and its interpreters have confused the questions at different levels. The remainder of this (paper) will discuss the meaning of death at these four levels.

The Formal Definition of Death

A strictly formal definition of death might be the following:

> Death means a complete change in the status of a living entity characterized by the irreversible loss of those characteristics that are essentially significant to it.

Such a definition would apply equally well to a human being, a non-human animal, a plant, an organ, a cell, or even metaphorically to a social phenomenon like a society or to any temporally limited entity like a research project, a sports event, or a language. To define the death of a human being, we must recognize the characteristics that are essential to humanness. It is quite inadequate to limit the discussion to the death of the heart or the brain.

Henry Beecher, the distinguished physician who chaired the Harvard committee that proposed a "definition of irreversible coma," has said that "at whatever level *we choose*..., it is an arbitrary decision" [italics added]. But he goes on, "It is *best* to choose a level where although the brain is dead, usefulness of other organs is still present" [italics added]. Now, clearly he is not making an "arbitrary decision" any longer. He recognizes that there are policy payoffs. He, like the rest of us, realizes that death already has a well-established meaning. It is the task of the current debate to clarify that meaning for a few rare and difficult cases. We use the term *death* to mean the loss of what is essentially significant to an entity—in the case of man, the loss of humanness. The direct link of a word *death* to

what is "essentially significant" means that the task of defining it in this sense is first and foremost a philosophical, theological, ethical task....

The Concept of Death

To ask what is essentially significant to a human being is a philosophical question—a question of ethical and other values. Many elements make human beings unique—their opposing thumbs, their possession of rational souls, their ability to form cultures and manipulate symbol systems, their upright postures, their being created in the image of God, and so on. Any concept of death will depend directly upon how one evaluates these qualities. Four choices seem to me to cover the most plausible approaches.

Irreversible Loss of Flow of Vital Fluids

At first it would appear that the irreversible cessation of heart and lung activity would represent a simple and straightforward statement of the traditional understanding of the concept of death in Western culture. Yet upon reflection this proves otherwise. If patients simply lose control of their lungs and have to be permanently supported by a mechanical respirator, they are still living persons as long as they continue to get oxygen. If modern technology produces an efficient, compact heart-lung machine capable of being carried on the back or in a pocket, people using such devices would not be considered dead, even though both heart and lungs were permanently nonfunctioning. Some might consider such a technological man an affront to human dignity; some might argue that such a device should never be connected to a human; but even they would, in all likelihood, agree that such people are alive.

"It is now possible to manipulate the dying process so that some parts of the body cease to function while other parts are maintained indefinitely."

What the traditional concept of death centered on was not the heart and lungs as such, but the flow of vital fluids, that is, the breath and the blood. It is not without reason that these fluids are commonly referred to as "vital." The nature of man is seen as related to this vitality—or vital activity of fluid flow—which man shares with other animals. This fluidity, the movement of liquids and gases at the cellular and organismic level, is a remarkable biological fact. High school biology students are taught that the distinguishing characteristics of "living" things include respiration, circulation of fluids, movement of fluids out of the organism, and the like. According to this view the human organism, like other living organisms, dies when there is an irreversible cessation of the flow of these fluids.

Irreversible Loss of the Soul from the Body

There is a long-standing tradition, sometimes called vitalism, that holds the essence of man to be independent of the chemical reactions and electrical forces that account for the flow of the bodily fluids. Aristotle and the Greeks spoke of the soul as the animating principle of life. The human being, according to Aristotle, differs from other living creatures in possessing a rational soul as well as vegetative and animal souls. This idea later became especially pronounced in the dualistic philosophy of gnosticism, where salvation was seen as the escape of the enslaved soul from the body. Christianity in its Pauline and later Western forms shares the view that the soul is an essential element in the living man. While Paul and some later theologian-scholars including Erasmus and Luther sometimes held a tripartite anthropology that included spirit as well as body and soul, a central element in all their thought seems to be animation of the body by a noncorporeal force. In Christianity, however, contrasting to the gnostic tradition, the body is a crucial element—not a prison from which the soul escapes, but a significant part of the person. This will become important later in this discussion. The soul remains a central element in the concept of man in most folk religion today.

"What the traditional concept of death centered on was. . .the flow of vital fluids, that is, the breath and the blood."

The departure of the soul might be seen by believers as occurring at about the time that the fluids stop flowing. But it would be a mistake to equate these two concepts of death, as according to the first fluid stops from natural, if unexplained, causes, and death means nothing more than that stopping of the flow which is essential to life. According to the second view, the fluid stops flowing at the time the soul departs, and it stops because the soul is no longer present. Here the essential thing is the loss of the soul, not the loss of the fluid flow.

Irreversible Loss of the Capacity for Bodily Integration

In the debate between those who held a traditional religious notion of the animating force of the soul and those who had the more naturalistic concept of the irreversible loss of the flow of bodily fluids, the trend to secularism and empiricism made the loss of fluid flow more and more the operative concept of death

in society. But man's intervention in the dying process through cardiac pacemakers, respirators, intravenous medication and feeding, and extravenous purification of the blood has forced a sharper examination of the naturalistic concept of death. It is now possible to manipulate the dying process so that some parts of the body cease to function while other parts are maintained indefinitely. This has given rise to disagreements within the naturalistic camp itself. In their report, published in 1968, the inter-disciplinary Harvard Ad Hoc Committee to Examine the Definition of Brain Death gave two reasons for their undertaking. First, they argued that improvements in resuscitative and supportive measures had sometimes had only partial success, putting a great burden on "patients who suffer permanent loss of intellect, on their families, on the hospitals, and on those in need of hospital beds already occupied by these comatose patients." Second, they argued that "obsolete criteria for the definition of death can lead to controversy in obtaining organs for transplantation."

These points have proved more controversial than they may have seemed at the time. In the first place, the only consideration of the patient among the reasons given for changing the definition of death was the suggestion that a comatose patient can feel a "great burden." If the committee is right, however, in holding that the person is in fact dead despite continued respiration and circulation, then all the benefits of the change in definition will come to other individuals or to society at large. For those who hold that the primary ethical consideration in the care of the patient should be the patient's own interest, this is cause for concern.

In the second place, the introduction of transplant concerns into the discussion has attracted particular criticism. Paul Ramsey, among others, has argued against making the issue of transplant a reason for updating the definition of death. . . .

Unfortunate Term

At first it would appear that the irreversible loss of brain activity is the concept of death held by those no longer satisfied with the vitalistic concept of the departure of the soul or the animalistic concept of the irreversible cessation of fluid flow. This is why the name *brain death* is frequently given to the new proposals, but the term is unfortunate for two reasons.

First, as we have seen, it is not the heart and lungs as such that are essentially significant but rather the vital functions—the flow of fluids—which we believe according to the best empirical human physiology to be associated with these organs. An "artificial brain" is not a present-day possibility, but a walking, talking, thinking individual who had one would certainly be considered living. It is not the collection of physical tissues called the brain, but rather their functions—consciousness; motor control; sensory feeling; ability to reason; control over bodily functions including respiration and circulation; major integrating reflexes controlling blood pressure, ion levels, and pupil size; and so forth—which are given essential significance by those who advocate adoption of a new concept of death or clarification of the old one. In short they see the body's capacity for integrating its functions as the essentially significant indication of life.

Second, as suggested earlier, we are not interested in the death of particular cells, organs, or organ systems, but in the death of the person as a whole—the point at which the person as a whole undergoes a quantum change through the loss of characteristics held to be essentially significant, the point at which "death behavior" becomes appropriate. Terms such as *brain death* or *heart death* should be avoided, because they tend to obscure the fact that we are searching for the meaning of the death of the person as a whole. At the public policy level, this has very practical consequences. A statute adopted in Kansas specifically refers to "alternative definitions of death" and says that they are "to be used for all purposes in this state...." According to this language, which has resulted from talking of brain and heart death, a person in Kansas may be simultaneously dead according to one definition and alive according to another. When a distinction must be made, it should be made directly on the basis of the philosophical significance of the functions mentioned above rather than on the importance of the tissue collection called the brain. For purposes of simplicity we shall use the phrase *the capacity for bodily integration* to refer to the total list of integrating mechanisms possessed by the body. The case for these mechanisms being the ones that are essential to humanness can indeed be made. Man is more than the flowing of fluids. He is a complex, integrated organism with capacities for internal regulation. With and only with these integrating mechanisms is homo sapiens really a human person.

Capacity for Integration

There appear to be two general aspects to this concept of what is essentially significant: first, a capacity for integrating one's internal bodily environment (which is done for the most part unconsciously through highly complex homeostatic, feedback mechanisms) and, second, a capacity for integrating one's self, including one's body, with the social environment through consciousness which permits interaction with other persons. Clearly these taken together offer a more profound understanding of the nature of man than does the simple flow of bodily fluids. Whether or not it is more a profound concept of man than that which focuses simply on the presence or absence of the soul, it is clearly a very different one. The ultimate test between the two

is that of meaningfulness and plausibility, that is, we see it as a much more accurate description of the essential significance of man and of what is lost at the time of death. According to this view, when individuals lose all of these "truly vital" capacities we should call them dead and behave accordingly.

"Terms such as brain death *or* heart death *should be avoided, because they tend to obscure the fact that we are searching for the meaning of the death of the person as a whole."*

At this point the debate may just about have been won by the defenders of the neurologically oriented concept. For the most part the public sees the main dispute as being between partisans of the heart and the brain. Even court cases like the Tucker suit and the major articles in the scientific and philosophical journals have for the most part confined themselves to contrasting these two rather crudely defined positions. If these were the only alternatives, the discussion probably would be nearing an end. There are, however, some critical questions that are just beginning to be asked. This new round of discussion was provoked by the recognition that it may be possible in rare cases for a person to have the higher brain centers destroyed but still retain lower brain functions including spontaneous respiration. This has led to the question of just what brain functions are essentially significant to man's nature. A fourth major concept of death thus emerges.

Irreversible Loss of the Capacity for Social Interaction

The fourth major alternative for a concept of death draws on the characteristics of the third concept and has often been confused with it. Henry Beecher offers a summary of what he considers to be essential to man's nature:

the individual's personality, his conscious life, his uniqueness, his capacity for remembering, judging, reasoning, acting, enjoying, worrying, and so on....

Beecher goes on immediately to ask the anatomical question of locus. He concludes that these functions reside in the brain and that when the brain no longer functions, the individual is dead. We shall take up the locus question later in this chapter. What is remarkable is that Beecher's list, with the possible exception of "uniqueness," is composed entirely of functions explicitly related to consciousness and the capacity to relate to one's social environment through interaction with others. All the functions which give the capacity to integrate one's internal bodily environment through unconscious, complex, homeostatic reflex mechanisms—respiration, circulation, and major integrating reflexes—are omitted. In fact, when asked what was essentially significant to man's living, Beecher replied simply, "Consciousness."

Thus a fourth concept of death is the irreversible loss of the capacity for consciousness or social integration. This view of the nature of man places even more emphasis on social character. Even, given a hypothetical human being with the full capacity for integration of bodily function, if he had irreversibly lost the capacity for consciousness and social interaction, he would have lost the essential character of humanness and, according to this definition, the person would be dead.

Even if one moves to the so-called higher functions and away from the mere capacity to integrate bodily functions through reflex mechanisms, it is still not clear precisely what is ultimately valued. We must have a more careful specification of "consciousness or the capacity for social integration." Are these two capacities synonymous and, if not, what is the relationship between them? Before taking up that question, we must first make clear what is meant by capacity.

"Where does one look if one wants to know whether a person is dead or alive?"

Holders of this concept of death and related concepts of the essence of man specifically do not say that individuals must be valued by others in order to be human. This would place life at the mercy of other human beings, who may well be cruel or insensitive. Nor does this concept imply that the essence of man is the fact of social interaction with others, as this would also place a person at the mercy of others. The infant raised in complete isolation from other human contact would still be human, provided that the child retained the mere capacity for some form of social interaction. This view of what is essentially significant to the nature of man makes no quantitative or qualitative judgments. It need not, and for me could not, lead to the view that those who have more capacity for social integration are more human. The concepts of life and death are essentially bipolar, threshold concepts. Either one has life or one does not. Either a particular type of death behavior is called for or it is not. One does not pronounce death halfway or read a will halfway or become elevated from the vice-presidency to the presidency halfway.

The Slippery Slope of Evaluation

One of the real dangers of shifting from the third concept of death to the fourth is that the fourth, in focusing exclusively on the capacity for consciousness or social interaction, lends itself much more readily to quantitative and qualitative considerations. When the focus is on the complete capacity for bodily integration, including the ability of the body to carry out spontaneous respiratory activity and major reflexes, it is quite easy to maintain that if any such integrating function is present the person is alive. But when the question begins to be, "What kinds of integrating capacity are really significant?" one finds oneself on the slippery slope of evaluating kinds of consciousness or social interaction. If consciousness is what counts it might be asked if a long-term, catatonic schizophrenic or a patient with extreme senile dementia really has the capacity for consciousness. To position oneself for such a slide down the slope of evaluating the degree of capacity for social interaction is extremely dangerous. It seems to me morally obligatory to stay off the slopes.

Precisely what are the functions considered to be ultimately significant to human life according to this concept? There are several possibilities.

The capacity for rationality is one candidate.... Consciousness is a second candidate that dominates much of the medical and biological literature....

Social interaction is a third candidate.

Importance of the Body

The concept presents one further problem. The Western tradition which emphasizes social interaction also emphasizes, as we have seen, the importance of the body. Consider the admittedly remote possibility that the electrical impulses of the brain could be transferred by recording devices onto magnetic computer tape. Would that tape together with some kind of minimum sensory device be a living human being and would erasure of the tape be considered murder? If the body is really essential to man, then we might well decide that such a creature would not be a living human being.

Where does this leave us? The earlier concepts of death—the irreversible loss of the soul and the irreversible stopping of the flow of vital body fluids—strike me as quite implausible. The soul as an independent nonphysical entity that is necessary and sufficient for a person to be considered alive is a relic from the era of dichotomized anthropologies. Animalistic fluid flow is simply too base a function to be the human essence. The capacity for bodily integration is more plausible, but I suspect it is attractive primarily because it includes those higher functions that we normally take to be central—consciousness, the ability to think and feel and relate to others. When the reflex networks that regulate such things as blood pressure and respiration are separated from the higher functions, I am led to conclude that it is the higher functions which are so essential that their loss ought to be taken as the death of the person. While consciousness is certainly important, man's social nature and embodiment seem to me to be the truly essential characteristics. I therefore believe that death is most appropriately thought of as the irreversible loss of the embodied capacity for social interaction.

The Locus of Death

Thus far I have completely avoided dealing with anatomy. Whenever the temptation arose to formulate a concept of death by referring to organs or tissues such as the heart, lungs, brain, or cerebral cortex, I have carefully resisted. Now finally I must ask, "Where does one look if one wants to know whether a person is dead or alive?" This question at last leads into the field of anatomy and physiology. Each concept of death formulated in the previous section (by asking what is of essential significance to the nature of man) raises a corresponding question of where to look to see if death has occurred. This level of the definitional problem may be called the locus of death.

The term *locus* must be used carefully. I have stressed that we are concerned about the death of the individual as a whole, not a specific part. Nevertheless, differing concepts of death will lead us to look at different body functions and structures in order to diagnose the death of the person as a whole. This task can be undertaken only after the conceptual question is resolved, if what we really want to know is where to look to determine if a person is dead rather than where to look to determine simply if the person has irreversibly lost the capacity for vital fluid flow or bodily integration or social interaction. What then are the different loci corresponding to the different concepts?

The *loci* corresponding to the irreversible loss of vital fluid flow are clearly the heart and blood vessels, the lungs and respiratory tract. At least according to our contemporary empirical knowledge of physiology and anatomy, in which we have good reason to have confidence, these are the vital organs and organ systems to which the tests should have applied to determine if a person has died. Should a new Harvey reveal evidence to the contrary, those who hold to the concept of the irreversible loss of vital fluid flow would probably be willing to change the site of their observations in diagnosing death.

Seat of the Soul

The locus, or the "seat," of the soul has not been dealt with definitely since the day of Descartes. In his essay, "The Passions of the Soul," Descartes pursues the question of the soul's dwelling place in the body. He argues that the soul is united to all the portions of the body conjointly, but, nevertheless, he concludes:

> There is yet . . . a certain part in which it exercises its functions more particularly than in all the others; and it is usually believed that this part is the brain, or

possibly the heart: the brain, because it is with it that the organs of sense are connected, and the heart because it is apparently in it that we experience the passions. But in examining the matter with care, it seems as though I had clearly ascertained that the part of the body in which the soul exercises its functions immediately is in no wise the heart, not the whole of the brain, but merely the most inward of all its parts, to wit, a certain very small gland which is situated in the middle of its substance. . . .

Descartes is clearly asking the questions of locus. His anatomical knowledge is apparently sound, but his conclusion that the soul resides primarily and directly in the pineal body raises physiological and theological problems which most of us are unable to comprehend today. What is significant is that he seemed to hold that the irreversible loss of the soul is the critical factor in determining death, and he was asking the right kind of question about where to look to determine whether a man is dead.

"One does not pronounce death halfway or read a will halfway or become elevated from the vice-presidency to the presidency halfway."

The fact that the Greek term *pneuma* has the dual meaning of both breath and soul or spirit could be interpreted to imply that the presence of this animating force is closely related to (perhaps synonymous with) breath. This gives us another clue about where holders of the irreversible-loss-of-the-soul concept of death might look to determine the presence or absence of life.

Locus of the Integrating Capacity

The locus for loss of capacity for bodily integration is a more familiar concept today. The anatomist and physiologist would be sure that the locus of the integrating capacity is the central nervous system, as Sherrington has ingrained into the biomedical tradition. Neurophysiologists asked to find this locus might reasonably request a more specific concept, however. They are aware that the automatic nervous system and spinal cord play a role in the integrating capacity, both as transmitters of nervous impulses and as the central analyzers for certain simple acts of integration (for example, a withdrawal reflex mediated through the spinal cord); they would have to know whether one was interested in such simple reflexes.

Beecher gives us the answer quite specifically for his personal concept of death: he says spinal reflexes are to be omitted. This leaves the brain as essentially the place to look to determine whether a man is dead according to the third concept of death. The brain's highly complex circuitry provides the minimal essentials for the body's real integrating capacity. This third concept quite specifically includes unconscious homeostatic and higher reflex mechanisms such as spontaneous respiration and pupil reflexes. Thus, anatomically, according to our reading of neurophysiology, we are dealing with the whole brain, including the cerebellum, medulla, and brain stem. This is the basis for calling the third concept of death *brain death,* and we already discussed objections to this term.

"This leaves the brain as essentially the place to look to determine whether a man is good."

Where to seek the locus for irreversible loss of the capacity for social interaction, the fourth conception of death, is quite another matter. We have eliminated unconscious reflex mechanisms. The answer is clearly not the whole brain—it is much too massive. Determining the locus of consciousness and social interaction certainly requires greater scientific understanding, but evidence points strongly to the neocortex or outer surface of the brain as the site. Indeed, if this is the locus of consciousness, the presence or absence of activity in the rest of the brain will be immaterial to the holder of this view.

The Criteria of Death

Having determined a concept of death, which is rooted in a philosophical analysis of the nature of man, and a locus of death, which links this philosophical understanding to the anatomy and physiology of the human body, we are finally ready to ask the operational question, What tests or measurements should be applied to determine if an individual is living or dead? At this point we have moved into a more technical realm in which the answer will depend primarily on the data gathered from the biomedical sciences.

Beginning with the first concept of death, irreversible loss of vital fluid flow, what criteria can be used to measure the activity of the heart and lungs, the blood vessels and respiratory tract? The methods are simple: visual observation of respiration, perhaps by the use of the classic mirror held at the nostrils; feeling the pulse; and listening for the heartbeat. More technical measures are also now available to the trained clinician: the electrocardiogram and direct measures of oxygen and carbon dioxide levels in the blood.

If Descartes' conclusion is correct that the locus of the soul is in the pineal body, the logical question would be, "How does one know when the pineal body has irreversibly ceased to function?" or more precisely, "How does one know when the soul has irreversibly departed from the gland?" This matter remains baffling for the modern neurophysiologist. If, however, holders of the soul-departing concept of death associate the soul with the breath, as suggested by the word *pneuma,* this might give us another clue. If respiration and specifically breath are the locus of the soul, then the techniques discussed above as applying to respiration might also be the appropriate criteria for determining the loss of the soul.

Harvard Criteria

We have identified the (whole) brain as the locus associated with the third concept of death, the irreversible loss of the capacity for bodily integration. The empirical task of identifying criteria in this case is to develop accurate predictions of the complete and irreversible loss of brain activity. This search for criteria was the real task carried out by the Ad Hoc Committee to Examine the Definition of Brain Death of Harvard Medical School; the simple criteria they proposed have become the most widely recognized in the United States:

1. Unreceptivity and unresponsitivity.
2. No movements or breathing.
3. No reflexes.
4. Flat electroencephalogram.

The report states that the fourth criterion is "of great confirmatory value." It also calls for the repetition of these tests twenty-four hours later. Two types of cases are specifically excluded: hypothermia (body temperature below 90°F) and the presence of central nervous system depressants such as barbiturates.

Other criteria have been proposed to diagnose the condition of irreversible loss of brain function. James Toole, a neurologist at the Bowman Gray School of Medicine, has suggested that metabolic products in the blood or cerebrospinal fluid could possibly be developed as well.

European Criteria

European observers seem to place more emphasis on demonstrating the absence of circulation in the brain. This is measured by angiography, radio-isotopes, or sonic techniques. In Europe sets of criteria analogous to the Harvard criteria have been proposed. G.P.J. Alexandre, a surgeon who heads a Belgian renal transplant department, reports that in addition to absence of reflexes as criteria of irreversible destruction of the brain, he uses lack of spontaneous respiration, a flat EEG, complete bilateral mydriasis, and falling blood pressure necessitating increasing amounts of vasopressive drugs. J.P. Revillard, a Frenchman, reportedly uses these plus angiography and absence of reaction to atropine. Even among those who agree on the types of measures, there may still be disagreement on the levels of measurement. This is especially true for the electroencephalogram, which can be recorded at varying sensitivities and for different time periods. The Harvard-proposed twenty-four-hour period is now being questioned as too conservative.

While these alternate sets of criteria are normally described as applicable to measuring loss of brain function (or "brain death," as in the name of the Harvard committee), it appears that many of these authors, especially the earlier ones, have not necessarily meant to distinguish them from criteria for measuring the narrower loss of cerebral function.

The criteria for irreversible loss of the capacity for social interaction are far more selective. It should be clear from the above criteria that they measure loss of all brain activity, including spontaneous respiration and higher reflexes and not simply loss of consciousness. This raises a serious problem about whether the Harvard criteria really measure "irreversible coma" as the report title indicates. Exactly what is measured is an entirely empirical matter. In any case, convincing evidence has been cited by the committee and more recently by a committee of the Institute of Society, Ethics and the Life Sciences that no one will falsely be pronounced in irreversible coma. In 128 patients who underwent autopsy, the brain was found to be "obviously destroyed" in each case. Of 2650 patients with isoelectric EEGs of twenty-four hours' duration, not one patient recovered ("excepting three who had received anesthetic doses of CNS depressants, and who were, therefore, outside the class of patients covered by the report").

Criteria Relationships

What then is the relationship between the more inclusive Harvard criteria and the simple use of electrocerebral silence as measured by an isoelectric or flat electroencephalogram? The former might be appropriate for those who associate death with the disappearance of any neurological function of the brain. For those who hold the narrower concept based simply on consciousness or capacity for social interaction, however, the Harvard criteria may suffer from exactly the same problem as the old heart- and lung-oriented criteria. With those criteria, every patient whose circulatory and respiratory function had ceased was indeed dead, but the criteria might be too conservative, in that some patients dead according to the "loss of bodily integrating capacity" concept of death (for which the brain is the corresponding locus) would be found alive according to heart- and lung-oriented criteria. It might also happen that some patients who should be declared dead according to the irreversible loss of consciousness and social interaction concept would be found to be alive according to the Harvard criteria. All discussions of the neurological criteria fail to consider that the criteria might be too inclusive, too conservative. The criteria might, therefore, give rise to classifying patients as dead according to the

consciousness or social-interaction conception, but as alive according to the full Harvard criteria. . . .

This leaves us with the empirical question of the proper criteria for the irreversible loss of consciousness which is thought to have its locus in the neocortex of the cerebrum. Brierley and his colleagues suggest that the EEG alone (excluding the other three criteria of the Harvard report) measures the activity of the neocortex. Presumably this test must also meet the carefully specified conditions of amplifier gain, repeat of the test after a given time period, and exclusion of the exceptional cases, if it is to be used as the criterion for death according to our fourth concept, irreversible loss of capacity for social interaction. The empirical evidence is not all in, but it would seem that the 2650 cases of flat EEG without recovery which are cited to support the Harvard criteria would also be persuasive preliminary empirical evidence for the use of the EEG alone as empirical evidence for the irreversible loss of consciousness and social interaction which (presumably) have their locus in the neocortex. What these 2650 cases would have to include for the data to be definitive would be a significant number of Brierley-type patients where the EEG criteria were met without the other Harvard criteria being met. This is a question for the neurophysiologists to resolve.

"It might also happen that some patients who should be declared dead according to the irreversible loss of consciousness and social interaction concept would be found to be alive according to the Harvard criteria."

There is another problem with the use of electroencephalogram, angiography, or other techniques for measuring cerebral function as a criterion for the irreversible loss of consciousness. Once again we must face the problem of a false positive diagnosis of life. The old heart and lung criteria may provide a false positive diagnosis for a holder of the bodily integrating capacity concept, and the Harvard criteria may give false positive indications for a holder of the consciousness or social interaction concept. Could a person have electroencephalographic activity but still have no capacity for consciousness or social interaction? Whether this is possible empirically is difficult to say, but at least theoretically there are certainly portions of the neocortex which could be functioning and presumably be recorded on an electroencephalogram without the individual having any capacity for consciousness. For instance, what if through an accident or vascular occlusion the motor cortex remained viable but the sensory cortex did not? Even the most narrow criterion of the electroencephalogram alone may still give false diagnoses of living for holders of the social interaction concept.

Complexities in Matching Concepts

It has been our method throughout this paper to identify four major concepts of death and then to determine, primarily by examining the empirical evidence, what the corresponding loci and criteria might be. But there are good reasons why the holders of a particular concept of death might not want to adopt the corresponding criteria as the means of determining the status of a given patient. These considerations are primarily pragmatic and empirical. In the first place, as a matter of policy we would not want to have to apply the Harvard criteria before pronouncing death while standing before every clearly dead body. It is not usually necessary to use such technical measures as an EEG, whether one holds the fluid-flow concept, the loss of bodily integration concept, or the loss of social interaction concept.

"There will be those who do not accept the correlated concept of death."

Reliance on the old circulatory and respiratory criteria in cases where the individual is obviously dead may be justified in either of two ways. First, there is the option implied in the new Kansas statute. . .of maintaining two operating concepts of death, either of which will be satisfactory. This appears, however, to be philosophically unsound, since it means that a patient could be simultaneously dead and alive. If the philosophical arguments for either of the neurological concepts are convincing, and I think they are, we should not have to fall back on the fluid-flow concept for pronouncing death in the ordinary case.

A second way to account for the use of the heart- and lung-oriented criteria is that they do indeed correlate empirically with the neurological concepts. When there is no circulatory or respiratory activity for a sufficient time, there is invariably a loss of capacity for bodily integration or capacity for consciousness or social interaction. Using circulatory and respiratory activity as tests is crude, and in some cases the presence of such activity will lead to a false positive diagnosis of life; but the prolonged absence of circulation and respiration is a definitive diagnosis of death even according to the neurologically oriented concepts. Their use is thus an initial shortcut; if these criteria are met, one need not go on to the other

criteria for the purpose of pronouncing death. This would appear to be a sound rationale for continuing the use of the old criteria of respiratory and circulatory activity.

A second practical difficulty is inherent in correlating concept and criteria. Let us examine this by asking why one might not wish at this time to adopt the EEG alone as a definitive criterion for pronouncing death. There are two possible reasons. First, quite obviously, there will be those who do not accept the correlated concept of death. They reject the irreversible loss of the capacity for consciousness or social interaction in favor of the irreversible loss of capacity for bodily integration or for fluid flow. Second, there are those who accept the concept of irreversible loss of consciousness or social interaction, but still are not convinced that the EEG unfailingly predicts this. If and when they can be convinced that the EEG alone accurately predicts irreversible loss of consciousness or social interaction without any false diagnosis of death, they will adopt it as the criterion. In the meantime they would logically continue to advocate the concept while adhering to the more conservative Harvard criteria, which appear to measure the loss of whole brain function. Since the distinction is a new one and the empirical evidence may not yet be convincing, it is to be expected that many holders of this concept will, for the time being and as a matter of policy, prefer the Harvard Committee's older and more conservative criteria for determining death.

Robert M. Veatch, Ph.D., is a professor of medical ethics at the Kennedy Institute of Ethics in Washington, D.C.

"In our litigious society, physicians and lawyers are understandably unwilling to go forward under the threat of civil or criminal liability."

Death Should Be Legally Defined

John J. Paris and Ronald E. Cranford

This March, 19-year-old Richard Berger was wheeled into the emergency room of the Smithtown (Long Island, N.Y.) General Hospital with a robber's bullet in his brain. Comatose as a result of massive brain damage, he had no reflex responses. His pupils were dilated and fixed; there was no response to light or intense pain. His electroencephalogram was flat. He was unable to breathe without a respirator. The boy's father had but one question: "Is he dead?" The physician replied: "He is brain dead." The father pressed further. Was his son legally dead? The physician's response is instructive: "Medically he is dead. Legally, I don't know. I am not a lawyer."

That confusion set up six days of agony for Richard's parents as physicians, lawyers, district attorneys and transplant coordinators tried to sift through the competing claims, hopes and expectations for the boy. The physicians, though convinced Richard was dead, would not pronounce him so unless the parents either sought a court order declaring him dead or decided to donate his organs. In the latter case the doctors and hospital believed they would be legally protected by the state's Uniform Anatomical Gift Act, which authorizes the removal of organs from brain-dead individuals.

The physicians explained the issues to the family and the complications resulting from the fact that in New York there was no determination of death statute. The district attorney compounded the family's woes by alerting them to the fact that the assailant probably would argue that the parents, not he, had caused their son's death. Though no court had ever accepted such a defense, that would not prevent things "from getting very, very ugly at the trial."

Yet a further burden for the parents, as they

watched their son breathing on the respirator, was the hope that though brain dead, he might somehow miraculously come out of the coma. That hope was finally dashed on the sixth day when Richard suffered a cardiac arrest. The parents were then confronted with the decision of immediately allowing the removal of his organs or facing the prospect of both his death and the destruction of his organs. At that point they determined that the miracle of life would go to the waiting recipient rather than to their son. They authorized the transplant.

Why, one might ask, did not the physician simply proceed on the basis of the medical evidence and pronounce Richard Berger dead? The attending physician, Dr. Arthur Rosen, a neurologist at University Hospital in Stony Brook, put it bluntly when he said, "Doctors will not pull the plug without a court order. The potential liability is just too great." It is indeed great in New York State where the famous Brother Fox case focused attention on the fact that some district attorneys believe "as things stand now, withdrawal of life support is homicide."

That comment by Robert L. Adams, first assistant district attorney of Rensselaer County, sent shock waves last fall through a large audience of medical personnel and attorneys attending a state-wide conference on "Legal and Ethical Aspects of Treatment for the Critically and Terminally Ill." Their trauma was intensified when Mr. Adams revealed that "there are D.A.'s in this state anxious to pursue such charges.... One told me he would see how many are enrolled in the Right to Life Party in his county, and he'd go from there."

Death Statutes

Such a question would not have been an issue for the Bergers in those 31 states that now have a brain-death statute. There, a brain-dead individual is dead. The New York legislature, however, has five times rejected attempts to pass a determination of death statute. It has done so under sustained pressure from the New York Catholic Conference, right to life groups and some Orthodox Jewish organizations which continue to insist that such legislation is morally repugnant, unnecessary and dangerous.

It is important to be clear on what determination of death statutes involve, how they have evolved and the need for them. It is equally important to understand the objections to such legislation, analyze and evaluate them, and devise a coherent public policy position on the issue. That policy must be medically sound, ethically appropriate and theologically acceptable.

"Doctors will not pull the plug without a court order. The potential liability is just too great."

Thirty years ago the definition of death was uniformly agreed upon and easy to assess: When the heart and breathing stopped, the patient was dead. Two technological developments have challenged that understanding: the advent of artificial life support systems and the possibility of organ transplants. The first allows the revival of patients whose hearts or breathing have stopped. If the patient had not suffered more than a few minutes of oxygen deprivation, he or she would resume a normal life. If, alternatively, the patient underwent prolonged oxygen deprivation (15-20 minutes), heart action might be restarted and breathing maintained by a respirator, but the destruction of the brain cells would mean that the patient would be unable to maintain either of those functions on his own.

Medical Determination

Neurological examinations are able to assess the extent of brain cell destruction and to distinguish patients who have suffered neocortical damage from those who have lost all brain functions including that of the brain stem. The first are in a persistent vegetative state. The overwhelming majority of the patients never regain mental functions of any type. Others may recover from the sleep-like coma after days to weeks and then have periods of wakefulness during which their eyes are open and move. There may even be rare instances of recovery of consciousness months or—as in the recently reported Minnesota case of Sgt. David Mack—almost two years after the initial trauma. All of these patients, including those like Karen Ann Quinlan who have suffered overwhelming destruction of the higher brain centers, continue to have functions of and circulation to the brain. They are clearly alive.

In contrast, brain-dead patients have no flow to the brain. Clinical examinations reveal no evidence of any brain functions. The pupils do not respond to light, nor are there any eye movements. Spontaneous respiration ceases because of the permanent destruction of the vital respiratory centers in the lower brain stem, and the patient is entirely dependent on mechanical respiratory support. Since cardiac functioning is not dependent on neural regulation from the brain, heartbeat can continue indefinitely in a respirator-supported brain-dead patient, though usually heart stoppage occurs within a few days. There are, however, published cases of confirmed brain-dead children being maintained for a month or more, and a recent *New England Journal of Medicine* article (1/7/82) contains the report of a 49-year-old New York man who survived 74 days in a brain-dead condition before the court-ordered removal of his respirator "terminated" his life.

With the ability to "sustain" patients through ventilator assistance came the realization that, with such technology, organs of brain-dead individuals could be kept "fresh" for transplant purposes. But in order to harvest the organs, the individual has to be dead. Physicians and society then faced two critical questions: When is the individual dead? And is it legitimate to ventilate the cadaver to preserve the organs? Moralists quickly agreed to an affirmative answer to the second query. The first proved more problematic.

Organ Harvests

That issue was sharply focused with the advent of cardiac transplant surgery. As is true with many medicomoral topics, it was the courts that first confronted the problem publicly. In the celebrated case of Tucker v. Lower (1977), a Virginia court had to determine whether the physicians who removed a brain-dead Bruce Tucker from a respirator and then transplanted his heart into a patient who was dying of cardiac failure were guilty of a wrongful death. The judge instructed the jury in a new definition of death: "In determining the time of death you may consider the following elements. . .among them the time of complete and irreversible loss of all function of the brain." The jury took less than an hour to return a verdict of not guilty.

To clarify the issue for physicians and families and to obviate the costly, burdensome and often traumatic trial of court battles, various states beginning with Kansas in 1970 enacted brain-death statutes. To date, some 31 states and the District of Columbia have followed suit.

To provide for greater uniformity on this subject and to avoid the strange situation of the same "body" being "alive" in one state and "dead" in the next, and the yet more paradoxical situation of a "body" being alive or dead in the same state depending on as extrinsic a factor as a signed anatomical gift card, the President's Commission for the Study of Ethical Problems in Medicine was charged by the Congress with developing a uniform determination of death statute. In its year and a half study, the commission heard testimony from a wide variety of medical, legal, ethical and religious viewpoints. Among the positions considered was Jean-Jacques Winslow's 18th-century text: "The Uncertainty of the Signs of Death and the Danger of Precipitate Interments" in which the author argued that putrefaction was the only sure sign of death.

President's Commission

From the outset the commission was determined to take "extreme caution" in formulating public policy in this area. Proposed changes in the existing laws would be designed to produce a minimal shift in the definition as well as a maximal acceptance among laymen, scientists and clinicians. To that end the commission took a very conservative posture in its hearings, in its findings and in its final report. It evaluated, but did not accept, the philosophical understandings of death as the loss of personality or personal identity. It likewise studied and rejected the proposal that "death" be defined as the permanent loss of higher brain functions. In its understanding, those who, like Karen Ann Quinlan, are in a persistent vegetative state are not dead.

The commission adopted as its position the widely accepted whole brain-death standard, i.e., death is established when "all functions of the brain including the brain stem have permanently and irreversibly ceased." Thus even if life continues in individual cells or organs, without the complex integration of the entire system, a person cannot properly be regarded as alive. It proposed the following Uniform Determination of Death Act (U.D.D.A.): "An individual who has sustained either 1) irreversible cessation of circulatory and respiratory functions, or 2) irreversible cessation of all functions of the entire brain, including brain stem, is dead. A determination of death must be made in accordance with accepted medical standards.

With such a careful and conservative formulation (one which had already been adopted with slight variation in 26 states, 10 state supreme courts and 13 nations and one which had the approval of the American Medical Association, the American Bar Association, the National Conference of Commissioners on Uniform State Laws and the American Academy of Neurology), it would seem that the remaining jurisdictions would quickly adopt the model statute.

Opposition to UDDA

Opposition, though, soon arose from several quarters. Various right-to-life groups and the Rev. Edward Bryce, chairman of the U.S. Bishops' Committee for Pro-Life Activities, released position papers denouncing the proposed statute as "unnecessary, dangerous and a stepping stone to euthanasia." Father Bryce's statements, which are a replay of the old arguments of the National Conference of Catholic Bishops against living-will legislation, have no application to brain-death statutes. They do reflect, though, the hysteria that exists among some of the right-to-life groups with regard to any attempt to deal with the subject of death and dying.

For example, the Minnesota Citizens Concerned for Life, a 25,000 member organization, testified at a legislative hearing that "it opposes not only brain-death legislation but any imposed definition of death." Such an action, contends Mary Winter, president of People Concerned for the Unborn Child, a powerful Pittsburgh-based antiabortion group, "would be the first step to the 'dehumanization' of the critically ill and to euthanasia." "Once you get that established," she continued, "you're on your way to a Holocaust."

People Concerned's memorandum attacking the U.D.D.A. shows the thinking behind their position. It begins by "exposing" support for the legislation by "euthanasia prone" groups and then it articulates their true worry: "As prolifers, we hold what science has proven: that human life begins at fertilization. A definition of death which refers to brain function is antilife because in the early stages of human development there is no brain. . . . A statute equating brain function with life would further legally dehumanize the unborn."

Failure to Make Crucial Distinctions

While the antiabortion stance is admirable, the statement fails to distinguish those with future potential for brain function from those who have exhausted that capacity.

"The commission adopted as its position the widely accepted whole brain-death standards."

In failing to make crucial distinctions, they follow the leading spokesman for their positions, Dr. Paul Byrne, a St. Louis pediatrician, and the Rev. Paul Quay, a St. Louis Jesuit who writes on medical issues. Dr. Byrne and Father Quay, together with the late Sean O'Reilly, authored a well-known article, "Brain Death—An Opposing Viewpoint" in *The Journal of the American Medical Association* (11/2/79) in which they maintain that destruction of the brain, not merely cessation of function, is required for death. Lest there be any doubt as to their standard for irreversible function, the authors provide examples of evidence of death: "If someone's head has been completely crushed by a truck or vaporized by a nuclear blast, or if his brain has been dissolved by a massive injection of sulfuric acid."

What, one might ask, would lead to such a demanding standard? Father Quay's testimony before the President's commission reveals a fear that physicians would be willing "to kill someone who is still alive" in order to obtain transplant organs. His standard of nuclear vaporization or "the total physical disintegration of the individual organs and tissues" not only precludes that grisly possibility, it guarantees no harvesting whatsoever. It also recalls Winslow's questionable criterion for certitude: putrefaction.

"Once you get that established, you're on your way to a Holocaust."

Dr. Byrne and Father Quay are not content to state their position. They claim that a brain function criterion "stands in flat contradiction to the religious beliefs of Christians, Jews, Moslems, Hindus and many others." A thorough search of the literature finds no Catholic moral theologian, no Protestant ethicist and but one Orthodox Jewish spokesman supporting their contention. Rabbi J. David Bleich of Yeshiva University opposes brain-death standards on the grounds that independent cardiac activity still occurs.

Rabbi Bleich, in fact, is the source of the Byrne-Quay dysfunction/destruction thesis. He articulated it at a 1977 conference on "Biomedical Ethics in the Perspective of Jewish Teaching" when he stated: "Dysfunction of the brain should not be confused with destruction of the brain. Only *destruction* of the brain can be entertained as a possible definition of death." Rabbi Moses Tendler (Rabbi Bleich's colleague at Yeshiva), Rabbi Seymour Siegal and Dr. Isaac Franck took issue with his interpretation of the tradition. They support the validity of total brain-death criteria for the determination of death.

Unfortunate Influence

None of this evidence dissuades the prolife forces from continued opposition to the legislation. They merely repeat the familiar refrain that legislation is unnecessary, dangerous and the road to euthanasia. The unfortunate aspect of that mantra is that it influences, if not determines, the political statements of many Catholic bishops. The bishops, in turn, influence and control the policy position of many legislators.

Speaking to that issue, State Senator Louis Bertonazzi of Massachusetts noted the fact that, "The mere presence of an auxiliary bishop of Boston speaking in opposition to the brain-death bill on 'moral grounds' has resulted in a fairly even split among members despite the fact that proponents outnumbered opponents." This, he observed, is not because of reasoned arguments advanced by the opponents but because of their well-known ability to punish or reward legislators. The fear of that punishment will become mobilized, Mr. Bertonazzi warns, if brain-death proposals become enmeshed with emotional cries against premature organ transplants or "pulling the plug."

That is precisely what happened in Minnesota where the Minnesota Citizens Concerned for Life held information meetings to demonstrate the evils of brain-death legislation. Their star witness was Dr. Paul Byrne who awed a dozen of the legislators with the story of a "brain-dead" patient rescued from a transplant surgeon's knife by a last minute movement of his Adam's apple. Dr. Byrne further dramatized the issue for the assembled lawmakers by describing the reality of "brain-dead" patients: "The heart is beating, there's blood pressure, they put out urine, they sweat, they're warm, they look like a human being and someone decides they're dead." After his presentation, no one in the Minnesota legislature wanted to decide they're dead. Not a single member wanted to sponsor the Uniform Determination of Death Act. This for a bill which in one form or another is already law in 31 states.

Similar influence was demonstrated this spring by the Missouri Catholic Conference when it opposed "any statutory definition of death." The bishops presented several objections: 1) There is no need for a statutory definition of death. No physician has ever been prosecuted for using brain criteria, and no Missouri case prohibits physicians from doing so. 2) There is strong disagreement among the medical profession about the acceptance of that standard. 3) There are foreseeable adverse consequences to patients, family rights, physician rights and the welfare of society from such a statute.

Inconsistent Assertions

On its face, points one and two are incompatible. If there is strong disagreement among physicians on the acceptance of a brain-death standard, to employ it as a criterion for death without legislative or judicial authorization would be cavalier, if not foolhardy. The Missouri Conference also acknowledges that there are physicians who, while accepting the criterion as valid, believe it is illegal to use it under the present circumstances. Consequently, they keep "dead" patients on respirators.

The assertion that there is strong medical disagreement on brain death needs close scrutiny. Once again, it is Dr. Byrne who is cited as the expert source. The St. Louis pediatrician is quoted as saying: "Brain death may be described as an esoteric creation of neurologists and neurosurgeons who are seeking to speed up the declaration of death for the purposes of transplants. The general practicing physician does not rely on those esoteric criteria in pronouncing a person dead." It is not the general pronouncement of death that is in doubt; it is the status of the brain-dead individual that is the subject of the debate.

On that topic there is no longer any doubt as to what are the medically accepted standards. "The Guidelines for the Determination of Death," a landmark document which reflects a summary of currently accepted medical practices, was published last fall in *The Journal of the American Medical Association* (11/13/81). It is signed by the nation's leading authorities in neurology, neurosurgery, critical care and legal medicine. It represents, in the words of the accompanying J.A.M.A. editorial, "a consensus that is truly a remarkable achievement, (one) of which the medical profession can be proud." That document endorses the Uniform Determination of Death Act.

Unreasonable Charges

The charge of impure motives on the part of neurologists and neurosurgeons likewise falters under examination. Dr. Shelley Chou, a neurosurgeon writing in *Lancet,* reports that at the University of Minnesota Hospital there are "about 20 brain-death cases per year and less than 50 percent of them become organ donors." A survey done in a major British hospital over a five-year period notes an even smaller percentage; 22.7 percent were donors. Similar figures are found in the President's Commission Report where we learn that "only seven of 38 subjects declared dead by neurological criteria in the commission's survey were organ donors."

The third cluster of concerns of the Missouri Catholic Conference is the least defensible. It objects that a legal definition of death would prevent the family of a brain-dead individual from continuing life support treatment if they so desired it; would assist hospitals in refusing to care for "dead bodies"; would aid insurance companies and the government in stopping payment for such care; and would inhibit the freedom of the individual physician from practicing medicine according to his own best judgment. Do the members of the conference really believe that the determination of death should be subject to the designs of families, the idiosyncratic judgments of physicians or the desires of third-party payers? The wishes, hopes or fantasies of the family or physician will not change the reality of death; nor should they influence its diagnosis.

In addition to the various Catholic conferences, the Catholic Hospital Association has given its attention to the subject. In a thoughtful and well-documented booklet entitled *Determination of Death,* the Rev. Albert S. Moraczewski, O.P., and J. Stuart Showalter explore the theological, medical, ethical and legal implications of brain death. They conclude their analysis with the statement: "We pose no legal or moral objection to U.D.D.A." Yet, they continue, "one cannot thereby simply assert that legislation of

such criteria is justified." To be justified, they assert, there must be evidence that the absence of legislation results in injustice to patients, families or physicians, evidence which they claim has not yet been established. They hold that the way to achieve public acceptance of the brain-death criteria is not by legislation—the usual way in which society codifies its social values—but by education.

Travesties of Justice

It is difficult to obtain public acceptance of a standard which is repeatedly attacked by some Catholic bishops as being morally suspect and potentially dangerous. It is yet more difficult to get physicians to follow the Moraczewski and Showalter exhortation that they should rely on their medical judgment rather than fret over legal liabilities. In our litigious society, physicians and lawyers are understandably unwilling to go forward under the threat of civil or criminal liability. A tragic example of that reality was the case of Melanie Bacchiochi, a 23-year-old Connecticut woman who was maintained in a brain-dead condition for 43 days until a court finally authorized the physician to follow the appropriate medical response to her condition.

"It is difficult to obtain public acceptance of a standard which is repeatedly attacked by some Catholic bishops as being morally suspect and potentially dangerous."

There have been yet other reported travesties of justice provoked by a lack of brain-death legislation. Last year, for example, the wife of a brain-dead New York policeman, who had been ambushed and shot in the head, was asked by the Queens County District Attorney not to disconnect the respirator lest that action jeopardize a potential first-degree murder conviction. The wife, a Catholic, replied she would never remove the respirator in such circumstances, saying: "It would be against my religion."

This year similar fears were expressed by the Nassau County District Attorney's Office in the Richard Berger case. And the physicians, afraid of potential liability, refused to remove the respirator without a court order or organ donor status. We are also familiar with several instances of families of confirmed brain-dead patients who, though told there is "no hope," refuse to authorize removal of the machines. Such authorization ought not be the burden of families.

If there were but a few such cases and if they all ended within a day or two, the misuse of the medical personnel and resources might be a tolerable price to pay for the family's adjustment to the death. But as a survey done by the President's commission indicates, there are 204 such cases per month in major medical centers. And the New England Journal article reveals that not all such patients succumb quickly to cardiac failure. In addition, we know that brain-dead children have substantial "survival rates." When these data are evaluated, it is apparent that the misallocation of resources, the financial costs and the emotional strain of continued "treatment" become vastly disproportionate to any putative benefits.

Shifts of Views

In the past few years there have been shifts in the stand taken by some prolife activists and Catholic conferences on the Uniform Determination of Death Act. Such well-known prolife spokesmen as Dr. Joseph Stanton, attorney Dennis Horan and Dr. C. Everett Koop have supported determination of death statutes. In the words of Dr. Koop, now the Surgeon General, "I think the Uniform Act addresses the critical issue of brain-stem death and therefore should be a piece of legislation which prolife groups could sincerely and honestly support."

It was that realization and the growing awareness that the idea of brain death "has become widely accepted in the medical profession" that led the Wisconsin Catholic Conference to withdraw its long standing opposition to a uniform determination of death act. This year, with the Wisconsin bishops no longer actively lobbying against the bill, the U.D.D.A. passed.

"There have been yet other reported travesties of justice provoked by a lack of brain-death legislation."

Yet more striking was the change in Pennsylvania where the Catholic conference has announced that it now supports the President's commission proposal. In a position paper explaining its shift, the Pennsylvania bishops provide a point by point refutation of the frequently repeated charge that such legislation is unnecessary, dangerous and the first step to euthanasia. They argue that technological changes make it imperative that we update our understanding of death. Then they declare it is far better to enact clarifying legislation than to leave the determination to the vagaries of court opinion and the burden of unnecessary litigation. If, as is possible, someone proposes a radical departure from the intent of this law in favor of euthanasia, then, they argue, that is the time to enter battle.

The Pennsylvania Catholic bishops have provided a model of how church involvement in the public policy process should proceed. Rather than merely join the chorus shouting "euthanasia" every time an issue involving death is raised, they have followed Archbishop John Roach's admonition that when the church enters the political arena, it must do so on the basis of reasoned argumentation. To provide this, the Pennsylvania bishops subjected the traditional charges against the legislation to critical analysis, found them inadequate and revised their position. Other state conferences should follow that example.

Acceptance of Responsibility

Within the past two years there have been several remarkable efforts to clarify the confusion existing on the difficult and trying issues of death and dying. The Vatican's splendid 1980 "Declaration on Euthanasia"—with its warning that "Today it is very important to protect, at the moment of death, both the dignity of the human person and the Christian concept of life, against a technological attitude that threatens to become an abuse"—set the agenda for study in this area. The exhaustive "Report on Defining Death," issued by the President's commission, and the authoritative "Guidelines for Determination of Death," by the nation's leading medical experts, provide the data on which to base a prudent public policy.

It is now the task of those who share the church's mission to understand the need for a sound public policy in this area, one which in the declaration's phrasing recognizes that "death is unavoidable; it is necessary therefore that we, without in any way hastening its hour, should be able to accept it with full responsibility and dignity." Acceptance of that responsibility necessarily involves an understanding of technology and medical developments as well as confidence in our ability to apply reasoned moral judgments to them. Thus our task and that of the bishops is to be informed on developments in medicine, to consult widely and wisely in this area, and to formulate positions that are both prudent and "in accordance with the plan of the Creator."

The authors requested that the following note be added to this viewpoint. It illustrates, again, the need to establish sound legal policies about death.

A May 1984 article in the New York *Daily News* quoted Queens District Attorney John Santucci who says that removing organs for transplantation from brain-dead patients is not legal. He issued this warning to physicians: "You are in potential violation of the law when you perform such organ removals and you might be subject to prosecution. You have no right to take the law into your own hands. Instead, you should be pressing for legislation to clarify the issues."

John J. Paris, S.J., is associate professor of ethics at Holy Cross College and the University of Massachusetts Medical School in Worcester. Ronald E. Cranford, M.D., is associate professor of neurology at the University of Minnesota Medical School and chairman of the ethics committee of the American Academy of Neurology.

viewpoint 83

Death Should Not Be Defined by Legislation

National Conference of Catholic Bishops, Committee for Pro-Life Activities

In 1977 a proposed resolution on death and dying was submitted to the Administrative Committee of the National Conference of Catholic Bishops by the Committee for Pro-Life Activities. This resolution states the committee's current policy with respect to certain legislative proposals: It firmly opposes all legalization of euthanasia, opposes so-called right-to-die and death-with-dignity laws because of the threat which they pose to the dignity and rights of dying persons and discourages the adoption of definition-of-death statutes. The section on definition of death reads as follows:

"Legislative proposals that attempt to define when death occurs are unnecessary. We oppose them because there is no demonstrated need for such laws, nor any assurance that they would accomplish the intended purpose. In addition they easily open the door to direct euthanasia legislation."

During the last few years several factors have changed in the legislative debate on this topic. The idea of brain death as a criterion for determining death has become widely accepted in the medical profession; more than half of our states' legislatures have adopted some form of brain-death legislation; in states where no such laws have been enacted the courts have sometimes taken an active role in legitimating the idea of brain death; and organizations such as the American Bar Association and the American Medical Association, originally wary of legislative proposals on brain death, now support legislation of this type. Some pro-life leaders and Catholic thinkers in various fields have also argued that there is a legitimate need for responsible Catholic involvement in the legislative debate on the determination of death and that the legitimate purposes of determination-of-death statutes can and

should be clearly distinguished from the issue of euthanasia.

Continued Questions

But despite the growing acceptance of brain-death legislation, many individuals and groups continue to raise questions about the claims on which such acceptance is based. These questions range from the theological and philosophical aspects of defining death, to the medical evidence marshaled in support of brain-death diagnoses, to the legal and political implications of definition-of-death statutes. Objections in these areas have led to a renewed debate both inside and outside the pro-life movement which has helped to clarify the moral and prudential issues involved in formulating a position on this kind of legislation.

The following report attempts to outline the major points of controversy in the current debate....

The complexity of the issue of determination-of-death legislation arises from the fact that it involves three different sets of questions and that these have often been blurred together in the legislative debate:

First, the basic conceptual question: Does brain death actually coincide with the death of the individual?

Second, two medical questions: Is the cessation of brain function an adequate indication of brain death? Do present criteria provide a reliable way of determining that brain function has totally and irreversibly ceased?

Third, a legislative question: If one can answer these other questions affirmatively, are there valid and compelling reasons for supporting legislation on the determination of death?...

The Conceptual Question

Catholic tradition speaks of death in terms of the separation of soul and body, and Thomistic philosophy describes the rational soul as the form of

"Resource Paper on Definition of Death Legislation," National Conference of Catholic Bishops. Reprinted with permission of the Bishops' Committee for Pro-Life Activities.

the body and the principle of its life. But these statements do not say anything directly about the empirical determination of death nor do they dictate any identification of the brain with the soul. The closest approximation to a papal statement on brain death is a set of remarks made by Pope Pius XII to an International Congress of Anesthesiologists in 1957....

The sections of Pius XII's address which relate to this question are as follows:

It remains for the doctor, and especially the anesthesiologist, to give a clear and precise definition of 'death' and the 'moment of death' of a patient who passes away in a state of unconsciousness. Here one can accept the usual concept of complete and final separation of the soul from the body; but in practice one must take into account the lack of precision of the terms 'body' and 'separation.' One can put aside the possibility of a person being buried alive, for removal of the artificial respiration apparatus must necessarily bring about stoppage of blood circulation and therefore death within a few minutes.

In case of insoluble doubt, one can resort to presumptions of law and fact. In general, it will be necessary to presume that life remains, because there is involved here a fundamental right received from the Creator, and it is necessary to prove with certainty that it has been lost....

Where the verification of the fact in particular cases is concerned, the answer cannot be deduced from any religious and moral principle and, under this aspect, does not fall within the competence of the church. Until an answer can be given, the question must remain open. But considerations of a general nature allow us to believe that *human life continues for as long as the vital functions—distinguished from the simple life of organs—manifest themselves spontaneously or even with the help of artificial processes.* A great number of these cases are the object of insoluble doubt, and must be dealt with according to the presumptions of law and of fact of which we have spoken.

Four Vital Points

Four features of Pius XII's address are of particular importance: 1) the recognition that this is a factual question having to do with the relationship between the brain and the vital processes of the rest of the human body; 2) the distinction between the "vital functions" of the human body and the "simple life of organs"; 3) the statement that vital functions may truly be the functions of a living human organism even when they are supported by artificial means; and 4) the insistence that, because this may literally be a life-and-death matter, diagnosis must be established with the greatest possible certainty.

This address is a helpful introduction to the conceptual debate over brain death, because one could accept its content and still ask: What role does the brain play in maintaining the life of the human organism? Does it play a central role in maintaining the body's "vital functions" to such an extent that only the "simple life of organs" remains once the brain is destroyed? Or is brain death the condition of a living but terminally ill patient whose other vital functions are being artificially supported?

"It remains for the doctor. . . to give a clear and precise definition of 'death' and the 'moment of death.'"

The majority of Catholic medical-moral experts in the United States now answer these questions in such a way as to affirm that brain death *is* the death of the human organism. Two lines of argument have been proposed to support this position: The first starts out from a philosophical understanding of the nature of biological life, while the second starts out from traditional medical practice and its way of determining death.

Organic Functioning

The philosophical argument is well represented by Germain Grisez and Joseph Boyle in [*Life and Death with Liberty and Justice* (1979)] a recent book on euthanasia:

Life often is said to be—in general—a certain kind of physicochemical process, and the life of an organism a collection of such processes. But an organism is more than a collection of processes; it is a coordinated system. From a thermodynamic point of view an organism is an unstable open system, but it continues because it is maintained in dynamic equilibrium by homeostatic controls. These controls are of various kinds, but in an organism which is complex enough to have a nervous system, this system coordinates and integrates the other control systems. This system is dispersed but centered in the brain; without some brain functioning, the whole system cannot be maintained. Thus when the whole brain ceases to function, the dynamic equilibrium is lost, the materials which were unified in the system begin behaving without its control, and decomposition begins.

Death, according to Grisez and Boyle, is "the irreversible loss of integrated organic functioning." This view avoids two false extremes: a reductionist identification of human life with the functions of individual organs, so that the human organism is seen merely as the material sum of its parts; and a dualistic identification of human life with the higher functions of reasoning or "social interaction," so that the human organism is "alive" by degrees (depending upon the ability to exercise specifically human functions). Grisez and Boyle also discuss the relationship of this view to the traditional criteria for determining death:

If death is understood in theoretical terms as the permanent termination of the integrated functioning characteristic of a living body as a whole, then one can see why death of higher animals is usually grasped in factual terms by the cessation of the vital functions of respiration and circulation, which correlates so well with bodily decomposition. Breathing is the minimum in 'social interaction.' However, considering the role of the brain in the maintenance of the dynamic equilibrium of any system which includes a brain, there is a compelling reason for defining death in factual terms as that state of affairs in which there is complete and irreversible loss of the functioning of the entire brain. To accept this definition is not to make a choice based on one's evaluation of various human characteristics, but is to assent to a theory which fits the facts....

"Without any change in the definition of death there has been a shift in the criteria for determining death."

If death can be correctly defined in factual terms as the complete and irreversible loss of the functioning of the entire brain, then this definition can be accepted and translated into operational and legal terms without any radical shifts in meaning, arbitrary stipulations or subjective evaluations. The problem which gave rise to the debate about the definition of death can be settled, and a good reason given for not proceeding to some other definition, proposed not to resolve vagueness but rather to alter the boundary of legal personhood in cases in which it has always been and still remains perfectly clear.

Redefinition Not Necessary

Thus if one defines death in terms of the loss of all brain functions, this is not a redefinition of death at all: It is a clarification of what actually happens in what has always been known as death. This clarification makes any redefinition of death unnecessary and exposes attempts at such redefinition as what they are: attempts to redefine and relativize the value of human life when it cannot exercise all the higher faculties.

A similar point is made by Dennis J. Horan, an attorney who is president of Americans United for Life. His starting point is slightly different, however. He begins with the traditional criteria for determining death and suggests that physicians have always implicitly used some notion of brain death in medical practice.

The traditional criteria rely on a prolonged cessation of respiratory and circulatory function, but

this cessation of vital functions is in fact linked to brain death in two ways. First, since the brainstem is the organ which integrates respiration and other spontaneous life-sustaining functions, the loss of spontaneous respiration and circulation is sometimes due to loss of brainstem function; second, since the brain will die within minutes of being deprived of oxygen under ordinary circumstances, the loss of respiration and circulation (from whatever cause) virtually assured death within minutes in an era which did not have artificial respirators for the continued oxygenation of the brain.

Shift in Criteria

After the development of artificial respirators physicians continued to diagnose death on the basis of respiratory and circulatory failure in most cases, but they knew that not all cessation of these functions assured death. Some patients who had stopped breathing could be revived and artificially sustained until they could resume spontaneous breathing, and patients with no pulse or heartbeat could be resuscitated if medical treatment were immediately available.

Therefore, claims Horan, without any change in the definition of death there has been a shift in the criteria for determining death. Patients are now considered dead only if there is *irreversible* cessation of (spontaneous) respiratory and circulatory functions. Furthermore, this irreversibility is often determined by asking whether these functions have ceased for a long enough period of time to assure the death of the brain through lack of oxygen.

The only problem here is with patients who have already been placed on respirators. What if a physician artificially forces air through the lungs of an unconscious patient by means of a respirator, but then finds that the patient's brain was already dead before the respirator was started or has stopped functioning at some point afterward? Horan claims that such a patient is already dead (in the sense that we have always meant the word "dead"), that the respirator is now simply delaying the inevitable process of decomposition by oxygenating the individual organs which remain alive. The reason why we now need determination-of-death legislation, Horan argues further, is not because brain-oriented criteria require a redefinition of death, but because the invalid linkage of this issue with the euthanasia issue has resulted in legislative abuses which must be fought legislatively.

"As Good as Dead"

Pro-life advocates for this view of brain death argue that it fundamentally differs from all ideologies which identify death with the cessation of cerebral function or the loss of the ability to engage in social interaction. Such ideologies do intend to redefine death in accordance with a quality-of-life ethic which tends to see as subhuman or as non-persons those who cannot exercise the higher functions.

For the proponents of such ideologies a brain-damaged individual is "as good as dead" although obviously not biologically dead. The viewpoint sketched above, on the other hand, recognizes that death occurs only with the irreversible loss of those functions which maintain the human being as a biological organism (that is, as an integrated whole rather than a mere collection of organs). Until this point, a patient may be terminally ill and even irreversibly comatose, but is still an individual who has full human dignity and rights. Thus there are two completely different reasons why artificial life-support techniques may sometimes be discontinued: with the consent of the patient or his family one may discontinue extraordinary treatment which will be of no benefit; or one may find that the patient is already dead, despite the artificial maintaining of the life of individual organs, and therefore discontinue treatment of a corpse as a matter of common sense.

The attempts of euthanasia advocates to confuse these two situations and redefine comatose patients as dead have cast a pall over what many see as legitimate attempts to update the means for diagnosing death.

When Life Begins

The line of argument proposed by Grisez, Boyle, Horan and others is also consistent with a recognition that each human life comes into existence at conception. This has not always been clear in the public debate. Ill-informed observers, some of them physicians, have claimed that if life ends with the death of the brain, it must begin only with the formation of the brain at approximately the eighth week after conception. This argument is invalid because the line of argument sketched above proposes that a member of the human species is alive as long as he or she performs the vital functions of circulation, respiration, etc. in an integrated fashion.

In the adult human being, one can argue that the brain is the integrating center for these vital functions to such an extent that its destruction coincides with the disintegration of the human organism into separate organs and organ systems; but the human organism performs its vital functions in an integrated fashion long before the brain is sufficiently developed to take over this integrating role. The human embryo is not a mere collection of protoplasm, but a thriving, integrated human organism at an early stage of development and therefore cannot plausibly be excluded from the category of human life simply because the requisite functions are organized by structures other than the brain.

At the level of medical practice, in fact, brain-death criteria are not often applied to very young children already born, because the child's brain reacts differently to trauma and resumes lost functions

more easily than the adult brain, yet these children cannot be described as not having human life. Any inconsistency here seems to lie with physicians and medical organizations which subscribe to the brain-death concept as described above, but deny that prenatal existence is part of the continuum of human life.

Minority View

While the approach of Grisez et al. is endorsed by the majority of medical-moral experts in the Catholic community, there is some dissent. The minority view has been most forcefully expressed by pediatrician Paul Byrne, philosopher Paul Quay and neurologist Sean O'Reilly, who have collaborated on several articles discussing this issue. This position, like the position to which it is opposed, can be considered at two levels: the level of philosophical reflection and the level of clinical practice.

The gist of the more abstract argument advanced by Byrne et al. is that the brain simply cannot be described as the integrating center for the vital functions of the body. Rather, the body's functioning involves a complex interaction of at least three organ systems—central nervous, circulatory and respiratory —no one of which is on a different plane from the others. If one of these systems is destroyed, this may initiate a dying process which is irreversible (at least under current medical knowledge and practice), but the patient is not dead until the other two systems have been destroyed. To revert to the words of Pope Pius XII, a brain-dead patient on a respirator is one whose vital functions "manifest themselves...with the help of artificial processes," not one in whom only the "simple life of organs" remains. To assert otherwise, they claim, is to elevate the brain to a status which it does not really have, making it the sole principle of human life and reducing the body's other integrating systems to mere collections of organs. Such an approach virtually equates the brain with the human soul.

"The brain simply cannot be described as the *integrating center for the vital functions of the body."*

This approach insists that the functioning of the human organism is more complex and decentralized than some presentations of brain death recognize. The respirator which helps to ventilate a brain-dead patient does not supplant the brain's integrating function, but simply pushes air into the lungs; exhalation takes place spontaneously, as does respiration at the cellular level. Heartbeat also continues spontaneously as long as the heart receives oxygen, since the brainstem does not direct the heart to beat, but only fine tunes its rate in accordance with the changing needs of the organism. This condition can continue for hours or days—some have claimed weeks or even months—after all observable brain functions have ceased; it is the condition not of a corpse, but of a mortally wounded body which has entered the last stage of the dying process.

"Presumably the brain-death concept would be discredited if a brain-dead patient had ever been found to recover."

Dr. Byrne and his colleagues also point to certain features of clinical practice with regard to brain-dead patients. Before the advent of the brain-death concept, the signs of death were clear to any physician: prolonged absence of pulse and heartbeat, fixed and dilated pupils, and so on. These events still occur, regardless of artificial life-support systems, at some point *after* observable brain functions have ceased (usually within a day or two). Between the time brain death is diagnosed and the time that vital functions break down, the patient breathes with artificial assistance, remains warm, has a pulse and is capable of developing conditions such as bed sores and pneumonia. Brain-dead patients are even prepared for the removal of their vital organs with the injection of a paralyzing drug, because spinal and other reflexes which remain would cause too much movement for transplant surgery to be feasible otherwise. Surely, they argue, one patient cannot die twice. If brain death is really death, then what is the state of a body on a respirator which, after spending hours or days in this condition, begins showing all the traditional signs of "death"? They suggest that only the second condition, in which circulation and respiration cease despite artificial life support, is really death.

Dr. Byrne's critics have replied that the residual functions to which he points are not significant, that without the integrating function of the brain they can no longer be considered as activities within a unified organism. Debate has continued on such points for several years, but it is increasingly clear that neither of the two positions under debate is a simple empirical claim which can be proved or disproved by an experimental study.

Assuming, for example, that brain-dead patients can (as some claim) be maintained for several weeks on life-support equipment, does this suggest that the human organism *can* function in an integrated fashion even after brain death (as Byrne *et al.* would claim)? Or does it show that we can keep the organs of a corpse alive and oxygenated for a considerable period after death, and therefore that legislation is needed to prevent medical resources from being directed to the mere delay of putrefaction in dead

patients?

Presumably the brain-death concept would be discredited if a brain-dead patient had ever been found to recover; but both sides in the debate agree that the destruction of the brain is incurable and irreversible. Patients have been known to recover after a diagnosis of brain death, but this has always been attributed to a flaw in the specification criteria used or in the way they were applied—and this could hardly be otherwise, since true brain death is irreversible *by definition.* But the problem of verification here is significant because of the need to "prove" the reliability of the brain-death concept "with certainty" (again using the words of Pius XII). One cannot be satisfied with the level of certainty characteristic of most medical theories and diagnoses because of the stakes involved. Vital organs are sometimes removed from brain-dead patients even before heartbeat and respiration have ceased, and this would be morally unacceptable if the patient were not truly dead.

Perhaps more disturbing is the evidence that even some medical professionals who favor legal approval of brain-oriented criteria to determine death share Dr. Byrne's skepticism as to whether brain death can be equated with the death of the human organism. Some of this evidence is attributable to ignorance, as when newspaper accounts refer to brain-dead patients as having "died" shortly after artificial life-support was removed. Even this careless use of language by journalists, however, indicates continued public confusion over a standard for determining death which runs counter to some common-sense intuitions. Much more serious are statements in professional publications such as the following:

1) The final report on brain death issued by the President's Commission for the Study of Ethical Problems admits that the "prevailing British viewpoint" considers tests for the cessation of brain function as "prognostic" tools (informing the physician that the "point of no return" has been reached in the dying process) rather than "diagnostic" tools (informing him that death has already occurred). Thus the Conference of the Royal Colleges and Faculties of the United Kingdom uses the absence of brain functions as a sign that support may be withdrawn, not necessarily as a sign that the patient is a corpse.

Professional Reservations

2) The same report of the president's commission notes that the Harvard criteria of 1968 offered "a definition of irreversible coma," along with a recommendation that irreversible coma be equated with death. The commission suggests that irreversible coma is simply a misleading phrase, that in fact "all individuals that meet 'Harvard criteria' are dead." Yet according to newspaper accounts, one of the authors of the Harvard criteria recently announced

that these criteria needed revising. Speaking at a conference on brain death, Dr. William Sweet noted that no one was ever known to regain consciousness after fulfilling these criteria, but claimed that they invalidly confused irreversible coma with the different condition of brain death. The medical literature offers evidence of several current conceptualizations of brain death, not all of which are clearly different from a simple state of vegetative coma.

3) In the editorial section of a major medical journal, Dr. Norman Fost recently commented on an article detailing research performed on a brain-dead patient. Fost distinguished between "patients whose brains have ceased to function but who are alive in most other respects" and patients who are "dead in the total sense." He went on to say:

A complete summary and refutation of the arguments equating brain death with death is beyond the scope of this commentary, but a few observations should be made. Although it is widely accepted that brain death is a valid indicator for discontinuing medical care, the reason is not necessarily because the patient is dead, but because the patient no longer has any interest in being maintained. In this sense brain death might simply be another in a long list of medical problems which make medical care pointless from the patient's and family's perspective. Other experiences and intuitions suggest that death of the brain is not the same as death in the traditional sense. A headless animal is clearly not dead on that basis alone. We would not feel right about burying someone with a beating heart even though he were brain dead. Brain death appears to be a critical juncture in the complicated process which constitutes death of the organism, but by itself it is not equal to death.

Dr. Fost concludes that there are good reasons for treating brain-dead patients differently from the way we treat either the clearly living or the clearly dead—e.g., their organs may be "harvested," "provided proper consent has been obtained," but there should be limitations on research using such patients.

Brain Dead, Somatically Alive?

4) Some remarkable comments along these lines were recently made by the editors of the Journal of the American Medical Association, an organization which supports the UDDA [Uniform Definition of Death Act]. The editors were commenting on an article detailing efforts to maintain a brain-dead pregnant woman on life-support equipment in order to deliver her child when it reached viability:

It has been known for some time that brain-dead patients, suitably maintained, can breathe, circulate blood, digest food, filter waste, maintain body temperature, generate new tissue and fulfill other functions as well. All of this is remarkable in a 'corpse.' Granted, these functions could not be maintained without artificial aid and, even so, will cease within a few weeks. However, many living patients depend on machines and will not live long; they are not thereby classified as (already) dead.

Now we are told that a brain-dead patient can nurture a child in the womb, which permits live birth several weeks 'post-mortem.' Perhaps this is the straw that breaks the conceptual camel's back. It becomes irresistible to speak of brain-dead patients being 'somatically alive' (what sort of 'non-somatic death' is the implied alternative?) of being 'terminally ill,' and eventually of 'dying.' These are different ways of saying that such patients (or at least their bodies) are alive. The death of the brain seems not to serve as a boundary; it is a tragic, ultimately fatal loss, but not death itself. Bodily death occurs later, when integrated functioning ceases.

> "Although it is widely accepted that brain death is a valid indicator for discontinuing medical care, the reason is not necessarily because the patient is dead."

We should clarify and delimit our claim. Clinicians who find it congenial to speak of brain-dead patients as 'terminally ill' (and the like) do not, in our interpretation, really view the bodies of these patients as dead. We endorse the view implicit in their use of these terms: The kind of functioning reported in these cases is that of bodies that are biologically alive. It must be emphasized, however, that these judgments apply to 'alive' and 'dead' as categories of biomedical science. Law and morality raise separate questions. In particular, we may hold, in all consistency, the *moral* view that brain-dead bodies ought not be maintained (except in unusual circumstances, such as those in these case reports). We may also endorse a brain-death law as a solution to a *legal* problem of liability and uncertainty. However, confusion and double-talk will persist unless these moral and legal issues are clearly distinguished from those of medical classification.

Legal Fiction

These editors seem to agree with the rejection of the brain-death concept by Byrne *et al.*, but then accept the concept as a legal fiction in order to facilitate organ transplants and protect physicians from legal liability. The idea that "law and morality" should define biologically alive but dying human beings as "dead" for reasons of social utility is, of course, completely unacceptable to both advocates and opponents of brain-death legislation within the pro-life movement.

To be sure, these statements are offset by others in the medical literature, in which brain death is clearly distinguished from irreversible coma and reasonable arguments are advanced for equating brain death with the genuine biological death of the human organism. But continuing disagreement on this point suggests that the consensus necessary for a law defining death might not exist. It is even more disturbing that some physicians claim that brain death is *not* death, but also claim that it should be equated with it for legal purposes. This approach suggests the same unacceptable quality-of-life ethic which redefines the unborn child as having something other than human life....

The Legislative Question

The opposition of the Committee for Pro-Life Activities to all definition-of-death statutes, aside from any doubts on philosophical or medical matters, has centered on the inappropriateness of *legislating* on such issues at all. There was thought to be no clear and legitimate motive for placing this topic in the legislative arena because there has never been a statutory definition of death in the United States and new criteria for diagnosing death would presumably win acceptance within the medical profession if they were medically valid.

Some of the support for legislation on the determination of death (and especially for new legislation on a definition of death) seemed to be motivated by non-medical concerns and especially by the concerns of death-with-dignity advocates who considered terminally ill and comatose patients as having useless or meaningless lives. Advocates of legalized euthanasia were in fact involved in the drive to make this a legislative issue, and their efforts made it impossible to support modernization of criteria for determining death without seeming to support a redefinition of death based on a quality-of-life ethic. Even in states where fairly restrictive laws were enacted, there was thought to be some danger that later amendments would covertly legalize a form of euthanasia. It was judged to be safer and more consistent (both logically and rhetorically) to oppose all introduction of legislation in this area whatever.

This situation has changed substantially in the last few years to such an extent that some strong advocates of a sanctity-of-life ethic claim compelling reasons for the enactment of brain-death legislation. Of course, those who have philosophical or medical objections to current brain-oriented criteria for determining death oppose all legislation in this area or support legislative proposals of their own—for example, Dr. Paul Byrne advocates legislation which would require destruction of the respiratory, circulatory and central nervous systems before death is declared. But even among those who find the medical and philosophical objections unconvincing,

there are at least three schools of thought on the subject of legislation.

Support for UDDA

Many have urged support for the UDDA, which (as a proposed uniform statute) seems likely to be a focus of attention for some years to come. The PCC [Pennsylvania Catholic Conference] took this stance (with the qualification mentioned earlier), based on its own study of the brain-death issue. Convinced that the brain-death concept is medically and philosophically sound, the PCC supports what it considers a restrictive brain-death statute in order to (a) give legal recognition to modern means for practicing good medicine with regard to the determination of death, and (b) protect comatose patients by preventing any judicial or legislative effort to authorize looser standards for brain death.

The PCC sees its stance as a defense of the sanctity-of-life ethic. Under the UDDA, it argues, only true physiological death of the human organism is defined as death, and this prevents the use of legal fictions to redefine death in accordance with a quality-of-life ethic. The PCC points out that brain-oriented criteria are already used to diagnose death in hospitals (including Catholic hospitals) throughout the country, even in states without brain-death legislation. The question is not whether such criteria will be used, but whether the law will set limits to prevent abuses.

"The concensus necessary for a law defining death might not exist."

The legal services office of the Catholic Health Association agrees that there is little difference in actual medical practice between states with the UDDA and states without it; but it draws a different conclusion from this information. The CHA's report on this issue suggests that there may be little or no need for such laws, and indeed that this may not be an appropriate subject for legislation. In light of recent judicial history and the strong concensus in the medical community in favor of the position advocated by the president's commission, it seems highly unlikely that any court dealing with this matter will accept a standard for brain death less strict than that of the UDDA. Without absolutely opposing legislative efforts, the CHA's report suggests that the education of physicians and the general public on medical and philosophical aspects of brain death is of a higher priority.

Minimal Standards

The third school of thought is that of the MCC [Missouri Catholic Conference]. The MCC sees a clear difference between definition-of-death laws such as the UDDA, which it opposes, and a determination-of-death statute which simply sets *minimal* standards for the medical diagnosis of death. Without denying that patients diagnosed in accordance with the UDDA are really dead, the MCC claims that by the very act of legally defining death as identical with a particular condition—something which our legal system has never done—the UDDA sets a dangerous precedent for laws which may not accord as well with medical fact. Thus the MCC's substitute is proposed as a way of avoiding this problem while meeting the valid concerns which the PCC and others have expressed: the legal recognition of valid medical practice and the protection against unacceptable definitions of death based on a quality-of-life ethic.

"There may be little or no need for [definition of death] laws."

Some state Catholic conferences and other groups endorse none of these three positions, maintaining that the medical and philosophical debates over brain death have not been satisfactorily resolved. These groups argue that the brain-death approach will certainly win legal and social acceptance if it proves to be medically valid and reliable. To endorse legislation in this area would be to substitute a legal definition prematurely for genuine knowledge in a rapidly changing area of research.

In one sense brain death involves questions of fact more directly than it involves moral issues. But the debate on this matter does have clear moral implications for anyone who would defend the dignity of human life during the last stages of the dying process. Among the moral problems raised by the foregoing analysis are the following:

1. If substantial doubt remains concerning the philosophical justification for the very concept of brain death, then endorsement of legislation which approves this concept is inappropriate and the use of the concept by physicians with or without the aid of legislation is cause for serious concern. If what is now called brain death may be only an irreversible stage of terminal illness, then discontinuance of life-support equipment may still be appropriate, but the removal of vital organs prior to the cessation of heartbeat and respiration is morally unacceptable.

2. If the concept of brain death is sound, but the diagnostic criteria currently in use do not reliably test for this condition, a more complex problem arises. Where criteria are of doubtful validity, a sound moral approach demands that the doubt be resolved in favor of life. Theoretically the UDDA should provide a legislative means to prevent the use of inadequate criteria for brain death; and the MCC's alternative

statute makes this restrictive intent even more clear. Yet neither has ever been enforced against physicians and it seems likely that the operative phrase in all such laws is the appeal to "accepted medical standards." The special problem here is that some widely used criteria may have been accepted out of medical ignorance, conceptual confusion or an unacceptable moral stance. The most appropriate action in this area might be further research and education on the issue, with public criticism (where necessary) of medical standards in this area which seem unproven or unreliable. In the meantime there is some risk that enactment of legislation such as the UDDA will be taken by some physicians as legal authorization for any set of brain-death criteria that has been advocated in the medical literature.

3. Even if the concept of brain death and the criteria for determining it are found to be valid, an additional problem is suggested by some of the literature quoted above. Some physicians and medical organizations apparently believe that brain death is not true biological death, but they support the UDDA as a useful legal fiction nevertheless. The disturbing implication here is that these physicians are willing to remove the vital organs from patients who they themselves believe (however wrongly) are still alive. As long as this attitude exists, to support a brain-death statute may be to help accustom such physicians to the idea of killing terminally ill patients for utilitarian purposes. There is a great need here for further education. Pro-life physicians who favor brain-death legislation may have to instruct their medical colleagues in the good reasons for supporting what they now support for the wrong reasons. Here also actual endorsement of a statute would seem premature until the educational process has proceeded further.

4. Finally, there are subtle prudential arguments concerning support for or opposition to particular forms of legislation. Is the UDDA a stepping-stone to euthanasia legislation or a bulwark against it? Does it prevent less restrictive brain-death definitions from being approved or set a dangerous precedent for them? It is sufficient here to note that the legal and political experts disagree on such matters and that a compelling need for such legislation has still not been demonstrated.

Because of continuing uncertainty on all these points, the Committee for Pro-Life Activities has decided not to reverse its earlier opposition to definition-of-death legislation.

In 1977, the Committee for Pro-Life Activities submitted a resolution on death and dying to the National Conference of Catholic Bishops. It recommended that the bishops oppose all legislation defining death, legalizing euthanasia, and supporting other death issues. This viewpoint is taken from the Committee's 1983 position paper which updates and reiterates its opposition to such legislation.

"Following a [living will] directive. . .fulfills the instrumental role of self-determination by promoting the patient's subjective, individual evaluation of well-being."

viewpoint**84**

Living Wills Assure Patients' Rights

President's Commission

An "advance directive" lets people anticipate that they may be unable to participate in future decisions about their own health care—an "instruction directive" specifies the types of care a person wants (or does not want) to receive; a "proxy directive" specifies the surrogate a person wants to make such decisions if the person is ever unable to do so; and the two forms may be combined. Honoring such a directive shows respect for self-determination in that it fulfills two of the three values that underlie self-determination. First, following a directive, particularly one that gives specific instructions about types of acceptable and unacceptable interventions, fulfills the instrumental role of self-determination by promoting the patient's subjective, individual evaluation of well-being. Second, honoring the directive shows respect for the patient as a person.

An advance directive does not, however, provide self-determination in the sense of active moral agency by the patient on his or her own behalf. The discussion between patient and health care professional leading up to a directive would involve active participation and shared decisionmaking, but at the point of actual decision the patient is incapable of participating. Consequently, although self-determination is involved when a patient establishes a way to project his or her wishes into a time of anticipated incapacity, it is a sense of self-determination lacking in one important attribute: active, contemporaneous personal choice. Hence a decision not to follow an advance directive may sometimes be justified even when it would not be acceptable to disregard a competent patient's contemporaneous choice. Such a decision would most often rest on a finding that the patient did not adequately envision and consider the particular

President's Commission for the Study of Ethical Problems in Medicine and Biomedical and Behavioral Research, "Deciding to Forego Life-Sustaining Treatment," March 1983.

situation within which the actual medical decision must be made.

Advance directives are not confined to decisions to forego life-sustaining treatment but may be drafted for use in any health care situation in which people anticipate they will lack capacity to make decisions for themselves. However, the best-known type of directive—formulated pursuant to a "natural death" act—does deal with decisions to forego life-sustaining treatment. Beginning with the passage in 1976 of the California Natural Death Act, 14 states and the District of Columbia have enacted statutory authorization for the formulation of advance directives to forego life-sustaining treatment. In addition, 42 states have enacted "durable power of attorney" statutes; though developed in the context of law concerning property, these statutes may be used to provide a legal authority for an advance directive.

Despite a number of unresolved issues about how advance directives should be drafted, given legal effect, and used in clinical practice, the Commission recommends that advance directives should expressly be endowed with legal effect under state law. For such documents to assist decisionmaking, however, people must be encouraged to develop them for their individual use, and health care professionals should be encouraged to respect and abide by advance directives whenever reasonably possible, even without specific legislative authority.

Existing Alternative Documents

Several forms of advance directives are currently used. "Living wills" were initially developed as documents without any binding legal effects; they are ordinarily instruction directives. The intent behind the original "natural death" act was simply to give legal recognition to living wills drafted according to certain established requirements. They are primarily instruction directives, although their terms are poorly enough defined that the physician and surrogate who will carry them out will have to make substantial interpretations. "Durable power of attorney" statutes are primarily proxy directives, although by limiting or describing the circumstances in which they are to operate they also contain elements of instruction directives. Furthermore, durable powers of attorney may incorporate extensive personal instructions.

Living wills. People's concerns about the loss of ability to direct care at the end of their lives have led a number of commentators as well as religious, educational, and professional groups to promulgate documents, usually referred to as living wills, by which individuals can indicate their preference not to be given "heroic" or "extraordinary" treatments. There have been many versions proposed, varying widely in their specificity. Some explictly detailed directives have been drafted by physicians—outlining a litany of treatments to be foregone or disabilities they would not wish to suffer in their final days. The model living wills proposed by educational groups have somewhat more general language; they typically mention "life-sustaining procedures which would serve only to artificially prolong the dying process." One New York group has distributed millions of living wills. The columnist who writes "Dear Abby" reports receiving tens of thousands of requests for copies each time she deals with the subject. Despite their popularity, their legal force and effect is uncertain. The absence of explicit statutory authorization in most jurisdictions raises a number of important issues that patients and their lawyers or other advisors should keep in mind when drafting living wills.

"Health care professionals should be encouraged to respect and abide by advance directives whenever reasonably possible."

First, it is uncertain whether health care personnel are required to carry out the terms of a living will; conversely, those who, in good faith, act in accordance with living wills are not assured immunity from civil or criminal prosecution. No penalties are provided for the destruction, concealment, forgery or other misuse of living wills, which leaves them somewhat vulnerable to abuse. The question of whether a refusal of life-sustaining therapy constitutes suicide is unresolved, as are the insurance implications of a patient's having died as a result of a physician's withholding treatment pursuant to a living will.

Yet even in states that have not enacted legislation to recognize and implement advance directives, living wills may still have some legal effect. For example,

should a practitioner be threatened with civil liability or criminal prosecution for having acted in accord with such a document, it should at least serve as evidence of a patient's wishes and assessment of benefit when he or she was competent. Indeed, no practitioner has been successfully subjected to civil liability or criminal prosecution for having followed the provisions in a living will, nor do there appear to be any cases brought for having acted against one.

Natural death acts. To overcome the uncertain legal status of living wills, 13 states and the District of Columbia have followed the lead set by California in 1976 and enacted statutes that formally establish the requirements for a "directive to physicians." The California statute was labeled a "natural death" act and this term is now used generically to refer to other state statutes. Although well-intended, these acts raise a great many new problems without solving many of the old ones. . . .

Opportunity to Reconsider

Some of the statutes attempt to provide patients with adequate opportunity to reconsider their decision by imposing a waiting period between the time when a patient decides that further treatment is unwanted and the time when the directive becomes effective. Under the California statute, for example, a directive is binding only if it is signed by a "qualified patient," technically defined as someone who has been diagnosed as having a "terminal condition." This is defined as an incurable condition that means death is "imminent" regardless of the "life-sustaining procedures" used. A patient must wait 14 days after being told of the diagnosis before he or she can sign a directive, which would require a miraculous cure, a misdiagnosis, or a very loose interpretation of the word "imminent" in order for the directive to be of any use to a patient. The statute requires that when a directive is signed, the patient must be fully competent and not overwhelmed by disease or by the effects of treatment, but a study of California physicians one year after the new law was enacted found that only about half the patients diagnosed as terminally ill even remain conscious for 14 days. There is an inherent tension between ensuring that dying patients have a means of expressing their wishes about treatment termination before they are overcome by incompetence and ensuring that people do not make binding choices about treatment on the basis of hypothetical rather than real facts about their illness and dying process. If a waiting period is deemed necessary to resolve this tension the time should be defined in a way that does not substantially undercut the objective of encouraging advance directives by people who are at risk of becoming incapacitated.

Although the California statute was inspired in part by the situation of Karen Quinlan, whose father had to pursue judicial relief for a year in order to authorize the removal of her respirator, it would not apply in a case like hers. [A.M. Capron stated in The Development of Law on Human Death that]

> The only patients covered by this statute are those who are on the edge of death *despite the doctors' efforts.* The very people for whom the greatest concern is expressed about a prolonged and undignified dying process are unaffected by the statute because their deaths are not imminent.

The class of persons thus defined by many of the statutes, if it indeed contains any members, at most constitutes a small percentage of those incapacitated individuals for whom decisions about life-sustaining treatment must be made. Although some statutes have not explicitly adopted the requirement that treatments may be withheld or withdrawn only if death is imminent whether or not they are used, this requirement is still found in one of the most recently passed natural death acts. Such a limitation greatly reduces an act's potential.

Some of the patients for whom decisions to forego life-sustaining treatment need to be made are residents of nursing homes rather than hospitals. Concerned that they might be under undue pressure to sign a directive, the California legislature provided additional safeguards for the voluntariness of their directives by requiring that a patient advocate or ombudsman serve as a witness. The Commission believes that health care providers should make reasonable efforts to involve disinterested parties, not only as witnesses to the signing of a directive under a natural death act, but also as counselors to patients who request such a directive to ensure that they are acting as voluntarily and competently as possible. Yet statutory requirements of this sort may have the effect of precluding use of advance directives by long-term care residents, even though some residents of these facilities might be as capable as any other persons of using the procedure in a free and knowing fashion.

Restricting Wishes

Paradoxically, natural death acts may restrict patients' ability to have their wishes about life-sustaining treatment respected. If health care providers view these as the exclusive means for making and implementing a decision to forego treatment and, worse, if they believe that such a decision cannot be made by a surrogate on behalf of another but only in accordance with an advance directive properly executed by a patient, some dying patients may be subject to treatment that is neither desired nor beneficial. In fact, although 6.5% of the physicians surveyed in California reported that during the first year after passage of the act there they withheld or withdrew procedures they previously would have administered, 10% of the physicians reported that they provided treatment they formerly would have withheld.

In addition, there is the danger that people will infer that a patient who has not executed a directive in accordance with the natural death act does not desire life-sustaining treatment to be ended under any circumstances. Yet the person may fail to sign a directive because of ignorance of its existence, inattention to its significance, uncertainty about how to execute one, or failure to foresee the kind of medical circumstances that in fact develop. Unfortunately, even the explicit disclaimer contained in many of these laws—that the act is not intended to impair or supersede any preexisting common-law legal rights or responsibilities that patients and practitioners may have with respect to the withholding or withdrawing of life-sustaining procedures—does not in itself correct this difficulty.

"The greatest value of the natural death act is the impetus they provide for discussions between patients and practitioners about decisions to forego life-sustaining treatment."

First, the declarations about the right of competent patients to refuse "life-sustaining procedures" take on a rather pale appearance since such procedures are defined by the statutes as those that cannot stop an imminent death. (In other words, competent patients may refuse futile treatments.) Second, it is hard to place great reliance on preexisting common law rights, since had the common law established such rights there would have been no real need for the statutes. Thus, if health care providers are to treat patients appropriately in states that have adopted natural death acts, they will need the encouragement of their attorneys—backed by sensible judicial interpretation of the statutes—to read the acts as authorizing a new, additional means for patients to exercise "informed consent" regarding life-saving treatment, but not as a means that limits decision-making of patients who have not executed binding directives pursuant to the act.

The greatest value of the natural death acts is the impetus they provide for discussions between patients and practitioners about decisions to forego life-sustaining treatment. This educational effect might be obtained, however, without making the documents binding by statute and without enforcement and punishment provisions....

Proposed Statutes

Various concerned groups have proposed statutes that might improve upon natural death acts, by being more generally applicable and authorizing proxy designation, as well as upon durable power of attorney statutes, by providing protections and procedures appropriate to health care decisionmaking. . . .

General Considerations in Formulating Legislation. The Commission believes that advance directives are, in general, useful as a means of appropriate decisionmaking about life-sustaining treatment for incapacitated patients. The education of the general public and of health care professionals should be a concern to legislators, as the statutes are ineffective if unknown or misunderstood. Many of the natural death and durable power of attorney statutes are less helpful than they might be. In the drafting or the amending of legislation to authorize advance directives, a number of issues need attention.

Requisites for a valid directive. Some way should be established to verify that the person writing a directive was legally competent to do so at the time. A statute might require evidence that the person has the capacity to understand the choice embodied in the directive when it is executed. The statute should clearly state whether the witnesses that are required attest to the principal's capacity or merely ensure that signatures are not fraudulent. Since such witnesses are likely to be laypeople, the standard of decision-making capacity they apply will rest on common sense, not psychological expertise. Furthermore, the standard they are asked to attest to may be as low as that used in wills, unless specified differently.

"Some way should be established to verify that the person writing a directive was legally competent to do so at the time."

The principal and the prospective proxy should recognize the seriousness of the step being taken, but this will be difficult to guarantee by statute. One way to increase the likelihood that due regard is given to the subject matter would be to provide that before a directive is executed, the principal (and proxy, where one is involved) must have had a discussion with a health care professional about a directive's potential consequences, in light of the principal's values and goals. This would also help ensure that any instructions reflect a process of active self-determination on the part of the patient.

Legal effect of directives. A statute should ensure that people acting pursuant to a valid directive are not subject to civil or criminal liability for any action that would be acceptable if performed on the valid consent of a competent patient. Since directives—particularly those including instructions—may contain unavoidable ambiguities, some recognition of the need for interpretation will be needed to provide

adequate reassurance for health care professionals and proxies. Some of the existing statutes speak of protection for actions taken in "good faith," which provides sensible protection. Some standard of reasonable interpretation of the directive may need to be imposed, however, on an attending physician's reading of the document, lest "good faith" offer too wide a scope for discretion. Such a standard might best be developed in case law and scholarly commentary rather than in the statute itself.

The wisdom or necessity of penalties for non-compliance (fines, for example, or suspension or revocation of professional licenses) depends upon the problem a statute is attempting to remedy. If health care professionals are unwilling to share responsibility with patients and, in particular, tend to overtreat patients whose physical or mental condition leaves them unable to resist, then—unless they are made legally binding—advance directives are unlikely to protect patients who want to limit their treatment. On the other hand, if health care professionals are simply unsure of what patients want, or if they are willing to share decisionmaking responsibility but are apprehensive about their legal liability if they follow the instructions of a person whose decisionmaking capacity is in doubt, then the threat of penalties would be unnecessary and potentially counter-productive by fostering an adversarial relationship between patient and provider. The evidence available at present does not clearly support substantial penalties. . . .

Administrative Aspects

Several procedural concerns probably need to be addressed in any statute for advance health care directives. A statute needs to specify how a directive becomes effective. Some of the natural death acts, as already mentioned, require that a directive be executed after the patient has been informed of a diagnosis, so that the person's instructions are arrived at in the context of the actual, rather than the hypothetical, choices to be made. Some statutes also provide that the directive be renewed every few years so that the signatory can reconsider the instructions or designation in light of changed circumstances or opinions.

The trigger for a valid directive becoming operative also needs to be specified. A statute may leave that question to the document itself, to be specified by the person executing the directive, or it may provide that a particular event or condition brings the document into play. In either case, the triggering event will require both a standard for action and a specification of who will determine that the standard is met. For example, a directive may become operative when a physician makes a particular prognosis ("terminal illness") or determines that a patient lacks decisional capacity regarding a particular health care choice. Provision must be made for the process and standard by which a document can be revoked. The value of self-determination suggests that as long as the principal remains competent, he or she should unquestionably have the power to revoke a directive. But what about an incompetent (incapacitated) person? The natural death acts have uniformly provided that *any* revocation by a principal negates a directive. In the context of foregoing life-sustaining treatment, that result may be sensible, since it would generally seem wrong to cease such treatment based upon a proxy's orders when a patient, no matter how confused, asks that treatment be continued. In other circumstances, however, allowing revocations by an incompetent patient could seriously disrupt a course of treatment authorized by a proxy. When the proxy intends to override the principal's contemporaneous instructions because the incompetent principal is contradicting earlier competent instructions and/or acting contrary to his or her best interests, the question of whether to follow the proxy or the principal may have to be resolved by an independent review.

"Institutions concerned with patient and practitioner education have an important role to play in encouraging patients to become familiar with and use advance directives."

In general, when disputes arise about such things as the choice made by a proxy or an attempted revocation by an apparently incapacitated principal, a review process will be an important safeguard for the patient's interests. In some circumstances the review mechanism need only judge whether the decision-making process was adequate. In other circumstances it may be advisable to review the health care decision itself and the application of the appropriate decisionmaking standard. In the absence of a special provision in the statute, questions of this sort should lead to intrainstitutional review and, as needed, to judicial proceedings.

Conclusions

The Commission commends the use of advance directives. Health care professionals should be familiar with their state's legal mechanisms for implementing advance directives on life-sustaining treatment and encourage patients to use these resources. In particular, practitioners can alert patients to the existence of durable power of attorney devices (in states where they exist) and urge them to discuss their desires about treatment with a proxy decisionmaker. In states without applicable legislation, practitioners can still inform their patients

of the value of making their wishes known, whether through a living will or or more individual instructions regarding the use of life-sustaining procedures under various circumstances.

Institutions concerned with patient and practitioner education have an important role to play in encouraging patients to become familiar with and use advance directives, and in familiarizing practitioners with the ethical and practical desirability of their patients using these mechanisms. Finally, legislators should be encouraged to draft flexible and clear statutes that give appropriate legal authority to those who write and rely upon advance directives. Such legislation needs to balance the provisions aimed at restricting likely abuses and those intended to allow flexibility and individuality for patients and proxies.

The President's Commission for the Study of Ethical Problems in Medicine and Biomedical and Behavioral Research began meeting in January 1980 to determine whether a federal statute defining death was necessary and to formulate such a statute if need was determined. In July 1981 the Commission submitted its report, from which this viewpoint is excerpted.

"The Living Will adds not one cubit to the rights the conscious patient already possesses, and it does...diminish... the patient's rights."

Living Wills Abuse Patients' Rights

Joseph R. Stanton

In late March of this year on a Wednesday morning, my telephone rang. It was a call from a friend in Rhode Island telling me that the "Living Will" bill was to be the subject of hearings that very afternoon before a committee of the state legislature. Having testified two weeks previously before the Massachusetts legislature, I agreed to change my plans for the day, and hurry to Rhode Island and testify. This I did because, as a physician, I believe the issue so very important to Senior Citizens is poorly understood. In the course of a long afternoon of testimony, a group of Senior Citizens appeared and testified. In essence, their message was, "When our time comes, we want to die with dignity—we want the Living Will to be law in this state."

Among many legislators, as also among many eldering citizens, there is a presumption that the Living Will is necessary for "death with dignity." "Death with dignity" is a catchy and appealing phrase, but that presumption is not backed by evidence.

Surely, all of us would like to live and die with dignity. Few of us, given our "druthers", would voluntarily choose prolonged suffering. Although, in fact, many of us have met physical suffering in the course of a lifetime, it is natural to wish for a painless passage when death is in fact inevitable.

Is the Living Will the right thing for Senior Citizens and legislators to support? Does it in fact bring death with dignity? Is it without problems? Is it a panacea to the problems of dying and death, those inevitabilities of human life? Or is it a Trojan horse?

History of "Living Will"

Of interest is the history of the "Living Will" concept. It is the baby of the Society for the Right to Die, Inc. of New York. The Society for the Right to

Die in turn is the offspring of the Euthanasia Educational Council, which in turn was sired by the Euthanasia Society of America.

Fifty-three years ago, in a trial balloon, the Euthanasia Society of America first proposed the direct killing of defective infants at birth.

Indeed, many people are surprised to learn that in the early decades of this century, there was a strong eugenics cult in America. Euthanasia, killing of defectives and those judged to be less than fully human as life was ending, had a substantial number of adherents. Attempts at legislating euthanasia were unsuccessful, however. In the late thirties and early forties, the actual killing of over 270,000 hospital patients termed "useless eaters" in the Third Reich put a quietus on the Euthanasia movement in this country that lasted for almost a quarter of a century.

In the late sixties and seventies, paradoxically, as medical science and the remarkable treatments of open heart surgery and cardio-pulmonary resuscitation have developed, there has been a parallel development of the concept of "death with dignity" and the Living Will.

"Death Control"

Today, we hear discussion both in medical and governmental circles of "Death Control." An editorial titled "A New Ethic for Society and Medicine" in the official journal of the California Medical Society in September, 1970 describes how a new medical attitude toward life is replacing the old Judeao-Christian reverence for human life ethic. It speaks of "Death Control" as follows:

Certainly this has required placing *relative values on human lives* and the impact of the physician to this decision process has been considerable. One may anticipate further development of these roles as the problems of birth control and birth selection are extended inevitably to *death selection and death control whether by the individual or by society*, and further public and professional determinations of when and when not to use scarce resources. (Italics added)

Joseph R. Stanton, "Should Senior Citizens Favor 'Living Will' Legislation? Is the Living Will a Trojan Horse?" Reprinted with permission of the author.

In a memo circulated in the Department of Health, Education and Welfare in 1979, government advocacy of the Living Will was suggested by a top financial analyst of the Department. He suggested pressuring states to pass Living Will legislation and wrote that if the Living Will was in operation in all fifty states that year, the Government could save 1.2 billion dollars. Statistically, the last year of a person's life is medically the most expensive year.

Would doctors ever carry out killing programs in America? A poll in *Modern Medicine* in May of 1976 affords some illumination. To the question, "Faced with a terminal patient whose suffering seems unbearable, can one consider *active euthanasia?*" 17% of the responding doctors replied "yes."

"No law can create dignity in dying by legislative fiat or Living Will."

Further, in the July/August, 1974 issue of *The Humanist*, there appeared an article by Thomas Furlow, M.D., "The Tyranny of Technology—A Physician Looks at Euthanasia." He writes, "At any event, the ideal agent for *active euthanasia* must be swift in action, highly lethal, and painless or even pleasurable if the patient is sentient. Particularly suited for euthanasia are the opiate analgesics (such as morphine), hypnotics (such as barbiturates), cardiac toxins (such as digitalis, potassium chloride), and paralyzing drugs (such as curare, succinyl choline). The first two groups would be most appropriate for awake patients, and the latter for mentally obtunded or comatose patients." Dr. Furlow was describing killing patients.

Euthanasia Increasingly Favored

Increasingly, articles and books favorable to euthanasia appear in the press. A doctor in England recently published a book detailing many acts of euthanasia, as reported in the *Boston Globe* 11/8/74. "The whole affair was conducted without fuss and was so civilized." Thus did Dr. George B. Marr of London, England explain the procedure of administering euthanasia by an injection of evipan (a barbiturate). He said in a telephone interview that it was "impossible" to estimate how many patients he has killed through euthanasia in his long career, but indicated the number was huge. "One gets a Freudian blackout on such an unpleasant activity."

I believe the dangers of the Living Will—the existence of the concept of "unwanted life" and "vegetables" as applied to human beings in our society—opens the doors to probable abuse of living wills. How paradoxical it would be if a Senior Citizen with a reversible condition was not treated just because he or she was old and had signed twenty years before a "Living Will." Yet, honest doctors will admit that all too often the first question asked by young doctors and nurses today when anybody over 60 is admitted to the hospital is, "Is she resuscitable if something unexpected happens?"

No Additional Rights

Every conscious patient presently possesses the right to accept or reject medical treatment and to retain or discharge his doctor. The Living Will adds not one cubit to the rights the conscious patient already possesses, and it does, in fact I believe, diminish and obfuscate the patient's rights. Living Wills may preclude for the conscious patient the right to informed consent. No one can make an intelligent decision to give informed consent in advance of unknown events. A Living Will requires consent to medical treatment or cessation of it before the patient has any idea of what the illness or condition may be, or what treatment may or may not be medically advisable. If that is an advance in patient "rights", its magic eludes me. The Living Will does nothing for the conscious patient.

For the mentally incompetent or unconscious patient, the Living Will is unnecessary to prevent patient suffering—unconscious patients are beyond suffering. Further, it is not good medical treatment to treat a patient with extraordinary means when the patient is dying and beyond hope.

Additionally, the Living Will gives legal immunity to the doctor for any action taken after the patient is certified as "terminally ill," unless the doctor is subsequently proved guilty of negligence. This would change the thrust of the law in a dangerous way.

At an hour when the time-honored sanctity of life ethic is under strong challenge by a quality of life ethic, the Living Will plays into the hands of those who seek the power of death control. The Sanctity of Life ethic has been the touchstone of that bond of trust between impaired patient and caring physician across recorded history. The Living Will does violence to that sacred relationship, and ultimately, it imperils both the patient and those charged with caring for the sick, the suffering and the dying.

No law can create dignity in dying by legislative fiat or Living Will. A dignified death is a phenomenon that comes most often to the human person who has lived well and who, in dying, is so cared for and with such compassionate concern, that he or she never loses the dignity inherent in the human person. It is the living, not the dying, who most often bring dignity to death.

Conscious patients and their families already possess the rights that the Living Will purports to bestow on them. The Living Will gives them nothing. However innocently offered or well-meant, the Living Will changes the thrust of the law, and does so in a potentially dangerous way.

Part of the Living Will for conscious patients depends on telling the patient he or she is "terminal." This would constitute a monstrous injustice that would adversely affect the care of many patients. It could remove hope, that inestimable asset which so often helps patients to beat incredible odds, or bear with grace and fortitude what you or I might find burdensome.

Medicine, today, is not a precise science, and prognostication is the most fallible of all the medical arts. Frankly, doctors are often wrong—well-meaning and careful, but wrong. Mistakes occur both in diagnosis and treatment. There are patients who have been given hopeless prognoses and who have lived; there are patients who have been assured, "you are perfectly all right," who have died. There are patients who have beaten incredible odds and have survived.

Living Wills speak of "no reasonable chance of recovery." Who defines what a reasonable chance is? The published data on cardiac resuscitation in cardiac arrest show a 19% chance of leaving the hospital. Is this "a reasonable chance of survival"? Supposing it was only 1% chance of survival? Forty-five years ago, when it was quite unusual, I walked out of an iron lung. I am surely delighted that no committee debated whether I had a *reasonable* chance of survival before caring people slipped me into that iron lung, or I would not presently write these lines.

"Terminal"

What will doctors inflict on conscious patients if they are obliged to tell them they are "terminal," as the Living Will would require? An editorial in the *Journal of the American Medical Association*, January 9, 1978, titled "Who Says It Is Terminal?" considers this. The Editor writes:

> Patients with advanced cancer are subjected to no greater cruelty than when referred to as having "terminal" cancer, or being a "terminal cancer patient." It is unjust to continue to use this term, which distorts the truth about cancer in an era when so much can be offered to these patients.
>
> Patients whose conditions are called terminal undergo severe emotional stress, and decisions are made on the assumption that death is imminent. However, many patients once so unjustly labeled have been successfully treated, resulting in prolonged survival and even cure.
>
> Physicians do not have the skill to predict accurately the course of events in the progress of cancer. Prediction of survival time in individual patients is rarely possible. Patients with advanced or metastatic cancer may eventually reach a state where no further definitive anti-cancer therapy is available, but with appropriate supportive therapies, long-term survival occurs.

Again, consider what Professor Donald. S. Kornfeld, M.D., Professor of Psychiatry at Columbia Presbyterian Hospital, New York, wrote, answering Sissela Bok in the *New York Times*, Tuesday, May 16, 1978.

> Mrs. Bok wants to make a case for telling "the truth," which suggests that physicians in fact know "the truth"; that we can tell someone, as they do on television, "I'm sorry, my dear, you have only six months to live." Unfortunately, medicine has not reached that stage of sophistication for any given patient. Outcome statistics for a sample of 100 patients do not provide any individual patient with the truth regarding his own outcome.
>
> However, to assume, even were "the truth" known, that all patients want that kind of truth, or would benefit from it, is a dangerous generalization. I have spoken to many patients who have been told "the truth," and have chosen to deny it. I have known others who have been told "the truth," and become depressed or anxious to the point where their last days, months or years were spent in terror of death. And, of course, there were those who have heard "the truth," and benefited from this knowledge, living out their days the better for having known it.
>
> What is needed is optimal understanding by physicians of the emotional needs of each patient and the ability to meet those needs. The art of medicine is the ability of a physician to know what psychological approach would be best for each of his patients. To suggest that we lay down arbitrary rules runs counter to the very plea for individual rights made by the author.

Dangers of "Passive Euthanasia"

The Living Will is advocated by some as "passive euthanasia," a conscious detoxification of the word "euthanasia." The greatest danger associated with well meaning legislation of this kind is that *once the concept of "passive euthanasia," implicit in present Living Wills, is codified in the law, there is danger that without any other action by the legislature, imperceptibly, the medical profession may move to acts of direct euthanasia.* The record of history on this point is not altogether reassuring. That danger should never be underestimated or discounted. Hitler did not order doctors to kill—he simply made it possible, and according to the Nuremberg trial data, 270,000 died.

"Patients with advanced cancer are subjected to no greater cruelty than when referred to as having 'terminal' cancer, or being a 'terminal cancer patient.'"

I do not believe that encoding Living Wills on the law books of any state in this nation is necessary, nor is it in the interest of either the state or of its impaired citizens, most particularly those on whose back the sun of life shines, and who are burdened with illness or approaching death. No doctor is presently required to invoke extraordinary measures to sustain life when death is imminent. The Living Will makes presumptions unwarranted by facts. It oversimplifies in what it promises. It does not add to conscious patients' rights. It is open to abuse. It diminishes the rights of the unconscious and the impaired.

In proposing a title for this article, I raised the question, "Is The Living Will a Trojan Horse?" Virgil recorded the fact that the Greeks, finding it impossible to overcome the battlements and walls of Troy constructed a gigantic wooden horse. Hidden within were Greek soldiers. The horse was left before the gates of Troy, and the Greeks withdrew. The curious Trojans dragged the horse through the gates and into the city. In the still of the night when Troy was asleep, the Greeks came out of the horse's belly, opened the city gates, and allowed the returning enemy army to enter and destroy the city.

"I believe the dangers of the Living Will—the existence of the concept of 'unwanted life' and 'vegetables' as applied to human beings. . . .—opens the doors to probable abuse of living wills."

Today, the words "meaningful," "wanted," and "cognizant and sapient" increasingly enter into public discourse as to whether a human life shall enjoy the protection of the law. Courts are increasingly allowing suits for "wrongful life." The word "vegetable" is not infrequently applied to human beings. The Supreme Court, in Diamond v. Chakrabarty, June 16, 1980, upheld the Court of Customs and Patent Appeals decision that a living thing may be patented. In the upheld Appeals Court decision is the bald statement that "life is largely chemistry." "We think," the patent appeals court said (Bergy, Coats and Malik in re Chakrabarty, 3/29/79), "the fact that micro-organisms are alive is a distinction without legal significance and that they should be treated no differently from chemical compounds."

Into a maelstrom such as presently exists in the American legal system with regard to questions of life and death, and wantedness, cognition and sapience, and quality of life, those of us who share the belief that each human life, no matter how young or old, perfect or imperfect, is the priceless and irreplaceable gift of God, we had best keep awake through the long night lest in enshrining in the law "Living Wills" and "Death with Dignity," we create a Trojan horse, which changes the roles of doctors and nurses from carers to evaluators of the quality of life, technicians deciding who shall live and who shall die.

Joseph R. Stanton, M.D., is a governing member of the Value of Life Committee Inc., a right to life organization.

Living Wills: A Model Bill

Yale Law School, Legislative Services Project

The following Model Bill was drafted at Yale Law School in a Legislative Services Project sponsored by the Society for the Right to Die. The use of * and ** is to indicate alternatives.

1. Purpose

The Legislature finds that adult persons have the fundamental right to control the decisions relating to the rendering of their own medical care, including the decision to have life-sustaining procedures withheld or withdrawn in instances of a terminal condition.

In order that the rights of patients may be respected even after they are no longer able to participate actively in decisions about themselves, the Legislature hereby declares that the laws of the State of _____ shall recognize the right of an adult person to make a written declaration instructing his physician to withhold or withdraw life-sustaining procedures in the event of a terminal condition.

2. Definitions

The following definitions shall govern the construction of this act:

(a) "Attending physician" means the physician selected by, or assigned to, the patient who has primary responsibility for the treatment and care of the patient.

(b) "Declaration" means a witnessed document in writing, voluntarily executed by the declarant in accordance with the requirements of Section 3 of this act.

(c) "Life-sustaining procedure" means any medical procedure or intervention which, when applied to a qualified patient, would serve only to prolong the dying process and where, in the judgment of the attending physician, death will occur whether or not

such procedures are utilized. "Life-sustaining procedure" shall not include the administration of medication or the performance of any medical procedure deemed necessary to provide comfort care.

(d) "Qualified patient" means a patient who has executed a declaration in accordance with this act and who has been diagnosed and certified in writing to be afflicted with a terminal condition by two physicians who have personally examined the patient, one of whom shall be the attending physician.

3. Execution of Declaration

Any adult person may execute a declaration directing the withholding or withdrawal of life-sustaining procedures in a terminal condition. The declaration shall be signed by the declarant in the presence of two subscribing witnesses *(who are not) **(no more than one of whom may be) (a) related to the declarant by blood or marriage, (b) entitled to any portion of the estate of the declarant under any will of declarant or codicil thereto then existing or, at the time of the declaration, by operation of law then existing, (c) a claimant against any portion of the estate of the declarant, or (d) directly financially responsible for the declarant's medical care.

It shall be the responsibility of declarant to provide for notification to his attending physician of the existence of the declaration. An attending physician who is so notified shall make the declaration, or a copy of the declaration, a part of the declarant's medical records.

The declaration shall be substantially in the following form, but in addition may include other specific directions. Should any of the other specific directions be held to be invalid, such invalidity shall not affect other directions of the declaration which can be given effect without the invalid direction, and to this end the directions in the declaration are severable.

Yale Law School, Legislative Services Project, "Medical Treatment Decision Act," from *Handbook of Enacted Laws.* Reprinted with permission of The Society for the Right to Die, 250 West 57th Street, New York, NY 10107, 212-246-6973.

DECLARATION

Declaration made this _____ day of _____ (month, year). I, _____, being of sound mind, willfully and voluntarily make known my desire that my dying shall not be artificially prolonged under the circumstances set forth below, do hereby declare:

If at any time I should have an incurable injury, disease, or illness certified to be a terminal condition by two physicians who have personally examined me, one of whom shall be my attending physician, and the physicians have determined that my death will occur whether or not life-sustaining procedures are utilized and where the application of life-sustaining procedures would serve only to artificially prolong the dying process, I direct that such procedures be withheld or withdrawn, and that I be permitted to die naturally with only the administration of medication or the performance of any medical procedure deemed necessary to provide me with comfort care.

In the absence of my ability to give directions regarding the use of such life-sustaining procedures, it is my intention that this declaration shall be honored by my family and physician(s) as the final expression of my legal right to refuse medical or surgical treatment and accept the consequences from such refusal.

I understand the full import of this declaration and I am emotionally and mentally competent to make this declaration.

Signed _____

City, County and State of Residence

_____

The declarant has been personally known to me and I believe him or her to be of sound mind.

Witness _____

Witness _____

4. Revocation

A declaration may be revoked at any time by the declarant, without regard to his or her mental state or competency, by any of the following methods:

(a) By being canceled, defaced, obliterated, or burnt, torn, or otherwise destroyed by the declarant or by some person in his or her presence and by his or her direction.

(b) By a written revocation of the declarant expressing his or her intent to revoke, signed and dated by the declarant. The attending physician shall record in the patient's medical record the time and date when he or she received notification of the written revocation.

(c) By a verbal expression by the declarant of his or her intent to revoke the declaration. Such revocation shall become effective upon communication to the attending physician by the declarant or by a person who is reasonably believed to be acting on behalf of the declarant. The attending physician shall record in the patient's medical record the time, date and place of the revocation and the time, date, and place, if different, of when he or she received notification of the revocation.

5. Physician's Responsibility: Written Certification

An attending physician who has been notified of the existence of a declaration executed under this act shall, without delay after the diagnosis of a terminal condition of the declarant, take the necessary steps to provide for written certification and confirmation of the declarant's terminal condition, so that declarant may be deemed to be a qualified patient, as defined in Section 1(d) of this act.

> *"Any adult person may execute a declaration directing the withholding or withdrawal of life-sustaining procedures in a terminal condition."*

An attending physician who fails to comply with this section shall be deemed to have refused to comply with the declaration and shall be liable as specified in Section 7(a).

6. Physician's Responsibility and Immunities

The desires of a qualified patient who is competent shall at all times supersede the effect of the declaration.

If the qualified patient is incompetent at the time of the decision to withhold or withdraw life-sustaining procedures, a declaration executed in accordance with Section 3 of this act is presumed to be valid. For the purpose of this act, a physician or health care facility may presume in the absence of actual notice to the contrary that an individual who executed a declaration was of sound mind when it was executed. The fact of an individual's having executed a declaration shall not be considered as an indication of the declarant's mental incompetency. *(Age of itself shall not be a bar to a determination of competency.)

In the absence of actual notice of the revocation of the declaration, none of the following, when acting in accordance with the requirements of this act, shall be subject to civil liability therefrom, unless negligent, or shall be guilty of any criminal act or of unprofessional conduct:

(a) A physician or health facility which causes the withholding or withdrawal of life-sustaining procedures from a qualified patient.

(b) A licensed health professional, acting under the

direction of a physician, who participates in the withholding or withdrawal of life-sustaining procedures.

7. Penalties

(a) An attending physician who refuses to comply with the declaration of a qualified patient pursuant to this act shall make the necessary arrangements to effect the transfer of the qualified patient to another physician who will effectuate the declaration of the qualified patient. An attending physician who fails to comply with the declaration of a qualified patient or to make the necessary arrangements to effect the transfer shall be civilly liable.

(b) Any person who willfully conceals, cancels, defaces, obliterates, or damages the declaration of another without such declarant's consent or who falsifies or forges a revocation of the declaration of another shall be civilly liable.

(c) Any person who falsifies or forges the declaration of another, or willfully conceals or withholds personal knowledge of a revocation as provided in Section 4, with the intent to cause a withholding or withdrawal of life-sustaining procedures contrary to the wishes of the declarant, and thereby, because of such act, directly causes life-sustaining procedures to be withheld or withdrawn and death to thereby be hastened, shall be subject to prosecution for unlawful homicide.

8. General Provisions

(a) The withholding or withdrawal of life-sustaining procedures from a qualified patient in accordance with the provisions of this act shall not, for any purpose, constitute a suicide.

"An attending physician who refuses to comply with the declaration of a qualified patient. . .[shall transfer] the qualified patient to another physician who will effectuate the declaration."

(b) The making of a declaration pursuant to Section 3 shall not affect in any manner the sale, procurement, or issuance of any policy of life insurance, nor shall it be deemed to modify the terms of an existing policy of life insurance. No policy of life insurance shall be legally impaired or invalidated in any manner by the withholding or withdrawal of life-sustaining procedures from an insured qualified patient, notwithstanding any term of the policy to the contrary.

(c) No physician, health facility, or other health provider, and no health care service plan, insurer issuing disability insurance, self-insured employee welfare benefit plan, or non-profit hospital plan, shall require any person to execute a declaration as a condition for being insured for, or receiving, health care services.

(d) Nothing in this act shall impair or supersede any legal right or legal responsibility which any person may have to effect the withholding or withdrawal of life-sustaining procedures in any lawful manner. In such respect the provisions of this act are cumulative.

(e) This act shall create no presumption concerning the intention of an individual who has not executed a declaration to consent to the use or withholding of life-sustaining procedures in the event of a terminal condition.

(f) If any provision of this act or the application thereof to any person or circumstances is held invalid, such invalidity shall not affect other provisions or applications of the act which can be given effect without the invalid provision or application, and to this end the provisions of this act are severable.

This model bill is being used by numerous state legislatures as an aid in drafting their own natural death statutes.

"We must come to recognize...that the funeral director has been, and is, an important caregiver in the American community."

Funeral Directors Serve the Community

Robert Fulton

In discussing the role of the caretaker of the dead, I think one should first be aware of a certain level of anticipation or even of anxiety that such a discussion generates. I think this is part and parcel of a general tension that is evident when such issues as death and dying are raised. Despite the belief that we have lifted the veil on this taboo topic, there is nevertheless a certain reluctance or uneasiness in addressing it openly.

General avoidance or denial of death, however, is often matched by a strong desire to probe and inquire into all the different aspects of the subject. My mother exemplified this ambivalence toward death as well as anyone. She used to nag my father about preparing his will, for example. On one occasion I overheard her say "Ed, put your paper down; I want to talk about something. We have avoided discussing our deaths long enough. Ed," she said, "whichever one of us dies first, I think I will go live in Florida."

There is a general reluctance to deal with the issues of dying and death, particularly as they relate to the aged. This is surprising when you consider that for the first time in the history of the world the elderly have a virtual monopoly on death: Statistically speaking, it is the elderly who are most likely to die in the United States, and for that matter throughout the industrialized nations of the world. It is critically important that gerontologists in particular recognize this fact and prepare to deal with its implications.

Death, of course, has always been among us, and ultimately all human beings, as well as all living things, die. All life ends in death and all relationships end in separation. Yet we resist these ideas today, just as the Neanderthals did 60,000 years ago. Even those primitive people ceremoniously laid out and buried their dead with symbols and artifacts

suggesting a belief in an afterlife. Since the time those graves were dug at Shanidar, Iraq, humankind has had ambivalent feelings about death, and about the human corpse. This is evident in the fact that we show great respect for the dead human body even as we try to avoid it.

On the one hand we believe death is purposeful—the will of God. On the other hand it is viewed as integral to our biological existence, and natural. From one perspective, death is only one experience in a series of experiences we can expect as humans, while from another perspective, there is only one life—and one death—and of the rest we know nothing. So from the time of Shanidar to the present one can observe a mixture of responses to the significance of death. And, as I have observed, associated with these ideas and reactions is an ambivalence toward the dead human body.

Rituals for the Dead

A cross-cultural view of the world will show, for instance, that while some societies abandon the body at the time of death as well as the place of death itself, other societies literally ingest the corpse. So from abandoning the body to eating it, we are made aware of the remarkable array of human responses to death.

The Egyptians embraced the idea of reincarnation by elaborately preparing the body in expectation of the soul's long journey and ultimate return. The Cairo Museum displays an embalming board that is over 46 centuries old. What that tells us, if nothing else, is that the idea of immortality, of humankind's belief in the persistence of existence, is historic.

To understand the role of the contemporary funeral director it has to be placed in such an historical and meaningful setting. Over the centuries, of course, the role of layer-out-of-the-dead or handler-of-the-dead has been assumed by different persons whose status has varied greatly—not only throughout Western

"The Role of the Funeral Director in Contemporary Society," by Robert Fulton in *Aging and the Human Condition,* edited by Lesnoff-Caravaglia, Human Sciences Press, 72 Fifth Avenue, New York NY, 10011, copyright 1982.

European society but in other cultures also.

Historically, and indeed up until the present day, Judaism has seen in the Hevra Kaddisha's, voluntary laying out of the dead, the most honorific gesture that one person can make toward another. It was, and is, considered the greatest of gifts—the greatest mitzvah—to lay out the dead. Again, the root of this attitude can be found in the belief that there is a spiritual risk in approaching or touching the dead human body. So again we observe an approach-avoidance relationship with the human corpse that is almost schizophrenic. We view it as something to be respected or revered at the same time that we attempt to avoid it or put it away.

In many religious communities throughout the world, mutilation of the corpse for the purpose of an autopsy is not tolerated. This attitude toward the sanctity of the dead human body is evidenced over thousands of years, from the time when the Egyptian priest-surgeon responsible for embalming the pharaohs risked physical harm as a result of what was considered a necessary but nevertheless sacrilegious act.

Among the Thlinget, a west coast Canadian tribe, the body is avoided so assiduously that its care is given over to another group entirely. The Thlinget, in turn, reciprocate when necessary.

> "For good or ill, the services provided by funeral directors reflect the manner and direction in which American society has moved in most other public services as well."

In France, since the medieval period, the few embalmers have all been physicians, whereas in America the role of embalmers appeared at the time of the Civil War with little or no academic or professional tradition behind him. Consequently, the status of the embalmer or layer-out-of-the-dead in America has been at best ambiguous, while at worst it has approximated the status of a public executioner.

The American Funeral Director

The emergence of the contemporary American embalmer, mortician, or, more recently, funeral director, is a consequence of many different forces. But it can primarily be attributed to the burgeoning of our industrial, technological society since World War I, with its emphasis on the division of labor, specialization, and efficiency. Urbanization, secularization, social mobility and family nucleation have also played their part in seeing that the care of the dying as well as the dead in America became the

responsibility of someone outside the family circle.

A survey I conducted some years ago found that while some funeral homes on the east coast have been in continuous operation for over 200 years, the average funeral home in the United States had been in existence about 55 years. Over this relatively short time the questions: who die, where do they die, and from what, have changed dramatically. Most deaths today are among the elderly rather than the young; they die in the hospital rather than at home; and they die from chronic and degenerative illnesses like heart disease and cancer rather than from infectious and contagious diseases. These demographic changes, among others, are integral to a discussion of the appropriate role of the contemporary American funeral director.

The different studies that I have conducted about death, funerals, and funeral directors have shown that in the last few decades, and particularly since World War II, criticism of funeral practices in the United States has been loud, persistent, and ubiquitous....

Without going into the specific issues at this time, I would like to spell out the social and attitudinal environment in which funerals are conducted today and in which funeral directors play their part, so that we might have a better sense of what they, as well as we, are about in the latter half of the twentieth century.

Religious Values and the Funeral

Generally speaking, in the eyes of many people the funeral director's role is in conflict with some of our religious values. To many, the emphasis he places on the body appears to take priority over the spirit. The funeral director, moreover, is charged with usurping the function of the clergy and presuming upon the role of the family, while the funeral itself is said to be held for its own sake with little regard to the needs or wishes of the bereaved. There is also great concern over the funeral director's alleged efforts to promote expensive and elaborate funerals while urging viewing and embalming upon grieving families. All of this is seen as contrary to our traditional beliefs and practices.

And yet, for good or ill, the services provided by funeral directors reflect the manner and direction in which American society has moved in most other public services as well. We have turned to the modern funeral home and the contemporary funeral director for services that once were the responsibility and right of the family. But this is true, as we know, of many other features of American life as well.

Any analysis of funeral practices, however, must begin with the recognition of the regional, ethnic, and religious variability found in America. Although there are now 22,000 funeral homes in the United States—an overabundance according to some—it must be recognized that like the small town with its different churches, American funeral homes serve different religious, cultural, and ethnic groups, as well as different social classes across many different regions of the United States. This not only makes for an apparent redundancy of facilities and services, it also makes it difficult to speak accurately about an average American funeral. In one community, moreover, there may be found a funeral home that has been in existence for three or four generations under the same family management, while in another community there may be a branch of a large conglomerate or funeral chain. These and other conditions affect the general situation and compel us to recognize the factors of variability and change that bear on this social phenomenon.

Elderly People and the Funeral Director

For instance, as I have mentioned, elderly persons now have the greatest probability of dying in the United States. Last year 70% of the persons who died were over 65. Less than 6% of the persons who died were under 15. By contrast, at the turn of the century children made up over half of all deaths, yet represented only one-third of the population. The elderly, on the other hand, made up 4% of the population and accounted for 17% of the deaths. Today, however, the elderly represent 11% of the population and account for more than two-thirds of all deaths.

The elderly, as we know, more often than not die away from home, away from their families, often isolated and alone. Most gerontologists are aware, as well as concerned, about the changing sets of relationships implicit in these developments as they affect family contacts, family commitments, and family continuity. It means, fundamentally, if the recent study we conducted at the University of Minnesota is at all an indicator, that attitudes toward the dying as well as the dead are changing in America—and changing significantly.

Our study, for instance, suggests that responses and reactions to death are now both variable and in flux, and that these changes are a function of changes in religious beliefs, social class and mobility, and family relationships. We found that while there are many basic similarities between the responses of survivors toward the death of a family member, the degree and nature of the relationships can be crucial to the specific reaction reported. That is, the response of a parent to the death of a son or daughter, or of a wife to the death of a husband, can be radically different from the response of an adult son or daughter to the death of an elderly parent.

Death in a Nursing Home

But as we have observed, not only are most people who die elderly, but they are a burgeoning age group in our society. Today over 23 million persons are over 65. Of this group 7 million are over 75, and

persons over 100 number now in the thousands. We also realize that America is a highly urbanized, mobile, and secular society, and that our families are increasingly nuclear in form and function. The death of an elderly person in a hospital or nursing home after a long illness is quite different from the sudden, unexpected death of a child by accident in his own home. How one responds, how one acts, or what is to be done with the body take on a different significance in these different contexts.

"He is performing a task that we ourselves choose not to do."

In San Diego in 1978, one sixth of all deaths was handled in the following manner: After the death, an organization called the Telephase Society was notified and arrangements were made to deliver the body from the place of death to a crematorium in an unmarked van. Encased in a rubberized bag, the body was then cremated, and the ashes were scattered or placed in a cardboard container for later disposition. A bill for this service was subsequently mailed to the surviving spouse or other responsible party.

Practically nothing is known of the survivors' emotional reactions to these deaths, or what arrangements, if any, were made to memorialize the dead. Nor do we know anything of the survivors' manner of grief.

We do know, however, from our research at the University of Minnesota, that the 40- to 60-year-old children of elderly persons who died reported muted or limited feelings of grief at the time of the death. In fact, a few men in the study reported that upon the deaths of their fathers they felt in no way bereaved. Nor did they commemorate their deaths in any way. For some of the respondents, their attitude was that their fathers had lived out their lives and now they were over. Any service or response other than the immediate disposition of the body was viewed as unnecessary or inappropriate. One respondent even wrote that, as far as he was concerned, his dead father's body was "just a hunk of meat." In our sample persons such as this responded to their loss in as minimal a way as possible. While responses like these were in a distinct minority, nevertheless they augur an increase of such sentiments and remind us again of the varied and problematical responses to death.

In the face of these and other developments still emergent in the United States, the question of the role of the contemporary funeral director is increasingly relevant to us all and particularly to gerontologists. The answer or answers to that question, however, are both difficult and contingent.

There is tremendous variability in the response to

loss by death. Death doesn't mean the same thing to all people. How one reacts to the death of another depends upon many different personal and social factors. What is the appropriate disposition of a dead human body? What should we expect of a funeral director or of a funeral? As I mentioned, in the San Diego area one of six bodies is being handled in a most direct and unceremonious manner. But the general practice across the country reflects degrees of relationship and levels of feeling and expectations different from what is occurring in this particular section of the country.

"This observation and the recurring question—what to do about death?—brings me back again to the important role the American funeral director plays in our lives."

What is the role of the funeral director under these circumstances, given that we are a highly secularized society and generally shielded from the more unpleasant conditions and experiences of life? Moreover, we run away from death as well as the place of death. Citizens in our society, as in many other societies, characteristically display an impulse to leave the place of death, to move and withdraw from friends and relatives. What is the role of the funeral director when we also consider, that in addition to such specific behavior, that one of every five families moves every year? What is the role of the funeral director when our survey of almost 600 survivors showed that less than 15% reported being contacted by a clergyman or other professional person following the death of a family member? What is the role of the funeral director in a highly urbanized community when great numbers of people live in isolated or nucleated states of existence?

What is the role of a funeral director when the general population is increasingly educated to live in our highly technological society, while the funeral director's education consists generally of a high school education plus two years of practical training? Although it is improving, the training the funeral director receives is probably not in keeping with the training of most of the younger members of the community, who sooner or later will seek out his services.

What is the role of the funeral director in a society in which the clergy views him as offending many of their cherished beliefs and traditions? To associate the contemporary funeral with historic Egyptian funeral customs, as some funeral directors do, does violence to traditional Christian theology. For a funeral director to participate in a Catholic service in the morning and a Protestant service in the afternoon is acceptable and desirable from an ecumenical point of view; nevertheless, for many clergymen the funeral director's acceptance of all faiths as spiritually equal by implication casts doubt on the presumed spiritual efficacy of their rites and rituals, as well as on the presumed primacy of sanctity of their respective faiths. For these and other reasons, the two functionaries most significantly associated with the disposition of the dead in American society are at odds with one another by the very nature of their commitments and obligations.

The Funeral Director's Services

But at the same time the funeral director is not wholly a businessman—a salesman. We must remember that at the same time we cast him into a macabre role or make him the object of droll humor, he also performs a mitzvah—albeit for a fee, like the doctor and the lawyer. His function parallels the traditional service of the Hevra Kaddisha—of laying out the community's dead. He is performing a task that we ourselves choose not to do, and he does so in a manner that conveys the respect we reserve for the dead. As a consequence he takes on a sacerdotal function, a priestly role, while at the same time he is a merchandizer of coffins and other accoutrements of the grave.

His role, therefore, is by its very nature contradictory. This contradiction becomes most clear when we realize that funeral directors are the only "businessmen," or persons without professional degrees, who are permitted to attend to a naked human body. There are exceptions of course—the artist is one—but for all intents and purposes the funeral director shares a sacerdotal function with the priest and physician, and to the extent that he does, his role is unique to American occupations and professions. Therein lies much of the confusion and conflict associated with our assessment of him as a functionary of the dead.

What role, then, can we assign to him when we question his motives and are confused about his rightful tasks? How difficult it is to attribute to him good intentions when at the same time we are ever fearful that he will exploit his client's grief for his own gain, particularly since we believe that one of the greatest things that you can do for a fellow human being is to offer help—without expecting compensation—when he or she has suffered the loss of a loved one.

Helping the Dead

These reasons, historically contradictory reasons, evoke so much emotion that we find the role of the American funeral director one of conflict. Yet we must ask ourselves, who is going to help at the time of death? Our surveys show that there are very few professional persons who now help the bereaved.

Who is going to be at the home of the bereaved first? Who is going to advise the grief-stricken? Who is going to inform the widow of her rights? There are very few sociologists or psychologists available. When a person dies in the hospital, the doctor views his job as over; so does the nurse. Only now with the rise of the hospice movement do we see a preliminary and tentative attempt to respond to a few of the issues implicit in my questions.

What we must come to recognize is that the funeral director has been, and is, an important caregiver in the American community. We must come to appreciate that inherent in his role and intrinsic to his skills and experience, are social opportunities and individual talents that must be channeled and employed even more. They must be galvanized and harnessed by the community so that the services he provides and the skills he possesses can be utilized to their fullest.

Skills and Services

What are the skills and services that the funeral director possesses and that the health care field must look at and reassess?

"If we begin to open up lines of communication with [the funeral director]. . .we will discover that there is much to be gained and little to be lost in the face of the great challenge that death presents to us all."

First, of all the different persons in the community to whom one can turn at the time of death, the funeral director is not only the most visible, but more often than not the most available. Simply, it is his business. That is what he is paid to do, and the fact that members of his family may have been serving the same community for two or three generations provides a basis of trust and security that is not readily appreciated or available among other members of a community's health care network. The studies of Charles Binger at the Langely Porter Institute and Colin Parkes at Harvard have shown that following a death the person who was designated as being helpful or an important social resource to the bereaved was the family funeral director.

There are many reasons for these findings. Experience, for one thing: The funeral director was frequently the only knowledgeable person who would speak about the dead person or who was relatively comfortable discussing the death with the bereaved. By way of contrast, it is reported that some nursing homes whisk dying patients out of the home to avoid the taint and stigma of a death. In Minneapolis, for example, one particular nursing home has advertised that the reason there was always a room available for occupancy was that residents got well and went home. In short, when we look clinically and less critically at funerals and funeral directors, we recognize that the person who is often identified as most knowledgeable about the problems associated with the death, who knows what to do and is helpful and supportive to the bereaved, is the funeral director.

Death and the Professionals

Let us consider for a moment the attitudes toward death and dying of gerontologists, academicians, doctors, nurses, and other concerned members of the network of health care in the community. On the one hand, they are profoundly committed to the idea of education and training, and all of the other things basic to good council and advice. On the other hand, they recognize that when someone dies their own avoidance of death, their shyness or anxiety about it, do not allow them as professional persons to intervene and support survivors any more than the neighbor or friend across the street. This observation and the recurring question—what to do about death?—brings me back again to the important role the American funeral director plays in our lives.

I would argue, moreover, that if we would begin to see him as a member of the community mental health team, we would recognize that he is virtually an untapped resource. And that if we begin to open up lines of communication with him in our capacity as health care practitioners, as members of the clergy, and as community social workers, we will discover that there is much to be gained and little to be lost in the face of the great challenge that death presents to us all.

Robert Fulton, Ph.D., is a professor of sociology and the director of the Center for Death Education and Research at the University of Minnesota in Minneapolis.

"Funeral men constantly seek to justify the style and cost of their product on the basis of tradition."

Funeral Directors Are Parasites

Jessica Mitford

Funeral directors are members of an exalted, almost sacred calling...the Executive Committee believed that a cut in prices would be suicidal, and notified the manufacturers that better goods, rather than lower prices, were needed.... A $1,000 prize was offered for the best appearing corpse after 60 days.... A resolution was passed requesting the newspapers in reporting the proceedings to refrain from flippancy.

—Sunnyside, 1885

These observations are culled from an 1885 report describing the proceedings of one of the earliest National Funeral Directors Association Conventions. Almost eighty years later, the problems they reflect continue to occupy the attention of the undertaking trade: how to be exalted, almost sacred, and at the same time to be successful businessmen in a highly competitive situation; how to continually upgrade their peculiar product; how to establish successful relations with press and public.

The special public relations problem that dogs the undertaker has existed for a long time, arising out of the very nature of his occupation. It is uphill work to present it attractively, but he tries, perhaps too hard. Of late years he has compounded his built-in dilemma by veering off in his own weird direction towards a cult of the dead unsanctioned by tradition, religion, or common sense. He has painted himself into a difficult corner. His major justifications for his practices fly in the face of reality, but he persists; the fantasy he has created, and in which he by now has so much cash invested, must somehow be made desirable to the buying public. And, like every other successful salesman, the funeral salesman must first and foremost believe in himself and his product.

He is in any case not just a funeral salesman. There is the creative aspect of his work, the aesthetically

rewarding task of transforming the corpse into a Beautiful Memory Picture. Pride of craftsmanship, fascination with technique and continuous striving for improvement shine through all that he writes on this subject.

Devoted Embalmers

The sort of passionate devotion it is possible to develop for embalming, the true Art for Art's Sake approach, is captured in a testimonial letter published as part of an advertisement for Cosmetic Tru-Lanol Arterial Fluid. Like any other craftsman, the embalmer gets satisfaction from rising to a challenge and often hates to part with his finished product. The letter describes an unusually difficult case: "The subject...was a 69-year-old lady, 5'2" tall with 48" bust and 48" hips. Death was a sudden heart attack. She lay 40 hours in a heated apartment prior to being moved." The writer goes on to mention other inauspicious circumstances surrounding the case, such as a series of punctures made in the center of circulation by some bungler in the Medical Examiner's office. However, Tru-Lanol comes to the rescue: "Surface penetration was slow and even, with excellent cosmetic results....By the fourth day, the swelling in the features was receding in a very uniform manner, and the cosmetic was still excellent. Honestly, I don't know of another fluid that would have done as good a job in this case, all things considered." He adds wistfully, "I wish I could have kept her for four more days." How poignant those last words! And, in a way, how very understandable.

Every craft develops its outstanding practitioners, those who seem to live for the sake of their work. Such a one is Elizabeth "Ma" Green, born in 1884, a true zealot of funeral services. *Mortuary Management*, in a recent tribute to this unusual woman, recalls that "Ma" got her start in a lifelong career of embalming as a teen-ager: "It was during this early period of her life that she became interested in caring for the dead.

As this interest increased, she assisted the village undertaker in the care and preparation of family friends who passed away." "Ma" never looked back. By the early twenties she had become a licensed embalmer, and later took a job as principal of an embalming college. She has been in this work, woman and girl, some sixty years: "It was obvious she had an almost passionate devotion to the Profession."

"In their constant striving for better public relations, funeral men are hampered by their inability to agree on what they are."

Funeral people are always saying that "funerals are for the living," yet there is occasional evidence that they have developed an eerie affection, a genuine solicitude, for the dead, in whose company they spend so much time. It is as though they really attribute feelings to these mute remains of humanity, much as a small child attributes feelings to his Teddy bear, and that they are actually concerned with the comfort and well-being of the bodies entrusted to their care. A 1921 issue of *The Casket* describes a chemical which "when sprayed into the mouth of a cadaver, prevents and stops the development of pyorrhea." An advertisement in the trade press for Flying Tiger Airlines is headed THIS TIGER CARES: "This kind of caring has made Flying Tigers the most experienced air shipper of human remains. There's Tigers' exclusive Human Remains log. . . ." In Massachusetts, proposed legislation approved by the funeral industry would make it an offense to "use profane, indecent or obscene language in the presence of a dead body."

When the funeral practitioner puts pen to paper on this favorite subject, the results are truly dreamy flights of rhapsody. Mr. John H. Eckels says in his textbook, *Modern Mortuary Science*, that "The American method of arterial embalming . . . but adds another laurel to the crown of inventiveness, ingenuity, and scientific research which the world universally accords to us. . . . In fact, there is no profession on record which has made such rapid advancement in this country as embalming. . . . In summing up this whole situation, the funeral profession today is one of the most vital callings in the cause of humanity. Funeral directors are the advance guards of civilization. . . ." These vivid metaphors, these laurels, crowns and advance guards, express with peculiar appropriateness the modern undertaker's fond conception of his work and himself. How to generate equal enthusiasm in the minds of the public for the "funeral profession" is a more difficult problem.

Educating the Public

Mr. Edward A. Martin, author of *Psychology of Funeral Service*, sees undertakers in a role "similar to that of a school teacher who knows and believes in his subject but who must find attractive ways to impress it indelibly upon his pupils. Our class consists of more than 150 million Americans, and the task of educating them is one that cannot be accomplished overnight." He adds, "Public opinion is based on the education of the public, which believes what it is told."

There is some evidence that while this great pedagogical process has taken hold most strongly among the funeral men themselves, it has left the public either apathetic or downright hostile. In other words, the funeral men live very largely in a dreamworld of their own making about the "acceptance" of their product in the public mind. They seem to feel that saying something often and loudly enough will somehow make it true. "Sentiment alone is the foundation of our profession!" they cry. "The new funeral director is a Doctor of Grief, or expert in returning abnormal minds to normal in the shortest possible time!"

But the public goes merrily on its way, thinking (when it thinks of the matter at all) that moneymaking is the foundation of the funeral trade, that the matter of returning abnormal minds to normal is best left in the hands of trained psychiatrists, that it has neither been asked for nor has it voiced its approval of modern funeral practices.

There are really two parts to the particular selling job confronting the funeral industry. The first is that of convincing people of the correctness and essential Americanism of the kind of funeral the industry wants to sell; convincing them, too, that in funerary matters, there is an obligation to adhere closely to standards and procedures established by the funeral directors—who, after all, should know best about these things. The second is that of projecting an ever more exalted image of the purveyors of funerals.

Justifying Funeral Tradition

Funeral men constantly seek to justify the style and cost of their product on the basis of "tradition," and on the basis of their theory that current funeral practices are a reflection of characteristically high American standards. The "tradition" theory is a hard one to put across, as we have seen; the facts tend to run in the opposite direction. Therefore certain incantations, Wise Sayings with the power of great inspiration, are frequently invoked to help along the process of indoctrination. There is one in particular which crops up regularly in mortuary circles: a quotation from Gladstone, who is reported to have said, "Show me the manner in which a nation or a community cares for its dead and I will measure with mathematical exactness the tender sympathies of its people, their respect for the law of the land and their loyalty to high ideals." One could wish he were with us in the twentieth century to apply his handy measuring tape to a calendar issued by the W.W. Chambers Mortuary. Over the legend "Beautiful Bodies by Chambers" appears an unusually well endowed, and completely naked, young lady. Another favorite soothsayer is Benjamin Franklin, who is roped in from time to time and quoted as having said, "To know the character of a community, I need only to visit its cemeteries." Wise old Ben! Could he but visit Forest Lawn today, he would have no need to go on to Los Angeles.

In their constant striving for better public relations, funeral men are hampered by their inability to agree on *what* they are, what weight should be given the various roles in which they see themselves, what aspect should be stressed both within the trade and to the public. Is the funeral director primarily merchant, embalmer, lay psychiatrist, or a combination of all these? The pronouncements of his leaders, association heads, writers of trade books and manuals, and other theoreticians of the industry betray the confusion that exists on this point.

The Need for Embalming

"Embalming is the cornerstone upon which the funeral service profession was founded and it has remained so through the years. It is the only facet of service offered by our industry that is not wholly based upon sentiment, with all its attendant weaknesses," editorializes the *American Funeral Director*. The authoritative Messrs. Habenstein and Lamers see it differently. They are of the opinion that funeral service rests primarily on "the psychological skills in human relations necessary to the proper handling of the emotions and dispositions of the bereaved." Still another journal sees it this way: "Merchandising is the lifeblood of the funeral service business...." And, in a laudable effort to reconcile some of these conflicting ideas, there is an article in the *American Funeral Director* headed "Practical Idealism in Funeral Directing," which declares, "The highest of ideals are worthless unless they are properly applied. The funeral director who thinks only in terms of serving would very likely find himself out of business in a year or less....And if he were compelled to close up his establishment what possible use would be all his high ideals and his desire to serve?" And so the Practical Idealist comes back full circle to his role as merchant, to "costs, selling methods, the business end of his costs."

Funeral people are always telling each other about the importance of ethics (not just any old ethics but usually "the *highest* ethics"), sentiment, integrity, standards (again, "the highest"), moral responsibility, frankness, cooperation, character. They exhort each other to be sincere, friendly, dignified, prompt,

courteous, calm, pleasant, kindly, sympathetic, good listeners; to speak good English; not to be crude; to join the Masons, Knights of Columbus, Chamber of Commerce, Boy Scouts, P.T.A.; to take part in the Community Chest drive; to be pleasant and fair-dealing with employees and clients alike; not to cuss their competitors; and, it goes without saying, so to conduct themselves that they will be above scandal or slander. In short, they long to be worthy of high regard, to be liked and understood, a most human longing.

Funeral Director's Contradictions

Yet, just as one is beginning to think what dears they really are—for the prose is hypnotic by reason of its very repetitiveness—one's eye is caught by this sort of thing in *Mortuary Management*: "You must start treating a child's funeral, from the time of death to the time of burial, as a 'golden opportunity' for building good will and preserving sentiment, without which we wouldn't have any industry at all." Or this in the *National Funeral Service Journal*: "Buying habits are influenced largely by envy and environment. Don't ever overlook the importance of these two factors in estimating the purchasing possibilities or potential of any family....Envy is essentially the same as pride....It is the idea of keeping up with the Joneses....Sometimes it is only necessary to say, '...Here is a casket similar to the one the Joneses selected' to insure a selection in a substantially profitable bracket."

Merchants of a rather grubby order, preying on grief, remorse and guilt of survivors, or trained professional men with high standards of ethical conduct?...

"There is hardly an issue of the many funeral trade publications that does not reflect some aspect of this sense of bitter persecution."

Possibly the vast gap between desire and reality on this question of professionalism—the contradiction between the high-flown talk of Ethical Values and vexatious commercial necessities—accounts in good measure for the painful sensitivity to criticism evidenced by the funeral men. The slightest suggestion of opposition to any part of their operation, the slightest questioning of their sincerity, virtue and general uprightness, produces howls of anguish and brings them running like so many Brave Little Dutch Boys to plug the holes in the dike.

It is as though generations of music hall jokes, ribald cartoons, literary bons mots of which the undertaker is the butt had produced a deep-seated persecution complex, sometimes bordering on an industry-wide paranoia. The very titles of their speeches reveal this uneasy state of mind. Topics for addresses at a recent convention were: "What Are They Doing To Us?" and "You Are Probably Being Talked About Right Now."

Relationship with the Community

In their relations with the community as a whole, the funeral men carry on a sort of weird shadowboxing, frequently wildly off the mark. There is an old act—possibly originated by the Marx Brothers?—in which a bartender is trying to get rid of a bothersome fly. He goes after it with his bar towel, knocking down bottles as he swings; soon the bar is a shambles. Finally the fly settles on his nose and the bartender takes a last swipe, this time with a full bottle—and succeeds in knocking himself out while the fly unconcernedly buzzes off. The funeral industry's approach to public relations is frequently reminiscent of that bartender.

Enemies seem to lurk everywhere—among competitors, of course, but also among the clergy, the medical profession, the tissue banks, the cemetery people, the press. There is hardly an issue of the many funeral trade publications that does not reflect some aspect of this sense of bitter persecution, of being deeply misunderstood and cruelly maligned.

Journalist Jessica Mitford reached instant fame with the publication of The American Way of Death. *The book was considered a* tour de force *and remains today one of the most searing indictments of the American funeral industry.*

"To be present at the death of a friend or a family member...often may confirm the idea that death is only a transition, a release."

viewpoint 89

A Home Funeral Consoles the Bereaved

Irene B. Seeland

During ten years of working with terminal patients, their families, and the hospital staff I have become increasingly aware of the problems that surround dying in the hospital. Particularly outstanding is the isolation of the terminal patient during the last days or hours of life. Limitations in visiting hours and hospital regulations make the participation of other than the closest family members difficult, if not impossible, and never enable children to be more than distant observers of an event that will deeply affect their lives and future.

Often patients die in the hospital alone, or in the company of a nurse or an aide. Usually, the family is notified shortly before or after the actual death; in some hospital settings, family members may be able to come to the hospital room to say goodbye to the deceased. Many times the body is removed to the hospital morgue as quickly as possible, partly because there is a functional need for the hospital bed, partly because the staff do not want to upset other patients, and partly because they want to remove the dead person from sight. Often a funeral director who may not be personally known to the family is notified. He then assumes the responsibility of taking the body from the morgue to the funeral home where he and his staff take care of all necessary preparations. The visit to the funeral chapel during specific hours enables the bereaved to spend some time with the body, and ceremonies appropriate to the religious belief and customs of the family usually take place in the chapel or at a later time in a church or temple.

The question of whether a more active participation of family members in the preparation for a funeral might be therapeutic in their own process of bereavement began to emerge during these years. The role of the funeral during the acute bereavement

period of a family's life came very strongly into personal focus when, over a period of nine months, I experienced the death of two persons who were close to me, as well as to a large number of friends.

Home Treatment

My husband, a 43-year-old director of an international educational institution, became acutely ill with acute lymphoblastic leukemia in July 1975. After an initial three weeks' hospitalization marked by serious complications, a short-term remission was achieved, and my husband, after extensive discussions with his physicians and family members, chose to proceed with the proposed lengthy chemotherapeutic treatment on an outpatient basis. Treatments continued over a period of 13 months, with three separate hospitalizations for central nervous system involvement and treatment. The illness progressed rapidly and remissions became increasingly shorter. Side effects of the chemo-therapeutic agents added to complications of the illness, and during the last four months of his life my husband was nearly completely paralyzed and needed 24-hour nursing care. His wish to remain at home was fulfilled and made possible by the dedicated care of a group of five friends who took turns with me in providing the necessary intensive home care. This group consisted of two psychiatrists, a lawyer, a medical student, and a psychology student, all of whom had been our close friends and co-workers for several years. The medical and nursing skills of these people improved quickly with the assistance of the primary physicians and several private duty nurses, and this team soon proved to be adequate to the rapidly growing medical and nursing care needs of my husband as his illness progressed. His two physicians, after some initial concern about whether adequate care could be provided in his home setting, did everything in their power to assist in this process and helped to overcome institutional barriers

Irene B. Seeland, "The Funeral as a Therapeutic Tool in Acute Bereavement," in *Grief: Counseling the Bereaved.* New York: Columbia University Press, 1981. Reprinted by permission.

in providing medication, blood tranfusions, and other means of support.

Throughout his illness my husband remained mentally alert and active and provided much-needed emotional stability and support to those caring for him. Friends, co-workers, and children had easy access to him, and he openly shared with those close to him his own process of preparing for his death, which he anticipated and accepted, yet which he did not give into without "putting up a good battle first."

Dying at Home

He died at home after 13 months of illness at the age of 44. A 24-hour period of coma preceded his death.

Two months prior to his death, when chemotherapeutic treatments were becoming increasingly ineffective, he had suggested to me that I should find a funeral director and begin to explore funeral arrangements. His only specific wish was to be cremated. He had no other particular preferences regarding funeral arrangements, but he agreed completely with the following suggestions: to have the body remain at home following his death until the time of cremation; to have a small, informal ceremony conducted in the home and not at the cemetery; and, in general, to keep the process simple.

Through friends, I made contact with a funeral director and discussed the situation with him. During the first meeting the specific wishes of my husband and our family were explored to see if they were possible and feasible. Our family's wish for the body to remain at home prior to cremation and to allow a minimum of 24 hours for a wake made embalming necessary. The funeral director, trained in home embalming by his father in an old Italian family business, felt that this could be done in a private home. Details regarding choice of other funeral arrangements, the casket, cremation site, and expenses were discussed and made final during this meeting. My husband was relieved to know that arrangements had been completed and that there would be no need for our family to deal with these issues, either shortly before or after his death when the stress of the situation would be taking its greatest toll on everyone.

On the day when my husband's death was obviously approaching, the closest family members and friends stayed with the comatose patient, spending the time in reflection and preparing for the death. Other friends were notified, and those who expressed a wish to be with the patient for a while were encouraged to do so. Our oldest son, nine years of age, and the seven-year-old son of close friends joined at the bedside for a brief period, with the clear awareness that it was to say a final goodbye. Our younger son, eight-years-old, who had been quite overwhelmed by the destructiveness of the illness on his father's physical appearance, felt unable to join but asked me to say goodbye for him.

After my husband's death those closest to him stayed with the body for a while before notifying the physicians and the funeral director, all of whom had previously been alerted to the impending death. When the funeral director arrived, I requested permission to remain with the body during the embalming process. When the embalming was completed, friends helped to wash and dress the body and assisted the funeral director in placing the body into the casket.

The Home Funeral

The open casket was placed in a large room that is used to exhibit some of the art pieces my husband had collected during his life, and it was surrounded by flowers and candles. This room, large enough to accommodate 40 people, was to become the central point for the family and friends over the next 36 hours. During the first night several friends offered to stay with the body so that the persons who had spent the last few months in taking care of my husband could rest or get some sleep. Some friends stayed to take care of the children, and others prepared food and notified friends and co-workers who had not yet been advised of the death.

On the next day there was opportunity to spend time in small or large groups with the body. Later in the day, when other friends and co-workers arrived, people were invited to read from scriptures, poetry, or other sources meaningful to them or to sing songs my husband had loved. Two of the children participated in most of these proceedings. Our younger son again felt too overwhelmed to participate, and his wish to share in the events only from a distance was respected.

"Small groups of family members and friends shared the wake. They found. . .an opportunity to acknowledge the reality of death."

During the second night small groups of family members and friends shared the wake. They found in these quiet hours an opportunity to acknowledge the reality of the death and to begin the process of dealing with their own grief. In the morning of the second day a brief final goodbye was said, and the casket was closed and taken to the crematorium. Only our family and our most intimate friends accompanied the casket. In the chapel of the crematorium we said a final prayer to send the body on its last journey.

Six months after the onset of my husband's illness, one of his closest friends, a 72-year-old, single woman and professor of education, had become seriously ill with metastatic ovarian cancer. After surgery she was placed on chemotherapy and had an excellent remission for a period of seven months. She participated in my husband's funeral with the full awareness that she was the most likely person to follow him in death.

Progression of Illness

After the relapse and fairly fast progression of her illness a few months later she also expressed a wish to spend as much of her remaining life as possible at home and not in the hospital. Since her only direct family was an elderly brother and his wife living in California, both of them retired and physically infirm, friends and co-workers decided to make use of the experience gained in taking care of my husband, and, with the assistance of an excellent Jamaican nurse's aide, they were able to provide 24-hour nursing coverage at the patient's home. This time the group of people caring for the patient was larger and included a number of younger people, as well as older friends, several of whom had had no previous close exposure to serious illness and death.

"The fact that the body of the deceased remained each time in a home setting made it possible for friends and family to spend time with the body."

This patient's progression toward death was slower and less dramatic, and she spent three weeks in a state of alternating semicoma and alertness before she died following a deep coma that lasted three days. Earlier in her illness she had expressed a wish to have a funeral similar to that of her friend, and so some time was spent exploring her specific concerns and wishes about funeral arrangements.

The patient died surrounded by all those who had cared for her, and her death provided a deeply moving experience for them. In particular, those people who had never previously witnessed a death and who were not likely, at least in their professional fields, to be part of the dying of another person expressed gratitude to be able to be present at her death.

Funeral's Impact on Children

The funeral, wake, and cremation mainly followed the process of the first funeral. Because the patient's studio apartment was too small for a large gathering of people, it was decided to use my home for the wake. Before this decision was made, the question of what impact a second funeral in the home would have on the children was explored. In view, however, of the fact that the patient was a very close friend of the family and godmother to my oldest son,

we felt that the children would understand the relevance of having the funeral in their father's home, especially since this had been the patient's hope.

During the wake, friends and co-workers again had time and opportunity to reflect on the life and the work of their friend, as well as to allow the reality of the loss of another close person, one who had contributed so much to their lives, to sink in. The two children who had participated in the first funeral joined again and shared actively in the wake and the periods of being together. My younger son initially stayed away from the room where the open casket was placed and stated that he was too frightened of the body to join the others. A brief exploration with me about his fears seemed to have little impact. Yet shortly thereafter he offered to escort a newly arrived friend into the room and joined the other people for the rest of the day. He stated with great relief that his fantasies about what a dead person looked like had been proved wrong, and he brought his most treasured toy, a toy raccoon, to keep his old friend company.

The rapidity and intensity of events during this period did not leave much space for reflection on and understanding of what impact the illness, death, and burial of these two persons had on the lives of those who had participated in some or all aspects of their care. In retrospect, however, it has become clear that much was gained and learned during this time, and during the many explorations following the death of these two people the essence of the learning process emerged. Learning had taken place in several fairly distinct processes.

The Illness

The decision to take care of both patients in their own home environment confronted every person involved with the process of progressive illness and the deterioration of the body on a day-to-day basis. This proved to be a painful and stressful experience for everyone, but acceptance was made possible through the unusual emotional equilibrium, sense of humor, and perspective that both patients demonstrated. Nevertheless, both patients were also subjected to periods of severe physical stress, pain, and sometimes discouragement and shared these as willingly with those around them as they had shared their times of peacefulness and resolution.

In both cases there was little doubt that the illness was incurable and would lead to death in the near future. The time available was, however, used intensely and was limited only by the progressive impairment of the patients' physical function. The fact that both patients knew their diagnosis and probable prognosis from the beginning of their illness made possible open communication, exploration, and planning for all concerned.

As the illness progressed and death approached, the reality of having to plan for a funeral became clear. The patient, his family, and friends had no particular precedent to follow, nor did they feel any social or specific religious obligations that might determine the format of a funeral. The freedom to plan without a prescribed form made it possible to allow an organic process to take place that expressed the needs and took into account the life realities of those participating in this life process. The willingness of the funeral director to be open to somewhat unconventional plans and to put his professional skills into creative use did much to allow arrangements to proceed without conflict or complications during a stressful time. The meetings with the funeral director several weeks prior to the actual death of the patients alleviated much anxiety and concern and also established a rapport and trust that proved to be invaluable at the time of death. At that point the funeral director was no longer a stranger and "businessman" proceeding with "his business" but a friend who had been willing to listen and offer advice and help.

The Death

At the time of death of both patients, those involved in their actual physical care were gathered around their bed for several hours and shared the actual death process. The fact that this took place in the home environment contributed much to making this a peaceful and constructive experience. It also enabled people to give each other support; to reflect on the life, the illness, and the death of the patients; and to begin slowly to prepare psychologically for the time after the death.

The actual moment of death was deeply experienced by those present and transmitted to everyone a strong sense of transition, not an end.

Some time after the death was spent in quietness and individual prayer. After this time the task of beginning with the more functional aspect of preparing for a funeral was taken up: notification of physicians, the funeral director, and friends and family members who were not in the immediate vicinity. Until the arrival of the physicians and the funeral director, we again spent time in quiet togetherness, sitting by the bedside of the deceased, allowing a process of accepting the long-anticipated and now finally actual fact of the death of a beloved person to begin. My decision to stay with the body during the embalming in both cases came from a strong feeling of not wanting to leave the bodily remains of these two close people without company during this time, and it was a purely personal choice.

After the embalming process several friends rejoined me, and together we washed and prepared the body for dressing. Although none in their lives had previously helped with this type of task, they all experienced a sense of participating in a beautiful,

ancient ritual, and they all felt that they could express one more time their love for the deceased by this last act of care. Upon completion of the dressing and placing of the body in the casket, the open casket was placed in the room chosen to function as the place for the wake for the next 24 hours.

The Wake

The decision to hold an "old-fashioned" wake had emerged from a sense that there was need for an opportunity to spend time with the body, to reflect, and to say personal goodbyes. A period of several hours during the next day was set aside for other friends and co-workers to come and join. This allowed for more private time for closer friends and immediate family, as well as for some time to be shared with other people.

"Just as the process of giving birth has...lost much of its threat...there is hope that death similarly will lose its terror for man."

The fact that the body of the deceased remained each time in a home setting made it possible for friends and family to spend time with the body between periods of rest; to take care of other people, especially the children; and in this way to allow for a more continuous and more natural process of accepting the fact of death. For the individual it gave space to sit by the body and review past times together, to deal with unresolved issues, to have times of sorrow and peacefulness—all in the presence of the body—and at all times to find confirmed the fact of death. The process of the wake in the home proved to be especially helpful to the children, who had an opportunity to approach death at their own rate of acceptance, to be with the body, or to be with the family not too far away from the body. They entered into a process of becoming familiar with death and observing others in their own process of dealing with it, all in their own familiar environment. In the case of the younger son this process was slower and more painful, and yet it came to a point of successful resolution at the time of the second death that the child had had to experience within nine months.

Those friends who kept watch at the casket during the nights expressed later that those hours had been very precious to them. When the time for ending the wake arrived, a feeling of completion had emerged, and the last moments with the body before closing the casket gave them the feeling of having said a final goodbye to a friend who was going on a long journey. At that point there was also a strong sense that what was to be cremated was not the old friend but only the physical remains.

The drive to the crematorium, both times in glorious sunshine, and the brief time in the crematorium's chapel were characterized by a feeling that a long and painful process had been brought to a point of completion. There was a strong sense of fullness or wholeness and a shared feeling that this process had left its participants richer.

"Close participation in the physical care of the patient can relieve the feeling of helplessness."

The days and weeks after each death confirmed the impression that the events surrounding and immediately following the death of these two persons had contributed much to help the bereaved to enter into their own process of acceptance, of separation, and of transition into a life now without these two friends who had contributed so much to everyone's life. The mourning process continued in its normal fashion with periods of sorrow, remorse, aloneness, and depression, and yet it was much helped by the fact that an important human experience had been shared with several people during the illness, death, and funeral of these two friends. During later times of exploration many of the friends expressed their own intense experience of participating in an aspect of human life that had added new and unexpected dimensions of understanding to their perceptions of life and of death.

One month after the death of these two people, a child was born to two other friends, and the continuity of life was confirmed in this joyful event.

Universal Human Needs

The events described here were in some respects specific to particular life situations and sequences of events. They were also an expression of the people who participated in them and of their lives and their work together. It would be difficult to extract these events out of the lives in which they occurred and develop them into a "model" for patient care or for planning for a funeral.

There are, however, certain aspects of the described process that may be an expression of more universal human needs and experiences and may, therefore, have greater relevance to other people. Active participation in the care of a terminal patient can have a variety of impacts on the participants. It creates the possibility for more closeness and openness, sharing of previous times and events, and a mutual giving. It may also bring into the open underlying conflicts and unresolved issues, both in the patient and in those around him, and, if dealt with appropriately, it can facilitate the resolution of

these issues before the patient's death and thus alleviate guilt and remorse in the survivors. Close participation in the physical care of the patient can relieve the feeling of helplessness and at the same time bring the progressive physical deterioration into clear perspective and give opportunity for the family to prepare themselves for the impending death of the patient. Death may then be experienced as a welcome and well-deserved release and respite for the suffering friend.

To be present at the death of a friend or a family member, which used to be a frequent occurrence in the past, enables the participants to witness for themselves the passage of the dying and often may confirm the idea that death is only a transition, a release. It may also help alleviate unrealistic fears and fantasies about the "agonies of death," for many patients die peacefully and not in a terrifying struggle.

Participating in Preparing the Body

Active participation in the preparation of the body for the funeral gives an opportunity to express a last act of care and love to the dead one. This also permits one to become familiar with the effect that death has on the human body. There is little chance to "make believe" that the dead person is only "sleeping," as the euphemism goes, when one assists in the washing and the dressing of a body; it confronts the participants with the finality of death, allowing them to move toward the next step in their mourning process. This confirmation of death continues for an extended period of time, during the process of the wake as the family and friends spend time with the body and have an opportunity to work through in themselves their own feelings, thoughts, and memories while still in the presence of the body.

Two other aspects of the two funerals seem to have a particular importance and deserve to be mentioned. The availability of the funeral director as a human being, as well as a helping professional, added much to the therapeutic effect of the funerals on the bereaved. His willingness to help plan and assist in arranging the funeral in such a manner that it could become an organic expression of the family's needs and wishes, made him a friend and caring helper instead of a distant outsider to whom a business was delegated. As emerged in later discussions, the participation of the family and friends in the preparation for the funeral also had a deep effect on the funeral director himself, who felt that he was included in the process that the family was undergoing and that he was invited and allowed to give of himself beyond his professional skills. A business transaction became a human interaction instead, and it enriched his own life in addition to giving a greater meaning to his professional activities.

The participation of a number of friends and co-workers in the care of the patients and in the preparation for their funerals provided much human support for all involved. It made possible periods of respite for the family and closer friends who carried the major burden of the physical care and who were also under serious psychological stress because of the impending loss of two important people in their lives. It allowed the growth of closer human bonds, and, as became evident after the death of both patients, it welded people together in the shared intense experience of caring and giving and participating together in one of the most important events in life.

"The participation of a number of friends and co-workers. . . . allowed the growth of closer human bonds."

The two funerals described here proved to be of deep human relevance for all who participated in them. They are looked back upon as cherished memories, and there is a consensus that they allowed for a resolution and healing. They were much more than an expression of grief and loss; they were a true celebration of the lives of those who had died by those who would go on with the task of living. Just as the process of giving birth has, in the last decades, lost much of its threat and has become a process in which both parents increasingly and consciously participate and which they experience as an intense and meaningful event in their lives, so there is hope that death similarly will lose its terror for man and begin to be shared as a meaningful and intensely experienced event of human existence.

This viewpoint is taken from the book Acute Grief, Counseling the Bereaved.

"Consumers do want changes. And only through their own Cooperative Funeral Homes can they see their visions take root."

viewpoint **90**

A Funeral Cooperative Meets Society's Needs

Raymond Paavo Arvio

"Dance on Saturday night at the Cooperative Funeral Home in memory of Bill Jervis."

"Sauerbraten Dinner, honoring the memory of our friend William Kinkel, to be held Tuesday at 7:00 P.M. at the Cooperative Funeral Home. Please come. Send your reservations to..."

"Poetry Reading in the Fireplace Room at the Cooperative Funeral Home on Thursday at 8:00 P.M. to recall the life and concerns of Melissa Blankton."

Strange announcements? Maybe to our untrained eyes. We are not used to associating these events with a funeral home.

But all things are possible. Simple self-determination, the taproot of our activity, says they are....

If a Cooperative Funeral Home takes the position that it wishes to provide a freedom of choice for consumers, then it must allow its facilities to provide the range of responses of which we humans are capable.

So depressed are many Americans by their experience with the typical funeral home, they may find it difficult to deal with other concepts. Yet a truly service-oriented Cooperative Funeral Home, it can be argued, needs to be open to the broadest possibilities.

Why should we conform at the time of death? Many people, trying to be as true to themselves as possible for a lifetime, don't want to go the way everyone else does. Their very last act should be true to their lives, they might well say; the funeral should not be a defeat but a last victory over the conforming forces of society, those forces that say there is only one way to do things, one way to live, one way to die. Break out. Live. Let the world know you are truly alive. We can hear those persons now! Sing out loud in public places: praise be to the souls who dare to be different!

Let us pursue some of the possibilities.

Rooms for Memorial Meetings

It will be difficult for the typical Cooperative Funeral Home to switch rooms back and forth from the funereal to the festive (yes, festive), wheeling out the casket after one kind of occasion and changing the drapes to suit the moods of those who might prefer a more vigorous and lighthearted kind of occasion. All-purpose rooms will take lots of work and lots of planning. It might be better, if facilities permit, to have different kinds of rooms for different kinds of purposes.

In our...discussion about memorial meetings, it became clear that variety is desirable. Thus a memorial meeting may require just a large plain room with lots of comfortable seats. A fireplace at one end is ideal, for fire is one of the universal symbols of warmth, of the mix of new life and old life accepted and cherished by many. As the fire dies down, the last speakers having shared their recollections, the attenders sit in silence as the fire draws its last strength from the wood that gave it life. The family rises, the signal for the group to shake hands, everyone strengthened by a beautiful experience of sharing.

Refreshments may be served now at one end of the room or in an adjoining room. The life, not the body and death, of the deceased friend, is with the group, as friends greet each other, receive the introductions of new people, and talk about the sights and sounds and recollections of the life they have been reviewing.

After food has been served and visitors have departed, the immediate survivors leave for the living of a different life. While the refreshment crew cleans up, the attendants of the Cooperative Funeral Home begin the process of setting up the chairs in the main

Fireplace Room for another meeting scheduled to begin soon.

An aficionado of folk dancing has died the week before, and his relatives and friends, faithful to his wishes, have arranged a folk dance at the Home for those who had shared in that interest. The chairs are placed along the walls, the rug is rolled up, the fire is relighted, and the record-playing system rolled into the room. Earlier, favorite dance records of the deceased person had been picked up by someone from the Home. A fresh urn of coffee is being made and a supply of apples and oranges laid out. That is the style of the folk-dance society; that will be today's style. Three hours have been reserved for the dance.

"Part of the magic of the Cooperative Funeral Home is that it provides a place where volunteer friends of the deceased can do their supportive work."

The folk-dance leader arrives a few minutes before the appointed time to check on arrangements. Then the guests begin to arrive. When a sizable group is assembled, the leader stands on a chair and says, slowly and clearly, "Our friend, Bill Jamison, loved to dance. Dancing was, in fact, his life. A student of folk dancing, a great teacher, he saw the world through the dancing feet of people who had set aside their worries and grievances to spend time following the patterns and paces of the folk art. Bill asked us to remember him with a last dance, here at the Home. He asked that we laugh and eat and dance, in the way we did when he was with us. This is the way he wants to be remembered. Turn up the music. Let's dance, to the memory of Bill Jamison!"

For almost three hours, the familiar music heightened the sense of Bill's presence. He was there dancing. One expected him to stand up and announce the next dance, the way he often did at the usual meetings of the group. The dance over, the exhausted friends left with a warm glow. Bill would not be forgotten.

While the dancers were in their third hour, a kitchen crew was working on the last preparations for a dinner scheduled in the Fireplace Room for six that evening. The dinner was to recall the life and memory of a man, Arthur Houser, who for years had taught math in the local high school but who nourished a private life as a splendid cook. His favorite, as his friends well knew from events he had hosted at the fraternal hall, was sauerbraten. On his planning forms, Arthur had said he did not want to have people look at his body or at his casket; he wanted, instead, a dinner in the Fireplace Room of

the Home for his friends. The menu was to be sauerbraten. He asked that his favorite "oom-pah" music be played over the room's loudspeakers and that German beer be served with the meal. He made it clear in his "Expression of Wishes" that he didn't want a lot of sad speeches during the meal. Between the meal and dessert, he said, he would like the high school principal, a good friend of his, to read a poem of which Arthur was particularly fond. That was all. The music turned on again, the eating and drinking continued. Every bite eaten, every drop of beer swigged became a reminder of Arthur's presence on earth among his friends.

It is nine o'clock now at the Home. The dinner group has left. The tables are being folded and the chairs stacked. The clatter of the last dishes being washed can be heard in the now quiet cooperative.

An Intimate Memorial

At 9:30, a small group is due to arrive. They want the fire burning and a circle of soft-cushioned chairs around the fireplace. Mostly elderly people, the group wants a silent meeting of recollection for ancient Aunt Jane, who had lived at the nearby Senior Citizens' Center. When she died, her body had been cremated, as she suggested. The handful of people who lived with her at the Center had been asked to come together a week later, to sit around the fireplace and to speak if they wished about her life.

The fireplace roaring at first, quieting into a steady rhythm of wind and puff and crackle, hosts the two dozen friends of Aunt Jane's. No one says anything at first. Then one person speaks of the first time, some ten years earlier, that she met Aunt Jane, the day she came to the Center to live. Aunt Jane was spunky then, a little irritated that she had to move in with what she called "crotchety old people." She found, instead, people like herself, full of games, good conversation, enjoyment of flowers. The years passed. The friend recalls speaking to Aunt Jane just a couple of weeks ago about her grand entrance ten years before. "Aunt Jane looked up at me," the speaker quietly says, "and told me that she wishes everyone of every age could have the good life she had had these past ten years. People *need* friends." Smiles of recognition pass around the gathered group. Another speaks of her "green thumb" with flowers, another of her unheralded work of comforting one or another of them who had a sudden feeling of loneliness and isolation, another reads a poem which reminds the speaker of Aunt Jane, another remembers the time Aunt Jane decorated the lobby of the Center for the expected arrival of relatives from Des Moines and how happy she was about the visit. An hour passes. There are gaps of peaceful silence between the messages. Betty Jo, as the reserved time draws to a close, says, "We will always remember Aunt Jane. Thank God for everything she has done for us." The group stands up slowly, puts on coats and walks out together, returning to the Center, their mutual home until death.

So much for the Fireplace Room. Its capacity to contain the souls of the living and the dead is clear, its infinite flexibility revealed through its actual uses. What the Spirit declared should be, can be.

The Cheerful Rooms

There is another workable dimension in an avant-garde facility, that is, one big enough to include a variety of rooms for other purposes. Why not cheerful rooms, decorated with bright yellow flowers and red stripes? Why not a bright blue room, a red room? These can be the focus for occasions with body display or with closed caskets as well. People might wish to pursue the conventional (perhaps for the sake of the family, a gentle recognition of debt to others), but to do it in an unconventional setting.

There may be a woman, the party-giver of the community, who will want bright streamers around her closed coffin and sent from corner to corner of the gaily decorated room. People thinking of her thought of parties. She had requested in her funeral planning forms that her Lutheran minister conduct a religious service for her, that the Flower and Stripes Room be used, that her friends be given, on entering the room, a specially printed copy of a poem she had written about the joys and gifts of friends and life. Her minister has a copy of her "Expression of Wishes"; he knows her special spirit and, while he is accustomed to thinking about funereal occasions in more somber settings, he knows that he had a character in Millicent Dunkin; he does a good job. Somehow the atmosphere, brimful of life and cheer and color (and potted live flowers around the room, her special request) makes his otherwise usually somber message about ashes to ashes and dust to dust seem almost a cheerful message. The gathering senses it; the weeping relatives sense it; the organist (a volunteer working at the Home) senses it. "This is the way Millie wanted it," friends said to each other, shaking hands after the service. They line up to shake the hands of the relatives and then proceed to the fleet of cars outside. Their destination is the Livingston Cemetery, some miles away, where the body, with the usual ceremony, will be placed in the Dunkin family plot.

Providing for the Deceased

People's lives are reflected in these occasions of death. Current practice takes bodies into environments unseemly for most people. The revolution of values occasioned by the new consumerism asks that the last public occasion be like life. Or be what was wanted. The purpose of the Home is to do the best it can to provide the occasion requested by the deceased, responding in good spirit to these last wishes. The Home, given its commitment to freedom of choice, could not criticize.

It is not in a position to criticize. It exists to serve.

The typical funeral home is organized to repress the individual and his requests. Only one atmosphere is permitted: somber, sobersides, straight. While the cooperative can provide that response if the consumer wishes it, there is no doubt but that the new availability of choice to consumers will prompt an easier and lighter flow of funeral events. Infinite varieties will appear. Mark death we must, but in our Home we shall have a role in determining how it shall be marked.

Part of the magic of the Cooperative Funeral Home is that it provides a place where volunteer friends of the deceased can do their supportive work: the meal, the party, the flowers. The less dependence on staff, the less costly the occasion. No private-profit funeral parlor permits the engagement of friends and relatives in the conduct of funeral occasions. Liberated consumers, operating in their own Home, have restored to them their fundamental right to create a last special time of recollection of their friend.

"The gaudy signs of death, the crosses and stars and crypts and angels with arms raised, would be replaced by nature itself, by signs of life."

One room can be devoted to music.

Another can be a Little Theater, where slides and films about the life of the deceased friend can be shown. Artistic performances can be viewed. "This Is Your Life" performances, offered by friends, can heighten the life of the dead by recalling in dramatic form events of times gone by.

Poetry readings, performances of Shakespeare, a violinist's rendition of loved music can take place if the Home has arranged facilities for them.

An adaptable facility, representing adaptable people, will be open to consumer choice. Splendid and healthy, it will replace the arthritic knee-bending sorrow of current practice. The mystery of funeral practice will disappear as consumers take over the practices related to death, conduct the occasions of sorrow and celebration. Death belongs to consumers. It is, after all, they who die. There is basic earth wisdom in their taking charge.

The Outside Occasion

The beauty of these variants is that they are all possible. Consumers do want changes. And only through their own Cooperative Funeral Homes can they see their visions take root.

There is always the possibility that private-profit funeral directors, sensing consumer interest in variants, will change their practices and offer more choice. That is splendid. More people—those whom we could never induce to cooperate with us—will have the benefit of our work. They may pay more, but they will have more options. It will be good to know that we have taken benefits to the general community, in fact influencing the quality of life and death.

The Cooperative Funeral Home, responsive to requests from its members, may wish to explore outside occasions.

An outdoor band pavilion, on the back lawn of the Home or perhaps in a special park at a distance, can be the site for funeral occasions. Many people would like outdoor band concerts to mark their departure. Why not? The music, sending its waves across the green lawns and upward among the leafy branches, will sing of a life well spent. The listeners, relatives and friends, hearing the music, will think of their mutual loss, their hearts stirred by music.

"The Cooperative Funeral Home is an educational institution. It is designed to teach, to open up the mind to the reality of death."

Speakers, in a formal program, can mount the steps of the pavilion and conduct traditional or not-so-traditional services. There can be a distribution of ashes in special flower gardens adjacent to the pavilion, in which the notion of life joining life will become vivid for those participating.

Memorial Gardens

Memorial gardens are an excellent idea and will draw response from many advanced consumers. Acres of gray tombstones are not an appealing last place of residence for most people. The distribution of ashes among selected flowers and shrubbery would provide a moving and beautiful occasion. Should cemeteries for earth burials fall within the purview and control of the Cooperative Funeral Home, they could include sections devoted entirely to flowers, which can be made available potted and cut for inside occasions at the Home. A small greenhouse can do the job in winter months. Such cooperative flower-growing can reduce the consumer's dependence on the expensive private-profit florist.

Should a large group of members wish the Home to own land for earth burials, new opportunities will arise. There is no reason why cemeteries should look the way they look. Bodies can be buried without regard to location, if the members wish that to be the practice. Unmarked graves, plotted only on an office wall at the cemetery office, can provide space for the rural beauty we miss in those rows and rows of

stones, reminding one of blocks of tenements in a crowded city, or of high-rise apartments in Gotham. As a final housing development and most cemeteries focus too much on dead bodies, some members will say. A plot of land can be divided between the stone-raisers and the gardeners, so that choice can be maintained. No one need be kept out, that is the primary rule. Or two plots of distant land, each with a different style and in different directions from the Home, can be owned by the Home.

The chartered bus opens up horizons for outside occasions. Arranged by the Home, a visit to a beach, mountainside or public campsite can provide a lovely way to celebrate someone's life. It could be a special visit to a cherished view, for example, followed by a sit-down picnic. How much better a few hours spent this way than in a dismal funeral parlor, in the old way.

The key to all of this, we have to say, is in the ability of the Home to respond to various wishes and needs. If some group in the Home rejects some idea, they do not have to participate in it. There should be understanding and tolerance in the development of Home programs, lest we move into divisive stances, forcing some members to leave the cooperative and start another one down the street: one Home for conventional cooperators, one Home for radical cooperators. What a loss of energy that would be! What a loss of buying power! Undoubtedly, both would decline, having lost the central spirit of Consumer Cooperation.

Let's think about that gentle mountainside, with that piece of woods someone knew was for sale. Let's leave it untouched, just the way it is. Could it serve some of our members?

It is conceivable that permission could be secured for it to become a place for earth burials. If so, the burial of bodies, uncasketed, in the nooks and crannies of such a site, would give life-strength, a natural fertilizer, lending it the natural beauty that life always gives to life. If such is not possible, it can become a marvelous Co-op Memorial Mountain, the resting place for ashes, the place for memorial tree plantings.

The Cemetery Gardens

Paths sliced through the deep woods would take the hiker up and down the piney paths. The higher the walk, the greater the view. Little waterfalls, chortling in and out of stony ruts along the way, lend light bubbles to the otherwise motionless scenario. Birds slice song into the hush. The visitor, thinking about a dead friend, would think only good and high thoughts. The mean and the crass would have gone their way, leaving only the reflection of a person's fine deeds, outgoing actions, cheerful ways, touching moments. This wooded cathedral would hold the souls of a countless number of cooperators, unencumbered by the sold-out signs of dismal stone-pocked cemeteries. There would always be room for more on the Memorial Mountain.

The ecology of life would be preserved through such a program. There would be no need, its advocates would argue, for setting aside hundreds and thousands of acres for burial plots. Conservationists, student ecologists, flower-lovers, Johnny Appleseeds could exult in the knowledge that a mountainside would stay forever a shrine to life—through its new role. The gaudy signs of death, the crosses and stars and crypts and angels with arms raised, would be replaced by nature itself, by signs of life.

What a place for spiritual retreats, for seminars, for events related to the thoughtful work of the Cooperative Funeral Home! A lodge, built near the roadway, not cutting into the deeper woods, could house a hundred occasions. Perhaps a single marker, inside the lodge or placed nearby, could hold the names of those whose bodies, ashes or perhaps souls alone have been consigned by survivors to this place of eternal rest.

Parallel developments could occur on a gentle plain, too, with a restful view toward a monumental elm in the middle of the field. Or along a stretch of coastline, whose beach property might become available to the Home. Or by a quiet river or lake. Family pilgrimages of remembrance to such beautiful memory-places could be delightful family picnics.

Food and Liquor

Death brings tension, an inward probing that is hard for most people to absorb. The sense of grief—the strange sorrow that overcomes a group in the midst of mourning—needs relief. Many members of the Cooperative Funeral Home might well inquire into the possibility that a portion of the huge basement (if there is one) be set aside for an eating-and-drinking place. There was a time when private homes were large enough for these occasions, when everyone attending the funeral would join the family for hours of good eating, good drinking and, finally, hearty laughter. Grief finds surcease in the new return to life marked by laughter, whose sounds end our pain and ease our sorrow.

Families whose backgrounds recall these occasions will yearn for them, as they themselves struggle with an understanding of death. Recalling the gatherings, they will intuitively know them to be sound, fulfilling, important. There will be those in the fellowship of the Cooperative Funeral Home who might resist this development, yet it should be explored for the sake of unity. The Home, if it is unable to incorporate such an activity in its buildings for legal reasons or because of fear of divisions within the membership, might have on its list of cooperating groups a local inn or eatery that would welcome a reserved-party night. The Home, in arranging for the celebration, either in its own facility

or outside, for those who feel more whole through its practice, is being true to its mandate to serve its members.

The Home as Educator of Adults

The Cooperative Funeral Home is an educational institution. It is designed to teach, to open up the mind to the reality of death. An active Home, accepting this task, will become engaged in a multiplicity of educational tasks in and out of its facility.

"The idea of a memorial society and its logical extension into the idea of a Cooperative Funeral Home are commended to people everywhere."

The idea of the cooperative as educator is a varient on the traditional scheme we have outlined. It suggests outreach, not necessarily with a view to drawing members into the cooperative (as in the public-relations or sales program), but with a view to challenging the community to become realistic about death, to become engaged in reevaluation of tradition and prescribed ways of handling it.

Some members emphasizing the Home as educator of adults will think of it as a mission station. It does its service job, but it also sends out missionaries to stir up the natives (philosophically), to arouse new concern, to elevate the insights of an entire community.

At the heart of an educational program there must be books and materials. The Home should be a bookseller, a purveyor of ideas. It might even do some printing and reprinting of materials by some of its members on the subject of death and death practices. A corner of the Home would have the literature in racks, with prices indicated. Some items would be free of charge.

The bookshop would be a resource for anyone, member or not, who wished to pursue the subject. Part of the bookshop might be a lending library, enabling materials to circulate freely among those who might not wish to buy materials or have the funds to do so.

Members of an education committee would develop a program designed to get discussions of death and death practices on the agendas of a hundred or more religious, fraternal and service organizations in the community. People on the committee would do research themselves, enabling them to become resource persons themselves, to sit on panel discussions, to participate in debates, to be interviewed on radio and television.

None of this, it is important to emphasize, is necessarily related to the matter of building up membership. If it happens, that is fine, but the purpose of each individual working on the educational committee ought to be (1) the encouragement of advance planning, (2) the public discussion of death and death practices, (3) the nurturing of discussion and study groups in existing organizations, (4) the wider distribution of educational materials on the subject and (5) the spreading of the idea that the Home is an educational resource in the field of death, death planning and death practices.

"The worst thing that can happen to the committee is that someone will say No, and that is not too dreadful to contemplate."

Members of such a committee, whose work would be truly unique in most communities, will want to spend considerable time with each other and with their books. They will have the expertise, but before they become teachers they must be learners. One by one, as each member reaches out to the community, experiences will return to the group, giving it a boost for yet greater activity.

The committee might wish to develop a master plan for its activity among adults. It should list the various groups in the community, identify those it knows most about (some committee members might also be members of those groups) as well as those it knows least. No group that has monthly meetings, discussions, public events for its membership need be exempt from the list. Death can be a compelling subject for everyone.

A basic service from the committee to the community would be a speakers' bureau type of activity. Hundreds of groups seek thoughtful and good speakers for their meetings; some may actively welcome the committee's unusual concern. Many will refuse interest and decline the opportunity. But momentum develops, always, if the committee does but persist. At some point, in the queer logic of these things, it will become fashionable to discuss death, and then you will not have enough time and energy to handle all the inquiries.

Many communities boast extension or evening schools for adults, sometimes in connection with the public high school or the local community college. The more informed leaders of the committee might consider preparing a syllabus on death education and presenting it to the evening school organizers as a possible course entry. Social workers, religious institutional personnel, teachers, senior-citizen-center staff members, psychologists, doctors, lawyers and ordinary citizens can use such seminar and classroom

experiences, for few have been taught even to talk about it themselves, much less talk about it with those asking for help.

Communication Task

If the committee can think of its task as opening up conversations about death wherever it seeks to have input, it will have many rewards. Even where the program might seem too advanced, too sticky, too disturbing for a group's membership, there will have been a conversation. In this sense, every outgoing effort by the committee will be productive. The worst thing that can happen to the committee is that someone will say No, and that is not too dreadful to contemplate. For many people who say No today will wind up saying Yes tomorrow. . . .

The Cooperative Funeral Home, like death itself, is a moment in time.

It can be used as a focus for growth. We have to choose how to use it.

By working together, by coming to the point where we recognize that the tasks of death are everyone's, we face death in a new way. We free ourselves from exploitation, from undignified obeisance to old and useless forms. We become a free people.

The idea of a memorial society and its logical extension into the idea of a Cooperative Funeral Home are commended to people everywhere. Beyond the Home is a better society.

Raymond Paavo Arvio is the author of The Cost of Dying and What You Can Do About It. *A former instructor at Queens College, he has lectured widely in the field of funeral reform, helped found memorial societies in New York State, and originated a public TV series on consumer education.*

Donating Your Body: A Difficult But Preferable Choice

David Owen

My wife recently told me she intends to donate her body to science. I found the proposition ghoulish, even though it would relieve me (I intend to survive her) of the expense of disposal. I said that I was determined to have a more traditional send-off: a waterproof, silk-lined, air-conditioned casket priced in the sports car range, several acres of freshly cut flowers, a procession of aggrieved school children winding slowly through some public square, a tape-recorded compilation of my final reflections, and, local ordinances permitting, an eternal flame. But after a bit of research, I have come around to her point of view.

Two powerful human emotions—the fear of death and the love of bargains—inexorably conflict in any serious consideration of what to do with an expired loved one, all the more so if the loved one is oneself. Most people secretly believe that thinking about death is the single surest method of shortening life expectancy.

On the other hand, the appeal of the bargain intensifies when a third (though essentially unheard of) emotion—the desire to do good for its own sake—is injected into the discussion. If, after one is entirely through with it, one's body can be put to some humane or scientific use, enabling life to be preserved or knowledge to be advanced, can one in good conscious refuse? And yet, the mortal coil recoils.

"No freezing in the winter. No scorching in the summer." Such are the advantages of booking space in an aboveground burial condominium, according to a flyer I received not long ago. Printed across the bottom of the page was this disclaimer: *"We sincerely regret if this letter should reach any home where there is illness or sorrow, as this certainly was not intended."* In

other words, if this information has arrived at one of the rare moments in your life when it would actually be of immediate use, please ignore it.

Unchanged Death Industry

That the funeral business is filled with smoothies, crooks, and con men has been well known since at least 1963, when Jessica Mitford published her classic exposé, *The American Way of Death.* Mitford's book is required reading for all mortals. Fit-A-Fut and Ko-Zee, she revealed, were the trade names of two styles of "burial footwear," the latter model described by its manufacturer as having "soft, cushioned soles and warm, luxurious slipper comfort, but true shoe smartness." The same company also sold special postmortem "pantees" and "vestees," enabling funeral directors to gouge a few extra dollars out of any family that could be dissuaded from burying a loved one in her own underwear.

Twenty years later, the death industry is unchanged in almost every particular except cost. Mitford found that the average funeral bill, according to industry figures, was $708. When I visited a local mortuary to price a simple burial for a fictitious ailing aunt, the director rattled off a list of probable charges that added up to more than $5,000, flowers and cemetery plot extra. His estimate included $110 for hauling her body two blocks to his establishment and $80 for carrying it back out to the curb. Pallbearing is a union job in New York City; family members can't lay a hand on a coffin without getting a waiver from the local. ("If they drop the casket, pal," a Teamsters spokesman told me, "you're gonna be in trouble.") Hairdresser, $35. Allowing "Auntie" (as he once referred to her) to repose in his "chapel" for one day—something he told me was mandatory, despite the fact that I said I didn't want a memorial service and that no relatives would be dropping by—would be $400.

The largest single charge we discussed was for the

casket. He used the word "minimum" as an adjective to describe virtually any model I expressed an interest in that cost less than $1,500. The single wooden coffin in his showroom was "very" minimum ($1,100). The whole genius of the funeral business is in making you believe you're buying a refrigerator or a sofa or even a car instead of a box that will be lowered into the ground and covered with dirt. Since there are no *real* criteria, other than price, for preferring one such box to another, you end up doing things like sticking your hands inside a few models and choosing the one with the firmest bedsprings. "Women seem to like the color coordination," my Charon said in reference to a 20-gauge steel model (I think it was called the Brittany) with a baby-blue interior. Since the women he was talking about are dead, that word "seem" is positively eerie.

The Popularity of Cremation

Cremation is becoming a fairly popular choice among people who think of themselves as smart shoppers. The funeral industry has responded to this trend by subtly discouraging its customers from considering cremation and by making sure that cremation is very nearly as expensive as burial in a box. A pamphlet called "Considerations Concerning Cremation," published by the National Funeral Directors Association, Inc., and distributed by morticians, pretends to be evenhanded but is actually intended to horrify its readers. "Operating at an extremely high temperature (a cremation oven) reduced the body to a few pounds of bone fragments and ashes in less than two hours.... Most of the cremated remains are then placed in an urn or canister and carefully identified." This last sentence is the funeral director's equivalent of "Most newborn babies are then sent home with their proper mothers." Earth burial, in contrast, is "a gradual process of reduction to basic elements."

If the funeral business dislikes cremation, it positively abhors the donation of bodies to medical schools, because in such cases the opportunities for profiteering are dramatically reduced—though not, to be sure, eliminated. There is virtually nothing you can do, short of being disintegrated by Martians in the middle of the ocean, to keep a funeral director from claiming a piece of the action when you die. Once again, a pamphlet tells the story: "...essential to avoid the possibility of disappointment...more bodies available than the maximum required... rejection *is* permitted by state law...you can expect your funeral director to be of assistance...."

One almost wishes one could die tomorrow, the sooner to savor the pleasure of taking one's business elsewhere.

Ernest W. April, associate professor of anatomy at Columbia University's College of Physicians & Surgeons, is the man in charge of superintending

Columbia's supply of cadavers. Dr. April shares his office with Rufus, a huge red dog who wandered into his yard one day and doesn't like to be left alone. Also in Dr. April's office are some skulls, an old-fashioned radio, a human skeleton, a spine, a paperback book with a picture of a skull on it, some more skulls, a few microscopes, some big bones on a shelf, and a small plastic bone on the floor (for Rufus).

Your Own Cadaver

"Most medical students look forward to receiving their cadaver," Dr. April told me. "Once they have their cadaver they are, from their point of view, in medical school. It's something tangible. There's anticipation, trepidation. In the first laboratory exercise, the students basically come up and meet the cadaver, almost as if it were a patient."

"The funeral industry has responded to this trend by subtly discouraging its customers from considering cremation by making sure that cremation is very nearly as expensive as burial."

As at all medical schools, Columbia's cadavers are donated. Prospective benefactors eighteen years of age and older fill out anatomical bequeathal forms and return them to the university. Hours, days, weeks, months, or years pass. "When the Time Comes," as one brochure puts it, the donor's survivors call the medical school's department of anatomy. "Within the greater metropolitan area," the brochure says, "arrangements for removal of the body can be made by the medical college. Alternatively, the family may engage a local funeral director to deliver the **unembalmed** body to the medical college at the address on the cover." Medical schools almost always require unembalmed bodies because ordinary cosmetic embalming, the kind sold at funeral homes, turns skins to the consistency of old shoes and doesn't hold off deterioration for more than a few days. Medical school embalming, on the other hand, is designed for the ages. "We've had some specimens that we've kept for over twenty years," one professor told me. "It's almost like the Egyptians."

Donated cadavers are stored in a refrigerated room until they're needed. Columbia has about 200 students in each class. The ideal student-cadaver ratio is four to one (which means "every two people get one of everything there's two of," a medical student explains). Contrary to what the funeral directors imply, Columbia, like many schools, has fewer bodies than it would like and so must assign five students to each. Ratios as high as eight to one are not unheard of. If the donor consents beforehand, a cadaver bequeathed to one institution may be transferred to another with greater need. New Jersey, for some reason, attracts almost as many cadavers as it does medical students and occasionally ships extras to New York. (That's extra cadavers, not extra medical students.) People who don't like the idea of being dissected by students at all can specify on their bequeathal forms that their bodies are to be used only for research.

Donation Programs

"If a person donates his remains for biomedical education and research," Dr. April says, "there's a moral obligation on our part to utilize the body on this premises if at all possible, and only for that purpose. The only exception is that we occasionally do make material that has been dissected available to art students because, going back to the time of Leonardo da Vinci, Raphael, Titian, and Michelangelo, artists have had a real need to know and understand anatomy." Subscribers to public television, among others, should find this prospect irresistible: a chance to benefit science *and* the arts.

"The ideal donor is a young man who has played a game of basketball, run a few miles, and then had a safe dropped on his head."

When Columbia's anatomy courses end, the cadavers are individually cremated and buried in a cemetery plot the university owns. All of this is done at the university's expense. (In comparison with funeral home rates, the cost of picking up, embalming, storing, cremating, and burying each cadaver is estimated by medical school officials at about $400.) If the family desires, the uncremated remains can be returned at the end of the course, as long as the family asks beforehand and agrees to cover any extra costs.

Nearly all medical schools operate donation programs much like Columbia's. All you have to do is call up the anatomy department at the nearest medical school and ask what the procedure is. A group called the Associated Medical Schools of New York, based at Manhattan's Bellevue Hospital, oversees donations to a dozen or so institutions around the state, including the New York College of Podiatric Medicine and the New York University School of Dentistry. You might think that a podiatry school and a dental school could happily share cadavers, but no school will take less than a whole body.

I sent away for donation information from dozens

of medical schools and state anatomical boards. Studying the resulting avalanche of brochures has given me more than a week of intense reading pleasure, making me feel at times like a young girl poring over brides' magazines in hopes of discovering the perfect honeymoon. Comparison-shopping for a place to send one's corpse, like all consumer activities, quickly becomes a joy independent of its actual object. There are many factors to consider.

Factors to Consider

For example, I knew an elderly man who pledged his body to Harvard. When he died last year, his wife contacted a local funeral home to make the arrangements and was told that it would cost about $1,000 above and beyond the standard fee paid by Harvard. When the widow properly balked (all they had to do was drive the corpse fifty miles), the mortician supplied an eight-page letter justifying his charge. Among other problems, he wrote, was "the possibility that a body may be rejected by the Medical School." This conjures up unwanted images of admissions committees, and obliquely suggests that if my friend had aimed a little lower in the first place, the problem might never have arisen.

Medical schools do reserve the right not to honor pledges. All schools turn down bodies that have been severely burned, for obvious reasons. Other requirements vary. Pennsylvania rejects bodies that are "recently operated on, autopsied, decomposed, infectious, mutilated or otherwise unfit." Contagious diseases are particularly worrisome; anatomists keep a careful watch for Jakob-Creutzfeldt disease, a slow-acting virus that kills not only the occasional medical student but also cannibals who dine on the brains of their victims. All schools, as far as I can tell, accept bodies from which the eyes and thin strips of skin have been removed for transplantation. Removal of major organs, however, is almost always unacceptable, which means that organ donors (see below) generally can't also be cadaver donors. The state of Pennsylvania is more lenient in this regard. Most other schools want their cadavers intact, although the University of Kansas will accept bodies from which no more than "one extremity has been amputated."

Stanford's brochure is full of high sentence and King Jamesian resonances, the sort of prose selective colleges use to dishearten the hoi polloi. One section lists five grounds for rejection, each beginning with the phrase "The Division of Human Anatomy will not accept...."One thing the Division of Human Anatomy will not stand for is "the body of a person who died during major surgery," which sounds like the medical equivalent of refusing to cross a picket line. The section concludes, *"In summary, the Division of Human Anatomy reserves the right to refuse any body which is, in the opinion of the Division, unfit for its use."*

Chances are, you have a long and healthy life to

live. But a lot of other people don't.... This strangely comforting thought comes from a pamphlet called "The Gift of Life," published by a Cleveland outfit called Organ Recovery, Inc. Since there's usually no way to tell whether your organs or your whole body will be more useful until When the Time Comes, the wisest course is to promise everything to everyone and leave it to the experts to sort things out later.

Organ donation has been given a lot of publicity in recent years. Drivers' licenses in most states now have tiny organ-pledge forms on the back. These forms don't have much legal meaning. At New York's Columbia Presbyterian Hospital, for instance, no one will remove an organ (or cart away a cadaver to a medical school) unless the next of kin give their consent. You could die with an organ-donor card in every pocket, and another one pasted on your forehead, and still no one would touch you if your current or separated but not divorced spouse, son or daughter twenty-one years of age or older, parent, brother or sister twenty-one years of age or older, or guardian, in that order, said no. Prince Charles carries a donor card; but if he dropped dead (God save the King) at Presbyterian, someone would have to get permission from Lady Di before removing anything. If you want to be an organ donor, carrying a card is much less important than making sure your relatives know your wishes.

No matter how thorough you are about clearing the way, however, the chances are slim that your heart, liver, kidneys, or lungs will ever be transplanted into somebody else. Only about one percent of all the people who die are potential kidney donors, for instance, and kidneys are actually removed from only one in five of these. The reason is that a suitable organ donor is that rarest of individuals, a person in marvelous health who is also, somehow, dead. Major organs for transplantation have to be removed while the donors' hearts are still beating, which means that all major-organ donors are brain-dead hospital patients on artificial respiration. The ideal donor is a young man who has played a game of basketball, run a few miles, and then had a safe dropped on his head.

Organ Recovery Programs

John M. Kiernan, organ recovery coordinator at Columbia Presbyterian, explains that Karen Ann Quinlan is not a potential organ donor, because she is not dead. She is breathing by herself and there is activity in her brain. Every organ donor must be pronounced utterly and irretrievably deceased by two separate physicians who will not be involved in the ultimate transplantation. They are not goners; they are gone. This requirement is meant to reassure people who fear that signing organ-donor cards is the rough equivalent of putting out Mafia contracts on their own lives. I used to share these fears; now they strike me as silly.

The bookshelves in Kiernan's office hold volumes with titles like *Brain Death: A New Concept or New Criteria?* Nearby are a few test tubes filled with darkish blood. Behind his door is a big blue-and-white picnic cooler that he uses to carry transplantable organs from donors to recipients. Big blue-and-white picnic coolers seem to be the industry standard for moving organs, whether across town or across the country. In a cover story on liver transplants last year, *Life* magazine published a picture of a man hoisting a cooler called a Playmate Plus into the back of a station wagon. The cooler contained a liver packed in ice.

If your major organs don't make it (because, say, you've lived a long time and faded away slowly in the comfort of your own bed), there's still hope for lesser service. Almost anyone can give skin, eyes, bone, often without hurting one's chances of getting into medical school. Small strips of skin (whose removal does not disfigure a cadaver) are used to make dressings for burn victims. These dressings help keep many people alive who might die without them. Several parts of the eye can be transplanted. There are perhaps 50,000 people now blind who would be able to see if enough of us followed the example of Henry Fonda and Arthur Godfrey and donated our corneas. Bone transplants eliminate the need for amputation in many cancer cases. The National Temporal Bone Banks Program of the Deafness Research Foundation collects tiny inner-ear bones and uses them in medical research.

None of these programs will save you burial costs the way donating your whole body will. Nor can you receive money for giving all or part of yourself away. Paying for bodies is widely held to be unseemly and is, in fact, against the law. On the other hand, physicians do not to my knowledge refuse payment for performing transplant operations. Maybe the law ought to be rewritten to include a little sweetener for the people who make the operations possible. On still another hand, the last thing Washington needs right now is a lobby for dead people, who only vote in Texas and Chicago as it is.

"I sort of like the idea of one day inhabiting the nightmares of some as yet (I hope) unborn medical student."

To find out more about these programs you can either ask your doctor or write to an organization called the Living Bank, P.O. Box 6725, Houston, Texas 77265. The Living Bank is a clearinghouse for organ and whole-body donation, coordinating anatomical gifts all over the country.

Making intelligent consumer choices usually entails

trying out the merchandise. In this case, a test drive is out of the question. But since I had never so much as clapped eyes on an actual dead person before, I asked Columbia's Ernest April if he would give me a tour of his anatomy classroom. He agreed somewhat reluctantly, then led me down precisely the sort of stairway you would expect to be led down on your way to a room full of bodies. The classroom, by contrast, was cool and airy and had a high-priced view of the Hudson River. Blue walls, green floor, bright lights, a big blackboard, a lighted panel for displaying X rays, videotape monitors hanging from the ceiling, lots of enormous sinks for washing up.

"Making intelligent consumer choices usually entails trying out the merchandise. In this case, a test drive is out of the question."

Also, of course, the bodies. There seemed to be about thirty of them, each one lying on a metal table and covered with a bright yellow plastic sheet. The only noticeable odor in the room was the odor of new plastic, familiar to anyone who has smelled a beach ball. Since the course was drawing to an end, the shapes beneath the sheets were disconcertingly smaller than expected: as dissection progresses, students tag the parts they're finished with and store them elsewhere. To demonstrate, Dr. April pulled back the yellow sheet on the table nearest us, causing a momentary cessation of my heartbeat and revealing the top of a skull, a set of dentures, a long striated purplish thing, some other things, I'm not sure what else. But no arm, the object of his search. Far across the room, a few students were huddled over a dark form that suggested nothing so much as the week after Thanksgiving. My initial queasiness subsided and, with a sort of overcompensating enthusiasm, I asked if I could bound across the room for a closer look. Dr. April gently persuaded me to stay put. "This is late in the course," he said softly. "It's not particularly pleasant."

The Transformation

Unpleasant, yes; but is it disgusting or unbearable? Many people say they can't stand the thought of being dissected; much better they say, to be fussed over by a funeral director and eased into a concrete vault, there to slumber intact until awakening by choirs of angels. But death is death, and every body, whether lying on a dissection table, baking in a crematorium, or "reposing" in a $10,000 casket, undergoes a transformation that doesn't lend itself to happy contemplation. In terms of sheer physical preservation, a medical school cadaver is vastly more enduring then the recipient of even the costliest

ministrations of a funeral director. No casket ever prevented anyone from following the road that Robert Graves described in *Goodbye to All That:* "The colour of the faces changed from white to yellow-grey, to red, to purple, to green, to black, to slimy." The transformation takes hours, days.

Morticians sew corpses' lips together, bringing the needle out through a nostril. Lips are pinned to gums. Eyes are covered with plastic patches, then cemented shut. Orifices are plugged. To prevent loved ones from belching, howling, or worse as the accumulating gases of deterioration escape through any and all available exits, funeral home employees press hard on the abdomen immediately before and after family "viewings." Makeup is slathered on. Abdomens are drained. Leaks are patched. Unsightly lumps and bulges are trimmed away.

The trouble with death is that *all* the alternatives are bleak. It isn't really *dissection* that appalls; it's mortality. It may be gross to be dissected, but it's no less gross to be burned or buried. There just isn't anything you can do to make being dead seem pleasant and appealing. And barring some great medical breakthrough involving interferon, every single one of us is going to die. We should all swallow hard and face the facts and do what's best for the people who will follow us.

Which is why you would think that doctors, who spend their entire lives swallowing hard and facing facts, would be the eagerest anatomical donors of all. But they are not. Of all the people I interviewed for this article—including several heads of anatomical donation programs, a number of medical students, physicians, even the chief medical examiner of New York—only *one* of them, Ernest W. April, had pledged any part of his body to scientific study or transplantation. And April is a Ph.D., not an M.D. "I don't know of any medical student who is going to give his body," a medical student told me.

Dreading Your Own Profession

Do doctors know something? Of course not. Every profession lives in secret horror of its own methods. Most reporters I know can't stand the idea of being interviewed. But society would crumble if we weren't occasionally better than those who believe themselves to be our betters.

Morbid humor at their expense is one thing future cadavers worry about. Medical schools are aware of this and take great pains to keep jokes to a minimum. Still, a certain amount of horsing around is inevitable. Michael Meyers, the man who played Ali McGraw's brother in *Goodbye, Columbus* and went on to become a physician, described some dissection hijinks in a book called *Goodbye, Columbus, Hello Medicine.* "By the second week of gross anatomy," Meyers wrote, "it was interesting to notice which members of the class really rolled up their sleeves and dug in (no pun intended—although one group of students did nickname their cadavers 'Ernest,' so they could always say that they were 'digging in Ernest')...'' and so on and so on. This is a level of comedy that I do not, to be perfectly frank, find intimidating. And a cadaver donor who wanted to have the last laugh could arrange to have an obscene or hilarious message (''Socialized Medicine''?) tattooed across his chest. Beat them to the punchline. Humorous tattoos don't seem to be grounds for rejection, even at Stanford.

As for dissection itself, it's about what you would expect. ''You work through the text,'' says a young woman just beginning her residency, ''and by Halloween you've gotten to the hands. Well, we had a girl in our group who wanted to be a surgeon, and she did the most amazing thing. She dissected off the skin *in one piece.* It was like a glove. It was beautiful. And then there was mine. It looked like someone had been cracking walnuts. Little flecks, you know? And then this graduate student comes up and says, 'Have you found the recurrent branch of the medial nerve?' And I start looking through my pile...''

''The trouble with death is that all *the alternatives are bleak.''*

A first dissection, like a sexual initiation, is likely to be a botched job: long on theory and good intentions, short on practical knowhow. Results improve with practice, but early impressions linger. No wonder medical students don't like the idea of being dissected. For many of them, anatomy class is their first real experience of death. Maybe it's a good thing if physicians develop, right from the beginning, an overpowering abhorrence of cadavers. We are all better served if our physicians devote their energies to keeping us from turning into the things they hated to dissect in medical school. Anatomy classes, in a sense, trick grade-grubbing premeds into developing something like a reverence for human life.

Donating one's body is an act of courage, but it's not a martyrdom. Medical students may not immediately comprehend the magnitude of the gift, but so what? I confess I sort of like the idea of one day inhabiting the nightmares of some as yet (I hope) unborn medical student. And if my contribution means that my neighborhood mortician will go to bed hungry, shuffling off to his drafty garret in the Fit-A-Fut coffin shoes I decided not to buy, then so much the better. Dying well is the best revenge.

David Owen is a freelance writer in New York. This viewpoint is taken from an article he wrote as a staff writer for Harper's *magazine.*

"Moody's study shows that experiences of something beyond this life happen far more often than most of us have imagined."

viewpoint **92**

Near-Death-Experiences Point to an Afterlife

Morton T. Kelsey

There is no question that the evidence for some kind of survival after death is a very important matter. It is important if there are some facts, and it is equally important if there are none. But it is practically impossible to deal with this evidence so long as we remain within a framework or world-view which does not allow for non-physical reality.

Most of the researchers in this field have noted the lack of serious scientific study of this subject. Ordinary textbook science does not admit the existence of a spiritual reality. Because of this, within the world-view held by most people, any scientific question about a person's continued existence after death is considered a non-question. It is literally a meaningless question or, in the philosophical language of Wittgenstein, "non-sense." In most instances not even psychologists can conceive of any value in asking such a question as this....

Our culture still keeps its materialistic prejudice. In spite of the fact that this research continues and evidence keeps on accumulating, people find it difficult to consider the reality of parapsychological experiences, and so they automatically rule out any idea of life separate from material reality. Therefore the possibility of continued existence after death is denied. *Unless we can be open to the possibility of some kind of existence different from the life we experience in the material world, which perhaps is even immeasurable, it is useless even to consider or study the question of survival after death....*

Let us now turn to the actual evidence, keeping in mind that we must look beyond the current popular understanding of God and the world around us in order to be able to evaluate these facts....

In various kinds of literature we find stories of people coming to the edge of death, getting a taste of what it is like and then returning to describe their experience....There is a widespread belief that the human soul goes on a journey after the body dies, but there are few literary accounts of people coming to the edge of death and then returning....Probably the most detailed and interesting story of such an encounter with death is that of George Ritchie in the book that he wrote with Elizabeth Sherrill, *Return from Tomorrow....*

Near Death Experiences

In 1965 Raymond Moody, an undergraduate student in philosophy, learned of Dr. Ritchie's experience and went to talk with him. He was impressed by the story and the stature of the man who told it. He mentally filed away the account. Later, he heard of other quite similar experiences and began to investigate the subject in depth. Raymond Moody went on to receive a Ph.D. in philosophy from the University of Virginia and then on to teaching philosophy. Afterward he decided to become a medical doctor and a psychiatrist. Both Dr. Moody and Dr. Ritchie discovered that when they described the near-death experience, someone in the listening group would usually come forward to share a similar experience. By the time Dr. Moody began his residency in psychiatry he was writing his first book, *Life After Life,* describing these experiences of other people in detail. This study shows that experiences of something beyond this life happen far more often than most of us have imagined....

The material for *Life After Life* came from interviews with about fifty people selected out of one hundred and fifty cases of near-death experiences. An over-all picture of what happened to them was given describing the fifteen typical elements in their accounts. The response to this book was almost overwhelming. Hundreds of letters poured in to contribute new examples. Out of this material Dr. Moody wrote a second book, *Reflections on Life After Life....*

In the two books we find nineteen elements in all which sometimes enter into these experiences. Only a few of these are common to all or most of the accounts, and so far there is none in which more than about half of these elements appear. There does not seem to be any rigidly pre-arranged order of occurrence. Most cases appear to be different in sequence, although some of the experiences are almost identical.

"There is no question that the evidence for some kind of survival after death is a very important matter."

Almost everyone spoke of the first, most common element: their experience was inexpressible. There was something about it which was more than could be described. It was more than they had words for. This is not surprising. We Western men and women seem to limit ourselves to expressing common experiences. When it comes to unusual or mystical experiences like this one, our language is poverty-stricken. The Greeks used at least twelve words to describe encounters with the non-physical world, and students of Sanskrit tell me that they have over twenty words for various nuances of spiritual experience, while we blush to use more than one or two. Yet perhaps the important part of such an experience for us is its ineffable quality or the fact that something we cannot express makes us certain that it is a genuine encounter and not something we have thought up on our own.

The next characteristic is also found in practically every experience of individuals who return from clinical death. They report knowing or hearing themselves declared dead. Usually they hear the voice of a doctor or nurse, or perhaps a spectator at the scene. However, they do not feel dead. Like people who are "slain in the spirit," they feel perfectly conscious even though they are unable to move their bodies. To the outside observer they appear to be in a coma, both mentally and physically inert. For instance, if shock or an injection is given to bring them back, they show no reaction of pain. And apparently pain is not felt during a near-death experience. At the same time the person may hear every word that is said, sometimes with abnormal clarity. It is important for people who visit the dying to realize this fact. Dr. Alan McGlashan brings this out in his book *Gravity and Levity* in which he discusses several instances of patients in a coma who knew everything that was being said and done.

At this stage many people report a sense of incredible peace, and often comfort or pleasant quiet. Any pain they had suffered has suddenly disappeared and instead they are filled with a sense of well-being and comfort. Nurses and those in religious orders who work with the terminally ill report the same thing. At the point of death there often comes a time of peace and quiet acceptance, even contentment. The unpleasantness we fear so much does not seem to be connected with actual dying, but with the devastating suffering which often leads to death.

The accounts generally describe that other kinds of things then begin to happen almost immediately. Many people tell of hearing some kind of noise once they are cut off from the direct awareness of their bodies. The noise can come in many different ways. Sometimes it is described as an unpleasant noise, a loud buzzing, roaring or banging which is absorbing and even grating. Some people hear a softer rush of wind, while others are drawn by a melodious ringing of bells or the sound of beautiful music. It is as if another realm of existence first breaks in upon dying people in a way that touches their senses and gets their attention.

Along with their experience of a noise, a great many descriptions tell of being drawn rapidly through a dark, tunnel-like space. To some people the area appears like a sewer or well, and there are other descriptions of a cylinder or funnel, a narrow valley or cave. However it is pictured, the experience seems to be that of being drawn through and out of one's body. These images all appear to imply separation from one kind of existence, from life in the physical body, and entrance into another realm and another kind of life.

"Out-of-the-Body Experience"

At this point in the course of most near-death experiences people seem to be separated or disengaged from their bodies. They are apparently able to observe their bodies from the outside and watch what is being done to them. Some individuals have been able to describe in detail the efforts to revive them, even though their physical senses were in no condition to see or hear anything that was happening. They described "hovering" or "floating" above their unconscious bodies and watching the scurry of activity. Sometimes they described the backs of nurses and doctors bending over them. Later, to the amazement of their physicians who corroborated the details, they reported exactly what went on, including complicated procedures that they had never actually *seen*.

This aspect of the near-death experience seems to be similar to the psychic phenomenon of clairvoyance known as an "out-of-the-body experience," in which the person seems to separate from his or her body and to get information about things that are completely out of range of sight, hearing, or other bodily senses. This kind of clairvoyance is discussed at some length by Charles Panati in his book *Supersenses* and also by Lyall

Watson in *The Romeo Error*.

According to some of the reports, people in this state of disembodiedness find it difficult to believe that they are dead. They have what seems to be a body, but not a physical one. They can see and hear people in the physical world and feel baffled because they cannot make contact with them. Time does not seem to exist for them, at least in the sense of clock time. They have unimpeded thought and movement and perception. They seem to pick up thoughts of others in a telepathic way rather than through hearing in the ordinary way. Sometimes they mention how difficult and depressing it was to be separated in this way from the world one has known.

In most cases, however, the sense of isolation apparently does not last very long. Meetings with friends who had already died, and also with some other kind of being, are described in quite a few of the accounts given to Dr. Moody. Arthur Ford in his own near-death report told of being greeted by many of the dead whom he had known. There are also many deathbed reports of dying persons who appeared to speak with someone who was not present in the room with them. We shall discuss this later.

In addition there is another element of encounter described by the people whom Dr. Moody interviewed which is even more significant. This encounter, in fact, seems almost too good to be true.

The Most Significant Element

People who are brought back from actual death often speak about coming into the presence of "a being of light" who is experienced with the same intensity the disciples felt when Jesus was transfigured before their eyes. In spite of the intensity of the light and the fact that this being appears to ask probing questions about the direction of the person's life, there is seldom anything painful reported about this experience. Instead, what is described is a sense of direct, personal communication and a feeling that the being of light is expressing love and concern for the person, even in asking about the quality of his or her life.

As one would expect, this experience has a tremendous impact on the individuals who encounter it. This element is so important that an example is needed to help us define and understand it. In one account presented by Dr. Moody the person related:

I floated . . . up into this pure crystal clear light, an illuminating white light. It was beautiful and so bright, so radiant, but it didn't hurt my eyes. It's not any kind of light you can describe on earth. I didn't actually see a person in this light, and yet it has a special identity, it definitely does. It is a light of perfect understanding and perfect love.

The thought came to my mind, "Lovest thou me?" This was not exactly in the form of a question, but I guess the connotation of what the light said was, "If you do love me, go back and complete what you began

in your life." And all during this time, I felt as though I were surrounded by an overwhelming love and compassion.

There are so many descriptions of contact with the divine as an encounter with light that we can mention only a few. The Quakers speak of their experiencing God as an experience of the inner light. In Greek Orthodox thinking *the Light* is considered a central description of the invisible God. One of the main elements of Paul's experience of God on the road to Damascus was the appearance of a great light. This experience of light, which also occurs frequently in the depth of meditation, seems to be one of the most common and most significant aspects of the near-death experience.

Life Review

This element of meeting the being of light seems to precipitate a review of the person's entire life. It appears from the accounts as if all the events and feelings and reactions of one's whole life are present, as in a rushing river flowing with incredible speed before the mind's eye. In some cases only the highlights seem to appear, while other people tell of feeling that they see everything that ever happened in their lives. Along with the review there seem to appear two standards for assessing the value of one's life, which are: Did one learn to love others, and did one acquire knowledge?

"There is widespread belief that the human soul goes on a journey after the body dies."

In addition to these most common elements of the experience there are several other aspects that often appear. Some people tell of suddenly seeming to be in touch with all wisdom and knowledge. The possession of knowledge seems to be a quality of "the being of light," and these individuals, without any effort, suddenly seem to share in it. They express a sense of contact with a mind which understands everything and puts them in touch with all of that knowledge. It is like having an infinite computer at one's fingertips. This is an ecstatic or visionary experience which is greatly valued by these individuals.

Then there is the "city of light" or "heaven" which some people described. Although Dr. Moody had few reports in his first book which could be thought of as describing a heaven, in his second book he included these accounts. They tell of seeing people in such a place, but in a form different from ordinary human existence. Apparently one does not see or hear them in the ordinary way but simply "knows" they are there. In the same way one "knows" that this is a place of vivid colors, flowers and fountains, beautiful scenery, with even the streets and buildings of a city. There is a sense of peace, of beauty, love and non-darkness. . . .

Reluctance to Return

The very quality of the near-death experience makes it difficult for many people to want to return to ordinary existence, and the return is often resisted. In the first moments of apparent death there seems to be an intense desire to get back into the body. But as one experiences more of what is available on the "other side," there is evidently less and less desire to return. Some people say that they do not know why they return, while others realize a need to do so because they still have unfinished business to accomplish in this life. Whether people say that they were forced to return, or that they had a choice, their attitude toward the experience is usually the same. Again and again one finds reports that this was the most vivid and real experience of a person's life. People often speak of how this experience stays with them, and they value it as Jung did, as an experience of absolute objectivity.

There is no doubt about the frustration in returning to normal life after a near-death experience. . . .

"There are so many descriptions of contact with the divine as an encounter with light."

Many people report that their lives have been changed by this encounter with near-death and something beyond. They seem to have a deeper sense of human values, particularly love, and a new sense of purpose and meaning in their daily lives. They take life more seriously, and yet playfully, and their fear of death is diminished. They have been near the edge and have found that life did not cease and there is even more meaning beyond death than on this side. And so they no longer see death as either the cessation or diminution of life, but as an entrance into a larger and more complete form of existence.

Two questions have been raised as to whether it is wise to make studies like this at all. In the first place many people have wondered if such reporting may not be a dangerous incentive to suicide. The answer to this question, interestingly enough, is found in Dr. Moody's study. Certain of the accounts he received were reports of near-death experiences after attempted suicide. These, without exception, were unpleasant experiences which contrasted sharply with the bulk of the descriptions. These accounts all suggest that people who try to get out of a difficult situation in this world through suicide find themselves in similar difficulty after they leave their physical existence behind. Persons who are tormented here apparently cannot solve their problem by electing to leave this life. The torment seems to go on with them.

Morton T. Kelsey is the author of the book Afterlife: The Other Side of Dying. *This viewpoint was excerpted from a chapter in that book.*

viewpoint **93**

Near-Death-Experiences Are Hallucinations

Ronald K. Siegel

The time is 1920. Thomas Edison has always been a believer in electrical energy. He once wrote that when a man dies, a swarm of highly charged energies deserts the body and goes out into space, entering another cycle of life. Always the scientist, Edison feels that some experiment demonstrating the immortal nature of these energies is necessary. In an interview in *Scientific American,* he states: "I have been thinking for some time of a machine or apparatus which could be operated by personalities which have passed onto another existence or sphere. . . . I am inclined to believe that our personality hereafter does affect matter. If we can evolve an instrument so delicate as to be affected by our personality as it survives in the next life, such an instrument ought to record something."

The time is 1978. The California Museum of Science and Industry opens an exhibit organized around the thesis that energy is indestructible, that consciousness can exist independent of the physical body, and that there is much evidence that consciousness continues after death. Designated "Continuum," the exhibit stresses the words of great philosophers who have supported the belief in life after death. Displays bombard the visitor with reports of visions of the dead and descriptions of the afterlife, in order to demonstrate that consciousness can exist without the physical body. However, the exhibit avoids the tricky philosophical problem posed by the fact that a conscious physical body is always the one to make such reports!

Popular Belief in Afterlife

Epistemological difficulties aside, the belief in life after death thrives. A recent Gallup poll reveals that approximately 70 percent of the people in the United States believe in the hereafter. An earlier survey conducted in the Los Angeles area indicates that 44 percent of the respondents claimed encounters with others known to be dead.

Suddenly, popular books abound with stories of reincarnation, mediums, spirits, ghosts, parapsychology, and other evidence for man's survival after death. Even the speculations of Maurice Maeterlinck on paranormal phenomena—including life after death—are reprinted for popular audiences.

Medical journals start publishing reports of patients who have had afterlife visions following near-death experiences. New therapeutic approaches to dying, based on a sympathetic assurance that life continues after bodily death, are developed. A major psychiatric periodical, *The Journal of Nervous and Mental Disease,* sets a precedent by publishing a literature review of the reincarnation and life-after-death research. Aware of the controversial nature of such a publication the *Journal* invites a commentary on the work. Regrettably, the commentary (written by a close friend of Stevenson's, an admitted "admirer" and colleague of 25 years) is not critical, but heavy with needless platitudes.

How should we judge such evidence? Should there be a trial by faith, or perhaps by combat—reminiscent of holy wars of bygone days? Perhaps a modern jury trial could weigh the evidence. Indeed, such a trial was conducted in 1969 (see *The Great Soul Trial,* by John Fuller), with the testimony of numerous expert witnesses supporting the belief in survival of the soul after death. The evidence to be presented here can be considered exhibits in a trial for scientific evidence of life after death. The reader, as trier of fact, must resist influence by the passionate and romantic pleadings of highly credentialed "expert" witnesses, since equally qualified experts of opposing viewpoints can always be found. For example, Freud wrote "our own death is . . . unimaginable, and

Ronald K. Siegel, "Accounting for 'Afterlife' Experiences," *Psychology Today,* January 1981. Reprinted with permission of the author.

whenever we make the attempt to imagine it we can perceive that we really survive as spectators" in the afterlife, and the German poet and scientist Goethe agreed that "the soul is indestructible...its activity will continue through eternity." Conversely, the equally famous philosopher Auguste Comte replied that "to search for the soul and immortality is a product of a childish phase of human development."

Modern "Evidence"

Nonetheless, man's concern with life after death has been more than a passing amusement of childhood. Modern writers who are "pro" life after death are not transparently unscientific in method or data. They acknowledge that their data arise spontaneously and are not subject to controlled experiments. They also note that "visits to the other side" can be stimulated by ingestion of hallucinogenic substances, but they curiously discount the possibility of controlled studies with these drugs. Rather, they endorse the use of parapsychological approaches. The bulk of the resultant data consists of phenomenological reports from individuals who have "experienced" life after death. There are a few surveys and questionnaire studies, but many of these are conducted on individuals who only observed dying patients and make inferences as to the nature of deathbed visions of the afterlife. Other studies use highly selective data, although the researchers are honest enough to say so. Better-documented studies—of physician Raymond Moody and parapsychologists Karlis Osis and Erlendur Haraldsson admit that the reported phenomena are open to several interpretations. Most researchers do not appear to be "cranks" who rationalize their interpretations with strong religious convictions, unjust attacks upon opposing viewpoints, or complex neologisms. A rare few compare themselves with Einstein, Colombus, or Galileo in respect to the unconventional investigation of sacred scientific doctrine. But unlike the pseudoscientists described by mathemetician Martin Gardner, who manifest strong compulsions to attack the greatest scientists and best-established theories, many current investigators of life after death try to accommodate their interpretations to established scientific thinking. These quasi-scientific orientations are all the more deserving of scrutiny because they give the appearance of valid scientific thought and testing.

Taken together, the evidence to be discussed here views life after death as a phenomenon involving physical, biological, behavioral, imaginal, experiential, cognitive, and cultural variables. But all nature presents itself to man primarily as phenomena with such attributes. In perceiving natural phenomena, man recognizes groups of events that share many cohesive features, in contrast to other events displaying less stability and persistence of pattern.

Historian Arnold Toynbee noted in 1975 that all living organisms that are subject to death exert themselves to stay alive, whether or not they have produced progeny. While many species grieve, as humans do, at the loss of mates or members of a social grouping, Toynbee echoes the popular notion that human beings are unique in being *qware* that death comes to all. Death, in terms of its physical sequels, is no mystery. After death the body disintegrates and is reabsorbed into the inanimate component of the environment. The dead human loses both his life and his consciousness. Toynbee asks the age-old question of what happens to consciousness after death, since both life and consciousness are invisible and intangible conditions.

"To search for the soul and immortality is a product of a childish phase of human development."

The most logical guess is that consciousness shares the same fate as that of the corpse. Surprisingly, this commonsense view is not the prevalent one, and the majority of mankind rejects the hypothesis of annihilation at death. Instead, they continue to exert their basic motivation to stay alive and formulate a myriad of beliefs concerning man's survival after death. Many of these beliefs revolve around the notion that the intact human personality survives in another dimension—an afterlife. Toynbee finds that idea suspicious, for although the body disintegrates, ghosts and spirits of the dead always appear in the familiar form of an embodied human: "Moreover, ghosts appear not naked, but clothed, and this sometimes in the dress of an earlier age than the ghost-seer's own....It seems more likely that the apparent visibility of a ghost is an hallucination." Conversely, Hans Holzer, a contemporary researcher of life after death, believes that the apparitions of the dead wish to be recognized and thus, considerately, appear as they did in physical life.

Other versions emphasize reincarnation, whereby humans have many successive lives in this world, each life with a different body, interrupted by short stays in another dimension. This idea of immortality through reincarnation seems to have been suggested to man both by his dreams and by inherited resemblances of the living to the deceased, resemblances in both physical and behavioral traits. Recent LSD research has also suggested that under suitable conditions individuals often have transpersonal experiences in which they experience their own identities but in different times, places or contexts. These experiences also include distinct feelings of reliving memories of a previous incarnation. However, the allied ability of these LSD subjects to identify with various animals or even inanimate objects strongly suggests that the reincarnation stories are little more than vicariously retrieved memories and fantasies. While some writers, like psychologist William James, have termed such experiences mere "dream creations," others have given serious philosophical and theological thought to the topic.

Afterlife and Sciences

Recently these beliefs in life after death have been related to several scientific disciplines, including physics and biology. Arthur Koestler has noted that the elementary particles of modern physics, like photos of light, can behave as both waves and particles. Similarly, he says that "the contents of consciousness that pass through the mind, from the perception of colour to thoughts and images, are unsubstantial 'airy nothings,' yet they are somehow linked to the material brain, as the unsubstantial 'waves' and 'fields' of physics are somehow linked to the material aspects of the sub-atomic particles." Furthermore, Koestler believes that such waves of consciousness can exist independent of brain matter, but he is unable to describe this association. He argues that perhaps ghosts and spirits are simply the reverberating waves of humans who, like radio transmitters, generate signals somewhere in the universe even after being turned off (dead). This idea is related to the "energy body" which parapsychologists claim leaves the physical body at death. Surely we can hear the sounds of distant dead stars through our radio telescopes. Koestler would have us believe that personalities or souls of dead humans persist in a similar way and, like the phantom limbs of amputees, can only be "felt" by those who have been attached to them in the past. With imperialistic zeal he carries speculation one step further and suggests that these dead souls go on to join some "cosmic mindstuff" which contains the record "of the creative achievements of intelligent life not only on this planet, but on others as well."

"Much of man's belief in the afterlife is manifested by nonverbal. . .behavior."

Charles Darwin wrote a scholarly paper in 1891 stating his belief that ghosts and spirits were *really* visions of the departed. He expressed the traditional assumption among biologists that man is the only living creature that entertains the idea of immortality. The idea was further examined by a German biologist, August Weisman, who mentioned the "continuity of the germplasm" and "the immortality of unicellular beings and of the reproductive cells of multicellular organisms." Weisman compared biological immortality to a certain form of perpetual motion, like the cycle of water evaporation and rain, whereby the cycle of life is repeating. While the individual and its body cells will "perish utterly" at death, the germ cells (genetic material) will maintain a continuity of life through reproduction—a type of immortality. But in the sense that a discrete soul or mind survives death, both Weisman and contemporary anthropologist Ashley Montagu reject the immortality principle. Montagu adds that man's belief in survival after death is probably related to some deep biological craving of the organism. The belief is maintained and strengthened, Montagu theorizes, because it contributes to the stability of social groups and other human endeavors.

Since nonhuman animals are governed by physical and biological principles similar to those governing man, the analysis of their behavior associated with dying and death may reveal important insights into related human behaviors. Much of man's belief in the afterlife is manifested by nonverbal, albeit overt, behaviors. These include religious ritual and ceremony, burying behavior, and the superstitious association of events in nature with ongoing acts.

Ancient Signs of Belief

Anthropologists cite the deliberate interments of the dead by Neanderthal man 100,000 years ago as the first evidence of man's belief in life after death. Excavations at the famous Shanidar cave in Iraq show evidence of Neanderthal funeral rites, including feasts, burials with flowers and food, and carefully prepared graves with markers. Even the skeletal remains of Cro-Magnon man are found buried in the fetal position, in line with the primitive myth that such a position facilitates rebirth. The study of allied behaviors in nonhuman animals provides an opportunity to understand their nature and function in man.

If deliberate burials are signposts of the belief in life after death for man, one cannot ignore the elaborate burying behavior of elephants as a similar sign of ritualistic or even religious behavior in that species. When encountering dead animals, elephants will often bury them with mud, earth, and leaves. Animals known to have been buried by elephants include rhino, buffalo, cows, calves, and even humans, in addition to elephants themselves. Other ethologists have observed elephants burying their dead with large quantities of food, fruit, flowers, and colorful foliage. Not only do these large animals display death rituals, but some of the smallest social insects also display stereotyped patterns of "necrophoric" behavior in regard to corpses. For example, sociobiologist Edward O. Wilson notes that ants of the genus *Atta* carry their dead into deserted nest chambers and galleries, and that the *Strumigenys lopotyle* of New Guinea "piles fragments of corpses of various kinds of insects in a tight ring around the entrance of its nest in the soil of the rain forest floor." Other types of funeral rites have been observed among both elephants and chimpanzees in Africa. Ethologist Eugene Marais describes an equally mysterious and quasi-religious behavior among South African baboons; they ritually huddle together with the setting of the sun, gaze at the western horizon, observe a period of silence, and "then from all sides would come the sound of mourning, a sound never uttered otherwise than on occasions of great sorrow—of death or parting."

Human Awareness

As do other animals, humans have a strong instinct to survive. Unlike other animals, humans are credited with the capability of realizing that death comes to all. And so, Richard Cavendish, a historian and folklorist, states: "The human solution to this grim dilemma is a life in some different world after death." Anthropologists have endorsed this solution, praising man for his "discovery" of the afterlife. Early man's awareness of his own repeating biological cycles, for example, regeneration of tissue or replacement of baby teeth with permanent teeth, may have provided a basis for this belief. Cavendish credits the belief in an afterlife to man's cognizance of season cycles, wherein death in winter is followed by rebirth in spring. And man may have been influenced by his observation of other natural cycles: the rising and setting of the sun, day and night, the waxing and waning of the moon, low and high tide, and so on. Indeed, many primitive peoples have religious ceremonies celebrating life after death in close association with natural seasonal events. The Hindus made the direct connection by comparing life after death with the flourishing of this year's grass and flowers, their dying, and their replacement by similar yet not identical grass and flowers in the next year. Ancient Egyptians believed in eternal life in association with the sun: "The sun rose each day in renewed strength and vigour, and the renewal of youth in a future life was the aim and object of every Egyptian believer." The sun was the symbol of the afterlife for the Aztecs, who believed that if you died properly, as in battle or sacrifice, you were reborn as a hummingbird or butterfly. Among many indigenous groups in South America, the mysterious cyclical appearances of mushrooms following rainstorms were considered gifts from the gods, and the hallucinations resulting from subsequent ingestion of certain species confirmed the reality of an afterlife.

Early man's inevitable ecological encounters with animal life suggested similar fates for nonhumans as well. The butterfly was an ancient Greek symbol of reincarnation, and St. Theresa of Avila used the metamorphosis of a caterpillar from gravelike cocoon to beautiful butterfly to symbolize resurrection. Contemporary psychiatrist Elisabeth Kubler-Ross tells her terminal patients that dying is like a butterfly's shedding its cocoon and emerging into a new life.

Man's study of life after death is highly dependent on the words, pictures, and other symbols used in description. Many of these words have sensory qualities and describe such properties as sights, sounds, tastes, and smells. Accident victims who have had near-death experiences often report visions of long, dark tunnels or sounds of ringing and buzzing. Surgical patients who are resuscitated following cardiac or respiratory failure frequently report floating out of their bodies and watching the operation from a distant perspective. Terminal patients often experience unbidden memory images of long-forgotten childhood events and deceased relatives. These images arise with such startling vividness that they often prompt the patient to react by speaking with the image or moving toward it. A British psychiatrist described such images as "mental representation so intense as to become mental presentation."

"Death in terms of its physical sequels, is no mystery. . . . The most logical guess is that consciousness shares the same fate as that of the corpse."

Many see a blinding white light and regard it as a higher being or god. In a similar way, the vivid visions and voices that often accompany epileptic seizures were once thought to be so mysterious that the sufferer believed "he really saw or heard an angel from heaven, or had a visit with the Holy Ghost, or was carried up into heaven or down into hell."

Many reports from individuals are generated from communication with the dead via mediums, spiritualists, ghosts, apparitions, automatic writing, clairvoyance, and allied techniques. If such methods appear tenuous to the skeptic, Allen Spraggett, a Canadian lecturer on the paranormal, typifies the field by responding that "if we are to examine the evidence for an afterlife honestly and dispassionately we must free ourselves from the tyranny of common sense." Accordingly, he argues that ghosts and apparitions are indeed hallucinations, but they are projected telepathically from the minds of dead people to those of the living! Both classic and contemporary literature are replete with these reports. In one report a dead man communicated to his living wife that the afterlife had "a lawn that would put any Earth golf club to shame. Flowers I've never seen before. Even new colors. And everywhere, people. Thousands of them. Happy people, doing things they really liked to do."

Other reports are less casual and present

descriptions in a more serious tone. A classic case that initiated much of the serious research in the field occurred in 1943. George Ritchie died of pneumonia for nine minutes (although there are no medical records to document this), was revived, and reported a journey to the afterworld where he met Jesus and was shown heaven and hell. David Wheeler provides an interesting collection of reports from the "clinically dead," those in near-death accidents, or who have had out-of-body experiences and deathbed visions. He acknowledges that it may be impossible to separate these reports from hallucinations, but he feels that hallucinations would be much more idiosyncratic and varied than these reports. His collected reports of the afterlife are highly consistent, which he argues is evidence of a singular separate reality in the hereafter.

Moody's Prototypical Vision

In his book, *Reflections on Life After Life*, Raymond Moody also attempted to describe that prototypical vision of life after death. Moody was neither the first to do so nor the most careful in his methods. But he has been the most popular author on the contemporary scene and, along with psychiatrist Elisabeth Kubler-Ross, can be credited with stimulating the current interest in the field. Moody collected a series of reports and interviews of near-death experiences, which he defines as "an event in which a person could very easily die or be killed (and may even be so close as to be believed or pronounced clinically dead) but nonetheless survives, and continues physical life." He was admittedly "sympathetic" to the people he interviewed and says, "in a couple of cases I did ask very loaded questions." Consequently, Moody is aware that his investigation is unscientific and does not even attempt to provide statistics or complete patient histories, which would have contributed greatly to the value of his work. Nonetheless, he has compiled an inventory of afterlife descriptions.

"All these phenomena bear a strong resemblance to those reported in drug-induced hallucinations."

According to Moody, the prototypical experience of dying includes the following common elements: ineffability (meaning that the experience is impossible to describe with words); hearing doctors or spectators pronouncing them dead; feelings of peace and quiet; a loud ringing or buzzing noise; a dark tunnel through which the person may feel himself moving; out-of-body experiences; meeting others, including guides, spirits, dead relatives, and friends; a glowing light

with a human shape; a panoramic review of one's life; a border or limit beyond which there is no return; visions of great knowledge; cities of light; a realm of bewildered spirits; supernatural rescues from real physical death by some spirit; a return or coming back with changed attitudes and beliefs.

Deathbed Visions

A few studies have verified this basic phenomenology of life-after-death experiences. In a questionnaire study, Karlis Osis obtained information from 640 physicians and nurses who observed the behavior of dying patients. A high frequency of deathbed visions was reported. These included the phenomena described by Moody and "scenes of indescribable beauty and brilliant colors resembling those experienced under the drug influence of mescaline or LSD." But Osis argued that the dying patient's otherwise clear sensorium indicated that the experiences were not hallucinations. However, it is important to note that hallucinations can occur in states where consciousness is "clear." Indeed, drug-induced hallucinations are frequently marked by heightened perceptual sensitivity. In addition, W.F. Mitchell has shown that hallucinations of dead relatives and friends can occur in states of clear consciousness when triggered by emotional states surrounding death, such as mourning.

Another study by Osis and Haraldsson, presents a more detailed examination of deathbed visions. Once again they confirm the typical phenomenology, which they argue only *appears* similar to dreams, hallucinations, or depersonalization experiences, but their evidence fails to present any significant differences. These authors remain convinced that there is a real "postmortem survival" out there somewhere, and they suggest that only those individuals sensitive to ESP and telepathy may experience it. But if deathbed visions are similar to other hallucinatory visions, they may have similar explanations that do not require beliefs in untestable constructs such as an afterlife, the soul, or extrasensory perception.

Explainable Experiences?

All these phenomena bear a strong resemblance to those reported in drug-induced hallucinations and in hallucinations produced by other conditions. For example, ineffability is a characteristic of peak religious and mystical experiences, including those induced by psychedelic drugs. These episodes are marked by suppression of verbal behavior, which has been related to states of central nervous system activity. The hearing of voices or other sounds is reminiscent of surgical patients recovering from anesthesia who often recall auditory stimuli that occurred during surgery. This is particularly common with the dissociative anesthetics nitrous oxide, ether, and ketamine, which allow sensory input to the brain.

The bright light is characteristic of many types of mental imagery; it is due to stimulation of the central nervous system that mimics the effects of light on the retina. It can also occur when the electrical activity in the brain is altered in such a way that the threshold for perception of phosphenes (electrical activity in the visual system) is lowered, and bright lights are seen in otherwise dark surroundings. This point can create a tunnel perspective. Compare the following reports from afterlife and drug hallucinations:

Tunnels in afterlife reports: "My awareness of the room dimmed, and the world immediately around me became like a tunnel with walls that glowed with a slight orange-red reflected light." "I felt like I was riding on a roller-coaster train at an amusement park, going through this tunnel at a tremendous speed." "I found myself in a tunnel—a tunnel of concentric circles...[a] spiraling tunnel."

Tunnels in drug hallucinations: "I'm moving through some kind of train tunnel. There are all sorts of lights and colors." "It's sort of like a tube, like I sort of feel...that I'm at the bottom of a tube looking up." "I am traveling into a tunnel and out into space."

The cities of light and other geometric patterns in afterlife visions resemble the geometric forms, often seen from aerial perspectives, which dominate early hallucinogenic intoxication and other hallucinatory experiences. Like the bright lights and tunnels, these geometric forms are partially produced by entoptic phenomena (structures within the eye) and electrical activity in the visual system. Consider the similarity of these accounts:

Cities and lights in afterlife reports: "There were colors—bright colors—not like here on earth, but just indescribable...I could see a city. There were buildings—separate buildings...a city of light." "I believe that it was at the very instant when I felt myself die that I started moving at very high speed toward a net of great luminosity and great brilliance."

Cities and lights in drug hallucinations: "There are tall structures all around me...it could be buildings, it could be anything...and in all colors." "Like extremely futuristic architecture, something like you would see at Expo '80 or something like that, like spheres and things constructed very differently." "And it seems like I'm getting closer and closer to the sun, it's very white...and there's like a geometric network or lattice in the distance."

Out-of-Body Experiences

The out-of-body experiences are common in a wide variety of altered states and hallucinations. Moody cites one respondent who lost part of a leg in a near-death accident: "I could feel my whole body, and it was whole. I know that. I felt whole, and I felt that all of me was there, though it wasn't." On the basis of this single case, Moody hastily concludes that severe damage to the physical body does not adversely affect the spiritual body. It seems more likely that the patient was reporting a "phantom limb" experience, a phenomenon common among recent amputees and associated with persisting neurological activity in sensory cerebral centers. The meeting of others is similar to hallucinatory states wherein guides will appear to lead the individual through novel and potentially anxious experiences. It is also similar to the appearance of "imaginary companions" who guide lonely explorers and shipwrecked sailors, and similar to the "imaginary playmates who amuse young and lonely children.

"The out-of-body experiences are common in a wide variety of altered states and hallucinations."

The guides and spirits are often dead relatives or religious figures whom Osis and Haraldsson label "other worldly messengers" from a "postmortem mode of existence." The fact that such relatives may be dead now or that such religious figures may never have existed does not prove they are alive and well in the hereafter. Rather, the experiences support the argument that these deathbed visions are retrieved memory images (or fantasy images) that were alive and well when originally stored. This could also account for the appearance of memory imagery common in both afterlife and drug visions. The panoramic review or "flash of life" is vivid, spontaneous, colorful, three-dimensional, kinetic, and genuine, all common features of hallucinations produced by states of central nervous system arousal. For example, compare the following description of this imagery in afterlife and drug visions:

Memory imagery format in afterlife reports: "It just flashed before me like a motion picture that goes tremendously fast, yet I was fully able to see it, and able to comprehend it." "The best thing I can think of to compare it to is a series of pictures like slides. It was just as if someone was clicking off slides in front of me, very quickly."

Memory imagery format in drug hallucinations: "Everything's changing really fast, like pictures in a film, or television, just right in front of me. I am watching it happen right there." "People standing in the office, appearing like slides that are crossing my field of vision."

The Nature of Hallucinations

Osis and Haraldsson assume that hallucinations will only portray information stored in the brain and, unlike real perceptions of the afterlife, could not portray what they consider "strange new environments" or novel experiences. But hallucinations (like dreams, images, thoughts, and fantasies) are often elaborate cognitive embellishments of memory images, not just mere pictorial replicas. This constructive aspect of hallucinations can be illustrated by a simple exercise. Recall the last time you went swimming in the ocean. Now ask yourself if this memory includes a picture of yourself running along the beach or moving about the water. Such a picture is obviously fictitious, since you could not have been looking at yourself, but images in the memory often include fleeting pictures of this kind. Hallucinations also include equally improbable images such as aerial perspectives, feelings of flying, and panoramic vistas of incredible beauty and novelty. As in hallucinations, the visions of the afterlife are suspiciously like this world, according to the accounts provided by dying patients themselves. Osis and Harraldsson report: "...beautiful surroundings where green grass and flowers grow. She seemed very pleased, happy that she could see these pleasant things. She said that it was like a garden with green grass and flowers. She was fond of flowers and had a garden at home."

"Even when individuals attribute reality to afterlife or drug visions, the reports possess all the elements of vivid dreams."

The researchers argue that the word *like* in this account indicates a glimpse of the beyond and not an actual garden. Here they are confusing similes with veridicality. The phrasing of *like, as if,* and *it is as though* are characteristic of hallucinatory reports when individuals do not perceive a reality to the images or when the images are modified sufficiently so as to prevent convenient description. Even when individuals attribute reality to afterlife or drug visions, the reports possess all the elements of vivid dreams, complete with feelings of flying and "supernatural" rescues. This is why hallucinations are sometimes called "waking dreams." Consider the following similar reports: Perceived reality in afterlife reports: "I floated down to a grassy field which had horses, cows, lions, and all kinds of wild and tame animals. It was a painting at first, then it became real. I was in that field looking at all those great things when you (indicating the doctors) pulled me back."

Perceived reality in drug hallucinations: "In fact, the scenes in my head are very real....I mean if you get right into it, it's as though you are there sort of like in a movie or something....That's a mental image, not a real one. I guess it's hard to tell the difference." "Now it looks like a comic book scene,

not at all vivid only I'm not daydreaming, I see these things!" "My mind left my body and apparently went to what some describe as the 'second state.' I felt I was in a huge, well-lit room, in front of a massive throne draped in lush red velvet. I saw nothing else but felt the presence of higher intelligence tapping my mind of every experience and impression I had gathered. I begged to be released, to return to my body. It was terrifying. Finally I blacked out and slowly came to in the recovery room. That's my ketamine experience."

The border or limit in afterlife reports is similar to states of "ego loss" or "psychological death" experienced in altered states of consciousness, including drug induced hallucinations. These experiences can include transcendence of space and time; awe, wonder, and a sense of sacredness; a deeply felt positive mood, often accompanied by intense emotions of peace and tranquility; a feeling of insight or illumination or some universal truth or knowledge (the "noetic" quality); and changed attitudes and beliefs that pass into an afterglow and remain as a vivid memory. Collectively these experiences constitute the ineffable mystical experience induced both by psychedelic drugs and by true religious experiences.

The Afterlife as Hallucination

The remarkable similarity of imagery in life-after-death experiences and in hallucinatory experiences invites inquiry about common mechanisms of action. The experiences can be considered as a combination of simple and complex imagery. The simple imagery consists of tunnels, bright lights and colors, and geometric forms. As discussed, they are probably caused by phosphenes, which are visual sensations arising from the discharge of neurons in structures of the eye. They also reflect the electrical excitation of organized groups of cells in the visual cortex of the brain.

Most of the investigators undertaking to explain complex imagery of people and places have described the visions as the result of an excitation of the central nervous system. As early as 1845 French psychiatrist Jacques Moreau was maintaining that hallucinations resulted from cerebral excitation that enabled thoughts and memories to become transformed into sensory impressions. Recent electrophysiological research has confirmed that hallucinations are directly related to states of excitation and arousal of the central nervous system, which are coupled with a functional disorganization of the part of the brain that regulates incoming stimuli. Behaviorally the result is an impairment of perceptions normally based on external stimuli and a preoccupation with internal imagery.

These states of excitation can be triggered by a wide variety of stimuli, including psychedelic drugs, surgical anesthetics, fever, exhausting diseases, certain injuries and accidents, as well as by emotional and physiological processes involved in dying. In studies with the fatally ill, Adrian Verwoerdt, a psychiatrist, has found that in the transition from health to fatal illness a patient passes through a period in which he is alone with his symptoms. Sensory signals from the body, though subliminal at times, trigger a mental awareness of feeling different or peculiar, followed by reactions of flights into fantasy and imagery in order to direct attention away from the physical concerns and escape into private comforting thoughts. Visions of the afterlife can be among these reactions. Psychiatrist Jack Weinberg describes a similar experience in the dying based on physiological changes. He notes that as organs degenerate, the perception of physical stimuli may not go beyond the point of sensory ceptor, and stimuli become blocked from awareness. Consequently, the individual becomes disengaged from physical concerns and turns attention inward to self-reflection, reminiscence, and thoughts of approaching death. These experiences may be coupled with a fear of death, a fear that is an effective trigger of altered states of consciousness in death and near-death situations. Such physiological and psychological triggers were undoubtedly present in many deathbed visions of afterlife, as Osis and Haraldsson report that 75 percent of their respondents suffered from cancer, heart attacks, or painful postoperative conditions.

"Angel Dust"

A classic example of a chemically triggered death experience can be found in intoxications with phencyclidine (also known as PCP or Angel Dust), a psychoactive drug with mixed excitatory, sedative, cataleptoid-anesthetic, and hallucinatory properties. Edward Domino, a psychopharmacologist, and Elliot D. Luby, a clinical psychologist, describe a salient feature of phencyclidine intoxication as reduced verbal productivity, the appearance of calm in the subjects, and reported experiences of sheer "nothingness." One subject reported lying in a meadow and described this meadow "as a place that he has often considered he would like to be buried in. The theme of death ran through most of his retrospective account of the episode. Possibly the experience of combined cutoff of interoceptive and exteroceptive cues is close to one's conception of what death must be like." Other common deathlike experiences in phencyclidine intoxication include ineffability of the experience and difficulty in verbal behavior; feelings of peace and quiet; disturbances in space and time perception; out-of-body phenomena (including ecstatic feelings of timelessness, weightlessness, peace, serenity, and tranquility); no perception of smells, odors, temperature, or kinesthesia; fear; and confusion. Naturally, this can lead to a concern with death and deathlike thoughts

for the phencyclidine-intoxicated individual. This state of preoccupation with death, termed *meditatio mortis*, may develop into a transient psychotic state that can predispose certain individuals to suicidal or homicidal behavior.

"These states of excitation can be triggered by a wide variety of stimuli, including psychedelic drugs, surgical anesthetics, fever."

The specific content of complex hallucinatory imagery is greatly determined by set (expectations and attitudes) and setting (physical and psychological environments). For many dying and near-death experiences, the sets (fear of approaching death, changes in body and mental functioning, etc.) and settings (hospital wards, accident scenes, etc.) can influence eschatological thoughts and images. Stanislov Grof, a psychiatrist, and Joan Halifax, an anthropologist, suggest that the universal theme of this imagery may be related to stored memories of biological events that are activated in the brain. Accordingly, they suggest that the feelings of peace and quiet may be related to the original state of intrauterine existence, when there is complete biological equilibrium with the environment. The experience of moving down a dark tunnel may be associated with the clinical stage of delivery in which the cervix is open and there is a gradual propulsion through the birth canal. The border or limit may be associated with the experience of incipient emergence from the mother, which is followed by delivery and feelings of transcendence. In a sense, Grof and Halifax are suggesting that the dying or near-death experience triggers a flashback or retrieval of an equally dramatic and emotional memory of the birth experience. Thus, the state of arousal present at death evokes memories or feelings associated with previous states of such arousal, as may have occurred during birth. Such a process would be similar to that which occurs when a specific song or melody spontaneously evokes an image of a loved one or when a child's behavior causes the remembrance of one's own long-forgotten childhood.

Released Perceptions

Perhaps the most integrated explanation of life-after-death hallucinations can be based on the perceptual-release theory of hallucinations, formulated by the British neurologist Hughlings Jackson in 1931. As updated by psychiatrist L.J. West, the hypothesis assumes that normal memories are suppressed by a mechanism that acts as a gate to the flow of information from the outside. An input of new information inhibits the emergence and awareness of previous perceptions and processed information. If the input is decreased or impaired while awareness remains—for example, as in dying or shock—such perceptions are released and may be dynamically organized and experienced as hallucinations, dreams or fantasies. Or if the storage of perceptions in the brain is sufficiently stimulated (by drugs or fear) and persists for a suitable time, the released perceptions can also enter awareness and be experienced as hallucinations.

> ## "Anthropological studies of afterlife concepts. . .are strikingly similar for all cultures of man."

West offered an analogy to illustrate the process. Picture a man in his living room, standing at a closed window opposite his fireplace and looking out at the the sunset. He is absorbed by the view of the outside world and does not visualize the interior of the room. As darkness falls outside, though, the images of the objects in the room behind him can be seen reflected dimly in the window. With the deepening of darkness the fire in the fireplace illuminates the room and the man can now see a vivid reflection of the room, which appears to be outside the window. As the analogy is applied to the perceptual-release hypothesis of life-after-death experiences, the daylight (sensory imput) is reduced while the interior illumination (the general level of arousal of the central nervous system) remains bright, so that images originating within the rooms of the brain may be perceived as though they came from outside the windows of the senses.

An Overview

From his early observations of animals burying their dead, through awareness of the seasonal cycles of nature, to recognition of the inherited resemblances of the living to the dead, man developed the concept of life after death in an effort to explain these behaviors and the feelings underlying them. Anthropological studies of afterlife concepts and of the soul's posthumous journey are strikingly similar for all cultures of man. The state of death may have idiosyncratic meanings for different individuals, but the experience of dying involves common elements and themes that are predictable and definable. These elements and themes arise from common structures in the human brain and nervous system, common biological experiences and common reactions of the central nervous system to stimulation. The resultant experience, universally accessible, is interpreted by self referential man as evidence of immortality, but this interpretation is little more than a metaphor to describe a common subjective state of consciousness. That subjective state can be remarkably real and convincing for many individuals. While satisfied that Western science may explain many elements of life-after-death phenomena, believers in the afterlife, like believers in other paranormal experiences, are nevertheless dubious when anyone dismisses the value of the total experience too readily.

Even if the experience of life after death doesn't lead to a "real" other world, the belief may very well change behavior in this one. Already the contemporary literature has glorified the afterlife trip. The popular writer Archie Matson titled a chapter "The Thrill of Dying" and makes the experience seem as harmless as an amusement-park ride. John Weldon and Zola Levitt begin a chapter in their book called "The Wonderful World of Death" by assuring the reader he will be born again.

In the past, death and dying were often accompanied by loneliness, as if the individual were possessed by Pan, the Greek god of lonely places and panic. The belief in life after death provided much comfort and security. Through the research discussed here we have begun to understand the nature of these life-after-death experiences as hallucinations, based on stored images in the brain. Like a mirage that shows a magnificent city on a desolate expanse of ocean or desert, the images of hallucinations are actually reflected images of real objects located elsewhere. The city is no less intriguing and no less worthy of study or visitation because it is not where we think it is. With such understanding we can counsel the dying to take the voyage, not with Pan at their side but with Athena, the goddess of wisdom. But, for the living, may the life after death rest in peace.

Ronald K. Siegel is an associate research psychologist in the department of psychiatry and biobehavioral sciences at the University of California in Los Angeles. He has published numerous articles on psychopharmacology and hallucinations.
A more complete version of this viewpoint by Dr. Siegel appeared in the October 1983 issue of American Psychologist *under the title "The Psychology of Life after Death." The* American Psychologist *version includes discussion of early anthropology, reports from individuals and several experimental studies. The editors recommend that the* American Psychologist *article be read in its entirety.*

"Evidence from . . . hypnosis strongly indicates that subconscious memories of past lives are carried by us all!"

Additional Lives Will Follow Death

Ian Currie

We know a good deal about what it is like to be dead. Yet there are some questions still to be asked. As the saying goes, "You're a long time dead." But *are* you? Do you stay dead "forever?" Surprisingly, this question can be answered with a fair degree of precision. *You can expect to stay dead about fifty-two years.*

Most people in the West regard the idea of reincarnation as a fantastic superstition, and find it difficult to imagine how such an outlandish doctrine could have developed. The basis for this "doctrine" is, however, *known*. It is the same basis from which all of the ideas in this book have been derived: *actual human experiences*. And there is only one kind of human experience which could be the basis for the idea of reincarnation—memories of past lives. . . .

Reincarnation Research

Research on reincarnation should not be undertaken lightly. The claim that we have all lived before is a profoundly disturbing one, and cannot responsibly be made without painstaking investigation. Such investigation has, in fact, been conducted over the past dozen years, with scrupulous objectivity. And from all of this research has come a single finding: reincarnation is not merely a theory; it is a fact.

The leading student of *conscious* memories of past lives is Dr. Ian Stevenson, a highly respected professor of psychiatry at the University of Virginia. He has collected 1,700 cases of persons who have definite memories of a life prior to their present one. These memories, typically very vivid, are absolutely convincing to those who carry them. And, although some do not recall enough detail for a definite identification of their former selves, a good many others do!

Ian Currie, *You Cannot Die: The Incredible Findings of a Century of Research on Death.* New York: Methuen/A Jonathan James Book, 1978. Reprinted with permission of the author.

In a typical instance, a child, as soon as he is old enough to talk (usually between the ages of two and three) begins to make persistent claims that he used to be someone else. Most parents make active efforts to discourage these revelations. But the child is adamant. He insists that what he says is true, even if he is punished repeatedly for doing so, and pleads to be taken to his former home, which he gives every sign of missing intensely. He will provide a great deal of detail about his former self, including his name and address. Where such claims have been checked, they usually turn out to be correct. Such a person did live and die where and how the child says he did. If the child is taken to his claimed former neighborhood, he will usually be able to take investigators to his former home, observing correctly any changes that have been made since his "death." The house, then white, is now green; a tree beside it has been cut down; a business across the street is no longer in existence. If ten friends and relatives of the dead man are lined up in front of him, along with ten people whom the dead man had never met, the child will be able to identify those he once knew. This identification often involves some very strong emotions. A three-year-old child may call his former wife correctly by a pet name, rush to embrace her, speak to her as a husband would to a wife, and state that he wishes to remain with her rather than with his parents. On encountering his children, who are of course a good deal older than he, he will address them and behave towards them in a way entirely appropriate to a parent. And in the most extraordinary cases, the child will bear on his body a birthmark closely resembling in shape and location a wound suffered by the dead man, either before or during his death.

Dr. Stevenson's meticulous investigation of thirty of the most convincing cases has established, beyond any doubt, that they are genuine. The person involved really did live, die, and become reembodied. But such vivid conscious memories of past lives, although certainly not rare, are not the rule. The majority of us clearly do not have them. And this poses an obvious problem. Why do only some of us recall past lives? If reincarnation is, as I have claimed, a fact, then why should it have happened to a mere thirty, or even to a mere 1,700, of all of the world's millions? The answer is that it hasn't. Evidence gathered from some 1,500 hypnotized persons shows, beyond any doubt, that *it has happened to us all.*

Conscious Memories of a Past Life

These memories can vary greatly in clarity and detail. Most commonly they appear as vivid fragments which do not contain enough detail to identify a specific historical personality. The memories may involve powerful emotions—often anguish—and are not sympathetically received by parents. . . .

"You can expect to stay dead about fifty-two years."

In the majority of cases, such memories, although intense, don't provide enough detail on the identity of the former personality to permit them to be linked to a specific individual who lived in the past. A minority, however, do. These cases show so clearly that reincarnation does occur. . . .

The Case of Corliss Chotkin Jr.

In the spring of 1946, in Angoon, Alaska, Victor Vincent, a fullblooded Tlingit Indian, died. During the last years of his life, he had a very close relationship with his niece, Mrs. Corliss Chotkin. About a year before his death he told her that he would return to her as her next son. And so that she would know him, he said, this son would have two scars on his body which he himself now had. Both of these scars were the result of surgical operations. One was at the base of his nose on the right side. The other was on his back and was quite distinctive, as it included round holes left by stitches. Eighteen months after Victor's death, his niece gave birth to a son. The boy was named Corliss Chotkin, after his father. He was born with two birthmarks on his body—exactly the same in appearance and location as the two scars borne by Victor Vincent.

Dr. Stevenson examined these birthmarks in 1962. They looked exactly like old scars. The one on Corliss's nose was darker than the surrounding skin, and was definitely indented. Of the birthmark on his back, the Doctor said:

> It was heavily pigmented and raised . . . [extending] about one inch in length and a quarter inch in width.

Along its margins one could . . . easily discern several small round marks outside the main scar. Four of these . . . lined up like the stitch wounds of surgical operations.

These birthmarks were interesting, to say the least. But they were followed by a series of even more extraordinary occurrences. When Corliss was thirteen months old and just beginning to talk, his family began trying to teach him his name. And one day when his mother was attempting to do this, a most startling event occurred. The little boy suddenly opened his mouth and said, in a Tlingit accent whose excellence was totally unexpected in a child of that age: "Don't you know me? I'm Kahkody." *"Kahkody" was the tribal name of the dead Victor Vincent.* And that was only the beginning.

When Corliss was two and being wheeled along a street in front of the docks, he suddenly saw someone and became greatly excited, jumping up and down and saying "There's my Susie." Susie was Victor Vincent's stepdaughter, and Corliss, in his present life, had never met her! What followed was just as strange. The two-year-old child hugged Susie affectionately, spoke (correctly) her Tlingit name, and kept repeating, excitedly, "My Susie, my Susie!"

Recognizing Past Relationships

A few weeks later Corliss was again out with his mother when he suddenly said, "There is William, my son." William Vincent was in fact the son of Victor Vincent and Mrs. Chotkin was unaware that he was in the immediate vicinity until Corliss spoke. At the age of three, his mother took him with her to a large meeting. Corliss remarked, "That's the old lady," and "There's Rose." Rose was Victor Vincent's widow, and Victor had always called her "the old lady." Corliss had picked her out of the crowd before his mother had noticed that she was present.

> On another occasion, Corliss recognized a friend of Victor Vincent, Mrs. Alice Roberts, who happened to be . . . walking past the Chotkins' house where Corliss was playing in the street. As she went by he called her correctly by her name, a pet name.

In a similarly spontaneous way he recognized, at various times, other friends of Victor Vincent. He would accost them, call them by name, and display a familiarity toward them which was not only highly unusual, in that Corliss had never seen them before, but quite inappropriate for a child. In addition, he showed an inexplicable familiarity with other aspects of Victor Vincent's life. For example, on one occasion:

> Mrs. Chotkin and Corliss were at the home formerly occupied by Mrs. Chotkin and her family during the life of Victor Vincent. The boy pointed out a room in the building and said: "When the old lady and I used to visit you, we slept in that bedroom there." This remark seemed all the more extraordinary since the building, which had formerly been a residence, had by that time been given over to other purposes and no

rooms in it could be easily recognized as bedrooms. But the room he indicated had in fact been occupied by Victor Vincent and his wife when they had visited the Chotkins.

All of these events occurred before the child was six. But by about the age of nine, Corliss began to make fewer statements about his previous life as Victor Vincent, and these memories apparently began to fade. By the time Dr. Stevenson met him in 1962, when he was fifteen, he said he no longer remembered anything of his previous life. (Dr. Stevenson's research shows that these memories usually begin to fade about the age of six, although they may be retained into adult life.) . . .

This case is typical of those involving conscious, verifiable memories of a past existence. Dr. Ian Stevenson has personally investigated dozens of such cases, and he has already published thirty in detail. His investigations have been scrupulous, painstaking, and time-consuming. Every alternative explanation to that of reincarnation, such as deliberate fraud or errors of memory, has been carefully considered, assessed, and eventually rejected.

A favorite counter-explanation offered by skeptics has been "genetic memory"—the idea that the experiences of the former personality have somehow been genetically recorded and passed down to the second personality, who falsely experiences them as conscious memories of his own past life. However, in the vast majority of Stevenson's cases, there is no genetic relationship whatever between the two personalities. . . .

Unconscious Memories of a Past Life

We don't really know how common conscious memories of a past life are, as there is plenty of reason for a family to conceal and repress them. In the East, such memories are usually felt by parents to be troublesome and embarrassing; they lead to fears that their child will leave them (as he frequently declares he wishes to), and they are often thought to indicate an early death. For all of these reasons, efforts are usually made to stop the child from talking about them. In the West, of course, such claims are regarded at best as highly fantastic, or at worst, as evidence of mental illness. But despite the high likelihood of widespread suppression of such memories by parents, it seems obvious that those who claim them are definitely in the minority. This, however, does not justify a complacent return to the notion that most of us "only live once"—*for evidence from regression hypnosis strongly indicates that subconscious memories of past lives are carried by us all!*

Experiments by psychologists have revealed that hypnosis can take people back in time. They need simply to be told to "go back." "Going back" means reliving past memories in vivid detail, sometimes in such detail that the present personality seems literally to become younger: at "age six" a hypnotized person

may write his name just as he did in first grade; at "age four," he may produce a child-like, preliterate scrawl. And where such memories can be checked, they turn out to be astonishingly accurate, right down to the wallpaper-pattern over the crib of a two-week-old baby. Taken back into the womb, subjects report warmth and darkness; some assume the fetal position. Progression forward to birth produces some painful memories: people writhe, twist, gasp, are crushed, squeezed and strangled, emerge into blinding light soaking wet and freezing cold, complain of being held upside down, and mourn that their mothers are unconscious and unable to cuddle them. And when they are taken back *beyond* the womb, *they begin to report in detail on past lives.*

Of every ten people, nine can be hypnotized, and will report in detail on past existences. Nor can this "reporting" be dismissed as mere fantasy, for subjects typically display a highly accurate knowledge of even the most obscure details of remote times and places where they claim to have lived. Verifying such memories may require the help of scholars who specialize in the history of the society involved, as well as an examination of obscure publications not available in English. *And almost always, these memories are verified as correct.* Deliberate efforts on the part of the hypnotist to persuade the subject to "change his story" are generally unsuccessful. Regressed subjects seem to tell the truth!

Fear of Hypnotism

And when the one of ten who "cannot" be hypnotized is given special treatment, we often discover that his subconscious mind has been saying "No!" for a very understandable reason. If he is reassured that he is safe and that the hypnotist will protect him from discomfort, pain, and danger during the regression, he *can* sometimes be hypnotized after all. *And if he is, it frequently turns out that he has recently died a very painful and traumatic death.*

"Every alternative explanation to that of reincarnation. . . has been carefully considered, assessed, and eventually rejected."

In examining the work of regression hypnotists who believe in reincarnation, I have been struck by the fact that, often, they seem to have become involved in this strange research because of personal experiences which have led them to believe that they and others have lived before. Hypnotherapist Arnall Bloxham reached this conclusion while still a child. Dreams are known to tap the subconscious, and his most vivid dreams were of the past, of people and of places completely unknown to him during his waking life. And then one day, on a vacation trip in the Cotswolds, he found himself in a place he recognized. It was a road which he had seen before, many times—*in his dreams;* a steep, tree-lined road, yellow and dusty. Bloxham knew that if he followed that road he would come to a castle. And he did—he came to Sudeley Castle. Bloxham recognized it. He knew the interior so well that he didn't need a guide. For he had lived there before—in another life. . . .

Hypnotic Regression and Historical Personalities

Memories of past lives may be conscious or unconscious, but the most convincing reports of either should contain the following features: First, they should involve a great deal of historical detail, which should, when researched, turn out to be correct. Secondly, it should be possible to prove that this historical detail was not already known to the present personality. If it were, then the regression could be a fantasy based on this knowledge and concocted under hypnosis. Thirdly, it is more convincing if the person whose life is described in the regression is completely obscure, and not someone so familiar to historians that books and articles have already been written about him. And finally, it should be possible to establish, through historical research, that this completely obscure personality from the past *actually did exist.*

"The most convincing reports. . .should involve a great deal of historical detail, which should, when researched, turn out to be correct."

In the case of *conscious* memories of past lives, all four criteria can often be met; a good deal of authentic detail about an obscure personality is often recalled. And the past personality can often be identified as well because only a few years have passed between the death of the first person and the birth of the second.

In the case of *unconscious* memories elicited by hypnosis, the first three criteria are almost always met—we are given historically authentic detail originating from an obscure personality. In fact, of some 1,500 past lives reported under hypnosis, nearly all concerned completely obscure individuals. But with the final criterion—proving that this obscure personality actually lived—we have a bit more trouble. In the case of hypnotically elicited memories, a lengthy period usually exists between the past death and the present birth. Although it can range

from a few months to several centuries, it is, on the average, fifty-two years. Given the total obscurity of the personalities involved, historical records are usually too poor to permit identification for periods seventy-five years or more in the past. . . .

"Xenoglossy"

When people are hypnotically regressed, they talk about past lives which they claim to have lived. And sometimes they do more than just talk. They talk *in a foreign language which they do not speak in this life.* And it is not just a matter of the recitation, under hypnosis, of a few words or phrases they may have picked up. They can carry on a fluent conversation with speakers of that language. This phenomenon is technically known as "responsive xenoglossy."

Needless to say, the foreign language spoken perfectly fits the place in which the person claims to be living in his past life. It also fits the time—for in cases in which the language has been subjected to expert analysis, it turns out to be an *archaic* form. *It is being spoken as it was centuries ago.* It is remarkable enough suddenly, to be able to speak a new language, but to speak an *archaic* form of it is more remarkable still. Additionally, these conversations often have a rather curious feature. The hypnotized person understands perfectly questions addressed to him in the language that he speaks in this life, and he can respond in this language. But he sometimes shows a *preference* for replying in the foreign tongue.

K.E., a Philadelphia doctor, occasionally made use of hypnosis in his general practice, and in 1955 began hypnotic experimentation with his thirty-seven-year old wife, T.E. He discovered that she readily went into a deep trance and he began some age regression experiments with her. During one of these, she began speaking broken English in a deep masculine voice, and with what seemed a Scandinavian accent. This masculine personality identified himself as "Jensen Jacoby" and sometimes replied to questions in what sounded like a Scandinavian language. T.E. was regressed to this personality eight times, and at some of these sessions native speakers of Scandinavian languages were present, including Dr. Nils G. Sahlin, a native speaker of Swedish and former Director of the American Swedish Historical Museum in Philadelphia.

Swedish Peasant

"Jensen" proved to understand modern Swedish, but himself spoke an archaic form of it. He described a life as a simple peasant farmer in Sweden centuries ago.

> He seemed to have little knowledge of his country beyond his own village and the trading center he visited. He had heard of English sailors landing. . . . He had heard of Russia and shared the common fear of Russians in Scandinavia. Apart from these scant references to international affairs, Jensen spoke only of the narrow round of life in his village, composed

of hard work and simple sensuous diversions. According to Jensen's account of himself, he lived in a place called Morby Hagar....This seems to have been his name for the place where his house was, evidently a tiny village at most....Some distance away—a day or two by horse—there was a town with a harbor called Havero. Here Jensen took his produce for sale....

Jensen...venerated a "ruler" called Hansen. The latter may have been a local hero or chief. Several times Jensen described Hansen as "forste man" *(first man or chief)*. In one session Jensen relived an incident occurring when he was sixty-two.... Engaged in some kind of fight with enemies, he waded into water (or was pushed into it) and then received a blow on the head which seems to have killed him.... Jensen showed an intense dislike of war. He delivered most of his answers to questions in a rather quiet voice.... But when an interpreter [interviewer who spoke Swedish] touched upon the subject of war, Jensen fairly shouted his disapproval...."Jensen also showed strong emotion in referring to his hero or chief, Hansen, the speaking of whose name he once accompanied by beating his own chest repeatedly and vigorously with both fists.

During another session, Jensen was asked to open his eyes and look at a number of objects and pictures, some borrowed from the American Swedish Historical Museum in Philadelphia. He was asked to identify them. Dr. Sahlin comments:

There were innumerable indications that Jensen was totally unacquainted with modern articles.... On the other hand, he showed immediate familiarity with...things dating back to and before the seventeenth century.... While Jensen...understood modern Swedish...without difficulty, he had no modern vocabulary, no words for things of exclusively modern date.

Ten scholars of the Swedish language examined transcripts of the tape-recorded, Swedish-speaking sessions with Jensen. *The consensus was that Jensen was a seventeenth-century Swedish peasant farmer who lived in southwestern Sweden near the Norwegian border. The Philadelphia housewife was speaking in a voice three hundred years old!*

Could she have "faked" it? Could this be some kind of fraud? Dr. Ian Stevenson conducted a scrupulously careful investigation of T.E.'s background. It took him some six years to complete. And he proved conclusively that T.E. knew nothing whatever of any Scandinavian language, much less seventeenth-century peasant Swedish!

Large-Scale Research Support for Reincarnation

Dr. Ian Stevenson has proven that reincarnation *does happen*— that *there are people alive today who once died.* And the regressions of hypnotists like Arnall Bloxham and Loring Williams *suggest* that the Stevenson cases are more than mere oddities, and that many people—perhaps most—have in fact reincarnated and can remember past existences. But it is the data derived from Dr. Helen Wambach's

regressions of over 1,000 people to some 1,100 past lives which proves, beyond any reasonable doubt, that we have all lived before.

One extremely consistent and very impressive finding emerges from the massive collection of data gathered by Dr. Wambach. In every respect, we get exactly what we should if people were actually recalling lives they had in fact lived in the past, rather than simply inventing fantasies based on normal sources of knowledge like books and movies. And as we are about to see, the detail in support of this statement is so intricate and so consistent that it simply cannot be explained away as mere fantasy.

"Most of the persons who lived and died in the past have been obscure persons who led extremely humble lives."

Dr. Wambach reasoned that no matter how convincing an *individual* regression might be, it could not produce the most valid proof of reincarnation. One could not rule out the possibility that what the person produced was a fantasy-life based on normally-acquired knowledge of a particular time and place. But if, on the other hand, she were to regress hundreds of people into the past, and hundreds claimed, when regressed, to have had a life in a particular time and place, with all consistently reporting the same obscure details of daily life, then this result would indeed be difficult to explain away as a fantasy. How could 100 people possibly have the *same* fantasy?

Hypnotized Groups

Dr. Wambach therefore began experimenting with groups of people, hypnotizing them simultaneously, and, once that was done, sending them back to particular times and places. Two basic techniques were used, a temporal and a geographical one. She would offer her hypnotized subjects a choice of dates from the past, and ask them to choose the one for which they got the most vivid imagery. Or she would ask them to visualize a map of the earth and tell them that they would feel themselves especially drawn to a certain place. They would then be asked a series of questions about the particular life they were experiencing.

I set up a series of questions that would help locate my subjects, and would also serve as a check on the validity of their recall. I asked them to see the color of their skin, whether their hair was curly or straight and what its color was, and I asked them about the landscape and climate they found themselves in. My purpose was to see if they were of the appropriate race for the place they had chosen, and whether the landscape and climate corresponded to what we know of the area.

I wanted to get information of the kind I could check in archeological texts and historical records. I asked my subjects to visualize the food they were eating . . . because there are many records of the kinds of foodstuffs eaten in each time period and place. I also asked them to see the eating utensil and other household objects they were using, because this too could be checked.

I decided to ask my subjects to go to a market to get supplies and to describe the market and the supplies that they bought. Money is also a clue to a place and time in the past, so I asked them to visualize the money they might have exchanged for goods.

Other areas that could be checked were the architecture they saw and the kind of clothing and footgear they wore. Not only could I see whether the clothing they described was accurate according to historical texts, but I could tell whether other subjects in the same time period and in the same place wore similar types of clothing.

And this method succeeded beyond her wildest dreams.

No Caesars and No Cleopatras

Most of the people who lived and died in the past have been obscure persons who led extremely humble lives. Critics of reincarnation have often claimed that people supposedly having memories of past lives are simply fantasizing about life as an historically prominent person. In fact, nothing could be further from the truth. In Dr. Wambach's 1,100 lives, we simply do not meet Caesar, Cleopatra, Henry the Eighth, George Washington, or, in fact, anybody of historical importance. That statement does have to be slightly qualified; there was *one*. A woman described a life in which she had been James Buchanan, fifteenth president of the United States, during the years 1857-61. In fact, she provided some exceedingly obscure details of his life which lent a good deal of authenticity to her claim. And there were a few people who claimed to have been kings or rulers who were not absolutely unknown to history, but they were obscure rulers in rather remote societies; not at all the sorts of people about whom historical romances are written.

"A great many reported past lives as members of races and sexes other than their own."

But with the exception of this tiny handful of persons, the overwhelming majority of the lives reported from the past were those of simple peasants, who led lives of extreme hardship, filled with unremitting toil, and maintained by a diet of the utmost dullness. And, in fact, a good many of them commented afterwards on how hard and restricted these lives were; the contrast with the relative luxury and openness of their present lives was dramatic.

Lovers of hamburgers and fries, rare roast beef, and pork chops smothered in mushroom gravy were more than a trifle astounded to have found themselves living in wretched huts and sustaining themselves on ground acorns and cereal grains mixed to a mush with water. This extremely rudimentary diet was reported to be enlivened by the occasional greasy rodent.

Dr. Wambach's subjects described very restricted lives, close to the soil and focused within small local groups. They usually had little or no knowledge of anything beyond their own communities, and the biggest event of their lives was the arrival of strangers. They also reported a great many deaths as infants, which is in fact exactly what did happen, though it is hardly the sort of life that one would be likely to fantasize. As Dr. Wambach put it:

Among my subjects, I find that hardly anybody is anybody! I have discovered that the vast majority of people were in their past lives so unlettered and so out of touch with what is recorded in the history books that I couldn't even tell when they were alive unless I suggested a time period. If I regressed them to the year 1600, say, and determined that they were in England and asked who was king, they wouldn't have the faintest notion and couldn't care less. I generally found that if I attempted to find out who was pope or what great battles had taken place—great historical events and that sort of thing—these matters were of no concern to them. They lived in their own little circles and were indifferent to people or events that were beyond their ken.

Other Races and Sexes

And further surprises were in store. Two of the most basic aspects of identity are one's sex and race. Research done on North Americans has shown that most people, if given a choice, would prefer to be white males. Therefore if reported "past lives" are the product of fantasy, we would expect lives as white males to predominate. But they don't. Although most of Dr. Wambach's subjects were white, *a great many reported past lives as members of races and sexes other than their own.* It is a biological fact that, throughout human history, approximately half of the population has been male, and half female. Therefore, if regressions really do reflect reality, we would expect to get roughly a fifty-fifty split between male and female lives for any reasonably-sized sample of regressed subjects. And in fact exactly this has proven to be the case! Of 1,100 past lives reported, 49.4 percent were as women, and 50.6 percent as men.

Dr. Wambach's first sample group of regressed subjects was 78 percent female:

Regardless of the sex they had had in the current lifetime, when regressed to the past, my subjects split neatly and evenly into 50.3 percent male and 49.7 percent female lives. When this finding emerged in my first sample group, I wanted very much to see if it would prove to be true in another sample group. It could be that 28 percent of my female subjects preferred to think of themselves as male, and that was why I had gotten the

50-50 ratio. So in my second sample group of three hundred cases, I had a much closer ratio of males to females in their here-and-now lives; 45 percent of my subjects were male in the second sample, and 55 percent female. But when I regressed them I once again found the virtual 50-50 split—this time, 50.9 percent male and 49.1 percent female. *This result, I feel, is the strongest objective evidence I have yet discovered that when people are hypnotized and taken to past lives, they are tapping some real knowledge of the past.*

When hypnotized and regressed, people simply don't report the kinds of lives that make any sense at all as wish-fulfilling fantasies....

Absolute Ordinariness

If any theme comes through clearly in Dr. Wambach's regressions it is the absolute ordinariness of these lives and deaths. A young woman named Frances was regressed to the 1700s. To her great surprise, she found herself wearing obviously masculine boots.

> Then, when I looked at my clothes and my hands, I realized that I was a man. I seemed to be some kind of laborer, because there was mud on my boots and my clothing was rough. My hands were calloused and work-worn. I was standing in a plowed field, but could see a small hut in the distance. Apparently, this was where I lived, because I found myself eating my evening meal in this small dark hut. I ate with a wooden spoon from a wooden bowl.... [My] death...was some kind of accident with horses....it happened very fast, and I was out of my body before I seemed to know what had happened....I was glad that that lifetime was over. It was a hard...life. The date of my death flashed as 1721, and the place where I lived was around Arles, France....

The Wambach regressions are filled with the most striking agreements among subjects who went to the same time and place. A young woman was regressed to 25 A.D. and found herself a male in northern Italy close to the Adriatic Sea. She was a carpenter of some kind, working with wood and tools. She found herself purchasing supplies with a very odd coin:

> **Subject:** "[It] was dark gray and had a hole in the middle. It seemed to be shaped like a square with the corners pounded to try to make it look round. I've never seen anything like it!"
> **Dr. Wambach:** "Did it seem to be crude around the edges?"
> **Subject:** "Yes, as though it had been hammered rather than molded."
> **Dr. Wambach:** "I've had that coin described to me at least twenty times before. It was used around the Mediterranean Sea in the time period 500 B.C. to 25 A.D."

This is certainly extraordinary. Twenty-one people, at different times and in different groups, went to the same place and time period and all found themselves using the same peculiar coin....

Population Statistics

Reincarnation requires human bodies. If these don't exist, then reincarnation quite obviously cannot occur. And hasn't the world's population increased enormously over the centuries? It certainly has. Scholars of human population trends estimate that the world's population doubled between the first century A.D. and 1500, doubled again by the nineteenth century, and has since quadrupled. Therefore, isn't reincarnation impossible?

"No contradiction of any kind exists between the regression data and world population statistics."

This is certainly a very powerful argument against reincarnation. Since Dr. Wambach asked her 1,100 subjects to specify the time-period to which they were regressing, were any "population trends" apparent in their choices? Indeed they were. And these trends display precisely what we would expect to find if reincarnation actually does occur: Dr. Wambach's subjects chose to be born into different time periods with a frequency which precisely paralleled scholars' estimates of the size of the human population at those times. Their past-life choices double from the first century to 1500, double again by the nineteenth century, and quadruple from then until the twentieth. In other words, reincarnation is entirely dependent on the availability of human bodies, and if we were to regress individual human beings from the present back, generation by generation, to the first century, they would report many lives when the population was large and few when it was small.

Therefore, no contradiction of any kind exists between the regression data and world population statistics.

Profound Possibilities

The regression data open up some stupendous possibilities, possibilities which will be profoundly shocking to most of us, who have been absolutely convinced by our experience in this life that we belong to one sex, one race, one social level, one nationality, and one ethnic group. For the regression data make it apparent that most of us have been, at different times, both men and women, black, white, yellow and brown, rich and poor, and a variety of nationalities and ethnicities. When individuals are regressed through a succession of lives (and this has been done with only a small sample), these lives are extremely varied with respect to sex, race, social level, and ethnic group. For example, Dr. Wambach says:

> Some were fairly wealthy in past lives, but the rich ones are not rich in their next lives. Often they are very poor. If they were important in one life, they didn't stay that way.

One of her subjects, for instance, a woman in her

present life, was in the 1400s a male athlete in Central America, who died at age 40; then a black male native of New Guinea in the 1500s who died young; a middle-class Venetian housewife who was born in 1540 and died in old age; a woman who lived in Normandy in the early eighteenth century and was a servant in a tavern or inn; a redheaded boy who lived in the eastern United States in the early nineteenth century and died at age eight of smallpox, and, between 1888 and 1916, a Norwegian seaman who died of an unspecified disease at the age of 28. No effort was made to make a complete inventory of her lives; these are probably only a few of them....

"It seems that this woman was receiving from everyone in this life the same treatment she had dealt to others in the previous life experience."

What are we to make of such a bewilderingly varied life-experience? Was there a developmental process linking these lives? As we will shortly see, a process of some sort can be found. At the very least, we can see powerful evidence of a claim sometimes made by discarnate communicators that the purpose of human life is to "learn" by acquiring highly varied experiences in all kinds of times, societies, and bodies. And from this there emerges one clear revelation, a revelation which, were it taken seriously, would introduce some profoundly new dimensions into human relationships. Human identity, and human animosities, are based on fundamental distinctions—of sex, of class, of religion, of nationality, of ethnicity. But regressions make it clear that we ourselves have been, or will be, all of that which we now are not, and even that which we now despise and hate. What could be more profoundly educational than to express, in one life, hatred and contempt for others different from oneself, and to then return, in a later life, as a member of the despised group, to endure that same hatred and contempt? Such considerations bring us to the ancient doctrine of *karma*.

Past Life Research and Karma

The doctrine of karma is a simple one. It holds that, through reincarnation, all human beings will eventually learn the "golden rule" the hard way: that injury and evil done to others will be atoned for by personal suffering in subsequent lives, while love and compassion shown to others will "return" as personal fulfillment....

Loring Williams, a hypnotist who has regressed many people, has some definite opinions about karma, based on those regressions. In a conversation with the writer Brad Steiger, he said:

> Karma is difficult to pin down unless you know a lot about your subject's background and you are able to obtain...a good many regressions from the same subject. In those cases where I have known something of my subject's history...and have been able to get a good detail on several of his past lives, I have seen a definite pattern of Karma.

Williams went on to illustrate his case by citing a regression which he had recently performed. A woman, regressed to 1800, claimed to be a governess in France.

> In that capacity she managed to meet and marry a wealthy older man. She was very selfish and obsessed by money, jewels, servants and power. She devoted many years to making her elderly husband just as miserable as possible, and she was delighted when he finally died and left her in control of the property and money.
>
> She was a tyrant in dealing with her servants, so much so, in fact, that she was finally murdered by one of her maids, who refused to be so thoroughly demeaned. This woman's present life has strongly borne out the Karma concept. The youngest of several girls, she was born into a very poor family. She was brought up with little money or luxuries. For some unexplainable reason, her mother and her sisters abused her. One of her sisters told me, "Poor Gloria spent her childhood crying. I don't know why, but we were always so mean to her. Even when she was a teenager there seemed to be an unspoken household conspiracy to give her the dirtiest jobs and to make her life miserable."
>
> It seems that this woman was receiving from everyone in this life the same treatment she had dealt to others in the previous life experience.

Was a person like Gloria, in his experience, doomed to persecution throughout all of a subsequent life? Not necessarily, it appears.

> When this girl grew up she was able to adjust emotionally and her family attitude changed. She is now...happily married...one seems to have the opportunity to overcome, or to adjust, to the conditions into which he is born. If he [does this successfully] there will be a corresponding improvement in the conditions into which he is born next time. In some cases, like that of Gloria, one begins to reap the harvest of his adjustment in the present life.

These are intriguing ideas: their implications are fascinating....

Choosing Life

Early in her research, Helen Wambach regressed a young man to a life in which he had died at the age of two. While he was still under hypnosis, she asked him why. His reply proved the idea for an entirely new aspect of regression research. He said he had realized he'd chosen the wrong parents, so he had just "left"—died.

This comment opened up some fascinating possibilities—could it be that people actually "chose" the life they were to lead, and that, in the deep levels of the subconscious, they retained the knowledge of how this choice had been made? Could it be that people actually carried with them the knowledge of why they were here on earth, and that this knowledge could be tapped in hypnosis? She decided to find out. She began hypnotizing subjects and asking them how they got into the particular body in which they found themselves. To her amazement, they answered her!

If people are asked, in their normal state of consciousness, why they were born and why they find themselves here on earth in a body, most will have no idea of the answer and many will find the question itself absurd. But when they are hypnotized and asked such questions, they respond in a dramatically different way. They give answers. They appear to ''know!''

''Did you choose to be born?''

''Yes, I chose.''

''Did anyone help you choose?''

''Lots of beings helped, but . . . I had to make the choice.''

''How do you feel about the prospect of being born into another lifetime?''

''I feel—sort of resigned.''

This is the voice of a regressed subject, who has been taken back in time to the period between his last death and his present birth. He's being asked to explain how he got into his present body. In a preliminary study, Dr. Wambach found that 38 percent of her subjects could not answer such questions. They ''lost'' her during the hypnosis and drifted into a sleep-like state, or they simply received no answers when such questions were put to them. She speculates that such subjects are similar to those who went ''blank'' and got nothing on past lives because they had suffered a recent, traumatic death. They receive no answers, she thinks, because their subconscious minds don't think they are ''ready'' for them. For those who are ready, however, karmic factors turn out to play a large role in their present lives.

Scientific Statistics

Dr. Wambach talked to four hundred and two regressed and hypnotized subjects about the processes that had led to their current lives. And, like the well-disciplined scientist that she is, she condensed the results of those conversations into statistics. But these are not the usual cut-and-dried statistics of scientific research. They are statistics to make the head spin.

Did you choose to be born?

Five percent said that they had not, that they simply found themselves in a fetus, being born. The other 95 percent stated that they had ''chosen'' their current lifetime.

> The great majority . . . said that they made their decision to be born on the basis of counseling by other entities during the between-life period. They were sometimes described as teachers, guides or gurus, but more often reported as friends and a group of kindred

spirits. One . . . reported: ''There's a large group. . . . We're all working together. . . . Some of us will experience life in [physical embodiment]—about a third of us—while others will not be born at this time.''

Did you want to be born?

While a majority—81 percent—felt they *needed* to be born in order to advance their personal development through the experiences of physical life, only 30% enjoyed physical life enough to really want it! One subject likened the decision to walking out onto the high board and trying to nerve yourself enough to dive off:

> It's like walking out on a high diving board, getting born. You know you want to do it to sharpen your skills, but when you get to the end of the board you want to turn around and go back and do it another day. But then it just seems as though there are people there who are coaching you and finally you just get pushed and—there you are. Born into life again.

Others phrased their reluctance in various ways.

> I feel very reluctant. . . . I don't want to be so restricted. I would rather be . . . in the between-life state . . . than in that small, confined body, but it is . . . something I have to do.

> Actual tears were running down my cheeks as you asked us to come to the time of decision about being born. It isn't so much sadness. . . . I don't feel sad. . . . [It's] just—well . . . life in a body is rough.

It was common for people who were regressed to the birth experience to say, immediately after birth:

> ''I want to go back home!'' By ''home'' they . . . meant life outside . . . a physical body.

''One subject likened the decision [to be born again] to walking out onto the high board and trying to nerve yourself enough to dive off.''

One expressed these feelings eloquently:

> The experience was . . . one of deep compassion. I felt compassion not only for the infant who was me, but for my mother and indeed everyone in the delivery room. . . . I was leaving a beautiful . . . place where many things were open to me, to come down into a very closed . . . environment. It seemed as though I knew all of the troubles that lay ahead, and I felt that it was such a waste that we humans don't understand . . . . I know that sounds strange. . . . Don't . . . understand *what?* Well . . . under the hypnosis, it seemed so clear to me that to be alive in the body is to be isolated from our true selves and away from the . . . knowledge that's available to us who are not in a body. I knew it was necessary to go through this experience. . . . Yet, it seemed such a tragedy that my mother, the doctor, and [the] others had no real understanding of what life is.

But the 30 percent who looked forward to physical embodiment made much more optimistic comments, many of them seeing the life to come as an adventure. One said:

It's like going on an expedition to a strange country. It's exciting.

Joining the Body

When did you join your body?

When asked this question, subjects answered, and the answers were rather startling. There was a general reluctance to join the fetus. Only 1 percent reported that they had entered it prior to the fourth month of pregnancy, and only 14 percent said they did between the fourth and eighth months. Thus, 85 percent joined their new bodies only after the eighth month of gestation! A large number (33 percent of the total) stated that they did not do so until just before the actual birth experience, and 15 percent, who particularly disliked becoming embodied again, said they did not join the fetus *until after birth had occurred!*

"It's like going on an expedition to a strange country. It's exciting."

Why are you being born?

The answers received to this question were nothing less than fascinating. Eighty-five percent stated that they already knew their parents and other important people in their present lives from relationships they had had with them in past lives! But even more extraordinary, as these relationships carry over from life to life, they do not remain the same but undergo every conceivable sexual and relational alteration. Thus, the subject's parents or children in the present life had been something very different in the past: present mothers and fathers might have been past sisters, brothers, friends, lovers, or children; the subject's present children often turned out to have been his parents in a past life. Relational and sexual change was the rule! For example, one subject said:

My mother had been my sister, my father and my child before.

Another stated:

My mother was my sister in a past life and my father was a lover. My first son had been a grandfather in one lifetime of mine, my second son had been a father, and my first daughter a friend. My second daughter I saw clearly as a mother of mine in a past life.

New perceptions about these intricate relationships elicited some powerful feelings. Many parents found themselves with a totally new view of their relationships with their children, perceiving them for the first time as independent individuals tied to them in complex ways through repeated lives, although dependent upon them at this particular time in the present life:

My daughter is an old friend of mine from another life. I sense...that her unborn child will be another old friend.

But what staggering learning prospects this opens! What conceivably better way to "know" someone than to have had a dozen different relationships with him—as parent, child, sibling, lover! In fact, precisely this, in karmic terms, was the stated purpose of these carry-overs. A majority of those who were aware of their purpose in choosing their present parents, and others with whom they would be closely involved, stated that this purpose was to work out karmic problems which had developed in past-life relationships, and, in particular, to learn to love them and to express love for them.

I did see why I was born, why I chose my parents. It was to help them in...their karmas.

Another subject observed:

This life seemed very burdensome. I came in with lots of burdens to clear up, especially...[with] my mother. I have to learn to love them, to give to them, my whole family. Having to be dependent on my mother was one of my challenges.

The decision to reincarnate in particular relationships was made, it was revealed, in consultation with spiritual "advisers" and/or in consultation with the other persons who were to be involved. *Thus karmic ties to others were the major single motivation for choosing to be born into a particular body.* But some subjects chose instead an environment which suited what they wished to achieve in the current life:

A few chose on the basis of the opportunities their genetic, environmental and emotional situation in that childhood would provide for them. The people who reported this type of choice generally had a clearer notion of the purpose they wanted to achieve in this lifetime than those who chose their family to work out past karma.

For example, one of these said:

This life is a test, a challenge: I'm purposefully setting up a scenario for learning what I want to know.

Another reported:

I was reluctant to be born.... I didn't want to go down and leave [the between-life state]...and feel cold and belittled. When I came through the birth canal...I felt afraid, vulnerable, alone. Lots of impersonal people and flashing light. My mother was asleep and no one held me or welcomed me and I felt that familiar longing for love. But when you asked the purpose...it was to go down and take some of that...peace and light [of the between-life state] and spread it around. To go into the confusion of this life, but at a time where my preoccupation didn't have to be survival. My purpose is to give out love as fully and freely as possible in whatever situation I get into.

And some of these subjects who had chosen their present life primarily for its "environment," rather than for its karmic ties, stated that the time period selected—the last half of the twentieth century—had been chosen because it offered unprecedented possibilities for personal growth:

I felt I needed to work out the female part of my entity. I chose this era because women will make great advances in my lifetime and I will help in that.

As another put it:

This will be my transcendent life, when I am able to know both physical and non-physical reality while still in the body.

Predetermination

Is your life predetermined?

The idea that you "choose" your life in advance in order to accomplish certain things raises a deeply disquieting question. Does this mean that your life is predestined in all its particulars, a script, in effect, that has already been written for a cast of "robots?" If you "choose" all of this in advance, then is any element of choice present while living this life, or do you merely go through predetermined motions? Fortunately, the data gathered by Dr. Wambach are such that this disturbingly important question can be answered. For it is clear from the comments of her subjects that what they have "chosen" is not predetermined at all, but only a "situation" with a certain potential, with certain possibilities which the individual may or may not be able to realize!

> *"Subjects frequently expressed grave doubt that they would be able to accomplish what they had chosen to achieve in their present life."*

Subjects frequently expressed grave doubt that they would be able to accomplish what they had chosen to achieve in their present life. They would report planning their current life, but it was common for them, when regressed to the period immediately after birth, to realize with a shock of dismay that they had underestimated the difficulties they would have to overcome if they were to achieve the goals they had set for themselves. Their courage would fail them, and they would yearn to go back to the between-life state. Again and again, they spoke of their chosen present lives as "challenges," as "tests" which they had to attempt, *clearly implying that failure was as probable an outcome of their efforts as success.*

> I have the stamina to do it...I can accept the challenges. It is necessary to develop my strengths through being alive in a body. They ["advisors" in the between-life state] said...that I should wait till a better time, with a smaller family, more time for you. But I felt that it has to be now. Someone has to start first but I told my friends, "Don't wait too long."

It is difficult to find words that can do justice to the revelations that have emerged from the research on which this chapter has been based. They are momentous, stunning, mind-blowing. And for those who are open enough to take them to heart, the world will never be the same.

Ian Currie is a Canadian writer and researcher on psychic subjects. A former teacher of sociology, he has also taught courses on death and dying in collaboration with colleagues from the fields of medicine, biology, geriatrics, theology, and psychology.

"The Kingdom of heaven is a perpetual spring festival, celebrating...the persistence of life as life, triumphing, however painfully, over death."

viewpoint **95**

A Joyous Heaven Will Follow Death

Andrew Greeley

Death is not the end of life; it is the experience of being cut off from Being. When we die it seems that not only our life ends but that we cease to be. We move into non-existence, our being is annihilated. Theologically this may be restated as the fear of being cut off from God. The death fear enters our lives very early, as the psychoanalysts have made clear. It is the fear of being cut off, of being alienated permanently. The Christian conviction of resurrection, experienced in the Easter symbol and ritual, says that nothing can cut us off from the love of God which is in Christ Jesus. We do not know very much about what happens after death—though as we shall see it is possible to speculate. The core of the Christian resurrection experience is the conviction, unshakable and irrefutable, that nothing can cut us off from God's love....

The resurrection of Jesus tells us that nothing can cut us off from that Ultimate Graciousness. From one point of view that may seem like a rather minimal belief. Nothing can cut us off from God's love. Is that all? Is there nothing more to Christianity? The only response possible is, "What more could there possibly be?"...

Hope and Curiosity

The hopeful person, then, is one who survives because he believes in survival; he lives because he believes he has something worth celebrating. He can afford to be more tolerant of others because others are less likely to threaten him. Diversity is not a challenge to his individuality or his freedom because he knows that nothing can really destroy that which is most uniquely and essentially himself. He is perhaps not any less afraid of death; we are all afraid of death. But he is not paralyzed by that fear, he will give up and quit, anticipating death by dying psychologically and humanly long before he dies physically. The hopeful person dies once. He lives strongly and vitally up to the point of death.

Hopefulness does not preclude discouragement, disillusion, frustration; it does preclude bitterness and cynicism. Hopefulness does not mean that we do not fall; but it does mean that we get up and walk on. Hopefulness says with T.S. Eliot, "Disillusion if persisted in is the ultimate illusion." Life is not a bowl of cherries, it is not a picnic, or even a parade; it is, quite literally, a deadly serious business. It is so serious that a Christian, obsessed as he is by hope, has no choice but to laugh about it. He says with Gregory Baum that "tomorrow will be different, even if tomorrow is the day after the last day of our lives." It may well rain on today's parade, but let's see about tomorrow.

And this expectation for what tomorrow may bring us is the final, most special, most distinctive aspect of the Christian "life before death." The Christian is curious, he wonders about tomorrow, he is intrigued by its possibilities and fundamentally unafraid of its terrors. John Shea has written that the best way a Christian can prepare for death is to develop a healthy capacity for surprise. It seems to me that that is the best description of the Christian life I have ever read. We are engaged in the business of developing our capacity of surprise. No matter how worn or weary or battered or frustrated or tired we may be, we still have an ability to wonder; we are still open, curious, expectant, waiting to be surprised. What will be around that next corner? Who lurks behind that bush? What is that Cheshire cat smile that just vanished in the leaves of yonder tree? Who is that knocking at the door? Who is messing around the garden? Who is trying to peek in through the latticework? Who is that making all that noise, leaping and bounding around over there in the hills? What's going on here? Is there some kind of

Andrew Greeley, *Death and Beyond*, 1976. © Andrew Greeley. Reprinted with permission of The Thomas More Press, Chicago, IL 60610.

conspiracy, some kind of plot? Who is the Plotter? There is something mysterious about this house. There's a Ghost in it, and he just went down the corridor. What the hell is going to happen next?

Ultimately, then, the universe is either an empty machine held together by some clever but essential brute force, or it is a haunted house spooked by playful ghosts. In the machine there is no wonder or mystery; in the haunted house there are a thousand puzzles, lots of tricks, and a surprise a minute. The best ghost stories are always comedies, so there is also a laugh a minute. Like Thomas More, we may even die laughing.

So the Christian goes to bed at night not afraid that he will wake up tomorrow to find himself dead, but curious as to what crazy fool surprise lays in store for him when he wakes up in this sometimes frightening, sometimes absurd, sometimes even vicious but always fascinating haunted house of a world.

Eternally Different Tomorrows

Or, to sum up the whole Christian argument, how do we know that tomorrow will be different? Every other tomorrow we have known has been different. Why shouldn't the next one?...

Imagine your own heaven if you will. If it is to be a Christian heaven, you can dispense with the Greek image of people sitting around plucking musical instruments and not doing much else but look vapid. The Christian heaven is active, dynamic, vigorous. It is not a place where life ends but rather a place where it continues.

"We do not know very much about what happens after death—though...it is possible to speculate."

In one sense it is not at all difficult to imagine what life after death will be like, for it will be, as I have argued repeatedly in this book, like life as we know it here on earth. It will be filled with the excitement, the wonder, the pleasures, the activity that makes life rewarding and exciting here on earth. Any sharp discontinuity between the two forms of life is completely foreign, I think, to the Christian resurrection symbolism. It was the same Jesus on Easter as before, transformed perhaps, glorious perhaps, but still Jesus. So it is with us, we believe, and the transformation will destroy nothing that is good or true or beautiful about human life. On the contrary, it will merely enhance what we already are.

On the other hand, we cannot even begin to imagine what our continued life will be like. Jesus himself has told us this: "Eye has not seen, nor has ear heard, nor has it entered into the heart of man those things which God has prepared for those who love Him." Our expectations, according to Maeterlinck, are all too modest. It will be life as we know it here on earth, but so transformed that we cannot even begin to imagine how splendid it will be. "Dream your most impossible dreams, hope your wildest hopes, fantasize your most impossible fantasies," Jesus tell us. "Then where they leave off, the surprises of my heavenly Father will only begin."

So we can look forward to both continuity and discontinuity, continuity of life but extraordinary transformation of the quality, the intensity, the richness, the splendor of life. It sounds like quite a show.

Surprises and Wonder

Most certainly this continued life of ours will be marked by surprises and by wonder. It is hard to imagine any kind of human life without surprises and wonder. If we have lost the child's capacity to delight in surprise, to be awed by the wonder, we have not become adult; we have become aged and senile. The fullness of life requires a highly sensitive awareness of the possibility of surprise and a powerful capacity for wonder. If life persistent is to be life at all, then it must be filled with surprises and wonder. John Shea's comment that the Christian prepares for death by developing his capacity for surprise is strictly and literally true. One simply cannot make it in the heavenly kingdom unless one is able to cope with surprise. Perhaps that's what Purgatory is all about; it's a place where we are given the chance to make up for the sense of wonder we did not develop and the capacity for surprise that we permitted to atrophy here on earth. Purgatory would then be less a place of suffering and more a place of preparation, a kind of spring training camp where we can learn to enjoy the wonderful, the marvelous, the unexpected.

Will hopefulness continue in the heavenly kingdom? I have argued throughout this book that that which is most authentically human in us is our hope. It is what enables us, forces us, to ask the religious questions and gives us the most powerful hint we have of the religious answers. It is that which most enables us to be ourselves, to release the full, rich, and vigorous potentialities of our personality, to take risks, to ask not why, but why not?

Will we have dispensed with hope when we come to the many mansions of the heavenly Father's kingdom?

The old catechetics said that we would, arguing that when one has achieved one's goal there is nothing left to hope for. Certainly St. Paul implied as much in his famous quotation in the first epistle to the Corinthians, chapter 13.

If one restricts hope to the human ability to assert that death is not the final answer, that when all the evil things that are possible have been done to us there is still yet one more word to be said, then obviously there is no more need for hope after that answer and after that last word. But hope can also mean a confidence of further growth, development, expansion, a challenge to more activity, a readiness for new adventures, an openness to new wonders. It is very hard to see how there can be human life without this kind of hope. So hope in this sense, or, as the sociologists would say, some kind of functional substitute for what we would call hope in our present state of life, would surely persist in our continued life after the transition point of death.

"Flow"

On the psychological level, I would suggest that what we will experience in our continued life will be what my colleague Mihaly Csikszentmihalyi calls "flow." He means that experience we enjoy when our capacities and talents are pushed to the limits but not beyond them. We experience "flow" not when we are doing something easy and routine, which requires little interest and generates little excitement, nor when we are doing something that is beyond our capacities and overwhelms us with complexities and demands. Rather we experience "flow" when we exercise the full vigor of our powers, when it is demanded of us that we do our best. Csikszentmihalyi describes how chess, sports, mountain climbing, surgery can all be "flow" activities for those who are skilled in them. It is almost as though an "automatic pilot" takes over, and one does what one must do with a rich, full, enjoyment, reveling in the challenge and one's capacity to meet it. . . .

"How do we know that tomorrow will be different? Every other tomorrow we have known has been different."

Each of us can think of our own "flow" experiences. Tennis, golf, cooking, singing, working with power tools are some examples perhaps. My guess is that "flow" experiences, which abound in our daily lives, are the best concrete, practical anticipations we get of what the delights of the heavenly life might be. . . .

Continued life, continued excitement, wonder, surprise, challenge, "flow," smashing great parties—those are the kinds of ordinary human experiences which best enable us, I think, to anticipate what our continued life will be. We can, of course, spend too much time reflecting on it. . . .

We prepare for the life that is to come not by fantasizing about it but by living hopefully, joyously, "flowingly," wonderfully in the present life. We prepare for the permanent resurrection festival by celebrating resurrection in the here and now. Each time we run the risk of dying to the old self so that we might rise to the new, we not only anticipate but we participate in that which is to come. . . .

The kingdom of heaven is a perpetual spring festival, celebrating, as do all spring festivals, the persistence of life as life, triumphing, however painfully, over death.

Woe to you party poopers and wet blankets, for you shall not enter into the kingdom of heaven—not without a long time in Purgatory, learning how to wonder, how to be surprised, how to celebrate.

And blessed are you who celebrate despite your tears, for yours is the kingdom of heaven.

Andrew Greeley, A Roman Catholic priest, is a noted lecturer, novelist, and journalist. He is a research fellow at the National Opinion Research Center of the University of Chicago and professor of sociology at the University of Arizona in Tucson.

"Belief in an afterlife remains...only a human wish."

An Afterlife Is Merely a Wishful Fantasy

Barbara J. Sowder

The exact time in history when the belief in an afterlife entered human thought is unknown. Some scholars postulate that man has believed in this concept for at least 100,000 years. Their hypothesis is based on excavations of Neanderthal graves in Iraq where the dead were buried with food and flowers and markers were carefully placed over their graves.

Some creationists, of course, would have difficulty with this hypothesis because they cannot concede that humankind existed before five or six thousand years ago. However, there are some more serious problems in inferring belief in an afterlife from the behaviors of deliberate burial and ritualism at death. One is that species other than man engage in deliberate burial and/or ritualistic and even religious-type behavior when encountering death. Second, ancient human societies—such as that of the biblical Hebrews—practiced deliberate burial and ritualism at death without seeming to believe in an afterlife.

Perhaps we will never identify the time in history when belief in an afterlife entered human thought. No doubt Atheists would like to see the concept dead, entombed in libraries, and resurrected only by scholars interested in the history of human beliefs and customs. But, the idea is very much alive, an active part of human beliefs and customs, and a favorite topic of religionists. For example, estimates from a 1978 Gallup poll indicate that 70% of Americans believe in a hereafter and the revival of fundamentalist Christianity in our nation has provided a new impetus for "pro-afterlifers" to preach the glories of heaven and the horrors of hell.

Hereafter, I will briefly address two questions: (1) What are some of the primary sources of "evidence" which religionists are likely to cite in defense of an afterlife?; and (2) What are some scientifically-based explanations for the phenomena that religionists may cite as "evidence"?

The source of "evidence" we are likely to hear most about, of course, comes from religious texts and teachings. The afterlife in these sources varies from culture to culture: from ghosts that hover about the living in preliterate societies, to a succession of reincarnations in eastern religions, to at least two types of immortality recorded in the book cited most often in our culture—the judaeo-christian bible.

Sources of "Evidence"

Consider for a moment the bible. Note that the notion of an afterlife entered Hebrew thought only around the 28th century, BP (before present), primarily through Persian influence. The lead came from isaiah (29:19) who declared: "The dead shall live, their bodies shall rise." This idea does not appear in the 22 books that precede "The book of isaiah." In "Genesis" (3:22) god casts adam and eve from the garden of eden lest they "...also take of the tree of life, and eat, and live forever." God says to adam: "You are dust, and to dust you shall return" (3:19). In these first 22 books, god and angels come to earth; man does not enter their realm. God promises one thing to all men—death. To the obedient, he promises long life, many descendents, and deliverance of enemies into their hands but *not* immortality. Isaiah changed all that by promising that the dead shall rise. Two centuries later, the writer of "The book of daniel" (12:2) qualified this promise by declaring that afterlife applied only to some, and then as a reward or punishment correlated with merit: "...many of those that sleep in the dust of the earth shall awake, some to everlasting life, some to shame and everlasting contempt." Such statements are the forerunners of the messianic doctrine embodied in the "kingdom of god" and preached by the jesus of the books of matthew, mark and luke, and elaborated upon by the writer of "The revelation

Barbara J. Sowder, "Life After Death," *American Atheist*, May 1982. Reprinted with permission from the American Atheist.

to john". The common thread in this doctrine is a physical resurrection of the dead body. Verses referring to this early Hebrew notion of a physical resurrection were retained in the "new testament", together with the later Greek and Roman overlays of the concept of an ethereal soul which ascends to heaven after death.

Christianity has never resolved these conflicting concepts of an afterlife. Believers merely choose the verses that best suit their belief system and declare them to be true because they are the divinely inspired "word of god". This argument is hardly scientific! It does, however, attest to man's tendency to embody language with absolute and supernatural origins and powers.

Psychic Powers

A second common line of "evidence" cited in support of an afterlife comes from the so-called psychical powers. Simply stated, this is a belief that certain humans, especially mediums, have a special power to communicate with the dead. This forms the cornerstone of modern parapsychology's study of an afterlife.

"Being evidence-oriented, we as Atheists can only continue to believe that life begins and ends with our short lifespan on this earth."

In the 1800's and early 1900's, prestigious scholars gathered the narrative accounts of people who had seen and/or communicated with the dead and subjected these reports to scientific scrutiny. These scholars concluded: (1) that most such reports were too weak to support the concept of life after death, (2) that some mediums were frauds; but (3) that a few accounts could not be explained scientifically. Those cases that could not be explained primarily involved reported instances where an apparition appeared 12 hours after his or her death to persons who had no knowledge of their death. Parapsychologists still tend to take psychic reports seriously; most scientists do not, and some have recently posed viable scientific explanations for such psychic phenomena. These explanations are the same as some of those posed for a third and relatively new type of "evidence"—the near-death experience.

The near-death experience has been of some research interest to physicians, psychologists, and psychiatrists for several decades. Professionals use these experiences to frame therapeutic approaches to dying, some of which are based on sympathetic assurance that life does indeed continue after death. Near-death experiences have been reported by the terminally ill and by individuals who have survived

clinical death and near-death accidents. Several common, prototypical experiences have been reported: meeting others, such as dead relatives and friends, spirits and guides; ineffability; feelings of peace and quiet; a loud ringing or buzzing noise; seeing a dark tunnel through which one may feel oneself move; out of body experiences; a being of light; a panoramic view of one's life; a border or limit beyond which there is no return; cities of light; visions of great knowledge; supernatural rescue from death by spirits; and a return or coming back with changed attitudes.

The data appeal to many christians because the experience sometimes results in a renewed interest in god and because the commonality of themes in these experiences has been said to substantiate the concept of an afterlife.

Near-Death Experiences

The near-death experience, however, is not the sole province of christians. Descriptions of death experiences and an afterlife are similar across cultures. And, these experiences are remarkably similar to drug-induced hallucinations and to sensory isolation experiences. For example, psychedelic drug hallucinatory episodes are marked by a suppression of verbal behavior; the hearing of voices and other sounds is similar to the reported experiences of patients recovering from anesthesia (especially nitrous oxide, ether, and ketamine); and, the bright lights reported in near-death experiences occur also in sensory isolation and in several nondrug hallucinatory states.

Such similarities can be illustrated by two examples of reported experiences:
1. *Tunnel in an Afterlife Report.*
   "My awareness of the room dimmed, and the world immediately around me became like a tunnel with walls that glowed with a slight orange-red reflected light."

2. *Tunnel in a Drug Hallucination.*
   "I'm moving through some kind of train tunnel. There are all sorts of lights and colors."

The "tunnel," as well as experiences like "cities of light," are probably caused by phosphenes, visual sensations that arise from the discharge of neurons in the eye structures. They also reflect the electrical excitation of organized groups of cells in the visual cortex of the brain. Various other near-death experiences also resemble hallucinations.

Recent electrophysical research has confirmed that hallucinations are related directly to excitation of the central nervous system. These excitation states are coupled with a functional disorganization of that portion of the brain that regulates incoming stimuli. What happens, essentially, is an escape inward into private thoughts.

This inward process may be accompanied by the

psychological defense mechanisms known as depersonalization and dissociation. Depersonalization produces, under threat of death, many of the reactions reported for near-death experiences. Depersonalization defends the endangered personality against the threat of death and also initiates an integration of that reality. This may be accompanied by visions of an afterlife, coupled with a sense of rebirth. Dissociation, on the other hand, usually operates unconsciously. It permits emotion and affect to be detached from an idea, object, or situation and has been postulated to underlie various psychical phenomena, including trance seances, automatic writing, and other behaviors that have yielded so many descriptions of an afterlife. Dissociation also produces hallucinations composed of many of the themes common to near-death experiences.

"No doubt Atheists would like to see the concept dead. . . . But, the idea is very much alive."

"The specific context of complex hallucinatory imagery is determined by set (expectations and attitudes) and setting (physical and psychological environments)." [Ronald K. Siegel] A set such as fear of death and a setting like a hospital ward may trigger eschatological thoughts and images. Some researchers have suggested that the universal themes in such imagery may be related to stored memories of intrauterine existence and birth. A more integrated explanation is based on the perceptual-release theory. This theory assumes that normal memories and perceptions are suppressed by some mechanism that inhibits the flow of information from the outside. If outside input is decreased while awareness remains, as in shock or dying, the old perceptions are released and may be dynamically organized and experienced as dreams, fantasies, or hallucinations. Or, if the perceptions stored in the brain are sufficiently stimulated for a long period of time by fear, drugs or other stimuli, the released perceptions can enter awareness and be experienced as hallucinations.

These major forms of "evidence" for the existence of an afterlife are hardly convincing! They attest, primarily, to the power of the human brain to translate a wish for eternal consciousness and a fear of eternal oblivion into dreams, fantasies, hallucinations, religious myths, and even quasi-scientific inferences. Belief in an afterlife remains, in the face of current knowledge, only a human wish and the ultimate promise of religions. Being evidence-oriented, we as Atheists can only continue to believe that life begins and ends with our short lifespan on this earth.

Barbara J. Sowder earned a Ph.D. in psychology from George Washington University. She is a research consultant in the Washington, D.C. area. This viewpoint is taken from a speech she addressed to the National American Atheist Convention in 1982.

"The vast amount of material I have examined leads me to believe that there is a certain pattern in the communications between the dead and the living."

viewpoint **97**

Communication with the Dead Is Proof of an Afterlife

Hans Holzer

The desire to communicate with the dead goes back to the beginning of mankind. It is usually the result of personal anxiety of one kind or another. The bereaved want to know that their loved ones still live. The weak hope for sage counsel from a departed who somehow is thought to know more than mortals. The nagging doubt about whether there is or isn't a Hereafter also drives many people to seek a form of communication with the dead. Only a small fraction of those seeking this link are motivated by scientific interest rather than personal curiosity....

There are two big groups of communications, as different as day and night in the way we relate to them. First, there are communications initiated by the dead. These are dramatic, often sudden, often surprising and occasionally frightening linkups between the two worlds. There are a number of reasons why I think the dead want to communicate with the living.

The advantage, from the scientific observer's point of view, in spontaneous phenomena of this kind is the state of mind of the recipient of the communication. Since he has not actively sought it, the elements of wish fulfillment are mostly absent. The unconscious does not play so large a part in this type of contact as it may play with induced communications, and the genuine emotional conditions that are usually behind such spontaneous contacts to begin with are present to their full extent. This is the sort of psychic phenomenon one cannot possibly reproduce in the laboratory because it involves unique, personal and deeply emotional experiences at both ends of the channel.

The "sender" in the non-physical world is motivated by some need or urge to communicate with the living person for whom the communication

is meant. The receiver is impressed emotionally by the content and form of the communication and the further implications of it; thus he is doubly involved in each and every communication from the Other Side. To create similar conditions artificially in a laboratory, with routine technicians or even with talented ESP subjects, is impossible. We are dealing here with far more complex situations than the mere reading of thoughts or the influencing of the fall of dice via psychokinesis. Dr. Joseph Rhine's experiments are great beginnings for a science that needed a first step in the right direction. Where the conservative parapsychologist and of course the large segment of hostile scientists are totally off the track is this area of communication: it is not even capable of confinement within a laboratory, much less capable of being artificially-created or recreated.

But there isn't any need for a laboratory. Many important events of nature are not susceptible to laboratory tests. The actual eruption of a volcano, or an underwater quake, or a major holocaust cannot be staged at will in the research center, yet the actual event may be observed on the spot by competent witnesses. Even the study of disease often simulates its subject rather than actually recreating it, for obvious moral reasons. And simulation is not duplication.

We do not as yet know all the laws that govern this communication. It may well be that what is required is the uniqueness and genuineness of the emotional situation. That is, unless there is real need for the communication to take place, the link is not established. If there were not some kind of restraining rule, I think we would have conversations between the dead and the living all day long and the phenomena would cease to be unusual. But they are unusual, and while the bulk of evidence is very heavy, they are by no means an everyday occurrence, nor is the establishing of channels an easy task. That, however, need not militate against scientific acceptance of these spontaneous communications. Many things in the universe are unusual or rare, and still are part of the orderly scheme of things. For instance, a nova—that is, a star imploding, or burning itself out and then falling into itself—occurs far fewer times than the creation of a new star or a comet or passing asteroid. Nevertheless, a nova is susceptible to proper observation and evaluation. Albinos occur among people and animals with some degree of regularity but are still considered unusual. Just the same, albinos are part of nature and by no stretch of the imagination can they be termed unscientific or unreal phenomena. Large numbers of examples do not necessarily make an occurrence scientifically valid, nor do few examples make it less so.

Communications Initiated by the Living

If we were able to control the spontaneous communication channels from the non-physical world, we would indeed have a major key in our hands. Perhaps the "board of directors" that runs all this does not want us to hold that key. On the other hand, nothing stops us from searching for our own channels, starting on our end.

Communications initiated by the living compose the second large group of communications. They too fall into many categories, depending on the nature of the channel used and on the approach by the individual making the contact, or attempting to make it.

The intermediary between a living person and the inhabitants of the non-physical world is called the instrument.

"The 'sender' in the non-physical world is motivated by some need or urge to communicate with the living person."

Putting aside here the notion that priests and ministers are intermediaries between man and the Divine—which they may or may not be—and reducing the attempt to communicate to its individual, personal level, we still have to have at least three elements or three persons: one who desires the contact, the instrument who makes the contact possible, and one who receives the communication. Once the initial contact is established, the receiver also turns sender, and the initiator of the contact becomes a receiver. But the instrument remains the same—an intermediary whose sole function is to make the contact possible as clearly and as untouched by the instrument's own personality as possible. This is not so easy as it may sound. The instrument's own personality cannot be set aside without proper training and discipline, and

even then there is always an element of that personality present in almost all communications between the two worlds.

The "Medium"

The instrument can be a professional or amateur "medium," a person with the gift of dissociation of personality, in the case of trance, clairvoyance, clairaudience, or clairsentience; if a so-called "mental" medium, the instrument does not lose consciousness during a "seance." The seance does not denote a mysterious ceremony in a darkened room when spirits descend upon the mortals to amaze them. Seance means to sit down with someone. Most communications are very simply held in a room, in normal light, with two or more people sitting quietly and trying to establish contact with the nonphysical world. Only in Hollywood movies does mumbojumbo enter the picture.

When a sitting utilizes the services of a trance medium, the departed will use the vocal chords of the medium to speak and may even rearrange his or her facial expression to approximate his or her own face. There may be physical movements by which the departed might wish to prove identity; specific phrases, words, nicknames and personal bits of information are given as a means of identification so that the one seeking the contact can be sure he has succeeded in establishing it with the right person....

Psychometrists

Among the mental mediums there are many who are called psychometrists. They are able to touch an object that was once the property of the departed and induce certain visions and impressions from it. Quite naturally, in using psychometric methods in attempting communication with the dead, one should be careful to disallow anything about the departed that might have been obtained by the medium from the touching of the object handed him or her.

But it is equally wrong to assume that *all* the information that may follow is obtained merely in this manner. I have witnessed a number of sittings where the touching of the object served as an opening door for the discarnate to enter and continue the sitting. Once the alleged dead is "present," the sitter will have to evaluate the messages received on their own merits. Although objects do carry a certain amount of information about their former owners, to my knowledge they do not contain complete biographies and detailed histories of that person. The only exceptions are cases where people died violently, or other forms of emotional trauma were present when the object was in the possession of the discarnate owner. Then the entire scene might very well have been imprinted on the object, and could be read by the psychic person.

But mediums are not easily found when a person lives in a rural area or small community outside the big cities. Still, the desire for communication is not confined to the "convenient" areas of the world. People who cannot obtain the services of psychics and who desire to initiate contact with departed ones have found alternative ways to do so.

There is, first of all, that most satisfying route of the direct communication. By training and by the sheer good fortune of having innate psychic talents, a person can establish a direct link with the world of the departed by developing his or her own mediumship. Depending again on the particular "phase" of that ability and the degree with which it is practiced, we find a number of do-it-yourself mediums enjoying contact with the Other World. The most common form of this contact is again through clairvoyance, clairaudience or clairsentience, but of the induced kind. Usually this is done through periods of withdrawal or regular meditation. Another form is automatic writing, wherein a dead person allegedly controls the hand of the medium and communicates through writing. I have examined many such cases and found that a fair number of the automatists are indeed controlled by the dead correspondents. The proof will be found in the nature and contents of the writings, the appearance of the handwriting and whether it is similar to the deceased person's own hand, and the absence of detailed knowledge of the dead person's life and habits on the part of the automatic writer....

Lastly, and perhaps least, there are the man-made instruments by which many seek communication with the world beyond. Whether it is called a planchette or a ouija board, a plain piece of wood inscribed with the letters of the alphabet and some figures serves as probably the best known apparatus of attempted communication....Ouija boards were created after World War I when a wave of Spiritualism swept England and America. The board was a way, it was thought, to contact the loved ones, and depending upon where the indicator—or a water glass, if one preferred—would point, the answer was either yes (oui,ja) or no.

The board has no supernormal faculties whatever. If any genuine communications result from its use by two or more people, then one must examine first of all whatever knowledge those present might have had of the subject.

Risks

Only when a person is found to communicate via the board who is totally unknown to all present and is afterwards found to have existed as a person, and in the way the communicator claims, do we have a reputable communication. For ouija boards, along with crystal balls, tea leaves and coffee grinds, merely serve as concentration points for the reader's own unconscious. It is the psychic ability of the ones using the board that makes the communication, if one occurs, possible.

On occasion genuine contacts with the dead do come about in this manner, but they are not common and represent perhaps five per cent of the total material obtained with the board....

"Death does not purify, but it does allow willing souls to learn something new."

There is also a certain risk involved in the indiscriminate use of the board. A person capable of deep trance mediumship and not aware of this potential ability might conceivably play with the board and "pick up" an undesired and undesirable discarnate person. Once an initial contact has been made, it is often difficult to get rid of the tie, and unless the involuntary medium has professional guidance, all sorts of difficulties could result. For that reason I hold a dim view of parlor games called ESP and the light touch given to what is essentially a very serious and important human faculty. Anyone who has had trance experience or who knows that he or she is a true medium should be very careful before using a ouija board alone, or without the assistance of a trained psychic researcher who might help break an unwanted trance state should this be required. It does not happen very often, but it can happen, and it represents a most undesirable form of communication between the two worlds....

Patterns

The vast amount of material I have examined leads me to believe that there is a certain pattern in the communications between the dead and the living. My research is based solely on first-hand cases that have come to my attention and does not include other researchers' cases, although I have studied most of the authoritative material available....

What is also new is my evaluation of these experiences in terms of motivation. Having disposed of the somewhat tiresome argument of hallucination by vigorously insisting on detailed accounts and properly evaluating my witnesses in terms of reliability and stability, I have accepted the cases I am about to present as genuine on the face of it because of some very important arguments.

To begin with, I can neither prove objectively nor disprove objectively what a man experiences and registers through his senses of sight, hearing, smell, etc. I must still rely upon his report, unless I am myself the recipient of the unusual experience. Any judgment of people's experiences along these lines must therefore rest on secondary evidence: the person's character, mental and physical health, general behavior patterns, past record, incentive to lie, if any, and a comparison of the descriptive detail of his experiences and the details given by large numbers of other witnesses whom he does not know and who do not know him. It is scientifically acceptable to consider as true evidence the testimonies given by a number of witnesses in various places and at various times if these witnesses are in no position to influence one another's testimony. The theory of hallucination, i.e., imaginary happenings which the person believes he is actually experiencing, will simply not cover the majority of cases where contact between the dead and the living has occurred.

It is quite farfetched to postulate that thousands of people in all sorts of circumstances hallucinate a dead relative under varying conditions, without any common denominator except that a psychic experience results. Far more logical is the assumption that an extraordinary ESP experience does indeed occur to these people, even if it is contrary to orthodox scientific beliefs *at that time*.

> *"It is quite farfetched to postulate that thousands of people in all sorts of circumstances hallucinate a dead relative."*

Parenthetically, one should remember that many situations nowadays taken for granted were contrary to scientific beliefs at one time. Television, radio, airplanes, photography, and many other human advances fall under that category. It is not true that science is at the zenith of knowledge today, with little if anything startling yet to come. Far from it. Science, as I define it, is merely a method of learning as much as one can about any given subject. It includes the proviso that one must change one's views and conclusions whenever new findings occur to alter earlier findings. Science is therefore a continually moving force that ought to be flexible and open-minded. It ought to welcome anyone with new ideas and investigate those new ideas. But it rarely does. Therein lies one of man's curious paradoxes: he wants to know desperately, but at the same time he fears any knowledge that might upset previously held beliefs.

Assurance of Hereafter

There are, I find, certain rules that seem to guide communications between the two worlds, and I have presented the material in what I consider the natural subdivisions.

First, there are communications from the dead who are motivated by the desire to let the living know that life continues beyond the Veil. This seems to be one of the most common overriding factors in all such communications, and little wonder it is, for our upbringing makes a belief in survival after physical death highly unlikely.

True, religion holds out the promise of a Hereafter to which we go either immediately or at a given point when the trumpets sound. But religion never specifies the nature, the methods, the concept of that transition. Rather does it clothe its promise in pious platitudes and vague promises that the good will be rewarded by being in heaven, and the bad by being relegated to hell. The first place is populated by ethereal beings of great beauty given mainly to uplifting pursuits, while the lower place resembles a low-class Turkish steambath with unfriendly attendants in red underwear. Religion, by and large, has seized upon the very real evidence for the existence of a Hereafter as a means to an end: promising heaven or threatening hell keeps the faithful in line.

Unfortunately, the large masses of people no longer *believe* this. Only a dwindling percentage of religiously oriented people actually accept these Hereafter concepts at face value. The majority I have questioned will admit only that they simply don't know if there is such a thing as a Hereafter, or they will deny outright that there *could* be. If they practice any religion at all, it is because of moral and social aspects, often even because of economic pressures to belong to an "in" group. But conservative religion on the one hand, and extremely liberal religion on the other, have both failed to satisfy man's external hunger for the truth about himself. If he is indeed endowed with an immortal soul, he wouldn't know it from his minister, priest or rabbi.

Ego and Altruism

But he just might glimpse a piece of the truth through psychic research....

There are two strong and compelling reasons why a dead person wants his family or friends to know that death is not the end, and that he or she is in fact very much alive in another dimension.

One reason is the continuing ego-consciousness of the dead person. He wants to let those closest to him know that he continues to exist as an entity and consequently that he wishes to be considered a continuing factor in their lives. This is for his own sake.

The second reason for this need to let the others know that life after death exists is for their sake. They too will eventually die. Why not give them the benefit of his experience? Why not teach them? Why not help those presumably ignorant of the true situation—that means nine out of ten of us—and do them the favor of letting them in on the world's greatest and most important secret: that man does not end at the grave?

Personal Encounter

My own encounter with this type of communication first came in the late fifties, when I happened to drop in at a meeting of the New York branch of the Cayce Foundation. This foundation is also known as the Association for Research and Enlightenment, and is dedicated to various forms of psychic and allied research. I sat quietly in the last row of the darkened room, in which there were a hundred or so people listening to a speaker. The lady was just ending her lecture-demonstration. The lights went on, and I was sorry to have come so late, but before I could leave, I noticed that the speaker was making her way through the crowd toward me.

"Are you Hans Holzer?" she asked. I nodded, thinking that someone had pointed me out to her. Nobody had, for in those days I was quite unknown. None of my books had yet appeared in this field. Quickly suppressing my ego and realizing that she could not possibly have known my name, I asked what she wanted to tell me.

"I'm Betty Ritter," she explained, "the medium. I have a message for you from an uncle." Well, I thought, bemused, I've got a lot of uncles. She must have felt my skepticism, for she added: "His initials are O.S., he's got a wife named Alice, and she's a blond."

Brief Message

Now I had had an uncle whose name was Otto Stransky; he had died tragically in a street car mishap in 1932, and though I had always respected him, I hardly knew him and had not thought of him in many years. His widow's name was and is Alice. At the time of his passing she was indeed a blond, but has long since turned gray.

There was no further message: this was it. He merely wanted me to know he *existed.* No alternate explanation would make sense. I had not been thinking of him, and if I had I would certainly not refer to my Aunt Alice as a blond, knowing full well that she had been gray for many years. Only in my uncle's memory would she still be a blond!...

The annals of psychic research are full of verified cases in which the dead come to bid the living a last good-bye. But the thought of separation is often overshadowed by the desire to announce the continuance of life. This, of course, is implied in the very fact of an appearance after death: only if the person survives can he come to say good-bye. Orthodox psychiatry has labored hard and long to explain most of these appearances as "hallucinations," but the fact is that the majority of cases show total ignorance on the part of the recipient that the person who communicates with him after death is no longer alive. You cannot hallucinate something you don't know....

Recurrent Dream

Mrs. G. Bigenko is a housewife living in a Pittsburgh suburb. She and her brother, Frank John Graziano, had been close in their childhood, which may be of some importance in the event I am about to relate. Whenever there exists an emotional bond between people, the communication between the world of the dead and that of the living seems to be easier. But this is by no means always the case, as even strangers have communicated in this way with each other.

"He merely wanted me to know he existed."

Frank Graziano and forty-one others were aboard a Navy transport flying over the ocean. On the nights of October 26, 27 and 28, 1954, Mrs. Bigenko had a vivid dream in which she felt someone was drowning. This recurrent dream puzzled her, but she did not connect it with her brother at the time, as she had no idea where he was or what he was doing at the moment. On October 30, 1954, she was awakened from sleep by the feeling of a presence in her room. This was not at her own home, but at the house of her in-laws. Her husband was sleeping in an adjoining room. As she looked up, fully awake now, she saw at the foot of her bed a figure all in white. A feeling of great sorrow came over her at this moment. Frightened, she jumped out of bed and ran to her husband.

The following evening, the telephone rang. Her brother Frank, crewman on an ill-fated air transport, had been lost at sea....

Contact with Dead

The desire to call up Uncle Joe in the great Beyond is as old as mankind. All the weaknesses inherent in such a daring proposition must be traced to the eagerness to make a contact *from this end,* rather than waiting for contact to happen, naturally and of necessity, from the other end of the "line."

Of course, not everybody considers it proper to make contact with deceased relatives; some people hold peculiar views about the propriety of such attempts. This is partly due to religious pressures and ingrained prejudices, and partly due to fear of the unknown. However, there is a substantial segment of the population that considers such contacts not only proper but even desirable. Their motives vary from greed to genuine spiritual curiosity. There isn't a day when my mail does not bring a request for an introduction to a good medium. The purpose is always personal; the goal is always some sort of contact with a loved one. Secondarily, people want to know their own future, and the loved ones are also asked advice about the future on the vague premise that a dead person knows more than a live one.

This does not follow. Passage into the non-physical world creates no wise men. It does not make angels out of sinners or saints out of good people merely because they happen to be dead. Death does not purify, but it does allow willing souls to learn something new, something the soul probably did not know until then: namely, that life continues, and that a person can expand his consciousness over there precisely as he can over here, if he is interested. Thus it is true that *some* individuals attain a higher degree of knowledge after their death, and this includes foreknowledge of future events. This happens because in the non-physical world the time and space barrier preventing everyday precognition on earth does not exist. Events shape up independently, and a clear-eyed person can look ahead in time and possibly speak to a living relative about it. But it does not follow that *all* dead can do this, or that being dead helps them to do this if the personal desire to learn is not present.

Among simple people there has grown up an almost mystical belief in the supernatural powers of the dead as if they were an army of soldiers ready to interfere in the lives of the flesh-and-blood world. Nothing could be further from the truth. The only difference between the living and the dead is the degree of density of their bodies, and consequently the greater maneuverability of the spiritual body in comparison with the clumsy physical "encasement."

"Of course, not everybody considers it proper to make contact with deceased relatives."

To seek contact with the dead, therefore, is a matter for only well-adjusted individuals to undertake. It is particularly ill suited for the unbalanced or too strongly bereaved, at least without proper instruction by a psychic researcher. The dangers are two-fold. To begin with, a person unable to accept the loss of a loved one may place too much emphasis on the life beyond and abandon himself to a concept for which he is not prepared. The physical body must have its due, and the dead cannot ever take the place of the living in human relations. A bereaved person might substitute a strong bond with the dead for the continuing search for relationships among the living, which nature has intended.

Hans Holzer is a popular writer in the field of parapsychology and the author of over twelve best-selling books on paranormal occurrences. He published How to Win at Life *in 1980.*

"There is indeed a world of spirits! But they are not the spirits of the dead."

Communication with the Dead Is Not Possible

Keith W. Stump

Recently, we received a curious tape recording from a *Plain Truth* reader.

The unusual recording purports to contain excerpts from actual voice conversations with persons who have died and "passed into the higher planes."

This two-way, telephone-like communication was reputedly accomplished by means of an electronic instrument invented by a group of American scientists and psychic investigators.

Many of you have probably seen newspaper or magazine articles about this alleged "breakthrough." Some may have heard the actual recordings. A few have written to *The Plain Truth* asking about this extraordinary device.

Is this—at last—concrete evidence of the continuance of conscious personality after death? Are these *really* the voices of the dead?

If not, what are they?

And what about "mediums" and "seances"? Can they really provide us with a link to the dead?

Invisible Hands

Few questions are as vitally important as that of man's ultimate destiny. *Is* there a life beyond the grave? If so, is it possible to communicate with those who have "passed over"?

Virtually all civilizations since the beginning of history have possessed some form of belief in an afterlife. And not surprisingly, attempts to communicate with the dead go back to earliest antiquity.

The belief that the spirits of those who have "passed over" can make contact with the living is known today as spiritualism or spiritism. Modern spiritism had its birth in Hydesville, New York, in the middle of the last century—specifically, March 31, 1848.

It is an interesting story. For several nights, mysterious rappings and strange noises had kept the Fox family awake. As far as John Fox could determine, the disturbing sounds could not be attributed to mice, rats or the wind. History is full of "haunted houses" of this type. But in this case, events took a unique turn.

On March 31, John Fox's two young daughters playfully issued a challenge to the noises—a challenge to repeat their own patterns of raps. Remarkably, their exact patterns were repeated—seemingly tapped out by invisible hands! The Fox sisters had established a dialogue with the unseen presence causing the noises!

Answering Raps

They then asked the presence questions that could be answered "yes" (one rap) or "no" (two raps). The presence willingly supplied answers.

Painstaking sessions employing various types of codes enabled the Fox sisters to acquire detailed information about the presence. Amazingly, it claimed to be the spirit of a dead peddler, Charles B. Rosma, murdered many years earlier in the basement of the cottage now occupied by the Fox family! For one reason or another, he had apparently been delayed in his progress into the "next world."

News of the goings-on in the Fox house spread rapidly, creating considerable stir. Neighbors were invited in to hear the "conversations." Many became convinced that the Fox sisters were in actual contact with the dead.

Modern spiritism was born.

Within a few decades, the controversial movement had gained millions of followers around the globe. Among them were many famous personages, such as Sir Arthur Conan Doyle—creator of the fictional detective Sherlock Holmes—and Sir William Crookes, the English physicist.

Death, the spiritists declared, is merely a door to

Keith W. Stump, "Communication with the Dead: Is it Possible?" *The Plain Truth*, April 1983. Permission to reprint by the Worldwide Church of God.

continuing life—in the "spirit world." Moreover, they said, we can establish communication with those on the "other side."

This contact is usually made through the agency of a medium at a seance. A seance (French for "a sitting") is a meeting for the purpose of obtaining spiritistic phenomena. The medium (usually a woman) is the focal point of a seance and acts as the organ of communication with "departed spirits."

Seances became the rage in fashionable society throughout Europe and America in the last century. In brief, a seance is conducted as follows:

A small group of people sit in a circle around a table, usually holding or at least touching hands. The room is quiet and dark. The medium then goes into a trance or semitrance, a state resembling deep hypnosis.

While in the trance, the medium purports to convey messages from the spirit world to those around the table. The messages often come by way of a "control," a departed spirit that associates itself with the medium and passes on messages from other spirits.

Truth or Fraud?

Sometimes the medium simply repeats to the participants around the table what she is told by her "control"—or describes what she sees in the spirit world. At other times, the control spirit or another spirit speaks directly through the medium.

On occasion, the participants themselves hear spirit voices coming from outside the medium, often from somewhere overhead. In rare instances, a spirit creates a vague visible form for itself and partially materializes—creating a ghostly apparition for all to see!

Many have come away from seances convinced of the authenticity of the phenomena. Others have suspected fraud. What is the truth?

Is communication between the "two worlds" possible?

Houdini

The famous stage magician Harry Houdini (1874-1926) sought an answer to this question. He threw out challenges to mediums to prove to his satisfaction the authenticity of their activities. He claimed he could duplicate by purely physical means any effect they produced in the course of a seance.

During the course of 30 years of witnessing alleged examples of communications with the "next world," Houdini declared he had not "found one incident that savored of the genuine."

What Houdini often did uncover were extremely clever frauds and skillful illusions perpetrated by charlatans and unscrupulous mediums on trusting victims.

Darkened rooms provided the perfect setting for fraud. Concealed microphones, wires, mirrors,

projectors, ventriloquism, sleight of hand and other ingenious techniques combined to produce a variety of spectacular effects convincing to the gullible. Houdini caught scores of embarrassed mediums red-handed in such frauds.

Based on his investigations, Houdini concluded that spiritism was riddled with trickery, deceit and fraud. Other investigators have agreed that the percentage of fraud is high.

But are *all* mediums fakes?

By no means!

There are many serious mediums who have stood up under the most rigorous scrutiny of investigators. Despite meticulous testing, they have given no evidence of any type of fraud.

Are these mediums, then, really in contact—as they believe—with the dead?

Spirit Photographs

The art of photography—in its infancy when modern spiritism was born—soon came to the aid of spiritists in convincing the public of life beyond the grave.

Hundreds of photographs have been taken over the decades purporting to show vaguely materialized spirits actually caught by the camera! Many spiritists consider such photos to be the outstanding proof of their beliefs.

"Few questions are as vitally important as that of man's ultimate destiny."

A large percentage of these photos, however, have been shown to be bogus—the results of "doctored" or retouched negatives, double exposures, trick lighting effects or other deceptions.

But others have stood up to the tests of investigators. I have personally examined scores of these photographs and am satisfied as to their overall genuineness.

But again—are these photos proof of life after death?

Electronic Communication

And now—a spectacular further development in the world of spiritism.

As mentioned at the beginning of this article, experimentation has reportedly produced an electronic device enabling the operator to engage in two-way, telephone-like conversations with the dead—a type of Ouija board with a voice!

It was the great inventor Thomas Edison who first conceived the possibility of instrumental communication with the dead. But experimenters had to admit failure in establishing an electronic link with the spirit world—until the late 1950s.

In 1959, the Swedish filmmaker and painter

Friedrich Jurgenson played back tapes of bird calls he had recorded in a Swedish forest. To his astonishment, he heard what he believed to be his dead mother's voice on the tape! This began a series of experiments to record spirit voices. Hundreds of voices have appeared on his tapes.

Other researchers have claimed to have recorded the spirit voices of Churchill, Hitler, Stalin, Tolstoy and many other famous men and women of history.

EVP

Many years of such research and experimentation have now produced the two-way machine previously mentioned. The device tunes in on certain radio frequencies that provide a channel over which "those in the higher planes"—the reputed dead—can convey their messages.

There is no apparent reason to doubt the sincerity or the integrity of those who have worked on this project or of other researchers in the field of EVP (electronic voice phenomena). It is unlikely that the voices have been faked in any way. There are no indications of fraud or hoax. It is apparent that the researchers are in actual voice contact with spirit entities.

"Houdini concluded that spiritism was riddled with trickery, deceit and fraud."

By what means does the device work? "It does work," remarks one of its inventors, "but we don't fully know those underlying laws yet." He also admits that mediumship is involved to some degree. "It [the device] requires an operator with a very special type of psychic energy."

Are these the voices of the dead?

Some investigators have suggested that these reputed "messages from the dead" might actually be coming somehow from the subconscious of the machine's operator himself, and not from the "other side." The same explanation has often been put forward to account for the messages of mediums in seances.

Many other explanations have been suggested for this and other spirit phenomena—all of which *at times* have probably played a role. But again, not all spirit phenomena can be adequately explained away by such theories. There remain certain manifestations for which no entirely satisfactory explanation has been offered—other than actual spirit contact.

But has contact been made with the dead? Or might there be another explanation?

No Immortal Soul

At the end of last year *The Plain Truth* published an article challenging the widely held belief in an "immortal soul." The age-old belief in the separate existences of the body and the soul was proved to be without support in the Bible!

That article explained the true scriptural definition of the word *soul*, demonstrating that "soul" designates man's physical life—that a soul is what man is, not something spiritual he has. Man has no inherent immortality. The soul is mortal and can die.

The article showed from the Bible that the dead "sleep" in insensibility in their graves until a future resurrection—a rising from the dead.

Many readers wrote in, inquiring how one can explain "ghosts," seances, spirit photography and related phenomena. If these are not the spirits of the dead—what are they?

The explanation is found in the Bible!

World of Spirits

The Bible reveals that there is indeed a world of spirits! But they are not the spirits of the dead—though some may masquerade as spirits of the dead! This spirit world is the world of angels—and demons (fallen angels).

Angels were created by God eons ago—long before the creation of the earth. The archangel whom we call Lucifer and one third of these created angels ultimately rebelled against God.

The disobedient Lucifer became Satan, "the Adversary." The angels who followed him in rebellion became demons. They remain subject to Satan, the "prince of demons."

Satan and his demonic cohorts exert enormous influence on this world. The Bible calls Satan "the god of this world." In that role, he has succeeded in deceiving the whole world.

Spiritual Darkness

Satan and his demons pretend to bring light. Demons have, for millennia, been turning mankind from truth into spiritual darkness, falsely calling that darkness "light." The Bible warns of the dangers of humans dabbling in the world of spirits....

Notice a biblical example of just how seriously God takes spiritism!

In I Samuel 28, we find an account of an ancient "seance" involving King Saul of Israel. Saul desired to know about the outcome of a great battle with the Philistines in which he was about to engage. He inquired of God, but received no answer. God refused to listen to Saul because of his rebellious attitude.

Saul then defied God's clear commands in the law and ordered his servants: "Seek me a woman that hath a familiar spirit, that I may go to her, and enquire of her."

Saul was told that there was a woman at Endor that had a familiar spirit. She is referred to as a witch in some translations, as a medium in others.

So Saul disguised himself and went to the woman by night and said: "I pray thee, divine unto me by the familiar spirit, and bring me him up, whom I shall name unto thee." The practice of "consulting the dead" was rife among ancient Israel's heathen neighbors. Saul had been influenced by their practices.

Deadly Impersonation

Now notice what happened:

The medium asked whom she should bring up. Saul said: "Bring me up Samuel."

The woman then saw a form that she believed to be Samuel. Saul himself did not see the spirit, for he asked the woman to describe it to him. As a result of the description, Saul "perceived that it was Samuel."

The spirit—still invisible to Saul—then spoke directly to Saul and prophesied of his impending defeat at the hands of the Philistines.

The spirit that appeared was not Samuel. Samuel was dead, and the "dead know not any thing." At death, one's thoughts perish—as the Bible plainly teaches.

"It is the world of demons. . .that is behind spirit manifestations."

Moreover, Scripture tells us that God refused to answer Saul by prophets. But Samuel was a prophet. The spirit that spoke to Saul thus could not have really been Samuel.

What had appeared to the medium and spoke to Saul was simply a form that *looked like* Samuel—a demon inpersonating Samuel! It was deception, however sincere the medium may have been. There is no other explanation within the teachings of the Bible!

Saul assumed the demon was Samuel—just as spiritists assume they are contacting the spirits of the dead. Spiritists would all do well to ask themselves the question posed by Hamlet in the play by William Shakespeare. Upon encountering a form claiming to be the ghost of his father, Hamlet thought to himself:

"The spirit that I have seen may be a devil, and the devil hath power to assume a pleasing shape."

Saul sinned by seeking a witch. God takes the sin of spiritism very seriously. "So Saul died for his transgression. . . ."

Works of Darkness

Demons are spirits of darkness. Spiritism is a work of darkness. Little wonder that it is normal spiritist practice to conduct seances in a darkened room. Strong light, say spiritists, hinders communications with the spirits. This fact in itself should tell them something about what kind of spirits they are dealing with!

One might also ask of spiritists why "afterlife" is apparently so concerned with such trivia as is often manifested in seances and "hauntings": knocks and rappings, eerie noises, screams, table levitating and the like. Is there not more to this alleged afterlife than the playing of childish pranks and usually trivial conversation?

The answer should be clear! It is not the dead with whom we are dealing!

The dead cannot communicate with the living! The reason? They're DEAD—not alive in some sort of "spirit world." No such survival is taught anywhere in the Bible!

It is the world of demons—seeking to perpetuate the false doctrine of the immortal soul—that is behind spirit manifestations in seances, spirit photographs and electronic voice phenomena. Masquerading as "spirits of the dead," they deceive the biblically unlearned—just as king Saul was deceived at Endor!

Such manifestations are accomplished by demon power—not by the Spirit of God! Most spiritists refuse to admit this possibility.

Man's True Destiny

There is only one mediator between God and man—Jesus Christ. Mediums and their familiar spirits are not the source of reliable spiritual knowledge, but rather perpetuate a false concept of man's destiny.

Keith W. Stump is a senior writer for The Plain Truth *magazine, a monthly publication of the Worldwide Church of God.*

"Without life after death, all of Christian faith would lose its significance."

Belief in an Afterlife Is Essential

Kenneth S. Kantzer

"When I die, I shall rot," Bertrand Russell declared. With dreadful honesty the famed British philosopher was drawing the logical conclusion of his own materialistic philosophy of life. Two thousand years earlier, the apostle Paul drew the same inevitable conclusion from an identical premise: "without hope," because "without God."

The most important question a person can ask is not, "Is there life after death?" but "Is there a God?" And a further question closely follows: "Am I accountable to Him?"

Without life after death, all of Christian faith would lose its significance. Clarence Macartney, brilliant Presbyterian preacher of a generation ago, wrote:

Meaningless Affirmations

"In certain respects the great article of the Apostles' Creed is the last: 'I believe in . . . the resurrection of the body, and the life everlasting.' Without that article, the other great affirmations have no meaning. Suppose one were to say, 'I believe in God the Father,' but not in life everlasting; or 'I believe in the Holy Ghost,' but not in the life everlasting; or, 'I believe in . . . the holy Catholic church, the communion of saints,' but not in the life everlasting. All those affirmations would be meaningless without the great chord struck in the final sentence of the Creed." He then notes that without that affirmation the creed would be like a great cathedral wrapped in the gloom of night. But with it, "the Creed is like a great cathedral illuminated by the sun and showing all the glory of the architect, sculptor, and painter."

Strangely, the Bible tells us little about heaven or the nature of life after death. Much is stated in only negative terms—no tears, no pain, no sorrow, no sighing. Life after death will be very unlike our

present life on earth. Yet for some of us, perhaps, eternal life would seem less attractive if God were to tell us a great deal about its nature. We are attracted by the more sensuous joys we find so desirable here on earth. They are the best our minds can grasp. And God condescends to use them to comfort us and woo us to the unimaginable delights that are now beyond our power to appreciate or comprehend.

Four Great Truths

The Bible's central teaching on everlasting life focuses on four great truths. First, we shall be like Christ. That is God's goal for each of us. We shall be good—like Christ.

In a recent poll, Americans were asked what they wanted most in life. The largest number wanted good health; next in order was a secure job. These are worthy goals. If we are honest, most of us will readily admit we should greatly like both. But if they are our highest goals, we are headed for disaster. Not everyone in this life will find either good health or a secure job. And with such goals we will be setting ourselves against God, since his ultimate goal for us is that we might be good like Christ.

Second, the Bible says everlasting life is with Christ and with God in his eternal kingdom. Though we know little about the furniture of heaven, we know it will be a perfect society of good people. Above all, it will be unending life with the One who is ultimately the source of all good.

What new and exciting tasks shall we be set to by God's infinitely creative mind? We have no way of conjecturing. We need not fear boredom, however—unless goodness itself is boring to us. Our own tiny corner of the universe with its inconceivable variety offers only a fascinating down payment on the infinite possibilities of the future. The wildest dreams of far-out science fiction cannot begin to hint at what the infinite creativity of the omnipotent, omniscient mind has in store for us.

Kenneth S. Kantzer, "The Good News the Resurrection Brings," *Christianity Today*, April 6, 1984. Copyright 1984 by CHRISTIANITY TODAY. Reprinted with permission.

Third, the Bible focuses on the integrity of our being. Everlasting life in the plan of God reveals his concern for the whole of each person's humanity—body and soul. In Scripture, therefore, the resurrection of the body marks our entrance into the eternal mode of existence.

We humans are neither matter nor spirit, but an essential unity of both. Death breaks that. True, the Bible speaks of an existence beyond the grave as the Spirit returns to its Creator, and we, though "absent from the body," are "present with the Lord." But Scripture qualifies this interim as an "unclothed" existence awaiting consummation at the grand day of resurrection. We humans can fulfill our destiny only as we are once again brought into wholeness by resurrection from the dead.

No doubt the idea of bodily resurrection brings as many problems to our minds as does human existence without a body. A famous atheist of a century ago, Robert Ingersoll, specially criticized the Christian doctrine that all bodies will one day be raised from the dead. With what body would they possibly be raised? He tried to disprove the doctrine by telling of a man who was buried in a churchyard beside an apple orchard. Later that year, an apple from a tree bordering the cemetery fell near his grave, and a seed sprouted and grew, sending roots into the grave. Eventually the tree bore apples, which the orchard's owner sold to nearby villagers.

Changing Atoms

"Now," Ingersoll asked, "whose body will be raised at the last day?" The chemical elements of the buried man's body entered through the roots of the tree into the apples, and ultimately became part of the bodies of a variety of villagers. Are we all going to be rather like Siamese twins in heaven?

Anticipating Ingersoll, ancient skeptics in Corinth had likewise raised similar objections, asking the apostle Paul, "With what kind of body will they [the resurrected believers] come?" Paul pointed out that we are aware of varied kinds of physical bodies. By his omnipotent power God will make us a body—a physical body of a kind exactly suited to us and to our new kind of existence in heaven. By his creative power God is not limited to any specific atoms—certainly not to those exact atoms in our body at the time of our death. He can create a new body from chemical elements of his choice, ones exactly suited to our needs, and to our spirit with which it will be rejoined in perfect unity.

This is really not so difficult to understand. Scientists tell us that the human body is constantly wearing away and simultaneously reproducing itself. The chemical elements in any part of our body are not the same as those of a few years ago. But except for the enamel of our teeth and the hardest parts of our large bones, the actual atoms that make up our body now are different from those in our body four

or five years ago. And the substance of the soft parts is completely exchanged every few months. Yet we know that our body is the identical one we had last year.

Perhaps the same thing will be true of our resurrection body. The same molecules will not compose it then. We do not know the chemical composition of that body, but we know it will be a body, not just a disembodied spirit. And in spite of changes, it will be just as much our body as our body today is the one we had a year ago. It will be our body because it will be perfectly suited to us and to our spirit. It will complete us by making us that unified whole of body and spirit God intended from the first.

Separation

The fourth scriptural focus regarding everlasting life is most disquieting. Awful as it seems, heaven is not for everyone: our heavenly Father makes it ready for those who are prepared to live in it. Painful as this is to contemplate, it is nevertheless difficult to see how in a moral universe things could be otherwise.

Character is formed and solidified in this life. By faith in Christ, so Scripture teaches, we are forgiven our sins and enter into life with God. Judicially, God receives us from the day we believe as being all we ought to be, since we possess the righteousness of Christ. The Bible calls this justification by faith. But this is only the first step in a process that prepares us for everlasting life in God's good kingdom. Bit by bit, our heavenly Father transforms our inward self into perfect Christlikeness. To do this he uses the process of life and death, climaxed when we are ushered into his immediate presence. Without this transformation, we would not be fitted to live with God in his good kingdom. We would not even enjoy it!

We are not puppets moved by divine caprice, but humans whose character is formed more and more surely through the experiences of life. Some choose evil, and their character is formed and solidified in evil. They unfit themselves for God and his holy kingdom. Only by destroying their personal integrity, trifling with their wills, and ignoring their moral character built over a lifetime could God transform them into beings suited to his perfect society. For reasons we do not fully understand, God allows them to forge their own evil destiny.

But for those God is preparing to dwell with him forever in his kingdom of the good, the old familiar words of the confession become a shout of triumph: "I believe in the resurrection of the body, and the life everlasting."

Kenneth S. Kantzer is advisory editor for Christianity Today, *a monthly magazine.*

"After careful analysis and reflection, I am convinced that belief in an afterlife brings no special peace to the dying."

Belief in an Afterlife Is Not Necessary

Robert E. Kavanaugh

Is there any kind of life after death? Can we ever know for certain?. . . Many times the question seems the most important in life and at other times too unimportant to ask. One thing is certain. No religion has yet succeeded in providing evidence sufficient to convince more than a fraction of mankind of its point of view, and only a somewhat larger fraction of its own followers. . . .

In short, we might easily conclude that nobody knows for certain about an afterlife. Instead, I choose to hold with Kierkegaard that every man knows for himself within his inner soul. Maybe nobody can ever know what to believe for anyone besides himself. Near death, true belief in what you sincerely hold will bring peace and any promise you need for your future. Scientists, philosophers and theologians are forever arguing each other into contradictions, and the man who claims to know what is correct for others to believe must leap across the centuries of conflicting and contradicting views. This conclusion makes far more sense to me than all the deathbed conversions where men tried to die in a faith unknown until the last, or in one they cared not or dared not to live by, a final greedy grasp, willing to pretend in order to steal a possible heaven. Just in case.

A major reason why Americans find it so easy to blithely dismiss all hint of an afterlife is that continued contentment seems possible in the present. Pain and poverty are far away from most and seem conquerable, while advances in medicine make death seem more distant. Life within an affluent society, or at least near one, dissipates so much of the human need to dream of heaven. The promise of plenty in this life, even if only made in movies and ads, blots out much thought of dying, perfuming all death,

distracting from afterlife with rich fantasies of now and tomorrow. Man madly concentrates on making heaven on earth, believing it possible, if only, if only. . . .

Present Feelings Sufficient

I am increasingly satisfied to only feel my present feelings, my fears, my pangs for more, my hopes, my panic, allowing them to rummage around inside, without running to my fantasies for a cure or an explanation. Then I begin to wonder if the whole question of an afterlife makes any difference at all. I find that I am no more or less moral by believing in it than I am by being indifferent, no happier, no kinder, no more peaceful. Maybe there is no life after death, only restful and dreamless sleep, and all we have is what we feel within us and what we see around us. Maybe there is nothing more than our bodies and minds, our friends, our work and hobbies, our growing older daily, our pains and wars, our human joys and death. And as I learn to love life and self and those nearby, finding new appreciation by study and reflection on death, maybe these are enough.

I am prepared to think momentarily with you that life here on earth is all we have. I can admit my own hopes for an afterlife are dreams that will never come true. Can you shed for the moment any myths about afterlife that might be lingering in your head? How would your life be changed? I think not much at all. The unhappily married think they might run to a divorce court. Teetotalers think they might tilt a few too many and the lusty envision risky affairs. The angry think they might murder someone in vengeance. On the contrary, I find by experience that men remain morally the same without belief in afterlife, and maybe nonbelievers work harder to make this world a moral and happier place because it is all they have.

Belief in any kind of an afterlife seems impossibly unreal even to those who claim unwavering faith. I

Robert E. Kavanaugh, *Facing Death.* New York: Nash Publishing Corporation, 1972. Reprinted with permission of Nash Publishing Corporation.

used to enjoy asking groups of staunch believers a series of questions. "How many believe in heaven?" All hands raised high. "How many believe heaven is eternal and perfect happiness?" Most hands this time. "How many are perfectly happy on earth?" Almost no hands. "How many want to leave for heaven today?" Never more than a few hands, usually wrinkled ones.

Would no afterlife alter the fears most men have of dying? I am convinced it would not change deathbed fears more than a tiny bit, probably reducing dying fears if anything, since dying believers reflect more anxiety over loss of life and possible punishment than a sense of joy at joining their God in heaven.

An afterlife where man lives pleasurably without his body is beyond my comprehension. I can admit its possibility but I cannot long for it or even know if I would want it. In sermons and lectures I used to describe life without a body, using Cardinal Newman's poem "The Dream of Gerontius" wherein he undertakes the formidable task of describing the moments after the soul leaves the body and ascends before Christ in particular judgment. With all of his considerable literary and philosophical skills, Newman failed. And I with him. Either we use figures of descriptive speech which demand a body or our explanations lose everyone except the deeply metaphysical.

"Any belief fashioned in life is a good belief for facing death provided it fits well enough to be one's own."

Poets and evangelists all face the same problem. So do novelists and preachers. Either they resort to an abstract imagery devoid of emotional and physical dimensions or they use that childlike imagery of fantasy which demands the presence of a body which lies molding in a grave or in the sea. Their heaven of abstraction has no attraction nor could any heaven delight a man without a body, as far as I can fathom. I think of the billions who have already died in the thousands of years man has inhabited this earth. Then I find little sense in turning on to tales of sylvan glens, mansions, verdant meadows, harp music, banquets or angelic choirs, not even to the humorous quips of black folk preachers who see heaven as "a never ending line of fried chicken, black-eyed peas and corn pone—without a white man in sight."

No Special Peace

After careful analysis and reflection, I am convinced that belief in an afterlife brings no special peace to the dying that cannot be found by firm adherence to any other belief. We meet religious people well enough disposed to die in dignity and in peace, yet we also meet nonreligious people with equal dispositions near death. It is not the content of a man's creed that makes him confident and peaceful near life's brink. It is more the quality of his act of believing that counts.

Faith or belief are not the sole privileges of religious people as I once thought. Faith is simply that total commitment of the entire person to an ideal, a way of life, a set of values, to anything or anyone beyond the narrow limitations of myself: God, mankind, the poor, science, human relations, growth and development, anything capable of bringing meaning and purpose to life.

Too readily we classify as believers only those who wish they were or claim to be, anybody who says "I believe." Belief can be surface or shallow, a childhood dream or a parental wish, a family tradition or what society demands. Or it can be deeply imbedded in every portion of one's personality and being. Belief can be thoughtless following, love for a preacher or a balm to our fears as easily as being what I considerately choose after prayer and reflection. True believers are those who internalize and live what they claim to believe. The truths they securely hold are wound tightly into the total self, altering every deed, coloring every view, influencing every relationship. Onlookers will know almost infallibly once they are in the presence of a true believer. He is not loud or defensive and has no need to argue pettily or to compel imitation. His firm belief in someone or something transcendent only invites admiration and imitation. This quality of believing is any man's major asset in facing his own death.

Difficulty of Commitment

Unfortunately, it is intensely difficult today for belief to go deeper than the lips. Commitment has become the rascal of our times, easily evading all but the truest of true believers. Believers in science will often leave their creed at the laboratory door and believers in God leave theirs in church. Those who claim to uphold the dignity of man will often hold up any man they can, while believers in eternal sleep sometimes live as if their life were to be measured by an avenging God. Many of us have differing sets of beliefs for any occasion. True belief that will bring solace near death is measured more in actions during life than by loud protestations.

Belief in any higher meaning or worth in life can lend a special beauty to a man's life, even when we violently disagree with the truth value of his creed. I can admire the glow on the face of the nun and the vibrations of sincerity from the Jehovah's Witness who pushes her frightened little boy to preach at my front door. I feel deep respect for the dynamism in the man for whom science is a mystical or religious experience and the serenity of one who finds his major meaning in learning to relate and better communicate with other men. The true believer, after I sort out my personal feelings toward the tenets in his creed, reflects to me a sense of inner worth, a spirit of mission and purpose, a confident conviction and a tranquil assurance. Near death the true believer knows why he lived and can face the unfinished tasks of his life with his vision in clear focus. Because true belief brought perspective into life, so will it endow death with a more satisfying point of view. And no matter how wonderful religion may be for many, it is only one of the many ways to gain this stature of true belief.

> *"Belief in any higher meaning or worth in life can lend a special beauty to a man's life, even when we violently disagree with the truth value of his creed."*

When death draws near, the dying frequently begin to wonder about the wisdom of a return to a childhood belief or a former faith, even about the quick adoption of a faith from someone they admire. Dying people confess to doubting whether they could make such a transition or if they might soon feel compelled to make a deathbed switch by the weight of fear and guilt. Their conflict is compounded by a human noble streak that makes many men reluctant, near death, to clutch desperately for truths they abandoned or denied in the heat of life. The dying will often appear bullheaded in their refusal to change beliefs when they are only attempting to be honest in not becoming a parasite for peace. There is nothing so wrong in a last minute switch to please a religious wife or husband, or maybe a mother, but I have great doubts about the faith and the love of a person who would occasion such a change for even the noblest of reasons.

Any Belief Is Good

Any belief fashioned in life is a good belief for facing death, provided it fits well enough to be one's own. Borrowing beliefs can be as risky as borrowing money. Any creed that has become a part of a person's life-style, that was sincerely held and lived by, that took the believer beyond the solipsism of self, can serve the dual purpose any belief seems to serve near death. First, it will grant purpose and meaning through the agony and pain, through the hopelessness and fear. Nothing ever seems quite so difficult if there is some reasonable purpose behind it. And any transcendent belief confers reason on life and its passing. Secondly, belief will prepare the dying to meet any God with whom they might be spending an eternity. Try as I might, I cannot conceive of any all-knowing, all-caring God of

whatever denomination who would admire a cheap and fearful switch near death more than a firm adherence to beliefs gained in the struggle of life.

Especially near death, the problem with making a commitment resurrects. No matter the beauty of the ideals or values we lived by, we always seem eager to wonder if something better will come, if a more rewarding creed is not around the corner. This deathbed version of the puritan ethic has become an American bug. In life, it nibbles away at enduring commitment, at marital vows, at job stability and at loyalty in friendship or fealty to country. And at death, it gnaws at the validity of our own beliefs.

Skeptics and agnostics can find peace at the end, plus assurance of safety in any possible hereafter, if their search is their creed and they are sincerely committed to it. When any quest for truth is real, not mere talk or laziness, not indifference or being too busy, it can reward the searcher with all the wealth found in true belief. We can help if we give him confidence in the validity of his own choice. One of the noblest styles of life conceivable is that of sincere searching for truth. No God I ever read about or could love would disown a creature who lived in honest quest for a purpose he could totally endorse. Nor would any God reject a creature who found out too late his searching was dishonest or his heart disinterested or distracted. When life is ebbing away, knowing that you tried is faith enough to still the very human fears at dying and to satisfy any God who allowed his people to become so confused and his world so confusing.

Robert E. Kavanaugh is a teacher and psychologist. A former priest, Mr. Kavanaugh has written several psychology textbooks as well as articles for publications such as Psychology Today.

organizations

Alternatives to Abortion International
46 N. Broadway
Yonkers, NY 10701
(914) 423-8580

AAI was founded in 1971 in Chicago. It is presently a World Federation of Pro-Life Emergency Pregnancy Service (EPS) Centers which assist persons involved in problem pregnancies and related distress. Its one mission is to reach all women in the world who have problem pregnancies, to offer them positive and life protecting services and support. Long-range solutions to problems and planning for the future are basic to these services. The organization publishes the quarterly *Heartbeat Magazine*.

American Association of Suicidology
2459 S. Ash
Denver, CO 80222
(303) 692-0985

Founded in 1967, the Association draws professionals and amateurs from various disciplines and fields of experience who share a common interest in the advancement of studies of suicide prevention and life-threatening behavior. It publishes the quaterlies *Newlink* and *Suicide and Life Threatening Behavior*.

American Civil Liberties Union
22 E. 40th Street
New York, NY 10016
(212) 944-9800

One of America's oldest civil liberties organizations, the ACLU was founded in 1920. It champions the rights of individuals in right-to-die and euthanasia cases as well as in many other civil rights issues. The Foundation of the ACLU provides legal defense, research, and education. The organization publishes the quarterly *Civil Liberties* and various pamphlets, books, and position papers.

American Council on Science and Health
1995 Broadway, 18th Floor
New York, NY 10023
(212) 362-7044

The Council, founded in 1978, provides consumers with scientifically balanced evaluations of food, chemicals, the environment, and human health. It publishes detailed reports on health risks and benefits associated with public health and environmental issues. Reports are based on reviews of current literature and supplemented by consultations with specialists from the fields of public health, medicine, nutrition, and the environmental sciences. Personnel also participate in regulatory and congressional hearings, radio and television debates, and other forums.

American Life Lobby, Inc.
P.O. Box 490
Stafford, VA 22554
(703) 690-2510

The Lobby, founded in 1979, is pro-life and opposes all forms of birth control other than the rhythm or sympto-thermal methods. Their primary goal is to secure passage of the Human Life Amendment and safeguard the constitutional right of the "personhood" of the unborn. They also fight against euthanasia, suicide, and government funding of family planning. The ALL publishes the newsletter *About Issues* as well as books, pamphlets, and information packets on current topics.

Americans United For Life
Legal Defense Fund
230 N. Michigan Avenue, Suite 915
Chicago, IL 60601
(312) 263-5029

This organization was created to meet the urgent need for active courtroom representation of the unborn. AUL has expanded its outreach to all areas where the sacredness of human life is challenged—handicapped newborns, the elderly, and comatose patients. The AUL Legal Defense Fund is the only full-time, pro-life law firm in the country. As such, it is vital to the ultimate success of the pro-life movement. This group has been involved in more than ten US Supreme Court cases, and many lower court battles. They publish a newsletter every six weeks, as well as the quarterly *Youth Crusaders News*.

Bay Area Cryonics Society
1259 El Camino Real, Suite 250
Menlo Park, CA 94025
(415) 858-0869

The Society, founded in 1969, is interested in life extension through cryonics: the practice of freezing a dead diseased human being in hope of bringing the person back to life when a cure for the disease is discovered. The Society's purposes are to promote education and to provide information about cryonic suspension and suspended animation; to encourage research, and to enable individuals to arrange for their own cryonic suspension. Write to the Society for more information.

Birthright U.S.A.
686 N. Broad Street
Woodbury, NJ 08096
(609) 848-1819

Birthright, a nonsectarian national organization, seeks to help pregnant women find alternatives to abortion. In addition, they provide childbirth education classes and parenting programs. They publish *The Life-Guardian*, a bimonthly newsletter, and various books.

Catholics for a Free Choice

2008 17th Street, NW
Washington, DC 20009
(202) 638-1706

This organization was founded in 1972 by Catholics who support personal freedom and who uphold the Supreme Court decision on abortion. Their goal is to preserve the right of women to choose abortion and contraception. A speakers bureau has been established whose participants express their view on being Catholic and pro-choice. The organization publishes a bimonthly newsletter *Conscience* and several monographs and pamphlets.

Center for Death Education and Research

1167 Social Science Building
University of Minnesota
267 19th Avenue S.
Minneapolis, MN 55455
(612) 373-3683

This pioneering program in death education, founded in 1969, sponsors original research into grief and bereavement as well as studies of the attitudes and responses to death and dying. The Center conducts television, newspaper, and university classes and workshops for the care-giving professions. A list of published materials and a description of the Center's Cassette Tape Program is available upon request.

Concern for Dying

250 W. 57th Street
New York, NY 10107
(212) 246-6962

This organization was founded in 1967 with the purpose of informing and educating the general public and medical, legal, and health care professionals on the problems and needs of terminally ill patients and their families. Their goal is to assure patient autonomy with regard to treatment, and the prevention of futile prolongation of the dying process. They publish *A Legal Guide to the Living Will, Euthanasia: A Decade of Change,* and the quarterly, *Concern for Dying Newsletter.*

Continental Association of Funeral and Memorial Societies, Inc.

2001 S Street NW, Suite 530
Washington, DC 20009
(202) 745-0634

The Association is a nonprofit organization of nearly 180 local societies which help people make simple, dignified, and economical funeral arrangements. Memorial societies work with local funeral directors and encourage members to plan (but not pay) in advance. Membership is open to all for a small lifetime fee and may be transferred if a member moves to another area. This organization publishes the quarterly *Bulletin,* the *Handbook for Funeral and Memorial Societies,* and the *Manual of Death Education and Simple Burial.*

The Cremation Society of Minnesota

4343 Nicollet Avenue S.
Minneapolis, MN 55409
(612) 825-2435

The Cremation Society of Minnesota chooses to dispense with costly and unnecessary pomp associated with conventional funerals and is committed to dignified disposition at the time of one's death. Write to the Society for more information on this process.

Cryogenic Society of America

c/o Huget Advertising
1033 South Blvd.
Oak Park, IL 60302

The purpose of the Society is to encourage the dissemination of knowledge of low temperature processes and techniques associated with cryogenics. In addition, the Society promotes research and development through its publications and professional contacts.

Foundation of Thanatology

630 W. 168th Street
New York, NY 10032
(212) 694-4173

This organization of health, theology, psychology, and social science professionals is devoted to scientific and humanist inquiries into death, loss, grief, and bereavement. The foundation, formed in 1967, coordinates professional, educational, and research programs concerned with mortality and grief. They publish annual directories and the periodicals *Advances in Thanatology,* and *Archives of the Foundation of Thanatology.*

The Hastings Center

360 Broadway
Hastings-on-Hudson, NY 10706
(914) 478-0500

Since its founding in 1969, The Hastings Center has played a central role in raising issues as a response to advances in medicine, the biological sciences, and the social and behavioral sciences. In examining the wide range of moral, social, and legal questions, the Center has established three goals: advancement of research on the issues, stimulation of universities and professional schools to support the teaching of ethics, and public education. It publishes perhaps the best periodical on the subject of death and dying, *The Hastings Center Report.*

Hemlock Society

P.O. Box 66218
Los Angeles, CA 90066
(213) 391-1871

Founded in 1980, the Society supports the active voluntary euthanasia for the advanced terminally ill and the seriously incurably ill. They seek to promote a climate of public opinion which is tolerant of the terminally ill individual's right to end his or her own life in a planned manner and to clarify existing laws on suicide and assisted suicide. They do not encourage suicide for any primary reason other than terminal illness; however, they do approve suicide prevention work. Furthermore, they believe that the final decision to terminate one's life is one's own. The Society publishes a Right to Die newsletter, and various books and monographs on the subjects of suicide and euthanasia.

Human Life International

418 C Street NE
Washington, DC 20002
(202) 546-2257

This organization serves as a research, educational, and service program offering positive alternatives to the anti-life/family movement. They provide research and conferences on topics such as: Christian sexuality, natural family planning, abortion, infanticide, and euthanasia. Their publications include *The Best of Natural Family Planning, Death Without Dignity,* and *Deceiving Birth Controllers.*

The International Association For Near-Death Studies, Inc.
University of Connecticut
Box U-2
Storrs, CT 06268
(203) 486-4170

The primary purpose of this organization is to encourage and promote the study of a phenomenon of world-wide interest: the near-death experience (NDE). This experience, which has now been reported in many parts of the world and has been documented in thousands of cases, may well serve to enrich understanding of the nature and scope of human consciousness itself and its relationship to physical death. They publish the quarterly *Vital Sign Newsletter*.

International Association for Suicide Prevention
c/o Charlotte P. Ross
Suicide Prevention and Crisis Center
1811 Trousdale Drive
Burlingame, CA 94010
(415) 877-5604

Founded in 1965, the association disseminates information about suicide prevention, arranges specialized training of persons in suicide prevention, and carries out research programs. The association publishes a quarterly newsletter.

Life Extension Foundation
1185 Avenue of the Americas
New York, NY 10036
(212) 575-8300

The foundation, founded in 1953, conducts research and education in the field of death prevention. It also studies and compiles statistics on various medical studies according to factors such as age, sex, occupation, and dietary standards.

Living Bank
P.O. Box 6725
Houston, TX 77265
(713) 528-2971

The Bank, founded in 1968, is an information center and registry created to help those persons who, upon their death, consent to donate all or part of their bodies for transplantation, therapy, medical research, or anatomical study. Persons interested in donating organs may register. Children under the age of 18 must have their parent's or guardian's signature. The headquarter's phone number is a 24-hour referral service. Write to the Bank for more information regarding this topic.

National Abortion Federation
900 Pennsylvania Avenue SE
Washington, DC 20003
(202) 546-9060

Founded in 1977, this national professional forum for all abortion service providers acts as a clearinghouse for information on the variety and quality of services offered. The federation publishes *Guidelines on How to Choose an Abortion Facility* and an annual membership directory.

National Abortion Rights Action League
1424 K Street NW
Washington, DC 20005
(202) 347-7774

The league's philosophy is to develop and sustain a pro-choice political constituency in order to maintain the right to legal abortions for all women. In addition, they initiate and coordinate political action of individuals and groups concerned with maintaining the 1973 Supreme Court decision affirming the choice of abortion as a constitutional right. The league also maintains a staff of lobbyists who brief members of Congress, testify at hearings on abortion, and organize affiliates across the country. They publish a newsletter four times a year.

National Funeral Directors Association
135 W. Wells Street
Milwaukee, WI 53203
(414) 276-2500

The Association, founded in 1882, maintains a speakers bureau as well as a library of over 400 volumes and films on subjects relating to dying, death, and bereavement. It publishes *The Director*, a bimonthly newsletter, for its members.

National Hospice Organization
1901 N. Fort Meyer Drive, Suite 402
Arlington, VA 22209
(703) 243-5900

The organization, founded in 1977, promotes the concept and care program of the hospice, ''a concept of caring for the terminally ill and their families which enable the patient to live as fully as possible, make the entire family the unit of care, and center the caring process in the home whenever appropriate.'' It maintains standards of care in program planning and implementation and monitors health care legislation and regulation relevant to the hospice movement. The organization plans to design a national policy for adoption by the federal government providing for care for the terminally ill and their families. It conducts educational and training programs in numerous aspects of hospice care for administrators and caregivers. They publish a *President's Letter* monthly.

National Organization for Women
425 13th Street NW, Suite 723
Washington, DC 20004
(202) 347-2279

NOW is the largest organization in the world devoted exclusively to women's rights. They oppose the human life amendment claiming it would destroy the personal freedom of Americans and ultimately eliminate effective and legal forms of birth control in the country. They publish a monthly newsletter, *National NOW Times*.

The National Pro-Life Political Action Committee
7777 Leesburg Pike, Suite 305
Falls Church, VA 22043
(703) 893-1440

The Committee's main objective is to help elect pro-life candidates to federal, local, and congressional offices from all 50 states who oppose the 1973 Supreme Court decision on abortion. They wish to amend the Constitution to protect every human life, born and unborn. A monthly newsletter, *Political Reporter Pro-Life*, summarizes the actions of the pro-life movement in the country.

National Research and Information Center
1614 Central Street
Evanston, IL 60201
(312) 328-6545

The Center publishes views of a wide and varied nature, including material on coping with grief and information about the funeral industry. Their newsletter, *National Reporter*, is published monthly.

National Right to Life Committee, Inc.
419 Seventh Street NW, Suite 402
Washington, DC 20004
(202) 638-4396

The Committee, founded in 1973, opposes both abortion and euthanasia. They provide ongoing public education programs on abortion, euthanasia, and infanticide and maintain a printed library with over 430 volumes. The committee lobbies before congressional committees urging legislation for a pro-life amendment. They publish *National Right to Life News*, a bimonthly periodical, and a pamphlet entitled *Challenge to Be Pro-Life*.

National Save-A-Life League
815 Second Avenue, Suite 409
New York, NY 10017
(212) 492-4668

This organization of professionals and trained volunteers was founded in 1906 to work toward the prevention of suicide and to counsel families of suicide victims. The organization maintains a crisis center, provides a speakers bureau, sponsors educational radio programs on suicide, and offers financial aid and referrals. The organization maintains a 24-hour hotline.

Planned Parenthood Federation of America
810 Seventh Avenue
New York, NY 10019
(212) 541-7800

This family planning organization was founded in 1921 with educational, research, and training interests. The local affiliates provide information, medical services, counseling, and referrals for contraception, abortion, voluntary sterilization, and infertility services. The federation operates over 700 centers in major cities in the US. They publish *Washington Memo*, books, pamphlets, newsletters, and an *Affiliate Directory*.

Pre-Arrangement Interment Association of America
1133 Fifteenth Street NW
Washington, DC 20005
(202) 790-5822

Founded in 1956, the association promotes burial and funeral pre-arrangement. In addition, they publish several pamphlets, including *I Don't Want to Think About It, An Introductory to Memorial Counselors*, available to members as they make their future funeral arrangements.

Religious Coalition for Abortion Rights, Inc.
100 Maryland Avenue NE
Washington, DC 20002
(202) 543-7032

The Coalition is comprised of 30 national religious organizations—Jewish, Protestant, Catholic, and others. Because each denomination approaches the issue of abortion from the unique perspective of its own theology, members hold widely varying views on when abortion is morally justified. But all agree that there are situations in which abortion may be a moral alternative. The Coalition operates on both national and state levels. Individuals may support Coalition activities by participation in its nationwide legislative alert network *Dispatch*, by subscribing to its monthly newsletter *Options*, and by working with its state affiliates.

Reproductive Rights National Network
17 Murray Street, Fifth Floor
New York, NY 10007
(212) 267-8891

The organization, founded in 1979, advocates reproductive freedom and supports the goals of abortion rights, adequate and safe birth control methods, child care, the right to live openly as a lesbian or a gay man, and freedom from sterilization abuse and from reproductive hazards on the job. They monitor legislation affecting reproductive rights and encourage the formation of new groups who promote reproductive freedom.

Saint Francis Center
1768 Church Street NW
Washington, DC 20036
(202) 234-5613

The Center provides a broad range of services to individuals, families, and professionals dealing with life-threatening illness, bereavement, and loss. Founded in 1973, the non-denominational Center has expanded its services from alternatives to commercial funeral practices to counseling, education, and support programs.

Society for Cryobiology
310 E. 67th Street
New York, NY 10021
(212) 570-3079

Founded in 1963, the Society investigates the field of low temperature biology. In addition, they promote an interdisciplinary approach to the study of freezing, hibernation, physiological effects of low environmental temperatures on plants and animals, and the medical applications of reduced temperatures. They publish a bimonthly newsletter.

Society for the Right to Die
250 W. 57th Street
New York, NY 10107
(212) 246-6973

The Society advances nationwide recognition and protection of an individual's right to die with dignity. It distributes "living will" forms and publishes legislative and judicial information. The organization serves as a clearinghouse for health professionals, educators, attorneys, lawmakers, the media, and the general public. It aids citizen committees to further patients' rights and conducts awareness campaigns to disseminate rights information.

TASH: The Association for Persons with Severe Handicaps
7010 Roosevelt Way NE
Seattle, WA 98115
(206) 523-8446

TASH is a national organization of parents, administrators, teachers, medical personnel, researchers, and other interested people dedicated to making appropriate education and services available for severely handicapped people from birth to adulthood. Write to the organization for more information.

JS Coalition for Life
Box 315
Export, PA 15632
(412) 327-7379

The Coalition was founded in September of 1972. It is an internationally recognized pro-life research and lobby agency. Its research projects cover a full range of concerns including abortion, population control, euthanasia, and fetal experimentation. The *Pro-Life Legislative Services* bulletin is published monthly.

The Value of Life Committee, Inc.
637 Cambridge Street
Brighton, MA 02135
(617) 787-4400

The Committee, founded in 1970, is concerned with fostering
respect for human life from fertilization to natural death. In
addition, they strive to inform the general public regarding issues
concerning life such as ethics, euthanasia, and genetics. The
committee disseminates dozens of articles and papers in support of
its position.

Voters for Choice
27 T Street NW, Suite 301
Washington, DC 20036
(202) 659-2550

This political action committee opposes the Human Life
Amendment to the Constitution and other bills before the US
Congress that would limit or prohibit abortions. The Committee
also focuses on raising money for pro-choice candidates and has
established a Legal Abortion Defense Fund for the critical defense
of legal abortions.

bibliography

The following bibliography of books, periodicals, and pamphlets is divided into chapter topics for the reader's convenience. The topics are in the same order as in the body of this *Opposing Viewpoint SOURCE*.

Abortion

Deborah Baldwin	"Abortion: The Liberals Have Abandoned the Poor," *The Progressive*, September 1980.
Edward Batchelor Jr., editor	*Abortion The Moral Issues.* New York: The Pilgrim Press, 1982.
Catholics United for Life	*Never to Live, Laugh or Love.* Pamphlet available from Heritage House 76, Inc., Pro-Family Pro-Life Resource Center, PO Box 730, Taylor, AZ 85939.
Christianity & Crisis	"Women, Abortion, and Autonomy," March 5, 1984.
Kenneth Cauthen	"The Legitimacy and Limits of Freedom of Choice," *The Christian Century*, July 1/8, 1981.
Judith Coburn	"Abortion: Will We Lose Our Right to Choose?" *Mademoiselle*, July 1981.
engage/social action	Special issue. "Abortion: The Debate Continues," March 1983.
Jane Furlong-Cahill	*Abortion: The Double Standard*, 1974. Pamphlet available from Catholics For A Free Choice, 201 Massachusetts Ave., NE, Washington, DC 20002.
Donald Granberg	"The Abortion Controversy," *The Humanist*, July/August 1981.
Donald Granberg	"What Does It Mean to Be Pro-Life?" *The Christian Century*, May 12, 1982.
Dena Kleiman	"When Abortion Becomes Birth: A Dilemma of Medical Ethics Shaken by New Advances," *The New York Times*, February 15, 1984.
John Krastel	"Return to Realism: A Prolife Agenda," *America*, February 7, 1981.
Catharine MacKinnon	"The Male Ideology of Privacy," *Radical America*, Vol. 17, No. 4, 1983.
Daniel C. Maquire	"Abortion: A Question of Catholic Honesty," *The Christian Century*, September 14/21, 1983.
Paul Marx	*From Contraception to Abortion.* Pamphlet available from Gloria Dei Enterprises, Inc., PO Box 593, Belmont, CA 94002.
Paul Marx	*The Death Peddlers*, 1971. Pamphlet available from Human Life Center, St. John's University, Collegeville, MN 56321. $1.95.
Mary Meehan	"In Things Touching Conscience," *The Human Life Review*, Winter 1984.
Andy Merton	"Bill Baird's Holy War," *Esquire*, February 1981.
James W. Prescott	"Abortion or the Unwanted Child: A Choice for a Humanistic Society," *The Humanist*, March/April 1975.
Marion K. Sanders	"Enemies of Abortion," *Harper's*, March 1974.
Libby Smith	"I'm a Criminal and Proud of It," *Mademoiselle*, August 1982.
Joseph Sobran	"The Averted Gaze: Liberalism and Fetal Pain," *The Human Life Review*, Spring 1984.

Infant Euthanasia

Kerby Anderson	"Infanticide and Baby Does," *Conserative Digest*, January 1984.
George J. Annas	"Baby Doe Redux: Doctors as Child Abusers," *The Hastings Center Report*, June 1983.
Diana and Malcolm Brahams	"The Arthur Case: A Proposal for Legislation," *Journal of Medical Ethics*, Vol. 9, 1983.
John J. Conley	"Baby Jane Doe: The Ethical Issues," *America*, February 11, 1984.
Eugene F. Diamond	"Treatment Versus Nontreatment for the Handicapped Newborn," *Infanticide and the Handicapped Newborn*. Provo, UT: Brigham Young University Press, 1982.
Jack Fincher	"Before Their Time," *Science*, 1982.
John Fletcher	"Attitudes Toward Defective Newborns," *The Hastings Center Studies*, Vol. 2, No. 1, January 1974.
Nat Hentoff	"Big Brother and the Killing of Imperfect Babies," *Voice*, December 8, 1983.
The Human Life Review	See all issues. Published by Human Life Foundation, Editorial Office, Room 840, 150 East 35th St., New York, NY 10016.
Marvin Kohl, editor	*Infanticide and the Value of Life.* Buffalo, New York: Prometheus Books, 1978.
Richard A. McCormick	"To Save or Let Die: The Dilemma of Modern Medicine," *Journal of the American Medical Association*, July 8, 1974.
Robert S. Morison	"The Human Fetus as Useful Research Material," *The Hastings Center Report*, April 1973.

John J. Paris and Richard A. McCormick — "Saving Defective Infants: Options for Life or Death," *America*, April 23, 1983.

Steve Rabey — "Koop's Compromise: A Step Toward Protecting the Baby Does of the Future," *Christianity Today*, February 17, 1984.

Carson Strong — "The Tiniest Newborns," *The Hastings Center Report*, February 1983.

Euthanasia

Patrick Derr — "Who Shall Live? Who Shall Die? Who Shall Play God? Some Reflections on Euthanasia," *Thought*, Vol. 57, No. 227, December 1982.

engage/social action forum-16 — Special issue on euthanasia, April 1976.

Euthanasia Educational Council — *A Living Will.* Pamphlet available from the Euthanasia Educational Council, 250 West 57th Street, New York, NY 10107.

James Gaffney — "The Vatican Declaration on Euthanasia & Some Reflections on Christian Ethical Methodology," *Thought*, Vol. 57, No. 227, December 1982.

Germain Grisez and Joseph M. Boyle — *Life and Death with Liberty and Justice: A Contribution to the Euthanasia Debate.* Notre Dame: University of Notre Dame Press, 1979.

Elizabeth Hall with Paul Cameron — "Our Failing Reverence for Life," *Psychology Today*, April 1976.

Allan J. Hamilton — "Who Shall Live and Who Shall Die?" *Newsweek*, March 26, 1984.

David Hilfiker — "Leaving the Debilitated to Die," *The New England Journal of Medicine*, March 24, 1983.

Dennis J. Horan and David Mall, editors — *Death, Dying, and Euthanasia.* Libertyville, IL: Kairos Books Inc., 1980.

Lawrence Maloney — "A New Understanding About Death," *U.S. News & World Report*, July 11, 1983.

Paul Marx — *Death with Dignity.* Pamphlet available from The Liturgical Press, Collegeville, MN, 56321.

Steven McGraw — "Brothers," *Guideposts*, February 1984.

John J. Paris and Richard A. McCormick — "Living-Will Legislation, Reconsidered," *America*, September 5, 1981.

Joy Hinson Penticuff — "Resolving Ethical Dilemmas in Critical Care," *Dimensions of Critical Care Nursing*, Vol. 1, No. 1, February 1982.

Val Ross — "The 'Mercy' Killers," *Maclean's*, November 21, 1983.

Jean Seligmann — "When Doctors Play God," *Newsweek*, August 31, 1981.

Jane J. Stein — *Making Medical Choices: Who Is Responsible.* Boston: Houghton Mifflin Company, 1978.

Samuel E. Wallace and Albin Eser — *Suicide & Euthanasia: The Rights of Personhood.* Knoxville: The University of Tennessee, 1981.

Suicide

American Association of Suicidology — *Suicide in Youth and What You Can Do about It.* This and other pamphlets available from Merck Sharp & Dohme, Division of Merck & Co., Inc., West Point, PA 19486.

American Association of Suicidology — *Before It's Too Late, Suicide—It Doesn't Have to Happen.* Pamphlets available from Merck Sharp & Dohme, Division of Merck & Co., Inc., West Point, PA 19486.

M. Pabst Battin — *Ethical Issues in Suicide.* Englewood Cliffs, NJ: Prentice-Hall, 1982.

M. Pabst Battin and David J. Mayo — *Suicide: The Philosophical Issues.* St. Martin's Press Inc., New York, 1980.

Patricia Blake — "Going Gentle into That Good Night," *Time*, March 21, 1983.

George Howe Colt — "Suicide in America," *Reader's Digest*, January 1984.

John Deedy — "Suicide: Learn to Hear the Sounds of Silence," *U.S. Catholic*, December 1983.

David Gelman and B.K. Gangelhoff — "Teen-age Suicide in the Sun Belt," *Newsweek*, August 15, 1983.

Peter Giovacchini — *The Urge to Die: Why Young People Commit Suicide.* New York: Macmillan Publishing Co., Inc., 1981.

Herbert Hendin — "A Saner Policy on Suicide," *Psychology Today*, May 1979.

John H. Hewett — *After Suicide.* Philadelphia: The Westminister Press, 1980.

Derek Humphry — *Let Me Die Before I Wake.* Los Angeles: The Hemlock Society, 1981, 1982.

Derek Humphry — *Jean's Way.* Los Angeles: The Hemlock Society, 1984.

Derek Humphry — *The Compassionate Crime.* Los Angeles: The Hemlock Society, 1982.

Jim Jerome — "Catching Them Before Suicide," *The New York Times Magazine*, January 14, 1979.

Ari Kiev — *The Courage to Live.* New York: Thomas Y. Crowell Publishers, 1979.

Francine Klogsburn — *Too Young to Die.* Boston: Houghton Mifflin Company, 1976.

Gene Lester and David Lester — *Suicide, the Gamble with Death.* Englewood Cliffs, NJ: Prentice Hall, 1971.

John E. Mack and Holly Hickler — *Vivienne.* Boston: Little, Brown & Company, 1981.

Arnold Madison — *Suicide and Young People.* New York: The Seabury Press, 1978.

Ronald Maris — "Why 30,000 Americans Will Commit Suicide This Year," *U.S. News & World Report*, April 2, 1984.

S.E. Sprott — *The English Debate on Suicide from Donne to Hume.* La Salle, IL: Open Court Publishing Company, 1961.

The Right to Die

Robert Bernstein — "Accept the Disabled," *The New York Times*, January 10, 1984.

Robert Bobrow — "The Choice to Die," *Psychology Today*, June 1983.

Glenn Collins — "The 'Right to Die': Is It Right?" *The New York Times*, April 25, 1983.

Max Ferber — "I Cried But Not for Irma," *Reader's Digest*, April 1976.

Marvin Glass — *Not Going to Hell on One's Own.* New York: Cambridge University Press, 1983.

Gloria Maxson — "Whose Life Is It Anyway? Ours, That's Whose!" *The Christian Century*, October 20, 1982.

Bruce L. Miller	"Autonomy & the Refusal of Lifesaving Treatment," *The Hastings Center Report*, August 1981.
Society for the Right to Die	*Handbook of Enacted Laws*, 1981. Pamphlet available from Society for the Right to Die, 250 West 57th Street, New York, NY 10107.
Susan Tifft	"Debate on the Boundary of Life," *Time*, April 11, 1983.
Edward Wakin	"Is the Right-to-Die Wrong?" *U.S. Catholic*, March 1978.

Coping with Death

Rodney Clapp	"Dying as a Way of Life," *Christianity Today*, March 18, 1983.
Lisl Marburg Goodman	*Death and the Creative Life.* Harmondsworth, Middlesex, England: Penguin Books, 1981.
David Hendin	*Death as a Fact of Life.* New York: W.W. Norton & Co., Inc. 1973.
Don W. Hillis	"How to Die Triumphantly," *Eternity*, November 1982.
Peter J. Kreeft	*Love Is Stronger than Death.* San Francisco: Harper & Row, 1979.
Elisabeth Kübler-Ross	*Living with Death and Dying.* New York: Macmillan Publishing Co. Inc., 1981.
Elisabeth Kübler-Ross	*Working It Through: An Elisabeth Kübler-Ross Workshop on Life, Death, and Transition.* New York: Macmillan Publishing Co. Inc., 1982.
Virginia Stem Owens	"The Necessity of Death," *Christianity Today*, April 6, 1984.
Frank E. Reynolds and Earle H. Waugh, editors	*Religious Encounters with Death: Insights from the History and Anthropology of Religions.* University Park, PA: The Pennsylvania State University Press, 1979.
Paul Robinson	"Five Models for Dying," *Psychology Today*, March 1981.
Patrick Francis Sheehy	*On Dying with Dignity.* New York: Pinnacle Books, 1981.
Peter Steinhart	"Leave the Dead," *Audubon*, January 1981.
Helmut Thielicke	*Living with Death.* Grand Rapids, MI: William B. Eerdmans Publishing Co., 1983.

Dealing with Grief

Jeanne Quint Benoliel	"Death Counseling and Human Development: Issues and Intricacies," *Death Education*, Vol. 4, 1981.
Joan Bordow	*The Ultimate Loss: Coping with the Death of a Child.* New York: Beauford Books, 1982.
Alla Bozarth-Campbell	*Life Is Goodbye Life Is Hello: Grieving Well Through All Kinds of Loss.* Minneapolis: Compcare, 1983.
Duncan B. Clark	"A Death in the Family: Providing Consultation to the Police on the Psychological Aspects of Suicide and Accidental Death," *Death Education*, Vol. 5, 1981.

Robert Fulton, David J. Gottesman, and Greg M. Owen	"Loss, Social Change, and the Prospect of Mourning," *Death Education*, Vol. 6, 1982.
Charles O. Jackson	*Passing.* Westport, CT: Greenwood Press, 1977.
Maurice Lamm	*The Jewish Way in Death and Mourning.* New York: Jonathan David Publishers, 1969.
Robert Jay Lifton	*The Broken Connection: On Death and the Continuity of Life.* New York: Basic Books, 1979.
Otto S. Margolis and others	*Acute Grief: Counseling the Bereaved.* New York: Columbia University Press, 1981.
National Reporter	"A Death in the Family: Parental Bereavement in the First Year-Part 1," November 1983. "Normal and Pathological Grief," August 1983. "Individual and Social Elements in Acute Grief," October 1983. Newsletters available from the National Research and Information Center, 1614 Central Street, Evanston, IL 60201.
Colin Murray Parkes	*Bereavement: Studies of Grief in Adult Life.* New York: International Universities Press Inc., 1972.
Judy Sklar Rasminsky	"When a Baby Dies," *Reader's Digest*, April 1984.
Peter Steinfels and Robert M. Veatch, editors	*Death Inside Out.* New York: Harper & Row, 1975.
Elaine Vail	*A Personal Guide to Living with Loss.* New York: John Wiley & Sons Inc., 1982.

Alternative Care of the Dying

Robert W. Buckingham	*A Special Kind of Love—Care of the Dying Child.* New York: The Continuum Publishing Corp., 1983.
Mary Reardon Castles and Ruth Beckman Murray	*Dying in an Institution: Nurse/Patient Perspectives.* New York: Appleton-Century-Crofts, 1979.
Norman Cousins	*Anatomy of an Illness.* New York: Bantam Books, 1979.
Deborah Duda	*A Guide to Dying at Home.* Santa Fe, NM: John Muir Publications, 1982.
Loma Feigenberg	*Terminal Care: Friendship Contracts with Dying Cancer Patients.* New York: Brunner/Mazel Publishers, 1980.
Harvey Humann	"Hospice," *New Realities*, Vol. IV, No. 3, September 1981.
Theodore H. Koff	*Hospice: A Caring Community.* Cambridge, MA: Winthrop Publishers Inc., 1980.
Benita C. Martocchio	*Living While Dying.* Bowie, MD: Robert J. Brady Co., 1982.
Anne Munley	*The Hospice Alternative.* New York: Basic Books, 1983.
National Reporter	"A Directory of Hospices—Part 1 & 2," *National Reporter*, November/December 1982. Pamphlets available from NRIC, 1614 Central Street, Evanston, IL 60201.
E. Mansell Pattison	"Helping with Dying," *The Experience of Dying*, Englewood Cliffs, NJ: Prentice-Hall, 1977.

Cicely Saunders	"Dying They Live: St. Christopher's Hospice," *New Meaning of Death,* edited by Herman Feifel. New York: McGraw-Hill Book Co., 1977.
Cicely Saunders	"Hospice in America: From Principle to Practice," *Hospice: The Living Idea.* London: Edward Arnold, 1981.
David H. Smith and Judith A. Granbois	"The American Way of Hospice," *The Hastings Center Report,* April 1982.
Sandol Stoddard	*The Hospice Movement.* Briarcliff Manor, New York: Stein & Day, 1978.
USA Today	"Relieving the Terminally Ill," June 1982.
Florence S. Wald	"Terminal Care & Nursing Education," *American Journal of Nursing,* October 1979.
Rosemary and Victor Zorza	*A Way to Die (Hospices).* New York: Alfred A. Knopf, 1980.

Delaying Death

Daniel Callahan	"Science: Limits & Prohibitions," *The Hastings Center Report,* November 1973.
James P. Carse	*Death and Existence.* New York: John Wiley & Sons Inc., 1980.
Dr. Thomas C. Chalmers and Alfred R. Stein	"The Staggering Cost of Prolonging Life," *Business Week,* February 23, 1981.
Thomas Donaldson	"A Brief Scientific Introduction to Cryonics," 1979. Pamphlet available from Trans Time, Inc., 1507 63rd Street, Emeryville, CA 94707.
Edward Edelson	"Cleansing the Blood," *Science,* October 1982.
Samuel Gorovitz	*Doctors' Dilemmas—Moral Conflict and Medical Care.* New York: Macmillan Publishing Co. Inc., 1982.
John K. Iglehart	"Transplantation: The Problem of Limited Resources," *The New England Journal of Medicine,* July 14, 1983.
Saul Kent	*The Life Extension Revolution.* New York: William Morrow and Company Inc., 1980.
Durk Pearson and Sandy Shaw	*Life Extension.* New York: Warner Books, 1982.
James Rachels	"Barney Clark's Key," *The Hastings Center Report,* April 1983.
Albert Rosenfeld	*Prolongevity.* New York: Alfred A. Knopf, Inc., 1976.
Arlene Sheskin	*Cryonics: A Sociology of Death and Bereavement.* New York: Irvington Publishers Inc., 1979.
Alvin Silverstein	*Conquest of Death.* New York: Macmillan Publishing Co. Inc., 1979.
Gordon Rattray Taylor	*The Biological Time Bomb.* Cleveland: World Publishing Co., 1968.
Roy L. Walford	*Maximum Life Span.* New York: W.W. Norton & Co., 1983.

Death and the Law

| *America* | "Brain Death: Responses to a Recent Article," March 26, 1983. |
| Harry Bernstein | "The Living Will," *The New York Times Magazine,* December 31, 1978. |

Samuel B. Burgess	"The Living Will: Another View," *Friends Journal,* May 1, 1984.
Edward Bryce	"Defining Death," *Origins NC Documentary Service,* August 13, 1981.
Paul A. Byrne, Sean O'Reilly, Paul M. Quay, and Peter Salsich Jr.	*Brain Death: The Patient, the Physician, and Society,* 1984. Pamphlet available from NCL Educational Trust Fund, PO Box 6501, Omaha, NE 68106.
Daniel Callahan	"On Feeding the Dying," *The Hastings Center Report,* October 1983.
James F. Childress	*Priorities in Biomedical Ethics.* Philadelphia: The Westminster Press, 1981.
Howard Fetterhoff	"Supporting a Determination of Death Bill," *Origins NC Documentary Services,* March 4, 1982.
Victor Fuchs	*Who Shall Live? Health, Economics, and Social Choice.* New York: Basic Books, 1983.
David Hellerstein	"The Slow, Costly Death of Mrs. K---," *Harper's,* March 1984.
Barbara Huttmann	"A Crime of Compassion," *Newsweek,* August 8, 1983.
Leon R. Kass	"Death as an Event: A Commentary on Robert Morison," *Science,* August 20, 1971.
Nancy Koster	"Brain Death: What Is It? Why Shouldn't It Be Legislated?" *MCCL,* January 1981.
Joann Lynn and James F. Childress	"Must Patients Always Be Given Food and Water?" *The Hastings Center Report,* October 1983.
Richard A. McCormick	*How Brave A New World? Dilemmas in Bioethics.* Garden City, NY: Doubleday & Company Inc., 1981.
Robert S. Morison	"Death: Process or Event?" *Science,* August 20, 1971.
Gerry Nadel	"Now They're Using a Scorecard to Determine Death," *Medical Economics,* May 10, 1971.
Jay F. Rosenberg	*Thinking Clearly about Death.* Englewood Cliffs, NJ: Prentice-Hall, 1983.
Bonnie Steinbock	"The Removal of Mr. Herbert's Feeding Tube," *The Hastings Center Report,* October 1983.
Phillip J. Swihart	*The Edge of Death.* Downers Grove, IL: Inter-Varsity Press, 1978.
Robert M. Veatch	"The Whole-Brain-Oriented Concept of Death: An Outmoded Philosophical Formulation," *Journal of Thanatology,* Vol. 3, 1975.
A. Earl Walker	*Cerebral Death,* 2nd Edition. Baltimore: Urban & Schwarzenberg, 1981.

The Funeral Industry

Raymond Paavo Arvio	*The Cost of Dying and What You Can Do.* New York: Harper & Row, 1974.
Editors of *Consumer Report*	*Funerals: Consumer's Last Rights.* New York: W.W. Norton & Co., 1977.
Jean Bethke Elshtain	"On Humanness & Honoring the Dead," *Commonweal,* March 1983.
Robert Fulton	*A Compilation of Studies of Attitudes Toward Death, Funerals, & Funeral Directors.* Pamphlet available from Center For Death Education and Research, Dept. of Sociology, University of Minnesota, Minneapolis, MN 55455.

Ruth Mulvey Harmer	*The High Cost of Dying.* New York: Crowell-Collier Press, 1963.
Donald Heinz	"The Last Passage: Re-Visioning Dying, Death and Funeral," *The Christian Century,* January 1982.
Paul E. Irion	*Cremation.* Philadelphia, PA: Fortress Press, 1968.
Paul E. Irion	*The Funeral, An Experience of Value,* 1956. Pamphlet available from Lancaster Theological Seminary, Lancaster, PA.
Roslyn Katz	"Preplanning Funerals: A Pastor's Initiative," *Christianity Today,* January 25, 1980.
National Reporter	"Implications of Cremation for Grief Adjustment," July 1983. "Perceptions of the Funeral Service & Post Bereavement Adjustment in Widowed Individuals: Part Two," January 1982. "Personality Characteristics of Elderly Attenders and Non-Attenders of Public Visitation and Viewing of the Body," January 1983. "Grief Resolution in Widowed Persons According to Funeral Chosen and Mode of Death and Demographic and Life Experience Variables: Part 1," March 1982. "Widows View the Helpfulness of the Funeral Service," February 1982. Newsletters available from NRIC, 1614 Central Street, Evanston, IL 60201.
Richard J. Obershaw	*Death, Dying, Grief & Funerals,* 1976. Pamphlet available from Grief Center, 1822 Hayes, Box 5, Minneapolis, MN 55418.
R. Larry Overstreet	"After the Funeral," *Moody Monthly,* May 1981.
James Ricci	"Kelly's Gift," *Reader's Digest,* June 1983.

After Life

H.N. Banerjee	*Americans Who Have Been Reincarnated.* New York: Macmillan Publishing Co. Inc., 1980.
Buff Bradley	*Endings: A Book about Death.* Reading, MA: Addison-Wesley Publishing Co. Inc., 1979.
James Breig	"Beyond the Pearly Gates: What US Catholic Readers Believe about the Afterlife," *U.S. Catholic,* May 1983.
Ian Currie	*You Cannot Die.* New York: Methuen Publications, 1978.
George Gallup Jr. and William Proctor	*Adventures in Immortality: A Look Beyond the Threshold of Death.* New York: McGraw-Hill Book Co., 1982.
Bruce Goldbert	*Past Lives, Future Lives.* North Hollywood, CA: Newcastle Publishing Co., Inc., 1982.
Joseph Head and S.L. Cranston	*Reincarnation: The Phoenix Fire Mystery.* New York: Julian Press/Crown Publishers, Inc., 1977.
Merrill Holtse	"Betting on a Hereafter," *The American Atheist,* January 1983.
Peter J. Kreeft	*Everything You Ever Wanted to Know About Heaven.* New York: Harper & Row, 1982.

Harold B. Kuhn	"Out-of-Body Experiences: Misplaced Euphoria," *Christianity Today,* March 13, 1981.
Hans Kung	*Eternal Life? Life after Death as a Medical Philosophical, and Theological Problem.* New York: Doubleday & Co. Inc., 1984.
Bruce Lockerbie	"Life and Death and the Marathon," *The Christian Century,* May 27, 1981.
Craig R. Lundahl	*A Collection of Near-Death Research Readings.* Chicago: Nelson-Hall Publishers, 1982.
McCall's	"Life After Death: What Americans Believe Now," June 1982.
Ruth Montgomery	*Strangers Among Us.* New York: Coward-McCann & Geoghegan, 1979.
Raymond A. Moody	*Life After Life.* Covington, GA: Mockingbird Books, 1976.
Mary Ann O'Roark	"Life After Death: The Growing Evidence," *McCall's,* March 1981.
Bruce R. Reichenbach	*Is Man the Phoenix? A Study of Immortality.* Washington, DC: Christian University Press, 1978.
Kenneth Ring	*Life at Death: A Scientific Investigation of the Near-Death Experience.* New York: Coward-McCann & Geoghegan, 1980.
D. Scott Rogo and Raymond Bayless	*Phone Calls from the Dead.* New York: Prentice-Hall, 1979.
Michael S. Sabom	*Recollections of Death: A Medical Explanation.* New York: Harper & Row, 1982.
Edwin Schneidmen	*Voices of Death.* New York: Harper & Row, 1980.
Susy Smith	*Life Is Forever.* New York: G.P. Putnam's Sons, 1974.
Jess Stearn	*The Search for a Soul: Taylor Caldwell's Psychic Lives.* Garden City, NY: Doubleday & Co. Inc., 1973.
Roy Stemman	*Spirits and Spirit Worlds.* Garden City, NY: Doubleday & Co. Inc., 1976.
Ian Stevenson	*Twenty Cases Suggestive of Reincarnation.* Charlottesville, NC: University Press of Virginia, 1974.
Helen Wambaugh	*Life Before Life: Choosing to Be Born.* New York: Bantam Books, 1979.
Helen Wambaugh	*Reliving Past Lives: The Evidence Under Hypnosis.* New York: Harper & Row, 1978.
William J. Whalen	"What Different Churches Believe about the Afterlife," *U.S. Catholic,* February 1984.
David R. Wheeler	*Journey to the Other Side.* New York: Tempo Books/Grosset & Dunalp/A Filmways Company, 1976.

index